Readings in Planning Theory

READINGS IN URBAN THEORY

SECOND EDITION

Edited by Susan S. Fainstein & Scott Campbell

DECEMBER 2001 I 418 PAGES
0-631-22344-4 HB I 0-631-22345-2 PB

Readings in
Urban Theory
SECOND EDITION
EDITED BY SUSAN S. FAINSTEIN AND SCOTT CAMPBELL

Blackwell
Publishing

Readings in Planning Theory

Second Edition

Edited by

Scott Campbell and Susan S. Fainstein

Blackwell Publishing

BLACKWELL PUBLISHING
350 Main Street, Malden, MA 02148-5020, USA
9600 Garsington Road, Oxford OX4 2DQ, UK
550 Swanston Street, Carlton, Victoria 3053, Australia

First edition published 1996
Second edition published 2003

9   2008

Library of Congress Cataloging-in-Publication Data

Readings in planning theory / edited by Scott Campbell and Susan S. Fainstein. – 2nd ed.
    p.   cm.
Includes bibliographical references and index.
ISBN 978-0-631-22346-7 (alk. paper); ISBN 978-0-631-22347-4 (pbk. : alk. paper)
1. City planning. I. Campbell, Scott, 1958– . II. Fainstein, Susan S.
HT165.5.R43   2003
307.1'216'0973 – dc21

2002066635

A catalogue record for this title is available from the British Library.

Set in 10/12 pt Sabon
by Kolam Information Services Pvt. Ltd, Pondicherry, India
Printed and bound in Singapore
by Markono Print Media Pte Ltd

The publisher's policy is to use permanent paper from mills that operate a sustainable
forestry policy, and which has been manufactured from pulp processed using acid-free and
elementary chlorine-free practices. Furthermore, the publisher ensures that the text paper
and cover board used have met acceptable environmental accreditation standards.

For further information on
Blackwell Publishing, visit our website:
www.blackwellpublishing.com

Contents

Contributors

Howell S. Baum
Robert A. Beauregard
Tim Brindley
Scott Campbell
Paul Davidoff
Susan S. Fainstein
Frank Fischer
Robert Fishman
Bent Flyvbjerg
Richard E. Foglesong
John Friedmann
Dolores Hayden
Patsy Healey
Jane Jacobs
Richard E. Klosterman
Norman Krumholz
John M. Levy
Charles E. Lindblom
William H. Lucy
David C. Perry
Yvonne Rydin
Leonie Sandercock
James C. Scott
Gerry Stoker
June Manning Thomas
Iris Marion Young

Acknowledgments

Baum, Howell S. Community and consensus: reality and fantasy in planning. *Journal of Planning Education and Research* 13, 1994.

Beauregard, Robert A. Between modernity and postmodernity: the ambiguous position of U.S. planning. *Environment and Planning D: Society and Space*, 7, 1989, pp. 381–95. Reprinted by permission of Pion Ltd, London.

Brindley, Tim, Rydin, Yvonne and Stoker, Gerry. "Popular planning: Coin Street, London" from *Remaking Planning: The Politics of Urban Change in the Thatcher Years*. Unwin Hyman, London, 1989.

Brindley, Tim, Rydin, Yvonne and Stoker, Gerry. "Postscript" from *Remaking Planning: The Politics of Urban Change* (2nd edn). Routledge, London, 1996.

Campbell, Scott. Green cities, growing cities, just cities? Urban planning and the contradictions of sustainable development. *Journal of the American Planning Association* 62(3), 1996. Reprinted by permission of the *Journal of the American Planning Association*.

Davidoff, Paul. Advocacy and pluralism in planning. *Journal of the American Institute of Planners* 31(4), 1965. Reprinted by permission.

Fainstein, Susan S. New directions in planning theory. *Urban Affairs Quarterly* 35(4), 2000. Reprinted by permission of Sage Publications Inc.

Fischer, Frank. Risk assessment and environmental crisis: toward an integration of science and participation. *Industrial Crisis Quarterly* 5(2), 1991. Reprinted by permission.

Fishman, Robert. "Urban utopias: Ebenezer Howard, Frank Lloyd Wright and Le Corbusier" from *Urban Utopias in the Twentieth Century: Ebenezer Howard, Frank Lloyd Wright and Le Corbusier* (ed. Robert Fishment). © 1977 by Basic Books, Inc. Reprinted by permission of BasicBooks Inc., a member of Perseus Books Group.

Flyvbjerg, Bent. *Rationality and Power: Democracy in Practice* (trans. Steven Sampson). The University of Chicago Press, Chicago, 1998.

Foglesong, Richard E. *Planning the Capitalist City.* © 1986 by Princeton University Press. Reprinted by permission of Princeton University Press.

Friedmann, John. Toward a non-Euclidian mode of planning. *Journal of the American Planning Association* 59(4), 1993. Reprinted by permission of the *Journal of the American Planning Association.*

Hayden, Dolores. *Redesigning the American Dream.* W. W. Norton Inc, New York, 1984.

Healey, Patsy. The communicative turn in planning theory and its implications for spatial strategy formation. *Environment and Planning B: Planning and Design* 23(2), 1996, pp. 217–34. Reprinted by permission of Pion Limited, London.

Jacobs, Jane. Extract from *The Death and Life of Great American Cities.* © 1961 by Jane Jacobs, used by permission of Random House, Inc. and Jonathan Cape, London.

Klosterman, Richard E. Arguments for and against planning. *Town Planning Review* 56(1), 1985. Reprinted by permission of Liverpool University Press.

Krumholz, Norman. Equitable approaches to local economic development. *Policy Studies Journal* 27(1), 1999. Reprinted by permission of Policy Studies Organization.

Levy, John M. What local economic developers actually do: location quotients versus press releases. *Journal of the American Planning Association* 56(2), 1990. Reprinted by permission of the *Journal of the American Planning Association.*

Lindblom, Charles E. The science of "muddling through." *Public Administration Review* 19, 1959. Reprinted with permission from *Public Administration Review* © by the American Society for Public Administration (ASPA), 1120 G Street NW, Suite 700, Washington DC 20005. All rights reserved.

Lucy, William H. APA's ethical principles include simplistic planning theories. *Journal of the American Planning Association* 54(2), 1988. Reprinted by permission of the Journal of the American Planning Association.

Perry, David C. "Making space: planning as a mode of thought" from *Spatial Practices: Critical Explorations in Social/Spatial Theory* (eds H. Liggett and D. C. Perry). Sage Publications Inc., 1995. Reprinted by permission of Sage Publications Inc.

Sandercock, Leonie. *Towards Cosmopolis. Planning for Multicultural Cities.* Wiley, 1998. Reprinted by permission of the author.

Scott, James C. Extract from *Seeing Like a State: How Certain Schemes to Improve the Human Condition Have Failed.* Yale University Press, New Haven, 1998, © 1998 by Yale University.

Thomas, June Manning. Educating planners: unified diversity for social action. *Journal of Planning Education and Research* 15(3), 1996.

Young, Iris Marion. Extract from *Justice and the Politics of Difference.* Princeton University Press, Princeton, 1990, © 1990 Princeton University Press. Reprinted by permission of Princeton University Press.

Introduction: The Structure and Debates of Planning Theory

Scott Campbell and Susan S. Fainstein

Planning theory is an elusive subject of study. It draws on a variety of disciplines and has no widely accepted canon. The purpose of this reader is twofold: (1) to define the boundaries of this area of inquiry and the works that constitute its central focus; and (2) to confront the principal issues that face planners as theorists and practitioners. It is organized by the questions that its editors raise, rather than by the chronological development of the field.

Compiling a reader in planning theory presents a tricky dilemma. One can either cautiously reprint the early postwar classics – thereby duplicating several past anthologies, including Faludi's popular 1973 reader – or else run the risk of prematurely elevating otherwise transient ideas. We take a different path; we have selected a set of readings – both "classic" and recent – that effectively address the pressing and enduring questions in planning theory.

We see the central question of planning theory as the following: *What role can planning play in developing the good city and region within the constraints of a capitalist political economy and a democratic political system?* The emphasis is not on developing a model planning process. Rather, we look for explanations and guides to planning practice based on analyses of the respective political economies of the United States and the United Kingdom. Our effort is designed to determine the historical and contextual influences and strategic opportunities that shape the capacity of planners to affect the urban and regional environment.

What is Planning Theory?

It is not easy to define planning theory: the subject is slippery, and explanations are often frustratingly tautological or disappointingly pedestrian. There are four principal reasons for this difficulty. First, many of the fundamental questions concerning planning belong to a much broader inquiry concerning the role of the state in social and spatial transformation. Consequently, planning theory appears to overlap with theory in all the social science disciplines, and it becomes hard to limit its scope or to stake out a turf specific to planning.

Second, the boundary between planners and related professionals (such as real estate developers, architects, city council members) is not mutually exclusive: planners don't just plan, and non-planners also plan. Failure to distinguish adequately the specific task of planning from the broader forces of urbanization makes it harder to recognize what can actually be done by planners. The most basic of questions too often remains unanswered: who exactly designs, builds, manages, and finally tears down cities? Ambitious, omnipotent planning theories often collide with the modest, constrained powers of actual planning practice.

Third, the field of planning is divided among those who define it according to its object (land use patterns of the built and natural environments) and those who do so by its method (the process of decision making). The result is two largely separate sets of theoretical questions and priorities that undermine a singular definition of planning.

Finally, many fields (such as economics) are defined by a specific set of methodologies. Yet planning commonly borrows diverse methodologies from many different fields, and so its theoretical base cannot be easily drawn from its tools of analysis. It is defined more by a shared interest in space and place, a commitment to civic community, and a pragmatic orientation toward professional practice. It is also a field defined by a series of both theoretical and practical questions, reflecting its somewhat ungainly straddling of both academic and professional causes.

Taken together, these considerable disagreements over the scope and function of planning and the problems of defining who is actually a planner obscure the delineation of an appropriate body of theory. Whereas most scholars can agree on what constitutes the economy and the polity – and thus what is economic or political theory – they differ as to the content of planning theory.

The abstract quality of planning theory means that practitioners largely disregard it. In this respect, planning resembles other academic disciplines. Most politicians do not bother with political theory; business persons generally do not familiarize themselves with econometrics; and community organizers do not regularly concern themselves with social theory. Planning as a practical field of endeavor, however, differs from other activities in its claim to be able to predict the consequences of its actions. Planners need to generalize from prior experience if they are to practice their craft. In their day-to-day work, planners may rely more on intuition than explicit theory; yet this intuition may in fact be assimilated theory. In this light, theory represents cumulative professional knowledge. Though many practicing planners may look upon the planning theory of their graduate education as inert and irrelevant – and see in their professional work a kind of homespun, in-the-trenches pragmatism – theory allows one to see the conditions of this "pragmatism." Just as Keynes warned of being an unwitting slave to the ideas of a defunct economist, we believe that it is also possible to be a slave to the ideas of a defunct planning theorist.

Why Do Planning Theory?

One of our prime motives in selecting the readings for this book is to enable practitioners to achieve a deeper understanding of the processes in which they are engaged than can be attained through simple intuition and common sense. Many in the field have decried the gap between theory and practice; yet we do not envision eliminating it completely. It is both unrealistic and inadvisable that planning practice and education become identical. We should no more expect practicing land use planners to implement the unadulterated arguments of the German philosopher Jürgen Habermas (who provides the conceptual foundations for communicative planning) in their jobs than expect graduate students to accept without question existing land-use practice. True, if the gap is *too big*, then planning education is irrelevant; but if there is *no* gap, then planning education is redundant. The role of planning theory should be to generate a creative tension that is both critical and constructive and that provokes reflection on both sides. In other words, its role is to create both the reflective practitioner and the practical scholar. These two need not think alike, but they should at least be able to talk to each other.

We therefore believe that theory can inform practice. Planning theory is not just some idle chattering at the margins of the field. If done poorly, it discourages and stifles; but if done well, it defines the field and drives it forward. We have consequently identified a set of readings that address themselves to the questions that planners must ask if they are to be effective, and we include case studies of planning in action with this purpose in mind.

Beyond this intention, we aim to establish a theoretical foundation that provides the field not only with a common structure for scientific inquiry, but also with a means for defining what planning is – especially in the intimidating company of more established academic disciplines. Theory allows for both professional and intellectual self-reflection. It tries to make sense of the seemingly unrelated, contradictory aspects of urban development and to create a rational system with which to compare and evaluate the merits of different planning ideas and strategies. It seeks the underlying conceptual elements that tie together the disparate planning areas, from housing and community development to transportation planning and urban design. Providing a common language is an important function of introductory theory and history courses for master's students, who gain a shared identity as planners with other students during their first year before veering into their sub-specialties in the second year. It can be both comforting and encouraging, when encountering the challenges of contemporary urban poverty, the lack of public space, the greed and shortsightedness of urban developers, to read Sam Bass Warner's (1987) account of nineteenth-century Philadelphia as a private city, or William Cronon's (1991) slaughterhouse vision of nineteenth-century Chicago. We not only know that we have been here before, but we also remind ourselves that in many ways urban life *has* improved, and planners and reformers can take some credit for this.

Because of this common language, planning theory is often the arena where the field of planning reassesses itself. Though too often this reflection degenerates into self-doubt (such as "if planning is everything, perhaps it is nothing"), it is not an exaggeration to say that planning theory is the philosophical conscience of the discipline. This self-critical function of planning theory therefore cuts both ways: one can use it to both claim legitimacy to others and question one's own legitimacy.

The language of planning theory also encourages planners to translate their specific issues into more general social-scientific theoretical language. It allows ideas and values from planning to find a broader audience, and it gives planning greater intellectual legitimacy. However, there is always the danger of intellectual grave robbing: of borrowing ideas from other disciplines that have been long dead in the discipline of origin. Or it may be that in borrowing from other fields, we sometimes are not up to speed: employing, for instance, a concept from Jürgen Habermas without understanding its deeper context in German intellectual history. So, planning theory should borrow, but with caution and rigor, avoiding out-of-date, oversimplified ideas taken out of context.

A well-developed theoretical foundation serves as a declaration of scholarly autonomy, often institutionalized in the form of a planning theory requirement for master's degree programs and professional certification in city planning. The relatively recent expansion of planning Ph.D. programs goes hand in hand with the rise of planning theory. Such programs not only support research within planning departments; they also encourage the development of the discipline's theoretical foundations. Ph.D. programs also use theory to distinguish and elevate themselves above master's programs and professional training.

Though theory helps planning assert its distinctiveness as an autonomous field, that field remains a diminutive newcomer surrounded by larger, more established disciplines. The result is that planning must define (and defend) itself by differentiating itself from its larger neighbors: if next to architecture, planning will emphasize the socio-economic city; in relation to geography, planning stresses the field's policy orientation; if adjacent to public policy, planners focus on space and local communities; and in contrast to economists, planners attend to issues of redistribution and market failures. These institutional boundary lines become crucial when planning shifts its academic alliances, such as from a school of architecture to a school of policy. This relational identity of planning shapes the debate regarding the "natural" institutional home of planning: should we go back to our architectural/land-use roots, push further ahead into social science, be subsumed into public policy, or strategically ally ourselves more closely with business and real estate? As a consequence of these issues, planning theory thus becomes an arbiter of the field's changing boundaries.

Our Approach to Planning Theory

Our approach is to place planning theory at the intersection of political economy and intellectual history. We do not see it, however, as mechanistically determined by these two forces. Those who misuse structural theory will inevitably fall victim to a sense of helplessness in the face of predestined social forces. Instead, the planner should use theory to view how the local and national political economy, in addition to the field's own history, influences the collective imagination of planning's possibilities, limitations, and professional identity. The challenge for this professional – and sometimes activist – discipline is to find the negotiating room within the larger social structure to pursue the good city.

We also place planning theory at a second intersection: that of the *city and region* as a phenomenon and *planning* as a human activity. Planning adapts to changes in the city and region, which in turn are transformed by planning and politics. This interaction is not a closed system. Planners not only plan places; they also negotiate, forecast, research, survey, and organize financing. Nor do planners have an exclusive influence over territories; developers, businesspersons, politicians, and other actors also shape urban and regional development. The result is that the discipline of planning is influenced by a wide variety of procedural and substantive ideas beyond its own modest disciplinary boundaries. Studies of planning refer to works in political science, law, decision theory, and public policy. Writings about cities and regions draw upon traditions primarily in urban history, urban sociology, geography, and economics. Though not always consistently, we use this practical distinction of substantive versus procedural theory to distinguish *Readings in Planning Theory* from its companion volume, *Readings in Urban Theory* (Fainstein and Campbell 2001).

Debates Define Theory: Five Questions of Planning Theory

No single paradigm defines the foundation of planning theory. Such a lack of agreement about planning priorities and planning ideologies is inevitable; yet this disagreement is mistakenly carried over into the classroom, leading to unnecessary conflict over how planning theory itself should be taught. As a result, many academic departments shy away from developing a rigorous, unified theory program. However, it is possible to agree on how to teach planning theory systematically even though planning itself may lack a systematic, uniform structure. To the contrary: the teaching of planning theory should explicitly explore the roots and implications of long-standing disputes in the field. Planning is a messy, contentious field; planning theory should provide the means to define and address these debates and understand their deeper roots.

In this light, we view planning theory as a series of debates. Here are five questions at issue.

I What are the historical roots of planning? (the role of history in planning theory)

The first question of theory is one of identity, which in turn leads to history. The traditional story told of modern city planning is that it arose from several separate movements at the turn of the century: the Garden City, the City Beautiful, and public health reforms. Three basic eras characterized its subsequent history: (1) the formative years during which the pioneers (Ebenezer Howard, Daniel Burnham, etc.) did not yet identify themselves as planners (late 1800s – *ca.* 1910); (2) the period of institutionalization, professionalization, and self-recognition of planning, together with the rise of regional and national planning efforts (*ca.* 1910–1945); and (3) the postwar era of standardization, crisis, and diversification of planning (Krueckeberg 1983).

This story, often repeated in introductory courses and texts, is useful in several ways. The multiplicity of technical, social, and aesthetic origins explains planning's eclectic blend of design, civil engineering, local politics, community organization, and social justice. Its status as either a quasi-, secondary, or pubescent profession is explained by its development as a twentieth-century, public-sector, bureaucratic profession, rather than as a late-nineteenth-century, private-sector profession such as medicine (Hoffman 1989).

At the most basic level, this framework gives the story of planning (at least modern professional planning) a starting point. Planning emerges as the twentieth-century response to the nineteenth-century industrial city (Hall 1996). It also provides several foundational texts: Howard's and Osborn's *Garden Cities of To-morrow: A Peaceful Path to Real Reform* (1945 [1898]), Charles Robinson's *The Improvement of Towns and Cities; or the Practical Basis of Civic Aesthetics* (1901), and Daniel Burnham's plan for Chicago (1909), as well as several defining events: the Columbia Exposition in Chicago (1893), which launched the City Beautiful Movement; the construction of Letchworth, the first English Garden City (1903); and the first national conference on city planning, held in Washington, D.C. (1909).

Yet this tale of planning's birth is also problematic. As the years go by and the planning pioneers fade from memory, the story is simplified and unconditionally repeated. Contingent or coincidental events and texts are elevated to necessary steps in the inevitable and rational development of modern planning. Even the best of tellers can succumb to repeating this tale of the "great men of planning history." The result is an essentialistic life-cycle model of planning's birth, growth, maturation, and mid-life crisis – a model that largely excludes the political, economic, and cultural forces that continually transform planning in both ideology and practice. In fact, such an uncritical acceptance of these early years of planning juxtaposes oddly with the soul-searching of the last quarter-century, especially after the failures of 1960s poverty programs and weariness of urban renewal created a crisis of confidence.

One path out of this debilitating historicism is to bridge benign past folklore and current skepticism through a reassessment of planning history in which both past and present are retold with the same critical (and sometimes revisionist) voice. Richard Foglesong's *Planning the Capitalist City* (1986) and Robert Fishman's *Bourgeois Utopias: The Rise and Fall of Suburbia* (1987) are but two of the better examples.[1] Some critical histories, however, are also narrow-minded, replacing the heroic stories of "the great men of planning history" with an equally unreflective disquisition on the historic logic of capital. The challenge is to write a planning history that encourages not only an accurate, but also a critical, subtle, and reflective understanding of contemporary planning practice. An effective planning history helps the contemporary planner shape his or her complex professional identity.

2   What is the justification for planning? When should one intervene?

Planning is intervention with an intention to alter the existing course of events. The timing and legitimacy of planned intervention therefore become questions central to planning theory: Why and in what situations should planners intervene? Implicit here is an understanding of the alternative to planning. Though it is most commonly assumed that the alternative is the free market, it could equally be chaos or myopic self-interest. Indeed, automatically assuming that we know the alternative to planning is dangerous. For some, the hope of rational planning is simply to replace the uncertainty of the market with the logic of the plan. Yet others hold the reverse belief: that the logic of the market should replace the chaos left by planning (Hayek 1944). Whereas the Great Depression seems to vindicate the former view, the collapse of Eastern European state socialism is frequently cited in support of the latter.

The duality between planning and the market is a defining framework in planning theory, and is the leitmotiv of classic readings in the field (such as Banfield 1968;

Dahrendorf 1968; Galbraith 1971). Evaluations of planning reflects his or her assumptions about the relationships between the private and public sectors – and how much the government should "intrude." The safe stance in planning has been to see its role as making up for the periodic shortcomings of the private market (Klosterman, chapter 4, this volume, Moore 1978). This approach creates a neat and tidy division between the public and private worlds, each with its unique comparative advantages. It treats planning as the patient understudy, filling in when the market fails but never presuming to replace the market permanently or change the script of economic efficiency. This way of legitimizing planning significantly limits creative or redistributive planning efforts, but it does make a scaled-down version of planning palatable to all but the most conservative economists (e.g. Friedman 1962).

Nevertheless, not everyone sees the market–planning duality as so clear-cut. For some, the function of planning is to confront the private market directly every step of the way (Harvey 1985); others see planning as helping the market along (Frieden and Sagalyn 1989). This debate becomes even murkier when one challenges the tidy separation between the public and private sectors, from either a relatively upbeat (Galbraith 1971) or a skeptical point of view (Lowi 1969). Public and private sectors no longer, if they ever did, represent mutually exclusive sets of actors, interests, or planning tools. The rise of public–private partnerships in the wake of urban renewal efforts also reflects this blurring of sectoral boundaries (Squires 1989). The growing number of planners working in the private sector further upsets the traditional professional role that planners play in the battles between public and private interests. Public-sector planners borrow tools developed in the private sector, such as strategic planning. The emergence of autonomous public authorities to manage marine ports, airports, and other infrastructures has created hybrid organizations that act like both a public agency and a private firm (Doig 1987; Walsh 1978). In addition, the growing non-profit or "third sector" demonstrates the inadequacies of viewing the world in a purely dichotomous framework of the government versus the market. Arguably more troublesome than this public–private blur, however, is the apparent appropriation of the public domain by the logic of privatization. Privatization of traditionally public services raises the question of whether only the public sector can serve the public interest or whether democratic citizenship – and all its rights and responsibilities – is being reduced to consumerism and consumer freedom.

3 "Rules of the game": What values are incorporated within planning? What ethical dilemmas do planners face?

This growing complexity and uncertainty in the planner's stance between the public and private sectors also renders problematic traditional ethical assumptions. As planners increasingly work in the private and quasi-private sectors, do they no longer owe loyalty to the public at large? As William Lucy outlines in this volume (chapter 22), planners are torn between serving employers, fellow planners, and the public (see also Marcuse 1976). In this terrain of contested loyalties, what remains of the once accepted cornerstone of planning: serving the public interest?

This dilemma is further complicated by the fact that planning's functions extend beyond merely technical activities to address larger social, economic, and environmental challenges. Within society at large the values of democracy, equality, and efficiency often clash. These conflicts are reflected in the choices that planners must make as they try to reconcile the goals of economic development, social justice, and environmental protection. Despite the long-term promises of sustainable development, this triad of goals has created deep-seated tensions not only between planners and the outside world but also within planning itself (Campbell, chapter 24, this volume).

Another ethical dimension arises from the difficulties surrounding the planner's role as expert. Questions concerning the proper balance between expertise and citizen input arise in issues like the siting of highways and waste disposal facilities, when particular social groups must bear the costs. They are played out, as Frank Fischer discusses (chapter 23, this volume), when experts seek to quantify risk, placing a monetary value on human life. They show up, as Martin Wachs argues, in the assumptions used by model builders when they forecast the future impacts of public facilities (Wachs 1982). Critics of those relying on expertise to justify policy doubt the legitimacy of ostensibly scientific methods, arguing that technical language disguises the values being interjected and obscures who wins and who loses. Nevertheless, the development of technical forecasting methods is necessary if planners are to fulfill their responsibility of designing policies for the long term.

4   The constraints on planning power – how can planning be effective within a mixed economy?

It is not enough to determine that planners should routinely intervene in the private market; that determination in itself raises the question of authority and power. Unlike some other professionals, planners do not have a monopoly on power or expertise over their object of work. Planners operate within the constraints of the capitalist political economy, and their urban visions compete with those of developers, consumers, and other more powerful groups. When they call for a type of development to occur, they cannot command the resources to make it happen. Instead, they must rely on either private investment or a commitment from political leaders. They also work within the constraints of democracy and of the governmental bureaucracy (Foglesong, chapter 5, this volume). Their goals, however, often have low priority within the overall political agenda. Thus, despite the planning ideal of a holistic, proactive vision, planners are frequently restricted to playing frustratingly reactive, regulatory roles.

The most powerful planners are those who can marshal the resources to effect change and get projects built (Doig 1987; Walsh 1978). They bend the role of the planner and alter the traditional separation between the public and private sectors. The resulting public–private partnerships make the planner more activist (Squires 1989); yet they also strain the traditional identity of the public planner and make many idealistic planners squirm. How else can one explain the uncomfortable mixture of disgust and envy that a lot of planners felt towards Robert Moses, who as the head of various New York City agencies had far more projects built than did all the traditional city planners he disparaged (Caro 1974)?

5 Style of planning: what do planners do?

The justification for planning is often comprehensiveness. Yet the ideal of comprehensiveness has suffered serious criticism. Standard accounts of planning theories explained comprehensive planning as the attempt to coordinate the multiple development and regulatory initiatives undertaken in a region or city. Success depended on a high level of knowledge and the technological capability to use it. It was ostensibly a worthy attempt, but failed on two accounts. First, it required a level of knowledge, analysis, and organizational coordination that was impossibly complex; critics questioned whether planners had any special capacity to coordinate all the specialists (Altshuler 1965). This critique led to the endorsement of incremental planning (Lindblom, chapter 10, this volume). Second, it presumed a common public interest, but in effect gave voice only to powerful interests and ignored the needs of the poor and the weak. This critique led to the call for advocacy planning (Davidoff, chapter 11, this volume).

The assault on comprehensive planning continued into the 1970s and 1980s. Strategic planning rejected comprehensive planning's impossibly general goals, and instead embraced the "lean and mean" strategies from the business and military sectors (Kaufman and Jacobs 1987; Swanstrom 1987). By contrast, equity planning emerged as a less combative form of advocacy planning that allowed planners to serve the interests of the poor from within the system (Krumholz, chapter 12, this volume; Krumholz 1996).

There are problems with writing a tidy obituary for comprehensive planning, however. First, many planners continue to use the comprehensive approach as the model of their work, both because they continue to believe in it, and because they dislike the alternatives (Dalton 1986). The primary task for many planners continues to be the writing and revising of comprehensive plans for their communities.

If the death notice of comprehensive planning may thus be premature, it may also misunderstand the theory's actual rise and fall. Planning theorists at times presume a dominance of comprehensive rational planning during the early postwar years that may never have actually existed. In retelling the history of planning, planners arguably are guilty of after-the-fact revisionism in their creation of a straw man out of comprehensive planning. Commentators on the comprehensive model remember a once united field that never truly existed; rather, what did exist was a young, diverse field seeking to define itself during a turbulent era. Even in the early postwar days of urban renewal and public housing construction, there were voices of skepticism and dissent in the planning community, long before Jane Jacobs's 1961 diatribe against modernist planning from her Greenwich Village stoop (chapter 2, this volume).

This is not to deny the importance of the comprehensive planning debate; but it should be seen as only one of several important debates that shaped the identity of the young field of planning theory. Unfortunately, much of this debate over comprehensiveness took place in a theoretical vacuum. Planners often argued about the proper role of planning based simply on the merits of the concepts themselves (e.g. large- versus small-scale; top-down versus bottom-up), while ignoring the vaster political and economic forces that shaped and constrained planning. The articulation and eventual challenge to comprehensive planning was thus part of a broader expansion of planning theory beyond land-use planning into social and economic policy.

The Continuing Evolution of Planning Theory

This historical revisionism of comprehensive planning – whether seen as either a defining moment in planning theory or as a mythic straw man – reflects a new period of critical reexamination. Planning theorists not only debate the relative merits of competing approaches to planning, but also question the selection of stories which the field uses to define itself. Challenges to the accepted standard list of iconic planners (including Howard, Burnham, Mumford, Moses, and Le Corbusier) and their projects (Garden Cities, City Beautiful, regionalism, and so forth) have opened up planning history to new voices and new iconic places; we are in the midst of a rethinking of the legitimate boundaries of planning history

Over a generation, the most significant advances in planning theory are a changing understanding of power (Brindley et al. and Flyvbjerg, chapters 16 and 17, this volume), of communicative action and the planner's role in mediating interactions among stakeholders (Healey, Baum, and Fischer, chapters 13, 15, and 23, this volume), of modernization/modernism (Beauregard and Scott, chapters 6 and 7, this volume), and of the complex links between diversity, equity, and community (Young, Thomas, and Sandercock, chapters 18, 19, and 21, this volume).

Even since the publication of the first edition of this reader (in 1996), the field has continued to shift. Postmodernism remains an important theme for planning theory, although some of the initial excitement has waned. Its enduring power has been to provide the idea of a historical break with the past, allowing the planning field to distance itself from the more unsavory aspects of twentieth-century planning by deeming them as by-products of modernism: disruptive urban renewal, dysfunctional high-rise public housing, the rejection of rich historical forms of reference, and an excessive zeal towards a universal norm of planning and design at the expense of local traditions and conditions. This engagement with the broader ideas of postmodernism can be seen in the assumption that we are entering a new historical period of post-industrialism, globalization, post-Fordism, and the "New Economy."

Communicative planning – the mediation of community discourse rather than the creation of a technically rational plan – has arguably also entered a new phase: it is simultaneously more accepted, differentiated, and criticized. Perhaps some of its early thunder is gone; despite the best efforts of its advocates, communicative action has not gained mass appeal as a totalizing new planning paradigm. Paradoxically, we have both internalized it as an accepted role for planning – "Haven't planners *always* communicated?" – but more clearly see its limitations as just one of many roles for planners. And despite the best intentions of communicative planners to construct beautiful narratives of a community's envisioned future from the "stories" of local residents, the graphs and financial reports from the rational, technocratic engineers, accountants, and developers still typically trump community vision.

A separate movement, called the "New Urbanism," promotes a revitalized vision of high-density, transit-and pedestrian-friendly neighborhoods as an antidote to faceless suburban sprawl. This movement has arguably influenced planning practice more than communicative theory, because of its more direct engagement with land use, design, real estate development, and environmentalism.[2] Indeed, the revitalized interest in innovative land-use planning (once seen as a stalwart but somewhat quiescent area of planning) can in part be traced to a more sophisticated environmentalism, vocal growth-containment movements, regional planning, and other elements of the new urbanism.

Like communicative action, New Urbanism has both proponents of its paradigm-shifting potential and vocal critics. Often the debate is a battle between two extreme camps: those who would run a narrow fence around New Urbanism and then proceed to criticize it for being too narrow, and those who would claim that *any* innovation in urban development (having to do with in-fill, preservation, transit orientation, neighborhood design, or ecology) is a victory for New Urbanism. Some planning theorists may have initially dismissed the movement as preoccupied with architectural design, possessing both a Disney-like unreality and a narrow, rose-colored nostalgia for small-town America. It also evokes an image of communitarianism that some find claustrophobic and intolerant (see, for example, Young, chapter 18, this volume). However, if New Urbanism continues to head in the direction of being a big, tolerant movement that embraces ideas of regionalism, sustainable development, affordable housing, environmental justice, communitarianism, and anti-sprawl – and thus builds alliances with both environmental and community and social justice groups – then it could emerge as a flexible, dynamic planning idea of substance and endurance.

If we assume that planning theory will evolve in response to changes in planning practice, the development of cities, and the rise of social movements, then we can speculate on future directions for planning theory. Planners urgently need a larger conceptual world view to understand the ramifications of the digital revolution of the Internet, massive data storage and retrieval, and geographic information systems (GIS). Theories of communicative action provide but an initial entrée to the shift from old school statistics and mechanistic optimization modeling to multimedia, web-based, interactive, participatory visualization modeling built upon theories of complex systems. If communicative action theory envisions planners as the facilitators of community self-definition, then in the age of the Internet this places planners not just at evening planning board meetings, but also as managers of local network-based interest groups, as webmasters, and as virtual chat-room monitors.

Theories of planning methodologies, once built upon the assumption of scarce, incomplete data, need to be revised to deal with the coming flood of data. The real-time tracking of flows in time–space coordinates (e.g. microchips and bar codes creating a world of geo-coded products, resources, and even people) creates new opportunities for planners to understand dynamic spatial processes, such as time–space-based user fees, development impact fees, and GIS-based performance zoning. But this data revolution will also thrust the field into the tricky ethical world of data privacy issues.

These prospects raise new dilemmas for planning: the field has traditionally focused on the design and management of physical, land-based networks (roads, sidewalks, rail, shipping routes) and nodes (zoning of residential, commercial, industrial, and public space). Does the rise of non-place-specific virtual networks threaten the traditional foundation of planning by bypassing the old planning infrastructure? If planning is traditionally tied to place, how might planning transform itself to remain relevant within the "space of flows" (Castells 2000)? Should planners claim "cyberspace" as a legitimate terrain for their tools of spatial analysis, coordination, and zoning?

Increasing globalization will force planning theory to incorporate different types of cities into what had been Euro-American models of urbanization: we will pay more attention to Shanghai, Tokyo, Mexico City, Mumbai, etc. in our theories. But this will likely come with a growing tension between the preservation of local communities and the acceleration of global networks, and will sharpen the divide between the priorities of place-based versus flow-based planning. In a paradoxical world that is simultaneously fragmenting and globalizing, local space is both so segregated, yet so highly permeable by the outside world, that traditional notions of an autonomous, self-determined local community do not easily endure. Nevertheless, we may cling to these notions for both good normative and empirical reasons (see, for example, Clavel and Kleniewski 1990; Shuman 1998). How might planning theory help us understand this hybrid global–local space?

All these examples suggest that the interaction between theory, urban change, and planning practice is symbiotic and often asynchronous. We would like to think that planning theory acts primarily as a kind of intellectual vanguard, pushing the professional field to rethink its outdated practices and the assumptions that underlie them. However, much of planning theory is instead an attempt to bring our thinking of planning up to date and in line with either urban phenomena (cyberspace, globalization, etc.) or social theories from other fields (such as postmodernism or critical theory). In addition, the theory–practice time lag may run the other way round: the task of planning theory is often to catch up with planning practice itself, codifying and restating approaches to planning that practitioners have long since used (such as disjointed incrementalism or dispute mediation). Planning theory can therefore alternately be a running commentary, parallel and at arm's length to the profession; a prescriptive avant-garde; or instead a trailing, reflective echo of planning practice.

If there is a persistent gap between grandiose theorizing and the modest accomplishments of the practicing planner, it may also be overly simplistic to attribute it to the distance between theory and practice. It may instead reflect the discrepancy between what the theorist rightfully envisions as the ideal social-spatial arrangement of the world (i.e. the good, just city) and the more modest contributions that planners can make towards this ideal (given the political-economic constraints posed on the profession). Planning scholars frequently conflate the two, imagining an ideal urban society and then making all its characteristics the goals of the planning agenda. But should the discipline be faulted for its lofty (and overreaching) ambitions?

The Enduring Question of the Public Interest

A generation ago, the engaging debates of planning theory involved the conflicts between comprehensive versus incremental planning, objectivity versus advocacy, centralization versus decentralization, top-down versus bottom-up leadership, and planning for people versus planning for place. These debates from the adolescence of planning theory now seem a bit tired and bypassed. It is not that they have been conclusively resolved, but rather that the field is so broadly scattered that each pole lives on. This current eclecticism reflects the fragmentation of planning itself. Nevertheless, these debates were arguably necessary for the intellectual development of the field, and the young planning theorist still needs to read and understand these controversies.

What has endured is the persistent question of the public interest. Planning continues to face the central controversy of whether there is indeed a single public interest and of whether planners recognize and serve it. Incremental planners claimed that the excessive complexity of the comprehensive public interest prevented the planner from serving it directly, while advocate planners argued that what was portrayed as the public interest in fact represented merely the interests of the privileged. More recently, postmodernists have challenged the universal master narrative that gives voice to the public interest, seeing instead a heterogeneous public with many voices and interests. Finally, the persistence of fundamentalist thinking and community identity based on religious, rather than secular, municipal values undermines the ability to find a consensual public interest (Baum, Chapter 15, this volume).

Nevertheless, planners have not abandoned the idea of serving the public interest, and rightly so. Postmodernists provided planning with a needed break from its preoccupation with a monolithic "public" (epitomized by Le Corbusier's and Robert Moses' love of the public but disdain for people); yet a rejection of Enlightenment rationality, shared values, and generally applicable standards leaves the planner without adequate methods for serving a fragmented population. Some have touted strategic planning and other borrowed private-sector approaches as the practical path for planning; but these approaches neglect the "public" in the public interest. A belief in the public interest is the foundation for a set of values that planners hold dear: equal protection and equal opportunity, public space, and a sense of civic community and social responsibility. The challenge is to reconcile these elements of a common public interest with the diversity (postmodern and otherwise) that comes from many communities living side by side. David Harvey looked to generally held ideas of social justice and rationality as a bridge to overcome this dilemma (Harvey 2001); similarly, Susan Fainstein (chapter 9, this volume) presents the model of the just city. The recent interest in communicative action – planners as communicators rather than as autonomous, systematic thinkers – also reflects an effort to renew the focus of planning theory on the public interest (Healey, chapter 13, this volume; Forester 1989; Innes 1998). Within this approach planners accept the multiplicity of interests, combined with an enduring common interest in finding viable, politically legitimate solutions. Planners serve the public interest by negotiating a kind of multicultural, technically informed pluralism.

In the end, the question of the public interest is the leitmotiv that holds together the defining debates of planning theory. The central task of planners is serving the public interest in cities, suburbs, and the countryside. Questions of when, why, and how planners should intervene – and the constraints they face in the process – all lead back to defining and serving the public interest, even while it is not static or fixed. The restructured urban economy, the shifting boundaries between the public and private sectors, and the changing tools and available resources constantly force planners to rethink the public interest. Planners have only begun to confront the challenge of defining the boundaries between public and private interests in cyberspace. This constant rethinking is the task of planning theory.

The Readings

We have selected the readings for this volume to represent what we think are the central issues in planning theory. In particular, they address the challenge and dilemma of planning as defined at the beginning of this introduction: *What role can planning play in developing the good city and region within the constraints of a capitalist political economy and a democratic political system?* We approach this question primarily through texts that address specific theoretical issues. However, we have also included several case studies that provide vivid and concrete illustrations of this question.

Planning theory is a relatively young field; yet one can already speak of "classic readings." Our guide has been to choose readings – both old and new – that still speak directly to contemporary issues. Most have been written in the past ten years, though some articles from the 1960s are still the best articulation of specific debates. Most draw upon experiences in the United States and the United Kingdom, though hopefully their relevance extends far beyond these boundaries.

This edition represents a substantial revision of the first edition of *Readings in Planning Theory* (1996). Over half the selections in this edition are new, reflecting more recent or more accessible statements of planning theories, or newly emerging themes. We have retained those readings from the first edition that students and teachers of planning theory continue to find useful and exciting.

We have organized the readings into six sections, each prefaced with a short introduction to the main themes. We begin with the foundations of modern planning, including both traditional and critical views of planning history. We then turn to two interrelated questions: *What is the justification for planning intervention?* and *How should planners intervene?* Addressing the political and economic justifications for planning, we have selected readings that examine the neoclassical, institutional, and Marxist arguments. They place planners in the larger context of the relationship between the private market and government (both local and national). Regarding the style of planning, the readings examine dominant planning approaches: comprehensive, incremental, advocacy, equity, and communicative planning. The case studies presented in the fourth section illustrate these opportunities for, and constraints on, planners in the United States and Europe.

Gender and racial politics have emerged as powerful, transformative forces in urban planning. The readings in the fifth section explore these themes of difference, discrimination, and inequality. These theories challenge planning to be more inclusive, to accept the city as home to divergent populations with radically different experiences and needs, to see how the existing city fabric perpetuates antiquated social and gender relations, and to pursue social justice more aggressively.

We conclude with three readings on planning ethics, professionalism, communication, and the environment. Each addresses a shortcoming of the traditional, rational-comprehensive model of planning, whether it is its simplistic conception of the public interest, its lack of subtlety about ethical conflicts, its presumption of privileged expert knowledge, or its inability to handle the politically charged issue of environmental sustainability. The emerging stance for planners involves a greater savvy about political conflicts, a proactive role in the communication of choices and risks, and an understanding of complex social and ecological systems.

NOTES

1 An excerpt from Foglesong's book is included in this volume (chapter 5), while an excerpt from Fishman's is included in the companion volume to this one (Fainstein and Campbell 2001).
2 Readings on the New Urbanism are contained in the companion volume to this one (Fainstein and Campbell 2001).

REFERENCES

Altshuler, Alan. 1965. The Goals of Comprehensive Planning. *Journal of the American Institute of Planning*, 31: 186–94.

Banfield, Edward C. 1968. Why Government Cannot Solve the Urban Problem. *Daedalus*, 97(4) (Fall): 1241–81.

Caro, Robert. 1974. *The Power Broker: Robert Moses and the Fall of New York*. New York: Alfred Knopf.

Castells, Manuel. 2000. *The Rise of the Network Society*, rev. edn. Oxford: Blackwell.

Clavel, Pierre, and Nancy Kleniewski. 1990. Space for Progressive Local Policy: Examples from the United States and the United Kingdom. In John R. Logan and Todd Swanstrom, eds, *Beyond the City Limits*, Philadelphia: Temple University Press, pp. 199–234.

Cronon, William. 1991. *Nature's Metropolis: Chicago and the Great West*, 1st edn. New York: W. W. Norton.

Dahrendorf, Ralf. 1968. *Essays in the Theory of Society*. Stanford, CA: Stanford University Press.

Dalton, Linda. 1986. Why the Rational Paradigm Persists: The Resistance of Professional Education and Practice to Alternative Forms of Planning. *Journal of Planning Education and Research*, 5(3): 147–53.

Doig, Jameson. 1987. Coalition Building by a Regional Agency: Austin Tobin and the Port of New York Authority. In Clarence Stone and Heywood Sanders, eds, *The Politics of Urban Development, Readings in Planning Theory*, ed. Lawrence: University Press of Kansas, pp. 73–104.

Fainstein, Susan S., and Scott Campbell (eds). 2001. *Readings in Urban Theory*, 2nd edn. Cambridge, MA: Blackwell.

Faludi, Andreas (ed.). 1973. *A Reader in Planning Theory*. New York: Pergamon Press.

Fishman, Robert. 1987. *Bourgeois Utopias: The Rise and Fall of Suburbia*. New York: Basic Books.

Foglesong, Richard E. 1986. *Planning the Capitalist City*. Princeton: Princeton University Press.

Forester, John. 1989. *Planning in the Face of Power*. Berkeley: University of California Press.

Frieden, Bernard, and Lynn Sagalyn. 1989. *Downtown Inc. How America Rebuilds Cities*. Cambridge, MA: MIT Press.

Friedman, Milton. 1962. *Capitalism and Freedom*. Chicago: University of Chicago Press.

Galbraith, John K. 1971. *The New Industrial State*. New York: New American Library.

Hall, Peter. 1996. *Cities of Tomorrow: An Intellectual History of Urban Planning and Design in the Twentieth Century*, updated edn. Oxford: Blackwell.

Harvey, David. 1985. On Planning the Ideology of Planning. In *The Urbanization of Capital*, Baltimore: Johns Hopkins University Press, pp. 165–84.

Harvey, David. 2001. Social Justice, Postmodernism and the City. In *Readings in Urban Theory*, ed. S. S. Fainstein and S. Campbell, 2nd edn, Cambridge, MA: Blackwell.

Hayek, Friedrich. 1944. *The Road to Serfdom*. London: Routledge.

Hoffman, Lily. 1989. *The Politics of Knowledge: Activist Movements in Medicine and Planning*. Albany: SUNY Press.

Howard, Ebenezer, and Frederic James Osborn. 1945 [1898]. *Garden Cities of Tomorrow*. London: Faber & Faber.

Innes, Judith E. 1998. Information in Communicative Planning. *Journal of the American Planning Association*, 64 (Winter): 52–63.

Kaufman, Jerome L., and Harvey M. Jacobs. 1987. A Public Planning Perspective on Strategic Planning. *Journal of the American Planning Association*, 53: 23–33.

Krueckeberg, Donald A. (ed.). 1983. The Culture of Planning. In *Introduction to Planning History in the United States*, ed. D. A. Krueckeberg, New Brunswick, NJ: Center for Urban Policy Research, pp. 1–12.

Krumholz, Norman. 1982. A Retrospective View of Equity Planning: Cleveland, 1969–1979. *Journal of the American Planning Association*, 48 (Spring): 163–74.

Lowi, Theodore J. 1969. *The End of Liberalism: Ideology, Policy, and the Crisis of Public Authority*. New York: Norton.

Marcuse, Peter. 1976. Professional Ethics and Beyond: Values in Planning. *Journal of the American Institute of Planning*, 42 (3): 264–74.

Moore, Terry. 1978. Why Allow Planners to Do What They Do?: A Justification from Economic Theory. *Journal of the American Institute of Planning*, 44 (4): 387–98.

Robinson, Charles Mulford. 1901. *The Improvement of Towns and Cities; or the Practical Basic of Civic Aesthetics*. New York: G. P. Putnam.

Shuman, Michael. 1998. *Going Local: Creating Self-Reliant Communities in a Global Age*. New York: Free Press.

Squires, Gregory D. (ed.). 1989. *Unequal Partnerships: The Political Economy of Urban Redevelopment in Postwar America*. New Brunswick, NJ: Rutgers University Press.

Swanstrom, Todd. 1987. The Limits of Strategic Planning for Cities. *Journal of Urban Affairs*, 9 (2): 139–57.

Wachs, Martin. 1982. Ethical Dilemmas in Forecasting Public Policy. *Public Administration Review*, 29 (Nov./Dec.): 562–7.

Walsh, Annmarie Hauck. 1978. *The Public's Business: The Politics and Practices of Government Corporations*. Cambridge, MA: MIT Press.

Warner, Sam Bass. 1987. *The Private City: Philadelphia in Three Periods of its Growth*, 2nd edn. Philadelphia: University of Pennsylvania Press.

Part I

Foundations of Twentieth-Century Planning Theory

Introduction

The readings in this first section examine the foundations of modern planning. They offer both traditional and critical views of planning history. We begin with Robert Fishman's examination of three foundational figures in planning history: Ebenezer Howard, Frank Lloyd Wright, and Le Corbusier. Fishman goes beyond the standard account of the three to examine the social history behind their distinctive utopias. Although all three were reacting to the grimy reality of industrial cities, each took a fundamentally different path towards planning their ideal urban society. Corbusier's Radiant City was mass-scaled, dense, vertical, hierarchical – the social extension of modern architecture. Wright went to the other extreme: his Broadacre City was a mixture of Jeffersonian agrarian individualism and prairie suburbanism, linked by superhighways. Howard's Garden Cities were scaled somewhere in between: self-contained villages of 35,000 residents held together by a communal cooperative spirit. The three utopias symbolize fundamental choices in the scale of human settlements: Corbusier's mass *Gesellschaft*, Howard's village-like *Gemeinschaft*, or Wright's American individualism. (Dolores Hayden will invoke this settlement triad later in this volume, in chapter 20.)

To complete the traditional foundation of city planning, one needs to include also the City Beautiful Movement at the turn of the previous century. With its origins in civic improvement, the Columbian Exposition of 1893 in Chicago, and Daniel Burnham's 1909 Chicago Plan, the City Beautiful Movement was an important catalyst for the rise of planning commissions, public–private partnerships, and civic aesthetic awareness. Yet the City Beautiful Movement also became an easy target of criticism: it was elitist if not totalitarian, advocating the beautification of the city surface while ignoring the poverty and inequality inherent in the political-economic structure of the city. (For further reading on the movement, see Foglesong 1986; Wilson 1989, 1996.)

Though these various foundations of intellectual planning history might represent distinctly different choices in imagining the ideal city, Jane Jacobs argues that they all suffer from a similar, dangerous misconception of how real cities actually operate. She summarily discredits these classic planning prototypes together under the label of the "Radiant Garden City Beautiful." She sees in Howard, Burnham, and Le Corbusier a shared uneasiness with actual cities, each of them seeking to replace the rich complexity of a real metropolis with the abstract logic of an idealized planned city. We include here the introductory chapter to her landmark 1961 critique of postwar American urban renewal, *The Death and Life of Great American Cities*. This book arguably makes unfortunate oversimplifications about the evils of planning, while both neglecting the destructive role of the private sector in urban renewal and romanticizing the capabilities of small, competitive, neighborhood businesses. Yet the book remains one of the most compelling and well-written arguments for encouraging diversity and innovation in big, dense, messy cities. It also signals the long transition of planning theory from an early faith in science and comprehensiveness to a more self-critical, incremental approach. It thereby anticipates a later interest in complexity. Jacobs demonstrates that the simple process of daily, intimate observation can lead to an understanding of the complexity of cities. (By contrast, many of the elaborate, mathematically minded urban models built by regional scientists and others led to a frustratingly simplistic view of cities.)

We conclude this section with a brief essay by John Friedmann, an influential and provocative voice in planning theory who taught for many years at UCLA. Friedmann resolutely pronounces the end of the old Euclidian world, and thus the collapse of the engineering mode of planning based on advanced decision making, blueprints, and scientific abstraction. In its place Friedmann argues for planning that links knowledge to action in the public domain. This non-Euclidian planning has five characteristics: it should be normative (not efficiency-based), innovative (not simply allocative), political (not neutral), transactive (not disempowering), and based on social learning (not closed, document-oriented activity). He offers a decentered view of planning, emphasizing the spaces of everyday life, and thus the local and regional scales, rather than the national or transnational. Friedmann is perhaps using a straw-man image of the old planning model to elevate the new model, and not all of it may in fact be new; but he does offer a compact statement of principles calling on planners to be engaged, entrepreneurial, left of center, locally committed, and transactive.

REFERENCES

Foglesong, Richard E. 1986. *Planning the Capitalist City*. Princeton: Princeton University Press.

Wilson, William H. 1989. *The City Beautiful Movement*. Baltimore and London: Johns Hopkins University Press.

Wilson, William H. 1996. The Glory, Destruction, and Meaning of the City Beautiful Movement. In *Readings in Planning Theory*, ed. S. Campbell and S. S. Fainstein, Cambridge, MA, and Oxford: Blackwell.

1

Urban Utopias: Ebenezer Howard, Frank Lloyd Wright, and Le Corbusier

Robert Fishman

Introduction

What is the ideal city for the twentieth century, the city that best expresses the power and beauty of modern technology and the most enlightened ideas of social justice? Between 1890 and 1930 three planners, Ebenezer Howard, Frank Lloyd Wright, and Le Corbusier, tried to answer that question.[1] Each began his work alone, devoting long hours to preparing literally hundreds of models and drawings specifying every aspect of the new city, from its general ground plan to the layout of the typical living room. There were detailed plans for factories, office buildings, schools, parks, transportation systems – all innovative designs in themselves and all integrated into a revolutionary restructuring of urban form. The economic and political organization of the city, which could not be easily shown in drawings, was worked out in the voluminous writings that each planner appended to his designs. Finally, each man devoted himself to passionate and unremitting efforts to make his ideal city a reality.

Many people dream of a better world; Howard, Wright, and Le Corbusier each went a step further and planned one. Their social consciences took this rare and remarkable step because they believed that, more than any other goal, their societies needed new kinds of cities. They were deeply fearful of the consequences for civilization if the old cities, with all the social conflicts and miseries they embodied, were allowed to persist. They were also inspired by the prospect that a radical reconstruction of the cities would solve not only the urban crisis of their time but the social crisis as well. The very completeness of their ideal cities expressed their convictions that the moment had come for comprehensive programs, and for a total rethinking of the principles of urban planning. They rejected the possibility of

Excerpts from Robert Fishman, *Urban Utopias in the Twentieth Century: Ebenezer Howard, Frank Lloyd Wright, and Le Corbusier*, pp. 3–20, 23–51, 64–75, 226–34. Copyright © 1977 by Basic Books, Inc. Reprinted by permission of Basic Books, a division of HarperCollins Publishers, Inc.

gradual improvement. They did not seek the amelioration of the old cities, but a wholly transformed urban environment.

This transformation meant the extensive rebuilding and even partial abandonment of the cities of their time. Howard, Wright, and Le Corbusier did not shrink from this prospect; they welcomed it. As Howard put it, the old cities had "done their work." They were the best that the old economic and social order could have been expected to produce, but they had to be superseded if mankind were to attain a higher level of civilization. The three ideal cities were put forward to establish the basic theoretical framework for this radical reconstruction. They were the manifestoes for an urban revolution.

These ideal cities are perhaps the most ambitious and complex statements of the belief that reforming the physical environment can revolutionize the total life of a society. Howard, Wright, and Le Corbusier saw design as an active force, distributing the benefits of the Machine Age to all and directing the community onto the paths of social harmony. Yet they never subscribed to the narrow simplicities of the "doctrine of salvation by bricks alone" – the idea that physical facilities could *by themselves* solve social problems. To be sure, they believed – and who can doubt this? – that the values of family life could be better maintained in a house or apartment that gave each member the light and air and room he needed, rather than in the cramped and fetid slums that were still the fate of too many families. They thought that social solidarity would be better promoted in cities that brought people together, rather than in those whose layout segregated the inhabitants by race or class.

At the same time the three planners understood that these and other well-intended designs would be worse than useless if their benevolent humanitarianism merely covered up basic inequalities in the social system. The most magnificent and innovative housing project would fail if its inhabitants were too poor and oppressed to lead decent lives. There was little point in constructing new centers of community life if the economics of exploitation and class conflict kept the citizens as divided as they had been in their old environment. Good planning was indeed efficacious in creating social harmony, but only if it embodied a genuine rationality and justice in the structure of society. It was impossible in a society still immured in what Le Corbusier called "the Age of Greed." The three planners realized that they had to join their programs of urban reconstruction with programs of political and economic reconstruction. They concluded (to paraphrase one of Marx's famous *Theses on Feuerbach*) that designers had hitherto merely *ornamented* the world in various ways; the point was to *change* it.

The ideal cities were therefore accompanied by detailed programs for radical changes in the distribution of wealth and power, changes that Howard, Wright, and Le Corbusier regarded as the necessary complements to their revolutions in design. The planners also played prominent roles in the movements that shared their aims. Howard was an ardent cooperative socialist who utilized planning as part of his search for the cooperative commonwealth; Wright, a Jeffersonian democrat and an admirer of Henry George, was a spokesman for the American decentrist movement; and Le Corbusier had many of his most famous designs published for the first time in the pages of the revolutionary syndicalist journals he edited. All three brought a revolutionary fervor to the practice of urban design.

And, while the old order endured, Howard, Wright, and Le Corbusier refused to adapt themselves to what planning commissions, bankers, politicians, and all the other authorities of their time believed to be desirable and attainable. They consistently rejected the idea that a planner's imagination must work within the system. Instead, they regarded the physical structure of the cities in which they lived, and the economic structure of the society in which they worked, as temporary aberrations that mankind would soon overcome. The three planners looked beyond their own troubled time to a new age each believed was imminent, a new age each labored to define and to build.

Their concerns thus ranged widely over architecture, urbanism, economics, and politics, but their thinking found a focus and an adequate means of expression only in their plans for ideal cities. The cities were never conceived of as blueprints for any actual project. They were "ideal types" of cities for the future, elaborate models rigorously designed to illustrate the general principles that each man advocated. They were convenient and attractive intellectual tools that enabled each planner to bring together his many innovations in design, and to show them as part of a coherent whole, a total redefinition of the idea of the city. The setting of these ideal cities was never any actual location, but an empty, abstract plane where no contingencies existed. The time was the present, not any calender day or year, but that revolutionary "here and now" when the hopes of the present are finally realized.

These hopes, moreover, were both architectural and social. In the three ideal cities, the transformation of the physical environment is the outward sign of an inner transformation in the social structure. Howard, Wright, and Le Corbusier used their ideal cities to depict a world in which their political and economic goals had already been achieved. Each planner wanted to show that the urban designs he advocated were not only rational and beautiful in themselves but that they embodied the social goals he believed in. In the context of the ideal city each proposal for new housing, new factories, and other structures could be seen to further the broader aims. And in general, the ideal cities enabled the three planners to show modern design in what they believed was its true context – as an integral part of a culture from which poverty and exploitation had disappeared. These cities, therefore, were complete alternative societies, intended as a revolution in politics and economics as well as in architecture. They were utopian visions of a total environment in which man would live in peace with his fellow man and in harmony with nature. They were social thought in three dimensions.

As theorists of urbanism, Howard, Wright, and Le Corbusier attempted to define the ideal form of any industrial society. They shared a common assumption that this form could be both defined and attained, but each viewed the ideal through the perspective of his own social theory, his own national tradition, and his own personality. Their plans, when compared, disagree profoundly, and the divergences are often just as significant as the agreements. They offer us not a single blueprint for the future but three sets of choices – the great metropolis, moderate decentralization, or extreme decentralization – each with its corresponding political and social implications. Like the classical political triad of monarchy – aristocracy – democracy, the three ideal cities represent a vocabulary of basic forms that can be used to define the whole range of choices available to the planner.

Seventeen years older than Wright and thirty-seven years older than Le Corbusier, Ebenezer Howard started first. His life resembles a story by Horatio Alger, except that Alger never conceived a hero at once so ambitious and so self-effacing. He began his career as a stenographer and ended as the elder statesman of a worldwide planning movement, yet he remained throughout his life the embodiment of the "little man." He was wholly without pretension, an earnest man with a round, bald head, spectacles, and a bushy mustache, unselfconscious in his baggy pants and worn jackets, beloved by neighbors and children.

Yet Howard, like the inventors, enlighteners, self-taught theorists, and self-proclaimed prophets of the "age of improvement" in which he lived, was one of those little men with munificent hopes. His contribution was "the Garden City," a plan for moderate decentralization and cooperative socialism. He wanted to build wholly new cities in the midst of unspoiled countryside on land that would remain the property of the community as a whole. Limited in size to 30,000 inhabitants and surrounded by a perpetual "greenbelt," the Garden City would be compact, efficient, healthful, and beautiful. It would lure people away from swollen cities like London and their dangerous concentrations of wealth and power; at the same time, the countryside would be dotted with hundreds of new communities where small-scale cooperation and direct democracy could flourish.

Howard never met either Frank Lloyd Wright or Le Corbusier. One suspects those two architects of genius and forceful personalities would have considered themselves worlds apart from the modest stenographer. Yet it is notable that Wright and Le Corbusier, like Howard, began their work in urban planning as outsiders, learning their profession not in architectural schools but through apprenticeships with older architects and through their own studies. This self-education was the source of their initiation into both urban design and social theory, and it continued even after Wright and Le Corbusier had become masters of their own profession. Their interests and readings flowed naturally from architecture and design to city planning, economics, politics, and the widest questions of social thought. No one ever told them they could not know everything.

Frank Lloyd Wright stands between Howard and Le Corbusier, at least in age. If Howard's dominant value was cooperation, Wright's was individualism. And no one can deny that he practiced what he preached. With the handsome profile and proud bearing of a frontier patriarch, carefully brushed long hair, well-tailored suits, and flowing cape, Wright was his own special creation. His character was an inextricable mix of arrogance and honesty, vanity and genius. He was autocratic, impolitic, and spendthrift; yet he maintained a magnificent faith in his own ideal of "organic" architecture.

Wright wanted the whole United States to become a nation of individuals. His planned city, which he called "Broadacres," took decentralization beyond the small community (Howard's ideal) to the individual family home. In Broadacres all cities larger than a county seat have disappeared. The center of society has moved to the thousands of homesteads that cover the countryside. Everyone has the right to as much land as he can use, a minimum of an acre per person. Most people work part-time on their farms and part-time in the small factories, offices, or shops that are nestled among the farms. A network of superhighways joins together the scattered elements of society. Wright believed that individuality must be founded on individual ownership. Decentralization would make it possible for everyone to live his chosen lifestyle on his own land.

Le Corbusier, our third planner, could claim with perhaps even more justification than Wright to be his own creation. He was born Charles-Édouard Jeanneret and grew up in the Swiss city of La Chaux-de-Fonds, where he was apprenticed to be a watchcase engraver. He was saved from that dying trade by a sympathetic teacher and by his own determination. Settling in Paris in 1916, he won for himself a place at the head of the avant-garde, first with his painting, then with his brilliant architectural criticism, and most profoundly with his own contributions to architecture. The Swiss artisan Jeanneret no longer existed. He had recreated himself as "Le Corbusier," the Parisian leader of the revolution in modern architecture.

Like other "men from the provinces" who settled in Paris, Le Corbusier identified himself completely with the capital and its values. Wright had hoped that decentralization would preserve the social value he prized most highly – individuality. Le Corbusier placed a corresponding faith in organization, and he foresaw a very different fate for modern society. For him, industrialization meant great cities where large bureaucracies could coordinate production. Whereas Wright thought that existing cities were at least a hundred times too dense, Le Corbusier thought they were not dense enough. He proposed that large tracts in the center of Paris and other major cities be leveled. In place of the old buildings, geometrically arrayed skyscrapers of glass and steel would rise out of parks, gardens, and superhighways. These towers would be the command posts for their region. They would house a technocratic elite of planners, engineers, and intellectuals who would bring beauty and prosperity to the whole society. In his first version of the ideal city, Le Corbusier had the elite live in luxurious high-rise apartments close to the center; their subordinates were relegated to satellite cities at the outskirts. (In a later version everyone was to live in the high-rises.) Le Corbusier called his plan "'the Radiant City,' a city worthy of our time."

The plans of Howard, Wright, and Le Corbusier can be summarized briefly, but the energy and resources necessary to carry them out can hardly be conceived. One might expect that the three ideal cities were destined to remain on paper. Yet, as we shall see, their proposals have already reshaped many of the cities we now live in and may prove to be even more influential in the future.

The plans were effective because they spoke directly to hopes and fears that were widely shared. In particular, they reflected (1) the pervasive fear of and revulsion from the nineteenth-century metropolis; (2) the sense that modern technology had made possible exciting new urban forms; and (3) the great expectation that a revolutionary age of brotherhood and freedom was at hand.

Caught in our own urban crisis, we tend to romanticize the teeming cities of the turn of the century. To many of their inhabitants, however, they were frightening and unnatural phenomena. Their unprecedented size and vast, uprooted populations seemed to suggest the uncontrollable forces unleashed by the Industrial Revolution, and the chaos that occupied the center of modern life. Joseph Conrad eloquently expressed this feeling when he confessed to being haunted by the vision of a "monstrous town more populous than some continents and in its man-made might as if indifferent to heaven's frowns and smiles; a cruel devourer of the world's light. There was room enough there to place any story, depth enough there for any passion, variety enough for any setting, darkness enough to bury five millions of lives."[2]

The monstrous proportions of the big city were relatively new, and thus all the more unsettling. In the first half of the nineteenth century the great European cities had overflowed their historic walls and fortifications. (The American cities, of course, never knew such limits.) Now boundless, the great cities expanded into the surrounding countryside with reckless speed, losing the coherent structure of a healthy organism. London grew in the nineteenth century from 900,000 to 4.5

million inhabitants; Paris in the same period quintupled its population, from 500,000 to 2.5 million residents. Berlin went from 190,000 to over 2 million, New York from 60,000 to 3.4 million. Chicago, a village in 1840, reached 1.7 million by the turn of the century.[3]

This explosive growth, which would have been difficult to accommodate under any circumstances, took place in an era of laissez-faire and feverish speculation. The cities lost the power to control their own growth. Instead, speculation – the blind force of chance and profit – determined urban structure. The cities were segregated by class, their traditional unifying centers first overwhelmed by the increase in population and then abandoned. Toward the end of the nineteenth century the residential balance between urban and rural areas began tipping, in an unprecedented degree, towards the great cities. When Howard, Wright, and Le Corbusier began their work, they saw around them stagnation in the countryside, the depopulation of rural villages, and a crisis in even the old regional centers. First trade and then the most skilled and ambitious young people moved to the metropolis.

Some of these newcomers found the good life they had been seeking in attractive new middle-class neighborhoods, but most were caught in the endless rows of tenements that stretched for miles, interrupted only by factories or railroad yards. Whole families were crowded into one or two airless rooms fronting on narrow streets or filthy courtyards where sunlight never penetrated. In Berlin in 1900, for example, almost 50 percent of all families lived in tenement dwellings with only one small room and an even smaller kitchen. Most of the rest lived in apartments with two tiny rooms and a kitchen, but to pay their rent some of these had to take in boarders who slept in the corners.[4] "Look at the cities of the nineteenth century," wrote Le Corbusier, "at the vast stretches covered with the crust of houses without heart and furrowed with streets without soul. Look, judge. These are the signs of a tragic denaturalization of human labor."[5]

Howard, Wright, and Le Corbusier hated the cities of their time with an overwhelming passion. The metropolis was the counterimage of their ideal cities, the hell that inspired their heavens. They saw precious resources, material and human, squandered in the urban disorder. They were especially fearful that the metropolis would attract and then consume all the healthful forces in society. All three visualized the great city as a cancer, an uncontrolled, malignant growth that was poisoning the modern world. Wright remarked that the plan of a large city resembled "the cross-section of a fibrous tumor"; Howard compared it to an enlarged ulcer. Le Corbusier was fond of picturing Paris as a body in the last stages of a fatal disease – its circulation clogged, its tissues dying of their own noxious wastes.

The three planners, moreover, used their insight into technology to go beyond a merely negative critique of the nineteenth-century metropolis. They showed how modern techniques of construction had created a new mastery of space from which innovative urban forms could be built. The great city, they argued, was no longer modern. Its chaotic concentration was not only inefficient and inhumane, it was unnecessary as well.

Howard, Wright, and Le Corbusier based their ideas on the technological innovations that inspired their age: the express train, the automobile, the telephone and radio, and the skyscraper. Howard realized that the railroad system that had contributed to the growth of the great cities could serve the planned decentralization of society equally well. Wright understood that the personal automobile and an elaborate network of roads could create the conditions for an even more radical decentralization. Le Corbusier looked to technology to promote an opposite trend. He made use of the skyscraper as a kind of vertical street, a "street in the air" as he called it, which would permit intensive urban densities while eliminating the "soulless streets" of the old city.

The three planners' fascination with technology was deep but highly selective. They acknowledged only what served their own social values. Modern technology, they believed, had outstripped the antiquated social order, and the result was chaos and strife. In their ideal cities, however, technology would fulfill its proper role. Howard, Wright, and Le Corbusier believed that industrial society was inherently harmonious. It had an inherent structure, an ideal form, which, when achieved, would banish conflict and bring order and freedom, prosperity and beauty.

This belief went far beyond what could be deduced from the order and power of technology itself. It reflected instead the revolutionary hopes of the nineteenth century. For the three planners, as for so many of their contemporaries, the conflicts of the early Industrial Revolution were only a time of troubles that would lead inevitably to the new era of harmony. History for them was still the history of progress; indeed, as Howard put it, there was a "grand purpose behind nature." These great expectations, so difficult for us to comprehend, pervaded nineteenth-century radical and even liberal thought. There were many prophets of progress who contributed to creating the optimistic climate of opinion in which Howard, Wright, and Le Corbusier formed their own beliefs. Perhaps the most relevant for our purposes were the "utopian socialists" of the early nineteenth century.

These reformers, most notably Charles Fourier, Robert Owen, and Henri de Saint-Simon, drew upon the tradition of Thomas More's *Utopia* and Plato's *Republic* to create detailed depictions of communities untainted by the class struggles of the Industrial Revolution. Unlike More or Plato, however, the utopian socialists looked forward to the immediate realization of their ideal commonwealths. Owen and Fourier produced detailed plans for building utopian communities, plans for social and architectural revolution that anticipated some of the work of Howard, Wright, and Le Corbusier. Two themes dominated utopian socialist planning: first, a desire to overcome the distinction between city and country; and second, a desire to overcome the physical isolation of individuals and families by grouping the community into one large "family" structure. Most of the designs envisioned not ideal cities but ideal communes, small rural establishments for less than two thousand people. Owen put forward a plan for brick quadrangles, which he called "moral quadrilaterals." One side was a model factory, while the other three were taken up with a communal dining room, meeting rooms for recreation, and apartments.[6] His French rival Fourier advanced a far more elaborate design for a communal palace or "phalanstery," which boasted theaters, fashionable promenades, gardens, and gourmet cuisine for everyone.[7]

The utopian socialists were largely forgotten by the time Howard, Wright, and Le Corbusier began their own work, so there was little direct influence from them. As we shall see, however, the search of each planner for a city whose design expressed the ideals of cooperation and social justice led him to revive many of the themes of his utopian socialist (and even earlier) predecessors. But one crucial element sharply separates the three planners' designs from all previous efforts. Even the most fantastic inventions of an Owen or a Fourier could not anticipate the new forms that twentieth-century technology would bring to urban design. The utopian socialists' prophecies of the future had to be expressed in the traditional architectural vocabulary. Fourier, for example, housed his cooperative community in a "phalanstery" that looked like the château of Versailles. Howard, Wright, and Le Corbusier were able to incorporate the scale and pace of the modern world into their designs. They worked at the dawn of the twentieth-century industrial era, but before the coming of twentieth-century disillusionment. Their imaginations were wholly modern; yet the coming era of cooperation was as real to them as it had been for Robert Owen. Their ideal cities thus stand at the intersection of nineteenth-century hopes and twentieth-century technology.

The three ideal cities, therefore, possessed a unique scope and fervor, but this uniqueness had its dangers. It effectively isolated the three planners from almost all the social movements and institutions of their time. In particular, it separated them from the members of two groups who might have been their natural allies, the Marxian socialists and the professional planners. The three ideal cities were at once too technical for the Marxists and too revolutionary for the growing corps of professional planners. The latter was especially intent on discouraging any suggestion that urban planning might serve the cause of social change. These architect-administrators confined themselves to "technical" problems, which meant, in practice, serving the needs of society – as society's rulers defined them. Baron Haussmann, that model of an administrative planner, had ignored and sometimes worsened the plight of the poor in his massive reconstructions of Paris undertaken for Louis Napoleon. But the plight of the poor was not his administrative responsibility. He wanted to unite the isolated sectors of the city and thus quicken the pace of commerce. The wide avenues he cut through Paris were also designed to contribute to the prestige of the regime and, if necessary, to serve as efficient conduits for troops to put down urban disorders. Haussmann's physically impressive and socially reactionary plans inspired worldwide imitation and further increased the gap between urban design and social purpose.[8]

Even the middle-class reformers who specifically dedicated themselves to housing and urban improvement were unable to close this gap. Men like Sir Edwin Chadwick in London bravely faced official indifference and corruption to bring clean air, adequate sanitation, and minimal standards of housing to the industrial cities. Yet these philanthropists were also deeply conservative in their social beliefs. Their rare attempts at innovation almost always assumed the continued poverty of the poor and the privileges of the rich. The model tenements, "cheap cottages," and factory towns that were commissioned in the second half of the nineteenth century were filled with good intentions and sound planning, but they never failed to reflect the inequities of the society that built them. When, for example, the English housing reformer Octavia Hill built her model tenements, she kept accommodations to a minimum so that her indigent tenants could pay rents sufficient not only to cover the complete cost of construction but also to yield her wealthy backers 5 percent annual interest on the money they had advanced her.[9] (This kind of charitable enterprise was known as "philanthropy at 5 percent.") Not surprisingly, designs put forward under these conditions were almost as bleak as the slums they replaced.

Howard, Wright, and Le Corbusier were not interested in making existing cities more profitable or in building "model" tenements to replace the old ones. These views might have been expected to have attracted the sympathetic attention of the Marxian socialists who then controlled the most powerful European movements for social change. Indeed, the *Communist Manifesto* had already recognized the necessity for radical structural change in the industrial cities by putting the "gradual abolition of the distinction between town and country" among its demands. Nevertheless, the socialist movement in the second half of the nineteenth century turned away from what its leaders regarded as unprofitable speculation. In an important series of articles collected under the title *The Housing Question* (1872), Friedrich Engels maintained that urban design was part of the "superstructure" of capitalist society and would necessarily reflect that society's inhumanities, at least until after the socialist revolution had succeeded in transforming the economic base. He concluded that any attempt to envision an ideal city without waiting for the revolution was futile and, indeed, that any attempt to improve the cities significantly was doomed so long as capitalism endured. The working class must forget attractive visions of the future and concentrate on immediate revolution, after which the dictatorship of the proletariat would redistribute housing in the old industrial cities according to need. Then and only then could planners begin to think about a better kind of city.[10]

Howard, Wright, and Le Corbusier could therefore look neither to the socialists nor to the professional planners for support. Initially, at least, they were forced back upon themselves. Instead of developing their ideas through collaboration with others and through practical experience, they worked in isolation on more and more elaborate models of their basic ideas. Their ideal cities thus acquired a wealth of brilliant detail and a single-minded theoretical rigor that made them unique. This isolation was no doubt the necessary precondition for the three planners' highly individual styles of social thought. Certainly their mercurial and independent careers showed a very different pattern from the solid institutional connections of, for example, Ludwig Mies van der Rohe or Walter Gropius. Mies, Gropius, and the other Bauhaus architects were also deeply concerned with the question of design and society; yet none of them produced an ideal city. They had more practical but also more limited projects to occupy them.[11] The ideal city is the genre of the outsider who travels at one leap from complete powerlessness to imaginary omnipotence.

This isolation encouraged Howard, Wright, and Le Corbusier to extend their intellectual and imaginative capacities to their limits, but it also burdened their plans with almost insurmountable problems of both thought and action. They had created plans that were works of art, but the city, in Claude Lévi-Strauss's phrase, is a "*social* work of art." Its densely interwoven structure is the product of thousands of minds and thousands of individual decisions. Its variety derives from the unexpected juxtapositions and the unpredictable interactions. How can a single individual, even a man of genius, hope to comprehend this structure? And how can he devise a new plan with the same satisfying complexities? For his design, whatever its logic and merits, is necessarily his alone. In imposing a single point of view, he inevitably simplifies the parts that make up the whole. Howard, Wright,

and Le Corbusier each filled his ideal city with *his* buildings; *his* sense of proportion and color; and, most profoundly, *his* social values. Would there ever be room
for anyone else? The three ideal cities raise what is perhaps the most perplexing
question for any planner: in attempting to create a new urban order, must he
repress precisely that complexity, diversity, and individuality that are the city's
highest achievements?

The problem of action was equally obvious and pressing. Deprived of outside
support, the three planners came to believe that their ideas were inherently powerful.
As technical solutions to urban problems and embodiments of justice and beauty, the
three ideal cities could properly claim everyone's support. By holding up a ready-
made plan for a new order, Howard, Wright, and Le Corbusier hoped to create their
own movements. This strategy, however, led directly to the classic utopian dilemma.
To appeal to everyone on the basis of universal principles is to appeal to no one in
particular. The more glorious the plans are in theory, the more remote they are from
the concrete issues that actually motivate action. With each elaboration and clarification, the ideal cities move closer to pure fantasy. Can imagination alone change
the world? Or, as Friedrich Engels phrased the question: How can the isolated
individual hope to *impose his idea* on history?

These two related problems of thought and action confronted Howard, Wright,
and Le Corbusier throughout their careers; yet they never doubted that ultimately
they could solve both. Each believed that if a planner based his work on the structure
inherent in industrial society and on the deepest values of his culture, there could be
no real conflict between his plan and individual liberty. Patiently, each searched for
that harmonious balance between control and freedom: the order that does not
repress but liberates the individual.

With equal determination, they sought a valid strategy for action. Their ideal
cities, they knew, could never be constructed all at once. But at least a "working
model" could be begun, even in the midst of the old society. This model would
demonstrate both the superiority of their architectural principles and also serve as a
symbol of the new society about to be born. Its success would inspire emulation. A
movement of reconstruction would take on momentum and become a revolutionary
force in itself. Rebuilding the cities could thus become, in a metaphor all three
favored, the "Master Key" that would unlock the way to a just society.

The three planners, therefore, looked to the new century with confidence and
hope. Against the overwhelming power of the great cities and the old order that built
them, Howard, Wright, and Le Corbusier advanced their designs for planned
growth, for the reassertion of the common interest and higher values, for a healthy
balance between man's creation and the natural environment. It would seem to be an
uneven contest. Nevertheless, the three planners still believed that an individual and
his imagination could change history. The revolution they were seeking was precisely an assertion of human rationality over vast impersonal forces. They resolved
that in the coming era of reconciliation and construction, the man of imagination
must play a crucial role. He would embody the values of his society in a workable
plan and thus direct social change with his prophetic leadership. For Howard,
Wright, and Le Corbusier, this next revolution would finally bring imagination to
power. "What gives our dreams their daring," Le Corbusier proclaimed, "is that they
can be achieved."[12]

Ebenezer Howard

The ideal city made practicable

Town and country *must be married*, and out of this joyous union will spring a new hope, a new life, a new civilization.   Ebenezer Howard (1898)

Of the three planners discussed here, Ebenezer Howard is the least known and the most influential. His *To-morrow: A Peaceful Path to Real Reform* (1898, now known under the title of the 1902 edition, *Garden Cities of To-Morrow*) has, as Lewis Mumford acknowledged, "done more than any other single book to guide the modern town planning movement and to alter its objectives."[13] And Howard was more than a theoretician. He and his supporters founded two English cities, Letchworth (1903) and Welwyn (1920), which still serve as models for his ideas. More important, he was able to organize a city planning movement that continues to keep his theories alive. The postwar program of New Towns in Great Britain, perhaps the most ambitious of all attempts at national planning, was inspired by his works and planned by his followers.

In the United States the "Greenbelt Cities" undertaken by the Resettlement Administration in the 1930s owed their form to the example of the Garden City. The best recent example of an American New Town is Columbia, Maryland, built in the 1960s as a wholly independent community with houses and industry. In 1969 the National Committee on Urban Growth Policy urged that the United States undertake to build 110 New Towns to accommodate 20 million citizens.[14] The following year, Congress created a New Town Corporation in the Department of Housing and Urban Development to begin this vast task.[15] So far, sixteen American New Towns have either been planned or are under construction. The most fruitful period of Ebenezer Howard's influence is perhaps only beginning.

If Howard's achievements continue to grow in importance, Howard the man remains virtually unknown. The present-day New Town planners are perhaps a little embarrassed by him. They are highly skilled professional bureaucrats or architects; Howard's formal education ended at fourteen, and he had no special training in architecture or urban design. The modern planners are self-proclaimed "technicians" who have attempted to adapt the New Town concept to any established social order. Howard was, in his quiet way, a revolutionary who originally conceived the Garden City as a means of superseding capitalism and creating a civilization based on cooperation. Howard's successors have neglected this aspect of his thought, and without it the founder of the Garden City movement becomes an elusive figure indeed. He shrank from the personal publicity that Frank Lloyd Wright and Le Corbusier so eagerly and skillfully sought. Throughout his life he maintained the habits and the appearance of a minor clerk. He once said that he enjoyed his chosen profession, stenography, because it enabled him to be an almost invisible observer at the notable events he recorded. Even at the meetings of the association he headed, he preferred to sit in an inconspicuous position behind the podium, where he could take down the exact words of the other speakers. Frederic J. Osborn, one of his closest associates, remembered him as "the sort of man who could easily pass unnoticed in a crowd."[16] He was, Osborn added, "the mildest and most unassuming of men...universally liked, and notably by children."[17]

Nonetheless, Howard succeeded where more charismatic figures failed. In 1898 he had to borrow fifty pounds to print *To-morrow* at his own expense. Five years later his supporters were advancing more than £100,000 to begin the construction of the first Garden City. The rapidity of this turn of events surprised Howard and is still difficult to explain. The root of the mystery is Howard himself. He had reached middle age before beginning his work on city planning and had never given any indication that he was capable of originality or leadership. His book, however, was a remarkable intellectual achievement. He concisely and rigorously outlined a new direction for the development of cities and advanced practical solutions that covered the whole range of city planning problems: land use, design, transportation, housing, and finance. At the same time, he incorporated these ideas into a large synthesis: a plan for a complete alternative society and a program for attaining it.

Howard, moreover, proved to be a surprisingly effective organizer. He was an indefatigable worker who bent with slavelike devotion to the task of promoting his own ideas. At cooperative societies, Labour Churches, settlement houses, temperance unions, debating clubs – at any group that would pay his railroad fares and provide a night's hospitality – he preached the "Gospel of the Garden City" under the title "The Ideal City Made Practicable, A Lecture Illustrated with Lantern Slides." He possessed a powerful speaking voice, and, more important, he was able to communicate an overwhelming sense of earnestness, an absolute conviction that he had discovered "the peaceful path to real reform." Mankind, he proclaimed, was moving inevitably toward a new era of brotherhood, and the Garden City would be the only fitting environment for the humanity of the future. His original supporters were not planners or architects but social reformers whose own dreams he promised would be realized in the Garden City. Patiently, he assembled a broad coalition of backers ranging from "Back to the Land" agrarians to George Bernard Shaw. Working constantly himself, he felt free to draw upon the resources and talents of others. He thus made his ideas the basis of a movement that, fifty years after his death, continues to grow. As one of Shaw's characters in *Major Barbara* observes, absolute unselfishness is capable of anything.

Inventing the Garden City

Howard never called himself a planner. His activities can be described in many words – theorist, organizer, publicist, city founder – and yet he always preferred to describe himself as an inventor. He was, he proudly proclaimed, the "inventor of the Garden City idea." The term is both appropriate and significant. In an image dear to the nineteenth century, Howard saw himself as one of those dreamers and backyard tinkerers who emerge from obscurity with one great idea, brave neglect and ridicule from the "practical" world, and finally see the skeptics confounded and the invention become an integral part of a better world. Howard in his moments of triumph was fond of comparing himself with George Stephenson, the self-taught engineer who built the first practical locomotive. The Garden City, he hoped, would be an equally significant innovation, revolutionary in itself and, like the early locomotive, capable of great improvement. It would be an engine of progress with the ability to unlock social energy and move society towards beneficent ends which even its inventor could not foresee.

The term "inventor" had one other meaning for him. As a devoted admirer of the great inventors and an occasional practitioner himself, he knew that the most important inventions were rarely the most original. They were, rather, uniquely serviceable applications of ideas that were already well known. This was precisely what Howard claimed for his innovation. In language borrowed from patent office applications he described the Garden City as a "unique combination of Proposals" that were already before the public. Howard was being truthful as well as modest. One can easily demonstrate that almost every aspect of the Garden City was borrowed from other schemes that were in existence at the time Howard began his work, some for the decentralization of cities, some for the democratization of wealth and power. This, however, would be to miss the point of Howard's achievement, for he alone saw the connection between the diverse ideas that went into his plan. With the ingenuity and patience of an inventor putting together a useful new machine out of parts forged for other purposes, Howard created a coherent design for a new environment and a new society.

Howard was able to assemble the disparate elements of the Garden City so successfully because he had a firm set of unquestioned beliefs that guided his actions. Unlike Wright and Le Corbusier, who were always emphasizing their own uniqueness, Howard was a remarkably typical product of his milieu. This prophet of decentralization was born in the center of London in 1850; his parents ran a small shop in the city. He left school at fourteen to become a junior clerk in a stockbroker's office. To better his prospects he taught himself the new Pitman system of shorthand and set up shop on his own.[18] He thus raised himself from the bottom of the hierarchy of clerkdom and joined that group of "little men" – petty entrepreneurs, commission salesmen, shopkeepers – who struggled to maintain a proud independence in the era before large organizations absorbed the white-collar class.

This success, however, never satisfied him. For Howard was touched by the great expectations of the nineteenth century. He wanted to contribute to the "unexampled rate of progress and invention" that he believed characterized his times. He started to tinker with gadgets: a keyless watch, a breech-loading gun, a typewriter that automatically allotted to each letter the space it occupied in print typography.[19] These projects, never successful, absorbed his attention and his ready cash. In his most unusual attempt to make his fortune he emigrated briefly to the United States, where a year spent as a homesteader in Nebraska convinced him of the virtues of stenography. He returned to London in 1876.[20]

After this episode his ambitions took a less material turn. While struggling to build up his stenography practice, he grew preoccupied with what was then called "the Social Question" – the origins and causes of all the poverty that daily surrounded him. Perhaps his own failure and temporary poverty in the United States had awakened his sympathy for the poor in his own country. The principles of moral duty he had learned in Sunday school and his own innate kindliness surely also played their part. In any case, he soon joined a series of reading and discussion groups with names like the "Zetetical Society." For him and the other members, these groups represented an opportunity to educate themselves in the great political and economic questions of the day. Together they taught themselves John Stuart Mill on political economy, Herbert Spencer on social science, Darwin and Huxley on evolution. There he met high-minded men and women with concerns similar to his own and was initiated into the world of middle-class London radicalism.

These genteel revolutionaries have rarely been appreciated or even understood in our time. They were amateurs and idealists in a field that has come to be dominated by professionals and politicians. Their plans for reconstructing society survive only in the pages of old pamphlets with titles in ornate type: *Brotherhood, Cooperation.* Photographs in these pamphlets show us their faces, which have no elegance and little humor but much hope and integrity; the men are in stiff white collars, the women in severely buttoned dresses. Under each picture is an identifying caption: "Secretary, Temperance Union and Cooperative Society" or "Spiritualist and Social Reformer." The Radicals had more than their share of cranks, but their movement was the home of much that was most humane in nineteenth-century British society, as well as the source of much that would prove most fruitful for the twentieth century. When Howard designed the Garden City in the 1890s, he followed unhesitatingly the social ideals he had learned as an obscure Radical of the 1870s and 1880s.

The Radicals believed that Victorian England was not the best of all possible worlds; that the economic life of the nation was corrupt, inhumane, inefficient, and immoral; and that political power, despite the appearance of democracy, was unjustly concentrated in the hands of a few. This concentration, they feared, would ruin the nation if allowed to continue. In the countryside the near-monopoly of landholding by large owners was bankrupting agriculture. Farm workers, deprived of any hope of owning their own land, were fleeing the land and swelling the urban slums. There they were easily exploited by "sweating" employers, whose sharp practices and monopolistic tactics were driving the honest "little person" out of business. If these trends were to continue, the result would be a society polarized between capital and labor. The Radicals were not Marxists, so they saw in this last prospect only violent conflict that would destroy both sides.

Their remedies for this dismal situation were democracy and cooperation. They wanted first to break the power of the landed gentry who controlled Parliament and to institute a thoroughgoing land reform. This would draw farm workers back from the slums and create a new class of yeoman smallholders, prosperous and independent. For the urban industrialized areas, the Radicals called for cooperation to replace large-scale capitalism. Profit sharing in production would gradually erase the distinction between worker and employer, thus ending class conflict. At the same time, cooperative stores would end profiteering and wasteful anarchy in distribution.

The Radicals devoutly believed in progress, and they held that humankind was evolving toward a higher stage of social organization – the cooperative commonwealth – in which brotherhood would become the basis of daily life. But while they were sure that humankind was capable of creating this better world, they had no definite strategy for achieving their goal. They rejected what were to be the two great engines of social change, government intervention and the labor movement. They rejected big government as a dangerous concentration of power, even if it were on their side. For the Radicals, independence and voluntary action were both means and ends. Nor did they support organizing the working class. As we have seen, they regarded class struggle as one of the evils of modern society.

Without a plan of action, the Radical movement alternated between long periods of discussion and short bursts of activity when the true path seemed to be found. One such burst accompanied the arrival in London in 1884 of Henry George, the American reformer whose proposal for a "single tax" of 100 percent of all rental income would, in effect, accomplish the Radical program of land reform at a stroke. George's ideas left their imprint on the Radical movement in general and, as we shall see, on Howard in particular, but they failed to win over the British electorate, and the enthusiasm subsided. Sometimes individuals or small groups would abandon their homes and businesses to form utopian colonies like Topolobampo in Mexico. There they hoped to create a "working model" of true cooperation to win over a skeptical world.

More frequently, the Radicals allowed themselves to hope that their small-scale cooperative enterprises might, through voluntary action alone, supplant their profit-making competitors. If the Trusts had grown great on the force of selfishness, why should not brotherhood prove even more powerful? Cooperative socialism could then prevail without any legislation. A good example of these hopes – and illusions – was a scheme propounded by two friends of Howard's, J. Bruce Wallace and the Reverend Bruce Campbell, to bring cooperative workshops and stores to the slum dwellers of London's East End. At the beginning of 1894 the co-ops, aptly named the Brotherhood Trust, had enrolled over one hundred customers. "Suppose," Wallace urged his supporters on February 1, 1894, "suppose one fresh customer gained monthly for every old customer." After some rapid calculations he was able to announce that by February 1, 1896, they would have over one hundred million enrolled. "In the third year the trade of the whole world would be in the hands of the Trust, for fraternal purposes."[21]

Wallace was quick to add: "I am not so sanguine as to believe that our little movement will actually spread with such rapidity."[22] Nevertheless, it was a revealing fantasy, the dream of a "little man" that his modest enterprise might one day change the world – without coercion. Slightly transposed, it was the same as an inventor's dream of worldwide success by virtue of having created a superior product. As we shall see, Howard's conception of the Garden City as "the peaceful path to real reform" combined elements of both dreams.

Throughout the 1880s, Howard continued to absorb both the principles and the problems of the Radical movement. He remained a follower, emerging from anonymity only once to deliver a speech on spiritualism at the Zetetical Society. His cogitations on interplanetary ether waves as the possible physical basis of spiritualist communication gave no hint of his coming concerns.[23] His period of quiescence ended suddenly, however, in 1888 with a single event that made him an activist for the rest of his life: he read Edward Bellamy's *Looking Backward*. Published in Boston in 1888, *Looking Backward* had won immediate popularity in the United States and exercised a profound influence over such men as Thorstein Veblen and John Dewey.[24] Written against the background of the industrial depression and growing labor unrest that engulfed both America and Europe in the third quarter of the nineteenth century, the book presented a graphic depiction of a society in which these problems had been overcome. The hero of the novel is a prosperous Bostonian who has the good fortune to sleep soundly from 1887 to 2000 and wake in a society organized on moral principles. Industry has been efficiently grouped into one government-owned cooperative Trust. Distribution has also been concentrated into one great Department Store, whose branches in every city and village sell everything the nation has produced. Competition has been replaced by centralized planning; poverty and unemployment are unknown; all citizens between twenty-one and forty-five occupy ranks in the "industrial army," and everyone receives an equal salary.

Although Bellamy's novel was only one of the genre of "utopian romances" that seemed as ubiquitous in their time as murder mysteries are in ours, it was by far the most effective in its critique of industrial capitalism and its imaginative demonstration that a better alternative could exist. *Looking Backward* was sent to Howard by an American friend. He read it at one sitting and was "fairly carried away." The next morning, as he later wrote

> I went into some of the crowded parts of London, and as I passed through the narrow dark streets, saw the wretched dwellings in which the majority of the people lived, observed on every hand the manifestations of a self-seeking order of society and reflected on the absolute unsoundness of our economic system, there came to me an overpowering sense of the temporary nature of all I saw, and of its entire unsuitability for the working life of the new order – the order of justice, unity and friendliness.[25]

Howard was sufficiently enthusiastic to believe that many others would share his revelation. He was especially impressed with Bellamy's use of an imaginative portrayal of an alternative to demonstrate the "absolute unsoundness and quite transitory nature" of existing society. In the absence of any other viable movement for change, Bellamy's vision of a better future could become the standard around which men of goodwill would unite. Howard claimed that he was responsible for persuading an English firm to publish *Looking Backward* in London in 1889.[26] In imitation of the Bellamy Clubs then forming in the United States, Howard soon began meeting with small groups to discuss Bellamy's ideas. In 1890 he participated in the formation of the English Nationalization of Labour Society, the counterpart of Bellamy's Nationalization Party in the United States.[27]

As *Looking Backward* won an enthusiastic readership in English Radical circles, Howard allowed himself the belief that the Nationalization movement was the plan for action the Radicals had been seeking. Even at the time of his greatest hope, however, he could not believe that the movement would have the power to take over the industry of Great Britain very soon. "This perception, naturally, led me to put forward proposals for testing Mr. Bellamy's principles, though on a much smaller scale."[28] Howard began to devise a model community of a few thousand people in which – as in *Looking Backward* – everyone would be employed by the community, whose directors would run every enterprise. If successful, this project would prove the efficacy of Bellamy's ideas to those who would not be moved by purely literary arguments, and thus speed the day when nationalization could occur on a national scale.

Characteristically, Howard's maiden attempt at planning was not an attempt to advance his own ideas but to adapt those of another. Nonetheless, as Howard began to work on the scheme, he came to realize that Bellamy's novelistic gifts had blinded him to the differences between his own goals and those advanced in *Looking Backward*. For Howard shared the Radical mistrust of all concentrations of power, whereas Bellamy made centralization the key to his reforms. Howard saw more clearly than many other readers that behind Bellamy's faith in control from above there was a strong authoritarian bias. Bellamy proudly compared his "industrial army" to the Prussian army. As for its leaders, he spoke grandly and vaguely of a small corps of managers who could plan the economy of the United States or any other nation in the year 2000. In his system, he claimed, the management of all American industry would be "so simple, and depending on principles so obvious and easily applied, that the functionaries at Washington to whom it is trusted require to be nothing more than men of fair ability."[29] Although Bellamy was realistic about the likely intelligence of the bureaucrats of the future, he had unlimited faith in their efficacy, a faith that Howard could not share. Bellamy had seized upon all the forces of concentration and centralization in late-nineteenth-century society and saw in them the possibility for a more humane order. Not only did Howard doubt the practicality of extreme centralization, but he also denied its desirability even if it could work.

Howard continued to work out the plan of a model community; now, however, it was designed to put forward and test his own ideas. The Garden City was not the simple result of Bellamy's influence on Howard. Rather, it grew out of Howard's attempt to correct Bellamy's authoritarian bias and to devise a community in which social order and individual initiative would be properly balanced.

He began with Bellamy's plan for "nationalization," the concept that the entire productive capacity of a nation could be managed as it if were one huge Trust, and all its stores and shops controlled as if they were branches of one great Department Store. In thinking about his own model community, Howard was particularly aware of the problems connected with farming. His own failure as a farmer had sufficiently sensitized him to the difficulties in that area, and he doubted that even a small community could successfully manage all its farms. He had, moreover, followed the decline of the Radical utopian colony in Mexico, Topolobampo, whose directors had controlled all productive activity. Their attempts at management had merely focused all the dissatisfactions of the colony on themselves and destroyed the experiment. Howard proposed, therefore, what would become the policy of the Garden City: that the community include both privately and collectively owned enterprise and leave to the citizens the choice of how they wished to work.

From this, Howard proceeded to an even more significant transformation: a critique of Bellamy's ideal of centralization. Bellamy believed that the industrial society of the future ought to be controlled by bureaucrats working from their command posts in the great cities. In opposing nationalization, Howard also began questioning the inevitability of centralization. Specifically, he began to modify his original view that the community he was designing was only a scale model of the centralized society of the future. Was the balance of individual society he was seeking possible in the metropolis? Or did the small decentralized community have an inherent value of its own?

In wrestling with this question, Howard was no doubt influenced by Peter Kropotkin, a Russian anarchist whose articles appeared in the widely read London journal *The Nineteenth Century* between 1888 and 1890.[30] These articles, later collected as *Fields, Factories, and Workshops* (1899), argued that while steam energy and the railroads had brought large factories and great cities, the dawning age of electricity would make possible a rapid decentralization. He saw the future in what he called "industrial villages," twentieth-century versions of the old crafts villages of the preindustrial era. There electrically powered, cooperatively owned cottage industries would turn out goods more efficiently than the old urban factories, while the workers' homes and gardens would be nestled in unspoiled countryside.

Kropotkin's views found a deep response in English Radical circles, especially his prediction that all the great urban concentrations of people and power were destined to disappear; his conviction that the future belonged to small-scale cooperators; and his belief that decentralization would make possible a society based on liberty and brotherhood. Howard, who called Kropotkin "the greatest democrat ever born to wealth and power,"[31] decisively abandoned his temporary infatuation with the centralized schemes of Edward Bellamy. Kropotkin had called his attention to the crucial importance of *scale* as a factor in social theory. "On a small scale," Howard proposed, "society may readily become more individualistic than now and more socialistic."[32] Conversely, he came to realize that the great city could never become the home of the cooperative civilization he was seeking. He was now ready to formulate the fundamental principle of the Garden City: *Radical hopes for a cooperative civilization could be fulfilled only in small communities embedded in a decentralized society.*

Howard thus turned to decentralization as a means of action, a way of voting with one's feet against the concentration of power and wealth that the cities represented. His anti-urbanism had nothing in common with the vague longings for a more natural life propagated by the "Back to the Land" movement, which was then enjoying one of its periodic revivals. He loved the excitement of London and deeply valued the social qualities of the great cities.[33] It was their economic and political role that disturbed him. "Palatial edifices and fearful slums are the strange, complementary features of modern cities."[34] Howard's identification of the metropolis with the extremes of wealth and power was the starting point of his analysis of the modern city and the real source of his antagonism toward it. He realized that the concentration of wealth and misery in the city would require an equally vast concentration of power to combat it. His favorite example of this was slum clearance. In a large city the inflated price of urban land and the vast numbers of slum dwellers meant that an effective program required a government with powers of taxation and confiscation that Howard, as a good Radical, shrank from even seeking. To accept the nineteenth-century metropolis as the inevitable context for modern life meant that either the force of vested interest would continue to prevail or an equally monstrous force based on class conflict would be raised to topple it.

Both alternatives affronted Howard's belief that mankind was moving to a higher stage of brotherhood. He drew the necessary conclusion: Large cities had no place in the society of the future. Surveying the "ill-ventilated, unplanned, unwieldy, and unhealthy cities – ulcers on the very face of our beautiful island,"[35] he proclaimed: "These crowded cities have done their work; they were the best which a society largely based on selfishness and rapacity could construct, but they are in the nature of things entirely unadapted for a society in which the social side of our nature is demanding a larger share of recognition."[36] Everything genuinely valuable in the social life of the city could and must be preserved in new communities designed so that the advantages of the town could be "married" to those of the country. "Human society and the beauty of nature are meant to be enjoyed together."[37] In communities of about 30,000 people based on small business and agriculture, everyone could enjoy the benefits of a healthy environment. Reduced to the scale of a Garden City, the gulf between capital

and labor would be narrowed, social problems would become amenable to cooperative solutions, and the proper balance of order and freedom could be achieved.

How could this great social transformation be achieved? Howard summed up his
response in his diagram of the "Three Magnets." Town and country were compared
to magnets, each with its particular drawing power, its particular combination of
attraction and repulsion. The town, with its excitement, high wages, and employment opportunities, suffered from high prices and poor living conditions. The beauty
of the countryside was vitiated by its economic backwardness and "lack of amusement." The task for the planner would be to create a third magnet, the Town-
Country magnet, the new community, which would have high wages and low
rents; beauty of nature but "plenty to do"; "bright homes and gardens" along with
freedom and cooperation.

In the diagram, "The People" are poised like iron filings between the magnets. This
aspect of the metaphor is unfortunate, for Howard's point is that people will respond
freely and rationally to the environment that gives them the most advantages. No one
had been drafted into the cities. The great migration from the countryside, which in
Howard's lifetime had brought seven million rural residents to the British urban
centers, occurred without legislative compulsion. Similarly, the great exodus from
the city to which Howard looked would require no coercive power.

What it required was planning. The Town-Country magnet had to be created
consciously to yield the combination of physical and social benefits that were
promised. This task Howard took upon himself. Although he had no training in
architecture or city planning, he did have the inventor's confidence that he could find
the better way. Working alone in the time he could spare from his stenography
practice, he set out to give the Radical movement not only a new goal but the
strategy for action it had been lacking. Building new towns, creating a new environment – that was the way to the cooperative commonwealth. Howard strove patiently to design that Third Magnet he called the Garden City, whose promise of a
better life would draw people away from the urban centers into a new civilization.

Design for cooperation

Between 1889 and 1892 Howard created the basic plan for his ideal community. He
envisaged his Garden City as a tightly organized urban center for 30,000 inhabitants, surrounded by a perpetual "greenbelt" of farms and parks. Within the city
there would be both quiet residential neighborhoods and facilities for a full range of
commercial, industrial, and cultural activities. For Howard did not conceive the
Garden City as a specialized "satellite town" or "bedroom town" perpetually serving
some great metropolis. Rather, he foresaw the great cities of his time shrinking to
insignificance as their people deserted them for a new way of life in a decentralized
society. No longer would a single metropolis dominate a whole region or even a
whole nation. Nor would the palatial edifices and giant organizations of the big city
continue to rule modern society. Instead, the urban population would be distributed
among hundreds of Garden Cities whose small scale and diversity of functions
embody a world in which the little person has finally won out.

Howard does not seem to have been familiar with the designs for geometric
cities that utopian socialists had put forward earlier in the nineteenth century.

Nonetheless, the perfectly circular, perfectly symmetrical plan he devised for the Garden City bears a distinct resemblance to some of these, notably James Silk Buckingham's cast-iron Victoria (1849).[38] The explanation, however, lies not in direct influence but in shared values. For Howard had inherited that tradition in English utopian thought in which it was assumed that society could be improved just as a machine could – through the appropriate adjustments. A properly functioning society would thus take on the precise and well-calculated look of a good machine.

For Howard, therefore, there was nothing merely "mechanical" in the relentless symmetry of the Garden City. He wanted to make the design the physical embodiment of his ideal of cooperation, and he believed that his perfectly circular plan would best meet the needs of the citizens. He promised that every building would be "so placed to secure maximum utility and convenience."[39] This "unity of design and purpose" had been impossible in old cities formed, in Howard's view, by "an infinite number of small, narrow, and selfish decisions."[40] In the Garden City, however, an active common interest would make possible a uniform, comprehensive plan. With selfish obstructions removed, the city could assume that geometric form that Howard believed was the most efficient and the most beautiful. The symmetry of the Garden City would be the symbol and product of cooperation, the sign of a harmonious society.

The only relevant book he remembered reading was written by a physician, Dr Benjamin Richardson, and entitled *Hygeia, A City of Health*.[41] It was an imaginative presentation of the principles of public sanitation in which Dr Richardson depicted a city whose design would be the healthiest for its inhabitants. He prescribed a population density of twenty-five people per acre, a series of wide, tree-shaded avenues, and homes and public gardens surrounded by greenery. "Instead of the gutter the poorest child has the garden; for the foul sight and smell of unwholesome garbage, he has flowers and green sward."[42] Howard was happy to follow this prescription. The public health movement, of which Dr Richardson was a prominent representative, was a vital force for civic action; it had persuaded the public that there was a strong correlation between the health of a community and its political and moral soundness. Howard maintained that the Garden Cities would be the healthiest in the nation. He incorporated the low population density, the wide avenues, and other features of *Hygeia* into the geometry of his own city.

The problem of health was especially important because Howard planned the Garden City to be a manufacturing center in which the factories would necessarily be close to the homes. In order to separate the residential areas and also to ensure that everyone would be within walking distance of the workplace, Howard put the factories at the periphery of the city, adjacent to the circular railroad that surrounds the town and connects it to the main line. Here one can find the enterprises appropriate to a decentralized society: the small machine shop, or the cooperative printing works, or the jam factory where the rural cooperative processes its members' fruits. As usual in the plan, physical location has a symbolic aspect. Industry has its place and its function, but these are at the outskirts of the community. Howard had little faith in the role of work – even if cooperatively organized – to provide the unifying force in society. This he left to leisure and civic enterprise.

There are two kinds of centers in the Garden City: the neighborhood centers and the (one) civic center. The neighborhoods, or "wards" as Howard called them, are slices in the circular pie. Each ward comprises one-sixth of the town, 5,000 people or about 1,000 families. Each, said Howard, "should in some sense be a complete town by itself" (he imagined the Garden City being built ward by ward).[43] The basic unit in the neighborhood is the family living in its own home surrounded by a garden. Howard hoped to be able to provide houses with gardens to all classes. Most residents would be able to afford a lot 20 by 130 feet; the most substantial homes would be arranged in crescents bordering Grand Avenue, a park and promenade that forms the center of the ward. In the middle of Grand Avenue is the most important neighborhood institution, the school. This, Howard commented, should be the first building constructed in each ward and will serve as a library, a meeting hall, and even as a site for religious worship. Churches, when they are built, also occupy sites in Grand Avenue.[44]

There are two cohesive forces that bring the residents out of their neighborhoods and unite the city. The first is leisure. The center of the town is a Central Park, which provides "ample recreation grounds within very easy access of all the people."[45] Surrounding the park is a glassed-in arcade, which Howard calls the "Crystal Palace": "Here manufactured goods are exposed for sale, and here most of that class of shopping which requires the joy of deliberation and selection is done."[46]

The Crystal Palace, in addition to providing an attractive setting for consumption, also permits the town, by granting or withholding leases, to exercise some control over distribution. Howard, as always, recommended a balance between individualism and central organization. He rejected the idea of one great cooperative department store run by the community, like the one in *Looking Backward*. Instead, he advocated that there be many small shops, but only one for each category of goods. If customers complain that a merchant is abusing his monopoly, the town rents space in the Crystal Palace to another shopkeeper in the same field, whose competition then restores adequate service. Whatever the merits of this solution, it aptly reflects the Radical ambivalence toward the trades that supported so many of them, the desire for economic independence without the self-destructive competition that accompanied it.

Important as consumption and leisure were in his system, Howard nonetheless reserved the very center of the Central Park to the second cohesive force, "civil spirit." He wanted an impressive and meaningful setting for the "large public buildings": town hall, library, museum, concert and lecture hall, and the hospital. Here the highest values of the community are brought together – culture, philanthropy, health, and mutual cooperation.

We might wonder what kind of cultural life a Garden City of 30,000 could enjoy, but this question did not bother Howard. He never felt the need of that intensification of experience – the extremes of diversity and excellence – that only a metropolis can offer. We must also remember, however, that Howard lived in a milieu that did not look to others to provide entertainment or enlightenment. The English middle class and a sizable part of the working class created its own culture in thousands of voluntary groups: lecture societies, choral groups, drama guilds, chamber symphonies. Here, as elsewhere, Howard disdained the kind of centralization that focused the life of a nation on a few powerful metropolitan institutions. He looked to small-scale voluntary cooperation not only for the economic base of the community but also for its highest cultural attainments.

The Garden City occupies 1,000 acres in the middle of a tract of 5,000 acres reserved for farms and forests.[47] This "Agricultural Belt" plays an integral role in the economy of the Garden City; the 2,000 farmers who live there supply the town with the bulk of its food. Because transportation costs are almost nonexistent, the farmer receives a good price for his produce, and the consumer gets fresh vegetables and dairy products at a reduced price. The Agricultural Belt, moreover, prevents the town from sprawling out into the countryside and ensures that the citizens enjoy both a compact urban center and ample open countryside. "One of the first essential needs of Society and of the individual," wrote Howard, "is that every man, every woman, every child should have ample space in which to live, to move, and to develop."[48] He added a new element to the rights of man – the right to space.

The Garden City in all its aspects expressed Howard's ideal of a cooperative commonwealth. It was the Zion in which he and his fellow Radicals could be at ease, the environment in which all the Radical hopes could be realized. Yet the Garden City was more than an image of felicity for Howard had carefully wedded his vision of the ideal city to a concrete plan for action. Indeed, he devoted relatively little attention to the details of the new city and a great deal to the means of achieving it. He wanted to show that there was no need to wait for a revolution to build the Garden City: it could be undertaken immediately by a coalition of Radical groups working within the capitalist system. The first successful Garden City would be a working model of a better society, and those that succeeded it would decisively alter English society. Building the Garden City was itself the revolution. The planned transformation of the environment was the nonviolent but effective strategy that the Radical movement had been seeking. The Garden City was, as Howard put it, "the peaceful path to real reform."

Howard wanted the building of the first Garden City to be an example of voluntary cooperation, and he devoted most of his book to outlining and defending his method. The key to Howard's strategy was his contention that building a new city could be *practical*, i.e., that money advanced for its construction could be paid back with interest. Funds could thus be solicited from high-minded and thrifty Radicals with the assurance that they would be both helping the cause and earning a modest return for themselves. The germ of Howard's scheme could be found in an article written in 1884 by the distinguished economist Alfred Marshall.[49] Marshall had pointed out that the rail networks that covered Great Britain rendered the concentration of so many businesses in London economically irrational. Many businesses could be carried out far more cheaply, efficiently, and pleasantly where land was inexpensive and abundant. Marshall proposed that committees be established to buy up suitable land outside London and coordinate the movement of factories and working people. The value of the land in these new industrial parks would rise sharply, and the committees that owned them would reap a handsome profit.

Howard, who knew both the proposal and its author,[50] took up this suggestion and transformed it to suit his own ends. He began by asking the reader to assume that a group of his supporters – "gentlemen of responsible position and undoubted probity and honor," as he hopefully described them – had banded together to form a nonprofit company. They would raise money by issuing bonds yielding a fixed rate (4 or 5 percent), purchase 6,000 acres of agricultural land, and lay out a city according to Howard's plans. They would build roads, power and water plants, and all other necessities, and then seek to attract industry and residents. The company would continue to own all the land; as the population rose, the rents too would rise from the low rate per acre for agricultural land to the more substantial rate of a city with 30,000 residents. All rent would go to the company and would be used to repay the original investors. Any surplus that remained after the financial obligations had been discharged would provide additional services to the community.[51]

Howard proposed, in other words, that the Garden City be founded and financed by philanthropic land speculation. The scheme was speculative because it was a gamble on the rise in values that would result from attracting 30,000 people to a plot of empty farmland, and philanthropic because the speculators agreed in advance to forgo all but a fixed portion of the expected profits. The concept was not original with Howard. "Philanthropy at 5 percent" was a familiar feature in English reform circles, and activists from the Owenites to the Christian Socialists made use of fixed-dividend corporations to raise money for cooperative stores and workshops. The Reverend Charles Kingsley, a Christian Socialist, aptly illustrated the spirit of this reconciliation of God and Mammon when he exhorted his followers to "seek first the Kingdom of God and his Righteousness with this money of yours and see if all things – profits and suchlike – are not added unto you."[52]

Howard did add a new emphasis to this method. He stipulated that part of the rental income each year be placed in a sinking fund and used to purchase the bonds of the original investors. As the number of bondholders decreased, the amount that the company had to pay each year to the ones remaining would also decrease. Meanwhile, income from rents would be constantly growing as the town grew; the surplus, as we have seen, was earmarked for community services. Eventually the Garden City would buy out all the original investors, and the entire income from rents could be used to benefit the citizens. Taxes would be unnecessary; rents alone would generously support schools, hospitals, cultural institutions, and charities.[53]

The residents of the Garden City would thus continue to pay rent, but landlords would be eliminated. The private ownership of land for the benefit of individuals would be replaced by collective ownership for the benefit of the community. Howard placed tremendous emphasis on this change. He, like almost every other Radical, believed that the "land question" – the concentration of the ownership of land in Great Britain in the hands of a few – was, as he put it, the "root of all our problems."[54] As late as 1873 an official survey had shown that 80 percent of the land in the United Kingdom was owned by less than 7,000 persons.[55] The spread of Garden Cities would transfer land ownership on a large scale from individuals to the community, thus inaugurating an economic and social revolution.

Howard's analysis of the crucial importance of the "land question" derived from the writings of the American reformer Henry George, a hero of English Radicals in the 1880s. George was probably the most influential man of one idea in nineteenth-century Anglo-American history. His panacea, the Single Tax (the appropriation of all rent by taxation) was based on his view that there was no real conflict between capital and labor. The "antagonism of interests," he argued, "is in reality between labor and capital on the one side and land ownership on the other."[56] The great landowners used their natural monopoly to demand exorbitant rents and thus appropriate without compensation the lion's share of the increased wealth from material progress that ought to go to the workmen and entrepreneurs who actually produced it. This perversion of the economic order impoverished the proletariat, imperiled the manufacturer, and upset the natural balance of supply and demand. It was the real cause of depression, class conflict, and the spreading poverty that seemed an inevitable companion to progress.

Characteristically, Howard accepted everything in George's theory that pointed toward reconciliation and rejected everything that promised conflict. He rejected the Single Tax because he saw that it meant the expropriation of a whole class. He accepted, however, George's view that the solution to the land question would restore the economy to a healthy balance and create the conditions for a reconciliation of capital and labor. He believed he had found the solution to the land question himself. The Garden City, he wrote, "will, by a purely natural process, make it gradually impossible for any landlord class to exist at all." Private landholding "will die a natural but not too sudden death."[57] Building Garden Cities would accomplish all of George's aims "in a manner which need cause no ill-will, strife or bitterness; is constitutional; requires no revolutionary legislation; and involves no direct attack on vested interest."[58] The Garden City company would, in fact, enjoy all the privileges of a profit-making concern. The legal forms that landlords had designed to protect their own interests would now foster the creation of a higher form of society.

The powers extended to the Garden City company as sole landlord would be greater than the legal authority possessed by any nineteenth-century English municipality. Through its control of all leases it could effectively enforce the ground plan and zone the community without special legal authority. Howard was a firm believer in "gas and water socialism," and he stipulated that the town's board of management should provide all utilities on a nonprofit basis. He also thought the town might well establish municipal bakeries and laundries.[59]

Although the Garden City company would have the legal right to own and operate all the industry in the Garden City, Howard favored a balance of public and private control. The large factories on the periphery were clearly to be established by private industry, though Howard hoped that through profit sharing they would eventually take on a cooperative character. They still would be subject to the authority that the town as sole landlord could impose: No polluters or employers of "sweated" labor would be allowed.[60] The board of management would also share responsibility for public services with private citizens. Howard hoped that individuals would establish a large group of what he called "pro-municipal enterprises." These were public services whose necessity was not yet recognized by the majority of the citizens, but "those who have the welfare of society at heart [would], in the free air of the city, be always able to experiment on their own responsibility, ... and enlarge the public understanding."[61] In addition to the more conventional charitable and philanthropic activities, "pro-municipal enterprises" included cooperative building and pension societies.

As income from rents grew, the municipality would gradually take over the services that voluntary cooperation had initiated. In industry, too, Howard believed that the evolutionary trend was toward greater public ownership and control. The most important principle, however, was that no one has the right to impose a degree of socialism for which the citizens were not ready. The elimination of landlord's rents would remove, in Howard's view, any immediate conflict of capital with labor and permit the peaceful coexistence of capitalist and socialist industry. The balance between the public and private sectors must shift slowly with the increasing capacity of the citizens for cooperation.

Howard had the patience to begin with imperfect forms because he had the capacity to see his ideal society evolving in time. He realized that a single Garden City of 30,000 was too small to provide the full measure of diversity that a genuine city must have. A Garden City could not, however, increase its size or density; that would spoil its plan. He proposed that it grow by establishing a new sister city beyond the Agricultural Belt. Howard believed that the cities should eventually organize themselves into "town clusters, each town in the cluster being of different design from the others, yet the whole forming one large and well-thought-out plan."[62] A diagram that appeared in *To-morrow* showed six Garden Cities arranged in a circle around a larger Center City. The plan had the cities connected by a circular canal, which provided power, water, and transportation. In the 1902 edition the canal was replaced by a more sober rapid transit system.[63]

The Social City, as Howard called each cluster of towns, represented his most advanced conception of the marriage of town and country; here "each inhabitant of the whole group, though in one sense living in a town of small size, would be in reality living in, and would enjoy all the advantages of, a great and most beautiful city; and yet all the fresh delights of the country...would be within a very few minutes' ride or walk."[64] With small communities already established as the basic units in society, these units could be arranged in planned federations to secure the benefits of larger size as well. Rapid communications between the towns meant greater convenience for trade, and, "because the people, in their collective capacity own the land on which this beautiful group of cities is built, the public buildings, the churches, the schools and universities, the libraries, picture galleries, theatres, would be on a scale of magnificence which no city in the world whose land is in pawn to private individuals can afford."[65] Once established, the Social City would become the base for still higher stages of evolution that Howard never ventured to describe.

Howard's reluctance to prescribe every detail or to foresee every contingency is one of the most important aspects of his method. The visionary planner can easily become a despot of the imagination. Working alone, deprived of the checks and balances of other minds, he is tempted to become the *roi soleil* of his realm and to order every detail of life of his ideal society. If Howard's geometric plans resemble a Baroque *Residenzstadt*, Howard himself was singularly free of the pretensions of a Baroque monarch. His plans, as he pointed out, were merely diagrams to be modified when put into practice.

The same may be said for his plans for social organization. In Howard's time the advocates of Socialism and Individualism (both usually capitalized) confronted each other like Matthew Arnold's ignorant armies. Bellamy, as we have seen, believed that the entire economy of the United States could be centrally directed by a few men of "fair ability." Herbert Spencer in his individualist phase held that the use of tax money to support public libraries was a step toward collectivist slavery.[66] Howard did not presume to judge this momentous debate. He made the spatial reorganization of society his fundamental demand because he believed that a new environment would open possibilities for the reconciliation of freedom and order that neither Bellamy nor Spencer could imagine. Howard sought to discover the minimum of organization that would secure the benefits of planning while leaving to individuals the greatest possible control over their own lives. He was a collectivist who hated bureaucratic paternalism and an apostle of organization who realized that planning must stay within self-imposed limits.

Building the Garden City

Howard's theories were now irrevocably tied to what happened on the more than 3,000 acres in Hertfordshire. The necessity of finding large sums of money to develop the new city made Howard increasingly dependent on the support of a few Liberal magnates like Cadbury and Lever. He never succeeded in building the broad coalition of reformist groups he had hoped to assemble – a fact that inevitably modified the tone and substance of his ideas. One source of working-class support that could have improved the balance was conspicuous in its absence: the coopera-tive movement. Howard looked to the "cooperators" to provide the leadership and experience for the working class to begin its own enterprises. "The true remedy for capitalist oppression where it exists," he wrote, "is not the strike of no work but the strike of true work. . . . If labor leaders spent half the energy in cooperative organiza-tion they now waste in cooperative disorganization, the end of our present unjust system would be at hand."[67]

The cooperative movement, moreover, was probably the only working-class or-ganization that had the resources to contribute significantly to the building of the Garden City. The movement had more than two million members organized into 1,600 local societies, which sold £92 million of goods in 1903 and distributed £10 million in profits.[68] The cooperative societies had either built or advanced the money for more than 37,000 houses by 1903, and the movement's factories manu-factured more than £10 million of goods annually.[69]

Howard's supporters in the movement hoped that cooperators would be the principal builders of the Garden City. At each of the annual Cooperative Congresses from 1900 to 1909 they argued that the next step toward the cooperative common-wealth was to organize the movement's stores, factories, and homes (which were now scattered over Great Britain) into the new environment that Howard prom-ised.[70] Despite influential support among the national leaders – J. C. Grey, Chair-man of the Cooperative Wholesale Society, was among the founders of the Manchester branch of the Garden City Association[71] – the congresses refused either to support First Garden City Ltd., or to build their own Garden City. The individual distributive societies were more anxious to preserve their independence than they were to create a new civilization. The cooperative counterbalance to capitalist investment and production at Letchworth never developed.

In the absence of any significant working-class support, the values of Neville and his fellow businessmen dominated First Garden City Ltd. For Howard, the Garden City was an environment in which capitalism could be peacefully superseded. Most of his supporters, however, looked to the Garden City as the place where capitalism could be most easily preserved.

Neville, who assumed the post of chairman of the executive of First Garden City Ltd., proposed to raise funds to begin construction by issuing £300,000 in shares, with the annual dividend not to exceed 5 percent of their par value. Neville believed that if the shares were to be sold, the company must purge itself of any utopian hopes and present itself at all times as a solid business venture and a good investment. "For mere philanthropy the money would not be forthcoming."[72] When Howard in his speeches mentioned the risks involved in starting a new city, Neville sternly reproached him. "I appreciate your reluctance to ask poor people to invest their savings, but there is all the difference in the world between refraining from enticing and deprecating investment."[73]

Faced with a board of prominent businessmen who were used to getting their own way, Howard was in danger of losing control of his own movement. The first test came over the land question. Howard proposed to retain the rise in land values for the community by disposing of all land in thousand-year leases that would provide for reassessment by an impartial committee every four years. If the value had increased over the last assessment, the rent would also be increased.[74] Howard hoped, as we have seen, that the rising income from rents would soon far exceed what was necessary to pay the 5 percent return to the stockholders and that the surplus could be used for community services.

Neville believed, however, that potential residents of Letchworth would be confused by the unfamiliar features of such a lease and would be frightened off by the fear of drastic rent increases. He therefore advocated a standard ninety-nine-year lease at a fixed rent.[75] The community, in other words, would have to wait one hundred years before negotiating a new lease at a higher rent and thus collecting its share of the "unearned increment."

The other businessmen on the board agreed with Neville. Howard, who was still earning his living as a stenographer, was no match for a cocoa millionaire or a soap magnate. He took the defeat in good spirits because he agreed with the businessmen that concern for details must not stand in the way of the speedy completion of the town. The prototype must first exist; it would then inspire others to more perfect efforts.

> The first result [of the building of Letchworth] will be that the number of people who favor the Garden City will be increased a hundredfold; and then a glorious task which an insignificant minority could not compass will be found quite easy by a majority of the nation. A splendid organization will be created and a City will then rise as superior in its beauty and magnificence to our first crude attempt as is the finished canvas of a great artist to the rough and untaught attempts of a schoolboy.[76]

In 1903 the company made perhaps its most important decision: It chose the firm of Parker and Unwin to be the architects of Letchworth. Barry Parker was a young architect from Derbyshire who began his career as a designer of textiles and wall-papers influenced by the arts-and-crafts movement.[77] Raymond Unwin, whose association with the Garden City was the start of a long career in city planning that would make him the leading British authority, was trained as an engineer and came to architecture under the influence of William Morris.[78] Both men were early supporters of Howard; as followers of Morris, they were engaged in a search that paralleled Howard's own. Morris had taught that the artist's efforts to create a beautiful society could not be separated from the activist's attempts to create a just one. "Before there can be a city greatly beautiful," wrote Unwin, "there must be some noble common life to find expression."[79]

But if Parker and Unwin sympathized with Howard's goals, they had no use for his rationalistic, geometric methods of town planning. They gave to the Garden City movement their own vision of the "city greatly beautiful," a vision derived from the medieval village as seen through the eyes of William Morris. They wanted to adapt what they believed were the still valid principles of traditional English town planning to the decentralized society of the future. Where Howard had expressed the architecture of cooperation in the mechanical symmetry of his original plan, Parker and Unwin sought instead what they called "organic unity."

They followed Howard's lead to the extent of clearly separating the town from the countryside that surrounded it. They placed the new city roughly in the middle of the Letchworth estate, setting aside 1,200 acres for the city proper and 2,800 acres for the Agricultural Belt that would surround it. Within the city, however, they rejected Howard's rigidly symmetrical diagrams and instead sought a more subtle "organic" sense of order suggested by the terrain. They took advantage of the positions of the hills, streams, an old Roman road, and even some of the larger trees to define the plan of the town. "The Crystal Palace" was replaced by a gently curving street of shops. Only the town center remained exactly what Howard intended it to be: a formal arrangement of municipal and cultural buildings.[80]

The contrast between Howard and his two architects was not, however, one simply between Howard's utilitarian bias and Parker and Unwin's aesthetic bent. If anything, Parker and Unwin were more practical than Howard. Industry, instead of forming a uniform periphery to Howard's circle, was grouped into an industrial park adjacent to the power plant and to the railroad. The tracks, in turn, separated industry from the residential area. The plan is effective without calling attention to itself through a calculated prettiness. In their quest for a natural unity Parker and Unwin succeeded – perhaps too well. As Herbert Read has pointed out, it is possible to visit Letchworth and even to live there without being aware that it is a conscious creation.[81]

Parker and Unwin believed that organic unity must extend up from the plan to embrace a common style of architecture. They saw the eclectic architecture of their time – in which a suburban villa tricked out with classical porticoes might be sandwiched between a Gothic extravaganza on the right and Renaissance palazzo on the left – as a horrible symptom of the chaotic individualism of their time. They held that the victory of cooperation in the Garden City could best be expressed in a consistent style derived from traditional village architecture, the brick and stucco, the gables and tile roofs of Hertfordshire. This was not mere antiquarianism, for Parker and Unwin "democratized" traditional architecture. Where other architects had used the vocabulary of picturesque gables and tiled roofs to glorify the suburban castles of the rich, Parker and Unwin employed traditional designs to express the unity of a cooperatively organized community of equals. In the context of their time, their designs for Letchworth stood for cleanliness, simplicity, and the honest use of materials – qualities the arts-and-crafts movement associated with the fourteenth century and hoped to revive in the twentieth. The fourteenth-century village, they believed, was the truest community that England had ever known, and its beauty was the expression of a unique balance of order and uniformity. This balance they hoped to recapture in that revitalized community of the future, the Garden City.

Parker and Unwin's designs thus bore little resemblance to Howard's plan for geometric boulevards and iron-and-steel Crystal Palaces. Nevertheless, both concepts derived from a common search for an architecture of cooperation. Parker and Unwin's plan was a sort of translation of Howard's original diagrams. It was, however, a loose translation that introduced some themes of its own. Unwin's hope that the Garden City would "give life just that order, that crystalline structure it had in feudal times,"[82] sounds a note of nostalgia for vanished stability not heard in Howard. Unwin's aesthetic glorification of the traditional village was also a glorification of the stable social relations he imagined existed there, and an implicit critique of the modern quest for change. For Unwin, the beautiful old English villages had "the appearance of being an organic whole, the home of a community" because they were "the expression of a corporate life in which all the different units were personally in touch with each other, consciously and frankly accepting their relations, and, on the whole, content with them."[83] Like the villagers themselves, "every building honestly confessed just what it was, and so fell into its place."[84] The Garden City, too, would be a community where everyone has his place and is content with it.

Parker and Unwin's concept of the Garden City thus had its reactionary as well as its forward-looking aspects. The two architects lacked Howard's confident faith in industrialization and the nineteenth-century world of rapid social change. For them, the Garden City was a place in which industrialization could be kept in its proper (subordinate) place and the incessant striving of modern times would yield to order and contentment. In their idealization of the English village, Parker and Unwin brought to prominence an element in the Garden City that had hardly existed in Howard: the fear of the great city and its social turmoil, the desire to discard the burdens of progress and return to the simple life. Their plans embodied the new stage in the Garden City movement, the stage in which Howard's influence was counterbalanced by Liberals like Cadbury, who looked back to an imagined paternalistic order. With their mixture of the enlightened and the medieval, Parker and Unwin reflected this split in the movement between an optimistic endorsement of the future and a nostalgic wish to escape from the modern world.

But Parker and Unwin, like the Garden City movement in general, ought to be judged not only on their realized plans but also on their aspirations. Their most revolutionary idea was never put into practice. In 1901, even before the decision to build a Garden City had been undertaken, Unwin proposed that the houses in the new city be organized cooperatively. His plan provided for "quadrangles" of homes in which three sides would be devoted to private apartments and the fourth to a common dining room, recreation room, and nursery. Food and coal would be purchased jointly, and the residents would share the cost of hiring cooks and maids. The quadrangle, he hoped, would become the basic unit of Garden City architecture, giving the city a "greater harmony and unity of effect" than would be possible where the land was carved into separate plots.[85]

Howard himself took up the plan in 1906 – "I believe the time has now come when [cooperation] can be successfully tried as one of the central ideas in domestic life,"[86] he wrote – but even his efforts resulted in only one quadrangle called Homesgarth.[87] Although Unwin modeled the quadrangle on an Oxford college, Homesgarth was too close in conception and design to communitarian experiments to be entirely respectable. Homesgarth, however, was no utopian scheme. "Its first object," Howard said, was "to provide a house of comparative comfort and beauty for the numerous folks of the middle class who have a hard struggle for existence on a mere budget – for those who require domestic help but can very ill afford it."[88] Homesgarth's small scale – only twenty-four families – and careful balance between family privacy and community functions is characteristic of Howard's pragmatic reinterpretation of the utopian tradition. In Howard's view, it was a piece of the new civilization and an important attempt to make cooperation part of the daily life of the Garden City.

Parker and Unwin hoped that even if First Garden City Ltd. would not support their plans for quadrangles, it would still provide funds to build the houses of Letchworth according to their designs. The company, however, was in serious financial difficulty. The original stock issue sold slowly; the directors bought £40,000, and some £60,000 was sold to the public in the first year, but it took three years to reach £150,000.[89] During those three years the company was forced to spend over £600,000 to provide the roads, gasworks, electrical generators, and other utilities the town needed.[90] The company was able to borrow the funds for these necessities, but it was unwilling to go more deeply in debt. Many of the first houses in Letchworth were built by speculative contractors whose designs introduced precisely those eccentricities that Parker and Unwin had wanted to banish from the town. These homes, however, were well suited to the tastes of Letchworth's first residents, many of whom were men and women of independent means and "advanced" opinions. Their enthusiasms included theosophy, vegetarianism, dress reform, and amateur theatricals; Letchworth was soon reputed to have more committees per person than any other town in England.[91] The company, fearing that Letchworth might soon get the reputation as a colony of cranks, then solemnly informed the press that only one resident habitually wore a toga and sandals.[92] When several men broke with convention by refusing to wear hats (which were then considered as necessary to outdoor attire as trousers), the town staged a public debate between the "Hatters" and the "No-Hatters." A company agent who believed that manufacturers would refuse to locate their plants where the norms of society were so openly questioned interrupted the proceedings and roundly denounced the "No-Hatters" as unpatriotic citizens who did not have the interests of Letchworth at heart.[93]

Despite the company's apprehensions, manufacturers did come to Letchworth. Only a few, like the cooperatively run Garden City Press Ltd., were attracted to the city for ideological reasons. Most came for precisely the practical reasons that Howard and especially Neville had foreseen. The rise in business activity in the first decade of the twentieth century created a demand for increased space that was hard to satisfy in London. Letchworth offered low rents, minimal taxes, and ample room to grow. When, for example, the publishing firm of J. W. Dent discovered that its London facilities offered no room for expansion, the publisher established a branch plant at Letchworth. The "Everyman" series of inexpensive classics was printed there.[94] Other enterprises began as the project of an amateur inventor and moved from a Letchworth garage to the industrial park. Light engineering and printing were the principal Garden City industries.[95]

The new factories promised to make Letchworth a self-supporting community. As houses and shops began to line the streets that Parker and Unwin had laid out, the social structure of the new town underwent a rapid change. A census taken of the 1,400 Letchworth residents in 1905 showed that almost all of them were from two groups: middle-class men and women of independent means (and their servants) and the skilled artisans who were building the new town.[96] By 1907 the population had more than doubled, and almost all the new residents were factory workers.[97]

Howard was now faced with the challenge to make good his claim that the Garden City would bring to working people health and living standards they could never have obtained in the old cities. Whatever the interests of his associates, he had not forgotten his belief that the Garden City would provide all the benefits that others were seeking from political and economic revolution. In practice, this challenge focused on housing. Could the Garden City accomplish what no other public or private organization in England had been able to do: construct decent dwellings that even the lowest-paid workers could afford? This meant, of course, building under existing social conditions. Howard had to assume that the tenants' wages would remain low, that interest on capital would continue to be paid, and that no government subsidy could be expected. If the Garden City would create good housing for all its citizens under these circumstances, then Howard's claim that it represented "the peaceful path to real reform" would receive powerful support.

Howard was convinced that planning, architectural ingenuity, and voluntary cooperation could solve the housing question. A cooperative building society, Garden City Tenants Ltd., was established in 1904 to raise capital for workers' housing.[98] As a stopgap measure, Thomas Adams persuaded the editor of *Country Life* to hold that magazine's "cheap cottage" competition at Letchworth. After the exhibition, the model cottages were sold very cheaply indeed to Letchworth workers.[99]

Garden City Tenants Ltd. then turned to Raymond Unwin for the multiunit dwellings the new town needed. Unwin's designs show the Garden City movement at its best – pragmatic, democratic, responsive to the needs of the people it served.[100] Unwin gave the same attention to these projects that other architects devoted to the rich man's villa. He made sure that every cottage got its share of sunlight, that every window and door was properly placed. That institutional bleakness that afflicts British (and not only British) architects when planning for the "lower orders" was completely absent from Unwin's work. Instead, there was a real sense of individual well-being and community solidarity, precisely the "organic unity" that Unwin had proclaimed.

The individual cottages were not left detached, as in the middle-class villas, but joined into rows of three to ten. These rows were then grouped around a central courtyard or field. This plan used far less land per unit than the villas and gave to each family the privacy of a two-story dwelling with its own garden. At the same time, there was substantial open space that could be shared in common. Within each cottage Unwin decided not to attempt to duplicate middle-class layouts, with their separate parlor, living room, dining room, and kitchen; on the small scale of the cottage this would have made the rooms claustrophobic. Moreover, Unwin wanted to design houses that "honestly confessed just what they were," not scaled-down copies of inappropriate models. He appreciated the fact that working-class family life traditionally centered around the hearth, and he therefore designed a combination living room–kitchen to be as comfortable, spacious, and open as possible.

At its best, Unwin's work represents that fruitful balance of individual and community which the Garden City stood for and which housing projects have seldom achieved since. It had, however, one great deficiency. When the costs of the new houses were added up, only skilled workers could afford them. The wages of the unskilled were simply too close to subsistence level for them to be able to pay the rent for any home that Unwin or Howard would call decent. As Howard later admitted, it was the bicycle that saved the situation. Workers who could not find housing in the Garden City bicycled each day from their jobs to apartments in the older towns beyond the Agricultural Belt, where cheap but substandard accommodations could be found.[101] One can hardly blame Unwin and Howard for their failure. If they were unable to build decent workers' housing without a subsidy, neither could anyone else.

These efforts in housing illustrate the real strengths and ultimate limitations of the Garden City idea as a social movement. By 1910 the practicality of Howard's basic concept had been proved. The new town of Letchworth was a clean, healthy, and well-planned environment; it had shown its capacity to attract industry and residents; and the First Garden City Ltd., though still financially pressed, was beginning to reap the rewards of its investment and declare its first dividend. The housing question, however, demonstrated that, despite Howard's hopes, the Garden City could not create its own oasis of social justice in an unjust society. Lower costs, better planning, community ownership of land – none of these could fully compensate for the inequities that were inherent in the social system of Howard's time. The path to real reform lay outside the Garden City.

By 1910, however, Howard was still looking to the future with confidence. He realized that Letchworth had its limitations, but Letchworth was only the first working model, which would surely inspire dozens and then hundreds of improved successors. But in 1910 the First Garden City was still the only Garden City, and no more were in the works. The problem for Howard was, where were the other Garden Cities that would begin to transform England?

Le Corbusier

The Radiant City

The Radiant City retained the most important principle of the Contemporary City: the juxtaposition of a collective realm of order and administration with an individualistic realm of family life and participation. This juxtaposition became the key to Le Corbusier's attempt to resolve the syndicalist dilemma of authority and participation. Both elements of the doctrine receive intense expression in their respective spheres. Harmony is in the structure of the whole city and in the complete life of its citizens.

The Radiant City was a more daring and difficult synthesis than the Contemporary City. In his effort to realize the contradictory elements of syndicalism, Le Corbusier made the Radiant City at once more authoritarian and more libertarian than its predecessor. Within the sphere of collective life, authority has become absolute. The Contemporary City had lacked any single power to regulate all the separate private corporations that accomplished the essential work of society; Le Corbusier had then believed that the invisible hand of free competition would create the most efficient coordination. The Great Depression robbed him of his faith. He now held that organization must extend beyond the large corporations. They had rationalized their own organizations, but the economy as a whole remained wasteful, anarchic, irrational. The planned allocation of manpower and resources that had taken place within each corporation must now be accomplished for society. In the Radiant City every aspect of productive life is administered from above according to one plan. This plan replaces the marketplace with total administration; experts match society's needs to its productive capacities.

The preordained harmony that Le Corbusier had called for in urban reconstruction would now be imposed on all productive life. The great works of construction would become only one element in the plan. This was a crucial extension of the concept of planning. Ebenezer Howard and Frank Lloyd Wright had believed that once the environment had been designed, the sources of disorder in society would be minimized and individuals could be left to pursue their own initiatives. This belief rested on a faith in a "natural economic order," a faith that Le Corbusier no longer shared. He confronted a world threatened by chaos and collapse. It seemed that only discipline could create the order he sought so ardently. Coordination must become conscious and total. Above all, society needed authority and a plan.

Syndicalism, Le Corbusier believed, would provide a "pyramid of natural hierarchies" on which order and planning could be based. The bottom of this pyramid is the *syndicat*, the group of workers, white-collar employees, and engineers who run their own factory. The workers have the responsibility of choosing their most able colleague to be their manager and to represent them at the regional trade council. Le Corbusier believed that although citizens would usually find it impossible to identify the most able man among a host of politicians, each worker is normally able to choose his natural leader. "Every man is capable of judging the facts of his trade," he observed.[102]

The regional council of plant managers represents the first step in the hierarchy. Each level corresponds to a level of administrative responsibility. The manager runs his factory; the regional leaders administer the plants in their region. The regional council sends its most able members to a national council, which is responsible for the overall control of the trade. The leader of this council meets with fellow leaders to administer the national plan. This highest group is responsible for coordinating the entire production of the country. If, for example, the national plan calls for mass housing, they allot the capital needed for each region and set the goals for production. The order is passed down to the regional council, which assigns tasks to individual factories and contractors. The elected representatives of the *syndicat* return from the regional council with instructions that determine his factory's role in the national productive effort.

This hierarchy of administration has replaced the state. As Saint-Simon had urged, an individual's power corresponds exactly to that person's responsibilities in the structure of production. The administrator issues the orders necessary for fulfilling the required quotas, and these orders provide the direction that society needs. The divisive issues of parliamentary politics cannot arise, for everyone shares a common concern that the resources of society be administered as efficiently as possible. Even the tasks of the national council are administrative rather than political. The members do not apportion wealth and power among competing interests groups. Their task, like that of all the other functionaries, is a "technical" one: they carry out the plan.

"Plans are not political," Le Corbusier wrote.[103] The plan's complex provisions, covering every aspect of production, distribution, and construction, represent a necessary and objective ordering of society. The plan is necessary because the Machine Age requires conscious control. It is objective because the Machine Age imposes essentially the same discipline on all societies. Planning involves the rational mastery of industrial process and the application of that mastery to the specific conditions of each nation. The plan is a "rational and lyric monument" to man's capacity to organize.

The plan is formulated by an elite of experts detached from all social pressure. They work "outside the fevers of mayors' and prefects' offices," away from the "cries of electors and the cries of victims." Their plans are "established serenely, lucidly. They take account only of human truths."[104] In the planner's formulations, "the motive forces of a civilization pass from the subjective realm of consciousness to the objective realm of facts." Plans are "just, long-term, established on the realities of the century, imagined by a creative passion."[105]

This plan for Le Corbusier was more than a collection of statistics and instructions; it was a social work of art. It brought to consciousness the complex yet satisfying harmonies of an orderly, productive world. It was the score for the great industrial orchestra. The plan summed up the unity that underlay the division of labor in society; it expressed the full range of exchange and cooperation that is necessary to an advanced economy.

Le Corbusier used the vocabulary and structures of syndicalism to advance his own vision of a beautifully organized world. His "pyramid of natural hierarchies" was intended to give the human structure of organization the same clarity and order as the great skyscrapers of the business center. The beauty of the organization was the product of the perfect cooperation of everyone in the hierarchy. It was the expression of human solidarity in creating a civilization in the midst of the hostile forces of nature. The natural hierarchy was one means of attaining the sublime.

People at work create a world that is truly human. But that world, once created, is a realm of freedom where people live in accord with nature, not in opposition to it. Like the Contemporary City, the Radiant City identifies the realm of freedom with the residential district. As if in recognition of the need to counterbalance the industrial realm's increased emphasis on organization, Le Corbusier has displaced the towers of administration from the central position they occupied in the earlier plan. The residential district stands in the place of honor in the Radiant City.

It is, moreover, a transformed residential district. Le Corbusier had lost the enthusiasm for capitalism that had led him originally to segregate housing in the Contemporary City according to class – elite in the center, proletariat at the outskirts. Now he was a revolutionary syndicalist, with a new appreciation of workers' rights. When he visited the United States in 1935, he found much to admire in the luxury apartment houses that lined Central Park and Lake Shore Drive, but he added, "My own thinking is directed towards the crowds in the subway who come home at night to dismal dwellings. The millions of beings sacrificed to a life without hope, without rest – without sky, sun, greenery."[106] Housing in the Radiant City is designed for them. The residential district embodies Le Corbusier's new conviction that the world of freedom must be egalitarian. "If the city were to become a human city," he proclaimed, "it would be a city without classes."[107]

No longer does the residential district simply mirror the inequalities in the realm of production. Instead, the relation between the two is more complex, reflecting Le Corbusier's resolve to make the Radiant City a city of organization *and* freedom. The realm of production in the Radiant City is even more tightly organized, its hierarchies of command and subordination even stricter than in the Contemporary City. At the same time, the residential district – the realm of leisure and self-fulfillment – is radically libertarian, its principles of equality and cooperation standing in stark opposition to the hierarchy of the industrial world. The citizen in Le Corbusier's syndicalist society thus experiences both organization and freedom as part of his daily life.

The centers of life in the Radiant City are the great high-rise apartment blocks, which Le Corbusier calls "Unités." These structures, each of which is a neighborhood with 2,700 residents, mark the culmination of the principles of housing that he had been expounding since the Dom-Inos of 1914. Like the Dom-Ino house, the Unité represents the application of mass-production techniques; but where the Dom-Ino represents the principle in its most basic form, the Unité is a masterful expression of scale, complexity, and sophistication. The disappointments of the 1920s and the upheavals of the 1930s had only strengthened Le Corbusier in his faith that a great new age of the machine was about to dawn. In the plans for the Unité he realized that promise of a *collective* beauty that had been his aim in the Dom-Ino design; he achieved a collective grandeur, which the Dom-Ino houses had only hinted at; and finally, he foresaw for all the residents of the Unité a freedom and abundance beyond even that which he had planned for the elite of the Contemporary City. The apartments in the Unité are not assigned on the basis of a worker's position in the industrial hierarchy but according to the size of his family and their needs. In designing these apartments, Le Corbusier remarked that he "thought neither of rich nor of poor but of man."[108] He wanted to get away both from the concept of luxury housing, in which the wasteful consumption of space becomes a sign of status, and from the concept of *Existenzminimum*, the design of workers' housing based on the absolute hygienic minimums. He believed that housing could be made to the "human scale," right in its proportions for everyone, neither cramped nor wasteful. No one would want anything larger nor get anything smaller.

The emphasis in the Unité, however, is not on the individual apartment but on the collective services provided to all the residents. As in the Villa-Apartment Blocks of the Contemporary City, Le Corbusier followed the principle that the cooperative sharing of leisure facilities could give to each family a far more varied and beautiful environment than even the richest individual could afford in a single-family house. These facilities, moreover, take on a clear social function as the reward and recompense for the eight hours of disciplined labor in a factory or office that are required of all citizens in a syndicalist society. The Unité, for example, has a full range of workshops for traditional handicrafts whose techniques can no longer be practiced in industries devoted to mass production. Here are meeting rooms of all sizes for participatory activities that have no place in the hierarchical sphere of production. There are cafés, restaurants, and shops where sociability can be cultivated for its own sake. Most important, in Le Corbusier's own estimation, the Unité provides the opportunity for a full range of physical activities that are severely curtailed during working hours in an industrial society. Within each Unité there is a full-scale gymnasium; on the roof are tennis courts, swimming pools, and even sand beaches. Once again, the high-rise buildings cover only 15 percent of the land, and the open space around them is elaborately landscaped into playing fields, gardens, and parkland.

The most basic services that the Unité provides are those that make possible a new concept of the family. Le Corbusier envisioned a society in which men and women would work full-time as equals. He therefore presumed the end of the family as an economic unit in which women were responsible for domestic services while men worked for wages. In the Unité, cooking, cleaning, and child raising are services provided by society. Each building has its day-care center, nursery and primary school, cooperative laundry, cleaning service, and food store. In the Radiant City the family no longer has an economic function to perform. It exists as an end in itself.

Le Corbusier and Frank Lloyd Wright were both intensely concerned with the preservation of the family in an industrial society, but here as elsewhere they adopted diametrically opposite strategies. Wright wished to revive and strengthen the traditional economic role of the family, to ensure its survival by making it the center both of the society's work and of its leisure. Wright believed in a life in which labor and leisure would be one, whereas Le Corbusier subjected even the family to the stark division between work and play that marks the Radiant City. The family belongs to the realm of play. Indeed, it virtually ceases to exist during the working day. When mother and father leave their apartment in the morning for their jobs, their children accompany them down on the elevator. The parents drop them off at the floor where the school or day-care center is located and pick them up after work. The family reassembles in the afternoon, perhaps round the pool or at the gym, and when the family members return to their apartment they find it already cleaned, the laundry done and returned, the food ordered in the morning already delivered and prepared for serving. Individual families might still choose to cook their own food, do their own laundry, raise vegetables on their balconies, or even raise their own children. In the Radiant City, however, these activities have become leisure-time hobbies like woodworking or weaving, quaint relics of the pre-mechanical age.

The Unité is thus high-rise architecture for a new civilization, and Le Corbusier was careful to emphasize that its design could be truly realized only after society had been revolutionized. He therefore never concerned himself with such problems as muggings in the parks or vandalism in the elevators. In the Radiant City, crime and poverty no longer exist.

But if the Unité looks to the future, its roots are in the nineteenth-century utopian hopes for a perfect cooperative society, the same hopes that inspired Ebenezer Howard's cooperative quadrangles. Peter Serenyi has aptly compared the Unité to that French utopian palace of communal pleasures, the phalanstery of Charles Fourier.[109] An early nineteenth-century rival of Saint-Simon, Fourier envisioned a structure resembling the château of Versailles to house the 1,600 members of his "phalanx" or rural utopian community. "We have no conception of the compound or collective forms of luxury," Fourier complained, and the phalanstery was designed to make up that lack.[110] He believed that in a properly run society all individual desires could find their appropriate gratification. The phalanstery, therefore, contains an elaborate series of lavish public rooms: theaters, libraries, ballrooms, and – Fourier's special pride – the dining rooms where "exquisite food and a piquant selection of dining companions" can always be found.

The phalanstery can be seen as the nineteenth-century anticipation and the Unité as the twentieth-century realization of architecture in the service of collective pleasure. Both designs represent what Le Corbusier termed "the architecture of happiness," architecture created to deliver what he was fond of calling "the essential joys." Fourier, however, could only express his vision in the anachronistic image of the baroque palace. Le Corbusier finds the forms of collective pleasure in the most advanced techniques of mass production. For him, the architecture of happiness is also the architecture for the industrial era.

The comparison of the phalanstery and the Unité suggests, finally, the complexity of Le Corbusier's ideal city. For Fourier was the bitter antagonist of Saint-Simon, whose philosophy is so central to Le Corbusier's social thought. The rivalry of the two nineteenth-century prophets was more than personal. Since their time, French utopian thought has been divided into two distinct traditions. The Saint-Simonian tradition is the dream of society as the perfect industrial hierarchy. Its setting is urban, its thought technological, its goal production, and its highest value organization. Fourier and his followers have envisioned society as the perfect community: rural, small-scale, egalitarian, dedicated to pleasure and self-fulfillment. In the Radiant City, Le Corbusier combines these two traditions into an original synthesis. He places a Fourierist phalanstery in the center of a Saint-Simonian industrial society. Community and organization thus find intense and appropriate expression: both are integral parts of Le Corbusier's ideal city for the Machine Age.

NOTES

1   For a fuller discussion of Frank Lloyd Wright, see Robert Fishman, *Urban Utopias in the Twentieth Century: Ebenezer Howard, Frank Lloyd Wright, and Le Corbusier* (New York: Basic Books, 1977).

2   Joseph Conrad, *The Secret Agent* (New York, 1953), p. 11. The quotation is drawn from the Preface, first published in 1921.

3   For statistics of urban growth, see Adna Ferrin Weber, *The Growth of Cities in the Nineteenth Century* (Ithaca, N.Y., 1899).

4   Hsi-Huey Liang, "Lower-class Immigrants in Wilhelmine Berlin," in *The Urbanization of European Society in the Nineteenth Century*, eds. Andrew Lees and Lynn Lees (Lexington, Mass., 1976), p. 223.

5   Le Corbusier, *La Ville radieuse* (Boulogne-Seine, 1935), p. 181.

6   For Owen, see J. F. C. Harrison, *Quest for the New Moral World* (New York, 1969).

7   For Fourier, see Jonathan Beecher and Richard Bienvenu, eds., *The Utopian Vision of Charles Fourier* (Boston, 1971).

8   For Haussmann and his influence see David H. Pinkney, *Napoleon III and the Rebuilding of Paris* (Princeton, N.J., 1958); Howard Saalman, *Haussmann: Paris Transformed* (New York, 1971); and Anthony Sutcliffe, *The Autumn of Central Paris* (London, 1970).

9   Peter H. Mann, "Octavia Hill: An Appraisal," *Town Planning Review* 23, no. 3 (Oct. 1953): 223–237.

10   Friedrich Engels, *Zur Wohnungsfrage*, 2d ed. (Leipzig, 1887).

11   See Barbara Miller Lane, *Architecture and Politics in Germany, 1918–1945* (Cambridge, Mass., 1968).

12   Le Corbusier, *Urbanisme* (Paris, 1925), p. 135.

13   Lewis Mumford, "The Garden City Idea and Modern Planning," introductory essay to F. J. Osborn's edition of *Garden Cities of To-morrow* (Cambridge, Mass., 1965), p. 29. Although Osborn's edition bears the title of the 1902 edition, his text restores portions of the 1898 text that were cut in 1902. Osborn's is therefore a "definitive" text, and I follow his usage in always referring to Howard's book as *Garden Cities of To-morrow*. All further references will come from Osborn's edition, abbreviated *GCT*.

14 See Donald Canty, ed., *The New City* (New York, 1969) for the details of this recommendation.
15 The New Towns, however, have had their problems. See "'New Towns' Face Growing Pains," *New York Times*, June 13, 1976, p. 26.
16 F. J. Osborn, Preface to *GCT*, p. 22.
17 Ibid., pp. 22–23.
18 Ebenezer Howard Papers, Hertfordshire County Archives, Hertford, England. Draft of an Unfinished Autobiography, folio 17.
19 C. C. R., "The Evolution of Ebenezer Howard," *Garden Cities and Town Planning* 2, no. 3 (March 1912): 46.
20 Howard Papers, folio 17.
21 J. Bruce Wallace, *Towards Fraternal Organization* (London, 1894), p. 19.
22 Ibid.
23 Howard Papers, folio 17.
24 For Bellamy's influence, see Sylvia E. Bowman, *The Year 2000: A Critical Biography of Edward Bellamy* (New York, 1958).
25 E. Howard, "Spiritual Influences Toward Social Progress," *Light*, April 30, 1910, p. 195.
26 E. Howard, "Ebenezer Howard, the Originator of the Garden City Idea," *Garden Cities and Town Planning* 16, no. 6 (July 1926): 133.
27 An account of the Nationalization of Labour Society can be found in Peter Marshall, "A British Sensation," in Sylvia Bowman, ed., *Edward Bellamy Abroad* (New York, 1962), pp. 86–118.
28 Howard, "Ebenezer Howard, the Originator of the Garden City Idea," p. 133.
29 Edward Bellamy, *Looking Backward* (New York, 1960), p. 127.
30 Peter Kropotkin, *Fields, Factories, and Workshops* (London, 1899).
31 Howard Papers, Draft of an Autobiography, folio 10.
32 *GCT*, p. 131.
33 Howard Papers, folio 10.
34 *GCT*, p. 47.
35 Ibid., p. 145.
36 Ibid., p. 146.
37 Ibid., p. 48.
38 James Silk Buckingham, *National Evils and Practical Remedies, with the Plan of a Model Town* (London, 1849). Although Howard mentions the utopian city of Buckingham in the text of *GCT* as one of the proposals he combined into the Garden City, he states in a footnote that in fact he had not seen Buckingham's plan until he had "got far on" with his project. *GCT*, p. 119.
39 Howard Papers, Early draft of *GCT*, folio 3.
40 Ibid.
41 Howard, "Spiritual Influences Toward Social Progress," p. 196. *Hygeia* was published in London in 1876.
42 Benjamin Ward Richardson, *Hygeia, A City of Health* (London, 1876), p. 21.
43 *GCT*, p. 76.
44 Ibid., pp. 50–56 and 71. Placing the churches along Grand Avenue means that no single church occupies the center of town. Howard's religious upbringing was Nonconformist.
45 *GCT*, p. 53.
46 Ibid., p. 54.
47 *GCT*, diagram #2. The diagram also shows such institutions as "convalescent homes" and the "asylums for blind and deaf" in the greenbelt. In an earlier version of his plan, Howard wanted the Agricultural Belt to cover 8,000 acres. See his "Summary of E. Howard's proposals for a Home Colony," *The Nationalisation News* 3, no. 29 (Feb. 1893): 20.

48 Howard Papers, Common Sense Socialism, folio 10.
49 Alfred Marshall, "The Housing of the London Poor," *Contemporary Review* 45, no. 2 (Feb. 1884): 224–231.
50 Howard Papers, folio 10. Howard recalled meeting Marshall in connection with stenography work he did for parliamentary commissions and discussing the Garden City idea with him. In a note added to *GCT* he claimed that he had not seen Marshall's article when he first formulated his ideas: *GCT*, p. 119.
51 *GCT*, pp. 58–88.
52 Howard Papers, quoted by Howard in an early draft of *GCT*, folio 3.
53 *GCT*, pp. 89–111.
54 Ibid., p. 136.
55 "Return of Owners of Land Survey," analyzed in F. M. L. Thompson, *English Landed Society in the Nineteenth Century* (London, 1963), pp. 317–319.
56 Henry George, *Progress and Poverty* (New York, 1911), p. 201.
57 Howard, quoted in W. H. Brown's interview with him, "Ebenezer Howard, A Modern Influence," *Garden Cities and Town Planning* 7, no. 30 (Sept. 1908): 116.
58 *GCT*, p. 131.
59 Ibid., pp. 96–111.
60 Howard Papers, Lecture to a Fabian Society, January 11, 1901, folio 3.
61 *GCT*, p. 104.
62 Ibid., p. 139.
63 I suspect the population of the Central City was put at 58,000 so that the whole complex would attain a population of exactly 250,000.
64 *GCT*, p. 142.
65 Ibid.
66 Ibid. Spencer held that public libraries in themselves were only "mildly communistic." See his "The New Toryism," *Contemporary Review*, 45, no. 2 (Feb. 1884): 153–167. These of course were Spencer's later views. A younger Spencer in *Social Statics* had called for the nationalization of the land. This permitted Howard to refer to Spencer as one of his influences: *GCT*, pp. 123–125.
67 *GCT*, p. 108.
68 *The Thirty-Sixth Annual Co-operative Congress* (Manchester, 1904), p. 63.
69 Ibid., pp. 65 and 83.
70 See especially Aneurin Williams, "Co-operation in Housing and Town Building," in *Thirty-Ninth Co-operative Congress* (Manchester, 1909), pp. 379–397.
71 Minutes of the Manchester Branch of the Garden City Association, April 1, 1902; now in the possession of the Town and Country Planning Association.
72 Howard Papers, Letter of Neville to Howard, November 13, 1903, folio 25.
73 Howard Papers, Letter of Neville to Howard, December 14, 1903, folio 25.
74 Howard Papers, Draft of 1,000-year lease dated "around 1902."
75 The details of Neville's position and the controversy that followed are in Aneurin Williams, "Land Tenure in the Garden City," Appendix A in C. B. Purdom, *The Garden City* (London, 1913).
76 E. Howard, "The Relation of the Ideal to the Practical," *The Garden City*, n.s. 2, no. 13 (Feb. 1907): 267.
77 See Barry Parker and Raymond Unwin, *The Art of Building a Home* (London, 1901), for the best record of the early careers and interests of both men.
78 See Walter L. Creese, ed., *The Legacy of Raymond Unwin: A Human Pattern for Planning* (Cambridge, Mass., 1967), especially the editor's introduction.
79 Raymond Unwin, "The Beautiful in Town Building," *The Garden City*, n.s. 2, no. 13 (Feb. 1907): 267.
80 Unwin, *Town Planning in Practice* (London, 1909).

81   Herbert Read, "A Tribute to Ebenezer Howard," *Town and Country Planning* 14, no. 53 (Spring 1946): 14.

82   Raymond Unwin, "On the Building of Houses in the Garden City," *Garden City Tract* no. 8 (London, 1901), p. 4.

83   Unwin, "Co-operation in Building," in Parker and Unwin, *The Art of Building a Home*, p. 92.

84   Ibid., p. 92.

85   Unwin, "Co-operation in Building," in Parker and Unwin, *The Art of Building a Home*, pp. 91–108. See also Raymond Unwin, *Cottage Plans and Common Sense*, Fabian Tract no. 109 (London, 1901).

86   E. Howard, "Co-operative Housekeeping," *The Garden City*, n.s. 1, no. 8 (Sept. 1906): 170.

87   Homesgarth was designed not by Unwin but by another architect associated with the Garden City movement, H. Clapham Lander. See his early advocacy of co-ops, "The Advantages of Co-operative Dwellings," *Garden City Tract* no. 7 (London, 1901).

88   Howard, "Co-operative Housekeeping," p. 171.

89   Aneurin Williams, "Land Tenure in the Garden City," p. 220.

90   First Garden City Ltd., *Prospectus*, 1909.

91   Charles Lee, "From a Letchworth Diary," *Town and Country Planning* 21, no. 113 (Sept. 1953): 434–442.

92   *Daily Mirror* (London), June 17, 1905.

93   Lee, "Letchworth Diary," pp. 439–440.

94   Ernest Rhys, *Everyman Remembers* (London, 1931).

95   C. B. Purdom, *The Building of Satellite Towns* (London, 1949), pp. 214–238.

96   *The Garden City* I, no. 3 (June 1905): 11.

97   Ibid., n.s. 1, no. 4 (Nov. 1907): 4.

98   Ibid., 1, no. 2 (Feb. 1904): 1.

99   Catalogue of the Cheap Cottage Exhibition at Letchworth (Letchworth, 1905).

100 The best source for Unwin's designs is his "Cottage Planning," in *Where Shall I Live?* (Letchworth, 1907), pp. 103–109.

101 Howard Papers, How the Bicycle Saved the City, folio 10; manuscript of an article, probably unpublished, by Howard.

102 Le Corbusier, *La Ville radieuse*, p. 192.

103 Ibid., title page.

104 Ibid., p. 154.

105 Ibid., p. 153.

106 Le Corbusier, *Quand les cathédrales étaient blanches* (Paris, 1937), pp. 280–281.

107 Le Corbusier, *La Ville radieuse*, p. 167.

108 Ibid., p. 146.

109 Peter Serenyi, "Le Corbusier, Fourier, and the Monastery at Ema," *Art Bulletin*, 49 (Dec. 1967): 277–286.

110 Charles Fourier, "An Architectural Innovation: The Street Gallery," in Jonathan Beecher and Richard Bienvenu, eds. and trans., *The Utopian Vision of Charles Fourier* (Boston, 1971), p. 243.

2

The Death and Life of Great American Cities

Jane Jacobs

This chapter is an attack on current city planning and rebuilding. It is also, and mostly, an attempt to introduce new principles of city planning and rebuilding, different and even opposite from those now taught in everything from schools of architecture and planning to the Sunday supplements and women's magazines. My attack is not based on quibbles about rebuilding methods or hairsplitting about fashions in design. It is an attack, rather, on the principles and aims that have shaped modern, orthodox city planning and rebuilding.

In setting forth different principles, I shall mainly be writing about common, ordinary things: for instance, what kinds of city streets are safe and what kinds are not; why some city parks are marvelous and others are vice traps and death traps; why some slums stay slums and other slums regenerate themselves even against financial and official opposition; what makes downtowns shift their centers; what, if anything, is a city neighborhood, and what jobs, if any, neighborhoods in great cities do. In short, I shall be writing about how cities work in real life, because this is the only way to learn what principles of planning and what practices in rebuilding can promote social and economic vitality in cities, and what practices and principles will deaden these attributes.

There is a wistful myth that if only we had enough money to spend – the figure is usually put at $100 billion – we could wipe out all our slums in ten years, reverse decay in the great, dull, gray belts that were yesterday's and day-before-yesterday's suburbs, anchor the wandering middle class and its wandering tax money, and perhaps even solve the traffic problem.

But look what we have built with the first several billions: low-income projects that become worse centers of delinquency, vandalism, and general social hopelessness than the slums they were supposed to replace. Middle-income housing projects

From Jane Jacobs, *The Death and Life of Great American Cities*, pp. 3–25. Copyright © 1961 by Jane Jacobs. Reprinted by permission of Random House, Inc.

that are truly marvels of dullness and regimentation, sealed against any buoyancy or vitality of city life. Luxury housing projects that mitigate their inanity, or try to, with a vapid vulgarity. Cultural centers that are unable to support a good bookstore. Civic centers that are avoided by everyone but bums, who have fewer choices of loitering place than others. Commercial centers that are lackluster imitations of standardized suburban chain-store shopping. Promenades that go from no place to nowhere and have no promenaders. Expressways that eviscerate great cities. This is not the rebuilding of cities. This is the sacking of cities.

Under the surface, these accomplishments prove even poorer than their poor pretenses. They seldom aid the city areas around them, as in theory they are supposed to. These amputated areas typically develop galloping gangrene. To house people in this planned fashion, price tags are fastened on the population, and each sorted-out chunk of price-tagged populace lives in growing suspicion and tension against the surrounding city. When two or more such hostile islands are juxtaposed the result is called "a balanced neighborhood." Monopolistic shopping centers and monumental cultural centers cloak, under the public relations hoo-ha, the subtraction of commerce, and of culture too, from the intimate and casual life of cities.

That such wonders may be accomplished, people who get marked with the planners' hex signs are pushed about, expropriated, and uprooted much as if they were the subjects of a conquering power. Thousands upon thousands of small businesses are destroyed, and their proprietors ruined, with hardly a gesture at compensation. Whole communities are torn apart and sown to the winds, with a reaping of cynicism, resentment, and despair that must be heard and seen to be believed. A group of clergymen in Chicago, appalled at the fruits of planned city rebuilding there, asked,

> Could Job have been thinking of Chicago when he wrote:
> Here are men that alter their neighbor's landmark . . .
> shoulder the poor aside, conspire to oppress the friendless.
> Reap they the field that is none of theirs, strip they the vine-yard wrongfully seized from
> its owner . . .
> A cry goes up from the city streets, where wounded men lie groaning . . .

If so, he was thinking of New York, Philadelphia, Boston, Washington, St. Louis, San Francisco, and a number of other places. The economic rationale of current city rebuilding is a hoax. The economics of city rebuilding do not rest soundly on reasoned investment of public tax subsidies, as urban renewal theory proclaims, but also on vast, involuntary subsidies wrung out of helpless site victims. And the increased tax returns from such sites, accruing to the cities as a result of this "investment," are a mirage, a pitiful gesture against the ever-increasing sums of public money needed to combat disintegration and instability that flow from the cruelly shaken-up city. The means to planned city rebuilding are as deplorable as the ends.

Meantime, all the art and science of city planning are helpless to stem decay – and the spiritlessness that precedes decay – in ever more massive swatches of cities. Nor can this decay be laid, reassuringly, to lack of opportunity to apply the arts of planning. It seems to matter little whether they are applied or not. Consider the Morningside Heights area in New York City. According to planning theory it should not be in trouble at all, for it enjoys a great abundance of parkland, campus, playground, and other open spaces. It has plenty of grass. It occupies high and pleasant ground with magnificent river views. It is a famous educational center with splendid institutions – Columbia University, Union Theological Seminary, the Juilliard School of Music, and half a dozen others of eminent respectability. It is the beneficiary of good hospitals and churches. It has no industries. Its streets are zoned in the main against "incompatible uses" intruding into the preserves for solidly constructed, roomy, middle-and upper-class apartments. Yet by the early 1950s Morningside Heights was becoming a slum so swiftly, the surly kind of slum in which people fear to walk the streets, that the situation posed a crisis for the institutions. They and the planning arms of the city government got together, applied more planning theory, wiped out the most run-down part of the area and built in its stead a middle-income cooperative project complete with shopping center and a public housing project – all interspersed with air, light, sunshine, and landscaping. This was hailed as a great demonstration in city saving.

After that Morningside Heights went downhill even faster.

Nor is this an unfair or irrelevant example. In city after city, precisely the wrong areas, in the light of planning theory, are decaying. Less noticed, but equally significant, in city after city the wrong areas, in the light of planning theory, are refusing to decay.

Cities are an immense laboratory of trial and error, failure and success, in city building and city design. This is the laboratory in which city planning should have been learning and forming and testing its theories. Instead the practitioners and teachers of this discipline (if such it can be called) have ignored the study of success and failure in real life, have been incurious about the reasons for unexpected success, and are guided instead by principles derived from the behavior and appearance of towns, suburbs, tuberculosis sanatoria, fairs, and imaginary dream cities – from anything but cities themselves.

If it appears that the rebuilt portions of cities and the endless new developments spreading beyond the cities are reducing city and countryside alike to a monotonous, unnourishing gruel, this is not strange. It all comes, first-, second-, third-, or fourthhand, out of the same intellectual dish of mush, a mush in which the qualities, necessities, advantages, and behavior of great cities have been utterly confused with the qualities, necessities, advantages, and behavior of other and more inert types of settlements.

There is nothing economically or socially inevitable about either the decay of old cities or the fresh-minted decadence of the new unurban urbanization. On the contrary, no other aspect of our economy and society has been more purposefully manipulated for a full quarter of a century to achieve precisely what we are getting. Extraordinary governmental financial incentives have been required to achieve this degree of monotony, sterility, and vulgarity. Decades of preaching, writing, and exhorting by experts have gone into convincing us and our legislators that mush like this must be good for us, as long as it comes bedded with grass.

Automobiles are often conveniently tagged as the villains responsible for the ills of cities and the disappointments and futilities of city planning. But the destructive effects of automobiles are much less a cause than a symptom of our incompetence at city building. Of course planners, including the highwaymen with fabulous sums of money and enormous powers at their disposal, are at a loss to make automobiles and cities compatible with one another. They do not know what to do with automobiles in cities because they do not know how to plan for workable and vital cities anyhow – with or without automobiles.

The simple needs of automobiles are more easily understood and satisfied than the complex needs of cities, and a growing number of planners and designers have come to believe that if they can only solve the problems of traffic, they will thereby have solved the major problem of cities. Cities have much more intricate economic and social concerns than automobile traffic. How can you know what to try with traffic until you know how the city itself works and what else it needs to do with its streets? You can't.

It may be that we have become so feckless as a people that we no longer care how things do work but only what kind of quick, easy outer impression they give. If so, there is little hope for our cities or probably for much else in our society. But I do not think this is so.

Specifically, in the case of planning for cities, it is clear that a large number of good and earnest people do care deeply about building and renewing. Despite some corruption, and considerable greed for the other man's vineyard, the intentions going into the messes we make are, on the whole, exemplary. Planners, architects of city design, and those they have led along with them in their beliefs are not consciously disdainful of the importance of knowing how things work. On the contrary, they have gone to great pains to learn what the saints and sages of modern orthodox planning have said about how cities *ought* to work and what *ought* to be good for people and businesses in them. They take this with such devotion that when contradictory reality intrudes, threatening to shatter their dearly won learning, they must shrug reality aside.

Consider, for example, the orthodox planning reaction to a district called the North End in Boston. This is an old, low-rent area merging into the heavy industry of the waterfront, and it is officially considered Boston's worst slum and civic shame. It embodies attributes that all enlightened people know are evil, because so many wise men have said they are evil. Not only is the North End bumped right up against industry, but worse still it has all kinds of working places and commerce mingled in the greatest complexity with its residences. It has the highest concentration of dwelling units, on the land that is used for dwelling units, of any part of Boston, and indeed one of the highest concentrations to be found in any American city. It has little parkland. Children play in the streets. Instead of superblocks, or even decently large blocks, it has very small blocks; in planning parlance it is "badly cut up with wasteful streets." Its buildings are old. Everything conceivable is presumably wrong with the North End. In orthodox planning terms, it is a three-dimensional textbook of "megalopolis" in the last stages of depravity. The North End is thus a recurring assignment for MIT and Harvard planning and architectural students, who now and again pursue, under the guidance of their teachers, the paper exercise of converting it into superblocks and park promenades, wiping away its nonconforming uses, trans-forming it to an ideal of order and gentility so simple it could be engraved on the head of a pin.

Twenty years ago, when I first happened to see the North End, its buildings – town houses of different kinds and sizes converted to flats, and four- or five-story tenements built to house the flood of immigrants first from Ireland, then from Eastern Europe, and finally from Sicily – were badly overcrowded, and the general effect was of a district taking a terrible physical beating and certainly desperately poor.

When I saw the North End again in 1959, I was amazed at the change. Dozens and dozens of buildings had been rehabilitated. Instead of mattresses against the windows, there were Venetian blinds and glimpses of fresh paint. Many of the small, converted houses now had only one or two families in them instead of the old crowded three or four. Some of the families in the tenements (as I learned later, visiting inside) had uncrowded themselves by throwing two older apartments together, and had equipped these with bathrooms, new kitchens, and the like. I looked down a narrow alley, thinking to find at least here the old, squalid North End, but no: more neatly repointed brickwork, new blinds, and a burst of music as a door opened. Indeed, this was the only city district I have ever seen – or have seen to this day – in which the sides of buildings around parking lots had not been left raw and amputated, but repaired and painted as neatly as if they were intended to be seen. Mingled all among the buildings for living were an incredible number of splendid food stores, as well as such enterprises as upholstery making, metalwork-ing, carpentry, food processing. The streets were alive with children playing, people shopping, people strolling, people talking. Had it not been a cold January day, there would surely have been people sitting.

The general street atmosphere of buoyancy, friendliness, and good health was so infectious that I began asking directions of people just for the fun of getting in on some talk. I had seen a lot of Boston in the past couple of days, most of it sorely distressing, and this struck me, with relief, as the healthiest place in the city. But I could not imagine where the money had come from for the rehabilitation, because it is almost impossible today to get any appreciable mortgage money in districts of American cities that are not either high-rent, or else imitations of suburbs. To find out, I went into a bar and restaurant (where an animated conversation about fishing was in progress) and called a Boston planner I know.

"Why in the world are you down in the North End?" he said. "Money? Why, no money or work has gone into the North End. Nothing's going on down there. Eventually, yes, but not yet. That's a slum!"

"It doesn't seem like a slum to me," I said.

"Why, that's the worst slum in the city. It has 275 dwelling units to the net acre! I hate to admit we have anything like that in Boston, but it's a fact."

"Do you have any other figures on it?" I asked.

"Yes, funny thing. It has among the lowest delinquency, disease, and infant mortality rates in the city. It also has the lowest ratio of rent to income in the city. Boy, are those people getting bargains. Let's see ... the child population is just above average for the city, on the nose. The death rate is low, 8.8 per thousand, against the average city rate of 11.2. The TB death rate is very low, less than 1 per ten thousand, can't understand it, it's lower even than Brookline's. In the old days the North End used to be the city's worst spot for tuberculosis, but all that has changed. Well, they must be strong people. Of course it's a terrible slum."

"You should have more slums like this," I said. "Don't tell me there are plans to wipe this out. You ought to be down here learning as much as you can from it."

"I know how you feel," he said. "I often go down there myself just to walk around the streets and feel that wonderful, cheerful street life. Say, what you ought to do, you ought to come back and go down in the summer if you think it's fun now. You'd be crazy about it in summer. But of course we have to rebuild it eventually. We've got to get those people off the streets."

Here was a curious thing. My friend's instincts told him the North End was a good place, and his social statistics confirmed it. But everything he had learned as a physical planner about what is good for people and good for city neighborhoods, everything that made him an expert, told him the North End had to be a bad place.

The leading Boston savings banker, "a man way up there in the power structure," to whom my friend referred me for my inquiry about the money, confirmed what I learned, in the meantime, from people in the North End. The money had not come through the grace of the great American banking system, which now knows enough about planning to know a slum as well as the planners do. "No sense in lending money into the North End," the banker said. "It's a slum! It's still getting some immigrants! Furthermore, back in the Depression it had a very large number of foreclosures; bad record." (I had heard about this too, in the meantime, and how families had worked and pooled their resources to buy back some of those foreclosed buildings.)

The largest mortgage loans that had been fed into this district of some 15,000 people in the quarter-century since the Great Depression were for $3,000, the banker told me, "and very, very few of those." There had been some others for $1,000 and for $2,000. The rehabilitation work had been almost entirely financed by business and housing earnings within the district, plowed back in, and by skilled work bartered among residents and relatives of residents.

By this time I knew that this inability to borrow for improvement was a galling worry to North Enders, and that furthermore some North Enders were worried because it seemed impossible to get new building in the area except at a price of seeing themselves and their community wiped out in the fashion of the students' dreams of a city Eden, a fate that they knew was not academic because it had already smashed completely a socially similar – although physically more spacious – nearby district called the West End. They were worried because they were aware also that patch and fix with nothing else could not do forever. "Any chance of loans for new construction in the North End?" I asked the banker.

"No, absolutely not!" he said, sounding impatient at my denseness. "That's a slum!"

Bankers, like planners, have theories about cities on which they act. They have gotten their theories from the same intellectual sources as the planners. Bankers and government administrative officials who guarantee mortgages do not invent planning theories nor, surprisingly, even economic doctrine about cities. They are enlightened nowadays, and they pick up their ideas from idealists, a generation later. Since theoretical city planning has embraced no major new ideas for considerably more than a generation, theoretical planners, financiers, and bureaucrats are all just about even today.

And to put it bluntly, they are all in the same stage of elaborately learned superstition as medical science was early in the last century, when physicians put their faith in bloodletting, to draw out the evil humors that were believed to cause disease. With bloodletting, it took years of learning to know precisely which veins, by what rituals, were to be opened for what symptoms. A superstructure of technical complication was erected in such deadpan detail that the literature still sounds almost plausible. However, because people, even when they are thoroughly enmeshed in descriptions of reality that are at variance with reality, are still seldom devoid of the powers of observation and independent thought, the science of bloodletting, over most of its long sway, appears usually to have been tempered with a certain amount of common sense. Or it was tempered until it reached its highest peaks of technique in, of all places, the young United States. Bloodletting went wild here. It had an enormously influential proponent in Dr Benjamin Rush, still revered as the greatest statesman-physician of our revolutionary and federal periods, and a genius of medical adminis-tration. Dr Rush Got Things Done. Among the things he got done, some of them good and useful, were to develop, practice, teach, and spread the custom of bloodletting in cases where prudence or mercy had heretofore restrained its use. He and his students drained the blood of very young children, of consumptives, of the greatly aged, of almost anyone unfortunate enough to be sick in his realms of influence. His extreme practices aroused the alarm and horror of European bloodletting physicians. And yet as late as 1851, a committee appointed by the State Legislature of New York solemnly defended the thoroughgoing use of bloodletting. It scathingly ridiculed and censured a physician, William Turner, who had the temerity to write a pamphlet criticizing Dr Rush's doctrines and calling "the practice of taking blood in diseases contrary to common sense, to general experience, to enlightened reason, and to the manifest laws of the divine Providence." Sick people needed fortifying, not draining, said Dr Turner, and he was squelched.

Medical analogies, applied to social organisms, are apt to be farfetched, and there is no point in mistaking mammalian chemistry for what occurs in a city. But analogies as to what goes on in the brains of earnest and learned men, dealing with complex phenomena they do not understand at all and trying to make do with a pseudoscience, do have a point. As in the pseudoscience of bloodletting, just so in the pseudoscience of city rebuilding and planning, years of learning and a plethora of subtle and complicated dogma have arisen on a foundation of nonsense. The tools of technique have steadily been perfected. Naturally, in time, forceful and able men, admired administrators, having swallowed the initial fallacies and having been provisioned with tools and with public confidence, go on logically to the greatest destructive excesses, which prudence or mercy might previously have forbade. Bloodletting could heal only by accident or insofar as it broke the rules, until the time when it was abandoned in favor of the hard, complex business of assembling, using, and testing, bit by bit, true descriptions of reality drawn not from how it ought to be but from how it is. The pseudoscience of city planning and its compan-ion, the art of city design, have not yet broken with the specious comfort of wishes, familiar superstitions, oversimplifications, and symbols – and have not yet embarked upon the adventure of probing the real world.

So in this chapter we shall start, if only in a small way, adventuring in the real world, ourselves. The way to get at what goes on in the seemingly mysterious and perverse behavior of cities is, I think, to look closely, and with as little previous expectation as is possible, at the most ordinary scenes and events and attempt to see what they mean and whether any threads of principle emerge among them. . . .

One principle emerges so ubiquitously, and in so many and such complex different forms, . . . [that it] becomes the heart of my argument. This ubiquitous principle is the need of cities for a most intricate and close-grained diversity of uses that give each other constant mutual support, both economically and socially. The compon-ents of this diversity can differ enormously, but they must supplement each other in certain concrete ways.

I think that unsuccessful city areas are areas that lack this kind of intricate mutual support, and that the science of city planning and the art of city design, in real life for real cities, must become the science and art of catalyzing and nourishing these close-grained working relationships. I think, from the evidence I can find, that there are four primary conditions required for generating useful great city diversity, and that by deliberately inducing these four conditions, planning can induce city vitality (something that the plans of planners alone, and the designs of designers alone, can never achieve)....

Cities are fantastically dynamic places, and this is strikingly true of their successful parts, which offer a fertile ground for the plans of thousands of people....

The look of things and the way they work are inextricably bound together, and in no place more so than cities. But people who are interested only in how a city "ought" to look and uninterested in how it works will be disappointed.... It is futile to plan a city's appearance, or speculate on how to endow it with a pleasing appearance of order, without knowing what sort of innate, functioning order it has. To seek for the look of things as a primary purpose or as the main drama is apt to make nothing but trouble.

In New York's East Harlem, there is a housing project with a conspicuous rectangular lawn that became an object of hatred to the project tenants. A social worker frequently at the project was astonished by how often the subject of the lawn came up, usually gratuitously as far as she could see, and how much the tenants despised it and urged that it be done away with. When she asked why, the usual answer was, "What good is it?" or "Who wants it?" Finally one day, a tenant more articulate than the others made this pronouncement: "Nobody cared what we wanted when they built this place. They threw our houses down and pushed us here and pushed our friends somewhere else. We don't have a place around here to get a cup of coffee or a newspaper even, or borrow fifty cents. Nobody cared what we need. But the big men come and look at that grass and say, 'Isn't it wonderful! Now the poor have everything!'"

This tenant was saying what moralists have said for thousands of years: Handsome is as handsome does. All that glitters is not gold.

She was saying more: There is a quality even meaner than outright ugliness or disorder, and this meaner quality is the dishonest mask of pretended order, achieved by ignoring or suppressing the real order that is struggling to exist and to be served.

In trying to explain the underlying order of cities, I use a preponderance of examples from New York because that is where I live. But most of my basic ideas come from things I first noticed or was told in other cities. For example, my first inkling about the powerful effects of certain kinds of functional mixtures in the city came from Pittsburgh, my first speculations about street safety from Philadelphia and Baltimore, my first notions about the meanderings of downtown from Boston, my first clues to the unmaking of slums from Chicago. Most of the material for these musings was at my own front door, but perhaps it is easiest to see things first where you don't take them for granted. The basic idea, to try to begin understanding the intricate social and economic order under the seeming disorder of cities, was not my idea at all, but that of William Kirk, head worker of Union Settlement in East Harlem, New York, who, by showing me East Harlem, showed me a way of seeing other neighborhoods, and downtowns too. In every case, I have tried to test out what I saw or heard in one city or neighborhood against others, to find how relevant each city's or each place's lessons might be outside its own special case.

I have concentrated on great cities, and on their inner areas, because this is the problem that has been most consistently evaded in planning theory. I think this may also have somewhat wider usefulness as time passes, because many of the parts of today's cities in the worst, and apparently most baffling, trouble were suburbs or dignified, quiet residential areas not too long ago; eventually many of today's brand-new suburbs or semisuburbs are going to be engulfed in cities and will succeed or fail in that condition depending on whether they can adapt to functioning successfully as city districts. Also, to be frank, I like dense cities best and care about them most.

But I hope no reader will try to transfer my observations into guides as to what goes on in towns, or little cities, or in suburbs that still are suburban. Towns, suburbs, and even little cities are totally different organisms from great cities. We are in enough trouble already from trying to understand big cities in terms of the behavior, and the imagined behavior, of towns. To try to understand towns in terms of big cities will only compound confusion.

I hope any reader will constantly and skeptically test what I say against his or her own knowledge of cities and their behavior. If I have been inaccurate in observations or mistaken in inferences and conclusions, I hope these faults will be quickly corrected. The point is, we need desperately to learn and to apply as much knowledge that is true and useful about cities as fast as possible.

I have been making unkind remarks about orthodox city planning theory, and shall make more as occasion arises to do so. By now, these orthodox ideas are part of our folklore. They harm us because we take them for granted. To show how we got them, and how little they are to the point, I shall give a quick outline here of the most influential ideas that have contributed to the verities of orthodox modern city planning and city architectural design.[1]

The most important thread of influence starts, more or less, with Ebenezer Howard, an English court reporter for whom planning was an avocation. Howard looked at the living conditions of the poor in late-nineteenth-century London and justifiably did not like what he smelled or saw or heard. He not only hated the wrongs and mistakes of the city, he hated the city and thought it an outright evil and an affront to nature that so many people should get themselves into an agglomeration. His prescription for saving the people was to do the city in.

The program he proposed, in 1898, was to halt the growth of London and also repopulate the countryside, where villages were declining, by building a new kind of town – the Garden City, where the city poor might again live close to nature. So that they might earn their livings, industry was to be set up in the Garden City; for while Howard was not planning cities, he was not planning dormitory suburbs either. His aim was the creation of self-sufficient small towns, really very nice towns if you were docile and had no plans of your own and did not mind spending your life among others with no plans of their own. As in all utopias, the right to have plans of any significance belonged only to the planners in charge. The Garden City was to be encircled with a belt of agriculture. Industry was to be in its planned preserves; schools, housing, and greens in planned living preserves; and in the center were to be commercial, club, and cultural places, held in common. The town and green belt, in their totality, were to be permanently controlled by the public authority under which the town was developed, to prevent speculation or supposedly irrational changes in land use and also to do away with temptations to increase its density – in brief, to prevent it from ever becoming a city. The maximum population was to be held to thirty thousand people.

Nathan Glazer has summed up the vision well in *Architectural Forum*: "The image was the English country town – with the manor house and its park replaced by a community center, and with some factories hidden behind a screen of trees, to supply work."

The closest American equivalent would probably be the model company town, with profit sharing, and with the parent-teacher associations in charge of the routine, custodial political life. For Howard was envisioning not simply a new physical environment and social life but a paternalistic political and economic society.

Nevertheless, as Glazer has pointed out, the Garden City was "conceived as an alternative to the city, and as a solution to city problems; this was, and is still, the foundation of its immense power as a planning idea." Howard managed to get two garden cities built, Letchworth and Welwyn, and of course Great Britain and Sweden have, since World War II, built a number of satellite towns based on Garden City principles. In the United States, the suburb of Radburn, New Jersey, and the depression-built, government-sponsored Green Belt towns (actually suburbs) were all incomplete modifications of the idea. But Howard's influence in the literal, or reasonably literal, acceptance of his program was as nothing compared to his influence on conceptions underlying all American city planning today. City planners and designers with no interest in the Garden City as such are still thoroughly governed intellectually by its underlying principles.

Howard set spinning powerful and city-destroying ideas: He conceived that the way to deal with the city's functions was to sort and sift out of the whole certain simple uses, and to arrange each of these in relative self-containment. He focused on the provision of wholesome housing as the central problem, to which everything else was subsidiary; furthermore he defined wholesome housing in terms only of suburban physical qualities and small-town social qualities. He conceived of commerce in terms of routine, standardized supply of goods, and as serving a self-limited market. He conceived of good planning as a series of static acts; in each case the plan must anticipate all that is needed and be protected, after it is built, against any but the most minor subsequent changes. He conceived of planning also as essentially paternalistic, if not authoritarian. He was uninterested in the aspects of the city that could not be abstracted to serve his utopia. In particular, he simply wrote off the intricate, many faceted, cultural life of the metropolis. He was uninterested in such problems as the way the great cities police themselves, or exchange ideas, or operate politically, or invent new economic arrangements, and he was oblivious to devising ways to strengthen these functions because, after all, he was not designing for this kind of life in any case.

Both in his preoccupations and in his omissions, Howard made sense in his own terms but none in terms of city planning. Yet virtually all modern city planning has been adapted from, and embroidered on, this silly substance.

Howard's influence on American city planning converged on the city from two directions: from town and regional planners on the one hand, and from architects on the other. Along the avenue of planning, Sir Patrick Geddes, a Scots biologist and philosopher, saw the Garden City idea not as a fortuitous way to absorb population growth otherwise destined for a great city but as the starting point of a much grander and more encompassing pattern. He thought of the planning of cities in terms of the planning of whole regions. Under regional planning, garden cities would be rationally distributed throughout large territories, dovetailing into natural resources, balanced against agriculture and woodland, forming one far-flung logical whole.

Howard's and Geddes's ideas were enthusiastically adopted in America during the 1920s, and developed further by a group of extraordinarily effective and dedicated people – among them Lewis Mumford, Clarence Stein, the late Henry Wright, and Catherine Bauer. While they thought of themselves as regional planners, Catherine Bauer has more recently called this group the "Decentrists," and this name is more apt, for the primary result of regional planning, as they saw it, would be to decentralize great cities, thin them out, and disperse their enterprises and populations into smaller, separated cities or, better yet, towns. At the time, it appeared that the American population was both aging and leveling off in numbers, and the problem appeared to be not one of accommodating a rapidly growing population but simply of redistributing a static population.

As with Howard himself, this group's influence was less in getting literal acceptance of its program – that got nowhere – than in influencing city planning and legislation affecting housing and housing finance. Model housing schemes by Stein and Wright, built mainly in suburban settings or at the fringes of cities, together with the writings and the diagrams, sketches, and photographs presented by Mumford and Bauer, demonstrated and popularized ideas such as these, which are now taken for granted in orthodox planning: The street is bad as an environment for humans; houses should be turned away from it and faced inward, toward sheltered greens. Frequent streets are wasteful, of advantage only to real estate speculators who measure value by the front foot. The basic unit of city design is not the street but the block and, more particularly, the superblock. Commerce should be segregated from residences and greens. A neighborhood's demand for goods should be calculated "scientifically," and this much and no more commercial space allocated. The presence of many other people is, at best, a necessary evil, and good city planning must aim for at least an illusion of isolation and suburbany privacy. The Decentrists also pounded in Howard's premises that the planned community must be islanded off as a self-contained unit, that it must resist future change, and that every significant detail must be controlled by the planners from the start and then stuck to. In short, good planning was project planning.

To reinforce and dramatize the necessity for the new order of things, the Decentrists hammered away at the bad old city. They were incurious about successes in great cities. They were interested only in failures. All was failure. A book like Mumford's *The Culture of Cities* was largely a morbid and biased catalog of ills. The great city was Megalopolis, Tyrannopolis, Nekropolis, a monstrosity, a tyranny, a living death. It must go. New York's midtown was "solidified chaos" (Mumford). The shape and appearance of cities was nothing but "a chaotic accident...the summation of the haphazard, antagonistic whims of many self-centered, ill-advised individuals" (Stein). The centers of cities amounted to "a foreground of noise, dirt, beggars, souvenirs, and shrill competitive advertising" (Bauer).

How could anything so bad be worth the attempt to understand it? The Decentrists' analyses, the architectural and housing designs that were companions and offshoots of these analyses, the national housing and home financing legislation so directly influenced by the new vision – none of these had anything to do with understanding cities or fostering successful large cities, nor were they intended to. They were reasons and means for jettisoning cities, and the Decentrists were frank about this.

But in the schools of planning and architecture – and in Congress, state legislatures, and city halls too – the Decentrists' ideas were gradually accepted as basic guides for dealing constructively with big cities themselves. This is the most amazing event in the whole sorry tale: that finally people who sincerely wanted to strengthen great cities should adopt recipes frankly devised for undermining their economies and killing them.

The man with the most dramatic idea of how to get all this anticity planning right into the citadels of iniquity themselves was the European architect Le Corbusier. He devised in the 1920s a dream city, which he called the Radiant City, composed not of the low buildings beloved of the Decentrists but instead mainly of skyscrapers within a park. "Suppose we are entering the city by way of the Great Park," Le Corbusier wrote. "Our fast car takes the special elevated motor track between the majestic skyscrapers: as we approach nearer, there is seen the repetition against the sky of the twenty-four skyscrapers; to our left and right on the outskirts of each particular area are the municipal and administrative buildings; and enclosing the space are the museums and university buildings. The whole city is a Park." In Le Corbusier's vertical city the common run of mankind was to be housed at 1,200 inhabitants to the acre, a fantastically high city density indeed, but because of building up so high, 95 percent of the ground could remain open. The skyscrapers would occupy only 5 percent of the ground. The high-income people would be in lower, luxury housing around courts, with 85 percent of their ground left open. Here and there would be restaurants and theaters.

Le Corbusier was planning not only a physical environment. He was planning for a social utopia too. Le Corbusier's utopia was a condition of what he called maximum individual liberty, by which he seems to have meant not liberty to do anything much, but liberty from ordinary responsibility. In his Radiant City nobody, presumably, was going to have to be his brother's keeper any more. Nobody was going to have to struggle with plans of his own. Nobody was going to be tied down.

The Decentrists and other loyal advocates of the Garden City were aghast at Le Corbusier's city of towers in the park, and still are. Their reaction to it was, and remains, much like that of progressive nursery school teachers confronting an utterly institutional orphanage. And yet, ironically, the Radiant City comes directly out of the Garden City. Le Corbusier accepted the Garden City's fundamental image, superficially at least, and worked to make it practical for high densities. He described his creation as the Garden City made attainable. "The garden city is a will-o'-the-wisp," he wrote. "Nature melts under the invasion of roads and houses and the promised seclusion becomes a crowded settlement... The solution will be found in the 'vertical garden city.'"

In another sense too, in its relatively easy public reception, Le Corbusier's Radiant City depended upon the Garden City. The Garden City planners and their ever-increasing following among housing reformers, students, and architects were indefatigably popularizing the ideas of the superblock; the project neighborhood; the unchangeable plan; and grass, grass, grass. What is more, they were successfully establishing such attributes as the hallmarks of humane, socially responsible, functional, high-minded planning. Le Corbusier really did not have to justify his vision in either humane or city-functional terms. If the great object of city planning was that

Christopher Robin might go hoppety-hoppety on the grass, what was wrong with Le Corbusier? The Decentrists' cries of institutionalization, mechanization, depersonalization seemed to others foolishly sectarian.

Le Corbusier's dream city has had an immense impact on our cities. It was hailed deliriously by architects and has gradually been embodied in scores of projects, ranging from low-income public housing to office-building projects. Aside from making at least the superficial Garden City principles superficially practical in a dense city, Le Corbusier's dream contained other marvels. He attempted to make planning for the automobile an integral part of his scheme, and this was, in the 1920s and early 1930s, a new, exciting idea. He included great arterial roads for express one-way traffic. He cut the number of streets because "cross-roads are an enemy to traffic." He proposed underground streets for heavy vehicles and deliveries, and of course like the Garden City planners he kept the pedestrains off the streets and in the parks. His city was like a wonderful mechanical toy. Furthermore, his conception, as an architectural work, had a dazzling clarity, simplicity, and harmony. It was so orderly, so visible, so easy to understand. It said everything in a flash, like a good advertisement. This vision and its bold symbolism have been all but irresistible to planners, housers, designers – and to developers, lenders, and mayors too. It exerts a great pull on "progressive" zoners, who write rules calculated to encourage nonproject builders to reflect, if only a little, the dream. No matter how vulgarized or clumsy the design, how dreary and useless the open space, how dull the close-up view, an imitation of Le Corbusier shouts, "Look what I made!" Like a great, visible ego it tells of someone's achievement. But as to how the city works, it tells, like the Garden City, nothing but lies.

Although the Decentrists, with their devotion to the ideal of a cozy town life, have never made peace with the Le Corbusier vision, most of their disciples have. Virtually all sophisticated city designers today combine the two conceptions in various permutations. The rebuilding technique variously known as "selective removal" or "spot renewal" or "renewal planning" or "planned conservation" – meaning that total clearance of a run-down area is avoided – is largely the trick of seeing how many old buildings can be left standing and the area still converted into a passable version of Radiant Garden City. Zoners, highway planners, legislators, land-use planners, and parks and playground planners – none of whom live in an ideological vacuum – constantly use, as fixed points of reference, these two powerful visions and the more sophisticated merged vision. They may wander from the visions, they may compromise, they may vulgarize, but these are the points of departure.

We shall look briefly at one other, less important, line of ancestry in orthodox planning. This one begins more or less with the great Columbian Exposition in Chicago in 1893, just about the same time that Howard was formulating his Garden City ideas. The Chicago fair snubbed the exciting modern architecture that had begun to emerge in Chicago and instead dramatized a retrogressive imitation Renaissance style. One heavy, grandiose monument after another was arrayed in the exposition park, like frosted pastries on a tray, in a sort of squat, decorated forecast of Le Corbusier's later repetitive ranks of towers in a park. This orgiastic assemblage of the rich and monumental captured the imagination of both planners and public. It gave impetus to a movement called the City Beautiful, and indeed the planning of the exposition was dominated by the man who became the leading City Beautiful planner, Daniel Burnham of Chicago.

The aim of the City Beautiful was the City Monumental. Great schemes were drawn up for systems of baroque boulevards, which mainly came to nothing. What did come out of the movement was the Center Monumental, modeled on the fair. City after city built its civic center or its cultural center. These buildings were arranged along a boulevard as at Benjamin Franklin Parkway in Philadelphia, or along a mall like the Government Center in Cleveland, or were bordered by park, like the Civic Center at St. Louis, or were interspersed with park, like the Civic Center at San Francisco. However they were arranged, the important point was that the monuments had been sorted out from the rest of the city and assembled into the grandest effect thought possible, the whole being treated as a complete unit, in a separate and well-defined way.

People were proud of them, but the centers were not a success. For one thing, invariably the ordinary city around them ran down instead of being uplifted, and they always acquired an incongruous rim of ratty tattoo parlors and secondhand-clothing stores, or else just nondescript, dispirited decay. For another, people stayed away from them to a remarkable degree. Somehow, when the fair became part of the city, it did not work like the fair.

The architecture of the City Beautiful centers went out of style. But the idea behind the centers was not questioned, and it has never had more force than it does today. The idea of sorting out certain cultural or public functions and decontaminating their relationship with the workaday city dovetailed nicely with the Garden City teachings. The conceptions have harmoniously merged, much as the Garden City and the Radiant City merged, into a sort of Radiant Garden City Beautiful, such as the immense Lincoln Square project for New York, in which a monumental City Beautiful cultural center is one among a series of adjoining Radiant City and Radiant Garden City housing, shopping, and campus centers.

And by analogy, the principles of sorting out – and of bringing order by repression of all plans but the planners' – have been easily extended to all manner of city functions, until today a land-use master plan for a big city is largely a matter of proposed placement, often in relation to transportation, of many series of decontaminated sortings.

From beginning to end, from Howard and Burnham to the latest amendment on urban renewal law, the entire concoction is irrelevant to the workings of cities. Unstudied, unrespected, cities have served as sacrificial victims.

NOTE

1   Readers who would like a fuller account, and a sympathetic account, which mine is not, should go to the sources, which are very interesting, especially *Garden Cities of To-morrow*, by Ebenezer Howard; *The Culture of Cities*, by Lewis Mumford; *Cities in Evolution*, by Sir Patrick Geddes; *Modern Housing*, by Catherine Bauer; *Toward New Towns for America*, by Clarence Stein; *Nothing Gained by Overcrowding*, by Sir Ray-mond Unwin; and *The City of Tomorrow and Its Planning*, by Le Corbusier. The best short survey I know of is the group of excerpts under the title "Assumptions and Goals of City Planning," contained in *Land-Use Planning, A Casebook on the Use, Misuse and Re-use of Urban Land*, by Charles M. Haar.

3

Toward a Non-Euclidian Mode of Planning

John Friedmann

We live in an unprecedented time, confronted by unprecedented problems. I suppose that every generation believes in the unprecedented nature of its time and place, and to some extent this belief is well founded. But what we are living through in the final decades of this century is something altogether different. It is nothing less than the collapse of the Euclidian world order of stable entities and common sense assumptions that have governed our understanding of the world for the past two hundred years. The engineering model of planning that served us during this period, with its penchant for advance decision making and blueprinting and its claims of superiority to other forms of decision making because of its scientific character, are thus no longer valid and must be abandoned. We are moving into a non-Euclidian world of many space-time geographies, and it is the recognition of this change that obliges us to think of new and more appropriate models.

Rethinking Planning

The conventional concept of planning is so deeply linked to the Euclidian mode that it is tempting to argue that if the traditional model has to go, then the very idea of planning must be abandoned. The only way around this dilemma – either Euclid or nothing – would be to define planning independently and distinct from the engineering sciences, which were its original inspiration. Such a definition involves the linking of knowledge to action: *Planning is that professional practice that specifically seeks to connect forms of knowledge with forms of action in the public domain.* Although fairly abstract, this definition allows us to reconceive planning as something other than engineering, where means are always efficiently related to given

Reprinted by permission of the *Journal of the American Planning Association*, 59(4) (Autumn 1993): 482–5. © American Planning Association, Chicago, IL.

ends, and blueprints lay out a course of action for others to pursue. The definition allows us to think of a non-Euclidian model of planning. What we need to do, then, is to rethink the questions of knowledge and action. What knowledge is relevant and with whose actions are we concerned?

To begin our excursion into this relatively uncharted terrain, we need first to consider the implications of the contemporary collapse of the time-space continuum. What would be the appropriate time and space of a non-Euclidian form of planning? The time of such a planning is the *real time* of everyday events rather than imagined future time. Planners would accordingly be more in the thick of things rather than removed from the actions that their planning under the old model was intended to guide. Viewed in this light, planning becomes less a way of preparing documents, such as analyses and plans, and more a way of bringing planning knowledge and practice to bear directly on the action itself. Central to a non-Euclidian planning model are planners acting as responsible, thinking urban professionals rather than as faceless bureaucrats engaged in the production of anonymous documents. Face-to-face interaction in real time is the new model of planning.

This is not to argue that it is altogether futile to imagine future time or useless to make projections, simulations, and other hypothetical studies about what might or ought to happen next year, or five or even fifty years from now. Human imagination cannot be confined to practical problem solving in the here and now. Being open to the future, the mind takes leaps in time. Concern with an imagined future will continue to play an important role in planning, but the emphasis in non-Euclidian planning should be on processes operating in actual or real time, because it is only in the evanescent and still undecided present that planners can hope to be effective.

As for the space of planning, we need to privilege *regional and local* over national and transnational space. This leads to a decentered view of planning. I am not saying that national and transnational planning are obsolete. Far from it. Planning is instituted at all levels of public decision making, but in thinking about a new model, where should the emphasis lie? There are several reasons for my choice of the regional and local scale. First, we must be more attentive than ever to regional and local variety and difference. The problems and conditions of planning are not everywhere the same, and it is the specificities of place that should be our guide. In other words, there is truth in the old adage that the solution should be as complex as the problem it proposes to solve. There are no simple solutions for problems in the public domain.

A second reason is the increasing presence of organized civil society in public decision making. This is a relatively new but increasingly salient phenomenon in the public life of cities and regions. It means that a space for participation must be found for a whole new set of actors in addition to the nation state and capital. Regions, cities, and neighborhoods are the places where meaningful citizen participation can take place. It is far less likely to occur at superordinate levels.

A third reason is that regions and localities are the spaces of people's everyday lives. National and transnational space is typically for corporate actions and super-ordinate bureaucracies. It is not the space where ordinary people can exert much influence on events. But ordinary people do affect the spaces where they earn their livelihoods and where their daily lives unfold. The quality of that space is exceptionally important to them.

A decentered planning is attractive for other reasons as well: the wider distribution of risks, the potential for social experimentation, and the revival of democratic practices. It is true, of course, that national and transnational conditions tend to constrain local and regional actions, and that structural changes at higher levels are often required before significant progress at local levels can occur. Neither politics nor planning can be abandoned at these superior levels of governance, and their role is indeed crucial. But changed or not, these conditions constitute merely the framework for everyday planning practice, and the bulk of most planners' attention should be focused on regions, cities, and neighborhoods.

Within the new continuum of real time and local space, a non-Euclidian planning model would have five characteristics. It would be normative, innovative, political, transactive, and based on social learning.[1] Before addressing each of these, it may be useful to contrast the new model with the familiar Euclidian or engineering model of planning. Whereas planning in the new model is normative, planning in the old model is normatively neutral in that its principal criterion is efficiency in the attainment of externally defined goals and objectives. Whereas planning in the new model is innovative ("setting something new into the world," would be a definition of action in this model), the old paradigm centers on the allocation of resources in budgets, land use maps, and the location of public facilities. Whereas the new model argues that planners should be political in the sense of being concerned with implementing strategy and tactics, the old model argues for strict adherence to the civil service code of affective neutrality and nonpolitical practice. And whereas the new model argues for a transactive, empowering planning style, the old centrist model is essentially disempowering in its impacts. Finally, whereas the new model is based on social learning, the old model is primarily a document-oriented activity that is largely closed to public scrutiny and therefore short on learning potential.

Planning should be normative

Whom should the practice of planning serve? One could, for example, argue that planners have an obligation to serve those who pay them. Such an answer, however, would be unacceptable as a guide to professional practice.

Teachers teach; lawyers serve justice; doctors heal. What do planners do? In every profession there is an ideal of service. Normative ideas for planning are difficult to define, because planners are active in a public – that is a political – domain where views and interests often clash. Thus, I cannot lay down a set of guidelines valid for every planner. There are, as we all know, both conservative and progressive planners; planners who serve special interests and those who would act in the interest of all humanity. Still, I would like to set forth my own considered values, which are grounded in a humanist vision. In the late twentieth century, the following values seem to compel serious consideration: the ideals of inclusive democracy; giving voice to the disempowered; integrating disempowered groups into the mainstream of economic and social life while preserving cultural diversity; privileging qualitative over quantitative growth, including the notion of sustainability; gender equality; and respect for the natural world. In this perspective, planning is well to the left of the political center. No doubt there will be argument on this point. On the other hand, since belief in the inevitability of historical progress is no longer tenable, the urgencies of the present world crisis and the specific values that they demand

– democracy, inclusion, diversity, quality of life, sustainability, equality of rights, and the multiple claims of the environment – need to inform planners' work.

Planning should be innovative

Innovative planning looks toward creative solutions to the social, physical, and environmental problems that rise to political consciousness in the public domain. Innovative planning is consequently focused rather than comprehensive in scope; present rather than future oriented; and concerned chiefly with institutional and procedural changes appropriate to the case at hand. Innovative planning is concerned more with resource mobilization than with central allocation. It operates in real rather than imaginary time. And above all, it is entrepreneurial. As such, it is well adapted to a decentered planning system that involves a concerting of the powers of many different actors. Therefore, innovative planning requires great skills in negotiation, mediation, and the art of compromise. It is a form of planning that, like entrepreneurship in the private sector, is prepared to take risks, even while remaining publicly accountable.

Planning should be political

In non-Euclidian planning, which takes place in real time, knowledge and action are so tightly looped that they appear not as two separate processes but as one. Implementation is therefore built into the planning process as a critical dimension, involving strategy and tactics designed to overcome resistance to change within the limits of legality and peaceful practice.

It is the common experience of humanity, however, that the new will be resisted, not because it is new, but because it threatens to displace something that already exists. The assumption on the part of welfare economists that certain changes ought to be preferred because they will make some people better off while making no one's position worse, is an empirical impossibility. Some people will always feel worsted by innovations, though not always in financial terms.

This being the case, planning entrepreneurs can expect to meet with opposition whenever they try to realize their intentions. Therefore, if they are to prevail, if only partially, they will need to think about their implementation strategies right from the start. Without the exigencies of implementation, planning designs remain empty forms. But to act strategically is already to act politically; it means taking power seriously as a crucial element in planning.

Planning should be transactive

In contemporary planning, two kinds of knowledge are especially pertinent in the search for solutions: expert and experiential knowledge. Planners are usually identified with the former; the latter is the uncodified knowledge of people who will be affected by potential solutions. If solutions are to be adequate to a problem, the two must be brought together. Indeed, the definition of the problem may result from linking expert with experiential knowledge in a process of mutual learning.

Because experiential knowledge is not codified, it becomes manifest primarily through speech. It is in the face-to-face transactions between planners and the affected population that a basis in knowledge adequate to the problem can be found.

Transactive planning is situation-specific and thus appropriate to decentered planning, which seeks a diversity of solutions at regional and local levels. Transactive planning seeks to draw potentially affected populations into the planning process from the very beginning, when problems still need defining. It is a participatory style with its own characteristics. Above all else, participation requires time. It also requires that both planners and citizens have the capacity to listen sympathetically and share the responsibility for problem definition and solution.

Transactive planning works best in small groups of up to twenty people. Because community representatives may not be empowered to speak for others, transactive planning is not an answer to the issue of democratic accountability. Its claim is more limited. Transactive planning brings more detailed and specific knowledge to bear on a situation than would be possible if only expert knowledge were used. In addition, it may also strengthen communal responses and channel them away from blind resistance into more constructive paths. Transactive planning seeks to tap into people's capacity for proactive practice and, where it is successful, may help create a sense of collective solidarity.

Planning should be based on social learning

In turbulent times, when little can be foreseen, there is a need to proceed cautiously and experimentally to learn from mistakes, to allow new information to guide the course of action, and to take immediate corrective actions as may be needed. Of course, long-term commitments must be made from time to time: rail transit systems, for example, must be designed on a substantial scale. Large-scale projects, however, are the exception rather than the rule, and increasingly, small-scale, flexible solutions are found to be the appropriate answer. For instance, small-scale power generation is becoming a technical and economic possibility. More flexible solutions than fixed rail systems are finding favor among transportation planners: share ride systems, jitney cabs, shuttle services.

The social learning model of planning argues for an open process with two main characteristics: critical feedback and a strong institutional memory. Openness requires democratic procedures. It favors open over closed meetings, and invites criticism and comment. The media and evaluative research both play an important role here. Planning in the public domain must be accountable. In a climate of secrecy, mistakes accumulate and, in the long term, almost certainly culminate in disaster.

Social learning systems require a confident leadership that is not afraid to admit mistakes. It also requires a political culture that does not seek immediate partisan advantage for every mistake committed. It is essential, however, to realize the broad implications of social learning. When action fails to satisfy expectations, questions must be raised concerning the strategy employed and, beyond that, the actor's image of reality, and even the ultimate values on which the action rests. To reconsider strategy, image, and values calls for the sort of courage that only planning entrepreneurs are likely to possess.

The New Urban Professional

The old planning model, rooted in nineteenth-century concepts of science and engineering, is either dead or severely impaired. Though still practiced, it has become largely irrelevant to public life. Though still taught in many parts of the academy, it has little of value to offer students.

In non-Euclidian planning, the planner is placed into the center of the activity we call planning as a responsible professional. This suggests a new and more aggressive role for planners seeking value-relevant changes within their spheres of competency. In this entrepreneurial role planners must be publicly accountable, as they preside over processes that are radically open to public inquiry.

Non-Euclidian planning is decentered, privileging regions and localities. It encourages the affected population to take an active part, and, thus, validates the experiential knowledge of ordinary people and promotes mutual learning between the planning expert and the affected population. The truth claims of planning, where knowledge is a combination of expertise and experience, are ultimately redeemed through intersubjective transactions between community participants and planners.

Non-Euclidian planning operates in real time by linking knowledge and action into a tightly looped process of strategic change. Planning entrepreneurs are primarily resource mobilizers who seek to concert public and private energies around innovative solutions to stubborn problems in the public domain. Such planning is oriented to values rather than profit. It is normative in its intent. Though planners remain free to choose, action in the public domain should be justified as that which furthers the cause of human flourishing and diversity throughout the world.

NOTE

1   I have discussed elements of this model in my writings over the past twenty years and they are brought together here for the first time as a comprehensive alternative to the rational decision-making model still championed by many planning theorists, most notably Andreas Faludi. Readers will find the following references useful: *Retracking America: A Theory of Transactive Planning* (Doubleday and Anchor, 1973); *The Good Society* (MIT Press, 1982); *Planning in the Public Domain: From Knowledge to Action* (Princeton University Press, 1987); and *Empowerment: The Politics of Alternative Development* (Basil Blackwell, 1992).

Part II

Planning: Justifications and Critiques

Introduction

The first two readings of this section (by Klosterman and Foglesong) directly address the question: What is the justification for planning intervention? They examine neoclassical, institutional, and Marxist arguments for and against planning, placing the profession in the political-economic context of the relationship between the private market and government (both the local and national states). The next two readings (by Beauregard and Scott) approach this question by examining the larger connection between modernism and the logic of planning. The final reading (by Perry) offers an alternative logic to delimit the task for planning.

Richard Klosterman provides a comprehensive overview of the justifications for planning in his 1985 article, "Arguments For and Against Planning." He evaluates political and economic arguments from both traditional and Marxist perspectives. He begins by outlining the standard market failure model, whereby planning steps in to address the periodic shortcomings of the free market system. This is perhaps the safest ground for planning, since it justifies government intervention based on its ability to improve and assist the functioning of an efficient market. Klosterman then examines three other arguments: planners address the shortcomings of the political system in fully representing the public interest; planners possess unique professional expertise and instrumental rationality; and planners either serve or challenge the capitalist system.

In a brief excerpt from his book, *Planning the Capitalist City*, Richard Foglesong provides his own Marxist perspective on the justification for planning. He departs from the market failure model's tidy and benign division of labor between the public and private sectors and instead sees a conflicted, contradictory relationship between government and business. The key dynamic to understanding the ambivalent role of planning in capitalist society is the "property contradiction": the contradiction between the social character of land and its private ownership and control. This conflict does not invariably lead to collapse or social upheaval, but it does create political conflict. The private sector naturally resists government intrusion into its affairs, yet at the same time needs government to socialize the control of land. For example, the private sector needs government to cope with externality problems, to help provide housing for the working poor, and to build and coordinate infrastructure. For Foglesong, this property contradiction is related to a more general contradiction: that between capitalism and democracy. Each interest has a separate agenda for land, and the role of planning is to maintain the balance between the two.

This regulation/laissez-faire dichotomy has been a staple of planning theory debates. More recently, it has been joined by the modernist/postmodernist divide. Many planning theorists were drawn to the emerging ideas of postmodernism during the 1980s; these ideas were novel enough to promote a burst of theoretical creativity and vague enough to tolerate imprecise planning polemics. The appeal was understandable: the transition from modernism to postmodernism provided an overall framework in which to critique the whole era of modernist planning. It thus allowed postmodernist analysts to distance themselves from modernism's monolithic obsession with the grid, the box, and the comprehensive plan (and led to much broadbrushed scapegoating of modernist icons such as Le Corbusier, Robert Moses, and Walter Gropius). Postmodernism's rejection of the master narrative in place of multiple discourses also provided theoretical support for the emerging interest in multiculturalism.

Robert Beauregard, in his 1989 article, "Between Modernity and Postmodernity: The Ambiguous Position of U.S. Planning," outlines the postmodern potential for planning. He argues that this transformation is neither smooth nor complete, and that planning is currently suspended between modernism and postmodernism. However, planners should not embrace postmodernism unconditionally but instead also redefine and incorporate the strengths of modernist planning. This reorientation should include a focus on the process of physical city building, a mediating role between capital, labor, and the state, and a greater push towards democracy.

The political scientist James Scott adds to the criticism of modernism – particularly what he calls "authoritarian high modernism." In an excerpt from his 1998 book, *Seeing Like a State: How Certain Schemes to Improve the Human Condition Have Failed*, Scott traces the link between modernism and the modern nation-state's efforts to simplify and standardize, while rejecting local context and initiative, to make the nation legible, measurable, and counted. This is how the modern state "sees." Scott identifies three elements common to disastrous abuses of modern state development: administrative ordering of nature and society through simplification and standardization ("high modernism"); the unrestrained use of the power of the modern state to implement these rational designs; and a civil society too weak to resist effectively. "Social engineering" becomes the consequence of high modernism and nation-state power, and the authoritarian tendencies of the single modernist voice of rationality displace all other forms of judgment.

Scott sees three effective resistances to authoritarian high modernism: the belief in a private sphere of activity outside the interference of the state (the idea of the private realm); liberal political economy (e.g. the ideas of Hayek); and, most importantly, civil society and democratic political institutions. What are the implications for planning? Plans should not be so ambitious and meticulous that they are closed systems. Smaller and reversible steps, flexibly open to both surprises and human inventiveness, will break with the hubris of modernist planning. In Scott's call for local initiative ("Metis"), as an alternative to state-level technocratic planning, one hears echoes of arguments also made by Jane Jacobs, Charles Lindblom, and others.

In the section's final essay, David Perry offers an alternative way to think about planning, emphasizing the field's spatial orientation to policy, or, in the current lingua franca, its "social production of space." He echoes Scott's concerns about the authoritarian logic of the abstract modernist gaze, and argues instead for a spatial view that is richly embedded in social relations. Planning is in tension between "the lived space and the abstract space of society." Perry argues that we should think of planning not as "making plans," but instead as "making space." This dichotomy hearkens back to the old debate between procedural and substantive planning. Because Perry shifts the traditional planning emphasis on physical or abstract space into the realm of "social space," he outlines a planning theory wherein space is also political and institutional and reflects the contradictions of the capitalist city. "[P]lanning should be thought of spatially as a changing and increasingly complex feature of the (social) relations of power, producing and reproducing the state and market, at both the institutional and the lived or everyday levels" (p. 151).

Perry laments the current confusion about planning, seemingly "at once ineffable and ubiquitous," that arises from its widely divergent local and regional contexts. The way out of this confusion lies therefore in shaping an identity for planning based on its spatial context in history. Rather than taking sides in the various and sundry planning debates (such as comprehensive versus incremental, reform versus utopian, top-down versus bottom-up, etc.), Perry takes a rather broad, inclusive definition of planning, viewing all approaches as components of a broader planning task of responding to spatial changes. There is no single definition of planning. Perry uses two examples – one at an unusually micro scale (homemaking), the other at a large scale (regionalism) – to highlight his point that "space making" is at the core of planning.

4

Arguments For and Against Planning

Richard E. Klosterman

Formal governmental attempts to plan for and direct social change have always been controversial. However, public and academic attention to planning peaked in the "great debate" of the 1930s and 1940s between proponents of government planning such as Karl Mannheim, Rexford Tugwell, and Barbara Wootton and defenders of "free" markets and laissez-faire such as Friedrich Hayek and Ludwig von Mises.[1] By the 1950s the debate had apparently been resolved: the grand issues of the desirability and feasibility of planning had been replaced by more concrete questions concerning particular planning techniques and alternative institutional structures for achieving society's objectives. Planning's status in modern society seemed secure: the only remaining questions appeared to be, Who shall plan, for what purposes, in what conditions, and by what devices?[2]

Recent events in Great Britain, the United States, and other Western societies indicate that planning's status is again being questioned and that the "great debate" had never really ended. National planning efforts have been abandoned in Britain and the United States; and the public agenda in both countries now focuses on deregulation, privatization, urban enterprise zones, and a host of other proposals for severely restricting government's role in economic affairs. Planning is increasingly attacked in the popular press, academic literature, and addresses to Parliament and Congress.[3] Graduate planning enrollments have declined dramatically, and government retrenchment around the world has severely reduced job opportunities for professional planners at all levels.[4] At a more fundamental level, practitioners, students, and academics increasingly view planning as nothing more than a way to make a living, ignoring its potential to serve as a vocation, filling one's professional life with transcending purpose.[5]

In this environment it seems essential to return to fundamentals and examine carefully the case for and against planning in a modern industrial context. This

Reprinted by permission of *Town Planning Review*, 56(1), (1985): 5–20.

article will critically examine four major types of argument that have been used as two-edged rhetorical swords both to criticize and defend government planning efforts and to consider the implications of these arguments for planning in the 1980s and beyond. The analysis will consider only formal governmental efforts at the local and regional level to achieve desired goals and solve novel problems in complex contexts, or what in Britain is called "town and country planning" and in America "city and regional planning."[6] As a result, the arguments considered below are not necessarily applicable to national economic planning or to the planning done by private individuals and organizations. Also not considered are the legal arguments for planning in particular constitutional or common-law contexts or arguments such as Mannheim's,[7] which have had little effect on the contemporary political debate.

Economic Arguments

Contemporary arguments for abandoning planning, reducing regulation, and restricting the size of government are generally accompanied by calls for increased reliance on private entrepreneurship and the competitive forces of the market. That is, it is often argued, government regulation and planning are unnecessary and often harmful because they stifle entrepreneurial initiative, impede innovation, and impose unnecessary financial and administrative burdens on the economy.

These arguments find their historical roots in the world of Adam Smith, John Stuart Mill, and others of the classical liberal tradition.[8] Emphasizing individual freedom, reliance on the "impersonal" forces of the market, and the rule of law, these authors called for minimal state interference in society's economic affairs to protect individual liberty and promote freedom of choice and action. On pragmatic grounds they argued that competitive markets could be relied upon to coordinate the actions of individuals, provide incentives to individual action, and supply those goods and services that society wants, in the quantities it desires, at the prices it is willing to pay.[9]

Building on these foundations, contemporary neoclassical economists have demonstrated mathematically that competitive markets are capable in theory of allocating society's resources in an efficient manner. That is, given an initial distribution of resources, a market-generated allocation of these resources cannot be redistributed to make some individuals better off without simultaneously making other individuals worse off.[10] However, this Pareto efficient allocation will occur only in perfectly competitive markets that satisfy the following conditions: (1) a large number of buyers and sellers trade identical goods and service; (2) buyers and sellers possess sufficient information for rational market choice; (3) consumer selections are unaffected by the preferences of others; (4) individuals pursue the solitary objective of maximizing profits; and (5) perfect mobility exists for production, labor, and consumption.[11]

The numerous obvious divergences between markets in the real world and economists' competitive market ideal justify a range of government actions fully consistent with private property, individual liberty, and decentralized market choice.[12] The need to increase market competition and promote informed consumer choice in a world of huge multinational firms and mass advertising helps justify restrictions on combinations in restraint of trade and prohibitions on misleading advertising.

Indicative planning efforts at a national level in France and elsewhere are likewise justified as providing the information required for rational market choice. The development of municipal information systems and the preparation of long-range economic forecasts are similarly justified as promoting informed market choice with respect to location decisions for which the relevant information is difficult to obtain, experience is limited, and mistakes can be exceptionally costly.[13]

More important, both classical and neoclassical economists recognize that even perfectly competitive markets require government action to correct "market failures" involving (1) public or collective consumption goods; (2) externalities or spillover effects; (3) prisoners' dilemma conditions; and (4) distributional issues.[14]

Public goods

Public goods are defined by two technical characteristics: (1) "jointed" or "nonrivalrous" consumption such that, once produced, they can be enjoyed simultaneously by more than one person; and (2) "nonexcludability" or "nonappropriability" such that it is difficult (in some cases impossible) to assign well-defined property rights or restrict consumer access.[15] Private goods such as apples, bread, and most "normal" consumer goods exhibit neither characteristic; once produced, they can be consumed by only one individual at a time. It is thus easy to restrict access to these goods and charge a price for their enjoyment. On the other hand, public goods such as open air concerts, television broadcasts, and a healthy and pleasant environment simultaneously benefit more than one individual, because one person's enjoyment does not prohibit another's enjoyment (except for any congestion effects). As a result, controlling access to these goods is either difficult (scramblers must be installed to restrict access to television broadcasts) or impossible (clean air).

Competitive markets can effectively allocate private goods that can be enjoyed only if they are purchased; as a result, the prices individuals are willing to pay for alternative goods accurately reflect their preferences for these goods. For public goods the benefit individuals receive is dependent on the total supply of the good, not on their contribution toward its production. Thus, in making voluntary market contributions to pay for, say, environmental protection, individuals are free to understate their real preferences for environmental quality in the hope that others will continue to pay for its protection – enabling them to be "free riders," enjoying a pleasant environment at no personal expense. Of course, if everyone did this, the money required to protect the environment adequately would no longer be available. Individuals may also underestimate others' willingness to contribute and "overpay," thereby ending up with more public goods and fewer private goods than they really desire. In either case the aggregated market preferences of individuals do not accurately reflect individual or social preferences for alternative public and private goods – the "invisible hand" fumbles.

Similar arguments can be made for public provision of quasi-public goods such as education, public health programs, transportation facilities, and police and fire protection, which simultaneously benefit particular individuals and provide shared, nonrationable benefits to society as a whole. As a result, public goods can be used to justify over 96 percent of public purchases of goods and services and an almost open-ended range of government activities.[16]

Externalities

Closely related to the concept of public goods are externalities or spill-over effects of production and consumption that are not taken into account in the process of voluntary market exchange.[17] The classic example is a polluting industrial plan that imposes aesthetic and health costs on neighboring firms and individuals not included in its costs of production. Similar spill-over effects are revealed by land developers who can freely ignore the costs of congestion, noise, and loss of privacy that high-intensity development imposes on neighboring landowners. Positive external economies include the increased land values associated with the construction of new transportation links and other large-scale improvements, which adjoining landowners can enjoy without compensation.

As is true for public goods, the divergence between public and private costs and benefits associated with externalities causes even perfectly competitive markets to misallocate society's goods and services. Profit-maximizing firms concerned only with maximizing revenues and controlling costs are encouraged to increase output even though the associated negative external costs vastly outweigh any increases in revenue because the external, social costs are not reflected in their production costs. Neighborhood beautification projects and similar goods with positive external effects similarly tend to be underproduced, because private entrepreneurs cannot appropriate the full economic benefits of their actions. In both situations the "invisible hand" again fails to reflect accurately the needs and desires of society's members.

Prisoner's dilemma conditions

Similar difficulties are revealed in circumstances in which individuals' pursuit of their own self-interest does not lead to an optimal outcome for society or for the individual involved. Consider, for example, the situation faced by landlords in a declining neighborhood who must decide whether to improve their rental property or invest their money elsewhere.[18] If landlords improve their property and others do not, the neighborhood will continue to decline, making the investment financially inadvisable. On the other hand, if the landlords do not improve their property and the others improve theirs, the general improvement of the neighborhood will allow landlords to raise rents without investing any money. As a result, it is in each individual's self-interest to make no improvements; however, if they all refuse to do so, the neighborhood will decline further, making things worse for everyone. An identical inevitable logic leads the competitive market to overutilize "common pool" resources with a limited supply and free access, such as wilderness areas and a healthy environment.[19]

The fundamental problem here, as for public goods and externalities, lies in the interdependence between individual actions and the accompanying disjunction between individual benefits and costs versus social benefits and costs. The only solution in all three cases is government action to deal with the public and external effects that are neglected in the pursuit of individual gain. Solutions for declining neighborhoods include compulsory building codes, public acquisition and improvement of entire neighborhoods, and "enveloping" – public improvements to neighborhood exteriors that will encourage private investments.

Distributional questions

As was pointed out above, economists have demonstrated that, given an initial distribution of resources, perfectly competitive markets will allocate those resources in such a way that no one can benefit without someone else being harmed. However, neither the initial nor the final distribution can be assumed to be in any way optimal. Both are determined largely by inherited wealth, innate talent, and blind luck and can range from states of perfect equality to extremes of tremendous wealth and abject poverty. Economic efficiency alone provides no criterion for judging one state superior in any way to another. As a result, given a societal consensus on the proper allocation of resources, for example, that all babies should receive adequate nutrition and that the elderly should be cared for, government tax collection and income transfer programs are justified to achieve these objectives with minimal market interference.[20]

Implications of the economic arguments

The preceding discussion has identified a range of government functions fully consistent with consumer sovereignty, individual freedom in production and trade, and decentralized market choice. Each of these functions justifies a major area of contemporary planning practice: first, providing the information needed for informed market choice through indicative planning, the development of urban information systems, and the preparation of long-range population, economic, and land-use projections: second, the provision of public goods through transportation, environmental, and economic development planning; third, the control of externalities and resolution of prisoner's dilemma conditions through urban renewal, community development and natural resources planning, and the use of traditional land regulatory devices; and lastly, health, housing, and other forms of social planning to compensate for inequities in the distribution of basic social goods and services. Specific government actions to reduce conflicts between incompatible land uses, coordinate private development and public infrastructure, preserve open space and historic buildings, and examine the long-range impacts of current actions can similarly be justified as needed to correct market failures revealed in the physical development of the city.

It must be recognized, however, that while *necessary* to justify government planning in a market society, these arguments are not *sufficient* to do so. This is true, first, because those activities that are the proper responsibility of government in a market society need not be *planning* matters at all. Government decisions concerning the provision of public goods, the control of externalities, and so on can be made in a number of ways: by professional planners, by elected or appointed public officials, by the proclamations of a divine ruler, or by pure happenstance involving no deliberate decision process at all. If planning is justified by the economic arguments for government alone, it is impossible to differentiate between government planning and government nonplanning – "government" is reduced to an undifferentiated mass.

More fundamentally, the inability of existing markets to allocate society's resources adequately does not necessarily imply that government provision, regulation, or planning are necessary or even advisable. Suitably defined and administered performance standards, building codes, and development requirements may guide the land development process more effectively than traditional master planning and zoning techniques; effluent charges can often control pollution discharges more efficiently than the direct enforcement of effluent standards; and public facilities and services may be provided more equitably by leasing and voucher systems than directly by government. Thus, in these and other areas, the appropriate role for planning may not be the preparation of formal end-state plans but the establishment and maintenance of an appropriate system of quasi-markets.[21]

As a result, the case for planning in a market society cannot be based solely on the theoretical limitations of markets outlined above. Popular dissatisfaction with the free enterprise system is based not on an appreciation of the various theories of market failure but on its inability to provide stable economic growth and an adequate standard of living for all of society's members. Conversely, the informed critiques of planning are made not in ignorance of the theoretical limitations of markets but in the belief that, despite these limitations, markets are still more effective than attempts at centralized coordination by government.[22] As a result, the case for planning in a modern market society cannot be made in the abstract but requires a careful evaluation of planning's effectiveness relative to alternative institutional mechanisms for achieving society's objectives.

Pluralist Arguments

Other arguments for and against planning emerged during the 1960s and 1970s to complement the economic arguments considered above. Accepting the economic arguments for government outlined above, Lindblom, Wildavsky, and other critics of planning suggest that government actions should not be guided by long-range planning or attempts at comprehensive coordination but by increased reliance on existing political bargaining processes.[23] Underlying these arguments is a political analogue to the economists' perfectly competitive market in which competition between formal and informal groups pursuing a range of divergent goals and interests is assumed to place all important issues on the public agenda, guarantee that no group dominates the public arena, maintain political stability and improve individuals' intellectual and deliberative skills. In this model government has no independent role other than establishing and enforcing the rules of the game and ratifying the political adjustments worked out among the competing groups. Thus, it is assumed, political competition, like market competition, eliminates the need for independent government action, planning, and coordination.[24]

Unfortunately, the pluralist model is subject to the same fundamental limitations that face the economic model of perfect market competition. Just as markets are dominated by gigantic national and multinational conglomerates, the political arena is dominated by individuals and groups who use their access to government officials and other elites to protect their status, privilege, and wealth and ensure that government acts in their interest. Particularly privileged are corporate and business leaders whose cooperation is essential for government's efforts to maintain full employment and secure stable economic growth. As a result, government officials, particularly at the local level, cannot treat business as only another special interest but must provide incentives to stimulate desired business activity, such as tax rebates and low-interest loans to attract new industry and downtown improvement projects to encourage retail and commercial activity in the central business district. Further supporting business's unique position in the group bargaining process is an unrecognized acceptance of the needs and priorities of business that pervades our political and governmental processes, media, and cultural and educational institutions.[25]

Systematically excluded from the group bargaining process are minority and low-income individuals and groups residing in decaying urban centers and rural hinterlands. Lacking the time, training, resources, leadership, information, or experience required to participate effectively in the political process, these groups have no effective voice in determining the public policies that shape their world. By thus tying individuals' political voice to underlying disparities in political power and resources, current political processes exacerbate existing inequalities in income and wealth and fail to provide adequate information for fully informed policy making.[26]

Group bargaining also fails adequately to provide collective goods and services that provide small benefits to a large number of individuals. In small groups, each member receives a substantial proportion of the gain from a collective good; as a result, it is clearly in their interest to ensure that the good be provided. For large groups, individual benefits are so small and organizational costs so large that it is in no one's immediate interest to provide for the common good. The result is an "exploitation of the great by the small" in which small groups with narrow, well-defined interests – such as doctors and lawyers – can organize more effectively to achieve their objectives than larger groups – such as consumers – who share more broadly defined interests. By turning government power over to the most interested parties and excluding the public from the policy formulation and implementation process, pluralist bargaining systematically neglects the political spill-over effects of government actions and policies on unrepresented groups and individuals.[27]

The limitations of pluralist bargaining, like the limitations of market competition, provide the theoretical justification for a wide range of planning functions. Accepting the critiques of comprehensive planning by Lindblom and others, some authors propose that planning be limited to the "adjunctive" functions of providing information, analyzing alternative public policies, and identifying bases for improved group interaction. The objective here, as for indicative planning, is improving existing decentralized decision processes by providing the information needed for more informed decision making.[28]

The pluralist model is incorporated directly into the advocacy planning approach, which rejects the preparation of value-neutral "unitary" plans representing the overall community interest for the explicit advocacy of "plural plans" representing all of the interests involved in the physical development of the city.[29] Recognizing the inequities of existing political processes, advocate planners have acted primarily as advocates for society's poor and minority members. Particularly noteworthy here are the efforts of the Cleveland Planning Commission to promote "a wider range of choices for those Cleveland residents who have few, if any, choices."[30]

Experience has demonstrated, however, that advocacy planning shares many of the limitations of the pluralist model on which it is based: (1) urban neighborhoods are no more homogeneous and the neighborhood interest no more easy to identify than is true at the community level; (2) group leaders are not representative of the group's membership; (3) it is easier to represent narrowly defined interests and preserve the status quo than to advocate diffuse and widely shared interests or propose new alternatives; and (4) public officials still lack the information required for adequate decision making.[31]

As a result, there remains a fundamental need for public sector planners who can represent the shared interests of the community, coordinate the actions of individuals and groups, and consider the long-range effects of current actions. This does not imply that the shared interests of the community are superior to the private interests of individuals and groups or that the external and long-term effects of action are more important than their direct and immediate impacts. It assumes only that these considerations are particularly important *politically*, because only government can ensure that they will be considered at all.[32] It is on these foundations that the traditional arguments for town and country planning have been made.

Traditional Arguments

The planning profession originated at the turn of the century in response to the widespread dissatisfaction with the results of existing market and political processes reflected in the physical squalor and political corruption of the emerging industrial city. The profession's organizational roots in architecture and landscape architecture were reflected in early views of planning as "do[ing] for the city what . . . architecture does for the home" – improving the built environment to raise amenity levels; increase efficiency in the performance of necessary functions; and promote health, safety, and convenience. The profession's political roots in progressive reform were reflected in arguments for planning as an independent "fourth power" of government promoting the general or public interest over the narrow, conflicting interests of individuals and groups. Others viewed planning as a mechanism for coordinating the impacts of public and private land uses on adjoining property owners and considering the future consequences of present actions in isolation from day-to-day operating responsibilities. Underlying all of these arguments was the belief that the conscious application of professional expertise, instrumental rationality, and scientific methods could more effectively promote economic growth and political stability than the unplanned forces of market and political competition.[33]

Implicit in these traditional arguments for planning are many of the more formal justifications examined above. The arguments for planning as an independent function of government promoting the collective public interest obviously parallel the economic and pluralist arguments for government action to provide public or collective consumption goods. The calls for planning as comprehensive coordination similarly recognize the need for dealing with the external effects of individual and group action. And the arguments for planning that consider the long-range effects of current actions likewise acknowledge the need for more informed public policy making. Noteworthy by its absence is any concern with the distributional effects of government and private actions, which were largely ignored in planners' attempts to promote a collective public interest.[34]

By midcentury, social scientists who had joined the ranks of academic planners began severely to question each of these arguments for public sector planning: Planners' concern with the physical city was viewed as overly restrictive; their perceptions of the urban development process seen as politically naive; their technical solutions found to reflect their Protestant middle-class views of city life; their attempts to promote a collective public interest revealed to serve primarily the needs of civic and business élites; and democratic comprehensive coordination of public and private development proven to be organizationally and politically impossible.[35]

Accompanying these critiques were new conceptions of planning as a value-neutral, rational process of problem identification, goal definition, analysis, implementation, and evaluation. In recent years the rational planning model has come under severe attack as well for failing to recognize the fundamental constraints on private and organizational decision making; the inherently political and ethical nature of planning practice; and the organizational, social, and psychological realities of planning practice. As a result, while the social need for providing collective goods, dealing with externalities, and so on remains, the planning profession currently lacks a widely accepted procedural model for defining planning problems or justifying planning solutions.[36]

Marxist Arguments

The recent emergence of Marxist theories of urban development has added a new dimension to the debate about the desirability and feasibility of planning.[37] From the Marxist perspective, the role of planning in contemporary society can be understood only by recognizing the structure of modern capitalism as it relates to the physical environment. That is, it is argued, the fundamental social and economic institutions of capitalist society systematically promote the interests of those who control society's productive capital over those of the remainder of society. The formal organization of the state is likewise assumed to serve the long-term interests of capital by creating and maintaining conditions conducive to the efficient accumulation of capital in the private sector, subordinating the conflicting short-run interests of the factions of capital to the long-run interests of the capitalist class, and containing civil strife that threatens the capitalist order. These actions are legitimized by a prevailing democratic ideology that portrays the state as a neutral instrument serving the interests of society as a whole.

Marxists argue that fundamental social improvements can result only from the revolutionary activity of labor and the replacement of existing social institutions benefiting capital by new ones serving the interests of society at large. Essential reforms include public ownership of the means of production and centralized planning, which would replace existing market and political decision processes by the comprehensive coordination of investment decisions and democratic procedures for formulating social priorities and restricting individual actions that conflict with the long-term interests of society.[38]

Applying this perspective to urban planning, Marxist scholars have been highly critical of traditional planning practice and theory. The arguments for and against planning examined above are dismissed as mere ideological rationalizations that fail to recognize the material conditions and historical and political forces that allowed planning to emerge and define its role in society. Accepting the limitations of market and political competition outlined above, Marxists interpret planners' actions in each sphere as primarily serving the interests of capital at the expense of the rest of society. Planners' attempts to provide collective goods and control externalities are assumed to serve the needs of capital by helping to manage the inevitable contradictions of capitalism revealed in the physical and social development of the city. Planners' attempts to employ scientific techniques and professional expertise are seen as helping to legitimize state action in the interest of capital by casting it in terms of the public interest, neutral professionalism, and scientific rationality. And planners' attempts to advance the interests of deprived groups are dismissed as merely coopting these groups, forestalling the structural reforms that are ultimately required to bring real improvement to their positions in society.[39]

While extremely valuable in helping to reveal the underlying nature of contemporary planning, the Marxist perspective has obvious limitations as a guide to planning practice.[40] A strict Marxist analysis, which sees all social relations and all government actions as serving the interests of capital, identifies no mechanism for reform other than a radical transformation of society, which is highly unlikely in the near future: if needed reforms can result only from the revolutionary action of labor and all attempts to help the needy merely delay necessary structural changes, there is no significant role for reform-minded planners who occupy an ambiguous class position between labor and capital. And rejection of planners' attempts to apply professional expertise and scientific methods to public policy making as merely legitimizing and maintaining existing social and economic relations deprives professional planners of their main political resource for dealing with other political actors – their claims to professional expertise.

As a result, as was true for the arguments for and against planning examined earlier, the Marxist arguments cannot be evaluated in the abstract but must be examined critically in the light of present economic and political realities. Thus, while it may be theoretically desirable to replace existing market and political decision processes, this is highly unlikely to happen in most Western democracies. The lack of a revolutionary role for planners in traditional Marxist analysis does not mean that they cannot work effectively for short-term reforms with other progressive professionals and community-based organizations. And while contemporary planning may indeed serve the interests of capital, it need not serve these interests alone and is clearly preferable to exclusive reliance on the fundamentally flawed processes of market and political competition.

Conclusions and Implications

The preceding discussion has examined a variety of arguments for and against planning in a modern industrial context. Underlying this apparent diversity is an implicit consensus about the need for public sector planning to perform four vital social functions – promoting the common or collective interests of the community, considering the external effects of individual and group action, improving the information base for public and private decision making, and considering the distributional effects of public and private action.

The first need is reflected in the economic arguments for government action to resolve prisoner's dilemma conditions and provide public or collective consumption goods, such as a healthy and pleasant environment, which cannot be provided adequately by even perfectly competitive markets. The second results from the inability of markets to deal with social costs and benefits of production and consumption that are not reflected in market prices or revenues. The third is reflected in the public and private need for improved information on the long-term effects of location decisions necessary for making adequately informed market decisions. And the fourth results from the fact that market competition alone is incapable in principle of resolving distributional questions in a socially acceptable manner.

From the pluralist perspective, planning is required to represent broadly defined interests that are neglected in the competition between organized groups representing narrower interests. And it is required to represent the external effects of political decisions on groups and individuals who are not directly involved in the political bargaining process. Improved information on the short- and long-term consequences of alternative public policies and actions is required to facilitate the group bargaining process. And planners are required to serve as advocates for society's neediest members, who are systematically excluded from the group bargaining process.

The traditional arguments for planning reflect the need for representing the collective interests of the community in the calls for planning as an independent function of government charged with promoting the public interest. The need for considering the external effects of individual action is reflected in the conception of planning as comprehensive coordination. From this perspective, planning is required to provide information on the physical development of the city and the long-range implications of current actions. Distributional questions were regrettably largely ignored in traditional planning's efforts to promote an aggregate public interest.

While largely critical of contemporary planning practice, the Marxist perspective recognizes each of the arguments for planning identified by the other perspectives. The need for representing the collective interests of the community is reflected in the Marxist prescriptions for replacing existing decentralized markets with centralized planning in the interests of society as a whole. The need for considering externalities is reflected in calls for the comprehensive coordination of investment decisions. From the Marxist perspective, traditional forms of planning information primarily serve the interests of capital; thus, to promote fundamental social change planners are called upon to inform the public of the underlying realities of capitalist society. And the need to correct the structural imbalances in power and wealth that shape contemporary society underlies the Marxist call for the radical reformation of society.

While all four perspectives propose that planning is required *in theory* to fulfill these fundamental social requirements, they each recognize in their own way that these theoretical arguments for planning are insufficient. Contemporary economists argue that market competition, properly structured and augmented, can be more efficient and equitable than traditional forms of public sector planning and regulation. Critics such as Lindblom have revealed planners' traditional models of centralized coordination to be impossible in a decentralized democratic society. And the social critics of the 1960s and 1970s and Marxist critics of today have demonstrated convincingly that traditional planning practice, while couched in terms of neutral technical competence and the public interest, has primarily served the interests of society's wealthiest and most powerful members.

An objective evaluation of sixty years' experience with town and country planning in Great Britain and the United States must recognize the tremendous gap between planning's potential and its performance. While there have been several remarkable successes, much of contemporary practice is still limited to the preparation of "boiler plate" plans, the avoidance of political controversy, and the routine administration of overly rigid and conservative regulations.[41] It is thus an open question whether planning, as currently practiced the world over, deserves high levels of public support or whether other professional groups and institutional arrangements can better perform the vital social functions identified above. As a result, the arguments for planning outlined above cannot be taken as a defence of the status quo in planning but must serve as a challenge to the profession to learn from its mistakes and build on new and expanded conceptions of the public interest, information, and political action to realize its ultimate potential.[42]

ACKNOWLEDGMENTS

I gratefully acknowledge the valuable comments received from Robert A. Beauregard of Rutgers University, Jay M. Stein of the Georgia Institute of Technology, and the anonymous reviewers of *Town Planning Review*.

NOTES

1 See, for example, Mannheim, Karl, *Man and Society in an Age of Reconstruction: Studies in Modern Social Structure*, New York, Harcourt, Brace, and World, 1944, pp. 41–75; Tugwell, Rexford G., "Implementing the General Interest", *Public Administration Review*, 1(1), Autumn 1940, pp. 32–49; Wootton, Barbara, *Freedom Under Planning*, Chapel Hill, University of North Carolina Press, 1945; Hayek, Friedrich A., *The Road to Serfdom*, Chicago, University of Chicago Press, 1944; and von Mises, Ludwig, *Planning for Freedom and Other Essays*, South Holland, Ill. Libertarian Press, 1952.

2 Examples here include Schonfield, Andrew, *Modern Capitalism*, New York, Oxford University Press, 1965, and Dahl, Robert A., and Lindblom, Charles E., *Politics, Economics, and Welfare*, New York, Harper and Row, 1953. The quotation is from Dahl and Lindblom, p. 5.

3 For recent critiques of planning see Friedman, Milton, and Friedman, Rose, *Free to Choose: A Personal Statement*, New York, Harcourt, Brace and Jovanovich, 1979; Simon, William E., *A Time for Truth*, New York, Reader's Digest Press, 1978; and Wildavsky, Aaron, "If Planning Is Everything, Maybe It's Nothing," *Policy Sciences*, 4(3), June 1973, pp. 277–295.

4 The dramatically declining enrollments in American planning schools are documented and analyzed by Krueckeberg, Donald A., "Planning and the New Depression in the Social Sciences," *Journal of Planning Education and Research*, 3(2), Winter 1984, pp. 78–86.

5 Friedmann, John, "Planning as a Vocation," *Plan (Canada)*, 6(2), April 1966, pp. 99–124, and 7(3), July 1966, pp. 8–26.

6 A similar definition of planning is proposed by Alexander, Ernest R., "If Planning Isn't Everything, Maybe It's Something," *Town Planning Review*, 52(2), April 1981, pp. 131–142.

7 Mannheim, op. cit.

8   These writers are "classical" liberals in that their views of government and liberty are fundamentally different from those associated with contemporary liberalism. Classical liberals define liberty in the negative sense in which freedom is determined by the extent to which individuals' actions are *externally* constrained by the actions of others; the wider the sphere of noninterference, the greater an individual's liberty. Thus to increase the (negative) liberty of individuals by decreasing the external interference of the state, classical liberals call for a sharply reduced role for government in the domestic and foreign economy. "Contemporary" liberals, on the other hand, view liberty largely in the positive sense in which individuals are free when no *internal* constraints such as a lack of knowledge, resources, or opportunities restrain their actions. From this perspective, increasing the (positive) liberty of individuals, particularly the most deprived, requires deliberate government action to promote social welfare and reduce the internal constraints on individual action, even though this may restrain the actions (and negative liberty) of some individuals. Compare Friedman, Milton, *Capitalism and Freedom*, Chicago, University of Chicago Press, 1962, pp. 5–6; and Finer, Herman, *Road to Reaction*, Boston, Little, Brown and Co., 1945, pp. 221–228. Contemporary examples of the classical liberal argument include Hayek, op. cit.; Friedman and Friedman, op. cit.; Friedman, op. cit.; and Sorensen, Anthony D., and Day, Richard A., "Libertarian Planning," *Town Planning Review*, 52 (4), October 1981, pp. 390–402.

9   Heilbroner, Robert L., *The Worldly Philosophers*, New York, Simon and Schuster, 1969 (3rd edn), pp. 48–61; Friedman and Friedman, op. cit., pp. 9–27.

10 See, for example, Bator, Francis M., "The Simple Analytics of Welfare Maximization," *American Economic Review*, 47 (1), March 1957, pp. 22–59.

11 Seventeen more restrictive assumptions including perfectly divisible capital and consumer goods and an absence of risk and uncertainty are identified by De V. Graaff, J., *Theoretical Welfare Economics,* London, Cambridge University Press, 1957.

12 For analyses of the many empirical limitations of real markets see Lindblom, Charles E., *Politics and Markets: The World's Politics-Economic Systems*, New York, Basic Books, 1977, pp. 76–89 and 144–157; and Heilbroner, Robert L., and Thurow, Lester C., *The Economic Problem,* Englewood Cliffs, N.J., Prentice-Hall, 1978 (5th edn), pp. 201–219.

13 Cohen, Stephen, *Modern Capitalist Planning: The French Model*, Cambridge, Mass., Harvard University Press, 1969; Foster, Christopher, "Planning and the Market," in Cowan, Peter (ed.), *The Future of Planning: A Study Sponsored by the Centre for Environmental Studies*, London, Heinemann, 1973, pp. 135–140; Meyerson, Martin, "Building the Middle-Range Bridge for Comprehensive Planning," *Journal of the American Institute of Planners*, 22 (1), 1956, pp. 58–64; and Skjei, Stephen S., "Urban Problems and the Theoretical Justification of Urban Planning," *Urban Affairs Quarterly*, 11 (3), March 1976, pp. 323–344.

14 Thus, for example, Adam Smith recognized that government must be responsible for (1) "protecting the society from the violence and invasion of other independent societies"; (2) "establishing an exact administration of justice"; and (3) "erecting and maintaining those public institutions and those public works, which... are ... of such a nature that profit could never repay the expense of an individual or small number of individuals": Smith, Adam, *An Enquiry into the Nature and Causes of the Wealth of Nations* (edited by Edwin Cannon), New York, Modern Library, 1937, pp. 653, 669, and 681; his third category of justified state functions is discussed on pages 681–740. Other government functions recommended by the classical economists include the regulation of public utilities, the establishment of social insurance systems, the enactment of protective labor legislation, and compensatory fiscal and monetary policy. See Robbins, Lionel, *The Theory of Economic Policy in English Classical Political Economy*, London, Macmillan, 1952, esp. pp. 55–61.

15 The literature on public goods is extensive. For excellent reviews see Burkhead, Jesse, and Miner, Jerry, *Public Expenditure*, Chicago, Aldine, 1971, and Head, John G., *Public Goods and Public Welfare*, Durham, N.C. Duke University Press, 1974, pp. 68–92 and 164–183. In the planning literature see Moore, Terry, "Why Allow Planners to Do What They Do? A Justification from Economic Theory," *Journal of the American Institute of Planners*, 44 (4), October 1978, pp. 387–398. The discussion below generally follows that in Bator, Francis M., *The Question of Government Spending: Public Needs and Private Wants*, New York, Collier Books, 1960, pp. 80–102.

16 Bator, op. cit., p. 104; Friedman and Friedman, op. cit., pp. 27–37. Similar arguments can be used to justify government provision of highways, dams, and other "decreasing cost" goods with large initial costs and decreasing marginal costs; see Bator, op. cit., pp. 93–95.

17 The relevant literature here is extensive as well. For excellent reviews see Mishan, E. J., "The Postwar Literature on Externalities: An Interpretive Review," *Journal of Economic Literature*, 9 (1), March 1971, pp. 1–28, and Head, op. cit., pp. 184–213. In the planning literature see Lee, Douglas B. Jr., "Land Use Planning as a Response to Market Failure," in de Neufville, Judith I. (ed.), *The Land Use Planning Debate in the United States*, New York, Plenum Press, 1981, pp. 153–154.

18 This example is adapted from Davis, Otto A., and Whinston, Andrew B., "The Economics of Urban Renewal," *Law and Contemporary Problems*, 26 (2), Winter 1961, pp. 106–117.

19 See the classic article by Garret Hardin, "The Tragedy of the Commons," *Science*, 162, 13 December 1968, pp. 242–248. For more general discussions see Luce, Duncan and Raiffa, Howard, *Games and Decision: Introduction and Critical Survey*, New York, John Wiley, 1957, pp. 88–154. In the planning literature see Moore, op. cit.,

20 Bator, op. cit., pp. 87–89; Musgrave, Richard S., *The Theory of Public Finance: A Study in Public Economy*, New York, McGraw Hill, pp. 17–22. These points do not, of course, exhaust the economic arguments for and against planning. Thus, while Friedman, op. cit., pp. 7–21, and Hayek, op. cit., pp. 43–118, defend unrestricted markets as necessary to protect individual liberty, Barbara Wootton, op. cit., argues that government planning is fully compatible with the whole range of cultural, civil, political, and economic freedoms. For other economic arguments for planning see Webber, Melvin M. "Planning in an Environment of Change, Part Two: Permissive Planning," *Town Planning Review*, 39 (4), January 1969, pp. 282–284; . . . and Lee, op. cit. More fundamental "Marxist" critiques of reliance on competitive markets are considered below.

21 See Webber, op. cit., pp. 284–295; Lee, op. cit., pp. 158–164; Friedman, op. cit., pp. 84–107; Moore, op. cit., pp. 393–396; and Foster, op. cit., pp. 153–165.

22 See, for example, Becker, Gary S., "Competition and Democracy," *Journal of Law and Economics*, 1, October 1958, pp. 105–109, and Wolf, Charles Jr., "A Theory of Non-market Failure: Framework for Implementation Analysis," *Journal of Law and Economics*, 22 (1), April 1979, pp. 107–140.

23 See, for example, Lindblom, Charles E., "The Science of Muddling Through," *Public Administration Review*, 19 (1), January 1959, pp. 79–88, and Wildavsky, op. cit.

24 Conolly, William E. (ed.), *The Bias of Pluralism*, New York, Atherton, 1969, pp. 3–13.

25 Lindblom, [*Politics and Markets*], pp. 170–233; Elkin, Stephen L., "Market and Politics in Liberal Democracy," *Ethics*, 92 (4), July 1982, pp. 720–732; Miliband, Ralph, *The State in Capitalist Society*, New York, Basic Books, 1969.

26 Gamson, William A., "Stable Underrepresentation in American Society," *American Behavioral Scientist*, 12 (1), November/December 1968, pp. 15–21; Skjei, Stephen S., "Urban Systems Advocacy," *Journal of the American Institute of Planners*, 38 (1), January 1972, pp. 11–24; also see Dye, Thomas R. and Zeigler, L. Harmon, *The Irony*

     of Democracy: An Uncommon Introduction to American Politics, North Scituate, Mass., Duxbury Press, 1975 (3rd edn), pp. 225–284.

27   Olson, Mancur, *The Logic of Collective Action: Public Goods and the Theory of Groups*, Cambridge, Mass., Harvard University Press, 1965; Lowi, Theodore J., "The Public Philosophy: Interest-Group Liberalism," *American Political Science Review*, 61 (1), March 1967, pp. 5–24. For an extensive discussion of other forms of "nonmarket failure" see Wolf, op. cit.

28   See, for example, Rondinelli, Dennis A., "Adjunctive Planning and Urban Policy Development," *Urban Affairs Quarterly*, 6 (1), September 1971, pp. 13–39; and Skjei, "Urban Problems and the Theoretical Justification of Planning."

29   Davidoff, Paul, "Advocacy and Pluralism in Planning," *Journal of the American Institute of Planners*, 31 (6), November 1965, pp. 331–338.

30   Krumholz, Norman, Cogger, Janice, and Linner, John, "The Cleveland Policy Planning Report," *Journal of the American Institute of Planners*, 41 (3), September 1975, pp. 298–304; Krumholz, Norman, "A Retrospective View of Equity Planning: Cleveland, 1969–1979," *Journal of the American Planning Association*, 48 (2), Spring 1982, pp. 163–174.

31   Peattie, Lisa R., "Reflections on Advocacy Planning," *Journal of the American Institute of Planners*, 34 (2), March 1968, pp. 80–88; Skjei, "Urban Systems Advocacy": Mazziotti, Donald F., "The Underlying Assumptions of Advocacy Planning: Pluralism and Reform," *Journal of the American Institute of Planners*, 40 (1), January 1974, pp. 38, 40–47.

32   Klosterman, Richard E., "A Public Interest Criterion," *Journal of the American Planning Association*, 46 (3), July 1980, p. 330; Barry, Brian, *Political Argument*, New York, Humanities Press, 1965, pp. 234–235.

33   For examples of each argument see (1) Robinson, Charles Mulford, *City Planning*, New York, G. P. Putnam's, 1916, pp. 291–303 (the quotation is from p. 291); (2) Howard, John T., "In Defense of Planning Commissions," *Journal of the American Institute of Planners*, 17 (1), Spring 1951, pp. 89–93; and Tugwell, op. cit.; and (3) Bettman, Alfred, *City and Regional Planning Papers* (edited by Arthur C. Comey), Cambridge, Mass., Harvard University Press, pp. 5–30, and Dunham, Allison, "A Legal and Economic Basis for City Planning," *Columbia Law Review*, 58, 1958, pp. 650–671.

34   The earliest example of this concern in the planning literature known to the author is Webber, Melvin M., "Comprehensive Planning and Social Responsibility: Toward an AIP Consensus on the Profession's Role and Purposes," *Journal of the American Institute of Planners*, 29 (4), November 1963, pp. 232–241.

35   For examples of these now-familiar critiques see Gans, Herbert J., "City Planning in America: A Sociological Analysis," in Gans, Herbert J., *People and Plans: Essays on Urban Problems and Solutions*, New York, Basic Books, 1963; Altshuler, Alan A., "The Goals of Comprehensive Planning," *Journal of the American Institute of Planners*, 31 (5), August 1965, pp. 186–195; Bolan, Richard S., "Emerging Views of Planning," *Journal of the American Institute of Planners*, 33 (4), July 1967, pp. 233–246; and Kravitz, Alan S., "Mandaranism: Planning as Handmaiden to Conservative Politics," in Beyle, Thad L., and Lathrop, George T. (eds), *Planning and Politics: Uneasy Partnership*, New York, Odyssey Press, 1970.

36   Critiques of the rational planning model have dominated the planning theory literature for the last decade. For reviews of this literature and their implications for contemporary planning practice see DiMento, Joseph F., *The Consistency Doctrine and the Limits of Planning*, Cambridge, Mass., Oelgeschlager, Gunn, and Hain, 1980, pp. 44–117; and Alexander, Ernest R., "After Rationality, What? A Review of Responses to Paradigm Breakdown," *Journal of the American Planning Association*, 50 (1), Winter 1984, pp. 62–69.

37 Examples here include Castells, Manuel, *The Urban Question: A Marxist Approach*, Cambridge, Mass., MIT Press, 1977; Harvey, David, *Social Justice and the City*, Baltimore, Johns Hopkins University Press, 1973, pp. 195–238; Paris, Chris (ed.), *Critical Readings in Planning Theory*, Oxford, Pergamon, 1982, and the articles cited in footnote 39 below.

38 Harrington, Michael, *Socialism*, New York, Saturday Review Press, 1972, pp. 270–307; Baran, Paul A., *The Longer View: Essays Toward a Critique of Political Economy*, New York, Monthly Review Press, 1969, pp. 144–149; Huberman, Leo, and Sweezy, Paul M., *Introduction to Socialism*, New York, Monthly Review Press, 1968, pp. 60–65.

39 See, for example, Fainstein, Norman I. and Fainstein, Susan S., "New Debates in Urban Planning: The Impact of Marxist Theory Within the United States," *International Journal of Urban and Regional Research*, 3 (3), September 1979, pp. 381–403; Beauregard, Robert A., "Planning in an Advanced Capitalist State," in Burchell, Robert W., and Sternlieb, George (eds), *Planning Theory in the 1980s: A Search for New Directions*, New Brunswick, N.J., Center for Urban Policy Research, 1978; Harvey, David, "On Planning the Ideology of Planning," in ibid.; Boyer, M. Christine, *Dreaming the Rational City: The Myth of City Planning*, Cambridge, Mass., MIT Press, 1983.

40 The discussion here draws heavily on that in Fainstein and Fainstein, op. cit.

41 See also Branch, Melville C., "Delusions and Defusions of City Planning in the United States," *Management Science*, 16 (12), August 1970, pp. 714–732, and Branch, Melville C., "Sins of City Planners," *Public Administration Review*, 42 (1), January/February 1982, pp. 1–5.

42 See Alexander, ["If Planning isn't Everything"], pp. 138–140; Klosterman, op. cit.; Forester, John, "Critical Theory and Planning Practice," *Journal of the American Planning Association*, 46 (3), July 1980, pp. 275–286; Clavel, Pierre, Forester, John and Goldsmith, William W. (eds), *Urban and Regional Planning in an Age of Austerity*, New York, Pergamon, 1980; and Dyckman, John W., "Reflections on Planning Practice in an Age of Reaction," *Journal of Planning Education and Research*, 3 (1), Summer 1983, pp. 5–12.

5

Planning the Capitalist City

Richard E. Foglesong

Capitalism and Urban Planning

David Harvey, a Marxist social geographer, has conceptualized urban conflict as a conflict over the "production, management and use of the urban built environment."[1] Harvey uses the term "built environment" to refer to physical entities such as roads, sewerage networks, parks, railroads, and even private housing – facilities that are collectively owned and consumed or, as in the case of private housing, whose character and location the state somehow regulates. These facilities have become politicized because of conflict arising out of their being collectively owned and controlled, or because of the "externality effects" of private decisions concerning their use. At issue is how these facilities should be produced – whether by the market or by the state, how they should be managed and by whom; and how they should be used – for what purposes and by what groups, races, classes, and neighborhoods. Following Harvey, the development of American urban planning is seen as the result of conflict over the production, management, and use of the urban built environment.

The development of this analysis depends on the recognition that capitalism both engenders and constrains demands for state intervention in the sphere of the built environment. First, let us consider some of the theories about how capitalism engenders demands for state intervention.

Sources of urban planning

Within the developing Marxist urban literature, there have been a variety of attempts to link urban conflict and demands for state intervention to the reproduction processes of capitalist society. Manuel Castells, one of the leading contributors to this literature, emphasizes the connection between state intervention in the urban development process and the reproduction of labor power.[2]

The Problem of Planning

The market system cannot meet the consumption needs of the working class in a manner capable of maintaining capitalism; this, according to Castells, is the reason for the growth of urban planning and state intervention. To the extent that the state picks up the slack and assumes this responsibility, there occurs a transformation of the process of consumption, from individualized consumption through the market to collective consumption organized through the state. This transformation entails not only an expansion of the role of the state, which is seen in the growth of urban planning, but also a politicization of the process of consumption, which Castells sees as the underlying dynamic of urban political conflict.

By contrast, David Harvey and Edmond Preteceille, writing separately, have related state intervention in the urban development process to the inability of the market system to provide for the maintenance and reproduction of the immobilized fixed capital investments (for example, bridges, streets, sewerage networks) used by capital as *means of production*.[3] The task of the state is not only to maintain this system of what Preteceille calls "urban use values" but also to provide for the coordination of these use values in space (for example, the coordination of streets and sewer lines), creating what he terms "new, complex use values."[4] François Lamarche, on the other hand, relates the whole question of urban planning and state intervention to the *sphere of circulation* and the need to produce a "spatial organization which facilitates the circulation of capital, commodities, information, etc."[5] In his view capitalism has spawned a particular fraction of capital, termed "property capital," which is responsible for organizing the system of land use and transportation; and urban planning is a complement and extension of the aims and activities of this group. In addition, and somewhat distinct from these attempts to relate urban planning to the reproduction processes of capitalist society, David Harvey has linked urban planning to the problems arising from the *uniqueness of land as a commodity*, namely the fact that land is not transportable, which makes it inherently subject to externality effects.[6]

The theories discussed above demonstrate that there are a variety of problems arising from relying upon the market system to guide urban development. At various times, urban planning in the United States has been a response to each of these problems. Yet these problems have different histories. They have not had equal importance throughout the development of planning. Moreover, not one of these problems is sufficient in itself to explain the logic of development of planning.

Constraints on urban planning

If the problems noted above arise from the workings of the market system, so that capitalism can be said to engender demands for state intervention in response to these problems, the capitalist system also constrains the realization of these demands. The operative constraint in this connection is the institution of private property. It is here that we confront what might be termed the central contradiction of capitalist urbanization: the contradiction between the social character of land and its private ownership and control. Government intervention in the ordering of the urban built environment – that is, urban planning – can be seen as a response to the social character of land, to the fact that land is not only a commodity but also a collective good, a social resource as well as a private right. Indeed, as the Marxist urban literature has sought to demonstrate, the treatment of land as a commodity fails to satisfy the social needs of either capital or labor. Capital has an objective interest in socializing the control of land in order to (1) cope with the externality problems that arise from treating land as a commodity; (2) create the housing and other environmental amenities needed for the reproduction of labor power; (3) provide for the building and maintenance of the bridges, harbors, streets, and transit systems used by capital as means of production; and (4) ensure the spatial coordination of these infrastructural facilities for purposes of efficient circulation. Yet the institution of private property stands as an impediment to attempts to socialize the control of land in order to meet these collective needs. Thus, if urban planning is necessary for the reproduction of the capitalist system on the one hand, it threatens and is restrained by the capitalist system on the other; and it is in terms of this Janus-faced reality that the development of urban planning is to be understood. Moreover, this contradiction is intrinsic to capitalist urbanization, for the impulse to socialize the control of urban space is as much a part of capitalism as is the institution of private property. Each serves to limit the extension of the other; thus, they are in "contradiction."[7] This contradiction, which will be termed the "property contradiction," is one of two that have structured the development of planning.[8]

The "property contradiction"   To state that capitalist urbanization has an inherent contradiction is *not* to predict the inevitable downfall of capitalism (although it does indicate a weakness in the capitalist structure of society that oppositional forces could conceivably exploit). Rather, it is assumed that capitalism is capable of coping with this contradiction, within limits, but that it is a continuing source of tension and a breeding ground of political conflict. Thus, our analytical interest is in the institutional means that have been devised to keep this contradiction from exploding into a system-threatening crisis. In recognizing this contradiction, we therefore gain a better appreciation of the importance, both politically and theoretically, of the institutional forms that urban planning has adopted over the course of its development, and of how (and how well) those institutional forms have responded to the contradiction between the social character of land and its private ownership and control.

In addition, recognizing this contradiction helps us to understand the patterns of alliance formation around planning issues, as well as the role of planners in mediating between different groups and group interests. For if the effort to socialize the control of urban land is potentially a threat to the whole concept of property rights, it is directly and immediately a threat to only one particular group of capitalists, those whom Lamarche terms "property capital." Included are persons who, in his words, "plan and equip space" – real estate developers, construction contractors, and directors of mortgage lending institutions.[9] It is this fraction of capital, in particular, that can be expected to oppose efforts to displace or diminish private control of urban development. Other capitalists, in contrast, may seek an expanded government role in the planning and equipping of space. For example, manufacturing capital may want government to provide worker housing and to coordinate the development of public and private infrastructure (such as utilities and railroads), and commercial capitalists may desire government restrictions on the location of manufacturing establishments. Likewise, nonowner groups have an interest in state intervention that will provide for or regulate the quality of worker housing, build parks, and improve worker transportation, for example. It is possible, therefore, for certain fractions of capital to align with nonowner groups in support of planning interventions that restrict the "rights" of urban landholders. The property contradiction thus manifests itself in the pattern of alliances around planning issues by creating, in intracapitalist class conflict, the possibility of alliances between property-owning and nonproperty-owning groups and allowing planners to function as mediators in organizing these compromises. Inasmuch as the property contradiction is inherent in the capitalist structure of society, existing independent of consciousness and will, recognition of this contradiction enables us to link the politics of planning to the structural ordering of capitalist society.

The "capitalist–democracy contradiction" The other contradiction affecting the development of urban planning is the "capitalist–democracy contradiction." If the property contradiction is internal to capitalism in that it arises out of the logic of capitalist development, the capitalist–democracy contradiction is an external one, originating between the political and economic structures of a democratic–capitalist society. More specifically, it is a contradiction between the need to socialize the control of urban space to create the conditions for the maintenance of capitalism on the one hand and the danger to capital of truly socializing, that is, democratizing, the control of urban land on the other. For if the market system cannot produce a built environment that is capable of maintaining capitalism, reliance on the institutions of the state, especially a formally democratic state, creates a whole new set of problems, not the least of which is that the more populous body of nonowners will gain too much control over landed property. This latter contradiction is conditioned on the existence of the property contradiction, in that it arises from efforts to use government action to balance or hold in check the property contradiction. Once government intervention is accepted, questions about how to organize that intervention arise: What goals should be pursued? How should they be formulated and by whom? This pattern of the capitalist–democracy contradiction following on the heels of the property contradiction is apparent in the actual history of planning, for while both contradictions have been in evidence throughout the history of planning in America, the property contradiction was a more salient generator of conflict in the earlier, pre-1940 period. The capitalist–democracy contradiction – manifested in the controversy over how to organize the planning process – has been a more potent source of conflict in the history of planning after World War II. It should also be emphasized that the capitalist–democracy contradiction is conditioned on the formally democratic character of the state, out of which the danger of government control of urban development arises. Were it not for the majority-rule criterion and formal equality promised by the state, turning to government to control urban development would not pose such a problem for capital.

Consideration of the capitalist–democracy contradiction leads us back to Offe's analysis of the internal structure of the state. Following Offe's analysis, it can be postulated that capitalism is caught in a search for a decision process, a method of policy making that can produce decisions corresponding with capital's political and economic interests. Politically, this decision process must be capable of insulating state decision making from the claims and considerations of the numerically larger class of noncapitalists, a task made difficult by the formally democratic character of the state. Economically, this decision process must be capable of producing decisions that facilitate the accumulation and circulation of capital (for example, promoting the reproduction of labor power and coordinating the building up of local infrastructure), a function that the market fails to perform and that capitalists do not (necessarily) know how to perform. Both of these problems are captured in the concept of the capitalist–democracy contradiction. The question we are led to ask, then, is, In what ways has the development of urban planning – viewed here as a method of policy formulation – served to suppress or hold in balance the capitalist–democracy contradiction in a manner conducive to the reproduction of capitalism?

NOTES

1   "Labor, Capital, and Class Struggle around the Built Environment in Advanced Capitalist Societies," p. 265.
2   *Urban Question*, pp. 460–61. Castells modifies his view in his most recent book, *The City and the Grass Roots*, which appeared after the manuscript of *Planning the Capitalist City* was essentially written. In this new book, Castells seeks to avoid the "excesses of theoretical formalism" that marked some of his earlier work (p. xvii). He also asserts that "although class relationships and class struggle are fundamental in understanding the process of urban conflict, they are by no means the only or even the primary source of urban social change" (p. xviii). My critical evaluation of Castells's earlier work is still valid and useful, however, since it lends emphasis and historical reference to some of Castells's own criticisms. Furthermore, my criticisms apply to a literature and a theoretical orientation that encompasses, as I point out, more than Castells's work.
3   Harvey, "The Political Economy of Urbanization in Advanced Capitalist Societies: The Case of the United States," p. 120; Preteceille, "Urban Planning: The Contradictions of Capitalist Urbanization," pp. 69–76. For Harvey, the need for a built environment usable as a collective means of production is only one of the connections between urban planning and capitalist development; he also recognizes the need for facilities for collective consumption to aid in reproducing labor power. See, e.g., his "Labor, Capital, and Class Struggle around the Built Environment."
4   Preteceille, "Urban Planning," p. 70.
5   "Property Development and the Economic Foundations of the Urban Question," p. 86.
6   *Social Justice*, chapter 5.
7   For a discussion of this use of *contradiction*, see Godelier, "Structure and Contradiction in *Capital*," pp. 334–68.
8   Cf. Michael Dear and Allen Scott's assertion that the "urban question" (a reference to the work of Castells) is "structured around the particular and indissoluble geographical and land-contingent phenomena that come into existence as capitalist social and property relations are mediated through the dimension of urban space." They also write that planning is "a historically-specific and socially-necessary response to the self-disorganizing tendencies of *privatized* capitalist social and property relations as these appear in urban space" ("Towards a Framework for Analysis," pp. 6, 13). Cf. also, in the same volume,

Shoukry Roweis's statement that "[u]rban planning in capitalism, both in theory and in practice, and whether intentionally or unknowingly, attempts to grapple with a basic question: how can *collective action* (pertinent to decisions concerning the social utilization of urban land) be made possible under capitalism?" ("Urban Planning in Early and Late Capitalist Societies," p. 170). These two theoretical analyses relate urban planning under capitalism to the problem of "collective control" – how to organize socially necessary forms of collective consumption and control in a society based upon private ownership – but they do not take note of the contradiction between capital's need for collective control in its own interest and the limits imposed by the internal structure of the *state*. This is the issue raised by Offe and which I capture in my concept of the "capitalist–democracy contradiction".

9 "Property Development," pp. 90–93.

FURTHER READING

Castells, Manuel. *The Urban Question.* Cambridge: MIT Press, 1977.

Dear, Michael, and Scott, Allen J., "Towards a Framework for Analysis." In *Urbanization and Urban Planning in Capitalist Society*, edited by Michael Dear and Allen J. Scott, pp. 3–18. London: Methuen, 1981.

Godelier, Maurice. "Structure and Contradiction in *Capital*." In *Ideology and Social Science*, edited by Robin Blackburn, pp. 334–68. New York: Vintage Books, 1973.

Harvey, David. "Labor, Capital, and Class Struggle around the Built Environment in Advanced Capitalist Societies," *Politics & Society* 6 (1976): 265–95.

——"The Political Economy of Urbanization in Advanced Capitalist Societies: The Case of the United States." In *The Social Economy of Cities*, Urban Affairs Annual, edited by Gary Grappert and Harold M. Rose, no. 9, pp. 119–63. Beverly Hills: Russell Sage, 1975.

——*Social Justice and the City.* Baltimore: Johns Hopkins University Press, 1973.

Lamarche, François. "Property Development and the Economic Foundations of the Urban Question." In *Urban Sociology: Critical Essays*, edited by Chris Pickvance, pp. 85–118. London: Tavistock Press, 1976.

Offe, Claus. "The Abolition of Market Control and the Problem of Legitimacy (I)." *Kapitalistate*, no. 1 (1973): 109–16.

Preteceille, Edmond. "Urban Planning: The Contradictions of Capitalist Urbanization." *Antipode* 8 (March 1976): 69–76.

Roweis, Shoukry. "Urban Planning in Early and Late Capitalist Societies." In *Urbanization and Urban Planning in Capitalist Society*, edited by Michael Dear and Allen J. Scott, pp. 159–78. London: Methuen, 1981.

6

Between Modernity and Postmodernity: The Ambiguous Position of U.S. Planning

Robert A. Beauregard

Introduction

From the early decades of the twentieth century through the 1960s, state planning in the United States of America was able to maintain the integrity of its modernist project.[1] In that project, planners strove to (1) bring reason and democracy to bear on capitalist urbanization, (2) guide state decision making with technical rather than political rationality, (3) produce a coordinated and functional urban form organized around collective goals, and (4) use economic growth to create a middle-class society. Planners took on the challenge of an industrial capitalism forged in the nineteenth century and shaped a response to the turmoil of modernization. They did so shrouded in modernism, the "*cultural* precipitates of this socio-historical period" (Schulte-Sasse 1987: 6).

By the 1980s, the modernist planning project was under attack. Some even talked about a crisis of state planning (Friedmann 1987) emanating from a series of profound changes involving urban restructuring, state politics, and cultural practices; each related to new activities and sensibilities often subsumed under a postmodern rubric. The landscape of postmodernity with its hypermobile capital, concentrations of advanced services, juxtaposition of vast wealth and extreme poverty, downscaled and customized production complexes, and deconcentrated central cities (Cooke 1988) poses novel and difficult problems for modernist planners. Moreover, the cultural practices of postmodernists undermine earlier commitments to a middle-class society, a disciplined urban form, the efficacy of rationalism, and political

Reprinted with permission from *Environment and Planning D: Society and Space*, 7 (1989): 381–95. Pion Limited, London.

neutrality. U.S. planning thus finds itself suspended between modernity and postmodernity, with its practitioners and theorists astride an ever-widening chasm.

In this chapter my objectives are threefold. My first is to examine the historical roots of state planning, highlighting its modernist elements. My second is to argue that the deconstruction of modernist planning represents a clash between new (postmodern) and old (modern) forms of urban political economies and of social thought. Last, I will offer suggestions as to how planning practitioners and theorists might respond critically to a postmodern capital restructuring and cultural transformation, heeding its calls to be flexible and open but not abandoning the modernist quest for a democratic and reformist planning and a commitment to the city.

Historical Backdrop

The roots of U.S. state planning lie in the late nineteenth and early twentieth centuries and within local responses to the modern city: its physical degradation, functional chaos, and the miseries suffered by the working class (Gans 1968; McKelvey 1963; Scott 1969; Sharpe and Wallock 1987). Although the planning of the built environment in the United States can be traced to the seventeenth-century European colonists (Foglesong 1986), the impetus for the institutionalization of planning grew out of social problems related to massive immigration, large-scale manufacturing, and the lack of controls over the built environment.

Planning took shape as part of a reform movement at the turn of the century, centered on the middle class and comprising diverse elements (Hofstadter 1955). One element was focused on the built environment and was mainly concerned with population congestion and public health. Reformers championed local legislation that would improve working-class slums by regulating the quality of the built environment through building and housing codes and instituted efforts to develop model, working-class housing (Fairbanks 1988). Public attention also turned to the provision of sanitation facilities and the imposition of public health regulations that would prevent the spatial diffusion of disease (Peterson 1983). These concerns intersected at the regulation of "nuisances" (for example, fire-prone laundries) that might create hazards and spread disease in residential areas.

Another group of reforms contributed to the establishment of state planning. Often referred to as "planners" rather than "housers," they concerned themselves, more broadly, with the emerging form of the industrial city and its chaotic juxtaposition of land uses (Boyer 1983). Joined with civic boosters, the planners supported rapid urban growth through the ordering of the built environment. Their actions were based on the notion that organized and physically coherent cities grounded in good functional and aesthetic principles are better than those that are not. This notion was inspired by an awareness of the anarchic qualities of capitalist urban development. Planners grasped early on that different capitalists pursue different spatial investment strategies in an uncoordinated fashion, thus creating an intracapitalist competition alongside a capital–labor struggle for control over the built environment. If the industrial city was to be an efficient mechanism for capital accumulation, and if labor was to be allowed respite from the ever-expanding oppression of the factory system and be given protection from unrestrained property capital (Walker 1978), someone had to bring order to its fragmented form.

The early planners thus undertook various "master planning" schemes that would arrange land-using activities in ways that achieved functional and aesthetic object-ives. The Chicago World's Fair of 1893 set forth one model of downtown design that could be used to situate public buildings (for example, library, post office, city hall) and capitalist infrastructure (for instance, railroad stations, office structures) around public spaces. The aesthetic was unabashedly "classical" – linear, holistic, and heroic – and the functional concerns unequivocally supportive of the production and circulation of capital and the emergence of a new pact between capital and the state. In this way, the emerging political economy of industrial capitalism would be manifested in a planned built environment, with the additional benefit of utilizing such a scheme to eradicate slums. Expanded and subdued, that paradigm became the "master plan," a document taking into account the functional and economic deter-minants of urban activities and their proper aesthetic and spatial interrelationships.

Through the early decades of the twentieth century, this mode of planning practice held sway with only minor variations. Restrictive legislation on housing was par-tially displaced by a call for public housing, the 1920s witnessed greater emphasis on highway and subdivision planning, and zoning as a local regulatory device began to displace the master plan. After World War II, housing, zoning, and transportation planning flourished. Urban renewal was added to the practice of planners, itself helping to revive, though only temporarily, the master planning tradition. During its spurt of growth in the 1960s, planning practice diversified into a multitude of specialties: environmental, manpower, social planning, health planning, transporta-tion, energy planning, and regional planning along with the traditional land use and housing (Beauregard 1986). Being a planner no longer meant regulating the spatial arrangements of land uses and providing housing. A variety of social planners challenged the increasingly specialized physical planners. As a result, planning practice underwent centrifugal disintegration. The common object of interest – the city – that had initially attracted "progressive" reformers was lost.

Theory and pedagogy

The history of practice, however, is only a partial history of planning. One must also pay attention to education and theory. University-based education for planners appeared in the late 1920s and remained relatively vocational until after World War II. At that time, planning education began to fracture into two camps: practi-tioners with professional degrees and theorists ordained as doctors of philosophy. Moreover, education became not only an occupational gateway but also a strong link between the practice and theory of planning, and between the actions of planners and the ideology that encased them.

Theoretically, planning has always been difficult to define; it can be said to have had only briefly a dominant paradigm and has remained on the fringes of critical social theory (Dear 1986; Friedmann 1987).[2] The planning extolled by the reformers of the Progressive Era was based on a mixture of common sense, emerging middle-class values of civic responsibility and organization, and selective elements of sociology and economics, all flavored with a strong sense of "classical" order related both to architecture and to the city. The central focus for reformers of housing and sanitation was the consequences for health of the slums, with theoretical understanding only partially advised by a rudimentary theory of disease. Those concerned with the city as a whole, people like Frederick Law Olmsted, organized their thinking mainly around organic analogies (Olmsted 1916), though many times the factory mentality induced the metaphor of the city as machine. During the interwar years (1918 to 1939), planning theory incorporated the Chicago school of sociology and human ecology to explain urban form and urban problems (Bailey 1975). Early planning theory was about the city and the built environment, and merged with practice; there were no "planning theorists," only reformers or practitioners with ideas about how the city should be structured.

After World War II, however, theory evolved as a specialization within planning (Beauregard 1987; Cooke 1983). The impetus was the Program in Education and Research in Planning at the University of Chicago (Sarbib, 1983). It was founded in 1947 with the goal of training Ph.D. students and thereby establishing planning as a legitimate academic discipline rather than solely as a profession. One result was to move planning education away from a "studio" model based upon learning by doing, the utilization of paradigmatic examples, and postgraduate apprenticeship under a "master planner." The replacement was the pedagogical model of the lecture and seminar; knowledge was fragmented into subdisciplines, and students learnt through texts rather than direct problem solving. Once graduated, only a dose of on-the-job training was needed.

The second result was to sever professional training from academic training by creating a career path for teachers of planning that did not necessarily intersect with planning practice. This allowed for the emergence of planning theorists who erected the intellectual base for planning practice but did not themselves act as practitioners. Dual career paths, however, undermined the contribution to practice; theorists looked for validation within academia rather than without. The combination of an academic pedagogical model, severance from practice, and creation of alternative career paths was fertile ground for the emergence of abstract theorizing distanced from the performative demands of practitioners.

Nonetheless, a dominant theoretical paradigm emerged in the 1950s and 1960s to define the contribution of planning (Beauregard 1984): a comprehensive, rational model of problem solving and decision making to guide state intervention. Theorists of this model believed that they had found the intellectual core of planning: a set of procedures that would generate conceptual problems for theorists, serve as a joint object for theory and practice, and guide practitioners in their daily endeavors. This view proved to be erroneous; while early postwar theorists articulated this "essence" of planning, the modernist project on which such an essence was based was being eroded.

The Modernist Project of Planning

The initial thrusts of the modernist project of planning were to diminish the excesses of industrial capitalism while mediating the intramural frictions among capitalists that had resulted in a city inefficiently organized for production and reproduction. Planners were to do this from within local and, less so, state governments. Their planning project was modernist because it engaged the city of industrial capitalism and became institutionalized as a form of state intervention. Underlying these concrete manifestations are procedural assumptions and substantive commitments that sealed the fate of planning as a modernist project.

Procedural assumptions

In the modernist planning project, reality that can be controlled and perfected is assumed. The world is viewed as malleable, and it is malleable because its internal logic can be uncovered and subsequently manipulated. Thus, modernist planners rejected the alienation that is often viewed as part of modernization (Schulte-Sasse 1987) yet adopted a viewpoint, also modernist, that overcomes alienation through a belief in the efficacy of human action and the importance of commitment (Kraushaar 1988; Orwell 1953). Modernist planners believe in a future in which social problems are tamed and humanity liberated from the constraints of scarcity and greed (Hutcheon 1987; Jencks 1985). Social control is wielded in order to drive society forward along a path of progress; planning is part of the modern "struggle to make ourselves at home in a constantly changing world" (Berman 1988:6).

Planners' involvement in this modernist struggle was not as people of action. Rather, their contribution was utilitarian understanding. Knowledge in planning would precede and shape the actions taken by investors, households, and governments. In effect, planning would liberate through enlightenment (Albertsen 1988; Friedmann 1987). Knowledge and reason would free people from fatalism and ideologies, allowing the logic intrinsic to an industrial society to be uncovered and exploited. Modernist planners thus situated themselves clearly within both a European rationalism and an American pragmatism (Hofstadter 1958; Scott and Shore 1979). To this extent, knowledge in planning had to be evaluated on a performative criterion, based as it was within a scientific mode of legitimation (Lyotard 1984). As such, planners were somewhat anti-intellectual; impatient with abstract theorizing and thus with social theory. Nevertheless, the aim of modernist planners was to act as experts who could utilize the laws of development to provide societal guidance.

Fostering the faith of modernist planners in the liberating and progressive potential of knowledge was their corresponding belief in their ability to maintain a critical distance (Bernstein 1987; Jameson 1984b). Planners laid claim to a scientific and objective logic that transcended the interests of capital, labor, and the state. This logic allowed modernist planners to disengage themselves from the interests of any particular group, avoid accusations of self-interest, and identify actions in the public interest, that is, actions that benefit society as an organic whole. Such an ideology served modernist planners in two ways: First, they could position themselves within the state without having to be labeled "political," and second, they could assert a mediative role between capital and labor.

Last, both the practice and theory of modernist planning revolves around the use of master narratives (Jameson 1984b). For practice, the narrative synthesizes developmental processes and the built environment into a coherent urban form that fulfills the functional necessities of the city. The text is the master plan. For theory, it involves the formulation of a dominant paradigm – comprehensive rationalism – that focuses the normal science of theorists. The "planning process" is its plot (Beauregard 1984). In essence, modernist planners believe in totalizing what planners call "comprehensive" solutions that have a unitary logic.

Substantive commitments

Such bowing to modernization is reflected in the substantive orientation of planning to the city and the state. As already mentioned, the modernist project is based upon a belief in the "synthetic" city; that is, the city of singular form invariant over time. This holistic and ahistoric perspective is derived from a revealed internal logic of how a city (under capitalism) functions. The task for planners is to take the fragments produced by the contradictions and struggles of capitalism and integrate them into a unique and orderly whole. As with modern art, "the unity of [planners'] work was assembled from fragments and juxtapositions" (Gitlin 1988: 35). This in turn enabled modernist planners to claim a privileged position in the realm of specialists; planners were to transcend specializations and provide the contextual integration for numerous experts involved in the reform of the industrial city.

The holism that modernist planners propounded was dependent both on the economic dynamics of the industrial city and on the parallel rise of a middle class. The "spatial paradigm" of modernist planning (Cooke 1988) was focused on the production of standard commodities for large markets, the importance of transportation infrastructure for the circulation of commodities, and the location of investment in proximity to labor. As well as disciplining the city for capital accumulation (Boyer 1983) and assuring an adequate supply of labor for the factories, however, planners had to meet the demands of a new administrative work force and an emerging professional stratum desirous of urban amenities (such as parks) and residential areas isolated from manufacturing districts. The contradiction between demands made on the work force by industrialists and the consumption demands of an emerging professional and managerial elite were reconciled in the minds of planners by a belief in the *embourgeoisement* of the working class. As capitalism was tamed, the city organized, and prosperity diffused socially and spatially, the lower classes would rise to affluence and take on the values and behaviors of the middle class (Gans 1968).

The expansion of the middle class also validated the belief that society was not riven by contradictions, and thus the city could be organized physically for "public" purposes. Invidious class distinctions were being erased by economic growth; thus the city could be viewed as the physical container for the workings of a conflict-free society (Hayden 1984). Modernization, and thus progress, meant that the good life diffused across all groups, natives and immigrants alike.

Moreover, modernization was possible because the state had progressive tendencies to be reformist and serve the long-run needs of all groups. From the "progressive" perspective, the state could be an instrumentality representative of the interests of all its citizens as disclosed by the expertise of planners. In this way, modernist planners skirt the ideological issue of the compatibility of planning and democracy (Aptheker 1967; Hayek 1944). Instead, they rest easy on the democratic pretensions of the state and their privileged insights into the public interest.

Intrinsic to this perspective is a need for functional equilibrium. The singular, organic, and totalizing view taken of the city leaves little leeway for chaos and indeterminacy.[3] For the great majority of planners involved with the "city functional," the efficient organization of the city was the preferred social interest (Hall

1989). Reason replaced greed, and a nonpartisan logic displaced self-regarding behavior. The public interest would be revealed through a scientific understanding of the organic logic of society.

In terms of its interest in growth and quest for efficiency, the logic of planning overlapped with that of capital, but it denied capital's way of achieving them. The ideology of planning was more attuned to political reform embedded within the state, thus reinforcing the substantive commitment to a state that is external to the economy, a further manifestation of the adherence to the idea of keeping a critical distance. Without this understanding, planners could not view themselves as interceding without bias in the workings of capitalism, nor could they be reformers and governmental employees. Modernist planners thus adopted the separation of the political from the economic – the capitalist trenches (Katznelson 1981) – that channels oppositional movements and enables the capitalist state to be viewed as an arena for reform.

In sum, the modernist project is derived from beliefs about knowledge and society and is inextricably linked to the rise of capitalism, the formation of the middle class, the emergence of a scientific mode of legitimation, the concept of an orderly and spatially integrated city that meets the needs of society, and the fostering of the interventionist state. Technical rationality is viewed as a valid and superior means of making public decisions, and information gathered scientifically is regarded as enlightening, captivating, and convincing. The democratic state contains an inherent tendency to foster and support reform, whereas its planners maintain a critical distance from specialized interests. Such beliefs repeat and mimic beliefs about enlightenment that are associated with the rise of capitalist democracies and with the modernist quest for control and liberation.

Modernist Planning Besieged

Modernist planning began to come apart in the 1970s and 1980s (Dear 1986). Novel political forms, economic relations, and restructured cities posed new difficulties for the premises that underlie practice. The critical distance that modernist planners attempted to maintain was radically altered, and the emancipatory potential of planning was virtually abandoned. Numerous commentators began to ask, "Who controls planning?" In turn, the theoretical quest for a master narrative that could be applied both to the city and to planning thought was brought to an end by eclecticism and a reluctance to embrace social theory. Such changes reflect the realities of a post-Fordist political economy and postmodern cultural sensibilities.[4]

Practice

There are numerous versions of the most recent round of capital restructuring (Beauregard 1989; Bluestone and Harrison 1982; Bradbury 1985; Castells 1985; Chase-Dunn 1984; Fainstein and Fainstein 1989; Harrison and Bluestone 1988; Peet 1987; Soja et al. 1983). One dominant interpretation is that Fordist means, techniques, and social relations of production have been superseded by post-Fordist and postmodern forms: high-technology products and processes, an expanded emphasis on the financial circuit of capital, more flexible procedures in the workplace, and a defensive and weakened labor force (Albertsen 1988; Cooke 1988). The state has become more ideologically conservative and more subservient to the needs and demands of capital, turning away from the simultaneous pursuit of both economic growth and welfare. Although the needs and demands of capital are (still) achieved through state assistance, the state has turned away from the simultaneous pursuit of welfare and economic growth (Kantor 1988; Smith 1988). Local politics, moreover, increasingly pivots around economic development and jobs (Stone and Sanders 1987). New spatial forms also have appeared (Conzen 1988; Cooke 1988): a postmodern city to join the postmodern political economy of flexible accumulation and the globalization of capital (Harvey 1987; Soja 1986).

Whether one accepts this or another version of "late capitalism", contemporary restructuring of capital has made the practice of modernist planning more precarious. On the one hand, planners are increasingly vulnerable to property and industrial capital through the state's deepening involvement in capital accumulation. Thus, planners are less able to maintain a desired critical distance. Economic development is so highly valued by elected officials that planners, even if they were not to share this ideology of growth, would find it difficult, if not impossible, to oppose the state's complicity. The result has been a peculiar form of nonplanning in which planners participate in individual projects, often attempting to temper the most egregious negative externalities, while failing to place these projects into any broader framework of urban development, a basic tenet of modernist planning (Fainstein and Fainstein 1987; Goldberger 1989).

The totalizing vision and the reformist tendencies of modernist planning have been undermined. Comprehensive planning that articulates the organic integrity of the city has become politically untenable. Such planning requires a balancing of interests and a taming of the excesses of capital, thereby hindering economic expansion. Planners, however, are less and less able to maintain even the facade of being concerned with those outside the "loop" of economic prosperity. No longer is the idea to improve society. The new strategy is to flee the problems of society by creating wider and wider circles of growth (Logan and Molotch 1987). Economic development, not reform, is the political aim of the 1980s, and it sacrifices regulation and the welfare state to the lure of new investment and jobs.

Under modernist planning, reform and growth were viewed as compatible even if they were not pursued equally. This distinguished planners from property developers. Now, the two groups have formed public–private partnerships. Even the schools train students in real estate development, the cutting edge of planning education. Planning has become entrepreneurial, and planners have become deal makers rather than regulators (Fainstein 1988). The critical distance cherished by modernist planners is eroding.

In turn, the proponents of policies to promote local growth attempt, often unsuccessfully, to conduct their business outside the realm of public scrutiny and debate. Private–public partnerships and public authorities isolate development politics from democratic politics (Friedland et al. 1978). Decisions about subsidies to private property, industrial investment, and public infrastructure are cast as technical decisions, and thereby depoliticized and confined to the deliberations of experts. Yet because planners still talk about the public interest and the negative consequences of development, if not reform, they are also kept to the fringes of the discussion. Development politics are for development-oriented individuals trained in business schools and housed in quasi-public economic development agencies.

More than the politics of the modernist project have been undermined by the recent capital restructuring. The form and dynamics of the city have changed to such an extent that the principles of modernist planning are less credible (Cooke 1988; Simonsen 1988; Soja 1986; Zukin 1988). First, whereas modernist planners had assumed that local actions were determinative of local conditions, thus partially justifying local planning, that fiction has been severely compromised. The heightened spatial mobility of capital has made large-scale property development and industrial investment into affairs of regional, national, and even international proportions. Locational determinants of investment are increasingly ephemeral. State subsidies are ubiquitous, and the quality-of-life factors that attract "advanced service" industries and educated labor are hardly confined to a few global cities.

In addition, and in order to attract capital investment, civic boosters and economic development officials attempt to commodify the "particularities of place" through public spectacles and festival marketplaces (Harvey 1987). To the extent that communities rely on cultural conditions and social amenities to generate growth, they are even more vulnerable to the influence of capital over consumption and "lifestyles." Accumulation and consumption have become more flexible and less place-bound (Harvey 1987), and planners lack the legal capacity and political weight to reshape the investment and employment prerogatives of capital.

Second, planners' grasp of a functional and unitary notion of urban development is even less justifiable. The expanding urban economies of "Progressive Era" cities and of metropolitan economies of the postwar period seemed to offer opportunities to maximize the interest of all classes, but the increasing fragmentation of capital and labor in the postmodern era and the failure of growth to eliminate or even ameliorate tenacious inequalities of class, race, and gender make ludicrous any assumption of unitary planning. The emergence of the modern city neither brought forth a society whose many groups participated equally in affluence nor erased the manifestation of past injustices. Rather, the postmodern city is layered with historical forms and struggled over by fractions of capital and labor, each of which is dependent upon economic activities that are industrial and postindustrial, formal and informal, primary and secondary (Davis 1987; Soja 1986). Under such conditions, it is difficult to maintain a modernist commitment to a conflict-free public interest.

National attempts to obliterate class distinctions through prosperity and collective consumption and the local attempts to provide events (for example, multiethnic affairs) that celebrate yet minimize differences have not led to the *embourgeoisement* of the working class. Neighborhoods of "displaced" blue-collar workers in marginalized households, recent immigrants from Asia and Latin America, and the extremely wealthy coexist in numerous cities. Even more compelling is the continued existence and expansion of the black "underclass" and the poverty and unemployment experienced by white and nonwhite working-class households alike (Wilson 1987). The fringes of black, Hispanic, and other immigrant areas, moreover, are increasingly the sites of racial confrontations.

Last, the lessening of state controls and the deepening obeisance to capital investment have exacerbated the negative consequences of rapid economic growth and have even intensified the "seesaw" effect of uneven development (Smith 1984). Fueled by the hypermobility of capital, cities like Houston have experienced prosperity but not without wide-ranging social and environmental costs (Feagin 1988). Such conditions thwart movement to an ideal city. Instead, the city functions as a locus of unending struggle around the distribution of the costs and benefits of growth and decline. The implications for modernist planning are profound. Without a conflict-free society and the possibility of a single textual response, the modernist planning project is cut adrift.

In essence, the master narrative of modernist planning is incompatible with a spatially problematic and flexible urban form whose articulations are intrinsically confrontational and whose purposes are more and more the ephemeral ones of consumption. Subsequently, a modernist striving for orderliness, functional integration, and social homogeneity is unlikely to succeed, as is the desire on the part of planners to maintain a critical distance and apply technical rationalism. Broadly cast, modernist planners are in the grip of a postmodern helplessness (Gitlin 1988).

Theory

Theoretically, planning remains in a modernist mode. The literature on planning theory is devoid of attempts to view planning theory through the lens of the postmodern cultural critique. Rather, this theoretical investigation has been initiated by urban geographers, mainly Michael Dear, Phillip Cooke, David Harvey, Edward W. Soja, and Edward Relph. This does not mean that planning theory has remained unaffected. The turmoil attendant to modernist planning practice reverberates into academe as planning theorists reflect upon the nature of planning practice and consider how to educate students. Moreover, the work of the above-mentioned urban geographers has begun to diffuse into the literature on planning theory, posing a postmodern challenge to planning theorists as they look toward the social sciences for theoretical guidance.

The postmodernist cultural critique is a complex one. It includes a turn to historical allusion and spatial understandings, the abandonment of critical distance for ironic commentary, the embracing of multiple discourses and the rejection of totalizing ones, a skepticism toward master narratives and general social theories, a disinterest in the performativity of knowledge, the rejection of notions of progress and enlightenment, and a tendency toward political acquiescence (Bernstein 1987; Cooke 1988; Dear 1986; Gregory 1987; Jameson 1984a; Jencks 1985; Lyotard 1984; Relph 1987; Soja 1989). Each aspect challenges modernist planning theory.

To begin, the postmodern interest in space and time would seem, at first glance, to be supportive of modernist planning. Planners have made location central to their work and have always had a strong need to relate past trends to future possibilities. The postmodern debate is filled with commentary on the new hyperspaces of capitalism (Jameson 1984a), with the more empirical literature extolling the uniqueness of localities. At the same time, postmodernism involves a turn to the past, particularly in terms of urban design and architectural styles.

Excluding neo-Marxist political economy, modernist planning has been dominated by procedural theories; that is, generic, paradigmatic theories meant to be applicable regardless of context, thus leaving space and time unattended. Moreover, the space and time of postmodernism are not the space and time of modernist planning. Planning theorists and practitioners cling to relativist and physically inert notions of space and a linear sense of time. The postmodern challenge is to conceive of space and time dialectically, socially, and historically; and to integrate such conceptions into a critical social theory. In turn, even though planning in the United States has been a local project, focusing mainly on communities, planning theorists have rejected materialist perspectives for idealistic ones and thus have difficulty relating to postmodern locality studies. Rather, too little attention is given to spatial scales and the interaction of the structural and the particular.

This theoretical stance indicates the way in which modernist planning theorists have interpreted the notion of maintaining a critical distance. With few exceptions (Davidoff 1965; Goodman 1971), they rejected the role of social critic. Despite the need for a radical critique of U.S. society, and the potential to do so when subsidized and protected by an academic position, theorists did not challenge the prevailing orthodoxy concerning the domestic benefits of economic growth. Rather, most retreated from political involvement, content to accept the "end of ideology" and thus to abandon a modernist commitment to reform. Prior to the 1960s, then, criticism centered on planning theories, specifically the comprehensive rational model. Modernist planning theorists turned away from the realities of planning practice and engaged in internal academic debates. Any commitment to being "public" was cast aside (Jacoby 1987). The critics within planning who emerged in the 1960s to debunk the conservative politics and middle-class bias of planning made explicit connections between the racism and inequality of U.S. society and planning, but they did not venture outside the profession to share their criticism with a wider public.

For theorists, the modernist commitment to a master narrative became at once easier and more difficult as academic forces increasingly distanced them from practitioners and isolated them from public debates. Practice no longer constrained their thoughts with pragmatic, political economic realities. As a body, planning theorists became highly eclectic, pursuing theoretical projects for their own sake. Collectively, they lost the object, the city, that had given planning its legitimacy. Their new objects – the planning process, policy making, decision making, and so on – were only tangentially the objects of practitioners; they were procedurally relevant, but not substantively so.

This postmodern fragmentation of planning theory would have been acceptable if it had paralleled a corresponding adoption of an integrative framework that critiqued society and advanced planning practice. Theorists did look toward economics, management science, and mathematics for a synthesis. However, the modernist disciplinary blinders that come with these bodies of knowledge only narrowed the theoretical perspectives of planners. The great nineteenth-century theories of Charles Darwin, Emile Durkheim, Sigmund Freud, and Max Weber, for example, have not been plumbed for their views on society and relevance for planning. References to twentieth-century grand theorists such as Michel Foucault, Claude Lévi-Strauss, Ferdinand Braudel, and even Lewis Mumford are just as rare.

Planning theorists operating with a leftist or neo-Marxist perspective have been more sensitive to integrative social theories and to broad and significant transformations under way in society. Friedmann (1987) is certainly attuned to deep intellectual currents, Forester (1989) has made major advances in planning theory by building on the ideas of Habermas, and Boyer's history of U.S. planning (1983) owes much to the structuralism of Foucault. The neo-Marxists (for example, Fainstein and Fainstein 1979; Harvey 1978) have prepared a powerful critique of the function of planning under capitalism but offer little guidance in practical affairs. Hayden's feminist analysis (1984) and Clavel's (1986) investigation of progressive planning have been successful in linking social theory to planning practice. Neither, however, has crystallized planning thought or attracted many adherents.

Planning theorists, with the above exceptions, have thus avoided the task of making sense of the post-Fordist economy and the postmodern city. They are silent about spatiality and treat planning ahistorically, despite a recent surge of interest in planning history. While other disciplines look outward (Dear 1988; Soja 1989), most planning theorists turn inward to planning pedagogy rather than to the social context of practice.

The postmodern cultural and literary theories that speak of the demise of the master narrative, the bankruptcy of positivism, and the political deficiencies of technical expertise are of little moment amongst planning theorists. A tinge of anti-intellectualism characterizes planning theory as a whole, at least if one interprets this as an unfamiliarity with and avoidance of current intellectual debates and the foundations of modern social thought. Planning theorists tend to carry on a dialogue among themselves, reflecting in their insularity the ambiguous and the peripheral social position of planning in the United States. The little enlightenment that is generated is thus confined to theorists rather than extended to practitioners and citizens. This further distances theorists from society and makes a clear political statement.

The postmodern debate, nonetheless, is not simply an issue of theoretical possibilities and cultural practices but also a political agenda, muddled though it is, that has implications for planning theory (Smith 1987). On the one hand, political and economic reform are not high on that agenda, and political acquiescence seems to extend from the celebration of multiple discourses. Such political inclinations coincide well with the directions taken by most modernist planning theorists, who have abandoned any critical role and turned to academic debates. To the extent that planning education, however, trains its students to think in terms of dampening the excesses of capitalism, improving society, and understanding the political role of the expert, a tension exists between modernist and postmodernist political sensibilities. On the other hand, the postmodern debate does offer a useful antidote to planners' belief in the *embourgeoisement* of the working class and the conflict-free homogeneity of social interests.

Overall, then, the modernist planning project has disintegrated but not disappeared. Practice has lost its "neutral" mediative position, forsaken its clear object of the city, abandoned its critical distance, and further suppressed reformist and democratic tendencies. Yet practitioners still cling to a modernist sensibility and search for ways to impose expertise on democracy and to integrate their many specialities around a grand vision such as the master plan. Theory, on the other hand, has undergone centrifugal disintegration without a corresponding refocusing of knowledge around social theories and a broadening of the planning debate. Neither does one find a theoretical commitment to more than a pragmatic political agenda. From this perspective, planning seems suspended between modernity and postmodernity, with practitioners and theorists having few clues as to how to (re)establish themselves on solid ground.[5]

Toward City-Centered and Democratic Planning

Though the modernist project of planning is under attack, and seemingly less and less viable as a response to contemporary social conditions and intellectual tendencies, one should not propose too hastily that planners should resolve the confusion by unconditionally adopting postmodernist alternatives. The modernist project needs to be reconstructed in a way that takes into account its strengths – the focus on the city, the commitment to reform, the mediative role within the state – and eradicates its weaknesses – the outmoded view of the city, the lack of democracy, an illiberal attitude toward narratives, and an insensitivity to the diversity of communities. Three modest suggestions are offered as a way to this reconstruction (see Beauregard 1990).

First, practitioners and theorists must rededicate themselves to the built environment as the object of action and inquiry. At present, the physical city exists within planning as a series of unconnected fragments rather than as a practical and theoretical synthesis of planning action and thought. The built environment is a source of capital accumulation, a place of consumption and reproduction, and a terrain of profound struggle. Moreover, the physical city is the object of practice and theory that historically enabled state planning to be established. To abandon it is to abandon the meaning of urban planning in the United States as well as the source of its legitimacy as a state activity.

Nonetheless, the "modernist" city of the unitary plan and the city of property capital have to be rejected. Instead, planners need to recognize the emergence of a post-Fordist city of dynamics and forms heretofore unaddressed. At the center of that perspective must be an object of integrative potential, substantive moment, and theoretical extension. One such object is the city-building process and its product, the built environment (Beauregard 1988). Such a focus can reintegrate the various specialties of planning around an object of historical significance and long-term legitimacy. It can provide substantive problems for grounding planning in the practicalities of everyday life and historical trends. Moreover, by understanding the way in which building a city is linked to political, economic, and cultural phenomena, planners can extend their reach (both practically and theoretically) and establish the basis for a critique of capitalist ideology and the politics of growth.

Second, planners need to take a mediative position between capital, labor, and the state. Although contradictory and certainly difficult to realize, such a position can be used to enhance political debate around the processes and outcomes of urban development. The idea is for planners to abandon political neutrality for a new "progressivism" linked simultaneously to the imperatives of the state and the needs of labor. Planning needs to be a countervailing power to capital, and it can do so under present conditions only by establishing a base within the community and by exploiting its institutional position within the state. Reaching out to the public with numerous opportunities for involvement in planning deliberations will enable planners to wield more influence within state channels (Benveniste 1977). Instead of hiding behind the cloak of expertise or remaining distant from controversy, planners must participate. The development of a constituency for planning is a prerequisite and a positive outcome; the enhancement of democracy would be its most important contribution.[6]

Practitioners and theorists, then, must open planning to a variety of constituencies. The United States is a multiplicity of communities and cultures. Theorists can support this by giving greater attention to broad social theories that offer explanations of current capital restructuring, critiquing existing epistemologies, and advancing new techniques and knowledge bases for thinking about practicing planning. Such theories must address more directly the conflicts within society and its social and cultural heterogeneity. In these ways, the modernist project of planning can be partially reconstructed while its links to postmodernism are enhanced. In order to establish a state planning concerned with the humanity of the city, a clear practical and theoretical discourse must be combined with political conviction and a respect for democracy.

ACKNOWLEDGMENTS

I extend my thanks to Michael Dear, Susan S. Fainstein, and an anonymous referee, each of whom provided extremely useful critiques of earlier drafts.

NOTES

1   Throughout the text, state planning is synonymous with planning undertaken by the various levels of government in the United States. When state planning refers to planning by the state-level government in contrast to the federal or local levels, the context will make the distinction clear. I use state in a similar fashion.

2   To this extent, I disagree with Soja (1989: 55, footnote 10, emphasis added) who claims that "the anglophonic tradition of planning education throughout the twentieth century has been one of the most important places for the preservation of practical geographical analysis, *critical social theory*, and the geographical imagination."

3   Pluralist political theorists in the postwar period, of course, interpreted this ostensible cacophony of voices as simply the workings of democracy.

4   For a similar argument concerning human geography, see Dear (1988) and Soja (1989).

5   This is also to say that postmodernism is not "modernism at its end" (Lyotard 1984); there is as much continuity as discontinuity. On this point, see Soja (1989) and the essays in the fourth 1987 issue of *Environment and Planning D: Society and Space* (*EPD* 1987).

6   Such a mediative position is politically vulnerable. That is no reason, though, to avoid it. Moreover, I do recognize the pedagogical issues here of how to train planning students to be socially and politically conscious (and critical), technically astute, and employable.

REFERENCES

Albertsen N, 1988, "Postmodernism, post-Fordism, and critical social theory" *Environment and Planning D: Society and Space* 6 339–365

Aptheker H, 1967, *The Nature of Democracy, Freedom and Revolution* (International Publishers, New York)

Bailey J, 1975, *Social Theory for Planning* (Routledge & Kegan Paul, Andover, Hants)

Beauregard R A, 1984, "Making planning theory: a retrospective" *Urban Geography* 5 255–261

Beauregard R A, 1986, "Planning practice" *Urban Geography* 7 172–178

Beauregard R A, 1987, "The object of planning" *Urban Geography* 8 367–373

Beauregard R A, 1988, "The city as built environment", paper presented at the International Sociological Association Research Committee on the Sociology of Urban and Regional Development Conference, "Trends and Challenges of Urban Restructuring," Rio de Janeiro; copy available from author

Beauregard R A, 1989, "Space, time, and economic restructuring," in *Economic Restructuring and Political Response* ed. R A Beauregard (Sage, Beverly Hills, CA) pp 209–240

Beauregard R A, 1990, "Bringing the city back in" *Journal of the American Planning Association* 56

Benveniste G, 1977, *The Politics of Expertise* second edition (Boyd and Fraser, San Francisco, CA)

Berman M, 1988, *All that is Solid Melts into Air* (Penguin Books, New York)

Bernstein C, 1987, "Centering the postmodern" *Socialist Review* 17 45–56

Bluestone B, Harrison B, 1982, *The Deindustrialization of America* (Basic Books, New York)

Boyer M C, 1983, *Dreaming the Rational City* (MIT Press, Cambridge, MA)

Bradbury J H, 1985, "Regional and industrial restructuring processes in the new international division of labor" *Progress in Human Geography* 9 38–63

Castells M, 1985 *High Technology, Space, and Society* (Sage, Beverly Hills, CA)

Chase-Dunn C K, 1984, "The world-system since 1950: what has really changed?", in *Labor in the Capitalist World-Economy* ed. C Bergquist (Sage, Beverly Hills, CA) pp 75–104

Clavel P, 1986, *The Progressive City* (Rutgers University Press, New Brunswick, NJ)

Conzen M P, 1988, "American cities in profound transition", in *The Making of Urban America* ed. R A Mohl (Scholarly Resources, Wilmington, DE) pp 277–289

Cooke P, 1983, *Theories of Planning and Spatial Development* (Century Hutchison, London)

Cooke P, 1988, "Modernity, postmodernity and the city" *Theory, Culture and Society* 5 475–492

Davidoff P, 1965, "Advocacy and pluralism in planning" *Journal of the American Institute of Planners* 31 596–615

Davis M, 1987, "Chinatown, part two?: the 'internationalization' of downtown Los Angeles" *New Left Review* 164 65–86

Dear M, 1986, "Postmodernism and planning" *Environment and Planning D: Society and Space* 4 367–384

Dear M, 1988, "The postmodern challenge: reconstructing human geography" *Transactions of the Institute of British Geographers* 13 262–274

EPD, 1987, "Reconsidering social theory: a debate" *Environment and Planning D: Society and Space* 5 367–434

Fainstein N I, Fainstein S S, 1979, "New debates in urban planning: the impact of Marxist theory" *International Journal of Urban and Regional Research* 3 381–401

Fainstein N I, Fainstein SS, 1987, "Economic restructuring and the politics of land use planning in New York City" *Journal of the American Planning Association* 53 237–248

Fainstein S S, 1988, "Urban transformation and economic development policy," paper presented at the annual meeting of the Association of Collegiate Schools of Planning, Buffalo, NY; copy available from author

Fainstein S S, Fainstein N I, 1989, "Technology, the new international division of labor, and location," in *Economic Restructuring and Political Response* ed. R A Beauregard (Sage, Beverly Hills, CA) pp 17–39

Fairbanks R, 1988, *Making Better Citizens* (University of Illinois Press, Champaign, IL)

Feagin J R, 1988, *Free Enterprise City* (Rutgers University Press, New Brunswick, NJ)

Foglesong R, 1986, *Planning the Capitalist City* (Princeton University Press, Princeton, NJ)

Forester J, 1989, *Planning in the Face of Power* (University of California Press, Berkeley, CA)

Friedland R, Piven F F, Alford R, 1978, "Political conflict, urban structure, and the fiscal crisis," in *Comparing Urban Policies* ed. D Ashford (Sage, Beverly Hills, CA) pp 175–225

Friedmann J, 1987 *Planning in the Public Domain* (Princeton University Press, Princeton, NJ)

Gans H (ed.), 1968, "City planning in America: a sociological analysis," in *Essays on Urban Problems and Solutions: People and Plans* (Basic Books, New York) pp 50–70

Gitlin T, 1988, "Hip-deep in post-modernism" *The New York Times* 6 December, pages 1, 35, and 36

Goldberger P, 1989, "When developers change the rules during the game" *The New York Times* 19 March, pages 36 and 38

Goodman R, 1971, *After the Planners* (Touchstone Books, New York)

Gregory D, 1987, "Postmodernism and the politics of social theory" *Environment and Planning D: Society and Space* 5 245–248

Hall P, 1989, "The turbulent eighth decade: challenges to American city planning" *Journal of the American Planning Association* 55 275–282

Harrison B, Bluestone B, 1988, *The Great U-Turn* (Basic Books, New York)

Harvey D, 1978, "On planning the ideology of planning", in *Planning Theory in the 1980s* eds R W Burchell, G Sternlieb (Center for Urban Policy Research, Rutgers University, New Brunswick NJ) pp 213–234

Harvey D, 1987, "Flexible accumulation through urbanization: reflections on 'postmodernism' in the American city" *Antipode* 19 260–286

Hayden D, 1984, *Redesigning the American Dream* (W W Norton, New York)

Hayek F, 1944, *The Road to Serfdom* (University of Chicago Press, Chicago, IL)

Hofstadter R, 1955, *The Age of Reform* (Vintage Books, New York)

Hofstadter R, 1958, *Social Darwinism in American Thought* (Beacon Press, Boston, MA)

Hutcheon L, 1987, "The politics of postmodernism: parody and history" *Cultural Critique* 5 179–207

Jacoby R, 1987, *The Last Intellectuals* (Farrar, Straus and Giroux, New York)

Jameson F, 1984a, "Postmodernism, or the cultural logic of late capitalism" *New Left Review* 146 53–92

Jameson F, 1984b, "Foreword," in *The Postmodern Condition* J F Lyotard (University of Minnesota Press, Minneapolis, MN) pp vii–xxi

Jencks C, 1985, *Modern Movements in Architecture* (Viking Press, New York)

Kantor P, 1988, *The Dependent City* (Scott Foresman, Glenview, IL)

Katznelson I, 1981, *City Trenches* (University of Chicago Press, Chicago, IL)

Kraushaar R, 1988, "Outside the whale: progressive planning and the dilemmas of radical reform" *Journal of the American Planning Association* 54 91–100

Logan J R, Molotch H L, 1987, *Urban Fortunes* (University of California Press, Berkeley, CA)

Lyotard J-F, 1984, *The Postmodern Condition* (University of Minnesota Press, Minneapolis, MN)

McKelvey B, 1963, *The Urbanization of America, 1860–1915* (Rutgers University Press, New Brunswick, NJ)

Olmsted F L, 1916, "Introduction," in *City Planning* ed. J Nolen (D Appleton, New York)

Orwell G, 1953, "Inside the whale," in *A Collection of Essays by George Orwell* (Harcourt Brace Jovanovich, New York) pp 210–252

Peet R, 1987, *International Capitalism and Industrial Restructuring* (Allen and Unwin, Winchester, MA)

Peterson J A, 1983, "The impact of sanitary reform upon American urban planning, 1840–1890," in *Introduction to Planning History in the United States* ed. D A Krueckeberg (Center for Urban Policy Research, Rutgers University, New Brunswick, NJ) pp 13–39

Relph E, 1987, *The Modern Urban Landscape* (The Johns Hopkins University Press, Baltimore, MD)

Sarbib J L, 1983, "The University of Chicago program in planning" *Journal of Planning Education and Research* 2 77–81

Schulte-Sasse J, 1987, "Modernity and modernism, postmodernity and postmodernism: framing the issue" *Cultural Critique* 5 5–22

Scott M, 1969, *American City Planning* (University of California Press, Berkeley, CA)

Scott R A, Shore A R, 1979, *Why Sociology Does Not Apply* (Elsevier, New York)

Sharpe W, Wallock L, 1987, "From 'great town' to 'non-place urban realm': reading the modern city," in *Visions of the Modern City* eds W Sharpe, L Wallock (The Johns Hopkins University Press, Baltimore, MD) pp 1–50

Simonsen K, 1988, "Planning on 'postmodern' conditions," paper presented at the International Sociological Association Research Committee on the Sociology of Urban and Regional Development Conference, "Trends and Challenges of Urban Restructuring," Rio de Janeiro; copy available from author

Smith M P, 1988, *City, State, and Market* (Basil Blackwell, New York)

Smith N, 1984, *Uneven Development* (Basil Blackwell, Oxford)

Smith N, 1987, "Rascal concepts, minimalizing discourse, and the politics of geography" *Environment and Planning D: Society and Space* 5 377–383

Soja E W, 1986, "Taking Los Angeles apart: some fragments of a critical human geography" *Environment and Planning D: Society and Space* 4 255–272

Soja E W, 1989, *Postmodern Geographies* (Verso, London)

Soja E W, Morales R, Wolff G, 1983, "Urban restructuring: an analysis of social and spatial change in Los Angeles" *Economic Geography* 59 195–230

Stone C N, Sanders H T, 1987, *The Politics of Urban Development* (University Press of Kansas, Lawrence, KN)

Walker R A, 1978, "The transformation of urban structure in the nineteenth century and the beginnings of suburbanization," in *Urbanization and Conflict in Market Societies* ed. K R Cox (Maaroufa Press, Chicago, IL) pp 165–205

Wilson W J, 1987, *The Truly Disadvantaged* (University of Chicago Press, Chicago, IL)

Zukin S, 1988, "The postmodern debate over urban form" *Theory, Culture and Society* 5 431–446

7

Authoritarian High Modernism

James C. Scott

Then, as this morning on the dock, again I saw, as if for the first time in my life, the impeccably straight streets, the glistening glass of the pavement, the divine parallelepipeds of the transparent dwellings, the square harmony of the grayish blue rows of Numbers. And it seemed to me that not past generations, but I myself, had won a victory over the old god and the old life.

Eugene Zamiatin, *We*

Modern science, which displaced and replaced God, removed that obstacle [limits on freedom]. It also created a vacancy: the office of the supreme legislator-cum-manager, of the designer and administrator of the world order, was now horrifyingly empty. It had to be filled or else. . . . The emptiness of the throne was throughout the modern era a standing and tempting invitation to visionaries and adventurers. The dream of an all-embracing order and harmony remained as vivid as ever, and it seemed now closer than ever, more than ever within human reach. It was now up to mortal earthlings to bring it about and to secure its ascendancy.

Zygmunt Bauman, *Modernity and the Holocaust*

. . . [S]tate simplifications . . . have the character of maps. That is, they are designed to summarize precisely those aspects of a complex world that are of immediate interest to the mapmaker and to ignore the rest. To complain that a map lacks nuance and detail makes no sense unless it omits information necessary to its function. A city map that aspired to represent every traffic light, every pothole, every building, and every bush and tree in every park would threaten to become as large and as complex as the city that it depicted.[1] And it certainly would defeat the purpose of mapping, which is to abstract and summarize. A map is an instrument designed for a purpose.

We may judge that purpose noble or morally offensive, but the map itself either serves or fails to serve its intended use.

In case after case, however, we ... [see] the apparent power of maps to transform as well as merely to summarize the facts that they portray. This transformative power resides not in the map, of course, but rather in the power possessed by those who deploy the perspective of that particular map.[2] A private corporation aiming to maximize sustainable timber yields, profit, or production will map its world according to this logic and will use what power it has to ensure that the logic of its map prevails. The state has no monopoly on utilitarian simplifications. What the state does at least aspire to, though, is a monopoly on the legitimate use of force. That is surely why, from the seventeenth century until now, the most transformative maps have been those invented and applied by the most powerful institution in society: the state.

Until recently, the ability of the state to impose its schemes on society was limited by the state's modest ambitions and its limited capacity. Although utopian aspir-ations to a finely tuned social control can be traced back to Enlightenment thought and to monastic and military practices, the eighteenth-century European state was still largely a machine for extraction. It is true that state officials, particularly under absolutism, had mapped much more of their kingdoms' populations, land tenures, production, and trade than their predecessors had and that they had become increas-ingly efficient in pumping revenue, grain, and conscripts from the countryside. But there was more than a little irony in their claim to absolute rule. They lacked the consistent coercive power, the fine-grained administrative grid, or the detailed knowledge that would have permitted them to undertake more intrusive experi-ments in social engineering. To give their growing ambitions full rein, they required a far greater hubris, a state machinery that was equal to the task, and a society they could master. By the mid-nineteenth century in the West and by the early twentieth century elsewhere, these conditions were being met.

I believe that many of the most tragic episodes of state development in the late nineteenth and twentieth centuries originate in a particularly pernicious combin-ation of three elements. The first is the aspiration to the administrative ordering of nature and society, an aspiration ... at work in scientific forestry, but one raised to a far more comprehensive and ambitious level. "High modernism" seems an appropri-ate term for this aspiration.[3] As a faith, it was shared by many across a wide spectrum of political ideologies. Its main carriers and exponents were the avant-garde among engineers, planners, technocrats, high-level administrators, architects, scientists, and visionaries. If one were to imagine a pantheon or Hall of Fame of high-modernist figures, it would almost certainly include such names as Henri Comte de Saint-Simon, Le Corbusier, Walther Rathenau, Robert McNamara, Robert Moses, Jean Monnet, the Shah of Iran, David Lilienthal, Vladimir I. Lenin, Leon Trotsky, and Julius Nyerere.[4] They envisioned a sweeping, rational engineering of all aspects of social life in order to improve the human condition. As a conviction, high modernism was not the exclusive property of any political tendency; it had both right- and left-wing variants, as we shall see. The second element is the unrestrained use of the power of the modern state as an instrument for achieving these designs. The third element is a weakened or prostrate civil society that lacks the capacity to resist these plans. The ideology of high modernism provides, as it were, the desire; the modern state provides the means of acting on that desire; and the incapacitated civil society provides the leveled terrain on which to build (dis)utopias.

We shall return shortly to the premises of high modernism. But here it is important to note that many of the great state-sponsored calamities of the twentieth century have been the work of rulers with grandiose and utopian plans for their society. One can identify a high-modernist utopianism of the right, of which Nazism is surely the diagnostic example.[5] The massive social engineering under apartheid in South Africa, the modernization plans of the Shah of Iran, villagization in Vietnam, and huge late-colonial development schemes (for example, the Gezira scheme in the Sudan) could be considered under this rubric.[6] And yet there is no denying that much of the massive, state-enforced social engineering of the twentieth century has been the work of progressive, often revolutionary elites. Why?

The answer, I believe, lies in the fact that it is typically progressives who have come to power with a comprehensive critique of existing society and a popular mandate (at least initially) to transform it. These progressives have wanted to use that power to bring about enormous changes in people's habits, work, living patterns, moral conduct, and world view.[7] They have deployed what Václav Havel has called "the armory of holistic social engineering."[8] Utopian aspirations per se are not dangerous. As Oscar Wilde remarked, "A map of the world which does not include Utopia is not worth even glancing at, for it leaves out the one country at which Humanity is always landing."[9] Where the utopian vision goes wrong is when it is held by ruling elites with no commitment to democracy or civil rights and who are therefore likely to use unbridled state power for its achievement. Where it goes brutally wrong is when the society subjected to such utopian experiments lacks the capacity to mount a determined resistance.

What is high modernism, then? It is best conceived as a strong (one might even say muscle-bound) version of the beliefs in scientific and technical progress that were associated with industrialization in Western Europe and in North America from roughly 1830 until World War I. At its center was a supreme self-confidence about continued linear progress, the development of scientific and technical knowledge, the expansion of production, the rational design of social order, the growing satisfaction of human needs, and, not least, an increasing control over nature (including human nature) commensurate with scientific understanding of natural laws.[10] *High modernism* is thus a particularly sweeping vision of how the benefits of technical and scientific progress might be applied – usually through the state – in every field of human activity.[11] If, as we have seen, the simplified, utilitarian *descriptions* of state officials had a tendency, through the exercise of state power, to bring the facts into line with their representations, then one might say that the high-modern state began with extensive *prescriptions* for a new society, and it intended to impose them.

It would have been hard not to have been a modernist of some stripe at the end of the nineteenth century in the West. How could one fail to be impressed – even awed – by the vast transformation wrought by science and industry?[12] Anyone who was, say, sixty years old in Manchester, England, would have witnessed in his or her lifetime a revolution in the manufacturing of cotton and wool textiles, the growth of the factory system, the application of steam power and other astounding new mechanical devices to production, remarkable breakthroughs in metallurgy and transportation (especially railroads), and the appearance of cheap mass-produced commodities. Given the stunning advances in chemistry, physics, medicine, math, and engineering, anyone even slightly attentive to the world of science would have almost come to expect a continuing stream of new marvels (such as the internal combustion engine and electricity). The unprecedented transformations of the nine-teenth century may have impoverished and marginalized many, but even the victims recognized that something revolutionary was afoot. All this sounds rather naive today, when we are far more sober about the limits and costs of technological progress and have acquired a postmodern skepticism about any totalizing discourse. Still, this new sensibility ignores both the degree to which modernist assumptions prevail in our lives and, especially, the great enthusiasm and revolutionary hubris that were part and parcel of high modernism.

The Discovery of Society

The path from description to presecription was not so much an inadvertent result of a deep psychological tendency as a deliberate move. The point of the Enlightenment view of legal codes was less to mirror the distinctive customs and practices of a people than to create a cultural community by codifying and generalizing the most rational of those customs and suppressing the more obscure and barbaric ones.[13] Establishing uniform standards of weight and measurement across a kingdom had a greater purpose than just making trade easier; the new standards were intended both to express and to promote a new cultural unity. Well before the tools existed to make good on this cultural revolution, Enlightenment thinkers such as Condorcet were looking ahead to the day when the tools would be in place. He wrote in 1782: "Those sciences, created almost in our own days, the object of which is man himself, the direct goal of which is the happiness of man, will enjoy a progress no less sure than that of the physical sciences, and this idea so sweet, that our descendants will surpass us in wisdom as in enlightenment, is no longer an illusion. In meditating on the nature of the moral sciences, one cannot help seeing that, as they are based like physical sciences on the observation of fact, they must follow the same method, acquire a language equally exact and precise, attaining the same degree of certainty."[14] The gleam in Condorcet's eye became, by the mid-nineteenth century, an active utopian project. Simplification and rationalization previously applied to forests, weights and measures, taxation, and factories were now applied to the design of society as a whole.[15] Industrial-strength social engineering was born. While factories and forests might be planned by private entrepreneurs, the ambition of engineering whole societies was almost exclusively a project of the nation-state.

This new conception of the state's role represented a fundamental transformation. Before then, the state's activities had been largely confined to those that contributed to the wealth and power of the sovereign, as the example of scientific forestry and cameral science illustrated. The idea that one of the central purposes of the state was the improvement of all the members of society – their health, skills and education, longevity, productivity, morals, and family life – was quite novel.[16] There was, of course, a direct connection between the old conception of the state and this new one. A state that improved its population's skills, vigor, civic morals, and work habits would increase its tax base and field better armies; it was a policy that any enlightened sovereign might pursue. And yet, in the nineteenth century, the welfare of the population came increasingly to be seen, not merely as a means to national strength, but as an end in itself.

One essential precondition of this transformation was the discovery of society as a reified object that was separate from the state and that could be scientifically described. In this respect, the production of statistical knowledge about the population – its age profiles, occupations, fertility, literacy, property ownership, law-abidingness (as demonstrated by crime statistics) – allowed state officials to characterize the population in elaborate new ways, much as scientific forestry permitted the forester to carefully describe the forest. Ian Hacking explains how a suicide or homicide rate, for example, came to be seen as a characteristic of a people, so that one could speak of a "budget" of homicides that would be "spent" each year, like routine debits from an account, although the particular murderers and their victims were unknown.[17] Statistical facts were elaborated into social laws. It was but a small step from a simplified description of society to a design and manipulation of society, with its improvement in mind. If one could reshape nature to design a more suitable forest, why not reshape society to create a more suitable population?

The scope of intervention was potentially endless. Society became an object that the state might manage and transform with a view toward perfecting it. A progressive nation-state would set about engineering its society according to the most advanced technical standards of the new moral sciences. The existing social order, which had been more or less taken by earlier states as a given, reproducing itself under the watchful eye of the state, was for the first time the subject of active management. It was possible to conceive of an artificial, engineered society designed, not by custom and historical accident, but according to conscious, rational, scientific criteria. Every nook and cranny of the social order might be improved upon: personal hygiene, diet, child rearing, housing, posture, recreation, family structure, and, most infamously, the genetic inheritance of the population.[18] The working poor were often the first subjects of scientific social planning.[19] Schemes for improving their daily lives were promulgated by progressive urban and public-health policies and instituted in model factory towns and newly founded welfare agencies. Subpopulations found wanting in ways that were potentially threatening – such as indigents, vagabonds, the mentally ill, and criminals – might be made the objects of the most intensive social engineering.[20]

The metaphor of gardening, Zygmunt Bauman suggests, captures much of this new spirit. The gardener – perhaps a landscape architect specializing in formal gardens is the most appropriate parallel – takes a natural site and creates an entirely designed space of botanical order. Although the organic character of the flora limits what can be achieved, the gardener has enormous discretion in the overall arrangement and in training, pruning, planting, and weeding out selected plants. As an untended forest is to a long-managed scientific forest, so untended nature is to the garden. The garden is one of man's attempts to impose his own principles of order, utility, and beauty on nature.[21] What grows in the garden is always a small, consciously selected sample of what *might* be grown there. Similarly, social engineers consciously set out to design and maintain a more perfect social order. An Enlightenment belief in the self-improvement of man became, by degrees, a belief in the perfectibility of social order.

One of the great paradoxes of social engineering is that it seems at odds with the experience of modernity generally. Trying to jell a social world, the most striking characteristic of which appears to be flux, seems rather like trying to manage a whirlwind. Marx was hardly alone in claiming that the "constant revolutionizing of production, uninterrupted disturbance of all social relations, everlasting uncertainty and agitation, distinguish the bourgeois epoch from all earlier times."[22] The experience of modernity (in literature, art, industry, transportation, and popular culture) was, above all, the experience of disorienting speed, movement, and change, which self-proclaimed modernists found exhilarating and liberating.[23] Perhaps the most charitable way of resolving this paradox is to imagine that what these designers of society had in mind was roughly what designers of locomotives had in mind with "streamlining." Rather than arresting social change, they hoped to design a shape to social life that would minimize the friction of progress. The difficulty with this resolution is that state social engineering was inherently authoritarian. In place of multiple sources of invention and change, there was a single planning authority; in place of the plasticity and autonomy of existing social life, there was a fixed social order in which positions were designated. The tendency toward various forms of "social taxidermy" was unavoidable.

The Radical Authority of High Modernism

> The real thing is that this time we're going to get science applied to social problems and backed by the whole force of the state, just as war has been backed by the whole force of the state in the past.
> C. S. Lewis, *That Hideous Strength*

The troubling features of high modernism derive, for the most part, from its claim to speak about the improvement of the human condition with the authority of scientific knowledge and its tendency to disallow other competing sources of judgment.

First and foremost, high modernism implies a truly radical break with history and tradition. Insofar as rational thought and scientific laws could provide a single answer to every empirical question, nothing ought to be taken for granted. All human habits and practices that were inherited and hence not based on scientific reasoning – from the structure of the family and patterns of residence to moral values and forms of production – would have to be reexamined and redesigned. The structures of the past were typically the products of myth, superstition, and religious prejudice. It followed that scientifically designed schemes for production and social life would be superior to received tradition.

The sources of this view are deeply authoritarian. If a planned social order is better than the accidental, irrational deposit of historical practice, two conclusions follow. Only those who have the scientific knowledge to discern and create this superior social order are fit to rule in the new age. Further, those who through retrograde ignorance refuse to yield to the scientific plan need to be educated to its benefits or else swept aside. Strong versions of high modernism, such as those held by Lenin and Le Corbusier, cultivated an Olympian ruthlessness toward the subjects of their interventions. At its most radical, high modernism imagined wiping the slate utterly clean and beginning from zero.[24]

High-modernist ideology thus tends to devalue or banish politics. Political interests can only frustrate the social solutions devised by specialists with scientific tools adequate to their analysis. As individuals, high modernists might well hold democratic views about popular sovereignty or classical liberal views about the inviolability of a private sphere that restrained them, but such convictions are external to, and often at war with, their high-modernist convictions.

Although high modernists came to imagine the refashioning of social habits and of human nature itself, they began with a nearly limitless ambition to transform nature to suit man's purposes – an ambition that remained central to their faith. How completely the utopian possibilities gripped intellectuals of almost every political persuasion is captured in the paean to technical progress of the *Communist Manifesto*, where Marx and Engels write of the "subjection of nature's forces to man, machinery, and the application of chemistry to agriculture and industry, steam navigation, railways, electric telegraphs, clearing of whole continents for cultivation, canalization of rivers, whole populations conjured out of the ground."[25] In fact, this promise, made plausible by capitalist development, was for Marx the point of departure for socialism, which would place the fruits of capitalism at the service of the working class for the first time. The intellectual air in the late nineteenth century was filled with proposals for such vast engineering projects as the Suez Canal, which was completed in 1869 with enormous consequences for trade between Asia and Europe. The pages of *Le Globe*, the organ of utopian socialists of Saint-Simon's persuasion, featured an endless stream of discussions about massive projects: the construction of the Panama Canal, the development of the United States, far-reaching schemes for energy and transportation. This belief that it was man's destiny to tame nature to suit his interests and preserve his safety is perhaps the keystone of high modernism, partly because the success of so many grand ventures was already manifest.[26]

Once again the authoritarian and statist implications of this vision are clear. The very scale of such projects meant that, with few exceptions (such as the early canals), they demanded large infusions of monies raised through taxes or credit. Even if one could imagine them being financed privately in a capitalist economy, they typically required a vast public authority empowered to condemn private property, relocate people against their will, guarantee the loans or bonds required, and coordinate the work of the many state agencies involved. In a statist society, be it Louis Napoleon's France or Lenin's Soviet Union, such power was already built into the political system. In a nonstatist society, such tasks have required new public authorities or "super-agencies" having quasi-governmental powers for sending men to the moon or for constructing dams, irrigation works, highways, and public transportation systems.

The temporal emphasis of high modernism is almost exclusively on the future. Although any ideology with a large altar dedicated to progress is bound to privilege the future, high modernism carries this to great lengths. The past is an impediment, a history that must be transcended; the present is the platform for launching plans for a better future. A key characteristic of discourses of high modernism and of the public pronouncements of those states that have embraced it is a heavy reliance on visual images of heroic progress toward a totally transformed future.[27] The strategic choice of the future is freighted with consequences. To the degree that the future is known and achievable – a belief that the faith in progress encourages – the less future benefits are discounted for uncertainty. The practical effect is to convince most high modernists that the certainty of a better future justifies the many short-term sacrifices required to get there.[28] The ubiquity of five-year plans in socialist states is an example of that conviction. Progress is objectified by a series of preconceived goals – largely material and quantifiable – which are to be achieved through savings, labor, and investments in the interim. There may, of course, be no alternative to planning, especially when the urgency of a single goal, such as winning a war, seems to require the subordination of every other goal. The immanent logic of such an exercise, however, implies a degree of certainty about the future, about means–ends calculations, and about the meaning of human welfare that is truly heroic. That such plans have often had to be adjusted or abandoned is an indication of just how heroic are the assumptions behind them.

In this reading, high modernism ought to appeal greatly to the classes and strata who have most to gain – in status, power, and wealth – from its world view. And indeed it is the ideology par excellence of the bureaucratic intelligentsia, technicians, planners, and engineers.[29] The position accorded to them is not just one of rule and privilege but also one of responsibility for the great works of nation building and social transformation. Where this intelligentsia conceives of its mission as the dragging of a technically backward, unschooled, subsistence-oriented population into the twentieth century, its self-assigned cultural role as educator of its people becomes doubly grandiose. Having a historic mission of such breadth may provide a ruling intelligentsia with high morale, solidarity, and the willingness to make (and impose) sacrifices. This vision of a great future is often in sharp contrast to the disorder, misery, and unseemly scramble for petty advantage that the elites very likely see in their daily foreground. One might in fact speculate that the more intractable and resistant the real world faced by the planner, the greater the need for utopian plans to fill, as it were, the void that would otherwise invite despair. The elites who elaborate such plans implicitly represent themselves as exemplars of the learning and progressive views to which their compatriots might aspire. Given the ideological advantages of high modernism as a discourse, it is hardly surprising that so many postcolonial elites have marched under its banner.[30]

Aided by hindsight as it is, this unsympathetic account of high-modernist audacity is, in one important respect, grossly unfair. If we put the development of high-modernist beliefs in their historical context, if we ask who the enemies of high modernism actually were, a far more sympathetic picture emerges. Doctors and public-health engineers who did possess new knowledge that could save millions of lives were often thwarted by popular prejudices and entrenched political interests. Urban planners who could in fact redesign urban housing to be cheaper, more healthful, and more convenient were blocked by real-estate interests and existing tastes. Inventors and engineers who had devised revolutionary new modes of power and transportation faced opposition from industrialists and laborers whose profits and jobs the new technology would almost certainly displace.

For nineteenth-century high modernists, the scientific domination of nature (including human nature) was emancipatory. It "promised freedom from scarcity, want and the arbitrariness of natural calamity," David Harvey observes. "The development of rational forms of social organization and rational modes of thought promised liberation from the irrationalities of myth, religion, superstition, release from the arbitrary use of power as well as from the dark side of our human natures."[31] Before we turn to later versions of high modernism, we should recall two important facts about their nineteenth-century forebears: first, that virtually every high-modernist intervention was undertaken in the name of and with the support of citizens seeking help and protection, and, second, that we are all beneficiaries, in countless ways, of these various high-modernist schemes.

Twentieth-Century High Modernism

The idea of a root-and-branch, rational engineering of entire social orders in creating realizable utopias is a largely twentieth-century phenomenon. And a range of historical soils have seemed particularly favorable for the flourishing of high-modernist ideology. Those soils include crises of state power, such as wars and economic depressions, and circumstances in which a state's capacity for relatively unimpeded planning is greatly enhanced, such as the revolutionary conquest of power and colonial rule.

The industrial warfare of the twentieth century has required unprecedented steps toward the total mobilization of the society and the economy.[32] Even quite liberal societies like the United States and Britain became, in the context of war mobilization, directly administered societies. The worldwide depression of the 1930s similarly propelled liberal states into extensive experiments in social and economic planning in an effort to relieve economic distress and to retain popular legitimacy. In the cases of war and depression, the rush toward an administered society has an aspect of *force majeure* to it. The postwar rebuilding of a war-torn nation may well fall in the same category.

Revolution and colonialism, however, are hospitable to high modernism for different reasons. A revolutionary regime and a colonial regime each disposes of an unusual degree of power. The revolutionary state has defeated the *ancien régime*, often has its partisans' mandate to remake the society after its image, *and* faces a prostrate civil society whose capacity for active resistance is limited.[33] The millennial expectations commonly associated with revolutionary movements give further impetus to high-modernist ambitions. Colonial regimes, particularly late colonial regimes, have often been sites of extensive experiments in social engineering.[34] An ideology of "welfare colonialism" combined with the authoritarian power inherent in colonial rule have encouraged ambitious schemes to remake native societies.

If one were required to pinpoint the "birth" of twentieth-century high modernism, specifying a particular time, place, and individual – in what is admittedly a rather arbitrary exercise, given high modernism's many intellectual wellsprings – a strong case can be made for German mobilization during World War I and the figure most closely associated with it, Walther Rathenau. German economic mobilization was the technocratic wonder of the war. That Germany kept its armies in the field and adequately supplied long after most observers had predicted its collapse was largely due to Rathenau's planning.[35] An industrial engineer and head of the great electrical firm A.E.G. (Allgemeine Elektricitäts-Gesellschaft), which had been founded by his father, Rathenau was placed in charge of the Office of War Raw Materials (Kriegsrohstoffabteilung).[36] He realized that the planned rationing of raw materials and transport was the key to sustaining the war effort. Inventing a planned economy step by step, as it were, Germany achieved feats – in industrial production, munitions and armament supply, transportation and traffic control, price controls, and civilian rationing – that had never before been attempted. The scope of planning and coordination necessitated an unprecedented mobilization of conscripts, soldiers, and war-related industrial labor. Such mobilization fostered the idea of creating "administered mass organizations" that would encompass the entire society.[37]

Rathenau's faith in pervasive planning and in rationalizing production had deep roots in the intellectual connection being forged between the physical laws of thermodynamics on one hand and the new applied sciences of work on the other. For many specialists, a narrow and materialist "productivism" treated human labor as a mechanical system which could be decomposed into energy transfers, motion, and the physics of work. The simplification of labor into isolated problems of mechanical efficiencies led directly to the aspiration for a scientific control of the entire labor process. Late nineteenth-century materialism, as Anson Rabinbach emphasizes, had an equivalence between technology and physiology at its metaphysical core.[38]

This productivism had at least two distinct lineages, one of them North American and the other European. An American contribution came from the influential work of Frederick Taylor, whose minute decomposition of factory labor into isolable, precise, repetitive motions had begun to revolutionize the organization of factory work.[39] For the factory manager or engineer, the newly invented assembly lines permitted the use of unskilled labor and control over not only the pace of production but the whole labor process. The European tradition of "energetics," which focused on questions of motion, fatigue, measured rest, rational hygiene, and nutrition, also treated the worker notionally as a machine, albeit a machine that must be well fed and kept in good working order. In place of workers, there was an abstract, standardized worker with uniform physical capacities and needs. Seen initially as a way of increasing wartime efficiency at the front and in industry, the Kaiser Wilhelm Institut für Arbeitsphysiologie, like Taylorism, was based on a scheme to rationalize the body.[40]

What is most remarkable about both traditions is, once again, how widely they were believed by educated elites who were otherwise poles apart politically. "Taylorism and technocracy were the watchwords of a three-pronged idealism: the elimination of economic and social crisis, the expansion of productivity through science, and the reenchantment of technology. The vision of society in which social conflict was eliminated in favor of technological and scientific imperatives could embrace liberal, socialist, authoritarian, and even communist and fascist solutions. Productivism, in short, was politically promiscuous."[41]

The appeal of one or another form of productivism across much of the right and center of the political spectrum was largely due to its promise as a technological "fix" for class struggle. If, as its advocates claimed, it could vastly increase worker output, then the politics of redistribution could be replaced by class collaboration, in which both profits and wages could grow at once. For much of the left, productivism promised the replacement of the capitalist by the engineer or by the state expert or official. It also proposed a single optimum solution, or "best practice," for any problem in the organization of work. The logical outcome was some form of slide-rule authoritarianism in the interest, presumably, of all.[42]

A combination of Rathenau's broad training in philosophy and economics, his wartime experience with planning, and the social conclusions that he thought were inherent in the precision, reach, and transforming potential of electric power allowed him to draw the broadest lessons for social organization. In the war, private industry had given way to a kind of state socialism; "gigantic industrial enterprises had transcended their ostensibly private owners and all the laws of property."[43] The decisions required had nothing to do with ideology; they were driven by purely technical and economic necessities. The rule of specialists and the new technological possibilities, particularly huge electric power grids, made possible a new social-industrial order that was both centralized and locally autonomous. During the time when war made necessary a coalition among industrial firms, technocrats, and the state, Rathenau discerned the shape of a progressive peacetime society. Inasmuch as the technical and economic requirements for reconstruction were obvious and required the same sort of collaboration in all countries, Rathenau's rationalist faith in planning had an internationalist flavor. He characterized the modern era as a "new machine order... [and] a consolidation of the world into an unconscious association of constraint, into an uninterrupted community of production and harmony."[44]

The world war was the high-water mark for the political influence of engineers and planners. Having seen what could be accomplished in extremis, they imagined what they could achieve if the identical energy and planning were devoted to popular welfare rather than mass destruction. Together with many political leaders, industrialists, labor leaders, and prominent intellectuals (such as Philip Gibbs in England, Ernst Jünger in Germany, and Gustave Le Bon in France), they concluded that only a renewed and comprehensive dedication to technical innovation and the planning it made possible could rebuild the European economies and bring social peace.[45]

Lenin himself was deeply impressed by the achievements of German industrial mobilization and believed that it had shown how production might be socialized. Just as Lenin believed that Marx had discovered immutable social laws akin to Darwin's laws of evolution, so he believed that the new technologies of mass production were scientific laws and not social constructions. Barely a month before the October 1917 revolution, he wrote that the war had "accelerated the development of capitalism to such a tremendous degree, converting monopoly capitalism into *state*-monopoly capitalism, that *neither* the proletariat *nor* the revolutionary petty-bourgeois democrats *can* keep within the limits of capitalism."[46] He and his economic advisers drew directly on the work of Rathenau and Mollendorf in their plans for the Soviet economy. The German war economy was for Lenin "the ultimate in modern, large-scale capitalist techniques, planning and organization"; he took it to be the prototype of a socialized economy.[47] Presumably, if the state in question were in the hands of representatives of the working class, the basis of a socialist system would exist. Lenin's vision of the future looked much like Rathenau's, providing, of course, we ignore the not so small matter of a revolutionary seizure of power.

Lenin was not slow to appreciate how Taylorism on the factory floor offered advantages for the socialist control of production. Although he had earlier denounced such techniques, calling them the "scientific extortion of sweat," by the time of the revolution he had become an enthusiastic advocate of systematic control as practiced in Germany. He extolled "the principle of discipline, organization, and harmonious cooperation based upon the most modern, mechanized industry, the most rigid system of accountability and control."[48]

The Taylor system, the last word of capitalism in this respect, like all capitalist progress, is a combination of the subtle brutality of bourgeois exploitation and a number of its great scientific achievements in the fields of analysing mechanical motions during work, the elimination of superfluous and awkward motions, the working out of correct methods of work, the introduction of the best system of accounting and control, etc. The Soviet Republic must at all costs adopt all that is valuable in the achievements of science and technology in this field.... We must organize in Russia the study and teaching of the Taylor system and systematically try it out and adapt it to our purposes.[49]

By 1918, with production falling, he was calling for rigid work norms and, if necessary, the reintroduction of hated piecework. The first All-Russian Congress for Initiatives in Scientific Management was convened in 1921 and featured disputes between advocates of Taylorism and those of energetics (also called ergonomics). At least twenty institutes and as many journals were by then devoted to scientific management in the Soviet Union. A command economy at the macrolevel and Taylorist principles of central coordination at the microlevel of the factory floor provided an attractive and symbiotic package for an authoritarian, high-modernist revolutionary like Lenin.

Despite the authoritarian temptations of twentieth-century high modernism, they have often been resisted. The reasons are not only complex; they are different from case to case. While it is not my intention to examine in detail all the potential obstacles to high-modernist planning, the particular barrier posed by liberal democratic ideas and institutions deserves emphasis. Three factors seem decisive. The first is the existence and belief in a private sphere of activity in which the state and its agencies may not legitimately interfere. To be sure, this zone of autonomy has had a beleaguered existence as, following Mannheim, more heretofore private spheres have been made the object of official intervention. Much of the work of Michel Foucault was an attempt to map these incursions into health, sexuality, mental illness, vagrancy, or sanitation and the strategies behind them. Nevertheless, the idea of a private realm has served to limit the ambitions of many high modernists, through either their own political values or their healthy respect for the political storm that such incursions would provoke.

The second, closely related factor is the private sector in liberal political economy. As Foucault put it: unlike absolutism and mercantilism, "political economy announces the unknowability for the sovereign of the totality of economic processes and, as a consequence, the *impossibility of an economic sovereignty.*"[50] The point of liberal political economy was not only that a free market protected property and created wealth but also that the economy was far too complex for it ever to be managed in detail by a hierarchical administration.[51]

The third and by far most important barrier to thoroughgoing high-modernist schemes has been the existence of working, representative institutions through which a resistant society could make its influence felt. Such institutions have thwarted the most draconian features of high-modernist schemes in roughly the same way that publicity and mobilized opposition in open societies, as Amartya Sen has argued, have prevented famines. Rulers, he notes, do not go hungry, and they are unlikely to learn about and respond readily to curb famine unless their institutional position provides strong incentives. The freedoms of speech, of assembly, and of the press ensure that widespread hunger will be publicized, while the freedoms of assembly and elections in representative institutions ensure that it is in the interest of elected officials' self-preservation to prevent famine when they can. In the same fashion, high-modernist schemes in liberal democratic settings must accommodate themselves sufficiently to local opinion in order to avoid being undone at the polls.

But high modernism, unimpeded by liberal political economy, is best grasped through the working out of its high ambitions and its consequences. It is to this practical terrain in urban planning and revolutionary discourse that we now turn.

NOTES

1   My colleague Paul Landau recalls the story by Borges in which a king, unhappy at maps that do not do justice to his kingdom, finally insists on a map with a scale of one-to-one. When complete, the new map exactly covers the existing kingdom, submerging the real one beneath its representation.
2   A commonplace example may help. One of the ordinary frustrations of the modern citizen, even in liberal democracies, is the difficulty of representing his unique case to a powerful agent of a bureaucratic institution. But the functionary operates with a simplified grid designed to cover all the cases that she confronts. Once a decision has been made as to which "bin" or "pigeonhole" the case falls into, the action to be taken or the protocol to be followed is largely cut-and-dried. The functionary endeavors to sort the case into the appropriate category, while the citizen resists being treated as an instance of a category and tries to insist, often unsuccessfully, that his unique case be examined on its singular merits.
3   I have borrowed the term "high modernism" from David Harvey, *The Condition of Post-Modernity: An Enquiry into the Origins of Social Change* (Oxford: Basil Blackwell, 1989). Harvey locates the high-water mark of this sort of modernism in the post-World War II period, and his concern is particularly with capitalism and the organization of production. But his description of high modernism also works well here: "The belief 'in linear progress, absolute truths, and rational planning of ideal social orders' under standardized conditions of knowledge and production was particularly strong. The modernism that resulted was, as a result, 'positivistic, technocratic, and rationalistic' at the same time as it was imposed as the work of an elite avant-garde of planners, artists, architects, critics, and other guardians of high taste. The 'modernization' of European economies proceeded apace, while the whole thrust of international politics and trade was justified as bringing a benevolent and progressive 'modernization process' to a backward Third World" (p. 35).
4   For case studies of "public entrepreneurs" in the United States, see Eugene Lewis's study of Hyman Rickover, J. Edgar Hoover, and Robert Moses, *Public Entrepreneurs: Toward a Theory of Bureaucratic Political Power: The Organizational Lives of Hyman Rickover, J. Edgar Hoover, and Robert Moses* (Bloomington: Indiana University Press, 1980). Monnet, like Rathenau, had experience in economic mobilization during World War I, when he helped organize the transatlantic supply of war material for Britain and France, a role that he resumed during World War II. By the time he helped plan the postwar integration of French and German coal and steel production, he had already had several decades of experience in supranational management. See François Duchene, *Jean Monnet: The First Statesman of Interdependence* (New York: Norton, 1995).
5   I will not pursue the argument here, but I think Nazism is best understood as a reactionary form of modernism. Like the progressive left, the Nazi elites had grandiose visions of state-enforced social engineering, which included, of course, extermination, expulsion, forced

sterilization, and selective breeding and which aimed at "improving" genetically on human nature. The case for Nazism as a virulent form of modernism is made brilliantly and convincingly by Zygmunt Bauman in *Modernity and the Holocaust* (Oxford: Oxford University Press, 1989). See also, along the same lines, Jeffery Herf, *Reactionary Modernism: Technology, Culture, and Politics in Weimar and the Third Reich* (Cambridge: Cambridge University Press, 1984), and Norbert Frei, *National Socialist Rule in Germany: The Führer State, 1933–1945*, trans. Simon B. Steyne (Oxford: Oxford University Press, 1993).

6 I am grateful to James Ferguson for reminding me that reactionary high-modernist schemes are about as ubiquitous as progressive variants.

7 This is not by any means meant to be a brief for conservatism. Conservatives of many stripes may care little for civil liberties and may resort to whatever brutalities seem necessary to remain in power. But their ambitions and hubris are much more limited; their plans (in contrast to those of reactionary modernists) do not necessitate turning society upside down to create new collectivities, new family and group loyalties, and new people.

8 Václav Havel, address given at Victoria University, Wellington, New Zealand, on March 31, 1995, reprinted in the *New York Review of Books* 42, no. 11 (June 22, 1995): 36.

9 Quoted in Zygmunt Bauman, *Socialism: The Active Utopia* (New York: Holmes and Meier, 1976), p. 11.

10 For an enlightening discussion of the intellectual lineage of authoritarian environmentalism, see Douglas R. Weiner, "Demythologizing Environmentalism," *Journal of the History of Biology* 25, no. 3 (Fall 1992): 385–411.

11 See Michael Adas's *Machines as the Measure of Men: Science, Technology, and Ideologies of Western Dominance* (Ithaca: Cornell University Press, 1989) and Marshall Berman's *All That Is Solid Melts into Air: The Experience of Modernity* (New York: Penguin, 1988). What is new in high modernism, I believe, is not so much the aspiration for comprehensive planning. Many imperial and absolutist states have had similar aspirations. What are new are the administrative technology and social knowledge that make it plausible to imagine organizing an entire society in ways that only the barracks or the monastery had been organized before. In this respect, Michel Foucault's argument, in *Discipline and Punish: The Birth of the Prison*, trans. Alan Sheridan (New York: Vintage Books, 1977), is persuasive.

12 Here I want to distinguish between advances in scientific knowledge and inventions (many of which occurred in the eighteenth century or earlier) and the massive transformations that scientific inventions wrought in daily material life (which came generally in the nineteenth century).

13 Witold Kula, *Measures and Men*, trans. R. Szreter (Princeton: Princeton University Press, 1986), p. 211.

14 Quoted in Ian Hacking, *The Taming of Chance* (Cambridge: Cambridge University Press, 1990), p. 38. A few years later, the Jacobins were, one could argue, the first to attempt to actually engineer happiness by transforming the social order. As Saint-Just wrote, "The idea of happiness is new in Europe." See Albert O. Hirschman, "Rival Interpretations of Market Society: Civilizing, Destructive, or Feeble," *Journal of Economic Literature* 20 (December 1982): 1463–84.

15 I am greatly indebted to James Ferguson, whose perceptive comments on an early draft of the book pointed me in this direction.

16 See, for example, Graham Buschell, Colin Gordon, and Peter Miller, eds., *The Foucault Effect: Studies in Governmentality* (London: Harvester Wheatsheaf, 1991), chap. 4.

17 Hacking, *The Taming of Chance*, p. 105. Hacking shows brilliantly how a statistical "average" metamorphosed into the category "normal," and "normal," in turn, into a "normative" standard to be achieved by social engineering.

18 By now, a great deal of historical research has made crystal clear how widespread throughout the West was the support for eugenic engineering. The belief that the state must intervene to protect the races' physical and mental characteristics was common among progressives and animated a well-nigh international social movement. By 1926, twenty-three of the forty-eight U.S. states had laws permitting sterilization.

19 See Gareth Stedman-Jones, *Languages of Class: Studies in English Working-Class History, 1832–1982* (Cambridge: Cambridge University Press, 1983). It is important to recognize that, among Western powers, virtually all the initiatives associated with the "civilizing missions" of colonialism were preceded by comparable programs to assimilate and civilize their own lower-class populations, both rural and urban. The difference, perhaps, is that in the colonial setting officials had greater coercive power over an objectified and alien population, thus allowing for greater feats of social engineering.

20 For a science-fiction account of the attempt to create a "technocratic and objective man" who would be free of "nature," see C. S. Lewis, *That Hideous Strength: A Modern Fairy Tale for Grown-Ups* (New York: Macmillan, 1946).

21 There is the interesting and problematic case of the "wild" garden, in which the precise shape of "disorder" is minutely planned. Here it is a matter of an aesthetic plan, designed to have a certain effect on the eye – an attempt to copy untended nature. The paradox is just as intractable as that of a zoo designed to mimic nature – intractable, that is, until one realizes that the design does not extend to allowing the critters to eat one another!

22 Karl Marx, from the *Communist Manifesto*, quoted in Berman, *All That Is Solid Melts into Air*, p. 95.

23 The airplane, having replaced the locomotive, was in many respects the defining image of modernity in the early twentieth century. In 1913, the futurist artist and playwright Kazimir Malevich created the sets for an opera entitled *Victory over the Sun*. In the last scene, the audience heard from offstage a propeller's roar and shouts announcing that gravity had been overcome in futurist countries. Le Corbusier, Malevich's near contemporary, thought the airplane was the reigning symbol of the new age. For the influence of flight, see Robert Wohl, *A Passion for Wings: Aviation and the Western Imagination, 1908–1918* (New Haven: Yale University Press, 1996).

24 The Jacobins intended just such a fresh start, starting the calendar again at "year one" and renaming the days and months according to a new, secular system. To signal its intention to create a wholly new Cambodian nation, the Pol Pot regime began with "year zero."

25 Quoted in Harvey, *The Condition of Post-Modernity*, p. 99.

26 In this section, the masculine personal pronoun is less a convention than a choice made with some deliberation. See Carolyn Merchant, *The Death of Nature: Women, Ecology, and the Scientific Revolution* (San Francisco: Harper, 1980).

27 See, for example, Margaret M. Bullitt, "Toward a Marxist Theory of Aesthetics: The Development of Socialist Realism in the Soviet Union," *Russian Review* 35, no. 1 (January 1976): 53–76.

28 Baruch Knei-Paz, "Can Historical Consequences Falsify Ideas? Or, Karl Marx after the Collapse of the Soviet Union," paper presented to Political Theory Workshop, Department of Political Science, Yale University, New Haven, November 1994.

29 Raymond Aron's prophetic dissent, *The Opium of the Intellectual*, trans. Terence Kilmartin (London: Secker & Warburg, 1957), is a key document in this context.

30 The larger, the more capital-intensive, and the more centralized the schemes, the greater their appeal in terms of power and patronage. For a critique of flood-control projects and World Bank projects in this context, see James K. Boyce, "Birth of a Megaproject: Political Economy of Flood Control in Bangladesh," *Environmental Management* 14, no. 4 (1990): 419–28.

31 Harvey, *The Condition of Post-Modernity*, p. 12.

32 See Charles Tilly's important theoretical contribution in *Coercion, Capital, and European States, A.D. 990–1992* (Oxford: Blackwell, 1990).

33 A civil war, as in the Bolshevik case, may be the price of consolidating the revolutionaries' power.

34 White-settler colonies (e.g., South Africa, Algeria) and anti-insurgency campaigns (e.g., Vietnam, Algeria, Afghanistan) have carried out huge population removals and forced resettlements. In most such cases, however, even the pretense that the comprehensive social planning was for the welfare of the affected populations has been paper-thin.

35 Here I am particularly indebted to the discussion of George Yaney, *The Urge to Mobilize: Agrarian Reform in Russia* (Urbana: University of Illinois Press, 1982), pp. 448–62.

36 Anson Rabinbach, *The Human Motor: Energy, Fatigue, and the Origins of Modernity* (Berkeley: University of California Press, 1992), pp. 260–71. In 1907, long before the war, Rathenau and a number of architects and political leaders had founded Deutsche Werkbund, which was devoted to fostering technical innovation in industry and the arts.

37 See Gregory J. Kasza, *The Conscription Society: Administered Mass Organizations* (New Haven: Yale University Press, 1995), especially chap. 1, pp. 7–25.

38 Rabinbach, *The Human Motor*, p. 290.

39 For recent assessments of the evolution of technology and production in the United States, see Nathan Rosenberg, *Perspectives on Technology* (Cambridge: Cambridge University Press, 1976); Rosenberg, *Inside the Black Box: Technology and Economics* (New York: Cambridge University Press, 1982); and Philip Scranton, *Figured Tapestry: Production, Markets, and Power in Philadelphia, 1885–1942* (New York: Cambridge University Press, 1989).

40 See the inventive article by Ernest J. Yanorella and Herbert Reid, "From 'Trained Gorilla' to 'Humanware': Repoliticizing the Body-Machine Complex between Fordism and Post-Fordism," in Theodore R. Schatzki and Wolfgang Natter, eds., *The Social and Political Body* (New York: Guildford Press, 1996), pp. 181–219.

41 Rabinbach, *The Human Motor*, p. 272. Rabinbach is here paraphrasing the conclusions of a seminal article by Charles S. Maier, "Between Taylorism and Technocracy: European Ideologies and the Vision of Industrial Productivity in the 1920s," *Journal of Contemporary History 5*, no. 2 (1970): 27–63.

42 Thorstein Veblen was the best-known social scientist expounding this view in the United States. Literary versions of this ideology are apparent in Sinclair Lewis's *Arrowsmith* and Ayn Rand's *Fountainhead*, works from very different quadrants of the political spectrum.

43 Rabinbach, *The Human Motor*, p. 452. For Rathenau's writings, see, for example, *Von kommenden Dingen* (Things to come) and *Die Neue Wirtschaft* (The new economy), the latter written after the war.

44 Walther Rathenau, *Von kommenden Dingen* (1916), quoted in Maier, "Between Taylorism and Technocracy," p. 47. Maier notes that the apparent harmony of capital and labor in wartime Germany was achieved at the cost of an eventually ruinous policy of inflation (p. 46).

45 Michael Adas, *Machines as the Measure of Men: Science, Technology, and Ideologies of Western Dominance* (Ithaca: Cornell University Press, 1989), p. 380. Sheldon Wolin, in *Politics and Vision: Continuity and Innovation in Western Political Thought* (Boston: Little, Brown, 1960), provides an extensive list of like-minded thinkers spanning the political spectrum, from fascists and nationalists at one end to liberals, social democrats, and communists at the other, and hailing from France, Germany, Austria-Prussia (the Prussian Richard von Moellendorf, a close associate of Rathenau and a publicist for a managed postwar economy), Italy (Antonio Gramsci on the left and fascists Masimo Rocca and Benito Mussolini on the right), and Russia (Alexej Kapitonovik Gastev, the "Soviet Taylor").

46 V. I. Lenin, *The Agrarian Programme of Social-Democracy in the First Russian Revolution, 1905–1907*, 2nd rev. ed. (Moscow: Progress Publishers, 1954), p. 195, written September 28, 1917 (first emphasis only added).

47 Leon Smolinski, "Lenin and Economic Planning," *Studies in Comparative Communism* 2, no. 1 (January 1969): 99. Lenin and Trotsky were explicit, Smolinski claims, about how electric centrals would create a farm population dependent on the center and thus make state control of agricultural production possible (pp. 106–7).

48 Lenin, *Works* (Moscow, 1972), 27: 163, quoted in Ranier Traub, "Lenin and Taylor: The Fate of 'Scientific Management' in the (Early) Soviet Union," trans. Judy Joseph, *Telos* 34 (Fall 1978): 82–92 (originally published in *Kursbuch* 43 (1976). The "bard" of Taylorism in the Soviet Union was Alexej Kapitonovik Gastev, whose poetry and essays waxed lyrical about the possibilities of a "union" between man and machine: "Many find it repugnant that we want to deal with human beings as a screw, a nut, a machine. But we must undertake this as fearlessly as we accept the growth of trees and the expansion of the railway network" (quoted in ibid., p. 88). Most of the labor institutes were closed and their experts deported or shot in the Stalinist purges of the 1930s.

49 Lenin, "The Immediate Tasks of the Soviet Government," *Izvestia*, April 28, 1918, cited in Maier, "Between Taylorism and Technocracy," p. 51 n. 58.

50 Graham Burchell, Colin Gordon, and Peter Miller, *The Foucault Effect: Studies in Governmentality*, with two lectures by and an interview with Michel Foucault (London: Wheatsheaf, 1991), p. 106.

51 This point has been made forcefully and polemically in the twentieth century by Friedrich Hayek, the darling of those opposed to postwar planning and the welfare state. See, especially, *The Road to Serfdom* (Chicago: University of Chicago Press, 1976).

8

Making Space: Planning as a Mode of Thought

David C. Perry

On the 110th floor [of the World Trade Center in New York City]...a poster, sphinx-like, addresses an enigmatic message to the pedestrian who is for an instant transformed into a visionary: It's hard to be down when you're up.

Michel de Certeau, 1984, p. 92

To decipher discourse through the use of spatial, strategic metaphors enables one to grasp precisely the points at which discourses are transformed in, through and on the basis of relations of power.

Michel Foucault, 1980, p. 70

The history of the evolution of planning roles can be understood as a global conversation between the planning profession and its situation.   Donald Schön, 1983, p. 205

A Spatial Approach to Planning

In his essay, "Walking in the City," Michel de Certeau recounts his visit to the top of the World Trade Center. From the top he describes the spectacular view one has of all other buildings, the streets, and the geographic boundaries and topographic fault lines, both natural and man-made, that compose the New York landscape. From this vantage point we join him in looking over the landscape, our eyes moving from one tall building down to a lower one, looking up toward midtown and beyond to Harlem and turning back down to Wall Street and the waterfront. Standing there it becomes clear that although this is a truly extraordinary view of the city, we still can't see what is going on in the buildings below or next to us – in fact we have no idea what is going on in the floors immediately beneath our feet. As for the streets, if we can see them at all, the activities of those walking and riding in them are, from this vantage point, effectively invisible. No matter how grand and far-reaching the view, we don't see *everything* from the top of the World Trade Center.

We cannot depend upon this singularly lofty position to get a clear sense of what is going on elsewhere; we have to get back on the elevator and go down a few floors, or go to another building and then another and so on. But such travels are not enough because our understanding of the city remains far from complete. No matter how many buildings we visit and how good our vantage points are, the views from above remain, by themselves, no more than particularized representations – "the exaltation of the scopic" of "vision" that is at once refreshing (in the difference of its view of the city), clean, and clear (in its removal from the relative chaos of the mobility and endless labyrinths of the street) and yet blind (to the views to be had from the tops of other buildings) and unresponsive (to the infinite array of patterns of individuated everyday life).

The sign at the top of the World Trade Center sums all this up: "It's hard to be down when you're up." So it is for planners. It's hard to produce a plan that at once captures the conditions of the society, city, or policy area and also meets the demands of each of the citizens experiencing the problems society is mobilized to process. It's hard to be both scopic and comprehensive and immediate and individually responsive.[1]

Modern urban life is carried out in a planned society – planned both up and down. All of us are citizens of what Spiro Kostof (1991) has called "the planned, or designed or created city... *la ville crée*" (p. 43). The source of such a social logic is authoritative – constituted through a set of power relations that manifest themselves spatially in both material and immaterial ways (Lefebvre, 1991). These plans are made all the more clear when they are placed in relief against our practices of another kind of city – *la ville spontanée* – the "chance-grown" or "geomorphic" (Kostof, 1991, p. 43), the "lived" or "everyday" (Lefebvre, 1991; de Certeau, 1984) urban space.[2] This latter space – the city of irregularity (Castagnoli, 1971, p. 124) – is both the object of planning and its anathema: planning mediates between the *freedom* of the city as ville spontanée and the orderly production of the city as ville crée. Together they are generative forces contributing to the far more complex "(social) production of space" (Lefebvre, 1991) as a whole.

In spite of this dialectical function of planning, there is still confusion over *how* to think about planning. Ironically it is planners themselves who appear to be the most confused about the role of planning as an agency/instrument of control enmeshed or embedded in the relations of power (see the conversation between Michel Foucault and Gilles Deleueze, 1977). At a time when there appears to be literally no end to the ways in which planning is being exercised in modern society, the planning profession itself is undergoing a crisis of professional identity. One observer laments that the profession is plagued by a seemingly limitless set of specialties and subspecialties, which has caused deep internal fractures among its members and so many different definitions that they are best captured in "mathematicians' notation... [suggesting that] there is really a Planning(1), Planning(2) ... Planning(n)" (Levy, 1992, p. 81). All of this has produced a nearly endless stream of conferences, techniques, and approaches while at the same time the number of professional planning jobs is drying up in reaction to economic and political forces beyond the control of the profession.

In summary, planning seems to be at once ineffable and ubiquitous, causing more than a few planners to look a bit nervously back at Aaron Wildavsky's 1973 essay (see Beauregard, 1989; Brooks, 1990; Levy, 1992; Lucy, 1994; Schön, 1983). After cataloging the various approaches planners take to their trade, Wildavsky (1973) concluded that "If Planning Is Everything, Maybe It's Nothing." William Lucy (1994), for one, marshaled a review of the various approaches to planning and suggested that "If Planning Includes too Much, Maybe It Should Include More." What joins both authors, quite surprisingly, is not the apparent debate over the "expansiveness" (Lucy, 1994) of planning, but their concern over how successfully planning activities either maintain or challenge the social order (the dominant relations of power). Wildavsky finds that planning is so unsuccessful as a practice that it should be read more as an "act of faith" than as a legitimate practice of power. William Lucy subscribes to the notion that planning, if it is properly defined in its role of system maintenance,[3] can actually be expanded to include even more features of social/policy formation.

Put another way, the more legitimate the planning mandate (that is, the more successfully the profession is embedded in the service of the dominant political economy), the more its activities can be expanded to successfully produce other relations of power. Lucy (1994), in his search for an acceptable (legitimating) definition, suggests that the core ingredient in an expansive planning practice is serving "healthy" people and places. Robert Beauregard (1990) calls for a synthetic "planning-as-development" theme of city building, targeting the real estate, industrial development, architecture, and investment nexus as the processal center of a "holistic" planning. Like-minded planning theorists and practitioners traverse between the two poles represented by Lucy and Wildavsky – in a conscious quest for a "common core" (Beauregard, 1990, p. 212) within which to root planning's legitimacy. Without such a common core or defining concept, contemporary planning scholars argue, planning will continue to be a profession with a "lost sense of identity, and purpose, as well as ... influence and legitimacy in the arena of policy-making and development" (Brooks, 1990, p. 219). The problem is planners never seem to arrive at a collectively agreeable core of action, much less theory. And, in all likelihood, such a paradigmatic core will not materialize because planning is one of those professions that is of its context born. "The institutional context of planning practice is notoriously unstable and there are many contending views of the profession, each of which carries a different image of the planning role and a different picture of the body of useful knowledge" (Schön, 1983, p. 204). The result, as read by critics and planning advocates alike, is a consistent marginality of the formal *profession* of planning in the real world and a collective malaise inside the profession.[4] Even from within a perspective where the legitimacy of planning is unproblematic there are endless debates among proponents of alternative definitions of planning.

Thinking about the History of Planning ... Spatially

Rather than set out on a similarly unsatisfactory quest for paradigmatic clarity and legitimacy, I will argue here that the search for the best definition of planning is better directed toward thinking differently: We should think about planning spatially. Instead of trying to come up with a politics and technology for planning that everyone can agree upon, I offer a spatial approach suggested by Foucault's work. Thinking spatially means seeing the various politics and technologies of planning – its various discourses – in their contextual place(s) in society. They become examples of particular relations of power that constitute the conditions of freedom and dominance in the socially produced urban space. Michael Dear and Allen Scott (1981) argue that planning, like urbanization, is a "social event," not a free-standing and independent moral and/or scientific occurrence. Planning is embedded in the dominant relations of social formation – deriving its spatial logic and historical meaning from "the general pattern of society as a whole" (Dear and Scott, 1981, p. 4). Therefore when we think of planning we should think of it as part of the production and reproduction of the social relations of power.

This approach ties the investigation of planning to its actual participation in the construction of social/physical space. Rather than insert the various types of planning into "abstract space" (or assertion of a singularly legitimate paradigm or politics)[5] in order to distance them from the "clutter of existing and competing ideas" (Smith, 1992, pp. 60–64), this approach seeks out that clutter as part of the space in which planning is generated. To leave planning in what Lefebvre calls abstract space is to render the very *idea* of planning less than complete. Planners do not so much climb up on the material abstraction of the tall building of comprehensive planning, for example, as they produce that space – that building – with all its vision and all its blindness. To think of planning spatially is to think of it not as the conceptualization of relations within the boundaries of abstract space but to see it as both the critical interrogation and affirmative intervention of such abstraction, as the "production of space."[6]

Against an approach that sees planning evolving through time into a singular planning profession, the history of planning can be viewed as sets of practices that have participated in the changes from mercantile to industrial and ultimately post-industrial urban forms. In the early years of the twentieth century, planners were identified with the creation of comprehensive master plans, carried out by corporatist, boardlike commissions with central responsibilities for the overall, apolitical planning of the city: "The planner framed his role at the center of a system for which he planned, in relation to agencies that would implement his plans and clients who would benefit from this" (Schön, 1983, p. 205). The product of such a process (the plan) was informed by these corporate relations of production as well. Perhaps the most famous master plan was and remains the Regional Plan of New York. The first volume of the plan, published in 1927 by the Regional Plan Association (RPA), begins with a description of the city and the purposes to which the city and planning are to be put:

> The metropolis, in one of its aspects, is essentially a piece of productive machinery competing with other metropolitan machines. It will prosper or decline as compared with other metropolises in rough proportion to the relative efficiency with which it can do economic work . . . that is, produce goods [and] services. The area of New York and its environs may be likened to the floor space of a factory. Regional planning designates the best use of this floor space – "the proper adjustment of area to uses." (RPA, 1927, p. 18)

However, just as planning practices offered plans that replicated and legitimated the relations of power found in the capitalist city, they also served to challenge the excesses of capitalism. Planning embodies the contradictions of capitalism, both as a practice of corporatist industrialism and a response to the chaos of the "wild city"

(Castells, 1976) such relations of production produce (Boyer, 1983). Frederick Howe (1926/1969), the legendary turn of the century reformer, lamented:

> The American city lags behind the work it should perform. It is negative in its function, rather than positive in its services. It has been stripped (by industrial capitalism) of power and responsibility. It is politically weak and lacks ideals of its possibilities. It has little concern for its people and they in turn have little concern for it. We have failed to differentiate between those activities that are private and those that are public. We have failed too to provide protection to the individual from inequalities of power and position, and have left him prey to forces as dangerous to his life and comfort as those against which the police are employed to protect. Further than this, we have failed to shift to society the burdens of industry that the coming of the city has created. We have permitted the sacrifice of low wages, irregular employment, and disease to be borne by the individual rather than the community. (p. v)

This is the city of "les classes dangereux" – who were at once the source of fear and paranoia and the object of righteous indignation over their conditions of oppression (Wilson, 1991, p. 7). They lived in a city where land uses, vehicles, races and ethnicites, men, women, and children were, in Howe's words, "inadequately planned." The very disorder, pain and chaos of the urban evoked an ideal alternative: the "rational city" (Boyer, 1983). "With the exception of Washington," Howe (1926/1969) opined, "there was no realization of the permanence of the city, of the importance of streets and open spaces, of building regulations, transportation, waterfronts and the physical foundations which underlie the city's life" (p. 194). In a very real sense, planning was also "a response to the turmoil of modernization" (Beauregard, 1989) – both as a responsive model of corporate capitalism and a challenge to the worst excesses of the very forces of privatism (Warner, 1974).

From the beginning, therefore, there was *no* clear or single definition of planning. Planning is a hard profession in the spirit of the poster at the top of the World Trade Center: both comprehensive and visionary (RPA [1927]) and at the same time critical and immediate. It is far more realistic to conceive of planning spatially – as a dialectically determined synchrony of public interventions generated by and in response to the order and chaos of the industrial city. Planning is seen then as less a product of clear mandate and agreeable paradigm of comprehensiveness than as a mixed dialectical response to the contradictions of the capitalist city. As Alan Altshuler (1965), writing a half a century later, observed, planning "is usually a contradiction and ambivalence" (p. 1).

From a spatial practice viewpoint, planning is not so much a response to the institutional contradictions of social formation as it is the embodiment of such conditions of contradiction and ambivalence (Perry, 1994). The planning literature on the roots of modern planning serves as de facto evidence of this point: Rather than think of planning spatially and synchronically, most practitioners and scholars search determinedly for *the* appropriate definition, *the* holistic paradigm of politics, practice, and technical expertise. Although many scholars argue that planning was really a movement toward comprehensiveness (Beauregard, 1989, 1990; Fainstein, 1991) and master planning, others are just as willing to suggest that planning was really a product of social reform and the desire for safe and healthy streets (Felbinger, 1995), homes, and workplaces (Howe, 1926/1969). Still others have suggested that planning was either an aesthetic impulse (Beard, 1926) or the product of a utopian movement captured in early visionary models such as Ebenezer Howard's "garden cities" and Tony Gariner's *cité industrielle* and continuing to Le Corbusier's mid-1920's Voison Plan for Paris or Clarence Stein's "sunshine village" (Barnett, 1986; Relph, 1987). In short, for all the boilerplate associated with the notion that planning in the first instance was a visionary exercise in comprehensive planning, there is equally strong evidence that planning was/is the product of strong street-level nostrums of social reform, revisionist utopian politics, applied scientific technologies of health and safety, and architectonic and landscape aesthetics. If we think of planning, from the outset, as essentially comprehensive – or as utopian or reformist or rational or aesthetic – then we miss the fact that these various discourses were (and still are) *all* planning and together composed the spatiality of early twentieth-century American planning as a social agency of legitimation and critique of the industrial city. They are all (in various discourses of consort, opposition, and internal contradiction) legitimating parts of and/or critical responses to the massive geographic and demographic changes (Fairfield, 1993), the emerging dominating logic of corporate and industrial capital, and the unhealthy and chaotic socioeconomic circumstances of human distress and poverty that were relational conditions of the late nineteenth century "private city" (Warner, 1974).

Charles Beard (1926) summarized the municipal planning movement as an aesthetic and scientific impulse to achieve that Holy Grail of industrial technologists, economic efficiency, and, in the process, to point out "enough waste and follies in any existing system of urban economy to arouse...advocates of urban planning...in the field of public health, the housing reformers and some social philosophers" (pp. 275–276). Robert Foglesong (1990) observes that planning quickly transformed from a political movement to a managerial one, where comprehensive plans became less efficacious, planners became managers and regulators, and the distinction between planner and administrator became exceedingly small. The management/planning of the city was grounded in the regulation of land use (Boyer, 1983): the public production of the legal logic of land employed as a factor of the capitalist mode of production. The economic use (Peterson, 1981) and the public definition of real property were joined. The proactive tools of land management became land use controls, plans, and zoning regulations. As a result John Levy (1992) concludes that even today, "the planner is part of the administrative apparatus of land development and a facilitator of community development" (p. 81). He adds that "for planning, this is an age when tactics are dominant and grand strategies and grand visions are much less prominent" (p. 81).

The transformation of early planning from highly visible vision and reform to relatively invisible and institutional tactics and regulation has been accompanied by parallel forays of other more centralizing tendencies to plan policies such as "urban renewal, urban and regional transportation, health services, public education, mental health and criminal justice" (Schön, 1983, p. 205). These forays, with their institutionalizing administrative structures, seem to specialize in

> plans designed to solve problems that either failed...or created problems worse than the problems they had been designed to solve. Some of the phenomena planners were most anxious to influence – poverty, crime, urban congestion and decay – seemed tenaciously resilient to intervention. (Schön, 1983, p. 205)

Planners seemed to be mistaken in the way they conceived of the problems, the plans, and the solutions. Their effectiveness at implementation of these plans was a failure at two levels: (a) the relative artificiality and inapplicability of the plans they offered and (b) the problematic position they held in the process of policy practice itself, due to their lack of direct expertise.

In the face of such deficiencies, a new planning practice joined the practices of master planning, management, regulation, and policy planning. Known variously as social planning, advocacy planning, or equity planning, this new form added an important and directly critical voice to planning – one that did not simply represent a critique of the social condition of the city and the political economy but a critique of planning itself. Here scholars as diverse as Donald Schön, Herbert Gans, Jane Jacobs, Frances Fox Piven, Norman Krumholz, Lisa Peattie, and John Friedmann set out to show how planners themselves were practitioners of the very relations of power that produced the social contradictions and economic inequities that composed much of the planning agenda. "Planners," wrote Donald Schön, "acting ostensibly in the public interest actually served the interests of real estate developers and large corporations by displacing the poor and ethnic minorities" (p. 208). What is important here is not the notion that somehow social planning replaced policy planning, but that planning, in its various manifestations of the production of space, now *included* a formally articulated critical position. Nor is it necessary to debate whether policy planning *displaced* land use planning or whether land use planning *replaced* comprehensive planning. What is significant is that the general discourse of planning – the overall spatiality of planning – *contains* all of these various planning(s). None of these notions of planning are whole or inclusive; they are all partial and constitutive of what planning was/is becoming. Again, to return to Foucault (in Foucault and Deleueze, 1977), each represents a different way in which planning facilitates (or confronts) and/or embodies the relations of power that produce the city/society.

A Spatial Approach to Current Planning Practice

Most recently the paradigmatic metaphor used most by practitioners and scholars to describe the planning profession has been development – in particular economic development. The economic development notion of planning has emerged, like progressive planning, out of the chaos of the city. Again changes in the capitalist mode of production in the city and globally have had profound effects on planning. Susan Fainstein (1991), in a recent issue of the *Journal of the American Planning Association*, put it bluntly:

> The foremost impetus driving new modes of planning has been the restructuring of the urban economy. In response to deindustrialization and the simultaneous expansion of the service sector, local governments have actively sought to attract new industries to their jurisdictions by offering packages of land and financing. Second, conservative national administrations have stressed market-based solutions to allocative questions and have promoted growth over redistribution. Third is a more proactive stance toward planning. (p. 22)[7]

The current definition of planning, born of this new economic era, has complex ramifications for some of the old conundrums of planning. Gone is stimulating reference to the contradictions of capitalism that triggered reformists like Frederick Howe and equity planners like Norman Krumholz. Even the tactics of traditional land use physical planners and public infrastructure planners, who were inclined to mystify – through regulations, bureaucracy and engineering and design technologies – the conflictual relationship they had with capital accumulation and the negative and inequitable impacts of such accumulation on the community, are minimized. The connection between the economic structure and planning legitimacy is now straightforwardly claimed, and the tactics developed to stimulate economic growth are frankly enumerated (Fainstein, 1991). Ideology – that is, democratic ideology – is no longer evoked to situate the planner's role: rather the contradiction between planning and capital is eliminated through a new mystification of the role of planner as developer – one who lives by the abstract code in which private advantage is equated with public benefit. Today, Fainstein (1991) observes, this planning merges in a context where "if the argument that what is good for business is good for everyone is not wholly accepted, neither is it opposed by a widely held alternative formulation" (p. 23). There is no longer a tension between accumulation and redistribution: It is assumed that accumulation will ultimately generate redistribution.

There is no illusion left as to where the "real" planners of the restructuring urban world are: They are not making abstract comprehensive plans that function in the public interest, they are "figuring out the local power structure and . . . [assuming] a role compatible with it" (Fainstein, 1991, p. 25). This role, if it is to be proactive, will be decidedly favorable to investment capital. The notion of planner as public advocate has been directly joined by the highly visible affirmation of planner as a facilitator, negotiator, and deal-maker – no longer to be found in the neutral "back room" of technological services and land use regulations, but in a highly entrepreneurial function serving the needs of investment capital, industrial and service sector firms, and labor. In some ways Fainstein is right, at least if you review the recent history of cities in the United States. In almost every city there can now be found a full range of new development specialists – in industrial development agencies and community development agencies, in Chambers of Commerce and a whole host of new not-for-profit private foundations and business groups, in public authorities and special district governments of all varieties.[8] The notion of planning as part and parcel of the development of the local, regional, and global economy has now captured almost every segment of institutional relations and has blurred boundaries of what used to be called the public and private sectors.

Yet just as the practice of planning as development has become more and more ubiquitous, crossing sectors of society as well as various agencies and levels of government, the notion that planning can be narrowed and defined within the confines of the development metaphor produces its own set of contradictions. As the politics of development and the planning of cities and their edges proceeds within this new restructuring logic of capital accumulation, new forms of the "wild city" materialize as well. These include heightened conditions of hopelessness, new forms of underemployment and unemployment, increased physical spaces of decline, and psychological as well as physical "zones of fear" (Davis, 1992). In addition, increased informalization of the economy and new migrations of people into and out of cities constitute a full array of issues that demand recurring perspectives of land use, management, comprehensive planning, reformist advocacy, and other practices of planning that challenge the dominant relations of production and social reproduction as much as they maintain them.

The splintering of urban space (McLean & Perry, 1994) – into "figured" (Boyer, 1995) spaces of tightly concentrated central city business districts, edge-city shopping malls, and mixed-use industrial and office parks; and "disfigured" (Boyer, 1995) spaces of declining social services, increasing hopelessness, uneven patterns of real estate, migration, unemployment, service delivery, poverty and unemployment – is both produced and reproduced in new global networks of capital, labor, and information (Casella, 1993). The notion that we can or should achieve a stable, inclusive profession or definition of planning in such an environment of splintered cities and rapidly changing, globalizing "spaces of flows" (Thrift, 1993) is more in question than ever before. If planning is born of its context, this fragmenting future should produce forms of planning that are even more spatially differentiated than the planning(s) of the past. In this non-Euclidian world (Friedmann, 1993 [ch.3]), which Casella (1993) calls "quantum," people now link

> knowledge to action, emphasize real time, and encourage appreciation of regional and local variety. In a quantum world there is also heightened concern over the long-term future, precisely because the future seems to be in danger of getting out of control. Planning must cope with the dislocations of rapid change and address the future too.
>
> (Casella, 1993, p. 485)

As a result planners like Casella and Stuart Meck (1990) argue for a form of planning that seems less connected to a centrally defined profession and more tied to accomplishing politically achievable results within the immediate context in which the planner is found. The tools of a planner's trade, Casella suggests, are increasingly technological, multidisciplinary, and intellectually free, meaning that planners will be even less likely to conceive of their profession through a discrete array of technologies; their disciplinary reach will be greater than ever before, given the rapid shifts in the splintering urban context; and given the swift and complex shifts of economic and social formation, they will be intellectually less tied to any preordained outcome.

All of this, contends Casella (personal interview, July 10, 1994), will be practiced increasingly by planners located outside bureaucracies altogether.[9] He estimates that the fastest-growing sector of planning activity is the individual consultant category, where planners are connected by computer, rather than bureaucratic position or proprietary function, to the (social) production of (urban) space. The agential place of planning, to say nothing of its metaphoric or paradigmatic space of function, is shifting rapidly. The dynamics, indeed the "cyber-spatiality" of planning is changing/ still becoming.

Seen spatially, planning is quite different from the postcard tourism that takes a visitor to the top of the World Trade Center, or at least it requires a different form of urban travel.[10] It is not impelled by a voyeuristic interest in "seeing all" of the city; it is the political mobilization of knowledge in the service of social order, where order is experienced differently and found to be different in the different spaces of the city. To think of planning as simply a scopic exercise of scale limits it to a single politico-technological snapshot of society, which invites criticism or rejection based on, among other things, alternative views or core definitions of planning representing other techniques or scalar appropriations of the social order.[11] Planning is not so much any one of these various approaches as *it is the diversely configured space of all of them – all the planning discourses of social formation – as they exemplify what Foucault (1980, p. 70) described as those "points where discourses are transformed in, through and on the basis of power"*. From this perspective the history of the approaches to planning can be viewed synchronically as well as critically. Planning is not so much a linear progression of practices – one displacing another – as it is an emerging *spatial practice* joining one new approach to another in the evolving production and reproduction of the relations of capital and the urban society attendant to it.

Making Space: What Planners Do

Spatial theory provides a useful approach to the question: What do planners, as instrumental practitioners of the social relations of power, do? Answering this question requires a consideration of planning as a *mode of thought* – a thinking that engenders/incorporates action. This requires a process different from the conventional characterizations of planning discussed previously, ones where planning is "rethought" in terms of new paradigms (of comprehensiveness or equity or social policy) or agencies of "societal guidance" (Beauregard, 1990, p. 210). To borrow from Immanuel Wallerstein (1991),[12] a bit of "unthinking" is in order here. The argument extends beyond a contribution to the critical thought that sees planning as part of the abstractions that produce relations of dominance. To consider planning as a *spatial practice* intent on the (social) production of space implies breaking down the mode of thinking that continues to separate the abstract spaces of social formation from the lived or everyday. In short the process of rethinking planning has traditionally allowed planners to think of what they do as essentially that of "making plans": the master plans, policies, or some other form of tool or agency of change. To think of planning, instead, as a spatial practice suggests that what planners do is *not* simply make plans but rather "make space."

   The first part of this chapter considered the spatiality of planning: That is, planning should be thought of spatially as a changing and increasingly complex feature of the (social) relations of power, producing and reproducing the state and market, at both the institutional and the lived or everyday levels. If this review of American planning tells us anything, it is that planning is always remaking itself as it is embedded in and responds to a world that itself is always in the process of being remade. That is, the various ways of planning are not so much displacements as they are transformative additions to planning in the face of urban change. As such the space of planning is best represented as a gerund – a verb-noun – both fixed in the social and physical relations (space) of the moment and changing in relation to both the past and the future (time). This means that planning is always more than one thing – it is both the planned and the unplanned, engaging the future (direction or goals) and the present, the distant and visionary, and the proximate and labyrinthine. Therefore planning infers not fixedness, but openness – this openness offering not a pluralism of positions or approaches, but the necessary "gerundic" state of a pluralized practice in the face of the time(s)/space(s) of contemporary social forma-tion(s). In this sense planning is more than a conceptual practice or intellectual technology whereby the lived and perceived experiences of society are joined. This version of planning is an example of what some critics call the production of an "abstract space" – a space scientifically or technologically grounded in a political-intellectual exercise of inclusiveness[13] – in which the various experiences of the city are rationally captured and attended to. As suggested above, such representations of urban space, grounded in the legitimating nostrums of the dominant political econ-omy, are always only partial. The limits of such conceptualization are uncovered in the face of "a world that is constantly remaking itself" (Grossberg, 1993, p. 1).

The practices of everyday life – those "street corners" of the urban scene that one can never see from the top of the World Trade Center – are aspects of planning most easily ignored, no matter how clear the day or finely tuned the technology of viewing. But to conceive of planning as a mode of thought is not only to consider its technology, rationality, ideology, and process but also to understand that the space planners make includes that which their technology excludes, their profes-sional distancing misses, and their processes actually confound. The notion of planning as a spatial practice – a dialectic of constant remaking in response to a world that is constantly being remade – grounds planning in everyday experience. This includes places or sites of spatial production – at all scales, the body, the family, the home, the workplace, the neighborhood, the city, the region, the world. Planning is always more or less comprehensive, developmental, equity-oriented, regulatory – a shifting, recursive spatiality that is characterized not only by the intellectual positions of planning, but also by the places or sites of intervention and the way in which such intervention travels. Planning then is a spatial practice that ensures continuity and some form of cohesion but, because of its dialectical and contradict-ory nature, not coherence.

Certain considerations are key to planning as a spatial practice: context, travel, connection, and scale. Planning, as suggested earlier, is of its *context* born – a social event, as Dear and Scott (1981) put it, that is both the product of and the producer of (social) space. Planning is a *lived* practice that is at once the genesis and the object of its *abstract practice* of design, strategy, policy, and regulation. And planning is also the practice of visible, geometric, physical, and ultimately *abstract relations* of social order (power) that "pass from the 'lived' to the abstract in order to project that abstraction onto the level of the lived" (Lefebvre, 1970, p. 241). The source of critical planning, advocacy, and equity rests most often in the everyday or lived complex and labyrinthine features of social phenomena, whose real significance (for a planning grounded in such phenomena) rests in their "fluidity and malleability" (Wallerstein, 1991, p. 71).[14]

The visit of de Certeau to the top of the World Trade Center is not only a helpful way to consider the spatiality of planning; it is also a heuristic of planning as a spatial practice. If the goal is to get beyond the boundaries of a planning defined as a professional, efficient, and technical "spatial science" (Gregory, 1994, p. 400) produ-cing abstract representations of space (Lefebvre, 1991) or "facsimiles" of the city (de Certeau, 1984) and to include the city as lived at different scalar levels (Smith, 1992), then the practice of planning must be considered a dialectic one, always *traveling* between the lived space and the abstract space of society. It is this travel that is at once most bothersome to planners and critics and the most important feature of practice.

Most scholars and theorists treat planners like the tourist who gets to the top of the World Trade Center and takes a picture of "the city," producing a product, a fixed facsimile of the urban – a technical, scientific, professionally produced replication and obvious abstraction of the lived experiences below. But, as practitioners will attest, planning is not a single tour to a fixed site – it is a traveling to many sites; not a visit *to* a place – it is the *making* of space. This making is a dynamic practice of traveling the distance between the abstract and the lived. Making (social) space for planners includes not only what is seen but what is unseen – what the plans include, theoretically, and what they exclude, what they abstractly represent through scientific logic and bureaucratic rationality and what is lived yet unrepresented. Understood this way, planning is at once a facsimile of power and an act of exclusion and domination that, if critically practiced, can also include the "other," which these acts tend to exclude. Planning, to repeat the words of the poster (de Certeau, 1984, p. 92), is "hard" – it is the practice of being "down when you are up." The irony of planning is that it at once promises such distance and is victimized by it: providing a distant vision of a better future and often excluding from the vision those who do not fit "productively" into the functions of the dominant political economy.

The notion of making space also implies *scale*.

> The continual production and reproduction of scale expresses the social as much as geographical contest to establish boundaries between different places, locations, and sites of experience. The making of place implies the production of scale insofar as places are made different from each other; scale is a criterion of difference not between places so much as between different kinds of places.   (Smith, 1992, p. 64)

Scale implies the territorialization of power across geographies of production and reproduction, such as the nation-state, the region, and global economic, informational, and financial networks. Scale also includes spaces of social activity; from the individual to the home and the neighborhood, these spaces are the grounded sites of both the material and metaphorical relations that represent social and cultural processes.

The ways in which the policies and practices of the nation-state and the city are connected to the social processes and relations of the individual are part and parcel of the critical spatial practices of planning. Making space implies scalar interconnectedness – a traveling between sites, a professional "jumping" of scales (Smith, 1992) in both the illumination of and the engagement with the contradictions planning intervention can produce and which such a traveling practice attempts to resolve.

The goal of planning today is to make/remake space in all its complexity. This includes the physical and relational sites of individual and collective experience: the home, work, neighborhood, city or region, nation, or globe. This is not to argue that the goal of the spatial practice of planning should be to produce "the nation" or "the home," for example. Rather than make products like housing plans, a planning practice that makes space links the policy to the everyday user of the housing unit and makes not the policy but a workable and working space – at once lived (in) and well-designed, built, financed, and regulated.

The process is a reflexive one that necessarily includes a wide range of relationships. For example, in the (social) production of (public) housing, this would include the dialectic among a number of components, including the contestation between users, local housing authority officials, and fiscal levels of government.

Planning, so conceived, is a recursive process. Whereas we can think of the urban designer as producing a physical design of the built geographic site and the architect as producing the design of the housing unit, planning is that gerundic process concerned with the ongoing making of the unit, the design of the housing project, the building of the unit, the actual inhabitants of the unit, the transformation of these units from projects to homes, the maintenance and rehabilitation of the units, the repopulation of the units with new tenants, the decline and destruction of the units, and so on. Contrary to the more narrow professional interventions of almost all others at the site or scale of the production of space, the planner's work is never done; it is, to repeat, a recursive spatial practice – meant to include both the design and building of physical infrastructure and the satisfactory use of the built space and the contested politics of what constitutes the public realm at the scale or site of the home. In sum, planners do not work on a different scale than the other design professionals so much as they make a different *kind* of space, informed as much by the experiences of the lived space of the users of the home or unit as by the institutional politics of budgets, regulations, and bureaucratic mandates.

Planning and the Production of Scale

Two examples of planning as the practice of making space are the scalar venues of home and region. The space of home is usually excluded from planning because it is too small and not easily represented in the abstract political relations of professional planning. The space of region is often excluded from economic planning in favor of the economistic notion of development, because it too has no effective proprietary or electoral territory of abstract political-economic representation.

Home

A typical approach to public housing is to work at the scale of housing policy, wherein the conditions of housing needs are defined, a plan devised, and the policy implemented. An alternative is to practice housing planning at the scale of the home, where the meaning of housing to individual householders is represented by planners first through the mediums of shared daily experience and then translated or traveled to the scale of housing policy produced by a public housing authority or other agency of the state. Jacqueline Leavitt and Susan Saegert (1988, 1989) report on a version of this planning practice, which they call the "community-household model." Grounded in the domestic work of the home, as practiced most often by women, this model integrates the lived experiences of everyday home life into housing and social service plans and programs. Housing planners using this model are required to travel between the lived experience of householders and the abstract institutional representations of housing authorities, master plans, and building and zoning regulations. The planners are oriented toward making better homes – their spatial practice becomes one of jumping scales as they undertake the hard process of carrying out the dialectics of comprehensive housing services that produce homes for individual families.

In a study of landlord-abandoned buildings in New York City conducted in the mid-1980s, Saegert and Leavitt (1988) found that the city was managing over 26,000 residential units in 4,000 abandoned buildings. They discovered that "such wholesale abandonment jeopardized the shelter security of the largely black and Latino, often female, low income tenants who inhabited the buildings" (p. 489). Through extensive interviews with the tenants of some of these buildings and with planners in the city housing agencies, they began to uncover a spatial practice of housing planning that was firmly embedded in both the lived conditions of the tenants and what they called the more abstract planning tools of community and government support. Their study

> shows that a combination of existing social networks, extensive technical involvement with technical assistance groups and political advocates, and programs that legitimate and provide resources for indigenous leaders' efforts while reinforcing tenant participation have led to successful, direct control by tenants of [these abandoned buildings].
> (Leavitt and Saegert, 1988, p. 495)

What started out, for housing professionals, as an apparently impossible situation of economic abandonment, social deprivation, and inflexible governmental programs was transformed significantly by an approach that defined planning as a long-term recursive process. This process incorporated the strategies poor people used to cope with landlord abandonment and devised successful tenant management and ownership programs. Leavitt and Seagert have schematized this hard process of being up and down into a five-stage community household model: Planning homes entails:

1   The mobilization of everyday domestic skills of coping/reacting to crisis.
2   The recognition of block or building-level networks of communication, goods sharing, and leadership development.
3   Community-level identification with the place of residence through the reinforcement of shared stories and memories of "place" or community.
4   Community-level identification with the neighborhoods and buildings where the tenants live through organizations such as churches, stores, clubs, gangs.
5   City-level response to the community-household representation of the housing or other social issue through putting plans and agencies in the direct service of these de facto community household-produced programs. (Leavitt and Saegert, 1988, p. 497).

Another example of planning as a spatial practice at the scale of the home is the long-term planning housing studio headed by Jacqueline Leavitt at UCLA. In 1989, Leavitt and her students entered into an agreement with the Resident Management Corporation (tenants' council) of the Nickerson Gardens housing project in Watts, a neighborhood of South Central Los Angeles, to conduct a pilot survey of tot-lots and laundry services in the project. Nickerson Gardens is, according to Leavitt (1993, p. 55), the largest public housing complex west of the Mississippi River, with 1,066 units housing 4,900 people, over 40% of whom are children. The majority of the families are African American, although there are now over 600 Latino families in Nickerson. An estimated 10% of the units are abandoned due to poor physical condition, and many of the remaining units are in various states of mechanical disrepair. The complex is plagued with poor maintenance, including overhead outside lights that have not been repaired in 14 years (Leavitt, 1992, p. 119), plumbing that shuts down all running water for long periods of time, broken recreational equipment, streets filled with potholes, and tot-lots, which, by day, were filled with glass, infected sand, and broken equipment and by night became "adult hangouts where raucous drinking was punctutated by drug deals" (Leavitt, 1992, p. 122).

Of all these issues, the ones that commanded the attention of the residents and convinced them to contract with professional planners to somehow help them bridge the gap between the policy-making administrators, architects, and planners of the Housing Authority of Los Angeles and themselves were tot-lots and laundromats. The studio was asked, on the basis of a survey, to prepare a report, financial proposals, and physical designs for both services: to rehabilitate the tot-lots and prepare designs for laundry facilities. The tot-lots were to be redesigned in line with the perceived needs of parents and children. The models for laundromats were to provide the residents and the Housing Authority with information on two different approaches: (a) decentralized laundries located throughout the housing complex and (b) a large free-standing, off-site facility that would serve Nickerson and the surrounding neighborhood, thereby acting as both a laundry and a training and revenue-development project for the RMC.

The initial experience of Leavitt and her students, as they tried to provide data for such revised plans, was quite frustrating. The cultural and experiential distance between the planners and the residents was quite wide. To reduce the distance and "travel" from the space of planner to tenant householder required that both Leavitt and her students spend long periods of time in Nickerson, in the lived space of the housing units.[15] Second, rather than use traditional survey methods of planning to abstractly represent the conditions of the housing units, they began, over weeks, to meet with the residents in their homes, in kitchens around potluck meals and door prizes, to discuss what it was like to live in the Gardens and what it would take to live better. Through such meetings they learned what should be included in the survey and then, rather than conduct the surveys themselves, they accompanied the leaders of the residential council to the units and acted as scribes (Leavitt, 1992, p. 123) while the residents conducted the surveys. The task of the planners then was to turn this information into technically useful physical designs and fiscally acceptable funding proposals that would fit into the plans of the Housing Authority and its architects, thereby creating a legitimate discourse between the residents and the planners over what sort of homes the units of Nickerson were and could be. In a community filled with the most powerful gangs, the highest rates of poverty, and dramatic differences between races and ethnicities, the physical condition of the housing units, while important, was less significant than the (social) production of a safe and comfortable home (space). Planning, as it was articulated here, had become a spatial practice: one of home making.

Over a period of years, rather than the originally projected 3-month graduate planning studio, the planning studio helped to facilitate a shift in the way housing policy would at a minimum be debated – the issues for the Housing Authority when considering the condition of Nickerson Gardens now included a full-scale consideration of tot-lots as an extended, safe, and accessible part of the home – where parents and children could visit and play, day and night. By 1992, two lots had been built with Housing Authority monies, and the residents and planners were developing proposals for others. Leavitt and the student planners had also designed proposals for the laundromats – both in the housing buildings and the larger commercial project. The residents were considering

> a variety of ideas for their laundry facility: a radio, television, vending machines, and a bathroom. More importantly, they have ideas for additional service that would be available while washing their clothes: having a baby-sitter, a playground for the children, a day care center, sewing workshops, ... books and a telephone.
>
> (Leavitt, 1993, p. 56)

In short the plans included making the space even more a home.

The community-household model treats the planning process as a recursive process that becomes part of the lived experience of householders, legitimates the demands of home making, uses technical designs of the professional planners, and informs and updates the master plans of the Los Angeles Housing Authority.

Region

Another way to look at planning is to consider it as part of the production of region. This is region in a broad sense, not only as a physical area but also a territorialization of politics and economics. The City of Buffalo and its surrounding region of Western New York (WNY) offer a case in point.

By the late 1970s, Buffalo was the clear victim of long-term deindustrialization. Unemployment in the region had reached double digits, the population had declined precipitously, per capita income was one fifth below that of comparable regions of the state, and the jobs provided by the manufacturing sectors of the economy had dropped from almost one half to barely one fifth of overall employment, as steel, machine, auto, and heavy metals production firms shut down or left the region (Perry, 1987; Stanback and Noyelle, 1982). Although many of the job losses were replaced by growth in the service sector, the rate of growth in these sectors remained uncompetitively below national rates (Kraushaar and Perry, 1990). What further complicated the state of the regional economy was the increased pattern of dependency that accompanied these changes – 60% of all local firms and 95% of all manufacturing firms employing over 100 employees were outside-owned, and almost all recent agreements in the transfer of ownership of firms benefited larger global and national outside capital. The fastest-growing parts of the economy were in the public sector, and the dependency of the region on increased social services, welfare, and other government mandated transfers to supplant the shaky regional wage was more pronounced than in any other region in the state. Last, all major capital investments in new firm startups or in expansions in excess of $750,000 included some form of governmental subsidy, such as loans and tax incentives.

The combined patterns of economic decline, rising social disparities, and distress were both served and exacerbated by increased economic dependency on outside ownership of the region's economy and increased subsidies from the public sector. The region's industrial economy was closing down, unable to function without the input of investment from outside capital and with almost complete dependence on public sector subsidies to retain, much less stimulate, firm-level activity. Taken together these relations of production and reproduction made for a region of powerlessness – a space of deindustrialization and dependency that embodied the contradictions and disparities of advanced industrial capitalism (Bluestone and Harrison, 1982; McLean and Perry, 1994; Perry, 1987; Smith and Feagin, 1987; Stanback and Noyelle, 1982).

Regional economic development planning in WNY was anything but regional. Instead it was a fragmented plethora of programs and organizations mobilized to meet the needs of capital on a firm-by-firm basis or the goals of local governments on a jurisdictionally competitive deal-by-deal or tax-abatement by tax-abatement basis. "The situation resembled an . . . [intra-regional] 'entrepreneurial economy' but with the public sector agencies playing the role of the entrepreneur . . . competing to 'cut the best deal' with private firms" (Perry, Kraushaar, Lines, and Parker, 1985, p. 28). As one economic development professional put it: "Our policy is the 'first firm through the door' gets the public support" (Perry et al., 1985, p. 29). In this environment there was no strategic analysis of the regional economy or interest in a more (globally) interactive and regional supportive economy. In fact, it had become quite the opposite: In the desperate days of structural economic change in this Rust Belt region, regional economic development was a form of "get your own as fast as you can" – cut a deal and cut out the competition whether it is overseas or over in the next county.

These policies had become the practice in many of the nearly 80 public and quasi-public agencies assigned to promote the economic development of the counties, towns, cities, and villages of WNY. Chambers of commerce, local development corporations, industrial development agencies, job training and assistance groups, and municipal development offices all had their own jurisdictions and their own separate mandates. In addition there were at least 26 different state departments and agencies administering economic development plans and programs. This intergovernmental profusion of agencies, incentives, and deals could require as many as 30 different state, federal, and local ports of call for a firm looking for help (Perry et al., 1985). In sum, the economic development process in the region could be as quick as a one-stop shop at the local industrial development agency (IDA) or an intergovernmental nightmare. Either way, the notion of *regional* economic development – where the firms, workers, and citizens of the WNY area could be spatially represented as a region of shared individually and collectively experienced economic decline and dependency – was lost.

In the early years of his administration, Governor Mario Cuomo, confronted with both statewide and regional variations of this economic decline, initiated the process of creating a statewide economic development plan. We, at the SUNY/Buffalo Department of Planning, were assigned the task of producing a draft of the section of the plan for distressed regions. Using Buffalo as an example, we defined the assignment as one of building/rebuilding the region, rather than establishing planning strategies to accomplish development. In addition to designing more traditional incentive and retention packages, our goal therefore was to define a process (a) embedded in networks of structural and global interdependence rather than dependency and (b) characterized by independent regional political power and internal clarity of communication rather than powerlessness and fragmentation. In short our plan was not organized around a series of developmental "end states"; instead we hoped to establish a recursive agential process that would make/remake the economy in a region being made/remade (Grossberg, 1993) during an era of economic restructuring.

We suggested the creation of a Regional Economic Development Corporation (REDC), a regional public authority serving the multi-county WNY area most identified with economic decline and social distress, political dependency, and fragmentation. The public authority model was chosen because of its independence. The clear fiscal and political independence of a public authority would go a long way toward turning around the externally perceived notion of regional political-economic powerlessness and would serve as a centralizing feature of the fragmented economic development efforts within the region. The REDC would be a legally independent agency under the state's public benefit corporation law, with its own bonding (both general and revenue) power, a board of directors with members appointed by the governor from the various levels of government, and agencies of development. As a public authority it would be able to hire its own technically skilled staff in finance, development, and human capital. It would have the ability to negotiate the sale of its own bonds, which in the tradition of many statewide authorities, would be tax exempt and secured by both state guarantees and a revenue-generating reserve fund. Finally, it would maintain institutional and fiscal ties to the larger statewide development authorities, such as the Urban Development Corporation (UDC) and the Job Development Authority.

The result, it was argued, would be the creation of a state policy that formally established regional economic development as a clear objective of statewide economic renewal. The "arm of the State" would be regional, not tied to bureaucratically cumbersome state agencies or to the myriad of locally circumscribed agencies, but responsive to the space of the region itself – a space defined by the contradictions of economic restructuring and growing political-economic dependency in the context of wider networks of politics and economics. The institutional power of an on-site, permanent, independent, and regionally circumscribed public authority, with the political legitimacy of state law and gubernatorial appointments to its board and the fiscal power that comes with dual access to state appropriations and the private bond markets, would give this regional authority the potential to travel the hard distance between up and down, between the powerful dependencies the region had in its relations with outside ownership and capital and the daily lived experienced of economic restructuring in the firms and workplaces of Buffalo and the rest of WNY.

This proposal to serve the region as a space of political and economic relations was shelved. Although the logic of placing a primary emphasis on the region had its proponents at the local level, the political leadership at the state level was not willing to take seriously the creation of a structure designed to put the political economy of a region, no matter how distressed, in a direct and privileged relationship with state resources and the bond markets. In the place of a REDC, WNY was left the newly formed Western New York Economic Development Corporation (WNYEDC). The only ostensibly regional public authority in New York, WNYEDC was maintained as a wholly owned subsidiary of the powerful statewide UDC. Although WNYEDC had some of the characteristics of the regional political economic process suggested in the REDC model, it had been created more for internal political reasons than as an agency of planning reform. Therefore, as a subsidiary of the UDC, WNYEDC was effectively a branch office of big government, rather than the bastion of regional planning independence we had suggested (Perry et al., 1985).

Even so, over the years WNYEDC has been the only agency actually engaged in the service and production of the economy as a region and has emerged as a center of communication and coordination – working to define political-economic relations between labor, capital, and the state in ways that are responsive to, but decidedly independent of, the proprietary relations of a particular firm or the politics of a particular jurisdiction. The authority's privileged, albeit dependent, subsidiary status within UDC has produced almost a decade of record receipts in terms of the traditional measures of jobs (90,000) and state loans, grants, and incentives (tens of millions of dollars annually) (Madore, 1994); the authority has also been able to marshal resources and staff to facilitate not plans but new networks/relations (or regions) of industry – a spatial discourse (in the most pragmatic sense) among producers, suppliers, labor, research, training, and education in such activities as food processing (WNYEDC, 1994), medical equipment (Liberante, 1994; WNYEDC, 1994), automobiles (Luria, 1992; WNYEDC, 1992), and wood products (WNYEDC, 1990).[16] "The goal," suggests WNYEDC President Judith Kossy (personal communication, August 24, 1994) "is to nurture and integrate these factors into new sectors [i.e., regions] of production." In a region where jobs and productivity have declined, the goal has been first and foremost to rebuild regional capacity. Therefore, the objective of the agency has been to establish/reestablish the *relations*, not only the product lines, of the actors in a particular economic activity. "Once the region becomes aware of the importance of the industry (as a geo-economic sector), we can help companies here become aware of each other with regard to product development, sales and research and development," said one official of the authority (Liberante, 1994).[17] From the work station to the classroom, to the investment bank, to the suppliers and retailers – the goal of the agency is to produce the recursive space, once more, of a *region* of economic activity. This region or space of material production is ultimately grounded in WNY – from down on the factory floor on up to the level of a new sector of production.[18] In this sense the agency, on a daily basis, embodies the very regional contradictions it seeks to confront; the relations of power and the issues of redefinition of the space(s) of dependency in the region.

Ironically what serves the WNYEDC well in this regard is its undemocratic independence from subregional electoral or local oversight. Its political independence from local control and its fiscal independence through its own state lines of finance serve to provide the region with a representative spatial practice.

Conclusion

The thread that winds its way through this chapter is that if we think of planning spatially, then planning is best practiced as making space. In this chapter I have attempted to provide a framework for such an analysis. I have tried to illustrate the spatiality of planning historically, and I have concluded with a brief discussion of some current examples of how to apply this approach to the conditions and conflicting forces of the planning context.

Instead of thinking of planning as a scopic practice of one or another certain science or knowledge of the urban (one tall building or another), it is far better to consider planning as a spatial, strategic discourse capable of representing its practice(s) or different discourses, like the city, as coming from different perspectives related to different scales of the urban. Applying such a notion of spatiality to the way we think about planning helps, I have suggested, situate planning as a mode of thought – as a spatial practice characterized neither by the "grand view" of a fixed or paradigmatic pinnacle nor the immediate fluidity of everyday life. The spatial practice of planning is the gerundic making of space – traveling the dialectic distance between abstract and concrete space. The spaces of home making and regionalism are not presented as the answer to what planning should be but as examples of what planning is.

ACKNOWLEDGMENTS

This chapter benefits greatly from the intellectual contributions found in the work of Robert Beauregard, Derek Gregory, and Neil Smith. However, my current interest in the spatiality of planning began, as does this chapter, with Michel de Certeau, Michel Foucault, and Henri Lefebvre. The critical and substantive support of Gilbert Chin and especially Helen Liggett has been very important, as was the institutional support I received while visiting Cleveland State University as the Albert A. Levin Chair of Urban Studies and Public Service.

NOTES

1   See, among others, Brooks (1990), Lucy (1994), and Levy (1992), who would all profess the need to establish some common core for planning.
2   There is a rich transdisciplinary literature on *la ville spontanée*. Recently much has been made of the work of Charles Baudelaire, especially the essays in the 1964 *The Painter of Modern Life and Other Essays*. Walter Benjamin has also studied the flaneur and the city – encouraging a whole range of scholars on the lived city – the city of everyday life (de Certeau, 1984) or the city as a labyrinth (Wilson, 1991).

    All of this leads to a similarly oriented literature in the social sciences on "politics at the street level" and the "figured/disfigured city." See also the work found in a collection of essays organized by Margaret Rosler (1991).
3   Lucy suggests that rather than carving planning up into particularly circumscribed professional and intellectual domains, that planning can actually be represented in the opposite way: in a "more expansive view" of the field. This expansiveness can only occur, Lucy suggests, if planning has a central principle from which to guide it. This principle for Lucy (1994) is "that healthy places nurture healthy people, and that public policies should aim at sustaining both healthy people and healthy places, not one or the other" (p. 305). In this way Lucy returns us to the metaphor of health – a broader more expansive version of the original reform goal of healthy people and places that first blended social reformers and engineers – or political change and technology in the planning of the chaotic political, economic, and social environment of the early industrial city.
4   The literature on planning may not have a collective identity but does seem to share a growing collective sense of what Brooks calls malaise over its identity, purpose, and legitimacy. See, among others, Peter Ambrose (1986), Thomas and Healey (1991), Boyer (1983), Perry (1994), Reade (1987), Altshuler (1965), Wildavsky (1973), Lucy (1994), and Levy (1992).

5 See Friedmann (1987) and Beauregard (1990) for a discussion of the morality of planning – its goals of social justice and redistribution and the fact that this morality should be grounded in an agreeable practice of intervention.

6 This is an important caveat because it allows for a different notion of how we (spatially) think about planning. To invoke the notion of the "production of space," writes Neil Smith (1992), is "to problematize the universal assumption of absolute space... also [rendering] problematic the whole range of spatial metaphors grounded in the assumption of absolute space" (p. 64).

7 Here Fainstein uses the notion of entrepreneurship developed by Peter Eisinger (1988).

8 See the collection of essays in Judd and Parkinson (1990). Also see the myriad reports and studies put out by the Council on Urban Economic Development, including CUED's journal, *Economic Development Commentary*, the *Economic Development Quarterly*, and the new studies of public and private not-for-profits and foundations put out by the Frey Foundation.

9 More than one half of the almost 30,000 members of the American Planning Association are not employed in the public sector, and this number is growing.

10 For a discussion of the notion of travel as an intellectual activity – one of theory and practice, see Edward Said's (1984) essay "Traveling Theory," pp. 226–247 in his collection *The World, the Text and the Critic*, and the wonderful discussion of the topic in the first chapter of Derek Gregory's (1994) book, especially pp. 9–14.

11 These other approaches to planning being examples of other visions or centers of what Foucault (1980) calls knowledge/power.

12 See Immanuel Wallerstein (1991) for a discussion of this notion of unthinking as compared to rethinking.

13 Wildavsky (1973) suggested that such an exercise was really one of "faith" rather than rationality, whereas Friedmann (1987) and Beauregard (1990) argue for planning as a responsive moral force and Brooks (1990) suggests a combination of political pragmatism and technology. Meck (1990) argues for an end to utopian comprehensiveness and a new hard-boiled pragmatism that comes from serving the interests at hand and therefore being "inclusive."

14 See Derek Gregory (1994, p. 9) for a wonderful introduction to contemporary spatial theory; also see James Clifford (1986, p. 22).

15 This section of the chapter is derived from a report on this project delivered in the form of a seminar conducted by Jacqueline Leavitt at SUNY at Buffalo as part of the Clarkson Chair week seminar on planning, Spring 1991, and an interview with Leavitt conducted on August 23, 1994.

16 It is impossible in the space here to describe, in any detail, the actual examples of this process including a new Medical Products Network of producers and suppliers, an automobile forum that links Detroit with producers and suppliers in a discourse on auto parts production activity in WNY, and an industrial effectiveness program that takes government and basic research to the site of production in new models and relationships of government, industry and university research. Further, WNYEDC is serving as a new space for coordinating overall planning activities for the regional and state planning agencies, as well as serving as the linkage between various sites of training and education and labor and industrial sector needs in a variety of areas.

17 Liberante, Carrie (1994, July 16). NY growth industry: Medical projects. *The Buffalo News*, pp. B1–B9. Reprinted with permission.

18 An example is the emergence of the Center for Industrial Effectiveness at SUNY, Buffalo, where research and expertise are actually taken to the factory floor in an attempt to include management, workers, and new research on efficiencies of production in sites of economic production.

REFERENCES

Altshuler, A. A. (1965). *The city planning process: A political analysis*. Ithaca, NY: Cornell University Press.

Ambrose, P. (1986). *Whatever happened to planning?* London: Methuen.

Barnett, J. (1986). *The elusive city: Five centuries of design, ambition and miscalculation.* New York: Harper & Row.

Baudelaire, C. (1964). *The painter of modern life and other essays*. New York: Da Capo Press.

Bluestone, B., and Harrison, B. (1982). *The deindustrialization of America: Plant closing, community abandonment, and the dismantling of basic industries*. New York: Basic Books.

Beard, C. (1926). Some aspects of regional planning. *American Political Science Review 20*, 273–283.

Beauregard, R. A. (1989). Between modernity and postmodernity: The ambiguous position of U.S. planning. *Society and Space, 7*, 381–395. [ch. 6 above]

Beauregard, R. A. (1990). Bringing the city back in. *Journal of the American Planning Association, 56*(2), 210–215.

Boyer, M. C. (1983). *Dreaming the rational city: The myth of American city planning.* Cambridge: MIT Press.

Boyer, M. C. (1995). The great frame-up: Fantastic appearances in contemporary spatial politics. In H. Liggett and D. C. Perry (eds.), *Spatial practices: New theories of social process* (pp. 81–109). Thousand Oaks, CA: Sage.

Brooks, M. P. (1990). The city may be back in, but where is the planner? *Journal of the American Planning Association, 56*(2), 218–220.

Casella, S. (1993). A quantum response to non-Euclidian planning. *Journal of the American Planning Association, 59*(4), 485.

Castagnoli, F. (1971). *Orthogonal town-planning in antiquity*. Cambridge: MIT Press.

Castells, M. (1976). The wild city. *Kapitalistate, 4–5*, 2–30.

Clifford, J. (1986). Introduction: Partial truths. In J. Clifford and G. Marcus (eds.), *Writing culture: The poetics and politics of ethnography* (pp. 1–26). Berkeley: University of California Press.

Davis, M. (1992). *The city of quartz*. New York: Vintage.

Dear, M., and Scott, A. J. (1981). *Urbanization and urban planning in capitalist society.* London: Methuen.

de Certeau, M. (1984). *The practice of everyday life* (S. Rendall, trans.). Berkeley: University of California Press.

Eisinger, P. (1988). *The rise of the entrepreneurial state*. Madison: University of Wisconsin Press.

Fainstein, S. S. (1991). Promoting economic development: Urban planning in the United States and Great Britain. *Journal of the American Planning Association, 57*(1), 22–33.

Fairfield, J. D. (1993). *The mysteries of the great city: The politics of urban design, 1877–1937*. Columbus: Ohio State University Press.

Felbinger, C. (1995). Conditions of confusion and conflict: Rethinking the infrastructure–economic development linkage. In D. C. Perry (ed.), *Building the public city: The politics, governance and finance of public infrastructure* (pp. 103–137). Thousand Oaks, CA: Sage.

Foglesong, R. E. (1990). Planning for social democracy. *Journal of the American Planning Association, 56*(2), 215–216.

Foucault, M. (1980). *Power/knowledge: Selected interviews and other writings 1972–1977* (C. Gordon, trans.). New York: Pantheon.

Foucault, M., and Deleuze, G. (1977). Intellectuals and power. In D. F. Bouchard (ed.), *Language, counter-memory, practice: Selected essays and interviews* (pp. 205–217). Ithaca, NY: Cornell University Press.

Friedmann, J. (1987). *Planning in the public domain*. Princeton, NJ: Princeton University Press.

Friedmann, J. (1993). Toward a non-Euclidian mode of planning. *The Journal of the American Planning Association, 59*(4), 482–485. [ch. 3 above]

Gregory, D. (1994). *Geographical imaginations*. [Oxford]: Basil Blackwell.

Grossberg, L. (1993). Cultural studies and/in new worlds. *Cultural Studies in Mass Communication, 10*, 1–22.

Howe, F. (1969). *The modern city and its problems*. College Park, MD: McGrath. (Original work published 1926.)

Judd, D., and Parkinson, M. (eds.). (1990). Leadership and urban regeneration. *Urban Affairs Annual Reviews, 37*.

Kostof, S. (1991). *The city shaped: Urban patterns and meanings through history*. Boston: Little, Brown.

Kraushaar, R., and Perry, D. (1990). Buffalo, New York: Region of no illusions. In R. D. Bingham & R. W. Eberts (eds.), *Economic restructuring of the American Midwest*. Norwell, MA: Kluwer Academic.

Leavitt, J. (1992). Women made fire: Public housing criticism in Los Angeles. *Frontiers, 13*(2), 109–130.

Leavitt, J. (1993). Shifting loads: From hand power to machine power to economic power. *Intersight, 2*, 53–57.

Leavitt, J., and Saegert, S. (1988). The community-household: Responding to housing abandonment in New York City. *Journal of the American Planning Association, 55*, 489–500.

Leavitt, J., and Saegert, S. (1989). *From abandonment to hope: The making of community-households in Harlem*. New York: Columbia University Press.

Lefebvre, H. (1970). *La Révolution urbaine*. Paris: Gallimand.

Lefebvre, H. (1991). *The production of space*. Oxford, UK: Basil Blackwell.

Levy, J. M. (1992). What has happened to planning? *Journal of the American Planning Association, 59*(1), 81–84.

Liberante, C. A. (1994, August 21.) WNY growth industry: Medical products. *Buffalo News*, pp. B1, B19.

Lucy, W. H. (1994). If planning includes too much, maybe it should include more. *Journal of the American Planning Association, 60*(3), 305–318.

Luria, D. (1992). *Auto forum*. Buffalo, NY: WNYEDC.

Madore, J. T. (1994, July 16). WNY gets record economic aid from state. *Buffalo News*, pp. B1, B9.

McLean, B., and Perry, D. C. (1994). *The splintering metropolis: New divisions of gender, race and economics in the northeastern production cities* (Policy Working Paper Series). Buffalo: State University of New York at Buffalo.

Meck, S. (1990). From high-minded reformism to hard-boiled pragmatism: American city planning faces the next century. *The Planner, 76*(6), 11–15.

Perry, D. C. (1987). The politics of dependency in deindustrializing America: The case of Buffalo, New York. In J. Feagin and M. Peter (eds.), *The capitalist city: Global restructuring and community politics* (pp. 113–137). Oxford, UK: Basil Blackwell.

Perry, D. C. (1994). Planning and the city: The turbulent practice. *Planning Theory, 10/11*, 23–42.

Perry, D. C., Kraushaar, R., Lines, J., and Parker, E. (1985). *Ending regional economic dependency: Economic development policy for distressed regions* (Studies in Planning and Design). Buffalo: Center for Regional Studies at State University of New York, Buffalo.

Peterson, P. E. (1981). *City limits*. Chicago: University of Chicago Press.

Reade, E. (1987). *British town and country planning*. Philadelphia: Open University Press.

Regional Plan Association (RPA) (1927). *Major economic factors in metropolitan growth and arrangement*. New York: Regional Plan of New York.

Relph, E. (1987). *The modern urban landscape*. Baltimore: The Johns Hopkins University Press.

Rosler, M. (1991). *If you lived here: The city in art, theory and social activism*. Seattle, WA: Bay Press.

Said, E. (1984). *The world, the text and the critic*. Cambridge, MA: Harvard University Press.

Schön, D. A. (1983). *The reflective practitioner: How professionals think in action*. New York: Basic Books.

Smith, M. P., and Feagin, J. R. (1987). *The capitalist city: Global restructuring and community politics*. Oxford, UK: Basil Blackwell.

Smith, N. (1992). Contours of a spatialized politics: Homeless vehicles and the production of geographical space. *Social Text, 33*, 55–81.

Stanback, T., and Noyelle, T. (1982). *Cities in transition*. Totowa, NJ: Allanheld, Osmun.

Thomas, H., and Healey, P. (eds.). (1991). *Dilemmas of planning practice: Ethics, legitimacy and the validation of knowledge*. Aldershot, UK: Avebury Technical.

Thrift, N. (1993). An urban impasse? *Theory, Culture and Society, 10*, 229–238.

Wallerstein, I. (1991). *Unthinking social science: The limits of nineteenth-century paradigms*. Cambridge: Polity.

Warner, S. B. (1974). *The private city: Philadelphia in three periods of its growth*. Philadelphia: University of Pennsylvania Press.

Wildavsky, A. (1973). If planning is everything, maybe it's nothing. *Policy Sciences, 4*, 127–153.

Wilson, E. (1991). *The sphinx in the city: Urban life, the control of disorder, and women*. London: Virago.

WNYEDC (1990). *Year-end report, 1989–1990*. Buffalo, NY: Author.

WNYEDC (1992). *Year-end report, 1991–1992*. Buffalo, NY: Author.

WNYEDC (1994). *Year-end report, 1993–1994*. Buffalo, NY: Author.

This article, written in 1995, makes reference to the World Trade Center and its once-popular observation desk. While the destruction of the WTC towers changes forever the meaning of such references, the conclusions drawn from that perspective, 110 floors up, remain relevant – at once reflecting the limits and opportunities of a scopic planning and the power and, now more than ever, the fragility of the built city. Therefore I have chosen to retain the references to the WTC that appeared in the original version of this chapter.

Part III

Planning Types

Introduction

We begin with a review essay by Susan Fainstein on "New Directions in Planning Theory." She examines the broader political context of three important movements in contemporary planning: the communicative model, the new urbanism, and the just city. All three offer alternatives to the existing mode of urban development, be it expert-based top-down planning, low-density market-driven sprawl, or the persistent inequality of capitalist urban development. Each represents an optimistic reassertion of social reform within planning theory, but ultimately Fainstein defends the just-city model as the best approach to create an effective political economic agenda for planning practice. By contrast, both communicative action and new urbanism suffer from an inability to adequately confront the underlying structural obstacles posed by capitalism and its political institutions. In the end, facilitating dialogue and promoting good design are significant but incomplete steps toward planning a just, sustainable, pluralistic city.

Underlying her argument is the assumption that planning theorists have too often worked in a political vacuum, assuming too much autonomy of planners to choose the best concept based on its intrinsic merits (Fainstein and Fainstein 1971, 1996). By linking the question of how best to plan with the question of what gives planners the power and legitimacy in society to intervene, she positions planners as part of the larger governmental bureaucracy and state power, rather than as independent, technocratic professionals directly serving the public interest. This perspective leads her to reassert the primacy of the progressive, political economic model.

The remaining essays in this section take a more detailed look at each of the dominant approaches to planning (including comprehensive, strategic, incremental, advocacy, equity, and communicative planning). To differentiate these various approaches, it is useful to begin with comprehensive planning (the rational, synoptic planning model based on setting far-reaching goals and objectives), and then view the alternative approaches as divergent responses to comprehensiveness. Incrementalism challenges the viability of large-scale, complex decision making and offers the much more modest approach of comparisons of discrete policy changes at the margins. Advocacy planning questions the existence of a single, consensual public interest and instead calls for the promotion of the particular interests of the disadvantaged. Strategic planning rejects trying to serve overly broad, vague social goals, instead proposing a targeted form of planning that takes constraints into account. Equity planning challenges the ability of traditional planning to get at the roots of poverty and inequality and makes redistribution its principal goal. Both incremental and strategic planning share a frustration with the unwieldiness and inefficiency of comprehensive planning, while both advocacy and equity planning presume that comprehensive planning does not go far enough to deal with the unfairness of cities. Finally, communicative action challenges comprehensive planning's preoccupation with the plan as expert document and instead sees planning as facilitating a public dialogue to define community issues and priorities.

An early and highly influential attack on the foundations of comprehensive planning was Charles Lindblom's 1959 article, "The Science of Muddling Through."[1] If comprehensive planning was to be the unifying paradigm for the emerging postwar field of planning, this consensus did not last long. Lindblom argued that the comprehensive model required a level of data and analytical complexity that was simply beyond the grasp and ability of planners. In fact, the actual practice of planners is rarely comprehensive; by default, planners fall back on a more modest, incremental approach. Lindblom argues that planners should abandon the comprehensive model and explicitly define their efforts as incrementalism, relying on "successive limited comparisons" to achieve realistic, short-term goals.

Incremental planning, however, has been criticized for being too timid and conservative, both reinforcing the status quo and thereby neglecting the need for transformative social change. It also shares the shortcoming of inductive thinking by assuming that short-term stimulus and response can replace the need for vision and theory. Nevertheless, the incrementalist stance has been a powerful and enduring counterargument to traditional master planning, and its ascendance reflects a fundamental transformation in planning thought. Where once it was grounded in a comprehensive vision of urban design and general forecasting models, planning is increasingly oriented to pragmatic politics and the marginal analysis of economic policy.

If incremental planning challenged comprehensive planning's reliance on massive information and complex analysis to serve the public interest, advocacy planning attacked the fundamental notion of a single, common "public interest." Paul Davidoff, in his classic and still definitive 1965 article, "Advocacy and Pluralism in Planning," argues that unitary planning perpetuates a monopoly over planning power and discourages participation. If planning is to be inclusive, it must not pretend that a single agency can represent the interests of a divergent and conflicted society. Instead, planning should promote equitable pluralism by advocating the interests of the disenfranchised. Traditional planning creates at least two barriers to effective pluralism. First, planning commissions are undemocratic and poorly suited to represent the competing interests of a pluralist society. Second, traditional city planning too narrowly addresses issues of physical planning, separating the physical from the social and thereby neglecting social conflict and inequality in the city. In this light, Davidoff's call for a move from land use to social-economic planning reflects a more general effort to shift the identity of the planner from the objective technocrat of the conservative 1950s to the engaged, social advocate of the contentious 1960s.

(Paradoxically, although teachers of planning theory lament that few actually practice Davidoff's ideas, his article remains one of the most frequently read essays in all
of planning.)

Later many planners would turn to strategic planning as a new model, which they
borrowed from the corporate and military worlds. Its appeal to planners lay in its
streamlined, efficient focus on specific tasks, rather than the often vague and broad
goals of comprehensive planning. It represented a way to privatize the style of public
planning while retaining public control. Yet it was also in part an abandonment
of the laudable comprehensive planning goal of serving a broad public interest
(Kaufman and Jacobs 1987; Swanstrom 1987).

Yet, the post-Great Society era was not simply a retreat to market-oriented
planning. A second group put forth the alternative of equity planning, which sought
to return planning to a more progressive path of both promoting the larger public
interest and directly addressing urban inequalities. Equity planning followed the
tradition of Davidoff's advocacy planning in both seeing the roots of urban development in socio-economic disparity in the nature of urban development and arguing
that planners have an explicit responsibility to help the disadvantaged. Equity
planning can be seen as a less combative form of advocacy planning: it is a "kinder
and gentler" form of advocacy planning consonant with the conciliatory, pragmatic
1980s, rather than the activist, sometimes revolutionary-minded 1960s. Equity
planning thus asserts a greater faith in finding a common ground of public interest
and working within the system of public-sector planning.

Norman Krumholz, the name most associated with equity planning, examines the
possibility of more progressive approaches to urban revitalization. He reflects on the
shortcomings of urban redevelopment strategies during the past several decades,
which have focused too much on downtown areas at the expense of the poor in
surrounding neighborhoods and which often lacked both a clear purpose and an
understanding of what worked and what did not. Krumholz sees these disparities in
his own Cleveland, whose poor continue to suffer disproportionately even in the
wake of new stadiums, museums, and other high-profile downtown development
projects. (Krumholz himself was planning director during the earlier era of deindustrialization in Cleveland – a period in which he courageously promoted equity
planning despite conventional wisdom maintaining that only thriving cities such
as San Francisco or Boston could "afford" social redistribution programs such as
inclusionary zoning and development linkages.)

Krumholz recognizes that progressive policies face opposition from growth coalition boosters who mouth free market rhetoric and resist funding for redistributional
purposes. Surveying equity-minded economic development efforts in various American cities, Krumholz nevertheless concludes that progressive local economic development is possible. Importantly, cities should emphasize public investment, build
upon existing strengths, and directly address redistributive issues. To push towards
equity planning, Krumholz encourages planning students and practitioners to
"broaden their traditional areas of concern beyond land use, zoning, and urban
design, and add a specific concern for the low-and moderate-income people of their
cities" (p. 234).

The last article in this section is by Patsy Healey, a leading proponent of communicative action-based planning (along with John Forester, Judith Innes, and others).
Communicative action emphasizes how people construct planning problems and

priorities through discussion, debate, and what Healey calls "inclusionary argumentation." Inspired by Habermas's intersubjective reasoning, communicative planners facilitate social learning and sorting through arguments within a democratic process. For Healey, the old style of planning based on instrumental rationality, material allocation, and a single omniscient perspective is out of date. The challenge facing planning is to articulate a common understanding of social problems in a world of multiple, divergent cultures, and communicative action is a way to make planning again more relevant.

After outlining this relatively recent planning theory, Healey examines how it can be used for spatial development strategies. The key is understanding how planning is "locally contingent": how the context of a community's politics and social circumstances shape policy. And these circumstances are becoming more complex, as polynuclear geographies and polymorphous communities replace old notions of central cities and homogenous populations. Despite the hypermobility of capital and information, space still matters: economic activities ultimately occur in a place, and communities are in competition with each other for highly skilled labor and growing companies. Healey delineates two types of community: one spatially based, and another, broader, stakes-based community. Understanding this plurality of interests means being open to a wider and changing range of stakeholders, as well as moving from distributive justice to inclusive diversity (a theme found in both Iris Marion Young's and June Manning Thomas's essays later in this volume, Chapters 18 and 19). Strategic spatial planning then becomes "a process of facilitating community collaboration in the construction of strategic discourse, in strategic consensus-building" (p. 251).

NOTE

1   Though Lindblom later revisited this issue in his 1979 article, "Still Muddling, not yet Through" (*Public Administration Review*, 39, pp. 517–26), the newer article was overly complex and itself muddled. The original remains the clearest statement of the argument.

REFERENCES

Fainstein, Susan S. and Norman I. Fainstein. 1971. City Planning and Political Values. *Urban Affairs Quarterly*, 6 (March): 341–62.

Fainstein, Susan S. and Norman I. Fainstein. 1996. City Planning and Political values: An Update View. In Scott Campbell and Susan S. Fainstein, eds, *Readings in Planning Theory*, Oxford: Blackwell, pp. 265–87.

Kaufman, Jerome L. and Harvey M. Jacobs. 1987. A Public Planning Perspective on Strategic Planning. *Journal of the American Planning Association*, 53: 23–33.

Swanstrom, Todd. 1987. The Limits of Strategic Planning for Cities. *Journal of Urban Affairs*, 9 (2): 139–57.

9

New Directions in Planning Theory

Susan S. Fainstein

The past decade has witnessed a reinvigoration of theoretical discussion within the discipline of planning. Inspired by postmodernist cultural critique and by the move among philosophers away from logical positivism toward a substantive concern with ethics and public policy, planning theorists have reframed their debates over methods and programs to encompass issues of discourse and inclusiveness. In the 1970s and 1980s, proponents of positivist scientific analysis battled advocates of materialist political economy. Although the divide between positivists and their opponents persists, other issues have come to define the leading edge of planning theory. Contemporary disagreements concern the usefulness of Habermasian communicative rationality, the effect of physical design on social outcomes (an old debate resurfaced), and the potential for stretching a postmarxist political economy approach to encompass a more complex view of social structure and social benefits than was envisioned by materialist analysis. Although discussions of communicative theory and political economy have transpired within academic journals and books,[1] the body of planning thought concerned with physical design has grabbed public notice and received considerable attention within popular media.[2] Building on widespread dissatisfaction with the anonymity and sprawl of contemporary urban growth, the "new urbanism" espouses an outcome-based view of planning based on a vision of a compact, heterogeneous city.

In this article, I discuss and critique contemporary planning theory in terms of its usefulness in addressing what I believe to be its defining question: What is the possibility of consciously achieving widespread improvement in the quality of human life within the context of a global capitalist political economy? I examine the three approaches referred to earlier under the rubrics of (1) the communicative model, (2) the new urbanism, and (3) the just city. In my conclusion, I defend the

Reprinted with permission from *Urban Affairs Review*, 35 (4) (March 2000): 451–78.

continued use of the just-city model and a modified form of the political economy mode of analysis that underlies it.

The first type, sometimes called the collaborative model, emphasizes the planner's role in mediating among "stakeholders" within the planning situation; the second, frequently labeled neotraditionalism, paints a physical picture of a desirable city to be obtained through planning; and the third, which derives from the political economy tradition, although also outcome oriented, is more abstract than the new urbanism, presenting a model of spatial relations based on equity. This typology of planning theories is not exhaustive – there remain defenders of the traditionally dominant paradigm of the rational model, as well as incrementalists who base their prescriptions on neoclassical economics, and Corbusian modernists, who still promote formalist physical solutions to urban decay. Nor are the types wholly mutually exclusive – each contains some elements of the others, and some theorists cannot be fit easily into one of the types. Nevertheless, each type can claim highly committed proponents, and each points to a distinctive path for both planning thought and planning practice.

Differences among the types reflect the enduring tension within planning thought between a focus on the planning process and an emphasis on desirable outcomes. In the recent past, neither tendency has fully dominated because theoretical orientations toward process and outcome have respectively affected different aspects of practice. Thus the concept of the rational model represented an approach based wholly on process, with little regard either to political conflict or to the specific character of the terrain on which it was working. As Beauregard (1987, p. 367) put it, "In its fullest development, the Rational Model had neither subject nor object. It ignored the nature of the agents who carried out planning and was indifferent to the object of their efforts [i.e., the built environment]." This model has provided the metatheory for planning activity in the decades since the 1960s, incorporating the faith in scientific method that swept through the social sciences during the cold war period. Within planning practice, it has primarily been used for forecasting impacts and for program evaluation. At the same time, however, as the rational model held sway among theorists, planning practitioners engaged in the development of zoning and environmental regulations, upholding an atheoretical, physical outcome-oriented vision of what Jacobs (1961, pp. 22–25) sarcastically termed the "radiant garden city."[3] Outcome-oriented physical planning has left its mark on metropolitan areas in the form of urban renewal, low-density development, and spatial and functional segregation.

Although the rational model and the physical master plan were the dominant, late twentieth-century modes of planning practice throughout the world, they did not escape a powerful critique. Their opponents, who decried the distributional consequences of these approaches, generally adopted a political economic analysis. From this standpoint, critics persistently inquired into who benefited from planning efforts and associated themselves with social movements seeking to block displacement of low-income urban inhabitants, build affordable housing, halt the movement of capital out of distressed cities, and ameliorate racial, ethnic, and gender disadvantage.

The recent theoretical moves involved in the typology sketched earlier represent a reaction both to previously dominant modes of thought and also to events "on the ground." Thus the communicative model responds to the imposition of top-down planning by experts deploying an Enlightenment discourse that posits a unitary public interest to be achieved through application of the rational model, the new urbanism is a backlash to market-driven development that destroys the spatial basis for community, and the just-city formulation reacts to the social and spatial inequality engendered by capitalism. In common with earlier critics of the rational model (see Fainstein and Fainstein 1979), theorists within all three schools doubt the applicability of the scientific method to urban questions; none of the three approaches relies on scientific justification as the rationale for its vision. Whatever their differences, they are all three postpositivist.

The Communicative Model

The communicative model draws on two philosophical approaches – American pragmatism as developed in the thought of John Dewey and Richard Rorty and the theory of communicative rationality as worked out by Jürgen Habermas.[4] The two strands differ somewhat in their methodologies. Neopragmatism tends toward empiricism, with its exemplars searching for instances of best practices within planning from which generalizations can be drawn. Thus

> The big question for the pragmatic analysts is how practitioners construct the free spaces in which democratic planning can be institutionalized. The idea... is to uncover examples of planning that are both competent and democratic, and then to explore who the practitioners were who did it, what actions they took to make it happen, and what sorts of institutional conditions helped or hindered their efforts.
>
> (Hoch 1996, p. 42)

Communicative rationality starts instead with an abstract proposition. According to Healey (1996, p. 239),

> A communicative conception of rationality... replaces[s] that of the self-conscious autonomous subject using principles of logic and scientifically formulated empirical knowledge to guide actions. This new conception of reasoning is arrived at by an intersubjective effort at mutual understanding. This refocuses the practices of planning to enable purposes to be communicatively discovered.

Pragmatism and communicative rationality emerge from different philosophical traditions. Whereas Dewey's work comes out of British philosophical realism and empiricism, Habermas's original approach traces back to Hegelian idealism and Marxist critical analysis and then later to Wittgenstein's scrutiny of language. Pragmatism and communicative rationality, however, converge when used to provide a guide for action to planners. This guide is the antithesis of Daniel Burnham's admonition to "make no small plans," an ambition that was once seen to embody the noblest aims of planning. Within communicative theory, the planner's primary function is to listen to people's stories and assist in forging a consensus among differing viewpoints. Rather than providing technocratic leadership, the planner is an experiential learner, at most providing information to participants but primarily being sensitive to points of convergence. Leadership consists not in bringing stakeholders around to a particular planning content but in getting people to agree and in ensuring that whatever the position of participants within the social-economic hierarchy, no group's interest will dominate.

Judith Innes (1998, p. 52) commented that "what planners do most of the time is talk and interact" and that "this 'talk' is a form of practical, communicative action." Innes (1995, p. 183) contended that the communicative model, which establishes the planner as negotiator and intermediary among stakeholders, has become so widely accepted as to form "planning theory's emerging paradigm."[5] Healey (1997, p. 29) summarized this theoretical turn as comprising the following emphases:

> (1) all forms of knowledge are socially constructed; (2) knowledge and reasoning may take many different forms, including storytelling and subjective statements; (3) individuals develop their views through social interaction; (4) people have diverse interests and expectations and these are social and symbolic as well as material; (5) public policy needs to draw upon and make widely available a broad range of knowledge and reasoning drawn from different sources.

Theoretical and practical deficiencies

In its effort to save planning from elitist tendencies, communicative planning theory runs into difficulties. The communicative model should not be faulted for its ideals of openness and diversity. Rather, its vulnerability lies in a tendency to substitute moral exhortation for analysis. Although their roots, via Habermas, are in critical theory, once the communicative theorists move away from critique and present a manual for action, their thought loses its edge. Habermas posited the ideal speech situation as a criterion by which to register the distortion inherent in most interactions. As such, it supplies a vehicle for demystification. But when instead ideal speech becomes the objective of planning, the argument takes a moralistic tone, and its proponents seem to forget the economic and social forces that produce endemic social conflict and domination by the powerful. There is the assumption that if only people were reasonable, deep structural conflict would melt away. Although unquestionably many disagreements can be ameliorated through negotiation – the attainment of exactions or planning gain[6] from developers by community groups offers an example – persistent issues of displacement as a consequence of modernization and siting of unwanted facilities proximate to weak constituencies are less susceptible to resolution. Even when relatively powerless groups may prevail in individual instances – usually as a result of threat, not simply acknowledgment of their viewpoint within a planning negotiation – they still suffer from systemic bias and typically end up with meager, often symbolic benefits.[7]

The communicative theorists make the role of the planner the central element of discussion. Both the context in which planners work and the outcome of planning fade from view.[8] Unlike the rational modelers, the communicative theorists have found a subject, but like them, they lack an object. Whereas in legal theory the object of analysis is the relationship between the legal system and society and in medical theory the concern is with the human body, in communicative planning theory the spotlight is on the planner. Instead of asking what is to be done about cities and regions, communicative planners typically ask what planners should be doing, and the answer is that they should be good (i.e., tell the truth, not be pushy about their own judgments). Like the technocrats whom they criticize, they appear to believe that planners have a special claim on disinterested morality:

> Planners must routinely argue, practically and politically, about desirable and possible futures.... They may be sincere but mistrusted, rigorous but unappreciated, reassuring yet resented. Where they intend to help, planners may instead create dependency; and where they intend to express good faith, they may raise expectations unrealistically, with disastrous consequences.
>
> But these problems are hardly inevitable. When planners recognize the practical and communicative nature of their actions, they can devise strategies to avoid these problems and to improve their practice as well.   (Forester 1989, pp. 138–39)

The present trend among communicative planning theorists is to avoid broad examinations of the relationship between planning, politics, and urban development.[9] Much recent work in planning theory has been devoted to examining the meanings of planners' conversations with developers and city officials, deconstructing planning documents, and listening to planners' stories:

> The challenge we face, as planners and policy analysts more broadly, is...to listen carefully to practice stories [i.e., stories of planning in practice] and to understand who is attempting what, why, and how, in what situation, and what really matters in all that. That challenge is not just about words but about our cares and constraints, our real opportunities and our actions, our own practice, what we really can, and should, do now.   (Forester 1993, p. 202)

Katha Pollitt (1999, p. 35), bemoaning a tendency toward solipsism among feminist writers, commented that

> "The personal is political" did not mean that personal testimony, impressions and feelings are all you need to make a political argument. The important texts of feminism have, in fact, been rather un-self-revealing. Simone de Beauvoir spent more than 700 pages in "The Second Sex" analyzing women's position in society through every conceivable lens: anthropological, economic, historical, literary, psychoanalytic, biological, philosophical, legal – except that of her own life.[10]

Similarly, the concern of communicative planning theory, itself influenced by feminism, has become subjective interpretation rather than the identification of causes, constraints, and substantive outcomes (see Campbell and Fainstein 1996). In fact, the search for explanation either gets lost in the thicket of hermeneutics or dismissed as totalizing (Milroy 1991; Beauregard 1991). The assumption is that explanation is necessarily reductionist. Yet even if we accept the premise that the purpose of planning theory is simply to tell planners what they ought to be doing, such knowledge depends on an accurate appraisal of the situation in which planners find themselves. Explanatory theory allows the observer to identify the general characteristics of a situation, and these characteristics cannot be inferred simply through the examination of discourse (Yiftachel 2001). This is not to deny the usefulness of experiential learning or of case analysis in contributing to understanding. But it does mean transcending individual experience, placing cases in a broad context, making comparisons, and not limiting analysis to exegesis.

In addition to questions of method, communicative theory runs into the fundamental issues of pluralist theory. Communicative theorists avoid dealing with the classic topic of what to do when open processes produce unjust results.[11] They also do not consider the possibility that paternalism and bureaucratic modes of decision making may produce desirable outcomes. Various studies of the European welfare states and of the New Deal in the United States have concluded that the principal measures for ensuring health and security were generated by state officials with little reference to interested publics (see Flora and Heidenheimer 1981; Mencher 1967; Skocpol 1985). Even though these measures would not have been approved without supportive constituencies and the threat of oppositional social movements, the actual formulation of policy (i.e., the planning of it) was highly insulated from stakeholder input.

Healey (1997) used the term *collaborative planning* to describe the process by which participants arrive at an agreement on action that expresses their mutual interests. She argued against a structuralist or political economy approach by contending that people do not have fixed interests. In other words, a particular structural position (e.g., capitalist) does not automatically produce a particular policy position (e.g., deregulation).[12] Discussion can lead capitalists to understand how they could benefit financially from environmental regulation when they might reflexively have opposed any attempt to restrict their freedom to pollute. And indeed, the vulgar Marxist view that interests can be immediately inferred from relations to the means of production is indefensible. The marked differences between the attitudes of American and European business executives toward the interventionist state, whereby Europeans are much more accepting of state leadership, indicates the extent to which interpretations of interest by groups in similar structural positions can vary. Nevertheless, the different perceptions of interest held by those in different structural positions are not resolved simply through the exchange of ideas. If European and American business leaders have different perceptions of interest, ideas alone are not the cause. Rather, they exist in different historical contexts and different fields of power. Major changes in perceptions of interest require restructuration as a consequence of crisis or of a social movement, not simply verbal assent (Lukács 1971).

Even if perceptions of interest are biased or misdirected by distorted speech and even if structures are socially constructed, changing speech alone does not transform structures. An intervening stage of mobilization is required. Ideas can give rise to social movements that in turn change consciousness, ultimately resulting in the adoption of new public policy, but this is more than a matter of negotiation and consensus building among stakeholders.[13] In the instances of both environmentalism and neoliberalism, discontent among influential fractions of the population became a social force when mobilized by a set of ideas that seemed to define a reason for feelings of dissatisfaction. The aroused consciousness that puts ideas into practice involves leadership and the mobilization of power, not simply people reasoning together. Moreover, transformative social movements, whether conservative like neoliberalism or progressive like environmentalism, themselves contain distortions. Marx and Engels (1947), in their critique of the Hegelians, asserted that the world was changed through struggle, not the force of ideas. They did not mean, as they are often misinterpreted, that economic structures automatically determine outcomes and that human agency is helpless to affect them. But they did mean that words will not prevail if unsupported by a social force carrying with it a threat of disruption. To put this another way, the power of words depends on the power of the speakers. To quote Bent Flyvbjerg (1998, p. 234), "When we understand power we see that we cannot rely solely on democracy based on rationality to solve our problems."

The theoretical lacunae of communicative theory reveal themselves in practice. Scrutiny of efforts to base planning on dialogue reveals serious problems of implementation and the continued dominance of the already powerful. Perhaps the most interesting contemporary example of a conscious effort toward meaningful, inclusive, consensual planning has been in South Africa. There the transitional situation, after the elimination of apartheid and before the establishment of new local governments, presented a unique opportunity for developing policies outside normally constraining structures. Preexisting policies and institutions did not require typical deference, and huge policy areas were open to new determinations. Yet, as described by Mary Tomlinson (1998, pp. 144–45),

> The loudly acclaimed "consensus" [on housing policy] supposedly hammered out by the stakeholders in the National Housing Forum which should have been achieved by hard bargaining among the parties was, in fact, the result of fudging vital differences between them. Faced with a conflict of vision between those who favoured a market-oriented strategy led by the private sector, and those who preferred a more "people-centred" approach in which "communities" would be the central players – or at least retain a veto – the forum parties opted for both, despite their incompatibility. Thus all parties wanted immediate and visible delivery – but some also wanted "empowerment." So both were included, despite the fact that they would prove to be contradictory in practice.
>
> By the second year of implementation of the housing subsidy scheme the consensus hammered out at the National Housing Forum had not, as its architects hoped, succeeded in binding all key housing interests to the policy: some key political actors had not been party to its formulation – and therefore did not feel bound by it – while crucial private interests proved ready to abandon it if it conflicted with their interests, or if it did not seem to produce the rate of delivery that [they] had hoped to achieve.

A study of the implementation of the economic development plan for South Africa's Western Cape, which was also devised in a policy forum, comes to a strikingly similar conclusion:

> Amongst the public of Cape Town, the plan [produced by the Western Cape Economic Development Forum] is probably better known than any before it: it is frequently referred to, usually in a positive light. It remains, however, a paper plan and an abstract vision. On the ground large-scale private investors have continued to follow their own locational logic, and low-income housing has continued to spread in low-density fashion on the city edge, where cheaper land is available. Certain of the well located parcels of land earmarked by the plan for low-income housing were allocated to Olympic sports facilities or other upmarket developments, others still stand empty.
>
> (Watson 1998, p. 347)

Innes (1996) used the example of the New Jersey State Plan to demonstrate the efficacy of the communicative model. Here stakeholders from throughout the state participated in a series of meetings that produced a document targeting some areas for growth or redevelopment and others for conservation. Implementation depended on "cross acceptance," whereby localities, rather than being forced to conform to the statewide plan, would agree to conduct their planning in accordance with it in return for certain benefits.

Yet the same issues that cropped up in South Africa affected the implementation of the New Jersey State Plan. To start with, to win approval of the various participants in the planning process, the plan contained only weak requirements for the construction of affordable housing, suburban integration, and compact development, even though lack of housing for low-income residents, suburban exclusion of the poor and minorities, and lack of open space were identified as the principal problems that planning was supposed to overcome. Then, despite the moderate nature of the plan and the cross-acceptance process, its implementation has been half-hearted at best and often strongly resisted by local planning boards. The principal result of consensual planning in New Jersey has been the continuance of a system whereby the market allocates land uses.[14]

These examples point to one problem of communicative planning in practice – the gap between rhetoric and action. The problem is perhaps most severe in the United States, where historic antagonism to a powerful administrative state has always limited the possibility of implementing any plan, regardless of how formulated (see Foglesong 1986). In Europe, where power is more centralized, corporatist bargaining has been institutionalized, and locally based interest groups are less able to block state action and the devolution of planning power to stakeholders; hence their assent to a plan is more likely to produce tangible results. Even there, however, agreement by participants to a document does not necessarily mean that anything will happen.

A second practical problem of communicative planning is the lengthy time required for such participatory processes, leading to burnout among citizen participants and disillusion as nothing ever seems to get accomplished. Cynical South Africans referred to the various policy forums as "talking shops." A third issue arises from the difficulties involved in framing alternatives when planners desist from agenda setting. Thus, for example, in Minneapolis, Minnesota, the city established a neighborhood planning process whereby residents formulated five-year plans for their neighborhoods and were allocated fairly substantial sums of money to spend. Planners assigned to facilitate the process were committed to a nondirective role and therefore only proposed actions when asked. The result was that some neighborhoods reached creative solutions, especially when participants were middle-class professionals, but others floundered in attempting to rank priorities and to come up with specific projects, sometimes taking as many as three years to determine a vague and hard-to-implement plan (Fainstein and Hirst 1996).

Finally, there is a potential conflict between the aims of communicative planning and the outcomes of participatory planning processes if planning is conducted within narrow spatial boundaries. The familiar specter of NIMBYism (not in my backyard) raises its head whenever participation is restricted to a socially homogeneous area.[15] Communicative theorists are committed to equity and diversity, but there is little likelihood that such will be the outcome of stakeholder participation within relatively small municipalities. Organizing planning across a metropolitan area to encompass diversity of class, race, and ethnicity requires extending the process through multiple political jurisdictions to escape the homogeneity imposed by spatial segregation. The obstacles to involving citizens in metropolitan-wide planning, however, are enormous, and doing so means sacrificing the local familiarity that is the rationale for participatory neighborhood planning.

The failures of planning during the heyday of massive urban renewal programs substantiate many of the objections to top-down, expert-driven planning and make desirable the communicative turn in planning. Nevertheless, the cruelties of massive clearance programs were not simply the result of deference to expertise. In the United States, business and political interests, not experts, constituted the power base on which the urban renewal endeavor was mounted, and the experts directing the programs were almost all physical determinists drawn from the design and engineering professions rather than planners and housing analysts (Gans 1968, chap. 18). The federal government terminated the program precisely when reforms, instigated by mobilized community groups and in reaction to urban civil disorder, had made it more sensitive to affected communities and less profitable for developers; this turn of events illustrates how problematic any policy is that circumvents power relations. Moreover, the present generation of planners is more likely to be responsive to the needs of neighborhood residents and ordinary citizens.[16] To the extent that they are not, the difficulty can only be partially remedied by open processes. City building for the benefit of nonelite groups requires empowering those who are excluded not just from discussions but from structural positions that allow them genuine influence. Ability to participate is one resource in the struggle for power, but it must be bolstered by other resources, including money, access to expertise, effective organization, and media coverage. Communicative theorists probably would not deny the importance of these resources, but neither do their analyses dwell on them. This omission constitutes the fundamental weakness of the theory.

The New Urbanism

New urbanism refers to a design-oriented approach to planned urban development. Developed primarily by architects and journalists, it is perhaps more ideology than theory, and its message is carried not just by academics but by planning practitioners and a popular movement.[17] New urbanists have received considerable attention in the United States and, to a lesser extent, in Great Britain.[18] Their orientation resembles that of the early planning theorists – Ebenezer Howard, Frederic Law Olmsted, Patrick Geddes – in their aim of using spatial relations to create a close-knit social community that allows diverse elements to interact. The new urbanists call for an urban design that includes a variety of building types, mixed uses, intermingling of housing for different income groups, and a strong privileging of the "public realm." The basic unit of planning is the neighborhood, which is limited in physical size, has a well-defined edge, and has a focused center: "The daily needs of life are accessible within the five minute-walk" (Kunstler 1996, p. 117).

The new urbanism stresses the substance of plans rather than the method of achieving them. In practice, it has stimulated the creation of a number of new towns and neighborhoods, of which Seaside, in Florida, is the best known.[19] Fundamental to its development has been a critique of American suburbia:

In the postwar era, suburbia became the lifestyle of choice for most Americans.

While this new way of living had many advantages, it also fragmented our society – separating us from friends and relatives and breaking down the bonds of community that had served our nation so well in earlier times. . . .

The costs of suburban sprawl are all around us – they're visible in the creeping deterioration of once proud neighborhoods, the increasing alienation of large segments of society, a constantly rising crime rate and widespread environmental degradation.

(Katz 1994, p. ix)

In this analysis, suburbia is responsible for far more than traffic congestion on the freeway and aesthetically unappealing strip-mall development. It is also the producer of crime and anomie.[20]

In its easy elision of physical form with social conditions, the new urbanism displays little theoretical rigor. Unlike other trends in planning, however, it is noteworthy for the popular response it has achieved. Although its appeal results partly from widespread dissatisfaction with suburban development and nostalgia for traditional forms, it also stems from the strong advocacy of its supporters, who have joined together in the Congress for the New Urbanism (CNU). The new urbanists do not fear playing the role disdained by the communicative theorists – that of persuasive salespersons for a particular point of view and deployers of strategies aimed at co-opting people. Thus Andres Duany unabashedly declared,

Now, although it's important to be flexible, open to new ideas, it's also important, when you confront the world, to maintain principles that are inviolate – one thing you can learn from Le Corbusier is that to influence and persuade, you must be polemical. You can't convince people by equivocating, by saying "Well, on the one hand this, on the other that." You'll bore them, and they'll chew you up. As a polemicist, you have to clarify matters. . . . And you have to attack. Whenever I'm invited to speak to the Urban Land Institute [an organization of property developers], I try to destabilize them with my certainty that they are wrong.   ("Urban or suburban?" 1997, p. 48)

Duany did make a gesture toward participatory planning in his endorsement of citizen involvement in the *charette*, the lengthy design workshop that furnished the details of his developments. But one suspects that the purpose is as much co-optive as informative. When asked whether his use of neotraditional architectural styles was "like your use of language, a way of concealing what you're doing," he replied, "Yes, exactly." He commented that architects who insist on using a style without mass appeal, by which he meant high modernism, are "separating themselves from where the power really is, which is the ability of architecture to transform society, to be of genuine social benefit" ("Urban or suburban?" 1997, p. 60).

Thus Duany and his confederates in the CNU did not fear distorted speech, nor did they shrink from using democratic procedures in responding to the public's stylistic preferences as a screen to achieve their desired socio-spatial arrangements.

Critique

The new urbanism is vulnerable to the accusation that its proponents oversell their product, promoting an unrealistic environmental determinism that has threaded its way throughout the history of physical planning. Harvey (1997, p. 1) praised certain aspects of the new urbanism – its emphasis on public space, its consideration of the relationship between work and living, and its stance toward environmental quality. Nevertheless, his endorsement was mixed:

> But my real worry is that the movement repeats at a fundamental level the same fallacy of the architectural and planning styles it criticizes. Put simply, does it not perpetuate the idea that the shaping of spatial order is or can be the foundation for a new moral and aesthetic order?...The movement does not recognize that the fundamental diffi-culty with modernism was its persistent habit of privileging spatial forms over social processes.   (Harvey 1997, p. 2)

As a consequence of its spatial determinism, the new urbanism runs into certain dangers. One frequently made criticism is that it merely calls for a different form of suburbia rather than overcoming metropolitan social segregation. Duany responded to this accusation by arguing that because most Americans are going to live in suburbs, planners need to build better suburbs. Moreover, he contended that it is not his philosophy but, rather, political opposition and obsolete zoning ordinances that prevent him from working in inner cities ("Urban or suburban?" 1997). And indeed, the effort to overcome the environmentally destructive, wasteful form of American suburban development constitutes the most important contribution of the new urbanism to the commonweal.

The movement is less convincing in its approach to social injustice. Harvey (1997) feared that the new urbanism can commit the same errors as modernism – of assuming that changing people's physical environment will somehow take care of the social inequalities that warped their lives. To be sure, with its emphasis on community, it is unlikely to commit the principal sin of modernist redevelopment programs – destroying communities to put people in the orderly environments that were thought to enhance living conditions. The real problem replicates the one that defeated Ebenezer Howard's radical principles in the construction of garden cities. To achieve investor backing for his schemes, Howard was forced to trade away his aims of a socialist commonwealth and a city that accommodated all levels of society (Fishman 1977). The new urbanists must also rely on private developers to build and finance their visions; consequently, they are producing only slightly less exclusive suburbs than the ones they dislike. Although their creations will contain greater physical diversity than their predecessors, their social composition will not differ markedly.

Harvey (1997) also worried that the new urbanist emphasis on community disre-gards "the darker side" of communitarianism. He claimed that "'community' has ever been one of the key sites of social control and surveillance bordering on overt social repression. . . . As a consequence, community has often been a barrier to rather than facilitator of progressive social change" (p. 3). He was apprehensive that the enforced conformity of community blocks the creativity arising from diversity and conflict. He thus raised issues that have been major points of debate in discussions of institutionalized community participation among supporters of redistributive meas-ures (see Fainstein 1990): Advocates argue that community power raises the self-esteem of members, whereas opponents fear that it produces parochialism and failure to recognize broader class interests (Katznelson 1981; Piven 1970).

Two problems come to the fore here. The classic and more important dilemma results from the two-edged quality of community, which in providing emotional sustenance to its members, necessarily excludes others. A second problem arises within theories of planning and urban design that urge the creation of exciting locales: Is planned diversity an oxymoron? Although Jacobs's (1961) critique of modernist planning undergirds much of the new urbanism, she would probably repudiate its effort to prescribe what in her view must be spontaneous. And truly, if one visits the world's planned new towns and downtown redevelopment projects, even those built with commitments to diversity and community, one is struck by their physical and social homogeneity:

> Sadly, the cornerstones of Jacobsian urbanism – picturesque ethnic shops piled high with imported goods, mustachioed hot-dog vendors in front of improvised streetcorner fountains, urban life considered as one enormous national-day festival – are cruelly mimicked in every Rouse market [i.e., festival marketplace developed by the Rouse Corporation] and historic district on the [American] continent. Contemporary developers have found it eminently easy to furnish such obvious symbols of urbanism, while at the same time eliminating the racial, ethnic, and class diversity that interested Jacobs in the first place.   (Boddy 1992, p. 126n)

At the same time, relying on the market for an alternative to planning will not overcome the problem of homogeneity. The failure of the market to provide diversity in most places means that if planners do not attempt to foster it, the outcome will be increasingly segregated neighborhoods and municipalities. Nevertheless, the new urbanism, with its focus on physical form, will not do the job either:

> The reification of physical models is used by the architects of New Urbanism as a strategy to create local community, by reproducing a physical environment that fosters greater casual social contact within the neighborhood. However, these architects fail to sufficiently consider segregation within the greater urban area according to class, race and ethnicity, and may, in fact, help perpetuate it.   (Lehrer and Milgrom 1996, p. 15)

Only a publicly funded effort to combine social groups through mixing differently priced housing with substantial subsidies for the low-income component can produce such a result. The new urbanists seek to create housing integration but, in their reliance on private developers, are unable to do so on a sufficient scale or across a broad enough range of housing prices to have a significant effect. However, a serious effort to attract public subsidy for the low-income component of their communities would involve the new urbanists in a political battle for which their architectural training and aesthetic orientation offer few resources. The appeal of Victorian gingerbread and Cape Cod shingle would not override the fear of racial and social integration.

For planning theory, the most interesting aspect of the new urbanism is that its assurance of a better quality of life has inspired a social movement. Its utopianism contrasts with communicative planning, which offers only a better process. Thus there is a model of planning practice that is based not on the picture of the sensitive planner who listens and engages in ideal speech but on the messianic promise of the advocate who believes in a cause and eschews neutrality. As in all such cases, the benefits are exaggerated. But there is an attraction to the doctrine, both because of its hopefulness and because the places it seeks to create do appeal to anyone tired of suburban monotony and bland modernism.

The Just City

In *Socialism: Utopian and Scientific*, Engels ([1892] 1935, p. 54) presented the Marxian critique of utopianism:

> The final causes of all social changes and political revolutions are to be sought, not in men's brains, not in man's better insight into eternal truth and justice, but in changes in the modes of production and exchange.

For Marx and Engels, social transformation could occur only when the times were ripe, when circumstances enabled the forces for social amelioration to attain their objectives. In their view, utopian thinkers, such as Robert Owen and Charles Fourier, could not succeed because they developed a social ideal that did not coincide with a material reality still dominated by capitalist interests. Only smashing the structure of class domination could create the conditions for achieving a just society. Attainment of this goal, however, would not result from a passive acquiescence to historical forces. Engels laid out a role for intellectual understanding in bringing about a desirable transformation, as well as a picture of the future that only avoided the label of utopianism through an assertion of historic inevitability – the claim that once the working class seized power, it inevitably would create a just society:

> Once we understand [social forces] . . . when once we grasp their action, their direction, their effects, it depends only upon ourselves to subject them more and more to our own will, and by means of them to reach our own ends. . . . But when once their nature is understood, they can, in the hands of the producers working together, be transformed from master demons into willing servants. . . . With this recognition at last of the real nature of the productive forces of today, the social anarchy of production gives place to a social regulation of production upon a definite plan, according to the needs of the community and of each individual.   (Engels [1892] 1935, pp. 68–69)

At the millennium's end, one can hardly be sanguine that the hegemony of any social grouping will produce outcomes that will fulfill "the needs of the community and of each individual." By considering such an outcome as an inevitable consequence of proletarian revolution, Marx and Engels could simultaneously dismiss a nonconflictual path to socialism as unrealizable and present their teleological vision of revolutionary socialism as both realistic and desirable. If one does not accept their theory of historical development, however, one must either face the problem of formulating goals and identifying agents or capitulate to whatever structure of social domination exists. In this situation, a rigorous belief that people are helpless before forces such as globalization, sectarianism, and the repressive apparatus of the state produces either stasis or, at best, simply resistance.[21]

This crisis of action has led to the revival of utopian thought among some thinkers on the Left. Harvey (2001), for example, has broken with the Marxian critique of utopian idealism despite his continued adherence to other aspects of marxian analysis.[22] In his introduction to *Justice, Nature, and the Geography of*

Difference (1996), he recounted his experience of attending an academic conference in an Atlanta hotel that was also hosting a convention of fundamentalist Christians. He was impressed by the much greater appeal of the Christians as compared to the academics, their greater joyfulness. Thus his new interest in utopias arises partly out of a recognition that creating a force for change requires selling a concept – as Duany so forthrightly pointed out – making people think that they want what you are offering.[23] Depicting a picture of a just city puts the planning theorist in the role of advocate – not necessarily the advocate for a particular group, as in Davidoff's concept of advocacy planning – but as the advocate of a program.

Just-city theorists fall into two categories: radical democrats and political economists. The former differ from communicative planning theorists in that they have a more radical concept of participation that goes beyond the involvement of stakeholders to governance by civil society, and they accept a conflictual view of society.[24] They believe that progressive social change results only from the exercise of power by those who previously had been excluded from power. Participation is the vehicle through which that power asserts itself. The political economy group, upon whom I shall focus in this section and among whom I include myself, takes an explicitly normative position concerning the distribution of social benefits. It goes beyond neo-Marxism, however, in analyzing distributive outcomes as they affect non-class-based groupings and refusing to collapse noneconomic forms of domination into class categories. Until recently, the political economy tradition involved a critique of urban and regional phenomena based on values that were rarely made explicit (Fainstein 1997; Sayer and Storper 1997). Although clearly the principal value underlying such analyses was equity, the discussion usually proceeded by identifying unfairness without positing what was fair. There has been, however, an effort of late, paralleling and drawing on work in philosophy (e.g., Nussbaum and Sen 1993; Young 1990), which has broken with positivism and with postmodernist relativism. The purpose of this project has been to specify the nature of a good city (Harvey 1992, 1996; Merrifield and Swyngedouw 1997; Beauregard 2000).

The audience for this endeavor has remained vaguely defined. By inference, however, one can deduce that the principal target group is the leadership of urban social movements. Because political economic analysis mostly condemns policy makers for being the captive of business interests, it is addressed primarily to insurgent groups, to officials in progressive cities (Clavel 1986), and to "guerrillas in the bureaucracy" (Needleman and Needleman 1974). Whereas the communicative planning theorists primarily speak to planners employed by government, calling on them to mediate among diverse interests, just-city theorists do not assume the neutrality or benevolence of government (Marcuse 1986). For them, the purpose of their vision is to mobilize a public rather than to prescribe a methodology to those in office.

A theory of the just city values participation in decision making by relatively powerless groups and equity of outcomes (see Sandercock 1998). The key questions asked of any policy by political economists have been, Who dominates? and Who benefits? The "who" has typically been defined by economic interest, but economic reductionism is not necessary to this mode of analysis; evaluation of outcomes can also be conducted with regard to groups defined by gender, race, and sexual orientation. Nor does the emphasis on material equality need to boil down to an expectation that redistribution should proceed to a point at which there is no reward to achievement.

The characteristic weakness of socialist analysis has been its dismissal of economic growth as simply capital accumulation that benefits only capitalists. Socialist doctrine fails to mobilize a following if it only ensures greater equality without also offering improved circumstances for most people. The market model and neoliberalism have proved popular because they promise increases in affluence for all even if within the context of growing inequality. Neo-Marxian analysis has shown that unregulated growth despoils the environment, primarily helps the upper echelons of the population, and even produces increased absolute deprivation at the bottom. Its attacks on the entrepreneurial state and its collaboration with private capital have delineated a collusion in which the interests of the majority have frequently been ignored (Squires 1989). Nevertheless, this critique did not point to a way in which the majority of the population can realize economic gains relative to their own previous position and, as a consequence, has lost popular support in the developed countries.

A persuasive vision of the just city needs to incorporate an entrepreneurial state that not only provides welfare but also generates increased wealth; moreover, it needs to project a future embodying a middle-class society rather than only empowering the poor and disfranchised. Whereas Marx dismissed the *lumpenproletariat* with contempt and placed his hopes with the working class, contemporary political economists tend to see society as consisting of the poor and the wealthy, ignoring the interests and desires of the vast middle mass and the aspirations for upward mobility of the working class. Yet, if substantive democracy is a constitutive element of a vision of social justice, then an antimajoritarian concept of society will not do. Recent work on industrial districts, social markets, local economic development, and national growth rates has pointed in a direction more sympathetic to middle-class aspirations (Storper 1997; Sayer and Walker 1991; Fainstein and Markusen 1993; Bluestone and Harrison 1997). Still, a great deal more attention needs to be paid to identifying a formula for growth with equity (Sanyal 1998).[25] And such an approach has to take into account the perseverance of a capitalist world economy and the evident success, at least for the moment, of a liberalized U.S. economy.

Participation in public decision making is part of the ideal of the just city, both because it is a worthy goal in itself and because benevolent authoritarianism is unlikely. At the same time, democracy presents a set of thorny problems that have never been theoretically resolved and can only be addressed within specific situations.[26] The almost exclusive preoccupation with participation that has come to characterize much of leftist thought since the demise of socialism in the Soviet bloc evades the problems that have vexed democratic theory throughout its history. Democratic pluralism, with its emphasis on group process and compromise, offers little likelihood of escape from dominance by those groups with greatest access to organizational and financial resources. Democratic rule can deprive minorities of their livelihood, freedom, or self-expression. Classic democratic theory deals with this problem through imbuing minorities with rights that cannot be transgressed by majorities. But what of the minority that seeks to exercise its rights to seize power and take away the rights of others in the name of religious authority or racial superiority? Democratic principles can easily accommodate ineffective or harmless minorities; they founder when confronted with right-wing militias, religious dogmatists, and racial purists. Thus the appropriate criterion for evaluating a group's claims should not be procedural rules alone; evaluation must comprise an analysis of whether realization of the group's goals is possible and, if so, whether such realization leaves intact the principle of social justice. Democracy is desirable, but not always.

Within a formulation of the just city, democracy is not simply a procedural norm but rather has a substantive content (see Pitkin 1967). Given the existing system of social domination, it cannot be assumed that participation by stakeholders would be transformative in a way that would improve most people's situation. Consequently, deliberations within civil society are not ipso facto morally superior to decisions taken by the state. Rather, "it is the double-edged nature of the state, its ability to effect both regressive or progressive social change, that must be stressed" (Yiftachel 1998, p. 400).

The state can do both good and bad, and likewise, so can the citizenry. As Abu-Lughod (1998, p. 232) put it,

> When one considers the wide range of associational groups within civil society that seek empowerment ... some of them are downright evil, while others seem very admirable. Furthermore, some forms of associational organization seem to be effective in achieving their goals whereas others, equally participatory, fail.

Storper (1998, p. 240) picked up on her theme:

> Abu-Lughod goes right to the heart of the matter in suggesting that the form of civil society – e.g. decentralized, embracing a diversity of voices – does not have a straightforward relation to the content of those voices. In this she mirrors an old debate in political philosophy, especially modern democratic political philosophy, between democracy as a set of procedures and democracy as content or substance.

Applying the just-city perspective, one must judge results, and furthermore, one must not forget that the results attainable through public policy are seriously constrained by the economy. Thus, even when the principal concern is not economic outcomes but ending discrimination or improving the quality of the environment, economic interests limit possible courses of action. To go back to the example of the New Jersey State Plan mentioned earlier, its primary purpose was environmental protection, not social integration or redistribution of land and property. Nevertheless, its content was affected by the state's dependence on private investors for new development and its implementation restricted by fears of landowners that their property values would be adversely affected by growth regulation. Thus economic interests impinge on planning even when the economy is not its foremost object.

As stated in the introduction to this article, the principal question of planning theory is the analysis of the possibility for attaining a better quality of human life within the context of a global capitalist political economy.[27] One way to approach this question is to frame a model of the good city and then to inquire how it is achievable. The model can be an abstract utopia – the cohesive city of the new urbanists' dreams – or be derived from the identification of places that seem to provide an exceptionally good quality of life (thus conforming to Hoch's 1996 description of pragmatic inquiry described earlier).

In a recent paper, I (Fainstein 1999) identified Amsterdam as comprising such an exemplar. Although not the embodiment of utopia, it contains many of the elements of the just city. If one considers the two other types of planning theory discussed here – communicative planning and the new urbanism – Amsterdam also conforms in many respects to their models. There is a highly consensual mode of decision making, with elaborate consultation of social groups and heavy reliance on third-sector organizations for implementation of policy. In conformity with the vision of the new urbanism, spatial forms are physically diverse, development is at very high density, and population is mixed by class and, to a lesser extent, ethnically. These achievements are within the context of a relatively equitable distribution of income, a very extensive welfare state, corporatist bargaining over the contours of the economy at the national level, and public ownership of urban land. All this came partly out of a tradition of planning and compromise but also out of militant struggle – by workers' parties for much of the century and by squatters and street demonstrators more recently.

Amsterdam is, of course, a wealthy Western city, and the theories discussed here derive primarily from a Western discourse rooted in the Enlightenment. Nevertheless, they are applicable to the developing world, where the goal of growth with equity has been a long-standing one. Despite the contention of various Asian dictators that the concepts of democracy and rights constitute Western values, the very active global human rights movement and the rapid spread of democratic ideas throughout much of the non-Western world indicate widespread acceptance of these values. Heller's analysis of the Indian state of Kerala supports this argument:

> Kerala is a striking example of equitable development: Successive governments in this southwestern state of 29 million inhabitants have successfully pursued social and redistributive strategies of development that has few, if any, parallels in the nonsocialist developing world. . . . The vigor and dynamism of civil society is matched only by the size and activism of the state. (Heller 1996, p. 1055)

In examining Amsterdam and Kerala, one can see that democratic procedure was crucial to their development but also that it was insufficient. Required also was a structural situation of relative material equality as both precondition and outcome of development and a culture of tolerance and commitment to equity. Put another way, both Amsterdam and Kerala operated within a mode of regulation that permitted private capital accumulation and a market economy while maintaining a large nonmarket sector. Citizens of Amsterdam and Kerala thus possess a set of social rights, not just political rights (see Marshall 1965).

Resurrecting Optimism

The three types of planning theory described in this article all embrace a social reformist outlook. They represent a move from the purely critical perspective that characterized much theory in the 1970s and 1980s to one that once again offers a promise of a better life. Whereas reaction to technocracy and positivism shaped planning theory of that period, more recent planning thought has responded to the challenge of postmodernism. It has therefore needed to assert the possibility of a guiding ethic in the face of the postmodernist attack on foundationalism:

> The disrupting, enabling meaning of the postmodern is derived from the critique of universalism and the placing of difference and heterogeneity in the foreground, but such an opening remains consistently incomplete for some differences we may want to struggle against when they encapsulate inequality, and the heterogeneous, plural or local do not of themselves carry any necessarily empowering or emancipatory meaning. Clearly, the locally or regionally particular can be as violently oppressive as the centrally or globally universal.   (Slater 1997, p. 57)

Communicative planning theory has evaded the issue of universalism by developing a general procedural ethic without substantive content. The new urbanists claim that their design prescriptions incorporate diversity and provide people what they really want rather than what archaic zoning laws and greedy developers impose on them. Thus, even though they have been criticized for imposing a particular formula on others, they defend themselves by arguing that their conception incorporates difference. Just-city theorists work from "the basic premise ... that any distributional conception of social justice will inevitably be linked to the broader way of life in which people engage" (Smith 1997, p. 21). The argument is that although there may be no universal standards of good and bad, there are criteria for judging better and worse (Smith 1997; see also Fainstein 1997).

The progressives of the previous period spent much of their energy condemning traditional planning for authoritarianism, sexism, the stifling of diversity, and class bias. More recent theorizing has advanced from mere critique to focusing instead on offering a more appealing prospect of the future. For communicative planning, this means practices that allow people to shape the places in which they live; for new urbanists, it involves an urban form that stimulates neighborliness, community involvement, subjective feelings of integration with one's environment, and aesthetic satisfaction. For just-city theorists, it concerns the development of an urban vision that also involves material well-being but that relies on a more pluralistic, cooperative, and decentralized form of welfare provision than the state-centered model of the bureaucratic welfare state.

At the millennium's end, then, planning theorists have returned to many of the past century's preoccupations. Like their nineteenth-century predecessors, they are seeking to interpose the planning process between urban development and the market to produce a more democratic and just society. The communicative theorists have reasserted the moral preoccupations that underlay nineteenth-century radicalism, the new urbanists have promoted a return to concern with physical form, and just-city theorists have resurrected the spirit of utopia that inspired Ebenezer Howard and his fellow radicals. Although strategic and substantive issues separate the three schools of thought described here, they share an optimism that had been largely lacking in previous decades. Sustaining this optimism depends on translating it into practice.

ACKNOWLEDGMENTS

I thank Frank Fischer for helping me clarify the ideas presented in this article, even though he is not in full agreement with them, and Norman Fainstein, David

Gladstone, Robert Beauregard, and Judith Innes for their comments on earlier drafts.

NOTES

1   See especially various issues of the journal *Planning Theory* and Lauria (1997).
2   An op-ed piece in the *New York Times* noted, "When [the chairman of the Metropolitan Atlanta Chamber of Commerce]...talks wistfully about the need to re-create the European town square in urban America, he is expressing sentiments that have spread through his entire business community with remarkable speed and intensity" (Ehrenhalt 1999).
3   By this she meant both the suburban legacy of Ebenezer Howard's garden city movement and the urban reconstruction schemes of Le Corbusier and the international movement.
4   The principal theorists who have developed communicative theory in planning are Judith Innes, John Forester, Jean Hillier, Patsy Healey, Charles Hoch, and Seymour Mandelbaum. See especially Mandelbaum, Mazza, and Burchell (1996) for an extensive collection of essays developing this theme. For critiques of communicative planning theory, see Flyvbjerg (1998), Yiftachel (2001), Lauria and Whelan (1995), and Tewdwr-Jones (1998).
5   See Muller (1998) for a critique of the applicability of Kuhn's concept of the paradigm to planning theory.
6   The terms *exactions* (in the United States) and *planning gain* (in the United Kingdom) refer to the granting of benefits – for example, contributions to a housing fund, building of a public facility, and so on – by developers in return for the right to develop.
7   Stone (1989) chronicled the minor victories and overall defeat of the African-American population of Atlanta within a series of planning decisions dominated by a business-oriented regime. Despite a black mayor and a significant black leadership cadre, "the [governing] coalition is centered around a combination of explicit and tacit deals. Reciprocity is thus the hallmark of Atlanta's regime, and reciprocity hinges on what one actor can do for another. Instead of promoting redistribution toward equality, such a system perpetuates inequality" (p. 241).
8   Healey (1997) is bothered by this aspect of the theory and seeks to overcome it. Her work is distinguished by greater attention to the object of planning than is the case for most of her colleagues in the communicative rationality group. Likewise, she is much less sanguine that good will triumph as a consequence of open discussion.
9   The first analytic case studies of planning were authored by political scientists (e.g., Altshuler 1965; Meyerson and Banfield 1955; Stone 1976) and did not contain this intense focus on the role of the planner.
10 It should be noted that much of Simone de Beauvoir's body of work did devote itself to an examination of her life; these writings, however, do not have the same theoretical importance or general applicability as *The Second Sex*. At the same time, they show the apparent contradictions between her general arguments and her life as lived, thereby raising important theoretical issues.
11 Healey (1997) again is an exception.
12 Lindblom (1990) took a similar position, arguing that interests are made, not discovered. He therefore preferred the term *volition* to interest.
13 The concept of stakeholder seems to imply that individuals and groups do have differing objective interests in a particular issue, even though the content of that interest is not fixed.

14 These conclusions are based on my own field observations.
15 American suburbs enjoy considerable autonomy and elicit substantial citizen participation in their planning processes. The outcome tends to be exclusionary zoning.
16 In a thesis examining four cases of military base conversion to peacetime uses, Hill (1998) found, contrary to her expectations, that in the most successful case, Boston's Charlestown Navy Yard, citizen participation did not play a significant role, but politicians and planners with a commitment to neighborhood development and environmental protection produced a desirable outcome.
17 Influential proponents of this body of thought include Peter Calthorpe, James Howard Kuntsler, Anton Nelessen, and especially Andres Duany and Elizabeth Plater-Zyberg.
18 Within the United Kingdom, Charles, the Prince of Wales, has been associated with the neotraditional movement and has sponsored development in accordance with principles of the new urbanism. In Britain and other parts of Europe, however, many of the tenets of the new urbanism have always formed the basis of planning regulation and thus do not represent as much of a reorientation as in the United States.
19 Katz's (1994) *The New Urbanism* contains pictures and plans of a number of these endeavors within the United States.
20 See Hamilton (1999) and Frantz and Collins (1999); these *New York Times* articles, published after the Littleton, Colorado, school massacre, traced problems of teenage alienation to suburban design and credited new urbanist forms with the potential to overcome them.
21 The reduction of oppositional action to simply resistance seems to be at the core of Foucault's philosophy. See Dreyfus and Rabinow (1983, p. 207).
22 Friedmann (2000) has also recently written a paper exploring this theme, as have I (Fainstein 1999).
23 According to Kumar (1991, p. 31), "In the abstract schemes of conventional social and political theory, we are told that the good society will follow from the application of the relevant general principles; in utopia we are shown the good society in operation, supposedly as a result of certain general principles of social organization."
24 John Friedmann and Frank Fischer fit into this category. See Friedmann (2000) and Fischer (2000).
25 Healey (1998) emphasized the importance of institutional forms that will support economic development and tried to show how this can occur within the framework of collaborative planning. Her formulation is more applicable to those countries that already engage in corporatist decision making under the auspices of a social democratic state than it does to the United States.
26 See Day (1997) for the particular difficulties the concept presents to planners.
27 I do not deal here with the obviously fundamental issue of how one measures the quality of life, but see Nussbaum and Sen (1993) for a set of seminal essays on this subject.

REFERENCES

Abu-Lughod, J. 1998. Civil/uncivil society: Confusing form with content. In *Cities for citizens*. edited by M. Douglass and J. Friedmann, 227–38. London: Wiley.
Altshuler, A. A. 1965. *The city planning process*. Ithaca, NY: Cornell Univ. Press.
Beauregard, R. A. 1987. The object of planning. *Urban Geography* 8 (4): 367–73.
——. 1991. Without a net: Modernist planning and the postmodern abyss. *Journal of Planning Education and Research* 10(3): 189–94.
——. Resisting communicative planning: An institutional perspective. 2000 Unpublished MS.

Bluestone, B., and B. Harrison. 1997. Why we can grow faster. *The American Prospect* 34: 63–70.

Boddy, T. 1992. Underground and overhead: Building the analogous city. In *Variations on a theme park*, edited by M. Sorkin, 123–53. New York: Hill and Wang.

Campbell, S., and S. S. Fainstein, eds. 1996. A discussion on gender. In *Readings in planning theory*, 441–74. Oxford, UK: Blackwell.

Clavel, P. 1986. *The progressive city*. New Brunswick, NJ: Rutgers Univ. Press.

Day, D. 1997. Citizen participation in the planning process: An essentially contested concept? *Journal of Planning Literature* 11(3): 421–34.

Dreyfus, H. L., and P. Rabinow. 1983. *Michel Foucault: Beyond structuralism and hermeneutics*. 2nd ed. Chicago: Univ. of Chicago Press.

Ehrenhalt, A. 1999. New recruits in the war on sprawl. *New York Times*, April 13.

Engels, F. [1892] 1935. *Socialism: Utopian and Scientific*. New York: International publishers.

Fainstein, S. S. 1990. The rationale for neighborhood policy. In *Neighborhood policy and programs*, edited by N. Carmon, 223–37. London: Macmillan.

———. 1997. Justice, politics and the creation of urban space. In *The urbanization of injustice*, edited by A. Merrifield and E. Swyngedouw, 18–44. New York: New York Univ. Press.

———. 1999. Can we make the cities we want? In *The urban moment*, edited by R. A. Beauregard and S. Body-Gendrot, 249–72. Thousand Oaks, CA: Sage.

Fainstein, S. S., and N. Fainstein. 1979. New debates in urban planning: The impact of marxist theory within the United States. *International Journal of Urban and Regional Research* 3: 381–403.

Fainstein, S. S., and C. Hirst. 1996. Neighborhood organizations and community power: The Minneapolis experience. In *Revitalizing urban neighborhoods*, edited by D. Keating, N. Krumholz, and P. Star, 96–111. Lawrence: Univ. Press of Kansas.

Fainstein, S. S., and A. R. Markusen. 1993. Urban policy: Bridging the social and economic development gap. *Univ. of North Carolina Law Review* 71: 1463–86.

Fischer, F. 2000. *Citizens, experts and the environment: The politics of local knowledge*. Durham, NC: Duke Univ. Press.

Fishman, R. 1977. *Urban utopias in the twentieth century*. New York: Basic Books.

Flora, P., and A. J. Heidenheimer, eds. 1981. *The development of welfare states in Europe and America*. New Brunswick, NJ: Transaction Books.

Flyvbjerg, B. 1998. *Rationality and power*. Chicago: Univ. of Chicago Press.

Foglesong, R. 1986. *Planning the capitalist city*. Princeton, NJ: Princeton Univ. Press.

Forester, J. 1989. *Planning in the face of power*. Berkeley: Univ. of California Press.

———. 1993. Learning from practice stories: The priority of practical judgment. In *The argumentative turn in policy analysis and planning*, edited by F. Fischer and J. Forester, 186–209. Durham, NC: Duke Univ. Press.

Frantz, D., and C. Collins. 1999. Breaking the isolation barrier. *New York Times*, May 6, F4.

Friedmann, J. 2000. The good city: In defense of utopian thinking. *International Journal of Urban and Regional Research* 24 (2): 460–72.

Gans, H. 1968. *People and plans*. New York: Basic Books.

Hamilton, W. L. 1999. How suburban design is failing teenagers. *New York Times*, May 6, F1, F4.

Harvey, D. 1992. Social justice, postmodernism and the city. *International Journal of Urban and Regional Research* 16: 588–601.

———. 1996. *Justice, Nature, and the Geography of Difference*. Oxford, UK: Blackwell.

———. 1997. The new urbanism and the communitarian trap. *Harvard Design Magazine*, Winter/Spring [Online]. Available: www.gsd.harvard.edu/hdm/harvey.htm.

———. 2001. The spaces of utopia. In *Between Law and Justice*, edited by L. C. Bower, D. T. Goldberg, and M. C. Musheno, Minneapolis: Univ. of Minnesota Press.

Healey, P. 1996. Planning through debate: The communicative turn in planning theory. In *Readings in planning theory*, edited by S. Campbell and S. S. Fainstein, 234–57. Oxford, UK: Blackwell.

——. 1997. *Collaborative planning*. Hampshire, UK: Macmillan.

——. 1998. Building institutional capacity through collaborative approaches to urban planning. *Environment and Planning A* 30: 1531–46.

Heller, P. 1996. Social capital as product of class mobilization and state intervention: Industrial workers in Kerala, India. *World Development* 24(6): 1055–71.

Hill, C. 1998. Re-use of former military bases: An evaluation of converted naval bases. Ph.D. diss., Rutgers University, New Brunswick, NJ.

Hoch, C. 1996. A pragmatic inquiry about planning and power. In *Explorations in planning theory*, edited by S. J. Mandelbaum, L. Mazza, and R. W. Burchell, 30–44. New Brunswick, NJ: Center for Urban Policy Research, Rutgers University.

Innes, J. 1995. Planning theory's emerging paradigm: Communicative action and interactive practice. *Journal of Planning Education and Research* 14(3): 183–89.

——. 1996. Group processes and the social construction of growth management: Florida, Vermont, and New Jersey. In *Explorations in planning theory*, edited by S. J. Mandelbaum, L. Mazza, and R. W. Burchell, 164–87. New Brunswick, NJ: Center for Urban Policy Research, Rutgers University.

——. 1998. Information in communicative planning. *Journal of the American Planning Association*, 14(3) (Winter) 52–63.

Jacobs, J. 1961. *The death and life of great American cities*. New York: Vintage.

Katz, P., ed. 1994. *The new urbanism: Toward an architecture of community*. New York: McGraw-Hill.

Katznelson, I. 1981. *City trenches*. New York: Pantheon.

Kumar, K. 1991. *Utopianism*. Minneapolis: Univ. of Minnesota Press.

Kunstler, J. H. 1996. *Home from nowhere*. New York: Simon & Schuster.

Lauria, M., ed. 1997. *Reconstructing urban regime theory*. Thousand Oaks, CA: Sage.

Lauria, M., and R. Whelan. 1995. Planning theory and political economy: The need for reintegration. *Planning Theory* 14: 8–33.

Lehrer, U. A., and R. Milgrom. 1996. New (sub)urbanism: Countersprawl or repackaging the product. *Capitalism, Nature, Socialism* 7(2): 1–16.

Lindblom, C. 1990. *Inquiry and change*. New Haven, CT: Yale Univ. Press.

Lukács, G. 1971. *History and class consciousness*. Cambridge: MIT Press.

[Maudelbaum, S. J., L. Mazza, and R. W. Burchell, eds 1996. *Explorations in planning theory*. New Bruswick, NJ: Center for Urban Policy Research, Rutgers University.]

Marcuse, P. 1986. The myth of the benevolent state. In *Critical perspectives on housing*, edited by R. C. Bratt, C. Hartman, and A. Meyerson, 248–58. Philadelphia: Temple Univ. Press.

Marshall, T. H. 1965. *Class, citizenship, and social development*. Garden City, NY: Doubleday Anchor.

Marx, K., and F. Engels. [1846] 1947. *The German ideology*. Reprint. New York: International Publishers.

Mencher, S. 1967. *Poor law to poverty program*. Pittsburgh: Univ. of Pittsburgh Press.

Merrifield, A., and E. Swyngedouw, eds. 1997. *The urbanization of injustice*. New York: New York Univ. Press.

Meyerson, M., and E. C. Banfield. 1955. *Politics, planning and the public interest*. Glencoe, IL: Free Press.

Milroy, B. M. 1991. Into postmodern weightlessness. *Journal of Planning Education and Research* 10(3): 181–88.

Muller, J. 1998. Paradigms and planning practice: Conceptual and contextual considerations. *International Planning Studies* 3(3): 287–302.

Needleman, M. L., and C.E. Needleman. 1974. *Guerrillas in the bureaucracy*. New York: John Wiley.

Nussbaum, M. C., and A. Sen, eds. 1993. *The quality of life*. Oxford, UK: Oxford Univ. Press.

Pitkin, H. F. 1967. *The concept of representation*. Berkeley: Univ. of California Press.

Piven, F. F. 1970. Whom does the advocate planner serve? *Social Policy*, May/June, 32–37.

Pollitt, K. 1999. The solipsisters. *New York Times Book Review*, 18 April, 35.

Sandercock, L. 1998. *Toward cosmopolis: Planning for multicultural cities*. New York: John Wiley.

Sanyal, B. 1998. The myth of development from below. Paper presented at the annual meeting of the Association of Collegiate Schools of Planning, Pasadena, CA, November.

Sayer, A., and M. Storper. 1997. Ethics unbound: For a normative turn in social theory. *Environment and Planning D: Society and Space* 15(1): 1–18.

Sayer, A., and R. Walker. 1991. *The new social economy*. Oxford, UK: Blackwell.

Skocpol, T. 1985. Bringing the state back in. In *Bringing the state back in*, edited by P. B. Evans, D. Rueschemeyer, and T. Skocpol, 3–43. Cambridge, UK: Cambridge Univ. Press.

Slater, D. 1997. Spatialities of power and postmodern ethics: Rethinking geopolitical encounters. *Environment and Planning D: Society and Space* 15: 55–72.

Smith, D. M. 1997. Back to the good life: Towards an enlarged conception of social justice. *Environment and Planning D: Society and Space* 15: 19–35.

Squires, G. D. 1989. *Unequal partnerships*. New Brunswick, NJ: Rutgers Univ. Press.

Stone, C. N. 1976. *Economic growth and neighborhood discontent*. Chapel Hill: Univ. of North Carolina Press.

——. 1989. *Regime politics*. Lawrence: Univ. Press of Kansas.

Storper, M. 1997. *The regional world: Territorial development in a global economy*. New York: Guilford.

——. 1998. Civil society: Three ways into a problem. In *Cities for citizens*, edited by M. Douglass and J. Friedmann, 239–46. London: John Wiley.

Tewdwr-Jones, M. 1998. Deconstructing communicative rationality: A critique of Habermasian collaborative planning. *Environment and Planning A* 30: 1975–89.

Tomlinson, M. R. 1998. South Africa's new housing policy: An assessment of the first two years, 1994–96. *International Journal of Urban and Regional Research* 22(1): 137–46.

Urban or suburban? 1997. A discussion held at the Graduate School of Design in July 1996, with invited commentary. *Harvard Design Magazine*, Winter/Spring, 47–61.

Watson, V. 1998. Planning under political transition: Lessons from Cape Town's Metropolitan Planning Forum. *International Planning Studies* 3(3): 335–50.

Yiftachel, O. 1998. Planning and social control: Exploring the dark side. *Journal of Planning Literature* 12(4): 395–406.

——. 2001. Can theory be liberated from professional constraints? On rationality and explanatory power in Flyvbjerg's *Rationality and Power*. *Planning International Studies, 6:* 251–6.

Young, I. M. 1990. *Justice and the politics of difference*. Princeton, NJ: Princeton Univ. Press.

10

The Science of "Muddling Through"

Charles E. Lindblom

Suppose an administrator is given responsibility for formulating policy with respect to inflation. He might start by trying to list all related values in order of importance, for example, full employment, reasonable business profit, protection of small savings, prevention of a stock market crash. Then all possible policy outcomes could be rated as more or less efficient in attaining a maximum of these values. This would of course require a prodigious inquiry into values held by members of society and an equally prodigious set of calculations on how much of each value is equal to how much of each other value. He could then proceed to outline all possible policy alternatives. In a third step he would undertake systematic comparison of his multitude of alternatives to determine which attains the greatest amount of values.

In comparing policies he would take advantage of any theory available that generalized about classes of policies. In considering inflation, for example, he would compare all policies in the light of the theory of prices. Since no alternatives are beyond his investigation, he would consider strict central control and the abolition of all prices and markets on the one hand and elimination of all public controls with reliance completely on the free market on the other, both in the light of whatever theoretical generalizations he could find on such hypothetical economies.

Finally, he would try to make the choice that would in fact maximize his values.

An alternative line of attack would be to set as his principal objective, either explicitly or without conscious thought, the relatively simple goal of keeping prices level. This objective might be compromised or complicated by only a few other goals such as full employment. He would in fact disregard most other social values as beyond his present interest and he would for the moment not even attempt to rank the few values that he regarded as immediately relevant. Were he pressed he would

Reprinted with permission from *Public Administration Review*, vol. 19 (1959): 79–88. © by the American Society for Public Administration (ASPA), 1120 G Street NW, Suite 700, Washington, DC 20005. All rights reserved.

quickly admit that he was ignoring many related values and many possible import-ant consequences of his policies.

As a second step, he would outline those relatively few policy alternatives that occurred to him. He would then compare them. In comparing his limited number of alternatives, most of them familiar from past controversies, he would not ordinarily find a body of theory precise enough to carry him through a comparison of their respective consequences. Instead he would rely heavily on the record of past experi-ence with small policy steps to predict the consequences of similar steps extended into the future.

Moreover, he would find that the policy alternatives combined objectives or values in different ways. For example, one policy might offer price level stability at the cost of some risk of unemployment; another might offer less price stability but also less risk of unemployment. Hence, the next step in his approach – the final selection – would combine into one the choice among values and the choice among instruments for reaching values. It would not, as in the first method of policy making, approximate a more mechanical process of choosing the means that best satisfied goals that were previously clarified and ranked. Because practitioners of the second approach expect to achieve their goals only partially, they would expect to repeat endlessly the sequence just described as conditions and aspirations changed and as accuracy of prediction improved.

By Root or by Branch

For complex problems the first of these two approaches is of course impossible. Although such an approach can be described, it cannot be practiced except for relatively simple problems and even then only in a somewhat modified form. It assumes intellectual capacities and sources of information that people simply do not possess, and it is even more absurd as an approach to policy when the time and money that can be allocated to a policy problem is limited, as is always the case. Of particular importance to public administration is the fact that public agencies are in effect usually instructed not to practice the first method. That is to say, their prescribed functions and constraints – the politically or legally possible – restrict their attention to relatively few values and relatively few alternative policies among the countless alternatives that might be imagined. It is the second method that is practiced.

Curiously, however, the literatures of decision making, policy formulation, planning and public administration formalize the first approach rather than the second, leaving public administrators who handle complex decisions in the position of practicing what few preach. For emphasis I run some risk of overstate-ment. True enough the literature is well aware of limits on human capacities and of the inevitability that policies will be approached in some such style as the second. But attempts to formalize rational policy formulation – to lay out explicitly the necessary steps in the process – usually describe the first approach and not the second.[1]

The common tendency to describe policy formulation even for complex problems as though it followed the first approach has been strengthened by the attention given to, and successes enjoyed by, operations research, statistical decision theory, and systems analysis. The hallmarks of these procedures, typical of the first approach, are clarity of objective, explicitness of evaluation, a high degree of comprehensiveness of overview, and – wherever possible – quantification of values for mathematical analysis. But these advanced procedures remain largely the appropriate techniques of relatively small-scale problem solving, where the total number of variable to be considered is small and value problems restricted. Charles Hitch, head of the Economics Division of RAND Corporation, one of the leading centers for application of these techniques, has written:

> I would make the empirical generalization from my experience at RAND and elsewhere that operations research is the art of sub-optimizing, i.e., of solving some lower-level problems, and that difficulties increase and our special competence diminishes by an order of magnitude with every level of decision making we attempt to ascend. The sort of simple explicit model which operations researchers are so proficient in using can certainly reflect most of the significant factors influencing traffic control on the George Washington Bridge, but the proportion of the relevant reality which we can represent by any such model or models in studying, say, a major foreign-policy decision, appears to be almost trivial.[2]

Accordingly I propose in this chapter to clarify and formalize the second method, much neglected in the literature. This might be described as the method of *successive limited comparisons*, I will contrast it with the first approach which might be called the rational-comprehensive method.[3] More impressionistically and briefly – and therefore generally used in this chapter – they could be characterized as the branch method and root method, the former continually building out from the current situation step by step and by small degrees; the later starting from fundamentals anew each time, building on the past only as experience is embodied in a theory, and always prepared to start completely from the ground up.

Let us put the characteristics of the two methods side by side in simplest terms (Table 10.1).

Assuming that the root method is familiar and understandable, we proceed directly to clarification of its alternative by contrast. In explaining the second we shall be describing how most administrators do in fact approach complex questions, for the root method, the "best" way as a blueprint or model, is in fact not workable for complex policy questions, and administrators are forced to use the method of successive limited comparisons.

Intertwining Evaluation and Empirical Analysis (1b)

The quickest way to understand how values are handled in the method of successive limited comparisons is to see how the root method often breaks down in *its* handling of values or objectives. The idea that values should be clarified, and in advance of the examination of alternative policies, is appealing. But what happens when we attempt it for complex social problems? The first difficulty is that on many critical values or objectives, citizens disagree, congressmen disagree, and public administrators disagree. Even where a fairly specific objective is prescribed for the administrator there remains considerable room for disagreement on subobjectives.

Table 10.1 Comparison of comprehensive versus incremental approaches

Rational-comprehensive (root)	Successive limited comparisons (branch)
1a Clarification of values or objectives distinct from and usually prerequisite to empirical analysis of alternative policies.	1b Selection of value goals and empirical analysis of the needed action are not distinct from one another but are closely intertwined.
2a Policy formulation is therefore approached through means-end analysis: First the ends are isolated, then the means to achieve them are sought.	2b Since means and ends are not distinct, means-end analysis is often inappropriate or limited.
3a The test of a "good" policy is that it can be shown to be the most appropriate means to desired ends.	3b The test of a "good" policy is typically that various analysis find themselves directly agreeing on a policy (without their agreeing that it is the most appropriate means to an agreed objective).
4a Analysis is comprehensive: every important relevant factor is taken into account.	4b Analysis is drastically limited: i) Important possible outcomes are neglected. ii) Important alternative potential policies are neglected. iii) Important affected values are neglected.
5a Theory is often heavily relied upon.	5b A succession of comparisons greatly reduces or eliminates reliance on theory.

Consider, for example, the conflict with respect to locating public housing, described in Meyerson and Banfield's study of the Chicago Housing Authority[4] – disagreement that occurred despite the clear objective of providing a certain number of public housing units in the city. Similarly conflicting are objectives in highway location, traffic control, minimum wage administration, development of tourist facilities in national parks, or insect control.

Administrators cannot escape these conflicts by ascertaining the majority's preference, for preferences have not been registered on most issues; indeed, there often *are* no preferences in the absence of public discussion sufficient to bring an issue to the attention of the electorate. Furthermore, there is a question of whether intensity of feeling should be considered as well as the number of persons preferring each alternative. By the impossibility of doing otherwise administrators often are reduced to deciding policy without clarifying objectives first.

Even when an administrator resolves to follow his own values as a criterion for decisions he often will not know how to rank them when they conflict with one another, as they usually do. Suppose, for example, that an administrator must relocate tenants living in tenements scheduled for destruction. One objective is to empty the buildings fairly promptly, another is to find suitable accommodation for persons displaced, another is to avoid friction with residents in other areas in which a large influx would be unwelcome, another is to deal with all concerned through persuasion if possible and so on.

How does one state even to himself the relative importance of these partially conflicting values? A simple ranking of them is not enough; one needs ideally to know how much of one value is worth sacrificing for some of another value. The answer is that typically the administrator chooses – and must choose – directly among policies in which these values are combined in different ways. He cannot first clarify his values and then choose among policies.

A more subtle third point underlies both the first two. Social objectives do not always have the same relative values. One objective may be highly prized in one circumstance, another in another circumstance. If, for example, an administrator values highly both the dispatch with which his agency can carry through its projects *and* good public relations, it matters little which of the two possibly conflicting values he favors in some abstract or general sense. Policy questions arise in forms that put to administrators such a question as: given the degree to which we are or are not already achieving the values of dispatch and the values of good public relations, is it worth sacrificing a little speed for a happier clientele, or is it better to risk offending the clientele so that we can get on with our work? The answer to such a question varies with circumstances.

The value problem is as the example shows always a problem of adjustments at a margin. But there is no practicable way to state marginal objectives or values except in terms of particular policies. That one value is preferred to another in one decision situation does not mean that it will be preferred in another decision situation in which it can be had only at great sacrifice of another value. Attempts to rank or order values in general and abstract terms so that they do not shift from decision to decision end up by ignoring the relevant marginal preferences. The significance of this third point thus goes very far. Even if all administrators had at hand an agreed set of values, objectives, and constraints, and an agreed ranking of these values, objectives, and constraints, their marginal values in actual choice situations would be impossible to formulate.

Unable consequently to formulate the relevant values first and then choose among policies to achieve them, administrators must choose directly among alternative policies that offer different marginal combinations of values. Somewhat paradoxically the only practicable way to disclose one's relevant marginal values even to oneself is to describe the policy one chooses to achieve them. Except roughly and vaguely, I know of no way to describe – or even to understand – what my relative evaluations are for, say, freedom and security, speed and accuracy in governmental decisions, or low taxes and better schools than to describe my preferences among specific policy choices that might be made between the alternatives in each of the pairs.

In summary two aspects of the process by which values are actually handled can be distinguished. The first is clear: evaluation and empirical analysis are intertwined; that is, one chooses among values and among policies at one and the same time. Put a little more elaborately one simultaneously chooses a policy to attain certain objectives and chooses the objectives themselves. The second aspect is related but distinct: the administrator focuses his attention on marginal or incremental values. Whether he is aware of it or not he does not find general formulations of objectives very helpful and in fact makes specific marginal or incremental comparisons. Two policies X and Y confront him. Both promise the same degree of attainment of objectives a, b, c, d, and e. But X promises him somewhat more of f than does Y, while Y promises him somewhat more of g than does X. In choosing between them, he is in fact offered the alternative of a marginal or incremental amount of f at the expense of a marginal or incremental amount of g. The only values that are relevant to his choice are these increments by which the two policies differ; and when he finally chooses between the two marginal values he does so by making a choice between policies.[5]

As to whether the attempt to clarify objectives in advance of policy selection is more or less rational than the close intertwining of marginal evaluation and empirical analysis, the principal difference established is that for complex problems the first is impossible and irrelevant, and the second is both possible and relevant. The second is possible because the administrator need not try to analyze any values except the values by which alternative policies differ and need not be concerned with them except as they differ marginally. His need for information on values or objectives is drastically reduced as compared with the root method; and his capacity for grasping, comprehending, and relating values to one another is not strained beyond the breaking point.

Relations between Means and Ends (2b)

Decision making is ordinarily formalized as a means–ends relationship: Means are conceived to be evaluated and chosen in the light of ends finally selected independently of and prior to the choice of means. This is the means–ends relationship of the root method. But it follows from all that has just been said that such a means–ends relationship is possible only to the extent that values are agreed upon, are reconcilable, and are stable at the margin. Typically, therefore, such a means–ends relationship is absent from the branch method, where means and ends are simultaneously chosen.

Yet any departure from the means–ends relationship of the root method will strike some readers as inconceivable. For it will appear to them that only in such a relationship is it possible to determine whether one policy choice is better or worse than another. How can an administrator know whether he has made a wise or foolish decision if he is without prior values or objectives by which to judge his decisions? The answer to this question calls up the third distinctive difference between root and branch methods: how to decide the best policy.

The Test of "Good" Policy (3b)

In the root method a decision is "correct," "good," or "rational" if it can be shown to attain some specified objective, where the objective can be specified without simply describing the decision itself. Where objectives are defined only through the marginal or incremental approach to values described above, it is still sometimes possible to test whether a policy does in fact attain the desired objectives; but a precise statement of the objectives takes the form of a description of the policy chosen or some alternative to it. To show that a policy is mistaken one cannot offer an abstract argument that important objectives are not achieved; one must instead argue that another policy is to be preferred.

So far the departure from customary ways of looking at problem solving is not troublesome for many administrators will be quick to agree that the most effective discussion of the correctness of policy does take the form of comparison with other policies that might have been chosen. But what of the situation in which administrators cannot agree on values or objectives, either abstractly or in marginal terms? What then is the test of "good" policy? For the root method, there is no test. Agreement on objectives failing, there is no standard of "correctness." For the method of successive limited comparisons, the test is agreement on policy itself, which remains possible even when agreement on values is not.

It has been suggested that continuing agreement in Congress on the desirability of extending old age insurance stems from liberal desires to strengthen the welfare programs of the federal government and from conservative desires to reduce union demands for private pension plans. If so, this is an excellent demonstration of the ease with which individuals of different ideologies often can agree on concrete policy. Labor mediators report a similar phenomenon: the contestants cannot agree on criteria for settling their disputes but can agree on specific proposals. Similarly, when one administrator's objective turns out to be another's means, they often can agree on policy.

Agreement on policy thus becomes the only practicable test of the policy's correctness. And for one administrator to seek to win the other over to agreement on ends as well would accomplish nothing and create quite unnecessary controversy.

If agreement directly on policy as a test for "best" policy seems a poor substitute for testing the policy against its objectives, it ought to be remembered that objectives themselves have no ultimate validity other than they are agreed upon. Hence agreement is the test of "best" policy in both methods. But where the root method requires agreement on what elements in the decision constitute objectives and on which of these objectives should be sought, the branch method falls back on agreement wherever it can be found.

In an important sense, therefore, it is not irrational for an administrator to defend a policy as good without being able to specify what it is good for.

Noncomprehensive Analysis (4b)

Ideally, rational-comprehensive analysis leaves out nothing important. But it is impossible to take everything important into consideration unless "important" is so narrowly defined that analysis is in fact quite limited. Limits on human intellectual capacities and on available information set definite limits to man's capacity to be comprehensive. In actual fact, therefore, no one can practice the rational-comprehensive method for really complex problems, and every administrator faced with a sufficiently complex problem must find ways drastically to simplify. An administrator assisting in the formulation of agricultural economic policy cannot in the first place be competent on all possible policies. He cannot even comprehend one policy entirely. In planning a soil bank program, he cannot successfully anticipate the impact of higher or lower farm income on, say, urbanization – the possible consequent loosening of family ties, possible consequent eventual need for revisions in social security and further implications for tax problems arising out of new federal responsibilities for social security and municipal responsibilities for urban services. Nor, to follow another line of repercussions, can he work through the soil bank program's effects on prices for agricultural products in foreign markets and consequent implications for foreign relations, including those arising out of economic rivalry between the United States and the USSR.

In the method of successive limited comparisons, simplification is systematically achieved in two principal ways. First, it is achieved through limitation of policy comparisons to those policies that differ in relatively small degree from policies presently in effect. Such a limitation immediately reduces the number of alternatives to be investigated and also drastically simplifies the character of the investigation of each. For it is not necessary to undertake fundamental inquiry into an alternative and its consequences; it is necessary only to study those respects in which the proposed alternative and its consequences differ from the status quo. The empirical comparison of marginal differences among alternative policies that differ only marginally is, of course, a counterpart to the incremental or marginal comparison of values discussed above.[6]

Relevance as well as realism

It is a matter of common observation that in Western democracies public administrators and policy analysts in general do largely limit their analyses to incremental or marginal differences in policies that are chosen to differ only incrementally. They do not do so, however, solely because they desperately need some way to simplify their problems; they also do so in order to be relevant. Democracies change their policies almost entirely through incremental adjustments. Policy does not move in leaps and bounds.

The incremental character of political change in the United States has often been remarked. The two major political parties agree on fundamentals; they offer alternative policies to the voters only on relatively small points of difference. Both parties favor full employment but they define it somewhat differently; both favor the development of water power resources but in slightly different ways; and both favor unemployment compensation but not the same level of benefits. Similarly, shifts of policy within a party take place largely through a series of relatively small changes, as can be seen in their only gradual acceptance of the idea of governmental responsibility for support of the unemployed, a change in party positions beginning in the early 1930s and culminating in a sense in the Employment Act of 1946.

Party behavior is in turn rooted in public attitudes and political theorists cannot conceive of democracy's surviving in the United States in the absence of fundamental agreement on potentially disruptive issues, with consequent limitation of policy debates to relatively small differences in policy.

Since the policies ignored by the administrator are politically impossible and so irrelevant, the simplification of analysis achieved by concentrating on policies that differ only incrementally, is not a capricious kind of simplification. In addition, it can be argued that given the limits on knowledge within which policy makers are confined, simplifying by limiting the focus to small variations from present policy makes the most of available knowledge. Because policies being considered are like present and past policies, the administrator can obtain information and claim some insight. Nonincremental policy proposals are therefore typically not only politically irrelevant but also unpredictable in their consequences.

The second method of simplification of analysis is the practice of ignoring important possible consequences of possible policies, as well as the values attached to the neglected consequences. If this appears to disclose a shocking shortcoming of successive limited comparisons, it can be replied that, even if the exclusions are random, policies may nevertheless be more intelligently formulated than through futile attempts to achieve a comprehensiveness beyond human capacity. Actually, however, the exclusions, seeming arbitrary or random from one point of view, need be neither.

Achieving a degree of comprehensiveness

Suppose that each value neglected by one policy-making agency were a major concern of at least one other agency. In that case, a helpful division of labor would be achieved and no agency need find its task beyond its capacities. The shortcomings of such a system would be that one agency might destroy a value either before another agency could be activated to safeguard it or in spite of another agency's efforts. But the possibility that important values may be lost is present in any form of organization, even where agencies attempt to comprehend in planning more than is humanly possible.

The virtue of such a hypothetical division of labor is that every important interest or value has its watchdog. And these watchdogs can protect the interests in their jurisdiction in two quite different ways: first by redressing damages done by other agencies; and second, by anticipating and heading off injury before it occurs.

In a society like that of the United States in which individuals are free to combine to pursue almost any possible common interest they might have and in which government agencies are sensitive to the pressures of these groups, the system described is approximated. Almost every interest has its watchdog. Without claiming that every interest has a sufficiently powerful watchdog, it can be argued that our system often can assure a more comprehensive regard for the values of the whole society than any attempt at intellectual comprehensiveness.

In the United States, for example, no part of government attempts a comprehensive overview of policy on income distribution. A policy nevertheless evolves and one responding to a wide variety of interests. A process of mutual adjustment among farm groups, labor unions, municipalities and school boards, tax authorities, and government agencies with responsibilities in the fields of housing, health, highways, national parks, fire and police accomplishes a distribution of income in which particular income problems neglected at one point in the decision processes become central at another point.

Mutual adjustment is more pervasive than the explicit forms it takes in negotiation between groups; it persists through the mutual impacts of groups upon each other even where they are not in communication. For all the imperfections and latent dangers in this ubiquitous process of mutual adjustment it will often accomplish an adaptation of policies to a wider range of interests than could be done by one group centrally.

Note, too, how the incremental pattern of policy making fits with the multiple pressure pattern. For when decisions are only incremental – closely related to known policies, it is easier for one group to anticipate the kind of moves another might make and easier too for it to make correction for injury already accomplished.[7]

Even partisanship and narrowness, to use pejorative terms, will sometimes be assets to rational decision making for they can doubly ensure that what one agency neglects, another will not; they specialize personnel to distinct points of view. The claim is valid that effective rational coordination of the federal administration, if possible to achieve at all, would require an agreed set of values[8] – if "rational" is defined as the practice of the root method of decision making. But a high degree of administrative coordination occurs as each agency adjusts its policies to the concerns of the other agencies in the process of fragmented decision making I have just described.

For all the apparent shortcomings of the incremental approach to policy alternatives, with its arbitrary exclusion coupled with fragmentation when compared to the root method, the branch method often looks far superior. In the root method, the inevitable exclusion of factors is accidental, unsystematic, and not defensible by any argument so far developed, while in the branch method the exclusions are deliberate, systematic, and defensible. Ideally, of course, the root method does not exclude; in practice it must.

Nor does the branch method necessarily neglect long-run considerations and objectives. It is clear that important values must be omitted in considering policy, and sometimes the only way long-run objectives can be given adequate attention is through the neglect of short-run considerations. But the values omitted can be either long-run or short-run.

Succession of Comparisons (5b)

The final distinctive element in the branch method is that the comparisons, together with the policy choice, proceed in a chronological series. Policy is not made once and for all; it is made and remade endlessly. Policy making is a process of successive approximation to some desired objectives in which what is desired itself continues to change under reconsideration.

Making policy is at best a very rough process. Neither social scientists nor politicians nor public administrators yet know enough about the social world to avoid repeated error in predicting the consequences of policy moves. Wise policy makers consequently expect that their policies will achieve only part of what they hope and at the same time will produce unanticipated consequences they would have preferred to avoid. If they proceed through a *succession* of incremental changes, they avoid serious lasting mistakes in several ways.

In the first place past sequences of policy steps have given them knowledge about the probable consequences of further similar steps. Second, they need not attempt big jumps toward their goals that would require predictions beyond their or anyone else's knowledge, because they never expect their policy to be a final resolution of a problem. Their decision is only one step, one that if successful can quickly be followed by another. Third, they are in effect able to test their previous predictions as they move on to each further step. Lastly they can often remedy a past error fairly quickly – more quickly than if policy proceeded through more distinct steps widely spaced in time.

Compare this comparative analysis of incremental changes with the aspiration to employ theory in the root method. People cannot think without classifying, without subsuming one experience under a more general category of experiences. The attempt to push categorization as far as possible and to find general propositions that can be applied to specific situations is what I refer to with the word "theory". Where root analysis often leans heavily on theory in this sense, the branch method does not. The assumption of root analysts is that theory is the most systematic and economical way to bring relevant knowledge to bear on a specific problem. Granting the assumption, an unhappy fact is that we do not have adequate theory to apply to problems in any policy area, although theory is more adequate in some areas – monetary policy, for example – than in others. Comparative analysis as in the branch method, is sometimes a systematic alternative to theory.

Suppose an administrator must choose among a small group of policies that differ only incrementally from each other and from present policy. He or she might aspire to "understand" each of the alternatives – for example, to know all the consequences of each aspect of each policy. If so the administrator would indeed require theory. In fact, however, he or she would usually decide that *for policy-making purposes*, it was essential to know, as explained above, only the consequences of each of those aspects of the policies in which they differed from one another. For this much more modest aspiration, the administrator requires no theory (although it might be helpful, if available), for the individual can proceed to isolate probable differences by examining the differences in consequences associated with past differences in policies, a feasible program because he or she can draw on observations from a long sequences of incremental changes.

For example, without a more comprehensive social theory about juvenile delinquency than scholars have yet produced, one cannot possibly understand the ways in which a variety of public policies – say on education, housing, recreation, employment, race relations, and policing – might encourage or discourage delinquency. And one needs such an understanding to undertake the comprehensive overview of the problem prescribed in the models of the root method. If, however, one merely wants to mobilize knowledge sufficient to assist in a choice among a small group of similar policies – alternative policies on juvenile court procedures, for example – one can do so by comparative analysis of the results of similar past policy moves.

Theorists and Practitioners

This difference explains – in some cases at least – why administrators often feel that outside experts or academic problem solvers are sometimes not helpful and in turn often urge more theory on them. And it explains why administrators often feel more confident when "flying by the seat of their pants" than when following the advice of theorists. Theorists often ask administrators to go the long way round to the solution of their problems, in effect ask them to follow the best canons of the scientific method when the administrators know that the best available theory will work less well than more modest incremental comparisons. Theorists do not realize that administrators are often in fact practicing a systematic method. It would be foolish to push this explanation too far, for sometimes practical decision makers are pursuing neither a theoretical approach nor successive comparisons, nor any other systematic method.

It may be worth emphasizing that theory is sometimes of extremely limited helpfulness in policy making for at least two rather different reasons. It is greedy for facts; it can be constructed only through a great collection of observations. And it is typically insufficiently precise for application to a policy process that moves through small changes. In contrast, the comparative method both economizes on the need for facts and directs the analyst's attention to just those facts that are relevant to the fine choices faced by the decision maker.

With respect to precision of theory, economic theory serves as an example. It predicts that an economy without money or prices would in certain specified ways misallocate resources, but this finding pertains to an alternative far removed from the kind of policies on which administrators need help. On the other hand, it is not precise enough to predict the consequences of policies restricting business mergers and this is the kind of issue on which the administrators need help. Only in relatively restricted areas does economic theory achieve sufficient precision to go far in resolving policy questions; its helpfulness in policy making is always so limited that it requires supplementation through comparative analysis.

Successive Comparison as a System

Successive limited comparison is, then, indeed a method or system; it is not a failure of method for which administrators ought to apologize. Nonetheless, its imperfections, which have not been explored in this chapter, are many. For example, the method is without a built-in safeguard for all relevant values and it also may lead the decision maker to overlook excellent policies for no other reason than that they are not suggested by the chain of successive policy steps leading up to the present. Hence it ought to be said that under this method, as well as under some of the most sophisticated variants of the root method – operations research for example – policies will continue to be as foolish as they are wise.

Why then bother to describe the method in all the above detail? Because it is in fact a common method of policy formulation and is, for complex problems, the principal reliance of administrators as well as of other policy analysts.[9] And because it will be superior to any other decision-making method available for complex problems in many circumstances, certainly superior to a futile attempt at superhuman comprehensiveness. The reaction of the public administrator to the exposition of method doubtless will be less a discovery of a new method than a better acquaintance with an old. But by becoming more conscious of their practice of this method, administrators might practice it with more skill and know when to extend or constrict its use. (That they sometimes practice it effectively and sometimes not may explain the extremes of opinion on "muddling through," which is both praised as a highly sophisticated form of problem solving and denounced as no method at all. For I suspect that insofar as there is a system in what is known as "muddling through," this method is it.)

One of the noteworthy incidental consequences of clarification of the method is the light it throws on the suspicion an administrator sometimes entertains that a consultant or adviser is not speaking relevantly and responsibly when in fact by all ordinary objective evidence the person is. The trouble lies in the fact that most of us approach policy problems within a framework given by our view of a chain of successive policy choices made up to the present. One's thinking about appropriate policies with respect, say, to urban traffic control is greatly influenced by one's knowledge of the incremental steps taken up to the present. An administrator enjoys an intimate knowledge of his past sequences that "outsiders" do not share, and his thinking and that of the outsider will consequently be different in ways that may puzzle both. Both may appear to be talking intelligently, yet each may find the other unsatisfactory. The relevance of the policy chain of succession is even more clear when an American tries to discuss, say, antitrust policy with a Swiss, for the chains of policy in the two countries are strikingly different, and the two individuals consequently have organized their knowledge in quite different ways.

If this phenomenon is a barrier to communication, an understanding of it promises an enrichment of intellectual interaction in policy formulation. Once the source of difference is understood, it will sometimes be stimulating for an administrator to seek out a policy analyst whose recent experience is with a policy chain different from his own.

This raises again a question only briefly discussed above on the merits of like-mindedness among government administrators. While much of organization theory argues the virtues of common values and agreed organizational objectives, for complex problems in which the root method is inapplicable, agencies will want among their own personnel two types of diversification: administrators whose thinking is organized by reference to policy chains other than those familiar to most members of the organization and, even more commonly, administrators whose professional or personal values or interests create diversity of view (perhaps coming from different specialties, social classes, geographical areas) so that even within a single agency, decision making can be fragmented and parts of the agency can serve as watchdogs for other parts.

NOTES

1   James G. March and Herbert A. Simon similarly characterize the literature. They also take some important steps, as have Simon's recent articles, to describe a less heroic model of policy making. See *Organizations* (John Wiley and Sons, 1958), p. 137.

2   "Operations Research and National Planning – A Dissent," 5 *Operations Research* 718 (October 1957). Hitch's dissent is from particular points made in the article to which his paper is a reply; his claim that operations research is for low-level problems is widely accepted.

    For examples of the kind of problems to which operations research is applied see C. W. Churchman, R. L. Ackoff and E. L. Arnoff, *Introduction to Operations Research* (John Wiley and Sons, 1957); and J. F. McCloskey and J. M. Coppinger (eds.), *Operations Research for Management*, vol. II (The Johns Hopkins Press, 1956).

3   I am assuming that administrators often make policy and advise in the making of policy and am treating decision making and policy making as synonymous for purposes of this chapter.

4   Martin Meyerson and Edward C. Banfield, *Politics, Planning and the Public Interest* (The Free Press, 1955).

5   The line of argument is, of course, an extension of the theory of market choice, especially the theory of consumer choice, to public policy choices.

6   A more precise definition of incremental policies and a discussion of whether a change that appears "small" to one observer might be seen differently by another is to be found in my "Policy Analysis," 48 *American Economic Review* 298 (June, 1958).

7   The link between the practice of the method of successive limited comparisons and mutual adjustment of interests in a highly fragmented decision-making process adds a new facet to pluralist theories of government and administration.

8 Herbert Simon, Donald W. Smithburg, and Victor A. Thompson, *Public Administration* (Alfred A. Knopf, 1950), p. 434.

9 Elsewhere I have explored this same method of policy formulation as practiced by academic analysts of policy ("Policy Analysis," 48 *American Economic Review* 298 (June, 1958)). Although it has been here presented as a method for public administrators, it is no less necessary to analysts more removed from immediate policy questions, despite their tendencies to describe their own analytical efforts as though they were the rational-comprehensive method with an especially heavy use of theory. Similarly, this same method is inevitably resorted to in personal problem solving, where means and ends are sometimes impossible to separate, where aspirations or objectives undergo constant development, and where drastic simplification of the complexity of the real world is urgent if problems are to be solved in the time that can be given to them. To an economist accustomed to dealing with the marginal or incremental concept in market processes, the central idea in the method is that both evaluation and empirical analysis are incremental.

Advocacy and Pluralism in Planning

Paul Davidoff

The present can become an epoch in which the dreams of the past for an enlightened and just democracy are turned into a reality. The massing of voices protesting racial discrimination have roused this nation to the need to rectify racial and other social injustices. The adoption by Congress of a host of welfare measures and the Supreme Court's specification of the meaning of equal protection by law both reveal the response to protest and open the way for the vast changes still required.

The just demand for political and social equality on the part of the African-American and the impoverished requires the public to establish the bases for a society affording equal opportunity to all citizens. The compelling need for intelligent planning, for specification of new social goals and the means for achieving them, is manifest. The society of the future will be an urban one, and city planners will help to give it shape and content.

The prospect for future planning is that of a practice openly inviting political and social values to be examined and debated. Acceptance of this position means rejection of prescriptions for planning that would have the planner act solely as a technician. It has been argued that technical studies to enlarge the information available to decision makers must take precedence over statements of goals and ideals:

> We have suggested that, at least in part, the city planner is better advised to start from research into the functional aspects of cities than from his own estimation of the values which he is attempting to maximize. This suggestion springs from a conviction that at this juncture the implications of many planning decisions are poorly understood, and that no certain means are at hand by which values can be measured, ranked, and translated into the design of a metropolitan system.[1]

While acknowledging the need for humility and openness in the adoption of social goals, this statement amounts to an attempt to eliminate, or sharply reduce, the

Reprinted by permission of the *Journal of the American Institute of Planners*, 31 (4) (1965): 544–55.

unique contribution planning can make: understanding the functional aspects of the city and recommending appropriate future action to improve the urban condition.

Another argument that attempts to reduce the importance of attitudes and values in planning and other policy sciences is that the major public questions are themselves matters of choice between technical methods of solution. Dahl and Lindblom put forth this position at the beginning of their important textbook, *Politics, Economics, and Welfare*.[2]

> *In economic organization and reform, the "great issues" are no longer the great issues, if they ever were. It has become increasingly difficult for thoughtful men to find meaningful alternatives posed in the traditional choices between socialism and capitalism, planning and the free market, regulation and laissez-faire, for they find their actual choices neither so simple nor so grand. Not so simple, because economic organization poses knotty problems that can only be solved by painstaking attention to technical details – how else, for example, can inflation be controlled? Nor so grand, because, at least in the Western world, most people neither can nor wish to experiment with the whole pattern of socioeconomic organization to attain goals more easily won. If for example, taxation will serve the purpose, why "abolish the wages system" to ameliorate income inequality?*

These words were written in the early 1950s and express the spirit of that decade more than that of the 1960s. They suggest that the major battles have been fought. But the "great issues" in economic organization, those revolving around the central issue of the nature of distributive justice, have yet to be settled. The world is still in turmoil over the way in which the resources of nations are to be distributed. The justice of the present social allocation of wealth, knowledge, skill, and other social goods is clearly in debate. Solutions to questions about the share of wealth and other social commodities that should go to different classes cannot be technically derived; they must arise from social attitudes.

Appropriate planning action cannot be prescribed from a position of value neutrality, for prescriptions are based on desired objectives. One conclusion drawn from this assertion is that "values are inescapable elements of any rational decision-making process"[3] and that values held by the planner should be made clear. The implications of that conclusion for planning have been described elsewhere and will not be considered in this chapter.[4] Here I will say that the planner should do more than explicate the values underlying his prescriptions for courses of action; he should affirm them; he should be an advocate for what he deems proper.

Determinations of what serves the public interest, in a society containing many diverse interest groups, are almost always of a highly contentious nature. In performing its role of prescribing courses of action leading to future desired states, the planning profession must engage itself thoroughly and openly in the contention surrounding political determination. Moreover, planners should be able to engage in the political process as advocates of the interests both of government and of such other groups, organizations, or individuals who are concerned with proposing policies for the future development of the community.

The recommendation that city planners represent and plead the plans of many interest groups is founded upon the need to establish an effective urban democracy, one in which citizens may be able to play an active role in the process of deciding public policy. Appropriate policy in a democracy is determined through a process of political debate. The right course of action is always a matter of choice, never of fact.

In a bureaucratic age great care must be taken that choices remain in the area of public view and participation.

Urban politics, in an era of increasing government activity in planning and welfare, must balance the demands for ever-increasing central bureaucratic control against the demands for increased concern for the unique requirements of local, specialized interests. The welfare of all and the welfare of minorities are both deserving of support: Planning must be so structured and so practiced as to account for this unavoidable bifurcation of the public interest.

The idealized political process in a democracy serves the search for truth in much the same manner as due process in law. Fair notice and hearings, production of supporting evidence, cross-examination, reasoned decision are all means employed to arrive at relative truth: a just decision. Due process and two (or more) party political contention both rely heavily upon strong advocacy by a professional. The advocate represents an individual, group, or organization. He affirms their position in language understandable to his client and to the decision makers he seeks to convince.

If the planning process is to encourage democratic urban government, then it must operate so as to include rather than exclude citizens from participating in the process. "Inclusion" means not only permitting citizens to be heard. It also means allowing them to become well informed about the underlying reasons for planning proposals, and to respond to these in the technical language of professional planners.

A practice that has discouraged full participation by citizens in plan making in the past has been based on what might be called the "unitary plan." This is the idea that only one agency in a community should prepare a comprehensive plan; that agency is the city planning commission or department. Why is it that no other organization within a community prepares a plan? Why is only one agency concerned with establishing both general and specific goals for community development, and with proposing the strategies and costs required to effect the goals? Why are there not plural plans?

If the social, economic, and political ramifications of a plan are politically contentious, then why is it that those in opposition to the agency plan do not prepare one of their own? It is interesting to observe that "rational" theories of planning have called for consideration of alternative courses of action by planning agencies. As a matter of rationality, it has been argued that all of the alternative choices open as means to the ends ought be examined.[5] But those, including myself, who have recommended agency consideration of alternatives have placed upon the agency planner the burden of inventing "a few representative alternatives."[6] The agency planner has been given the duty of constructing a model of the political spectrum and charged with sorting out what he conceives to be worthy alternatives. This duty has placed too great a burden on the agency planner and has failed to provide for the formulation of alternatives by the interest groups who will eventually be affected by the completed plans.

Whereas in a large part of our national and local political practice contention is viewed as healthy, in city planning, where a large proportion of the professionals are public employees, contentious criticism has not always been viewed as legitimate. Further, where only government prepares plans and no minority plans are developed, pressure is often applied to bring all professionals to work for the ends espoused by a public agency. For example, last year a federal official complained to a meeting of planning professors that the academic planners were not giving enough support to federal programs. He assumed that every planner should be on the side of the federal renewal program. Of course government administrators will seek to gain the support of professionals outside government, but such support should not be expected as a matter of loyalty. In a democratic system opposition to a public agency should be just as normal and appropriate as support. The agency, despite the fact that it is concerned with planning, may be serving undesired ends.

In presenting a plea for plural planning I do not mean to minimize the importance of the obligation of the public planning agency. It must decide upon appropriate future courses of action for the community. But being isolated as the only plan maker in the community, public agencies as well as the public itself may have suffered from incomplete and shallow analysis of potential directions. Lively political dispute aided by plural plans could do much to improve the level of rationality in the process of preparing the public plan.

The advocacy of alternative plans by interest groups outside government would stimulate city planning in a number of ways. First, it would serve as a means of better informing the public of the alternative choices open, *alternatives strongly supported by their proponents.* In current practice those few agencies that have portrayed alternatives have not been equally enthusiastic about each.[7] A standard reaction to rationalists' prescription for consideration of alternative courses of action has been, "It can't be done; how can you expect planners to present alternatives of which they don't approve?" The appropriate answer to that question has been that planners, like lawyers, may have a professional obligation to defend positions they oppose. However, in a system of plural planning, the public agency would be relieved of at least some of the burden of presenting alternatives. In plural planning the alternatives would be presented by interest groups differing with the public agency's plan. Such alternatives would represent the deep-seated convictions of their proponents and not just the mental exercises of rational planners seeking to portray the range of choice.

A second way in which advocacy and plural planning would improve planning practice would be in forcing the public agency to compete with other planning groups to win political support. In the absence of opposition or alternative plans presented by interest groups, the public agencies have had little incentive to improve the quality of their work or the rate of production of plans. The political consumer has been offered a yes/no ballot in regard to the comprehensive plan; either the public agency's plan was to be adopted, or no plan would be adopted.

A third improvement in planning practice that might follow from plural planning would be to force those who have been critical of "establishment" plans to produce superior plans, rather than only to carry out the very essential obligation of criticizing plans deemed improper.

The Planner as Advocate

Where plural planning is practiced, advocacy becomes the means of professional support for competing claims about how the community should develop. Pluralism in support of political contention describes the process; advocacy describes the role performed by the professional in the process. Where unitary planning prevails, advocacy is not of paramount importance, for there is little or no competition for the plan prepared by the public agency. The concept of advocacy as taken from legal practice implies the opposition of at least two contending viewpoints in an adversary proceeding.

The legal advocate must plead for his own and his client's sense of legal propriety or justice. The planner as advocate would plead for his own and his client's view of the good society. The advocate planner would be more than a provider of information, an analyst of current trends, a simulator of future conditions, and a detailer of means. In addition to carrying out these necessary parts of planning, he would be a *proponent* of specific substantive solutions.

The advocate planner would be responsible to his client and would seek to express his client's views. This does not mean that the planner could not seek to persuade his client. In some situations persuasion might not be necessary, for the planner would have sought out an employer with whom he shared common views about desired social conditions and the means toward them. In fact one of the benefits of advocate planning is the possibility it creates for a planner to find employment with agencies holding values close to his own. Today the agency planner may be dismayed by the positions affirmed by his agency, but there may be no alternative employer.

The advocate planner would be above all a planner, responsible to his or her client for preparing plans and for all of the other elements comprising the planning process. Whether working for the public agency or for some private organization, the planner would have to prepare plans that take account of the arguments made in other plans. Thus, the advocate's plan might have some of the characteristics of a legal brief. It would be a document presenting the facts and reasons for supporting one set of proposals, and facts and reasons indicating the inferiority of counter proposals. The adversary nature of plural planning might, then, have the beneficial effect of upsetting the tradition of writing plan proposals in terminology that makes them appear self-evident.

A troublesome issue in contemporary planning is that of finding techniques for evaluating alternative plans. Technical devices such as cost – benefit analyses by themselves are of little assistance without the use of means for appraising the values underlying plans. Advocate planning, by making the values underlying plans more apparent, and definitions of social costs and benefits more explicit, should greatly assist the process of plan evaluation. Further, it would become clear (as it is not at present) that there are no neutral grounds for evaluating a plan; there are as many evaluative systems as there are value systems.

The adversary nature of plural planning might also have a good effect on the uses of information and research in planning. One of the tasks of the advocate planner in discussing the plans prepared in opposition would be to point out the nature of the bias underlying information presented in other plans. In this way, as critic of opposition plans, the planner would be performing a task similar to the legal technique of cross-examination. While painful to the planner whose bias is exposed (and no planner can be entirely free of bias) the net effect of confrontation between advocates of alternative plans would be more careful and precise research.

Not all the work of an advocate planner would be of an adversary nature. Much of it would be educational. The advocate would have the job of informing other groups, including public agencies, of the conditions, problems, and outlook of the group he or she represented. Another major educational job would be that of informing clients of their rights under planning and renewal laws, about the general operations of city government, and of particular programs likely to affect them.

The advocate planner would devote much attention to helping the client organization to clarify its ideas and to give expression to them. In order to make clients more powerful politically the advocate might also become engaged in expanding the size and scope of his or her client organization. But the advocate's most important function would be to carry out the planning process for the organization and to argue persuasively in favor of its planning proposals.

Advocacy in planning has already begun to emerge as planning and renewal affect the lives of more and more people. The critics of urban renewal[8] have forced response from the renewal agencies, and the ongoing debate[9] has stimulated needed self-evaluation by public agencies. Much work along the lines of advocate planning has already taken place, but little of it by professional planners. More often the work has been conducted by trained community organizers or by student groups. In at least one instance, however, a planner's professional aid led to the development of an alternative renewal approach, one that will result in the dislocation of far fewer families than originally contemplated.[10]

Pluralism and advocacy are means for stimulating consideration of future conditions by all groups in society. But there is one social group that at present is particularly in need of the assistance of planners. This group includes organizations representing low-income families. At a time when concern for the condition of the poor finds institutionalization in community action programs it would be appropriate for planners concerned with such groups to find means to plan with them. The plans prepared for these groups would seek to combat poverty and would propose programs affording new and better opportunities to the members of the organization and to families similarly situated.[11]

The difficulty in providing adequate planning assistance to organizations representing low-income families may in part be overcome by funds allocated to local antipoverty councils. But these councils are not the only representatives of the poor; other organizations exist and seek help. How can this type of assistance be financed? This question will be examined below, when attention is turned to the means for institutionalizing plural planning.

The Structure of Planning

Planning by special interest groups

The local planning process typically includes one or more "citizens" organizations concerned with the nature of planning in the community. The Workable Program requirement for "citizen participation"[12] has enforced this tradition and brought it to most large communities. The difficulty with current citizen participation programs is that citizens are more often *reacting* to agency programs than *proposing* their concepts of appropriate goals and future action.

The fact that citizens' organizations have not played a positive role in formulating plans is to some extent a result of both the enlarged role in society played by government bureaucracies and the historic weakness of municipal party politics. There is something very shameful to our society in the necessity to have organized "citizen participation." Such participation should be the norm in an enlightened democracy. The formalization of citizen participation as a required practice in localities is similar in many respects to totalitarian shows of loyalty to the state by citizen parades.

Will a private group interested in preparing a recommendation for community development be required to carry out its own survey and analysis of the community? The answer would depend upon the quality of the work prepared by the public agency, work that should be public information. In some instances the public agency may not have surveyed or analyzed aspects the private group thinks important; or the public agency's work may reveal strong biases unacceptable to the private group. In any event, the production of a useful plan proposal will require much information concerning the present and predicted conditions in the community. There will be some costs associated with gathering that information, even if it is taken from the public agency. The major cost involved in the preparation of a plan by a private agency would probably be the employment of one or more professional planners.

What organizations might be expected to engage in the plural planning process? The first type that comes to mind are the political parties; but this is clearly an aspirational thought. There is very little evidence that local political organizations have the interest, ability, or concern to establish well-developed programs for their communities. Not all the fault, though, should be placed upon the professional politicians, for the registered members of political parties have not demanded very much, if anything, from them as agents.

Despite the unreality of the wish, the desirability for active participation in the process of planning by the political parties is strong. In an ideal situation local parties would establish political platforms, which would contain master plans for community growth, and both the majority and minority parties in the legislative branch of government would use such plans as one basis for appraising individual legislative proposals. Further, the local administration would use its planning agency to carry out the plans it proposed to the electorate. This dream will not turn to reality for a long time. In the interim other interest groups must be sought to fill the gap caused by the present inability of political organizations.

The second set of organizations that might be interested in preparing plans for community development are those that represent special interest groups having established views in regard to proper public policy. Such organizations as chambers of commerce, real estate boards, labor organizations, pro- and anti-civil rights groups, and anti-poverty councils come to mind. Groups of this nature have often played parts in the development of community plans, but only in a very few instances have they proposed their own plans.

It must be recognized that there is strong reason operating against commitment to a plan by these organizations. In fact it is the same reason that in part limits both the interests of politicians and the potential for planning in our society. The expressed commitment to a particular plan may make it difficult for groups to find means for accommodating their various interests. In other terms, it may be simpler for professionals, politicians, or lobbyists to make deals if they have not laid their cards on the table.

There is a third set of organizations that might be looked to as proponents of plans and to whom the foregoing comments might not apply. These are the ad hoc protest associations that may form in opposition to some proposed policy. An example of such a group is a neighborhood association formed to combat a renewal plan, a zoning change, or the proposed location of a public facility. Such organizations may seek to develop alternative plans, plans that would, if effected, better serve their interests.

From the point of view of effective and rational planning, it might be desirable to commence plural planning at the level of citywide organizations, but a more realistic view is that it will start at the neighborhood level. Certain advantages of this outcome should be noted. Mention was made earlier of tension in government between centralizing and decentralizing forces. The contention aroused by conflict between the central planning agency and the neighborhood organization may indeed be healthy, leading to clearer definition of welfare policies and their relation to the rights of individuals or minority groups.

Who will pay for plural planning? Some organizations have the resources to sponsor the development of a plan. Many groups lack the means. The plight of the relatively indigent association seeking to propose a plan might be analogous to that of the indigent client in search of legal aid. If the idea of plural planning makes sense, then support may be found from foundations or from government. In the beginning it is more likely that some foundation might be willing to experiment with plural planning as a means of making city planning more effective and more democratic. Or the federal government might see plural planning, if carried out by local anti-poverty councils, as a strong means of generating local interest in community affairs.

Federal sponsorship of plural planning might be seen as a more effective tool for stimulating involvement of citizens in the future of their community than are the present types of citizen participation programs. Federal support could be expected only if plural planning were seen not as a means of combating renewal plans but as an incentive to local renewal agencies to prepare better plans.

The public planning agency

A major drawback to effective democratic planning practice is the continuation of that nonresponsible vestigial institution, the planning commission. If it is agreed that the establishment of both general policies and implementation policies are questions affecting the public interest and that public interest questions should be decided in accord with established democratic practices for decision making, then it is indeed difficult to find convincing reasons for continuing to permit independent commissions to make planning decisions. At an earlier stage in planning, the strong arguments of John T. Howard[13] and others in support of commissions may have been persuasive. But it is now more than a decade since Howard made his defense against Robert Walker's position favoring planning as a staff function under the mayor. With the increasing effect planning decisions have upon the lives of citizens, the Walker proposal assumes great urgency.[14]

Aside from important questions regarding the propriety of allowing independent agencies far removed from public control to determine public policy, the failure to place planning decision choices in the hands of elected officials has weakened the ability of professional planners to have their proposals effected. Separating planning from local politics has made it difficult for independent commissions to garner influential political support. The commissions are not responsible directly to the electorate, and the electorate in turn is at best often indifferent to the planning commission.

During the last decade, in many cities power to alter community development has slipped out of the hands of city planning commissions, assuming they ever held it, and has been transferred to development coordinators. This has weakened the professional planner. Perhaps planners unknowingly contributed to this by their refusal to take concerted action in opposition to the perpetuation of commissions.

Planning commissions are products of the conservative reform movement of the early part of this century. The movement was essentially anti-populist and pro-aristocracy. Politics was viewed as dirty business. The commissions are relics of a not-too-distant past when it was believed that if men of goodwill discussed a problem thoroughly, certainly the right solution would be forthcoming. We know today, and perhaps it was always known, that there are no right solutions. Proper policy is that which the decision-making unit declares to be proper.

Planning commissions are responsible to no constituency. The members of the commissions, except for their chairperson, are seldom known to the public. In general the individual members fail to expose their personal views about policy and prefer to immerse them in group decision. If the members wrote concurring and dissenting opinions, then at least the commissions might stimulate thought about planning issues. It is difficult to comprehend why this aristocratic and undemocratic form of decision making should be continued. The public planning function should be carried out in the executive or legislative office and perhaps in both. There has been some question about which of these branches of government would provide the best home, but there is much reason to believe that both branches would be made more cognizant of planning issues if they were each informed by their own planning staffs. To carry this division further, it would probably be advisable to establish minority and majority planning staffs in the legislative branch.

At the root of my last suggestion is the belief that there is or should be a Republican and Democratic way of viewing city development; that there should be conservative and liberal plans, plans to support the private market and plans to support greater government control. There are many possible roads for a community to travel, and many plans should show them. Explication is required of many alternative futures presented by those sympathetic to the construction of each such future. As indicated earlier, such alternatives are not presented to the public now. Those few reports that do include alternative futures do not speak in terms of interest to the average citizen. They are filled with professional jargon and present sham alternatives. These plans have expressed technical land-use alternatives rather than social, economic, or political value alternatives. Both the traditional unitary plans and the new ones that present technical alternatives have limited the public's exposure to the future states that might be achieved. Instead of arousing healthy political contention as diverse comprehensive plans might, these plans have deflated interest.

The independent planning commission and unitary plan practice certainly should not coexist. Separately, they dull the possibility for enlightened political debate; in combination they have made it yet more difficult. But when still another hoary concept of city planning is added to them, such debate becomes practically impossible. This third of a trinity of worn-out notions is that city planning should focus only upon the physical aspects of city development.

An Inclusive Definition of the Scope of Planning

The view that equates physical planning with city planning is myopic. It may have had some historical justification, but it is clearly out of place at a time when it is necessary to integrate knowledge and techniques in order to wrestle effectively with the myriad of problems afflicting urban populations.

The city planning profession's historical concern with the physical environment has warped its ability to see physical structures and land as servants to those who use them.[15] Physical relations and conditions have no meaning or quality apart from the way they serve their users. But this is forgotten every time a physical condition is described as good or bad without relation to a specified group of users. High density, low density, green belts, mixed uses, cluster developments, centralized or decentralized business centers are per se neither good nor bad. They describe physical relations or conditions but take on value only when seen in terms of their social, economic, psychological, physiological, or aesthetic effects upon different users.

The profession's experience with renewal over the past decade has shown the high costs of exclusive concern with physical conditions. It has been found that the allocation of funds for removal of physical blight may not necessarily improve the overall physical condition of a community and may engender such harsh social repercussions as to severely damage both social and economic institutions. Another example of the deficiencies of the physical bias is the assumption of city planners that they could deal with the capital budget as if the physical attributes of a facility could be understood apart from the philosophy and practice of the service conducted within the physical structure. This assumption is open to question. The size, shape, and location of a facility greatly interact with the purpose of the activity the facility houses. Clear examples of this can be seen in public education and in the provision of low-cost housing. The racial and other socioeconomic consequences of "physical decisions" such as location of schools and housing projects have been immense, but city planners, while acknowledging the existence of such consequences, have not sought or trained themselves to understand socioeconomic problems, their causes or solutions.

The city planning profession's limited scope has tended to bias strongly many of its recommendations toward perpetuation of existing social and economic practices. Here I am not opposing the outcomes, but the way in which they are developed. Relative ignorance of social and economic methods of analysis have caused planners to propose solutions in the absence of sufficient knowledge of the costs and benefits of proposals upon different sections of the population.

Large expenditures have been made on planning studies of regional transportation needs, for example, but these studies have been conducted in a manner suggesting that different social and economic classes of the population did not have different needs and different abilities to meet them. In the field of housing, to take another example, planners have been hesitant to question the consequences of locating public housing in slum areas. In the field of industrial development, planners have seldom examined the types of jobs the community needed; it has been assumed that one job was about as useful as another. But this may not be the case when a significant sector of the population finds it difficult to get employment.

"Who gets what, when, where, why, and how" are the basic political questions that need to be raised about every allocation of public resources. The questions cannot be answered adequately if land-use criteria are the sole or major standards for judgment.

The need to see an element of city development, land use, in broad perspective applies equally well to every other element, such as health, welfare, and recreation. The governing of a city requires an adequate plan for its future. Such a plan loses guiding force and rational basis to the degree that it deals with less than the whole that is of concern to the public.

The implications of the foregoing comments for the practice of city planning are these. First, state planning enabling legislation should be amended to permit planning departments to study and to prepare plans related to any area of public concern. Second, planning education must be redirected so as to provide channels of specialization in different parts of public planning and a core focused upon the planning process. Third, the professional planning association should enlarge its scope so as not to exclude city planners not specializing in physical planning.

A year ago at the American Institute of Planners (AIP) convention it was suggested that the AIP constitution be amended to permit city planning to enlarge its scope to all matters of public concern.[16] Members of the Institute in agreement with this proposal should seek to develop support for it at both the chapter and national level. The constitution at present states that the institute's "particular sphere of activity shall be the planning of the unified development of urban communities and their environs and of states, regions and the nation *as expressed through determination of the comprehensive arrangement of land and land occupancy and regulation thereof.*"[17]

It is time that the AIP delete the words in my italics from its constitution. The planner limited to such concerns is not a city planner, but a land planner or a physical planner. A city is its people; their practices; and their political, social, cultural, and economic institutions as well as other things. The city planner must comprehend and deal with all these factors.

The new city planners will be concerned with physical planning, economic planning, and social planning. The scope of their work will be no wider than that presently demanded of a mayor or a city council member. Thus, we cannot argue against an enlarged planning function on the grounds that it is too large to handle. The mayor needs assistance, in particular the assistance of a planner, trained to examine needs and aspirations in terms of both short- and long-term perspectives. In observing the early stages of development of Community Action Programs, it is apparent that our cities are in desperate need of the type of assistance trained planners could offer. Our cities require for their social and economic programs the type of long-range thought and information that have been brought forward in the realm of physical planning. Potential resources must be examined and priorities set.

What I have just proposed does not imply the termination of physical planning, but it does mean that physical planning be seen as part of city planning. Uninhibited by limitations on their work, city planners will be able to add their expertise to the task of coordinating the operating and capital budgets and to the job of relating effects of each city program upon the others and upon the social, political, and economic resources of the community.

An expanded scope reaching all matters of public concern will not only make planning a more effective administrative tool of local government, it will also bring planning practice closer to the issues of real concern to the citizens. A system of plural city planning probably has a much greater chance of operational success where the focus is on live social and economic questions instead of rather esoteric issues relating to physical norms.

The Education of Planners

Widening the scope of planning to include all areas of concern to government would suggest that city planners must possess a broader knowledge of the structure and forces affecting urban development. In general this would be true. But at present many city planners are specialists in only one or more of the functions of city government. Broadening the scope of planning would require some additional planners who specialize in one or more of the services entailed by the new focus.

A prime purpose of city planning is the coordination of many separate functions. This coordination calls for planners with general knowledge of the many elements comprising the urban community. Educating a planner to perform the coordinator's role is a difficult job, one not well satisfied by the present tradition of two years of graduate study. Training urban planners with the skills called for in this article may require both longer graduate study and development of a liberal arts undergraduate program affording an opportunity for holistic understanding of both urban conditions and techniques for analyzing and solving urban problems.

The practice of plural planning requires educating planners who would be able to engage as professional advocates in the contentious work of forming social policy. The person able to do this would be one deeply committed both to the process of planning and to particular substantive ideas. Recognizing that ideological commitments will separate planners, there is tremendous need to train professionals who are competent to express their social objectives.

The great advances in analytic skills, for example in techniques of simulating urban growth processes, portend a time when planners and the public will be better able to predict the consequences of proposed courses of action. But these advances will be of little social advantage if the proposals themselves do not have substance. The contemporary thoughts of planners about the nature of individuals in society are often mundane, unexciting, or gimmicky. When asked to point out to students the planners who have a developed sense of history and philosophy concerning the place of individuals in the urban world, one is hard put to come up with a name. Sometimes Goodman or Mumford might be mentioned. But planners seldom go deeper than acknowledging the goodness of green space and the soundness of proximity of linked activities. We cope with the problems of the alienated citizen with a recommendation for reducing the time of the journey to work.

Conclusion

The urban community is a system composed of interrelated elements, but little is known about how the elements do, will, or should interrelate. The type of knowledge required by the new comprehensive city planner demands that the planning profession comprise groups of people well versed in contemporary philosophy, social work, law, the social sciences, and civic design. Not every planner must be knowledgeable in all these areas, but each planner must have a deep understanding of one or more of these areas and must be able to give persuasive expression to this understanding.

As members of a profession charged with making urban life more beautiful, exciting, creative, and just, we have had little to say. Our task is to train a future generation of planners to go well beyond us in its ability to prescribe the future urban life.

ACKNOWLEDGMENTS

I wish to thank Melvin H. Webber for his insightful criticism and Linda Davidoff for her many helpful suggestions and for her analysis of advocate planning. Special acknowledgment is made of the penetrating and brilliant social insights offered by the eminent legal scholar and practitioner, Michael Brodie, of the Philadelphia Bar.

NOTES

1 Britton Harris, "Plan or Projection," *Journal of the American Institute of Planners*, 26 (November 1960) 265–272.

2 Robert Dahl and Charles Lindblom, *Politics, Economics, and Welfare* (New York: Harper and Brothers, 1953) p. 3.

3 Paul Davidoff and Thomas Reiner, "A Choice Theory of Planning," *Journal of the American Institute of Planners*, 28 (May 1962) 103–115.

4 Ibid.

5 See, for example, Martin Meyerson and Edward Banfield, *Politics, Planning and the Public Interest* (Glencoe: The Free Press 1955) pp. 314 ff. The authors state: "By a *rational* decision, we mean one made in the following manner: 1. the decision-maker considers all of the alternatives (courses of action) open to him; ... 2. he identifies and evaluates all of the consequences which would follow from the adoption of each alternative; ... 3. he selects that alternative the probable consequences of which would be preferable in terms of his most valued ends."

6 Davidoff and Reiner, op. cit.

7 National Capital Planning Commission. *The Nation's Capital: a Policies Plan for the Year 2000* (Washington D.C.: The Commission, 1961).

8 The most important critical studies are Jane Jacobs, *The Life and Death of Great American Cities* (New York: Random House, 1961); Martin Anderson, *The Federal Bulldozer* (Cambridge: MIT Press, 1964); Herbert J. Gans, "The Human Implications of Current Redevelopment and Relocation Planning," *Journal of the American Institute of Planners*, 25 (February 1959) 15–26.

9 A recent example of heated debate appears in the following set of articles: Herbert J. Gans, "The Failure of Urban Renewal," *Commentary* 39 (April 1965) p. 29; George Raymond, "Controversy," *Commentary* 40 (July 1965) p. 72; and Herbert J. Gans, "Controversy," *Commentary* 40 (July 1965) p. 77.

10 Walter Thabit, *An Alternate Plan for Cooper Square* (New York: Walter Thabit, July 1961).

11   The first conscious effort to employ the advocacy method was carried out by a graduate student of city planning as an independent research project. The author acted as both a participant and an observer of a local housing organization. See Linda Davidoff, "The Bluffs: Advocate Planning," *Comment*, Dept. of City Planning, University of Pennsylvania (Spring 1965) p. 59.

12   See Section 101(c) of the United States Housing Act of 1949, as amended.

13   John T. Howard, "In Defense of Planning Commissions," *Journal of the American Institute of Planners*, 17(2) (Spring 1951) 89–95.

14   Robert Walker, *The Planning Function in Urban Government*, second edition (Chicago: University of Chicago Press, 1950). Walker drew the following conclusions from his examination of planning and planning commissions. "Another conclusion to be drawn from the existing composition of city planning boards is that they are not representative of the population as a whole" (p. 153). "In summary the writer is of the opinion that the claim that planning commissions are more objective than elected officials must be rejected" (p. 155). "From his observations the writer feels justified in saying that very seldom does a majority of any commission have any well-rounded understanding of the purposes and ramifications of planning" (p. 157). "In summary, then, it was found that the average commission member does not comprehend planning nor is he particularly interested even in the range of customary physical planning" (p. 158). "Looking at the planning commission at the present time, however, one is forced to conclude that despite some examples of successful operations, the unpaid board is not proving satisfactory as a planning agency" (p. 165). " ... (it) is believed that the most fruitful line of development for the future would be replacement of these commissions by a department or bureau attached to the office of mayor or city manager. This department might be headed by a board or by a single director, but the members or the director would in any case hold office at the pleasure of the executive on the same basis as other department heads" (p. 177).

15   An excellent and complete study of the bias resulting from reliance upon physical or land-use criteria appears in David Farbman, "A Description, Analysis and Critique of the Master Plan," an unpublished mimeographed study prepared for the Univ. of Pennsylvania's Institute for Urban Studies, 1959–1960. After studying more than one hundred master plans Farbman wrote:

> As a result of the predominantly physical orientation of the planning profession many planners have fallen victims to a malaise which I suggest calling the "Physical Bias." This bias is not the physical orientation of the planner itself but is the result of it ...
> The physical bias is an attitude on the part of the planner which leads him to conceive of the principles and techniques of *his profession* as the key factors in determining the particular recommendations to be embodied in his plans ...
> The physically biased planner plans on the assumption (conviction) that the physical problems of a city can be solved within the framework of physical desiderata: in other words, that physical problems can be adequately stated, solved and remedied according to physical criteria and expertise. The physical bias produces both an inability and an unwillingness on the part of the planner to "get behind" the physical recommendations of the plan, to isolate, examine or to discuss more basic criteria ...
> ... There is room, then, in plan thinking for physical principles, i.e., theories of structural inter-relationships of the physical city; but this is only part of the story, for the structural impacts of the plan are only a part of the total impact. This total impact must be conceived as a web of physical, economic and social causes and effects. (pp. 22–26)

16   Paul Davidoff, "The Role of the City Planner in Social Planning," *Proceedings of the 1964 Annual Conference*, American Institute of Planners (Washington D.C.: The Institute, 1964) 125–131.

17   Constitution of AIP, Article II "Purposes," in *AIP Handbook & Roster – 1965*, p. 8.

12

Equitable Approaches to Local Economic Development

Norman Krumholz

The Development Process

Local economic development is a process by which local governments manage resources to stimulate private investment opportunities in order to generate new jobs and taxes. Local government may try to execute its own plans and initiatives or, more likely, enter into partnerships with private enterprises or Community Development Corporations (CDCs). The core of locally based economic development is "the emphasis on 'endogenous development' policies using the potential of local human, institutional and physical resources" (Blakeley, 1989, p. 59).

The local economic development process is broken into a number of tasks. Blakeley (1989) lays these tasks out to include: data gathering and analysis; selecting local development goals, strategies, and criteria; selecting local development projects; building action plans and analyzing financial alternatives; specifying feasibility and project details; preparing the overall development plan; and scheduling its implementation.

The process assumes rational planning and a broad range of technical studies of labor markets and tax bases, interrelationships of land use and transportation, impact of employment growth on housing market, and financial feasibility. Other technical studies might include the need for new or improved capital facilities, cost-benefit analyses, and industrial quotients to target various industries. Yet, regardless of the form of local economic development or the specific technical studies, local economic development has the primary goal of creating new jobs for local residents and providing a net tax increase to the local coffers. These elements provide the entire "public purpose" for the use of public subsidies to stimulate private investment.

This textbook model of local economic development seems deeply flawed in practice. Surveys find that practitioners spend most of their time not on research

Reprinted with permission from *Policy Studies Journal*, 27 (1)(1999) 12 83–95.

and analysis, but on public relations, marketing, advertising, and sales. The process seems largely untouched by systematic planning or targeting (Levy, 1990). Leadership is provided by private developers or real estate entrepreneurs seeking their own objectives, rather than public officials and citizens seeking public objectives.

Significantly, the effectiveness of public subsidies in local development is unknown in terms of net new jobs or taxes. As Matthew Marlin (1990, p. 15) has noted: "despite billions of dollars and an ongoing controversy, practitioners and academics have generated surprisingly little empirical evidence regarding the effectiveness of economic development incentives or subsidies in promoting economic growth." The probusiness Committee for Economic Development (Holland, 1982) has written that: "although we advocate the use of public incentives to stimulate private investment, we question the real value of local tax incentives."

The success of local economic development in the 1980s and 1990s has consisted largely of new real estate developments downtown. If a city developed a new festival market shopping mall, new office towers, and a new hotel, it was considered to be revitalized. If circumstances warranted and the local public-private partnership was sufficiently powerful and well organized, cities might add a new sports stadium or an arena, an aquarium, or a cleaned-up waterfront. These were the essential elements in city "renaissance," and they emerged unplanned and piecemeal as circumstances and funding provided, one project at a time (Frieden & Sagalyn, 1989).

The process of economic development in city after city was quite similar. Cities contributed part of their Community Development Bloc Grant and Urban Development Action Grant funds to big downtown projects; abated property taxes; floated industrial revenue bonds; negotiated tax increment financing deals; built streets, sewers, and other capital improvements; and provided whatever public subsidies were necessary to encourage private investment. Often these arrangements resulted in land deals, financing schemes, and tax breaks so complicated that only the handful of attorneys working on the contracts could understand them. This raised problems of public accountability.

Further problems of accountability and oversight often arose from the implementing structure used in each project. To speed the development process and "take it out of politics," cities supported the formation of new, quasi-public, nonprofit development corporations whose books were closed to the public. As a result, a sports authority would be responsible for building the new stadium or arena, and a waterfront development corporation, run like a private corporation but empowered to receive and expend both public subsidies and private investments, would build waterfront facilities (Eisinger, 1988). Not surprisingly, it became less clear over time just what was public and what was private. Few seemed to care; the process was working, at least in terms of producing new buildings and private sector profits.

Harborplace in Baltimore, Quincy Market in Boston, Renaissance Center in Detroit, Peachtree Plaza in Atlanta, Pike Place Market in Seattle, Bunker Hill in Los Angeles, Horton Plaza in San Diego, Union Station in St. Louis, Gateway in Cleveland, and dozens of similar projects transformed the skylines of U.S. cities. In some cities the building of these "big-bang" projects displaced lower-income residents of older but still fashionable urban neighborhoods, but in other projects displacement was minimal. A constant, however, was support from the local media, who acted like cheerleaders, finding colorful and positive copy in pictures and stories of new construction, redevelopment, and the arrival of upper-income residents downtown.

Amid all of the new construction and the obvious regeneration of parts of the business district, nagging questions of equity, purpose, and effect remained. First, the spillover effect in the neighborhoods surrounding downtown seemed negligible with the exception of some housing developed by the CDCs. Second, local economic development did not seem to be satisfying its stated purpose, which was to generate new jobs for unemployed city residents and net tax increases with which to address other city problems. "Success" in downtown development did not seem to translate into lower poverty and unemployment rates for city residents (Squires, 1989; Wolman, Ford, and Hill, 1994). In 1980 about 16.5% of the population in central cities lived in poverty; a decade later the figure was 18.7%, and the rise of poverty took place even in the cities most successful with downtown development (Frieden and Sagalyn, 1989). Despite the tangible successes of downtown-focused public-private partnerships, suburban job growth during the 1980s ran well ahead of job growth in central cities.

Other questions surfaced around other issues: Who gains and who loses as a result of downtown development? How many jobs do these projects actually produce? Are they permanent or temporary? Who gets the jobs – city residents or suburbanites? Should public funds be engaged in real estate development or job generation? How is the public interest served when the city trades uncollected property taxes that provide social and educational services for lower-income people, for physical development that provides benefits for higher-income people? Should public investment aim at preserving manufacturing jobs versus investing in service jobs? Should more emphasis focus on new opportunities for minority and female businesses, rather than market and economic efficiency? Should quasi-public development corporations be accountable since they are spending public money? Unfortunately, these vexing questions went largely unaddressed.

Cleveland, Ohio, presents a compelling compendium of these issues. The city has been hailed in the local and national media as a "comeback" or "renaissance" city rising phoenixlike from the depths of the city's 1978 default (Magnet, 1989). The city's civic and political leaders forged powerful public-private partnerships and successfully developed new hotels and office buildings in downtown, new stadiums for the baseball Indians and football Browns, an arena for the basketball Cavaliers, a Rock and Roll Hall of Fame and Museum signature building, and a Great Lakes Science Museum. They also restored a faded train station into an upscale mall and redeveloped four old theaters into a theatrical center at Playhouse Square. All of this was accomplished with the lavish expenditure of public funds and property tax abatements largely at the expense of the Cleveland school district. Abatements cost the school district about $21 million a year ("Seeking to shield," 1997). Cleveland's Growth Association estimated that $3.6 billion had been invested downtown between 1990 and 1996.

At the same time, by many indices Cleveland was in deep trouble ("Local yearbook 1993," 1993). Cleveland's population dropped 11.9% from 1980 to 1990; by 1997 the population was down to approximately 490,000, about the size of the city in 1900. Cleveland, once the nation's sixth largest city, now ranks 25th in size. The elegant marquees of the theaters at Playhouse Square look out over empty sidewalks. In terms of personal income, Cleveland ranks next to the rockbottom, 99th out of 100. Only the residents of Hialeah, Florida, have lower incomes. The city is on the high end, however (third highest in the nation), in percentage of households receiving public assistance. Here it ranks behind only Detroit and Newark. Cleveland ranked seventh highest in percentage of unemployment. In 1990, Cleveland's African-American unemployment rate exceeded 20%, the highest of any major city in the nation, while the nonemployment rate (unemployed, discouraged, and not looking for work, or in jail) for African-American men aged 25 to 54 hovered near 50%. Only three cities in the United States – Detroit, New Orleans, and Miami – have higher levels of poverty than Cleveland; over 40% of all Cleveland families live under the poverty line, and the number is rising rapidly. Cleveland stood 96th out of 100 in percentage of persons over 25 who are high school graduates. In 1995, the Cleveland public high schools graduated only 38% of the students who enrolled in the ninth grade four years earlier. In 1995, a Federal judge put the 70,000-student school system under state control after it ran out of money halfway through the year ("Seeking to shield," 1997).

It seems clear that local economic development successes have failed to improve the quality of life of many Cleveland residents. While much was built downtown, the city failed to make an effective effort to leverage downtown investment in favor of its troubled residents. Rather, as in most American cities, the public-private partnerships doing local economic development focused massive public subsidies on downtown real estate deals that provided tangible benefits to developers, land owners, building trade unions, politicians, and development officials. But benefits in the form of jobs for poor and unemployed residents could not be demonstrated, and net benefits to the overall fiscal condition of these cities was questionable (Fainstein, Fainstein, Hill, Judd, and Smith, 1983; Squires, 1989).

An exception to this exclusively downtown focus was the work of neighborhood-based CDCs. In city after city, CDCs have demonstrated substantial competence in developing affordable housing, managing it efficiently, and maintaining a sustained flow of support and resources, although their budgets represent only a small fraction of the resources devoted to downtown development (Krumholz, 1997; Vidal, 1992).

Are such outcomes inevitable? Obviously, resources and power are concentrated among political and civic elites who prefer to control development for their ends within a centralized, top-down economic development model. But in some cities, reform-minded politicians and progressive urban planners and other administrators have constructed alternative policies in economic development that have led to a more equitable distribution of project costs and benefits. The cases below drawn from field research (Krumholz and Clavel, 1994) offer a sampling of what they have accomplished.

Examples of Equitable Approaches to Local Economic Development

Boston, Massachusetts

In November 1983 Raymond Flynn was elected mayor of Boston. The Flynn administration was elected with the support and assistance of neighborhood and housing activists. It believed it had a mandate to share the benefits of Boston's downtown economic boom with the city's neighborhoods (Krumholz and Clavel, 1994). Peter Dreier, a professor and housing activist, joined the Flynn administration as director of housing for the Boston Redevelopment Authority.

The Flynn administration strengthened Boston's rent control ordinance, imposing a linkage requirement on housing whereby developers had to use some of their profits from market-rate units to subsidize affordable units within the same development and executing a redlining study with an implied challenge under the Community Reinvestment Act. The result was to encourage Boston banks to set up a pool of $400 million earmarked for lending to disinvested neighborhoods and CDCs.

The Flynn administration was particularly active on the neighborhood level, greatly increasing city support for nonprofit CDCs and conveying the right of eminent domain to assist the Dudley Street Neighborhood Initiative, a low-income minority neighborhood, in its redevelopment plan ("Current topic: Dudley Street initiative," 1997). The administration did not limit itself to micropolicies; it also helped shape national housing policy. Dreier helped draft a proposal for a national community-based housing partnership program that would provide federal matching grants to support innovative partnerships of nonprofit housing developers, local governments, and private investors that formed in Boston and other cities during the 1980s. This proposal was incorporated by Congress into the 1990 National Affordable Housing Act, which reversed (for a time) the trend of federal cutbacks in spending for low- and moderate-income housing.

Cleveland, Ohio

In 1975 the Cleveland City Planning Commission published the *Cleveland Policy Planning Report* (Krumholz, Cogger, and Linner, 1975; Krumholz and Forester, 1990). The central goal statement of the Report diverges substantially from the land use, zoning, and transportation focus of the plans of most U.S. cities. It states (Krumholz et al., 1975, p. 9) that "equity requires that locally responsible government institutions give priority attention to the goal of promoting a wider range of choices for those Cleveland residents who have few, if any, choices."

The Cleveland plan downplays land use and zoning issues and instead diagnoses the root problems of the city as concentrated poverty and racial segregation. The plan aimed to improve services, neighborhoods, and quality of life for poor and working-class Cleveland residents; citizens who had "few, if any, choices." These objectives led Cleveland planners to negotiate successfully for lower fares and better service for the city's poor, elderly, and otherwise transit-dependent population in the negotiations that led to the establishment of Cleveland's Regional Transit Authority in 1975 (Krumholz, 1982).

The planner's policy "to invest in private redevelopment efforts where it can be shown that such investment will provide a return to the city in the form of jobs for city residents, net increases in revenues for the city and/or improved services for low-income residents" also led the planning commission to disapprove a $350 million downtown development proposal called Tower City (Krumholz, 1982, p. 168). The commission found that the proposal asked the city to waive important rights it held to the development site, to agree to underwrite millions in capital improvements that were not the city's responsibility, and to provide property tax abatements for 20 years, without providing any quid pro quo. The planners asked the developer to pay for the capital improvements on his own account and to forego tax abatement. As a condition of public subsidy, the developer also was asked to guarantee a certain number of jobs to city residents and a net increase in property taxes, or alternatively to support projects in Cleveland's neighborhoods. The developer declined on all counts, and the planners disapproved the Tower City proposal.

It should be clear that the planners were not opposed to new development per se. They realized new development might keep firms downtown that otherwise might have left the city completely, that development provides short-term construction jobs, and that it adds to the tax base (unless new tax revenues are abated). They wanted new development to leverage clear benefits to Cleveland's poor and working-class people and not simply exchange new bricks for old at substantial cost to the public treasury. This negotiation was an early model for linkage arrangements, which have proved useful in other cities.

Oakland, California

In the 1980s, the city of Oakland set as its top priority the employment of minority youth (Mier, 1984). Initially, as in other cities, Oakland approached the issue by entering into partnerships with the private sector. Thirty local corporations joined to acquire a majority partnership in a new hotel development to be managed by the Hyatt Hotel chain. The city supported this development with an Urban Development Action Grant loan covering 12.5% of the development costs, but then Oakland's bargaining took a more progressive turn.

Oakland insisted that their return from their Hyatt investment be used to capitalize a revolving loan fund available only to neighborhood-oriented small businesses. Then the city council adopted a policy to promote minority participation in publicly assisted development projects. The policy states that any project receiving any form of public subsidy should strive for minority set-asides for the following: (a) 26% of all construction expenditures for minority firms, (b) 50% of all construction jobs to minorities, and (c) 40% of all professional work to minorities. The policy also insists on extensive joint-venturing between private developers and neighborhood-based CDCs.

The city of Oakland has had substantial success in realizing these goals in the construction of a new convention center adjoining the Hyatt Hotel and in new office buildings. Minority firms also own 6% of the Hyatt Hotel and 8% of the new $21 million Third Office Building in the Civic Center complex.

Jersey City, New Jersey

In 1985, Mayor Anthony Cucci appointed Rick Cohen, a housing and planning consultant, to the post of Director of Jersey City's Department of Housing and Economic Development (HED). When Cohen arrived on the job, he was greeted with a rapidly inflating rental market, a spillover from the overheated housing market of New York City (Krumholz and Clavel, 1994). Cheap rental apartments were being converted to upscale condominiums, and other apartments that offered the prospect of future condominium conversion were being cleared of tenants and mothballed. Cohen's department immediately introduced an anticondominium conversion bill to preserve as many affordable rental units of housing as possible.

A linkage program to provide support for low-income housing was next on the agenda. Developers were asked either to include affordable housing units in their development proposals or to contribute to a low-income housing trust fund. As a direct result, 18% of the units in the $10 billion Newport development on the Hudson River are reserved for lower-income families.

By the time Cohen was finished with his four-year stint as director of HED, Jersey City had a $14 million trust fund for low-income housing and a newly instituted shelter system for the homeless. The city also had helped expand the base of neighborhood participation and power by broadening its funding of neighbor-hood-based CDCs. Cohen also had increased the racial and ethnic diversity of his staff. At the time he was appointed, only one professional project manager at HED was African-American; by the time he left more than half of the project managers were members of minority groups.

Chicago, Illinois

Perhaps the most aggressive model for a more equitable approach to local economic development is the *1984 Chicago Economic Development Plan* prepared by the late Robert Mier and his staff. Mier, a planner, academic, and neighborhood activist, established the Center of Urban Economic Development at the University of Illinois, Chicago. He also assisted in the mayoralty campaign of Harold Washington, who ran on a platform of neighborhood-based economic development and a broad concern for social justice. When Washington won the mayor's office in 1983, he appointed Mier to head Chicago's Department of Economic Development. How Mier and the other planners thought about their responsibilities is shown below in the goals and policies of their plan.

Goal: increase job opportunities for Chicagoans.
Policies: (a) target business investment in support of job development, (b) local preference in buying and hiring, (c) skilled labor force development, (d) infra-structure investment for job development, (e) affirmative action.
Goal: promote balanced growth.
Policies: (a) balanced growth between downtown and neighborhoods, (b) public-private partnerships, (c) strengthened tax base, (d) equitable distribution of the tax burden.
Goal: assist neighborhoods to develop through partnership and coordinated in-vestment.
Policies: (a) neighborhood planning, (b) expanded housing opportunities, (c) linked development, (d) expand funding for CDCs.
Goal: enhance public participation in decision making.
Policies: (a) increased citizen access to information, (b) increased opportunities for citizen involvement.
Goal: pursue a regional, state, and national legislative agenda.

The *Chicago Economic Development Plan* focused narrowly on running the city of Chicago for the benefit of its people. Its vision was driven by the notion that questions of economic equity – that is, who gets what kind of jobs and the resultant income – were bound inextricably to the practice of public urban economic development planning.

The plan proposed to use the full weight of the city's leverage – tax incentives, public financing, city purchasing, infrastructure improvements, and the like – to generate jobs for Chicago residents. City resources were seen as public investments with a targeted rate of return in the form of the number of jobs provided for Chicagoans. Specific hiring targets for minority and female employment were set, 60% of the city's purchasing was directed to Chicago businesses, and 25% of this spending was to be done with minority and women-owned firms.

The plan also sought to encourage balanced or linked growth between downtown and city neighborhoods. Public support was offered to private developers building projects in "strong" market areas if they were willing to help neighborhood economic development projects in "weaker" market areas. The help could be provided through technical or legal assistance to local CDCs, joint venturing on neighborhood projects, or through contributions to a low-income housing fund. As a final objective, the plan drew up a regional, state, and federal legislative agenda to advocate its interests. This was a reminder that the best-laid and most equitable of city plans can be undercut by state priorities and congressional budgets.

Lessons and Future Possibilities

As these cases (and other cases in other cities) make clear, more progressive approaches to local economic development are possible. These strategies can open government to previously excluded constituencies, link downtown development to neighborhood development, and more equitably distribute the costs and benefits of the economic development process (Keating, 1986; Mier, 1984; Mier, Moe, and Sherr, 1987). This is not to say that challenging the present focus of local economic development is easy; it is not. After all, the more progressive alternatives confront the boosterism of the public-private growth coalition, challenge the rational voice of the market, and bring into question the allocation of public subsidy for private profit. Yet it can be done, and politicians and administrators who initiate progressive reforms not only may survive, they may prosper. Moreover, the reforms they put in place often will outlast their own administration, thus shaping future economic development plans in a more progressive direction.

Three essential principles make up the basis for these progressive, alternative strategies. The first of these is a shift from real estate speculation to public investment, including investment into a city's deteriorating capital plant and major new investments in nurturing a better-educated work force. Cities, states, and nations must come to realize that education is the single most important economic development activity. Compared with improving education, tax incentives and other conventional development "tools" are insignificant.

Second is the need to build upon strengths. Instead of giving tax abatements and other public inducements to all large developers without discrimination, cities must find a market niche where they have natural advantages. To use the Cleveland example again, after a history as a manufacturing center and one of the great producers of durable goods in the world, Cleveland now is trying to reshape itself into a major tourist and convention destination. It is doubtful that the city has any

natural advantages in this area; the city's physical plant is suffering from obsoles-
cence – especially as compared with newer competitive structures in newer regions;
crime is high and racial transition is continuing; and Cleveland has a cold, gray
climate not conducive to attracting tourists in our hedonistic leisure-oriented culture. However, Cleveland is very strong in the metalworking and forging industries,
where over 35,000 workers were employed in 1985 (Regional Economic Institute,
1987). The presence of these strong industries and trained labor force gives Cleveland an advantage that could be built upon, especially since manufacturing provides
better-paying jobs and is tied to research and development that spins off new
processes and investments.

The third part of a progressive strategy is the need to address redistributive issues.
When economic development provides outcomes in which some groups always win
and other groups always lose, where some are asked to bear the property tax burden
and others evade the burden, the legitimacy of government policy is called into
question. It strains our sense of justice to observe that the beneficiaries of all the
tax-abated, publicly subsidized projects are among the richest families in America
while the owners of modest $40,000 homes in the city extend great efforts to pay their
property taxes. Moreover, the city – and especially the city schools – foot the bill for
tax abatement while suburban workers benefit directly from downtown development. Democracies must work toward what is considered efficient and fair; class
hostility and alienation are not good either for economic growth or for democratic
government, but the question is less one of strategy than politics: Who is likely to call
for such alternative economic development strategies and under what circumstances?

One possible approach for alternative economic development policies was offered
by Rob Mier. Mier modified the popular public-private partnership metaphor into a
more progressive public-regarding model called cooperative leadership (Mier, 1993,
chap. 10). This concept is seen as potentially a more successful and longer-lasting
approach to collaborative problem solving than the elite-based and centralized
public-private partnership model now generally in use and that generally is focused
on big development projects. The current model offers generic approaches to specific
problems, focuses exclusively on the production of wealth, and ignores redistributive and social justice issues. In the process, other participants and objectives are
ignored and those who are not consulted may become disaffected and block solutions to a problem.

Mier suggested that what is needed to replace current approaches is a "new
leadership," in which cooperation and collaboration with diverse groups would be
broadened, participating groups would be encouraged to seek their own objectives,
and ultimately negotiated agreements would be reached that would satisfy all
participants. Bridging all these sectors, Mier believed, would promote civic progress
in the most inclusive way. Communities, he argued, are increasingly diverse, and
urban economies are undergoing rapid change. This fluid situation creates unexpected problems that can be resolved best by new interorganizational linkages
incorporating traditional civic and political leadership along with economic development professionals, but also including megaindustries, academics, labor unions,
nonprofit philanthropies, urban residents, and neighborhood CDCs.

But, as is all too possible, professionalized leadership may undermine grass-roots
action, and cooperative leadership may be co-opted by centralized, top-down
approaches and ignore redistributive issues. It would seem that the only guarantee

of the success of cooperative leadership aimed at equitable objectives would be the organization, participation, and support of a majority of urban voters. Any attempt at long-term equity planning or economic development in our cities along these lines must enlist the electoral support of the large number of city voters who would benefit by such policies.

A second possibility for modifying the top-down, self-serving system that now runs economic development in most of our cities lies in broader participation by urban planners and other public administrators who truly are concerned about the plight of the lower-income and working-class people of their cities. This is not to suggest that urban planners single-handedly can change the political economy of our cities. Only broader social movements with consistent voter support can accomplish this, but planners and other public administrators can make more of a difference in the face of inequality, poverty, and human suffering than we now expect. They can do this by working hard and vocally, with technical skill and persistence, on issues involving equity, fairness, legitimacy, and justice and by exploiting the institutional openings offered by city government.

Contrary to popular belief, city hall is not monolithic but a web of networks and coalitions upon which power and influence rest. City charters and local politics rarely give the planning staff much power; instead they provide much ambiguity. The nonmonolithic character of urban politics, the ambiguity of planning mandates, the need of others for planning analyses, and the potential for problem-framing and public discussion all provide institutional opportunities for urban planners to make more progressive responses. Such openness in the system allows planners to develop ties to elected and appointed officials throughout city government. It allows them, at their many private meetings and at their required public meetings, to put meaningful issues on the public agenda, to frame the issues in a meaningful way, and to organize influential coalitions in support of their positions.

Just "what the planning problem is" in many cases is rarely clear. For example, garbage dumping in city parks can be a crime problem, a financial problem, or an environmental problem. In the same way, the demand by an important sports team for a new publicly subsidized stadium may be seen by some as an economic issue (funds needed for the subsidy), by others as a question of local priorities (the schools come first), and by still others as a political issue (will the mayor be responsible for losing the team?). Facing this rich ambiguity of problem interpretation, planners have an opportunity to frame most problems. They could well ask publicly: What consequences do the demands by the team have for the city's poor and vulnerable populations? What public subsidies for private benefits are at stake? How will this proposal affect the provision of essential public services?

Their public questioning can help establish negotiating positions to improve equity outcomes. For example, in reviewing the public sector's financing of facilities used by professional sports, the planners can ask whether the plans include revenues a community could generate to finance a facility with lower taxes such as taxing the income of players, establishing the stadium within a special taxing district, capturing the public's portion of the increased value of the team produced by the new facilities and leases, or assessing fees for the broadcast and telecast of games. Such questions may cause sharp public discussion, but they can never be wrong.

Because virtually any planning problem can be stated in a variety of ways, the ambiguity planners face is an essential part of their work and their potential for doing more than many do. Even when severely constrained by relations of power, the planning questions remain: What can and should be done? What if? Should the city allow? What advantages and disadvantages come with each alternative? How will this improve or injure the future for our city's vulnerable populations?

This is not to misstate the constraints on a planners' freedom to act; they are formidable. Yet we too easily presume planners' powerlessness. In the process, we often fail to explore the limits and vulnerabilities of those who appear more powerful. Constraints exist, but opportunities do, too, even when planning mandates provide little specific guidance. Planning problems of housing, parks, economic development, and transportation are poorly defined, messy, open-ended, and ambiguous; they can be defined and open to interpretation in many ways, including ways that promise more benefits to the weak and vulnerable populations of the city.

What is suggested here is that urban planners, through their training and the ethics of their professional organizations, be encouraged to broaden their traditional areas of concern beyond land use, zoning, and urban design, and add a specific concern for the low- and moderate-income people of their cities. City planners are not master builders, but they can be educators and organizers as well as technicians. They can use the information they command and their political literacy to ask key questions publicly, command and organize attention, and raise key issues with respect to the future of their cities and their people. Working within coalitions of like-minded citizens, politicians, and professionals toward progressive ends, planners might improve the outcomes of the local economic development process.

A final source of support for economic development schemes that address redistributive issues is demographic: the rapidly changing diverse nature of many of our major cities. New York, Chicago, Los Angeles, Atlanta, Washington D.C., Baltimore, New Orleans, and many other major cities now have "majority minority" populations. In the next decade, these cities probably will be joined by several states, including New Mexico, Arizona, Texas, and California, the last two being very important to presidential politics. There is no reason to imagine that the speed or scope of this population shift will change. Along with massive shifts of population from central cities to suburban regions and widening economic disparities (Hughes and Sternberg, 1992; United States Department of Housing and Urban Development, 1995) there has come to the United States an immigration flood on a scale never seen before. Since the passage of the Immigration and Nationality Act of 1965, some 20 million immigrants have entered the United States, most from Mexico (the largest single source of new immigrants) and Asia.

Mexican immigration is concentrated heavily in the Southwest, where Mexican-Americans now make up 28% of the population of Texas and 31% of the population of California. Their concentration is unique in U.S. history: They have sufficient numbers and coherence in a defined region to elect local, state, and national politicians of their choice, and alter existing patterns of culture and education, if they so choose. Further, given the open border with Mexico, immigration can be maintained indefinitely.

It seems inevitable, therefore, that "minority majority" cities and states may become more and more commonplace. As in the past, politicians seeking to represent minorities will be likely to push for greater voter registration and participation by their ethnic supporters. In time, it is reasonable to expect that many of them will be successful. The politicians who emerge from minority constituencies will not see the world in the same way any more than Carl B. Stokes governed in the same way as Richard Hatcher, Tom Bradley, or Coleman Young. But all of them will want to do more for their supporters, and the most politically adept will develop sufficient cultural cohesiveness and political strength to insist on new ways for their states and perhaps U.S. society to organize their affairs. In this event, which seems highly probable, local economic development will become a subset of the broader state and national politics of redistribution.

REFERENCES

Blakeley, E. J. (1989). *Planning local economic development*. Newbury Park, CA: Sage.
Current topic: Dudley Street initiative. (1997, April). *Planning*, pp. 6–7.
Eisinger, P. K. (1988). *The rise of the entrepreneurial state*. Madison, WI: University of Wisconsin Press.
Fainstein, S. S., Fainstein, N. I., Hill, R. C., Judd, D., and Smith, M. P. (1983). *Restructuring the city*. New York: Longman.
Frieden, B. J., and Sagalyn, L. B. (1989). *Downtown, inc.: How America rebuilds cities*. Cambridge, MA: MIT Press.
Holland, R. C. (1982, June 9). Speech given to the Committee for Economic Development.
Hughes, M. A., and Stemberg, J. (1992). *The new metropolitan reality*. Washington, D.C.: The Urban Institute Press.
Keating, W. D. (1986). Linking downtown development to broader community goals: An analysis of linkage policies in three cities. *Journal of the American Planning Association, 52* (2), 133–141.
Krumholz, N. (1982, Spring). A retrospective view of equity planning. *Journal of the American Planning Association, 48*, 163–174.
Krumholz, N. (1997). The provision of affordable housing in Cleveland. In W. Van Vliet (ed.), *Affordable housing and urban redevelopment in the U.S.* (pp. 52–72). Thousand Oaks, CA: Sage.
Krumholz, N., and Clavel, P. (1994). *Reinventing cities: Equity planners tell their stories*. Philadelphia, PA: Temple University Press.
Krumholz, N., Cogger, J., and Linner, J. (1975, Fall). The Cleveland policy planning report. *Journal of the American Planning Association, 41* (5), 298–304.
Krumholz, N., and Forester, J. (1990). *Making equity planning work*. Philadelphia, PA: Temple University Press.
Levy, J. M. (1990, Spring). What local economic developers actually do: Location quotients vs. press releases. *Journal of the American Planning Association, 56* (2), 153–160.
Local yearbook 1993. (July). *Governing*, pp. 42–51.
Magnet, M. (1989, March 27). How business bosses saved a sick city. *Fortune,* 119 (7), 106–111.
Marlin, M. R. (1990, February). The effectiveness of economic development subsidies. *Economic Development Quarterly,* 4, 15–22.
Mier, R. (1984). Job generation as a road to recovery. In P. Porter and D. Sweet (eds.), *Rebuilding America's cities: Roads to recovery* (pp. 160–172). New Brunswick, NJ: Center for Urban Policy Research.
Mier, R. (1993). *Social justice and local economic development*. Newbury Park, CA: Sage.
Mier, R., Moe, K. J., and Sherr, I. (1987). Strategic planning and the pursuit of reform: Economic development and equity. In H. Goldstein (ed.), *The state and local industrial policy questions* (pp. 161–175). Chicago, IL: The Planners Press.

Regional Economic Institute. (1987, February). *The bridge*. Cleveland, OH: Case Western Reserve University.

Seeking to shield schools from tax breaks. (1997, May 21). *New York Times*, pp. A1, A16.

Squires, G. D. (1989). *Unequal partnerships*. New Brunswick, NJ: Rutgers University Press.

United States Department of Housing and Urban Development. (1995). *Empowerment: A new convenant with America's communities*. Washington, D.C.: United States Government Printing Office.

Vidal, A. C. (1992). *Rebuilding communities: A national study of community development corporations*. New York, NY: New School for Social Research.

Wolman, H. L., Ford, C. C., III, and Hill, E. (1994). Evaluating the success of urban success stories. *Urban Studies*, 31 (6), 835–850.

13

The Communicative Turn in Planning Theory and its Implications for Spatial Strategy Formation

Patsy Healey

The Context

There is a widespread consciousness these days that economic and political orders have changed substantially. This is felt intensely at the level of "places", of urban regions and city neighborhoods. Where once we could assume some kind of "spatial coherence" (Harvey, 1985) to urban orders, places now seem to have fragmented into an amalgam of "bits and pieces", "niches and nodes". This reflects the disintegration of the economic and governance relations relied on in the postwar era, the "Fordist" economy and a managed approach to its development and supporting social welfare strategies (Jessop et al., 1991). In their place, urban regions have become containers within which coexist a diversity of social and economic relations, linking people in a place with those in other places, but not necessarily with those in the same place. The results in urban regions are tensions and conflicts, as the dynamics and values of different relational networks jostle together. The actions of one may consciously or unwittingly undermine the opportunities of another. Protest groups hold up the development process. Development projects trample on the fine-grained neighborhood resources of those who move in a spatially confined lifeworld. Traffic growth severs people on either side of streets and destroys the shared resource of clean air. Our urban regions seem to be becoming less interrelated and less understandable in simple models of land-value surfaces sloping downwards and outwards from a central core, or in the gravity models used to describe traffic

Reprinted with permission from *Environment and Planning B: Planning and Design*, 23 (1996): 217–34. (Note: An earlier version of this paper is published in *Are Local Strategies Possible?*, (ed. T Pakarinen, Department of Architecture, Tampere University of Technology, Tampere, Finland, 1995), under the title "The argumentative turn in planning theory and its implications for spatial strategy formation."

movements or the location of retail spending. At the same time, the quality of places has become important in regional economic development and in the struggle to avoid further environmental deterioration. Urban regions are now set in competition with each other, as people and companies seek locations with the institutional capacity to resolve conflicts, reduce tensions, and deliver local environments which can promote both healthy local economies and biospheric sustainability (Amin, 1994; Cooke and Morgan, 1993; Healey et al., 1995).

As a result, there is increasing interest in Europe in the spatial organization of urban regions and in spatial strategy (European Commission, 1995; Healey, 1994). But in the Western world, we seem to have lost confidence in our political systems, in our mechanisms for conflict mediation and for the strategic management of our collective affairs. So how are we to arrive at a spatial strategy? How do we get to *understand* the complex and diffused dynamics of urban regions? How do we get to *agree* on what the problems are, and on what we want to promote and safeguard? How can we translate agreement into *influence* on the ongoing flow of activities through which our regions are continually being reshaped?

It is in this context that the new ideas about public argumentation and communicative policy practice being developed in the field of planning theory have something to offer. In this chapter I first summarize the sources of these ideas and how they are being developed in the planning field, before discussing their implications for new strategic planning practices, and their capacity to address the above questions.

Public Policymaking as Communicative Argumentation

A new wave of ideas is sweeping over the field of planning and policy analysis. Of course there are always new theories and interpretations, new policy proverbs and management 'tricks' being provided as academic and practical reflection proceeds. But now and again, as Kuhn (1962) has shown us, we begin to see that many small contributions add up to a sea change in the parameters of our thinking, producing what Kuhn referred to as a paradigm shift. In the early stages, these are difficult to see. Only as they gather momentum and seem to come at us from several different directions at once do we recognize them for what they are, a sort of strategic resetting of our mental lenses. In the second half of this century, two such waves have swept across the planning field. The first brought with it the vocabulary of instrumental rationality and regional economics aligned to a management science which promoted strategic planning processes based on modeling the dynamics of urban systems and managing them with strategies developed through the so-called comprehensive rational planning process (for example, McLoughlin, 1969). This gave us a methodological and institutional inheritance of strategic planning designed in the heady days of rational planning in the 1960s and 1970s. The second gave us a substantive understanding of the power relations of urban region economies, through the analysis of the structuring dynamics of economic and political relations. This *political economy* of urban regions gave us aggressive critique of much public policy and planning activity. It also provided the foundations for new ways of analyzing the complex layering of different economic dynamics in our urban regions and their vulnerability to external influence (Amin et al., 1992; Massey, 1984).

But these ideas constructed policy processes in terms of power struggles, between capital and community, between fractions of capital, between economic growth and environmental quality. They had little to say about the fine grain of economic and social relations, about the diversity of ways of using and valuing places, and were uncomfortable in the face of rising concern about the destruction of the natural environment and the biospheric conditions for the survival of the planet's species mix. Their focus was heavily on material conditions, and on who should get what, not on how people come to understand and value the qualities of their environments. They were therefore ill placed to recognize the cultural diversity in our midst.

The new wave speaks to this diversity. It seeks to escape from the strait-jacket of a narrow instrumental rationality in its approaches to how to identify problems in need of strategic attention and how to act on them. It searches for ways of going beyond a preoccupation with the distribution of material resources. It starts from the recognition that we are diverse people living in complex webs of economic and social relations, within which we develop potentially very varied ways of seeing the world, of identifying our interests and values, of reasoning about them, and of thinking about our relations with others. The potential for overt conflict between us is therefore substantial, as is the chance that unwittingly we may trample on each other's concerns. Faced with such diversity and difference, how then can we come to any agreement over what collectively experienced problems we have and what to do about them? How can we get to *share* in a process of working out how to coexist in shared spaces?

The new wave of ideas focuses on how we get to discuss issues in the public realm. It seeks to develop normative principles which we might use to judge our discussions and to build interrelations across our differences which will enable us to undertake strategic consensus-building work through which to create interculturally sensitive strategies for managing our common concerns in urban region space. These ideas draw upon multiple sources of inspiration. A powerful intellectual influence is the work of Habermas. He is deeply committed to reconstructing a public realm which more fully reflects the range of our ways of knowing and reasoning than the narrow diminished world of instrumental rationality and the dominant interests of economic and bureaucratic power. He shows us that we are not autonomous subjects competitively pursuing our individual preferences, but that our sense of ourselves and of our interests is constituted through our relations with others, through communicative practices. Our ideas about ourselves, our interests, and our values are socially constructed through our communication with others and the collaborative work this involves. If our consciousness is dialogically constructed, surely we are deeply skilled in communicative practices for listening, learning, and understanding each other. Could we not harness these capacities explicitly to the task of discussion in the public realm about issues which collectively concern us? Habermas believes that we can. Further, he argues that implicit in our communicative acts is a normative judgment that people should relate to each other in ways that aim for comprehensibility, sincerity, legitimacy, and truth. These are his principles for the much misunderstood principle of an ideal speech situation. Of course, we all know that we let each other down on these criteria. But we do know how to judge each other when we do this. So could we not judge public discussion like this too? (See Habermas, 1984; 1987; 1993.)

These ideas, and other contributions within philosophical debate, focus on ways of reconstructing the meaning of a democratic practice, away from the paternalism of traditional representative notions, to more participatory forms based on *inclu-sionary argumentation*. By this term is implied public reasoning which accepts the contributions of all members of a political community and recognizes the range of ways they have of knowing, valuing, and giving meaning. Inclusionary argumenta-tion as a practice thus underpins conceptions of what is being called participatory democracy (Fischer, 1990; Held, 1987) or discursive democracy (Dryzek, 1990). Through such argumentation, a public realm is generated through which diverse issues and diverse ways of raising issues can be given attention. In such situations, as Habermas argues, the power of the 'better argument' confronts and transforms the power of the state and capital.

But it is not just in the arena of philosopy that such ideas are evolving. Similar concepts are embodied as practical strategies in the arena of environmental medi-ation. Here the challenge of getting people to agree about complex environmental conflicts has led to an interest in developing discursive forms of argumentation which encourage participants to move from zero-sum solutions to zero-plus reso-lutions (Forester, 1992). This means building strategies which do not merely add together and balance out the amalgam of interests. Through creative encounter, interests are reformed around new ideas. Strategy-making thus 'adds value' to the policy process. Similar innovations are occurring in efforts in consensus-building about strategies for managing environmental change in some U.S. states. Innes et al. (1994) describe collaborative strategy-building processes which generate *social and intellectual capital*. Within the field of management, reflecting a recognition that the human relations of the workplace may make a difference to how well people work, there is now a rich debate on how to build collaborative working relations and create cooperative work cultures.

From another direction, academics in the humanities have for some time been preoccupied with the study of language and meaning. Their emphasis has been on *deconstructing* discourses, to reveal the hidden values and understandings which lie behind the surface of language, art, and music. This work provides help in appreci-ating what is being communicated in any social situation. It alerts us to the hidden systems of power which may be conveyed through language. This connects to the approach of the sociologist Foucault on the way power relations are embedded in the fine grain of our social interactions (Rabinow, 1984). Of particular value in the deconstruction of social intercourse is the work of feminist academics in a wide range of fields. This has shown just how deeply invisible the categorizing and marginalization of women in our societies has been. By revealing this, it makes such practices open for inquiry and review. Feminist work also highlights how the thought world of instrumental rationality, and the neoclassical economics to which it is related, emphasizes competitive behavior and power as conflict. It tends to marginalize collaborative behavior, of the kind common in households or in com-munity enterprises, just as it has ignored gender generally in its discussion of policy processes (Huxley, 1993; Young, 1990). These contributions not only provide critical resources with which to recognize and resist many traditional policy prac-tices. They also offer ideas about how to collaborate across differences to construct new public discourses, derived from more richly inclusionary practices.

These ideas are interrelating with new directions in the theorization of social relations and the dynamics of social and economic change. Drawing on the political economy of power structures, on phenomenological understanding of the social construction of knowledge and meaning, and on ethnographic inspiration in the approach to the way human agency enacts and transforms social structure in the flow of daily life, this new *institutionalist* approach provides ways of analyzing the webs of social relations within which we live and work, their cultural diversity, and the way they overlap and intersect within particular spaces (Giddens, 1984). The problems of coexistence in shared spaces thus become those of managing these relational intersections. Creating a public discourse through which to discuss such problems means finding *arenas* within which to construct a 'public realm' and finding *modes of discourse* within which inclusionary discussion can take place. An inclusionary discussion in this context means one which draws upon the knowledge and understandings, the values and capacities, of the relational webs 'represented' within any political community.

These strands of thought have been evolving rapidly over the past twenty years, and increasingly draw inspiration from each other. In the planning field, they are represented in particular in the work of democratic and collaborative planning processes, notably that by Forester (1993a), Flyvbjerg (1996), and Sager (1994), who are searching for ways of realizing Habermasian ideas of communicative process; by myself (Healey, 1992a), Hillier (1993), and Hoch (1992), who have explored the micropolitics of policy talk and text in the planning field; by Bryson in his work on management principles for collaborative strategic planning in the public realm (Bryson and Crosby, 1992); and by Innes, who is exploring what makes for successful consensus-building in strategic planning work (Innes, 1992; Innes et al., 1994). Other work has developed a vigorous critique of 'modernist' rational planning and 'functionalist' social engineering (Boyer, 1983) to move beyond the class-based analysis of urban political economy, to explore 'postmodern' conceptions of the assertion of diversity and difference and the critique of 'ordering' efforts in public policy (Dear, 1986; Goodchild, 1990; Moore Milroy, 1991). Another line of analysis, drawing on feminist inspirations, has uncovered the power relations lying behind the imagery used in public discourse on planning issues, the rhetorical forms in which discussion takes place, and the assumptions locked into planning practices (Hillier, 1993; Huxley, 1993; Tait and Woolfe, 1991; Throgmorton, 1992). In recognition of the collective significance of these strands of thinking, reviewers who identify a new approach to planning have recently labeled it as an interpretive approach (Innes, 1995) or a communicative one (Sager, 1994).

Key themes to emerge from this work in relation to the challenge of finding new forms of strategic planning are:

1   How is it possible to distinguish between forms of argumentation, of discourse about planning matters, which *reinforce* existing relations of power and conventional understandings of issues and those which have the potential to *transform* these relations, in ways which are more relevant to the way we live now, and which have the capacity to open up the public realm to 'inclusionary argumentation' (Forester especially).

2   If we aim for 'inclusionary argumentation', what practices will help achieve this, given the diversity of those sharing spaces in urban regions? Recognizing that this diversity is not merely about interests, but about ways of conceiving of interests, ways of knowing, understanding, and valuing, how do we get to

communicate "across" these cultural differences? (Forester, Innes, and Healey especially).

3   What specific tasks are involved in the work of strategic consensus-building and strategy development which seeks to promote inclusionary argumentation, and what kinds of facilitating skills are needed to perform them? (Bryson and Crosby, Innes).

In reviewing these developments in the early 1990s, I concluded that their implications for planning could be summarized under ten points (Healey, 1992a; 1993). Planning, in this new wave of ideas, emerges as (1) an interactive and interpretative process, (2) undertaken *among* diverse and fluid "discourse communities", or cultures, (3) in ways which require "respectful" interpersonal and intercultural discussion, searching out ways of recognizing and valuing what we are trying to say to each other within the public realm. This enterprise focuses our attention (4) on the arenas where public discussion takes place and where problems and strategies are identified and evaluated and conflicts mediated, (5) on the multiple claims made for policy attention and the different forms in which these claims are made, (6) on ways of developing a critical, reflexive capacity which has both evaluative and creative potential, generating ideas about what to do and how, as well as testing them against the values of the diverse community members, and (7) on ways of opening out such strategic discourse in forms which are as inclusionary as possible. Through such new styles of planning discourse, it is hoped not only (8) that participants will learn new things about themselves, their relations, their interests, values, and understandings, but that, with such knowledge, they will (9) collaborate to change the way things are. In this way, such inclusionary argumentation has the power to *transform* situations, through the power of the better argument (Habermas, 1984), and the power of ideas, metaphors, images, and stories (Forester, 1992; Nussbaum, 1990). As Pierre Bourdieu says (1990), how we talk about things helps us to bring them about. Planning, as an explicit exercise in imagining the future, is thus about (10) "dreaming the possibility of change", imagining how to "start out on a journey" in mutually acceptable ways, rather than, as in the ideas of the urban designer planners, "dreaming the destination". If there is a destination implied, it is a process dream, of a democratic society which respects difference but yet collaborates, and which can live sustainably within its economic and social possibilities and environmental parameters.

A Communicative Approach to Spatial Strategy Formation

Much of the work of spatial and environmental planning activity is focused on managing the fine grain of change in local environments or promoting particular projects or objectives. But these actions embody assumptions about what is valued about local environments, how these values might be threatened, about why certain projects or policies are desirable, and who is supposed to benefit. These assumptions are often left implicit as the flow of "management" proceeds. As the work referred to in the previous section emphasizes, such implicit strategies may not only lock the flow of planning work into actions which are irrelevant or at odds with the ways economic and social relations within urban regions are changing, leaving planning systems as a kind of "relict apparatus" (Dear, 1995). They may also serve to entrench the power and interests of powerful groups, and make life difficult for others. Yet attempting to review and create new spatial strategies is an extraordinarily difficult task, and even more so if the objective is to do this in inclusionary ways, providing voice and respect to all members of the political community of an urban region. It requires ways of "giving voice" to all members, even though they cannot all be "present" in any discussion. It requires sorting through an array of issues – problems, arguments, claims for policy attention, ideas about what to do, fears of what will happen – to identify those which, for the various members, it makes sense to pay attention to. It involves moving beyond learning about the ways of understanding, and the agenda of ideas already available among community members, to developing new ideas about what to think, what to care about and what to do. It seems almost an impossible challenge in our dynamic, differentiated, complex, and conflictual urban regions.

The planning literature already referred to is beginning to provide us with interesting ways of thinking about this. I organize these ideas under five headings. Listed like this, there is a parallel with the step-by-step models of conventional rational planning processes. But, although the headings represent dimensions of strategic planning processes which need to be accomplished in some way, they are not presented here as a sequence of tasks to perform. Rather, they should be seen as questions which a political community contemplating a strategic planning initiative should ask itself.

1   **Where** is discussion to take place, in what forums and arenas; how are community members to get access to it?
2   In what style will discussion take place? What styles will most likely be able to "open out" discussion to enable the diversity of "languages" among community members to find expression?
3   How can the jumble of issues, arguments, claims for attention, and ideas about what to do which arise in discussion be **sorted out**?
4   How can a strategy be created that becomes a **new discourse** about how spatial and environmental change in urban regions could be managed?
5   How can a political community get to **agree** on a strategy, and maintain that agreement over time while continually subjecting it to **critique**?

Arenas for argumentation

The traditional way of discussing where policymaking takes place is to consider the arenas of formal political, administrative, and legal systems. These create formal arenas and allocate rights to be represented and heard in these arenas. Their form privileges some and marginalizes others. Analysis has until recently tended to concentrate on who wins and loses through the form of such systems, and how the "politics of voice", of articulate interests, challenges the power of "bureaucracy" and "capital". The perspective of inclusionary argumentation moves beyond this. Yet it cannot proceed without attention to where discussion takes place. The value of the traditional ideas is that they focus attention on how the arenas are constructed and where their legitimacy comes from. The impetus for spatial strategy formation does not just appear out of the ether. It arises from particular institutional situations. There needs to be a moment of opportunity, a crack in the power relations, a situation of contradiction and conflict, which encourages people to recognize that they need to reflect on what they are doing, that they need to work with different people, that they need to evolve different processes.

One of the critical resources at this stage is the capacity to read the cracks, to see the opportunities for doing things differently, and to be able to widen a crack into a real potential for change. Bryson and Crosby (1992) assign a key role to "leaders" in recognizing moments of opportunity and networks around the idea of an effort in strategy-making. But such activators need not necessarily be in formal leadership positions. They may arise in all kinds of institutional settings and relationships, and are merely those with the capacity to see and articulate to others a strategic possibility. Behind this skill lies the capacity for an acute sense of the relation between the structural dynamics of local economic, social, and political relations and how these are manifest in what particular people in a place are bothered about. The few accounts we have of planners talking about their work provide rich evidence of this capacity at work (for example, Krumholz, in Krumholz and Forester, 1992; or Crawley, 1991).

But having read the opportunity, which could occur in many nodes of local institutional arrangements, one needs careful thought about where to find the arenas where discussions can take place. One possibility could be to use existing organizational arrangements, for example, where urban region government already exists. But these may have become moribund and discredited. Or they may be difficult to unhitch from the control of a narrow range of interests. So another strategy may be to create new arrangements for mobilizing community voice (see Hillier, 1993; Innes et al., 1994).

A key problem here is the definition of "community", or the "universe" of those with a stake in an issue. The meaning of community used here is not that of the traditional place-based *Gemeinschaft*. Rather it refers to two meanings of community. The first is spatially based, all those in a place who share a concern and/or are affected by what happens there. The second is stake based, that is, all those who, directly or indirectly, have an interest in or care about what the people in the first community are doing in a place. These may be those who value the historic assets, or environmental qualities of a place, or who go there to shop; or they may be those affected by the adverse consequences of what a community in the first sense gets up to. An inclusionary strategic planning exercise needs to attend to both, the political community oriented to acting on a set of problems, and the wider community of stakeholders.

Mapping the stakeholders is an important task in any strategic planning process which operates in a world with a plurality of interests and sources of power (see Bryson and Crosby, 1992; Christensen, 1993; Hull, 1995). For an inclusionary sensibility, this means keeping open the potential that new stakeholders will be discovered, and respecting the ways in which their stakes are manifest.

The ethical challenge at this stage is that discussion gets started before the members of a political community have had a chance to work out what kind of arenas they would prefer or who the stakeholders are. As a result, some carry responsibility for the initial moves. Two ideas may help to distinguish these first moves which have inclusionary democratic potential and those which may entrench the dominance of a few powerful people. The first refers to an "inclusionary ethic". This emphasizes a moral duty to ask, as arenas are being set up, who are members of the political community, how are they to get access to the arena in such a way that their points of view can be appreciated as well as their voices heard, and how can they have a stake in the process throughout. This means moving beyond simple conceptions of distributive justice (everyone has equal standing) to a recognition of diversity (all groupings of people should have equal ability to put over their views) (Young, 1990). To perform such a moral duty effectively will be helped by access to a rich experiential political and social knowledge about community members, as well as perhaps analytical knowledge about the potential ways in which different people get involved in the public realm.

The second idea recognizes that the "where" of strategic discussion may shift about, and use different arenas at different times. Not only may it be helpful to encourage discussion in several institutional places at the early stages of a strategic planning exercise (for example, council chambers, business clubs, community halls, schools, radio phone-ins). The arenas may change in nature as discussion proceeds. Bryson and Crosby (1992) argue that the policy-innovation cycle moves through three types of setting: "forums", where strategic values and directions are articulated; "arenas", where policies are more precisely defined and converted into specific programs; and "courts" where outstanding disputes are articulated. They argue that each has its own distinctive styles and politics. This recognizes that, over time, discussion moves from discursive "opening out" to consolidation around particular ideas and consequential actions and values. But the danger is that such discursive closure loses touch with the rich manifestation of concerns raised earlier on. The important quality of an inclusionary approach is that the style and ethics of the discussion setting enables awareness of the stakeholder range to be sustained throughout the process and maintains opportunity for the assertion of all stakeholder claims for attention throughout as well.

The scope and style of discourse

A second set of considerations concerns what gets discussed and how. Bryson and Crosby (1992) refer to this as "searching". The practice of environmental appraisal contributes the term "scoping" for this task. In the planning tradition, we used to call this activity the "survey" stage. But an inclusionary effort in rethinking spatial strategy is much more than merely identifying what is going on and what the issues are. It involves opening out issues, to explore what they mean to different people, and whether they are really about what they seem to be or about something else. It requires a sort of mental "unhooking" from previous assumptions and practices, to try to see issues in new ways; even if only to allow us to recognize that some of our old ways are quite useful in new worlds.

This is a critical and delicate operation. It can easily be undertaken in ways which reinforce stereotypes, which narrow agendas, and which alienate many interested parties. But undertaken with inclusionary commitment, it can have enormous power in helping people learn about each others' concerns, about problems and possibilities, in ways which reach out across our cultural differences. Although there is now a considerable body of practical advice on how to engage in such discourse within the context of small groups, the challenge of collaborative discussion about urban region futures is more complex. Not only are the cultural differences among members of the relevant political communities likely to be large, with the consequence that the potential for misunderstanding is substantial. The issues themselves often involve making difficult chains of connection between what bothers people, what causes this, and what could be done about it.

Three aspects of this dimension are of particular interest. The first concerns its *style*. The possibility of inclusionary argumentation is barely satisfied merely by ensuring everyone has "voice" or a "route to voice". The material referred to in the previous section is rich with examples of the way voices are ignored or misheard, and of the problems of getting to speak in alien surroundings (Davoudi and Healey, 1995; Hillier, 1993). There are many possible styles of collective discourse. They vary in how people prepare themselves, how rooms are arranged, how communicative routines are set up (who speaks when and how), how discussion is concluded, remembered, and called up at a later time. Forester refers to these as the rituals of policy discussion (Forester, 1993b). The problem for strategic spatial planning exercises is that different participants may have different expectations of such routines, learned from local politics, from company management, from the practices of labor unions, from household collaboration, or from community-organization initiatives. An inclusionary approach will therefore mean actively discussing and choosing a style of discussion, and recognizing that not everyone will be comfortable in it to begin with. The growth of facilitators in environmental mediation and community development is an illustration of the importance of this work, where such facilitation moves beyond getting the issues out to considering how to discuss them.

The second aspect concerns its *language*. Participants may try hard to give each other respect and to follow routines which give space for everyone. But they may still "talk past" each other through using different ways of expressing things. These differences are not merely a matter of metaphors and imagery. Such images may have a particular meaning for those in one cultural frame of reference but be quite strange to another. Ironical and ambiguous expression from a speaker may be richly appreciated by some and completely missed by others. The differences also apply to the way statements are made. Some people are familiar with the language of consequences, grounded in economic reasoning or scientific evidence. Others are more accustomed to the language of belief or the political assertion of rights. Others again may be more comfortable with the expression of fears and dangers (Healey and Hillier, 1995). The challenge for strategic argumentation is to accept them all, but to recognize that translation may be needed and even then there are limits to intercultural communication, as Geertz (1983) shows in his discussion of *Local Knowledge*.

The third aspect concerns how the members of a political community are "called up" as discussion proceeds – that is, how they are accorded *respect*. Depending on how decisions about discussion arenas have been made, the discussion may take place in meeting rooms, in a mixture of meeting rooms and working groups, through videoconferencing or whatever ways participants can think of for spreading involvement. Yet, however energetically the opportunity to give voice is pursued in a community, some will be more actively involved than others, and a few will play key roles in shaping discussion, sorting out arguments, and developing a strategic discourse. But that does not mean that the others are inevitably marginalized. Any analysis of a conversation will typically reveal that more people are present than are actually speaking. It may also show that some people are present but not able to find expression. Analysis of discourse in sociology and linguistics illustrates how we construct, through our talk and our nonverbal language, definitions of ourselves and others, of me, of you, of we/us, you and them (for example, Boden, 1994; Silverman, 1993). Further, we 'call upon' other people in conversation, to legitimate a view, or to ground a point (Healey, 1992b). If these processes of defining who 'we' are, and of calling up nonpresent others are going on routinely in our everyday conversation, can we not make use of them in our discussions about matters of strategic spatial concern? This suggests that a key quality of inclusionary strategic argumentation is the capacity to keep under explicit review the various ways the members of a political community describe, to each other, both themselves, and the "others" of significance to them, as they engage in discussion. This needs to be accompanied by the ability to maintain active respect and appreciation for those members who for one reason or another are "not present". In any strategic discussion on urban region futures, it will always be the case that those not present will outnumber those present. The inclusionary challenge is to prevent those not present being absent from the discussion.

Sorting through the arguments

If the arenas for strategic spatial planning take the inclusionary forms proposed here, pursued through the open style suggested, the result can be that a huge array of issues are brought up for attention. A visual and verbal record of what goes on in such interactions would show an argumentative jumble of statements about facts, about values, about claims for attention, about fears, about consequences and apocalyptic disasters (Healey and Hillier, 1995). But these are more than just statements. They indicate how speakers feel about things, who they most relate to, and who they are trying to get to listen. As Forester (1993a) argues, how a point is made or a story is told tells people about how the speaker conceives of things, about the power relations they perceive around them, about the languages they use.

In conventional strategic planning exercises, such material is translated into, and filtered through, the technical language used by planning analysts and the administrators of planning systems. This will almost immediately reduce a person's speech into a "point", to join other points in a structured analytical framework through which the planners seek to "make sense" of what is going on. The argumentative jumble is translated into the familiar "analysis" work of spatial planning.

In a process of inclusionary argumentation, such analytical work needs to be much richer and more widely shared. Participants need to be encouraged to probe the meaning of the different points raised and to test out in discussion their implications for the concerns of other people. As discussion opens out and works through the issues raised, participants learn about what the issues are and about each other's ways of thinking and acting. Analysis is thus not an abstract technical process but an active enterprise in mutual sorting through the arguments and learning about possibilities. This sorting out process is not just about exploring and working out what are problems and why, and how conditions may be changed. It is more than developing an analysis of urban and regional change. It involves working out what people value in moral and aesthetic terms as well as in a material sense, and how values are affected. It requires attention to rights, and to the legitimacy of the multiplicity of claims for policy attention.

The role of expertise in this context, where experts act not merely as 'participants' with a point of view, is to facilitate the process of learning about and sorting through arguments and claims. It involves asking questions to the discussion members which help to open up meanings, or making links between an issue raised by one member and its potential implications for another. It may also involve offering key organizing ideas to help the discussants focus their thinking. This of course raises critical ethical questions about the way this is done. An inclusionary approach to argumentation demands that such expert facilitation offers up 'organizing ideas' for critical scrutiny, and avoids proposing them too early in the discussion, before people have had time to understand each other. This contrasts sharply with the current convention on how to approach public consultation on strategic planning matters. This argues that there is no point going out to consultation until after analysis has been undertaken and at least the parameters for option choice identified. This involves 'fixing' the issue agenda in advance and often much of the policy agenda. In contrast, a critical skill in facilitating inclusionary argumentation processes is knowing when to start sorting through arguments more formally, when to shift from trying to grasp different points of view on things, to trying to draw out common threads. This applies even more so to moving from "learning to understand", to "working out what to do".

Creating a new discourse

In many strategic planning exercises, broadly based discussion takes place in defined stages, before or after strategies have been articulated. Politicians or experts "invent" the strategic ideas. In the past, we acknowledged this when talking of Abercrombie's plan for London, or Hall's Strategy for South-east England. Later, it was said that plans were produced "by planners for planners". How can a strategy emerge from the collaborative, discursive processes described here? It requires a capacity to reach some agreement across differences as to what the issues are, the purposes of action, and the way the consequences, the costs and benefits of action, should be assessed. But it also represents a feat of collective imagining of possible courses of action and what these could achieve. Making a strategy according to these new ideas involves a collaborative effort in selecting from among possibilities, and sharpening up the selected strategies so that they make sense, both operationally in relation to resource allocation and regulatory power, and in terms of general understanding. The first is necessary to meet criteria of effectiveness, the second of legitimacy.

One way of thinking of this task of inclusionary spatial strategy-making is as a collaborative task in creating a new *policy discourse*. Here the term discourse is understood sociologically rather than linguistically (Silverman, 1993), as a system of meaning embodied in a strategy for action. The system of meaning begins its evolution as the argumentative jumble is scrutinized. As ideas about possible action come forward, new ways of thinking about the issues raised in argumentation are likely to emerge. The processes of sorting through and discourse creation are thus interactive. This might suggest that they can proceed in parallel, and in practice this often happens. However, as noted above, a strategic planning process which aims to open out discussion to enable new ways of looking at issues to emerge needs to avoid consolidation of the options for action too early in the process, before people know each other and the issues. Otherwise, debate can quickly regress to adversarial argument about entrenched positions. Further, policy discourses can become very powerful, imposing organizing concepts and a vocabulary of images and terms through which issues are discussed.

The way policy discourses develop is well described in recent studies of environmental issues. In a valuable review of approaches to the analysis of policy discourses, Hajer (1995) highlights the importance of the new understandings, or concepts, which provide the *discursive key* which "turns" the discussion from one conception to another. He argues that this phenomenon can be put to normative use, in the process of strategy development, shifting the "storyline" of policy debate from one account to another. The debate in the United Kingdom on the meaning of environmental sustainability in relation to spatial planning provides a good illustration of the evolution of policy discourse, with a broad but vague conception of sustainability as an inheritance to pass on to the future gradually consolidating into two competing conceptions, one focusing on the maintenance of an environmental asset stock, the other on containing development within biospheric carrying capacities (Healey and Shaw, 1994; Owens, 1994).

The power of such policy discourses in the planning field has been identified in recent studies examining planning "talk" and text. Policy ideas, once accepted, may have enormous longevity, as in the British green belt and the principles of urban containment, or the "district centres" strategies pursued for many years in Australian cities (McLoughlin, 1992). In describing the longevity of Dutch spatial planning ideas, Faludi and van der Valk (1994) develop the concept of a *planning doctrine* to describe these enduring conceptions. The vocabulary of such policies may enter popular consciousness, with public debate structured by the terminology of the policy and its practice (Grant, 1994; Hillier, 1993). Strategically perceptive planners and politicians may be very conscious of their role in creating new discourses. The defining quality of an inclusionary strategic discourse is that, within its storyline, there are parts for most people, and there is acknowledgment, where relevant, that some suffer more and some benefit more as the story proceeds. Any story has its regrets and little tragedies. In the rational planning mode, these were ignored. An inclusionary approach demands explicit attention to them (Forester, 1993b), to what cannot be achieved and what the costs of this may be, as well as what can be done. For an inclusionary and democratic approach to strategic spatial planning, the work of discourse creation is therefore both the most important and the most dangerous part of the process. Once a policy discourse has gained attention, it carries forward with it a distinctive storyline, about what is and should be, about what are seen as good or bad arguments, and about appropriate modes of argument and claims for policy attention. It gives meaning and significance to issues, problems, and actions, and focuses the setting of priorities for action. Once momentum has been achieved, policy discourses spread out and may come to influence a wide sphere of social action, sometimes achieving 'hegemonic' status. It is this persuasive power of discourse embedded in existing practices, and pursued by the powerful, which an inclusionary discursive form of strategic argumentation seeks to challenge, yet at the same time to acknowledge and use.

The formation of policy discourses carries dangers, therefore, because a policy discourse is a selective simplification of the issues in discussion and because it gains momentum by exaggeration. A strong discourse provides legitimate reasons for ignoring some evidence, some values, and some claims for policy attention. A cautious policymaking exercise might seek to avoid the production of such an organizing conception. But this would be to reduce its power to influence events. The challenge for an inclusionary approach to strategic spatial planning is to experiment with and test out strategic ideas in initially tentative ways, to open out possibilities for both evaluation and invention of better alternatives, before allowing a preferred discourse to emerge, and crowd out the alternatives. As Bryson and Crosby (1992) note, the timing of problem definition in a policymaking process is a critical issue. This suggests a discursive process is needed which explicitly explores different storylines about possible actions and offers up different discursive keys for critical attention, maintaining a critical attitude until there is broad support for a new strategic discourse. Having thus generated a knowledgeable consensus around a particular storyline, the task of consolidating the discourse and developing its implications can then proceed. The discourse community can be said by this time to have collaboratively chosen a strategy, over which they are then likely to have some sense of "ownership".

Agreement and critique

The objective of strategic inclusionary argumentation on urban region futures is a rich policy discourse which expresses a storyline which makes sense of many puzzles people have, and which proposes ways forward likely to make sense and bring benefits to as many participants as possible. But there will always be some people who will be unhappy with the story, or who have objections which cannot be resolved in debating arenas. Procedures are needed to provide a fair way to deal with objections and disagreements. As Bryson and Crosby (1992) argue, some form of *court* provides the locus for such arbitration. Courts, in judicial or semijudicial form, have an important role in most spatial planning systems. But such courts are more than merely a legal backstop to be used when the collaborative process reaches limits. An inclusionary form of argumentation needs to agree at the start how such disagreements will be addressed and keep these under critical review throughout. It also needs to pay attention to the terms in which such challenges are to be discussed. Formal courts tend to have their own styles and processes, often very alien to other people. It may be that the preoccupation of established legal systems, such as the British, with "fairness" and "reasonableness" is a valuable resource for arbitrating on local environmental disputes. But if not, some alternative principles need to be adopted as a matter of policy. Effective consensus-building thus builds on a clear understanding of rights to challenge the consensus, and the terms on which such challenges can be addressed. The right to criticize is thus an essential underpinning of inclusionary consensus-building strategies.

The "right to challenge" can become a "duty to challenge" as the selected strategy begins to have effects. The importance of this duty arises from the power of strategic discourse once it has gained acceptance, and from the potential to reinterpret a strategy selectively as it is called upon in subsequent situations. Strategies affect the dynamics of social relations through contributing to the way people frame how they think about how to act, and through generating constraints or barriers to action in one form or another. To have effects, a spatial strategy needs to influence the locational choices of those investing in places. It also needs to frame the work of those involved in regulating spatial change. It also needs to influence the way public action, investment, and regulation is legitimated. It should provide a store of reasoning and arguments to draw upon when exploring and justifying what has been done. But this framing role involves continual reinterpretation of the meaning of the strategy and selection from its elements. A rich strategic debate which includes those whose actions are to be influenced by the strategy may have the benefit that, with greater general understanding of what the strategy means and the reasons for it, the interpretative distortion will be minimized. A powerful discourse, energetically diffused, has the capacity to change what people think and what they do, and to maintain these changes. But inevitably over time there will be some interpretative drift. Further, conditions may change and new bases of power may evolve to confront and undermine the strategy.

For all these reasons, a strategic policy discourse needs to be subjected to continual reflexive critique. In rationalist methodology, this was understood as 'monitoring'. However, such monitoring focused on changes in context and their implications for strategy, and on whether specified policy objectives were being achieved (Reade, 1987). A reflexive critique of a strategic policy discourse needs to attend to these matters but also to keep an eye on whether a strategy still makes sense, whether its storyline still rings true, whether it still provides parts for most members of a political community, whether a new storyline has emerged over time, and whether this is as inclusionary as the old. A formal commitment to continual critique does not mean that a strategy is always being changed. As discussed, many strategic policy ideas endure for a long time. What is involved is a regular attention to critique, in which regard is had to the fundamental premises of the strategy, drawing on the understandings which produce it. This could involve periodic review of parameters, to help to maintain an active consciousness of what they are and what they mean, to counteract the tendency for broad assumptions to become invisibly embedded in established practices, or to fade away unnoticed. By keeping the parameters alive and in the open in this way, it also makes it possible to think more freely about changing them when community members begin to feel this might be needed.

Conclusions

The spatial planning tradition emphasized planning's role in spatial ordering, supported by rationalist methodologies of technical analysis and evaluation designed to achieve "public interest" goals (Boyer, 1983). In the more pluralist conditions of the later 20th century, this became transformed into a role in environmental conflict mediation, searching for the zero-sum solution. The approach outlined in this paper presents strategic spatial planning as a process of facilitating community collaboration in the construction of strategic discourse, in strategic consensus-building.

This approach in some respects revisits the activities of the well-known rational planning process. It involves review of issues (survey), sorting through findings (analysis), exploring impacts in relation to values (evaluation), inventing and developing new ideas (choice of strategy), and continuous review (monitoring). But these activities are approached in a very different way. They are undertaken inter-actively, often in parallel rather than sequentially; they deal explicitly in the everyday language of practical life, treating technical language as but one among the many languages to be listened to; as a result, the approach extends the reasoning process beyond instrumental rationality, to allow debate in moral and emotive terms. They involve active discursive work by the parties involved, facilitated by planners or other relevant experts, rather than being undertaken by planners themselves. And they are founded on principles of participatory democracy, underpinned by legal 'rights to be heard' and 'inclusionary terms' in which claims for attention must be redeemed, rather than the hierarchical forms of representative democracy. They derive from a normative concern to reshape the abstract systems within which we live in the mold of our everyday lives (Nord, 1991) or lifeworlds (Habermas, 1987).

These differences can clearly be seem from a summary of the methodological tasks identified under each of the headings discussed above.

1 Arenas for discussion
       reading the opportunity for strategic review
       setting up arenas
       adopting an inclusionary ethic
2 The scope and style of discussion
       selecting an inclusionary style
       working with multiple languages
       calling into presence nonpresent members
3 Sorting through the arguments
       acknowledging facts, values, and rights
       grasping different points of view
       drawing out common threads
4 Creating a new discourse
       using discourse keys
       exploring different storylines
       checking who belongs in a story
       acknowledging what is ignored in a strategy and why
5 Agreement and critique
       developing an explicit approach to conflict resolution at the start
       building in rights of challenge to the position of the consensus
       adopting principles for redeeming such challenges
       building in opportunities for regular reflexive challenge to the consensus

The approach outlined here, as with other approaches to strategic spatial plan-ning, is presented as a normative proposal, an idea about how we could go about strategic spatial planning in a better way. As an approach, however, it offers less a specific process and more a set of questions to help political communities invent their own processes. It represents an ideal to strive for. Realizing it in any particular circumstances would involve shaping it pragmatically to the social relations and political possibilities of particular situations. Every context will have distinctive power relations of division, domination, and exclusion which will have to be confronted and reduced through development of communicative practices. The result will inevitably be a locally specific process. But if its invention is informed by the inclusionary ethic which underpins the approach, its form should allow both voice and influence to be more evenly distributed among those with a stake in issues than is common in most strategic planning exercises these days.

Many will see this approach as too radical and too idealistic for our present times. Fearful of environmental risks and of economic decline, we may turn to our old hierarchical and technical habits, hoping these will deliver us safety and security at least, if not democracy and an open society. In some countries, notably Britain, it seems difficult to imagine building a collaborative open society on the ashes of our paternalist imperial state and the confusion of the array of contemporary neoliberal initiatives emphasizing individual responsibility and competitive behavior. Yet even here, consensus-building work is bubbling up, in regional strategic alliance formation and in work on Local Agenda 21. The practice is beginning to happen. The planning community, as a collection of experts involved in advising strategic debates and of academics reflecting on planning practices, needs to engage in vigorous debate and research on the forms and methodologies of this emerging approach.

For, though this inclusionary communicative approach to strategic argumentation emphasizes the direct involvement of community members, either through their active involvement or by their being accorded respect by those involved, it is methodologically complex to make it work. It is easy to get stuck in old adversarial habits. It is difficult to see the connections between phenomena. The implication of different knowledge claims may need clarification. Bringing the not-present into presence may need active "recognition" work. All this can be helped by experts who have built up a store of knowledge about the processes of urban and regional change and of collaborative strategic consensus-building processes. But to be useful to these processes, experts need to know much more about such processes. The development of appropriate expertise needs to be grounded in an ethics of service, of inclusion, of knowledgeability and of dynamic, reflexive critique. A major task for planning theory and planning education is to help prepare the experts of the future for this task.

REFERENCES

Amin A (ed.). 1994 *The Geography of Post-Fordism* (Basil Blackwell, Oxford)

Amin A, Charles D, Howells J, 1992, "Corporate restructuring and cohesion in the new Europe" *Regional Studies* 26 319–331

Boden D, 1994 *The Business of Talk* (Polity Press, Cambridge)

Bourdieu P, 1990 *In Other Words: Towards a Reflexive Sociology* (Polity Press, Cambridge)

Boyer C, 1983 *Dreaming the Rational City* (MIT Press, Cambridge, MA)

Bryson J, Crosby B, 1992 *Leadership for the Common Good: Tackling Public World* (Jossey Bass, San Francisco, CA)

Christensen K, 1993, "Teaching savvy" *Journal of Planning Education and Research* 12 202–212

Cooke P, Morgan K, 1993, "The network paradigm: new departures in corporate and regional development" *Environment and Planning D: Society and Space* 11 543–564

Crawley I, 1991, "Planning practice and politics", in *Dilemmas of Planning Practice* eds H Thomas, P Healey (Avebury, Aldershot, Hants) pp 101–114

Davoudi S, Healey P. 1995, "City challenge: sustainable process or temporary gesture?" *Environment and Planning C: Government and Policy* 13 79–95

Dear M. 1986, "Postmodernism and planning" *Environment and Planning D: Society and Space* 4 367–384

Dear M, 1995, "Prologomena to a postmodern urbanism", in *Managing Cities* ed. P Healey (John Wiley, Chichester, Sussex) pp 27–44

Dryzek J S, 1990 *Discursive Democracy: Politics, Policy and Political Science* (Cambridge University Press, Cambridge)

European Commission, 1995 *Europe 2000+: Cooperation for European Territorial Development* (Commission of the European Union, Luxembourg)

Faludi A, van der Valk A, 1994 *Rule and Order in Dutch Planning Doctrine* (Kluwer, Dordrecht)

Fischer F, 1990 *Technocracy and the Politics of Expertise* (Sage, London)

Flyvbjerg B, 1996 *Rationality and Power* (Avebury, Aldershot, Hants)

Forester J, 1992, "Envisioning the politics of public sector dispute resolution", in *Studies in Law and Society*, volume 12 eds S Sibley, A Sarat (JAI Press, Greenwich, CT) pp 83–122

Forester J, 1993a *Critical Theory, Public Policy and Planning Practice* (State University of New York Press, Albany, NY)

Forester J, 1993b, "Beyond dialogue to transformative learning: how deliberative rituals encourage political judgment in community planning process", paper presented to Workshop on "Evaluating the theory – practice and urban – rural interplay in planning", Bari, Italy, November; copy available from the author. Department of City and Regional Planning, Cornell University, Ithaca, NY

Geertz C, 1983 *Local Knowledge: Further Essays in Interpretive Anthropology* (Basic Books, New York)

Giddens A, 1984 *The Constitution of Society* (Polity Press, Cambridge)

Goodchild B, 1990, "Planning and the postmodern debate" *Town Planning Review* 61 119–137

Grant J, 1994 *The Drama of Democracy: Contention and Dispute in Community Planning* (University of Toronto Press, Toronto)

Habermas J, 1984 *The Theory of Communicative Action*, volume 1: *Reason and the Rationalization of Society* (Polity Press, Cambridge)

Habermas J, 1987 *The Philosophical Discourse of Modernity* (Polity Press, Cambridge)

Habermas J, 1993 *Justification and Application* (Polity Press, Cambridge)

Hajer M, 1995 *The Politics of Environmental Discourse: A Study of the Acid Rain Controversy in Great Britain and the Netherlands* (Blackwell, Oxford)

Harvey D, 1985 *The Urbanisation of Capital* (Basil Blackwell, Oxford)

Healey P, 1992a, "Planning through debate: the communicative turn in planning theory and practice" *Town Planning Review* 63 143–162

Healey P, 1992b, "A planner's day: knowledge and action in communicative practice" *Journal of the American Planning Association* 58 9–20

Healey P, 1993, "The communicative work of development plans" *Environment and Planning B: Planning and Design* 20 83–104

Healey P (ed.), 1994, "Trends in development plan-making in European planning systems". WP42, Department of Town and Country Planning, University of Newcastle, Newcastle upon Tyne

Healey P, Hillier J, 1995, "Community mobilization in Swan Valley: claims, discourses and rituals in local planning", WP 49, Department of Town and Country Planning, University of Newcastle, Newcastle upon Tyne

Healey P, Shaw T, 1994, "The changing meaning of 'environment' in British town planning" *Transactions of the Institute of British Geographers*, New Series 19 425–438

Healey P, Cameron S, Davoudi S, Graham S, Madani Pour A (eds), 1995 *Managing Cities* (John Wiley, Chichester, Sussex)

Held D, 1987 *Models of Democracy* (Polity Press, Cambridge)

Hillier J, 1993, "Discursive democracy in action", paper presented to Association of European Schools of Planning Congress, Lodz, Poland, July: copy available from the author, School of Architecture and Planning, Curtin University, Perth, Australia

Hoch C, 1992, "The paradox of power in planning practice" *Journal of Planning Education and Research* 11 206–215

Hull A, 1995, "New models for implementation theory: local strategies for renewable energy in England and Wales" *Journal of Environmental Planning and Management* 38 285–306

Huxley M, 1993, "Panoptica: utilitarianism and land use control", in *Postmodern Democracies* eds S Watson, K Gibson, Department of Geography, University of Sydney, Sydney, pp 269–284

Innes J, 1992, "Group processes and the social construction of growth management: the cases of Florida, Vermont and New Jersey" *Journal of the American Planning Association* 58 275–278

Innes J, 1995, "Planning theory's emerging paradigm: communicative action and interactive practice" *Journal of Planning Education and Research* 14 128–125

Innes J, Gruber J, Neuman M, Thompson R, 1994. "Coordination through consensus-building in growth management", report to California Policy Seminar, Department of City and Regional Planning, University of California, Berkeley, CA

Jessop B, Kastandiek H, Nielsen K, Pedersen O, 1991 *The Politics of Flexibility: Restructuring the State and Industry in Britain, Germany and Scandinavia* (Edward Elgar, Aldershot, Hants)

Krumholz N, Forester J, 1992 *Making Equity Planning Work* (Temple University Press. Philadelphia, PA)

Kuhn T, 1962 *The Structure of Scientific Revolutions* (University of Chicago Press, Chicago, IL)

McLoughlin J B, 1969 *Urban and Regional Planning: A Systems Approach* (Faber and Faber, London)

McLoughlin J B, 1992 *Shaping Melbourne's Future?* (Cambridge University Press, Cambridge)

Massey D, 1984 *Spatial Divisions of Labour* (Macmillan, London)

Moore Milroy B, 1991, "Into postmodern weightlessness" *Journal of Planning Education and Research* 10 181–187

Nord, 1991 *The New Everyday Life – Ways and Means* (Research Group for the New Everyday Life) (Allmänna Fölaget, Stockholm)

Nussbaum M, 1990 *Love's Knowledge* (Oxford University Press, New York)

Owens S, 1994, "Land, limits and sustainability: a conceptual framework and some dilemmas for the planning system" *Transactions of the Institute of British Geographers*, New Series 19 439–456

Rabinow P. 1984 *The Foucault Reader* (Penguin Books, Harmondsworth, Middx)

Reade E, 1987 *British Town and Country Planning* (Open University Press, Milton Keynes)

Sager T, 1994 *Communicative Planning Theory* (Avebury, Aldershot, Hants)

Silverman D, 1993 *Integrating Qualitative Data: Methods for Analysing Talk: Text and Interaction* (Sage, London)

Tait A, Wolfe J, 1991, "Discourse analysis and city plans" *Journal of Planning Education and Research* 10 195–200

Throgmorton J, 1992, "Planning as persuasive storytelling about the future: negotiating an electric power rate settlement in Illinois" *Journal of Planning Education and Research* 12(1) 17–31

Young I M, 1990 *Justice and the Politics of Difference* (Princeton University Press, Princeton, NJ)

Part IV

Planning in Action: Successes, Failures, and Strategies

Introduction

The case studies presented in the fourth section illustrate the opportunities and constraints to planners in the USA, the UK, and continental Europe. Though the planning literature has an abundance of dramatic tales of failure (such as Hall 1980; Pressman and Wildavsky 1984; Reisner 1993; Scott 1998), the four cases in this reader develop a more complex picture of planning outcomes. A common theme is the frequent deviation of planning practice from the logic and outcomes of the "rational planning model." In "What Local Economic Developers Actually Do: Location Quotients versus Press Releases," John Levy argues that the primary work of economic developers is selling, rather than traditional planning. His survey of economic development directors reveals that agencies spend most of their time in public relations, advertising, outreach to existing firms, and the like, with far less time devoted to "rational model" activities such as planning, research, and project development. Although this sales work serves as self-promoting advertising for the economic development agency and director, it is nonetheless useful in land markets with imperfect information. Indeed, Levy argues that this local promotion is not necessarily a case of zero-sum smoke-stack chasing among communities, but actually may have an overall positive contribution by improving the dissemination of information relevant to locational decisions. The resulting challenge to planning theory is to incorporate into community planning models the dominance of this sales role and the need for high-visibility activities with political payoffs.

The gap between planning theory and practice arises not only with the traditional comprehensive model, but also with more recent approaches such as strategic planning. In "Community and Consensus: Reality and Fantasy in Planning," Howell Baum examines a strategic community planning process in Baltimore, specifically an effort to increase financial participation in the Associated Jewish Community Federation of Baltimore. Baum investigates how the psychological group dynamics of community identity and conflict negotiations undermine the search for consensus: people don't always say what they mean, they are not always aware of their intentions, and their conscious aims conflict with their unconscious aims. Reflecting the techniques emphasized by communicative planning theorists, Baum pays particular attention to the dialogue in meetings and the ways in which participants articulate opinions about education and community. This process is especially complex in an environment where not only are religious and secular notions of community in conflict, but differences exist between the Orthodox and the non-Orthodox. If there is no consensus as to what "community" itself means, then achieving consensus on community priorities and goals is bound to fall short. For Baum, "community diversity challenged the aim of planning by consensus" (p. 277).

Not all case studies in planning are about failure. Tim Brindley, Yvonne Rydin, and Gerry Stoker offer an upbeat tale of popular planning success from London. The neighborhood surrounding Coin Street is located on the south bank of the Thames River, near the National Theatre, with Waterloo Station the dominant neighborhood feature. Redevelopment activity had essentially bypassed the area until the 1980s, when the expansion of the commercial area of central London created a tension between local residents and outside development interests. The story can be seen as a David and Goliath battle between "planning from below" and corporate office development. But it is also an instructive story of how local community organizations were able to actively engage in and change the direction of development in their backyard, bringing needed housing and local employment.

Popular planning is often advocated, but rarely implemented throughout all stages of the development process. The key to effective participation is not just opposition to a plan, but also the ability to consult, create, and present plans of one's own – that is, to become a "community developer," not just a protestor. The Coin Street neighborhood effectively achieved this dual strategy through two separate community groups, one more outspokenly activist and the other more institutionally grounded in the planning process. The Coin Street case is also a story of the way in which political changes at the national level (the switch of power between the Tories and the Labour Party) shaped the local planning climate. Community organizations were successful in their planning efforts in part because they flexibly and strategically adapted to these changing political circumstances.

In the final case of this section, Bent Flyvbjerg offers a cautionary tale from Denmark about the collision of planning and political power. Planning theory often steps awkwardly around the issue of power. It is as if many planning theorists embraced the idea of rational order to conquer the messy political stuff, writing for an audience of civil servants rather than political operators. Hence, "implementation" has been frustrating (and puzzling) for so many planning theorists, since turning rationality into action requires political power. This may explain why much of the effort to address the traditional shortcomings of planning theory has been to infuse the field with a greater awareness – and stance-taking – about political power (Pressman and Wildavsky 1984).

The confrontation of the grand, unifying plan with petty, fragmented power and its often undemocratic consequences is the theme of Flyvbjerg's book *Rationality and Power* and its final chapter (included here), "Power Has a Rationality that Rationality Does Not Know." Observing the flawed "Aalborg Project" in Denmark, Flyvbjerg questions the belief that "knowledge is power": "Planners, administrators, and politicians thought that if they believed in their project hard enough, rationality would emerge victorious; they were wrong" (p. 318). Though Flyvbjerg's story is one of planning failure, it is not the standard tale of incompetence, corruption, or excessive egocentric ambitions. Flyvbjerg develops ten insightful and sobering propositions for the constrained role of rationality in the real-world context of local politics, and in doing so, provides a more dynamic, nuanced understanding of the interaction between rationality and power than that typically implicit in traditional models of local planning.

REFERENCES

Hall, Peter. 1980. *Great Planning Disasters*. Berkeley: University of California Press.

Pressman, Jeffrey, and Aaron Wildavsky. 1984. *Implementation*, 3rd edn. Berkeley: University of California Press.

Reisner, Marc. 1993. *Cadillac Desert: The American West and its Disappearing Water*, rev. edn. New York: Penguin.

Scott, James C. 1998. *Seeing like a State*. New Haven: Yale University Press.

14

What Local Economic Developers Actually Do: Location Quotients versus Press Releases

John M. Levy

The activities of local economic developers fall into two general categories: "rational model" activities (after the planner's rational model) and sales activities. In the rational model a problem is defined, facts are gathered and analyzed, goals are chosen, courses of action are selected, programs are implemented, and the results are analyzed for future guidance (Banfield 1973). Thus, a rational model approach to local economic development might begin with defining the economic problem to be addressed. The problem might be seen, for example, as poor labor market conditions, or as the deterioration of the downtown area, or as tax base inadequacy.[1] If labor market conditions are the problem, the issue might be specified in terms of unemployment or underemployment, low wage rates in the local economy generally, low wage rates in certain occupations, or problems with seasonal fluctuations or cyclical instability. After the problem has been defined, facts would be gathered and analyzed, goals (for example, so many jobs of certain types) would be selected, and detailed strategies for achieving these goals would be developed. Strategies might include infrastructure development schemes, subsidization policy, marketing programs, and the like. The choice of both goals and strategies would be informed by calculations of costs as well as benefits, both monetary and nonmonetary.

Thus, rational model activities include studies of labor markets and tax bases, studies of traffic and environmental impacts and the effects of employment growth on housing markets, financial feasibility analysis, cost–revenue studies, and industry studies for targeting purposes. Rational model activities, of course, also include land use, transportation, and capital facilities planning. A successful economic development program is likely to promote population growth whether or not this is a desired effect. Thus, one could argue that virtually all the usual elements of comprehensive

Reprinted by permission of the *Journal of the American Planning Association*, 56 (2) (1990): 153–60.

planning have some relevance to a rational model approach to economic development planning.

The foregoing description implies a full-blown rational model approach. The more limited approaches, such as those that Malizia (1985) characterizes as "contingency" and "strategic" planning, would also fall on the rational side of the rational model/sales dichotomy. In fact, Malizia notes that these more limited approaches may serve as elements in a more comprehensive approach.

Sales activities ("marketing" would be an equally good term) are those activities that do not alter the physical, financial, or demographic realities of the community but rather inform and persuade firms and investors. They include calls on firms, speeches to rotary clubs, public relations, advertising, writing and dissemination of brochures, attendance at trade shows and other events, and "networking."

Though rational model and sales activities are conceptually separable, they are related. The "selling" that the economic developer does is generally highly factual and therefore makes use of at least some of the same data that would be necessary for a rational model planning approach. Then, too, techniques associated with the rational model might be used in designing sales and marketing strategies.

In most of the scholarly literature on local economic development, the emphasis is on rational model activities. If one had no acquaintance with the field other than through the scholarly literature, one would be likely to perceive local economic development as a rather systematic process akin to municipal planning. Bendavid-Val (1980), Friedman and Darragh (1988), Malizia (1985), and Moriarty and Cowen (1980) all treat local economic development in this manner. For the local economic development practitioner, however, the rational model activities definitely are secondary to sales activities. The process, as its practitioners report it, is far closer to sales than it is to planning.

This article examines survey data from the directors of local economic development agencies to determine how their agencies actually allocate effort and what activities they find to be most and least effective. It then offers speculations on why practitioners give more attention to sales activities than to planning activities and why there seems to be a certain cognitive dissonance between practitioner's behavior and the majority of scholarly literature.

A Survey of Economic Development Agencies

The survey was a mail questionnaire sent to the directors of 320 economic development agencies in February 1989. The agencies were randomly selected from the 1989 Economic Development Directory in the October 1988 issue of *Area Development*, the most widely read practitioner-orientated publication in the local economic development field. The survey excluded chambers of commerce, consulting firms, profit-making development organizations, and specialized agencies like port authorities and foreign trade zones, on the grounds that they generally do not perform a complete range of development functions.

Slightly more than half of the respondents were from governmental agencies, and the remainder were from quasi-public agencies.[2] Replies were received from 121 agency directors (37 percent). Of these replies, 112 (34 percent of the survey group) were usable and coded.[3] The mean full-time staff size of the responding agencies, exclusive of the director, was 6.2. Of the 107 respondents who answered the question on staff size, 52 indicated a staff size of 3 or less and 55 a staff size of 4 or more. Seventeen of the 107 respondents to the staff-size question indicated a full-time staff of more than 10.

The statistical results reported in this article should be regarded as indicative rather than definitive. The sampling frame, the Area Development Directory, may not be perfectly representative of the field, in that larger and better-known agencies have a greater probability of being included. Then, too, a number of the questions asked were open-ended. Therefore, tabulating them required some grouping and interpretation. Despite these limitations, the results are sufficiently strong and the responses to different questions sufficiently consistent to seem worthy of dissemination.

How Developers View their Activities

Selling activities clearly predominate over rational model activites. Most economic developers describe the selling side of their jobs as the most important, the most time-consuming, and the most productive part of their work. Tables 14.1 through 14.5 show their responses in greater detail.

As table 14.1 indicates, economic development directors view the sales activity – "publicizing the area and providing information" – as the single most important function that their agencies perform. In fact, the number of responses showing the sales function as the most important one is virtually equal to the total of all other responses combined.

As table 14.2 demonstrates, economic development agency directors also rank sales activities (represented by "public relations, advertising, provision of data, and response to inquiries") as the single biggest consumer of agency time. The second item in the table, "outreach to existing firms," combines large elements of sales and public relations with a certain amount of ombudsman activity, such as soothing relations between firms and government. In the rational model/sales dichotomy, outreach clearly falls on the sales side. The other items in the table fall into the

Table 14.1   Economic developers' opinions of the most important function of their agency

Function	Percentage of responses
Publicizing the area and providing information (S)	65
Providing sites (R)	23
Financing (R)	23
Joint ventures (R)	2
Obtaining grants (R)	6
Other	11

Notes: The question was "What would you say is the most important function of your agency?" and the choices were those shown in the table. The numbers add to more than 100 percent because approximately one-fifth of the respondents checked more than one item.
(S) denotes "sales" activity. (R) denotes "rational model" activity.

Table 14.2 The single activity on which economic development agencies spend most of their time

Activity	Percentage of respondents
Public relations, advertising, provision of data, and response to inquiries (S)	42
Outreach to existing firms (S)	32
Planning and research (R)	8
Site and project development and operations (R)	6
Financing (R)	6
Applications for grants (R)	4
Other	6

Notes: This table and table 14.3 are derived from the same question. Respondents were asked to use their own words to indicate, in descending order, the five items on which their agencies spend the most time. The responses were then grouped by the author. This table indicates the percentage of respondents who listed each of the above activities as the number-one time consumer. In the small number of cases where "administration" was listed as number one, the number-two item was substituted. This adjustment was made on the grounds that all agencies must spend time on administration and that it is, in effect, overhead to be spread across all specific activities. (S) denotes "sales" activity. (R) denotes "rational model" activity.

Table 14.3 Percentages of respondents naming various activities among the top five consumers of time

Activity	Percentages of respondents
Public relations, advertising, provision of data, and response to inquiries (S)	80
Outreach to existing firms (S)	70
Planning and research (R)	59
Applications for grants (R)	30
Site and project development and operation (R)	14
Financing (R)	11
Other	29

Notes: This table is derived in the same manner and from the same data as table 14.2. (S) denotes "sales" activity. (R) denotes "rational model" activity.

rational model category. Table 14.3 shows the percentage of respondents who listed the activities shown in table 14.2 among the top five time-consumers. Again, the preponderance of sales, as opposed to rational model responses is evident. The combined 150 percent for the first two items (sales) in the table...exceeds the combined 143 percent for the other five activities (rational model).

Table 14.4 indicates those activities that the directors of economic development agencies find the most and least useful. The responses are essentially consistent with the

Table 14.4   The most and least productive activities of economic development agencies

Activity	Percentage of responses	
	Most productive	Least productive
Advertising, public relations, providing data, responding to inquiries (S)	26	10
Outreach to firms now in the jurisdiction (S)	26	2
Deal making, financing, and assisting new businesses (R)	9	1
Research and planning (R)	8	1
Networking (S)	6	1
Site and project development (R)	5	0
Grant applications and compliance and reporting to higher levels of government (R)	3	15
Events and meetings (S)	2	14
Promoting tourism and convention business (S)	2	1
Dealing with politics (O)	0	8
Outside prospecting and overseas marketing (S)	1	3
Other	11	12

Notes: Respondents replied in their own words to the questions, "Over the last several years what do you think was the most (least) productive use of your professional time?" The replies were grouped by me. The terms used in grouping are as close as possible to the language used by the respondents. Several respondents indicated more than one most or least productive activity, and many respondents replied to the "most productive" question but left the "least productive" question blank. Thus, the two column totals are not the same. The "other" category includes a miscellany of replies that were obviously unique or that could not be readily coupled to a final activity – for example, "attending seminars" or "installing a computer system." (S) denotes "sales" activity. (R) denotes "rational model" activity. (O) denotes an organizational necessity that does not fit the rational model/sales dichotomy.

data in the previous tables. Note the large number of replies for the first two items in the "most productive" column.

Several items that drew predominantly "least productive" responses are worth discussing. One item, grant applications, was grouped with "compliance and reporting to higher levels of government" because so much compliance and reporting is connected with the receipt of grant monies. Roughly half of the respondents in the negative category indicated the application process itself as least productive, and the remainder listed the postgrant-reporting and compliance procedures as least productive. In answering this question, one economic development director cited "working on grant applications which did not have a chance of being funded but [which we] needed to do for political reasons." A number of respondents who indicated "events and meetings" as least productive noted that they spend much time at events they know will be unproductive because it is politically necessary. The response to "dealing with politics" is self-explanatory.

Targeting firms for recruitment purposes might be regarded as a prototypical rational model activity. Data on place characteristics can be matched against industry

Table 14.5 Degree of sectoral targeting specificity

Level of specificity	Percentage of respondents
No targeting	22
Targeting at the 1-digit SIC level	25
Targeting at the 2-digit SIC level	34
Targeting at the 3- or 4-digit SIC level	10
Indicated targeting but supplied no specifics	8

Notes: This table is based on replies to the questions, "Do you actively recruit firms? (yes) (no), If yes, do you target particular types of firms or particular industries? Please specify." The characterizations in the table are based on the Standard Industrial Classification (SIC) code, but since respondents replied in their own terms rather than SIC terms some interpretation was necessary. A reply like "corporate headquarters," "manufacturing," or "light manufacturing" would be recorded as 1-digit SIC level. A reply like "metalworking industries" or "food processing" would be recorded as 2-digit SIC level. Any response more specific like "medical instruments" would be listed in the 3- or 4-digit SIC category. Totals do not add to 100 because of rounding.

requirements and industrial sectors then targeted with a high degree of specificity. This seems to be the sensible way to maximize the effect of the selling effort. The conceptual tools for doing it – for example, location theory and financial analysis – are available. However, as table 14.5 indicates, the amount of targeting performed by most economic development agencies is modest. Although one director responded to the targeting question with "four digit SIC code and specific company parameters," answers like "manufacturers in the Northeast and upper Midwest" were more common. Most economic development directors who know their own areas should be able to reach the two-digit SIC code almost intuitively. Yet only 10 percent of the respondents went beyond the two-digit level.[4] Only two respondents mentioned having had professional studies done to select targeting categories. In response to the question, "Do you target?" a few respondents indicated that they did not target but intended to or thought they should. One director responded, "Technically yes, practically no."

The Focus on Sales

The survey included four related questions regarding the rational model/sales dichotomy. These can be summarized as follows:

1. What do you think is your agency's most important function? (Table 14.1)
2. On what activities does your agency spend most time? (Tables 14.2 and 14.3)
3. What activities are most and least productive for your agency? (Table 14.4)
4. How specifically do you target for recruiting purposes? (Table 14.5)

The responses to all four questions showed a consistent emphasis on the sales activities rather than the rational model activities. This response is not what most of the literature would lead us to expect. Consequently, for the remainder of this article we turn to the questions of whether the sales emphasis makes sense from a local perspective and whether or not it is useful when viewed from a national perspective.

Does emphasizing sales make sense?

One goal of the economic developer, though not the only one, is to achieve concrete results. To understand why the sales emphasis is likely to be more effective than a rational model emphasis, consider the economists' concept of the "perfect market." One requirement for the perfect market is that both buyers and sellers have complete information (Hirshleifer 1980). In this regard the market for commercial and industrial sites and structures is very far from perfect. Consider, for example, a task like "Find the best county within overnight trucking distance of Philadelphia in which to locate a widget-making plant of 500,000 square feet." The amount of data on taxes, wage rates, utility costs, construction costs, land availability and cost, shipping costs, environmental and land-use regulations, cost of living, housing costs and availability, amenities, and quality-of-life considerations that would be needed for each of several hundred counties would be formidable indeed. Narrowing the task to the municipal or site level would increase the data requirements still further. In a world of imperfect information, it is no wonder that public relations, promotion, advertising, sales, and related activities can become extremely important.

As the survey results indicate, local economic developers do find the offering of grants and financial incentives productive, but not nearly so useful as the sales aspect of their work. This should not be surprising. Most studies of location decisions do not show tax concessions and other financial incentives to be major factors. This is true of both recent studies (Hack 1988; Tosh et al. 1988; Wolkoff 1985) and older studies (Hellman et al. 1976; Reigeluth and Wolman 1979; Schmenner 1982; Vaughn 1980). To a considerable extent, similar incentives are offered by a wide range of localities. For example, in response to another question on financial programs in the survey, respondents by a large margin listed industrial revenue bonds (IRBs) as the most useful financial incentive.[5] In the 1980s IRBs were available in forty-seven out of fifty states (Richardson 1981). Although the details of their issuance varied somewhat from state to state, the basic process was necessarily similar. This is because all agencies that issued IRBs did so pursuant to the same provisions in the IRS code.

It is thus hard for the economic developer to be a winner through incentives, though it is possible to be a loser by failing to offer them when most of one's rivals do. In fact, much local economic development activity may be defensive. A community may maintain a program simply to stay even and to protect what it has from the depredations of other communities' economic developers. There might well be some mutual savings to be had from "disarmament," but the institutions for arranging it do not exist.

The emphasis on the sales role serves the economic developer in another important purpose that, to my knowledge, has been generally ignored in the literature. Namely, it helps the economic developer to keep his or her job. Economic development is not usually regarded as an absolutely essential community function in the sense that, say, police or fire protection is. Further, the educational and experiential qualifications for doing economic development are not usually defined with great specificity. It may be a statutory requirement that the commissioner of public works have a professional engineer's license and that the commissioner of planning have a planning degree, but it is not likely that there will be a comparable requirement for the director of economic development.[6] For these reasons, the field is characterized by high turnover. Thus, an economic developer who wants to maintain a hold on his or her position must participate in high-visibility activities. If a new firm opens a plant in town, the economic developer needs to be prominently associated with that event. If a firm is about to leave town, the economic developer must be seen as having fought a determined battle to prevent this unhappy event. For how else do the director and his or her staff justify their lines in the municipal budget? If the body politic does not know what the economic developer is doing, he or she may not be doing it much longer – no matter how good the developer may be.

Another reason high-visibility activity is advantageous to the local economic developer is that it is useful to the administration that pays the developer's salary. In a political climate in which government does not always enjoy high repute among the citizens and in which many politicians campaign for office by running against government, maintaining an economic development operation enables government to present itself in a very attractive light. The image of government allying itself with business to bring its citizens lower taxes and more jobs is quite a change from government's normal, ogrelike roles of taxing and regulating. However, this political gain can be had only if the operation is highly visible. In my experience as an economic development agency director in the late 1970s, this handshake with government is well understood by many in the economic development profession.

Is emphasizing sales useful?

Having argued that the pattern of behavior shown in the tables makes sense, we turn to the question of whether it is useful. Certainly, at the municipal level successful economic development efforts are useful. They deliver gains both to capital and to labor. Often, but not inevitably, they reduce property tax rates (McGuire 1987).

At the national level, it is not quite so evident that all this activity is useful. At first glance, the combat over who gets what firm might be considered a zero-sum game. Assume that community X, through its more competent development program, induces Acme Widget to locate there instead of in community Y, as it would otherwise have done. Is it not possible that the gain for X minus the loss for Y nets out to zero? Is it possible, in fact, that, when the costs of running the winning and the losing program are added in, the process becomes a negative sum game?

Orthodox economic theory suggests, however, that all this combat may actually perform a useful function when viewed at macroeconomic level. The net effect of all the advertisements, brochures, data sheets, press releases, talks to rotary clubs, calls on firms, liaison activity between firms and local governments and the like is to disseminate massive amounts of information relevant to location decisions. To the extent that this information improves the market, and to the extent that improved markets allocate resources more efficiently, a useful function is being performed. If, in a $5-trillion economy, we spend a few billion on a process that promotes better decision making, we may well be getting our money's worth.

In fact, one can argue that improving the market is the main, perhaps even the only, contribution that local economic development efforts make to national economic performance. It is true that the variety of financing incentives and tax expenditures provided in connection with local economic development efforts constitute a subsidy to capital formation and may thus accelerate the growth of GNP. However, it is hard to believe that an equal stimulus to capital formation could not be achieved at far lower cost by changes in the federal tax code. Some authors deny that local economic development efforts are at all connected with national economic performance (Kirby 1985). Others, on the basis of commonly accepted principles of economics, have asserted for a number of years that the effect of subsidization is to distort business decision making and thus to produce a net loss. Goffman (1962) has observed, "What a subsidy does, then, is to make it profitable for a company to locate in a less than optimal location."

Whether there are net equity gains from the sum of all local economic development activity is an open question. It is unlikely that more needy places generally outcompete less needy places for new industry. Two observers have recently suggested that, in fact, more affluent communities make more efficient use of their expenditures on economic development than do poorer municipalities (Rubin and Rubin 1987). Whether even the giving of subsidies, taken by itself, has the net effect of promoting equity is far from certain. At the federal level, grant sources like the Urban Development Action Grant Program and Economic Development Administration programs are guided at least in part by such considerations as poverty and unemployment rates. However, it would be naive to believe that need considerations are the only, or necessarily even the major consideration in determining the winners in the competition for grants (Gatons and Brintall 1984; Gist and Hill 1981, 1984). The very large tax expenditure in the form of IRB financing is not needs-based (Richardson 1981).[7] At the state and local level, both wealthy and poor jurisdictions can use more jobs and a larger tax base, and so both offer them. It would be amazing if there were not a great many canceling effects.

Consider a group of firms competing with one another in the national "widget" market. Firm A has been subsidized by the EDA. It competes with firm B, which has been subsidized with a UDAG grant. They both compete with firm C, which is located in an affluent suburb that is ineligible for both EDA and UDAG monies. However, firm C's capital costs were lowered by means of an IRB. These firms all compete with firm D, which received a state investment tax credit to encourage it to move from a less affluent to a more affluent state. Another competitor, firm E, does not benefit from any state or federal program or tax expenditure. However, it receives a substantial municipal property tax abatement. And so on. When one contemplates the multiplicity of grant programs and tax expenditures, as well as the large number of firms benefiting from one or more of them, it is evident that estimating the net effect would be a formidable task indeed. Thus, paradoxically, it may well be that the part of the local development process that lies more or less outside the rational model framework delivers the major, or possibly the only, aggregate benefit.

If the sales side of economic development looms so large to the practitioner, why is it so often slighted in the literature? One possible explanation is that, until recently, the field of economics generally has not taken much interest in advertising (or related activities like public relations). It is often regarded as overhead or as a phenomenon that exists only because of market imperfections. The fact that advertising makes nonrational as well as rational appeals may make it fit rather awkwardly into a discipline that takes as an axiom the existence of a rational "economic man." This situation is beginning to change in the scholarly literature (Nichols 1985). However, the fact that advertising is still not well integrated into the field can be verified by looking up the subject in any mainstream introductory text and noting that it is either covered very lightly or not mentioned at all.

Many scholars who have written about local economic development come from a planning or economics background. Thus, they tend to focus on the planning and economic aspects of the field – its rational model side – rather than on its selling side. Perhaps, more generally, scholars, being committed to systematic rationality, naturally tend to focus on the rationalistic and the quantifiable.

An Approach for Planners

It would be the subject of another chapter or perhaps a book, to convert these findings regarding practitioner behavior into detailed proposals for local economic development policy. However, some general comments are appropriate. Local economic development efforts, as reported by practitioners, are a relatively untargeted intermunicipal sales or marketing competition. As such, their connections with specific municipal planning goals will generally be tenuous. The fact that programs tend to have a sales rather than planning basis explains why so few programs are terminated. Were programs based on a rational model planning effort, one would occasionally observe a community saying, in effect, "We've reached our goal, let's stop." The dominance of the sales perspective may also explain why one sees economic development pursued when it cannot be justified in rational model terms. The affluent suburb that has low unemployment rates, labor shortages in some categories, low vacancy rates, tight controls on residential construction, and sky-high housing prices, but still assiduously pursues its own economic development is a case in point. So far as housing is concerned, this is not a new observation. Almost two decades ago Wilbur Thompson (1973) stated, "It is irresponsible to promote local industrial expansion without coupling this action to a low income housing policy which picks up the pieces. But we do it all the time." There is no reason to believe that his words are any less apropos today than in 1973.

The results of the game may be given an overall shape by the structure and requirements of state and national funding. But most practitioners do not regard such funding as a major element in the game. Then, too, as already noted, there is a very large potential for randomization due to the canceling effects among the myriad of grant and tax expenditure programs offered by various levels of government. For these reasons the shaping effect of federal and state programs is likely to be quite small.

It would certainly be desirable if we could integrate local economic development programs into the community planning process. When successful, the economic developer's efforts change the community. Obviously, it would be better for this to be done by design than by accident. But as responses to the questionnaires indicated, we are very far from that point. And it must be admitted that the mechanisms by which economic developers' efforts could be closely tied into the overall process of community planning and development are not evident.

Vigorous intermunicipal economic competition is here to stay. It would remain even if every cent of federal and state subsidy for local economic development were withdrawn. One task for the planner is to try to integrate local economic development efforts into a larger planning framework – not as is done in much of the literature but in the reality of municipal growth and development.

The academician who wishes to increase the usefulness of his or her contribution to the practice of economic development at the local level, or to make useful suggestions regarding state or national policy directed to local economic development, must recognize the dominance of the sales side of the process in the practitioner's work. Efforts to tie local economic development efforts into the broad context of community planning must be fitted into a setting in which sales is likely to remain the dominant mode. Such an approach is likely to be more effective than one that ignores sales activity or relegates it to a secondary role. It is also important to recognize the heavily political nature of the process and to concede that high-visibility activities with political payoff will inevitably have a prominent place.

ACKNOWLEDGMENTS

I would like to express my appreciation for very useful comments on survey technique by my colleague Patricia K. Edwards. I would also like to thank another colleague, Timothy Fluck, for numerous useful and perceptive comments on both the substance and the structure of this paper.

NOTES

1 Tax base considerations have not generally been counted directly in federal criteria for funding economic development. In my suburban experience they are, nonetheless, the most common motivation. This makes sense in that, if the jurisdiction is small relative to the metropolitan labor market, it cannot hope to capture most of the employment gains from new activity. However, it can capture the property tax gains.

2 "Public" means here an agency that is part of the structure of government and whose staff are government employees. "Quasi-governmental" means a public benefit corporation set up by and perhaps partially funded by government, but not part of the structure of government, and not staffed by government employees. There were no statistically significant differences in response between the two groups and therefore they were not disaggregated.

3 Several replies were rejected because they were from chambers of commerce, consultants, or agencies so new that they were unable to answer the questions.

4 In the Standard Industrial Classification (SIC) system the broadest categories of economic activity (manufacturing, trade, etc.) are one-digit codes. Each of these categories is then disaggregated. Within manufacturing there are twenty two-digit codes. For example, chemicals and allied products are SIC code 28; industrial inorganic chemicals are SIC code 281. Within that category, alkalies and chlorine are SIC code 2812, industrial gases are SIC code 2813, and so forth. The system is described in detail in *Standard Industrial Classification Manual* (U.S. Department of Commerce, 1987, and earlier editions).

5   Respondents were asked to classify a variety of federal and state programs on a three-part scale: most useful, somewhat useful, and least useful or no experience. IRBs received a 73 percent "most useful" response. The next largest "most useful" programs were revolving loan funds at 48 percent and interest rate reductions at 44 percent.

6   The American Economic Development Council gives a Certified Industrial Developer (CID) certificate, but it is generally not required as a condition of employment or responsibility, nor is it universally known in the field.

7   Perhaps these comments on EDA, UDAG, and IRBs should be cast in the past tense. The UDAG Program operated in fiscal 1989 entirely on "recaptured" funds, and at this writing further appropriations are not expected. EDA's budget for 1989 was about $200 million, or less than half of what it was in the 1970s. The Reagan administration repeatedly tried to eliminate the agency entirely and, at this writing, the Bush administration appears likely to pursue the same course. Industrial revenue bonds are likewise on the way out at this writing. The Tax Reform Act of 1986 eliminated IRBs for most uses other than manufacturing. Their use for manufacturing is scheduled to be terminated December 31, 1989. Only use for a limited range of public purposes such as sewage treatment will be permitted after 1989. But even before the 1989 phaseout, IRB effectiveness had been reduced simply by the reductions in marginal tax rates under the various Reagan administration tax bills.

REFERENCES

Banfield, Edward C. 1973. Ends and Means in Planning. In *A Reader in Planning Theory*, edited by Andreas Faludi. New York: Pergamon.

Bendavid-Val, Avrom. 1980. *Local Economic Development Planning: From Goals to Projects*. PAS Report no. 353. Washington, D.C.: American Planning Association.

Friedman, Stephan B., and Alexander J. Darragh. 1988. Economic Development. In *The Practice of Local Government Planning*, 2d ed. Washington, D.C.: International City Management Association.

Gatons, Paul K., and Michael Brintall. 1984. Competitive Grants: The UDAG Approach. In *Urban Economic Development*, vol. 27, *Urban Affairs Annual Reviews*, edited by Richard D. Bingham and John P. Blair. Beverly Hills, CA: Sage.

Gist, John R., and J. Carter Hill. 1981. The Economics of Choice in the Allocation of Federal Grants: An Empirical Test. *Public Choice* 36, 1: 63–73.

———. 1984. Political and Economic Influences in the Bureaucratic Allocation of Federal Funds: The Case of Urban Development Action Grants. *Journal of Urban Economics* 16, 2: 158–72.

Goffman, Irving. 1962. Local Subsidies for Industry: Comment. *Southern Economic Journal* 29, 2: 112–14.

Hack, Gordon D. 1988. Location Trends: 1958–1988. *Area Development*, October: 12.

Hellman, Daryll A., Gregory H. Wassall, and Laurance H. Falk. 1976. *State Financial Incentives to Industry*. Lexington, MA: Lexington Books, D. C. Heath.

Hirshleifer, Jack. 1980. *Price Theory and Applications*, 2d ed. Englewood Cliffs, NJ: Prentice-Hall.

Kirby, Andrew. 1985. Nine Fallacies of Local Economic Change. *Urban Affairs Quarterly* 21, 2: 207–20.

Malizia, Emil E. 1985. *Local Economic Development: A Guide to Practice*. New York: Praeger.

McGuire, Therese J. 1987. The Effect of New Firm Locations on Property Taxes. *Journal of Urban Economics* 22, 2: 223–29.

Moriarty, Barry M., and David J. Cowen. 1980. *Industrial Location and Community Development*. Chapel Hill: University of North Carolina Press.

Nichols, L. M. 1985. Advertising and Economic Welfare. *American Economic Review* 75, 1: 213–18.

Reigeluth, George A., and Harold Wolman. 1979. *The Determinants and Implications of Communities' Changing Competitive Advantage: A Review of Literature*. Working Paper no. 1264–03. Washington, D.C.: Urban Institute.

Richardson, Pearl. 1981. *Small Issue Industrial Revenue Bonds*. Washington, D.C.: Congressional Budget Office.

Rubin, Irene S., and Herbert J Rubin. 1987. Economic Development Incentives: The Poor (Cities) Pay More. *Urban Affairs Quarterly* 23, 1: 15–36.

Schmenner, Roger W. 1982. *Making Business Location Decisions*. Englewood Cliffs, NJ: Prentice-Hall.

Thompson, Wilbur. 1973. Problems Which Sprout in the Shadow of No Growth. *AIA Journal*, December 1973.

Tosh, Dennis E., Troy A. Festervard, and James R. Lumpkin. 1988. Industrial Site Selection Criteria: Are Economic Developers, Manufacturers and Industrial Real Estate Brokers Operating on the Same Wavelength? *Economic Development Review* 6, 3: 62–67.

Vaughn, Roger J. 1980. How Effective Are They? *Commentary*, National Council for Urban Economic Development. January 8: 12–18.

Wolkoff, Michael J. 1985. Chasing a Dream: The Use of Tax Abatements to Spur Urban Economic Development. *Urban Studies* 22, 4: 305–15.

15

Community and Consensus: Reality and Fantasy in Planning

Howell S. Baum

Strategic Planning in Community Organizations

Strategic planning is the effort to define an organizational mission, translate that mission into strategic goals, and implement those goals programmatically. Originally developed in the corporate sector, strategic planning emphasizes analyzing stakeholders' interests, opportunities and threats, strengths and weaknesses, and potential competitors before formulating a mission (Bryson and Roering 1987). With increasing financial stringency and fiscal and political uncertainty, nonprofit organizations have turned to strategic planning to delineate courses of action (Bryce 1992; Bryson 1988; Espy 1986; Miller 1989; Nutt and Backoff 1992).

The incorporation of a private sector planning approach into nonprofit organizations raises two questions. One is whether conceptual and methodological emphases on profit contradict nonprofits' service missions. Voluntary associations need to be fiscally sound, but are often deliberately altruistic. The second question concerns the fact that many nonprofit or voluntary organizations represent communities. In comparison with many firms, most nonprofit organizations have a wider range of stakeholders and are more susceptible to outside influences, including public political processes. Bryson (1988; Bryson and Einsweiler 1987) cautions that organizational planning methods must be modified for use with communities.

Both public and nonprofit sector planners ask what is new about strategic planning (Kaufman and Jacobs 1987). For all the talk about action, strategic planning is strikingly reminiscent of traditional models of comprehensive rationality. Strategic planners have learned that people have cognitive limitations and conflicting interests, but they still assume that people will eagerly cooperate in sharing their problems; collect information to test their assumptions; and, when a high-level principle

Reprinted with permission from *Journal of Planning Education and Research*, 13 (1994: 251–62). Copyright © 1994 Association of Collegiate Schools of Planning.

suggests terms for agreement, relinquish private interests. Yet no matter how long the lists of planning tasks, the trick is still to design a process that includes a wide range of stakeholders and encourages them to talk honestly about their desires, confront conflicts, and make painful decisions.

What is missing from the strategic planning literature is psychology. Not only do people not always say what they mean, but often they are not consciously aware of their intentions, and some of their unconscious interests conflict with their conscious aims, collaboration, and agreement on any collective purposes. Writers on strategic planning cite Mitroff's (1983) *Stakeholders of the Organizational Mind* for his argument that strategic planning should include many stakeholders, but they forget his observation that some important stakes are emotional or even unconscious. Argyris and Schön (1978; Argyris 1982; Schön 1982) have made little impact with their repeated findings that people in organizations resist analyzing or solving problems. Altogether unacknowledged is the evidence that workers have unconscious wishes and conflicts that can interfere not only with planning, but with the day-to-day activities that require and implement plans (Baum 1987; Hirschhorn 1988; Hirschhorn and Barnett 1993; Kets de Vries and Associates 1991).

A Case Example

This article examines a strategic planning effort by a nonprofit community organization, The Associated Jewish Community Federation of Baltimore. The story shows that participants held partly unconscious, putatively undiscussable assumptions about the community that hindered realistic examination of differences in belief and interest and led to decisions that displeased a majority of participants. The case is an example of the general phenomenon that people may prefer acting on fantasies about organizations or communities to realistically addressing conflicts and planning (see Schwartz 1990).

I developed this case in a study of strategic planning at The Associated. I approached the organization with an interest in how people talk about their communities while planning for them. After discussing research interests and organizational concerns, the planning director offered access to meetings and documents, as well as introductions to planning participants. The case is based on interviews, observations at meetings, and analysis of documents. The Associated's planning director and senior vice president published an account of the strategic planning that discusses their aims, the process, and recommendations (Levin and Bernstein 1991). The implementation activities described here follow the period covered in that article.

The Associated Jewish Community Federation of Baltimore

The Associated, formed in 1920 from a merger of several charitable organizations, is one of approximately 200 local Jewish community federations in the United States and Canada. It is a community organization with quasi-governmental roles, and it supports local Jewish agencies and national and international Jewish organizations, mainly through fund-raising campaigns and endowments. The 19 local agencies The

Associated supports include education, housing, recreation, vocational, counseling, health, refugee resettlement, and geriatric programs.

The Associated calls itself the central address of the Baltimore Jewish community, and occasionally speaks for the Jewish community on public issues. The Associated has a culture of "consensus" decision making, which emphasizes seeking positions that all active community interests can support. About 92,000 Jews live in metropolitan Baltimore in 36,000 households (Tobin 1986, p. 8). In the 1992–1993 annual campaign, 17,000 individuals or families contributed $22.5 million to the federation (all donors of $25 or more are considered members). However, approximately 75 families gave more than half of the $22.5 million, and power is centralized on the board and its executive committee, whose members include the largest contributors. Members of all federation committees are usually significant contributors. A professional staff of 45, headed by a president, manages the organization.

In the late 1980s, despite fund-raising success, The Associated faced two challenges. One was the growing requests from agencies for funds, particularly for fixing up old facilities. In addition, while the federation was raising more money each year, it was relying on a declining number of contributors. It was succeeding as a fund raiser but losing community involvement.

In 1986 The Associated hired a new president who initiated strategic planning. The primary aim was to increase financial participation in the federation. Secondly, Associated leaders wanted to expand their role as a community institution. Significantly, one result of planning was to put "community" in the organization's name. The plan is titled "Building a Stronger Community." The plan proclaims The Associated a community builder (Strategic Planning Committee 1989). Yet community diversity challenged the aim of planning by consensus.

Background: The Baltimore Jewish Community

The first Jewish settler came to Baltimore in 1772. German immigrants arrived in the mid-nineteenth century, succeeded in manufacturing and commerce, and created the first Jewish institutions. Russians arrived at the turn of the century, had a harder time adjusting to urban American conditions, and formed their own institutions. After living separately for decades, the two groups have mixed fairly well. National differences were once associated with religious differences, with most Russians adhering to traditional practices and most Germans choosing modern alternatives (Fein 1971). Now religious differences are largely independent of national heritage.

The three main denominational groups, Orthodox, Conservative, and Reform, lie along a continuum from traditional to modern. Among Baltimore Jews, 20% are Orthodox (the highest proportion in an American city), 35% are Conservative, and 29% are Reform, with 12% being other (Tobin 1986, p. 10). The most significant differences, religiously and politically, follow a rough line between Orthodox and non-Orthodox.

Yet there are important religious differences between traditional (also, ultra-) Orthodox and modern Orthodox. The ultra-Orthodox fiercely hold to religious and social traditions of seventeenth, eighteenth, and nineteenth century Eastern Europe. They guide their lives by traditional interpretations of the Torah (the Five

Books of Moses), and in Baltimore this fast growing group has built synagogues, schools, and charitable institutions.

Modern Orthodox are more lenient in their approach to belief and ritual practice and are more likely to be involved in secular educational institutions and the modern work world (Heilman 1992; Heilman and Cohen 1989; Liebman 1973, 1988). Yet politically, as Orthodox Jews, they follow the leadership of the traditional Orthodox, most of whose rabbis refuse to participate in the secular federation world but invoke religious authority and their greater numbers to direct modern Orthodox rabbis who do participate.

Non-Orthodox Jews hold a broad range of beliefs and practices but tend to converge on community political views that contrast with those of the Orthodox in three related ways. First, the Orthodox base their positions on biblical interpretation, while non-Orthodox are more likely to rely on contemporary political thinking, with the result that Orthodox often take positions defined currently as more conservative than those of non-Orthodox.

Second, the Orthodox consider the Torah a guide for public as well as private life. More accurately, traditional Orthodox recognize no distinction between a private religious sphere and a public civil domain. In contrast, non-Orthodox see religion as one institution among many in their lives and draw a boundary between the public world of work, politics, and society, and a private religious life.

Third, for traditional Orthodox the Torah defines not only correct political positions, but also a decision method – textual interpretation – which points to single right views on issues. In contrast, most non-Orthodox, as modernists and as liberals, are pluralists. They assume that several positions may be legitimate, and they expect to make decisions by bargaining toward a consensus that includes many interests.

Because liberalism is so familiar in American politics, it is important to hear an Orthodox rabbi explain how the Orthodox see decisions differently:

> Consensus is difficult for the Orthodox. In traditional Judaism there is no democracy. In traditional Judaism decisions are dictated by the Torah – the written Torah and the oral Torah. And set down in the guidelines of the *Shulchan Aruch* [a guide to everyday life]. People could vote out putting on *Tefillin* [prayer amulets] in the morning. It could be a majority, or consensus, or unanimous vote, but it wouldn't mean anything. When the decision comes to the floor, the question is, what does the *Shulchan Aruch* tell us?

It is difficult to imagine compromise between non-Orthodox who are willing to recognize the Orthodox as one interest among several and Orthodox who do not consider themselves an interest so much as the authoritative interpreters of holy word. Yet the Orthodox minority often prevail. Some of their success is attributable to distinctly modern political skills. In addition, they have exploited liberals' desire to include everyone. Finally, they have gained from a peculiar psychological dynamic. On the one hand, non-Orthodox may ridicule the traditional Orthodox for imitating a past way of life from Eastern Europe and resent their efforts to impose it on others. On the other hand, because they firmly adhere to religious law and keep alive a tradition, many Jews feel Orthodoxy is the only right way to be Jewish. Many who compromise with modernity feel guilty they have given away too much, fear they believe too little, and, consequently, support the Orthodox even when they disagree with them.

Moreover, the Orthodox are more successful than the non-Orthodox in continuing their community. Orthodox children are more likely to marry other Orthodox and stay in the Orthodox community, while many non-Orthodox children, including those in wealthy and prominent families, are moving away from Jewish religious practices and institutional life (Kosmin et al. 1991; Tobin 1986).

The Associated and the Community

One might ask how many Baltimore Jewish communities there are; whether The Associated represents one encompassing community, several communities, or one community among several; and, as the federation articulated its goal of Jewish continuity, how many communities this meant strengthening.

Associated staff and lay leaders resist publicly recognizing differences. They describe the Baltimore Jewish community as uniquely homogeneous among American Jewish communities. It has long traditions and is both physically concentrated and socially cohesive. The generations in Baltimore Jewish families have grown up and done business together, they feel a strong attachment to the city, and the children stay in the community. In this view, the centrality of The Associated reflects the community. The annual campaign is highly successful, not simply because of local wealth, but because of unusual generosity. Representatives of prominent families make up a cohesive leadership. Unlike in other cities, there are no divisive feuds, and all leaders come together to address common problems.

This account is condensed in an Associated fundraising slogan, "We are one." All Baltimore Jews are one community, yet some Orthodox answer simply, "We are not one." And a non-Orthodox rabbi, speaking with Associated staff and leadership, amended the phrase to say, "We are one, but we are many." A top staff member answered, "We are different, and we are the same." Though acknowledging differences, he concludes with sameness.

Asked how strategic planning participants resolved this question, a top staff member explained,

> There was agreement by everybody that there is one community. There were elements of different communities, but absolutely there is one community. In Baltimore it is one community. There is central giving and participation. Everyone from every segment is involved with The Associated, the organized Jewish community. Except for the unaffiliated. *Community* is used in the singular because of the concept of peoplehood. It is inclusionary. The Law of Return [that grants Israeli citizenship to any Jew emigrating to Israel]. Every member of the Jewish people is a member of the Jewish community in whatever area he resides. That is a geographic definition. Even the unaffiliated are members of the Jewish community.

In this complex argument, he acknowledges "different communities" but asserts "absolutely there is one community," although "the unaffiliated," who neither contribute to the federation nor belong to a synagogue, do not belong to it. In this account, *community* has a different meaning from *communities*. The latter is a sociological concept, referring to different patterns of worship, socializing, and institutional loyalty. In contrast, the "one community" is "The Associated, the organized Jewish community." For the community organization, the organization is the community. The community does not exist except where it is affiliated with the organization, and hence even those not affiliated with it are potential members. This is the sense in which The Associated sees only one community. This is a self-interested political argument.

This argument is supplemented by another, which invokes "the concept of people-hood," that is so inclusionary as to make even the unaffiliated members of the Jewish community. The first argument deals in social reality. It acknowledges different communities but argues that the current organization is the sole locus for commu-nity membership and citizenship. While a critic may reject the organization's ambi-tions, there is no question about its reality. In contrast, the second argument is abstract. It appeals to a peoplehood of common history and experience (Kaplan [1934] 1981). Even those who choose not to affiliate with the organized community are members of this community. Although the fact of nonaffiliation, as well as different Orthodox and non-Orthodox experiences, should challenge this claim, the argument stands beyond this evidence.

The second argument reinforces the political agenda of The Associated, but it has its own history. For the Orthodox it invokes the belief that all Jews were present at Mt. Sinai. It also fits the experience of many non-Orthodox, by redefining Jews from a religious community within which there are real disagreements, to an ethnic community which is seen as whatever its members are and do.

This argument also has psychological motives. For some, particularly older gen-erations, it reflects a real shared history. For them and many others it expresses a wish that all Jews could make up one people, or community; that all would care for one another; that the community would be strong. Seeing the community this way responds to the memory of the Holocaust and the history of persecution to which it belongs. It relates to current incidents of anti-Semitism. It offers security in a world that does not always accept Jews. Strategically, in religious and ethnic politics, a cohesive community matters. But beyond this, a single community is symbolically, unconsciously essential to security in the world, and any split endangers all.

For political and psychological reasons The Associated does not recognize signifi-cant differences among Jews. Rather, it both sees and denies the differences, as in the words of the staff member. How would this ambiguity affect strategic planning for community continuity?

Reality and Fantasy in Planning

Planners often try to identify goals representing community-wide interests. Their success depends on their responses to how people see their interests and what they want from planning. To be realistic and legitimate, decisions must follow rules that recognize different beliefs and interests.

If differences are relatively small and conflicts mild or infrequent, consensus decision making is appropriate. Searching for unanimity affirms and encourages articulation of common interests, and uncoerced unanimity may occur under several conditions. First, some problems have good solutions, and parties with overlapping interests may find a mutually satisfactory course of action. Second, people may feel unanimity is inherently good and decide to go along with the majority to affirm and create emotional unity. Third, people may so empathize with others' concerns that they go along with what others want, particularly when others feel their desires deeply (Mansbridge 1983).

When differences are greater, when parties are more self-interested or more intransigent, and when conflicts are frequent, majority rule may better lead to decisions. Its effectiveness requires that all participate voluntarily, have relatively equal power, and agree on the legitimacy of every interest. Each party can expect to be in the majority a sufficient number of times so as not to be aggrieved by any majority that overrules it.

Several conditions make majority rule difficult. First, if power is so concentrated that some interests have little or no chance to be part of a majority, the excluded may regard ostensible or even real majority decisions as illegitimate. Second, expertise or doctrine may persuade some parties that only certain positions are legitimate and lead them to oppose majority decision making that could include other positions. Third, actors may be so firmly invested in one view of their interests that they cannot compromise. If, nevertheless, all parties share an interest in acting together, they will need to create and negotiate other procedures for acting together. Their success depends on being willing to examine what they believe separates them. Otherwise, some may choose to act independently, even against others.

Consensus decision making is most likely to work in small, relatively homogeneous, face-to-face communities. A consensus culture in larger, more diverse groups may discourage minorities from pressing their views and encourage them to acquiesce when they do not really agree. Majority rule can work in communities with considerable diversity if managed by a central institution everyone considers legitimate. Still, when the community is large and issues are complex, institutional managers may be tempted to narrow the definitions of issues and the range of groups they involve in order to reach agreements, and excluded interests may rebel or withdraw.

Thus The Associated, in initiating strategic planning, especially with community continuity on the agenda, had to select a decision procedure that fits community dynamics.

The psychological meanings of decision rules

Communities or organizations may choose decision rules not only for their realistic fit with social conditions, but also for their tacit messages about acceptable personal motives and safety in decision making.

Under conditions of conflict that may make majority rule appropriate, people must act both caringly and aggressively. Caring helps to build coalitions on shared interests, but aggression is necessary to articulate interests, to force others to take them seriously, to bargain for a fair place for one's interests, and to defeat others with conflicting interests.

While creating coalitions can be gratifying, the aggression surrounding such alliances can be unsettling. One may fear doing battle. One may be afraid of losing – not just of being injured, but also of being shamed after exposing one's wants and then not being strong enough to prevail. One may be anxious about winning – feeling guilty about successfully influencing or harming others or afraid of reprisal. One may also feel anxious about the burdens of winning – being responsible for a policy which will be judged, and being responsible for other persons.

Majority rule presents leaders with other dangers. It assumes differences and directs parties to see differences. It reinforces individualism and group autonomy. By formally identifying winners and losers, majority rule not only shames consistent losers, but brands them as deviants and makes them potential dissidents. It becomes easy for them to move from criticizing policy to challenging the ground rules and leaving.

In contrast, consensus norms reassuringly assume a harmony of interests. They imply a world in which caring far outweighs aggression. People are similar, they easily join together, and their collective power strengthens all. No one will feel weak or ashamed about inadequacies. There will be no dangerous conflict, and no one need be anxious about battle. Consensus focuses attention on dissidents but defines them as eventual allies. Consensus rules give minorities power; by holding their ground, the minorities can force the majority to move toward them or prevent a decision. Deliberation may be aggressive, but it will be guided by reason. The end is a caring agreement – no one is a loser, no one is defeated, and no one is shamed.

These assumptions are psychologically reassuring to people who are anxious about aggression and conflict. They are politically reassuring to leaders who want control.

Organizations or communities may reasonably use consensus decision making to affirm common interests. But they may unrealistically adopt consensus rules with the aim of giving everyone a self-protective veto (Mansbridge 1983). Because the conflicts that necessitate such vetoes are inconsistent with a reality of common interests, a group that requires vetoes will rarely discover common interests. However, the group may never recognize that consensus rules do not fit their conditions if they want to be reassured by the fantasies that accompany the rules. They imagine that difference, conflict, and aggression dissolve under consensus rules. Wishful thinking may substitute for realistic planning and decision making. This was the risk The Associated faced in adopting consensus rules in strategic planning.

Strategic Planning for Community Continuity

The Associated created a Strategic Planning Committee in January, 1988, with subcommittees on services, relationships, and finances. The committee produced a plan in June, 1989. A Strategic Planning Implementation Council began work in July, 1989, with six task forces. The Services Task Force, taking up the work of the services subcommittee, gave rise in 1990 to a Commission on Jewish Education, which began work on a strategic plan for Jewish education. The commission was made a standing committee and also given budgetary responsibility. This case examines the part of strategic planning that focused on Jewish education as a means for promoting continuity of the Jewish community.

Planning

The strategic plan proclaimed the importance of Jewish education:

> Along with an experience of Israel, Jewish education is the most powerful bonding force among American Jewry; it powerfully strengthens Jewish identity and hence the Jewish community. At a time when many of the social, economic and ideological forces affecting Jewish life tend to weaken the sense of a distinctive history and shared values, Jewish education is vital to the preservation of the legacy.
>
> (Strategic Planning Committee 1989, p. 8)

This language covered over a major disagreement. Jewish education is broadly defined. Formal education includes both full-time day schools and part-time, after-school and/or Sunday supplementary religious education. Informal education comprises a range of loosely structured educational and social programs that lead participants to identify with the Jewish community. It includes, for example, trips to Israel and participation in Jewish Community Center recreational programs.

Most supporters of day schools are Orthodox. Six of seven day schools assisted by the federation at the time were Orthodox, one Conservative; a new Orthodox school and a new Reform school did not get aid. Supplementary programs are Conservative or Reform. Some non-Orthodox support day schooling but do not want it for their own children. Instead, the experience of Israel is a centerpiece in a largely non-Orthodox agenda to promote informal education.

Informal education advocates disagree with the Orthodox on educational content because they disagree about what a member of the community should know, do, and be. Orthodox emphasize religious belief and consider day schools the only valid form of Jewish education. Most non-Orthodox focus on a sense of belonging and believe many forms of education evoke this feeling. Taking an ethnic view, they see community as an intrinsic end, while many Orthodox, taking a religious view, see community as a support for individual practice.

Educational disagreements raised policy issues for strategic planning. Enrollment in supplementary programs was declining while enrollment in day schools was growing. Teaching in many supplementary programs was considered weak, but few non-Orthodox wanted day schools. Were day schools the reason fewer Orthodox married outside the community? While The Associated was committed to investing more in education, where should it put its money? Should it give more to the Orthodox day schools, which refused to account for funds, or more to informal education? How much should it get involved in educational planning and coordination to assure good use of funds?

Conflicts over education roughly followed denominational lines. Debate often simplified alternatives by pitting formal against informal education, with largely Orthodox on one side and non-Orthodox on the other. This argument reflected educational disagreements, but became a vehicle for expressing broader Orthodox–non-Orthodox conflicts.

The first draft of the services subcommittee report acknowledged the centrality of conflict between Orthodox and non-Orthodox:

[An argument against Associated involvement with schools is that] such support may raise difficult and potentially divisive questions of disproportionate subsidization of Orthodox over Conservative and Reform institutions; the substantial support from the Associated would imply an Associated voice in educational priorities, an influence the schools would strongly resist.

[It might be reasonable to support schools according to the amount of day school curriculum that is specifically Jewish.] Even so, such a formula would provide more support to Orthodox than to Conservative or Reform institutions. That might prove a source of contention. It would also seem to ignore one of the principal criteria for subsidy adopted by this subcommittee – namely, that priority should go to services addressed to persons at risk of not retaining their Jewish identity. Children of Orthodox homes are probably least likely to fall into this category. Should the formula then prefer children from least affiliated families? Or from poorer families? Or should we allocate support in proportion to the relative sizes of the Orthodox, Conservative and Reform communities? Or to the size of their youth populations?

The subcommittee's final report did not mention denominational conflicts. The strategic plan only offered general recommendations, deferring decisions to implementation. The plan recommended increasing funding for Jewish education, supporting day and supplementary education differently, and establishing a single entity to assess educational needs, evaluate programs, and decide on allocating Associated resources.

Implementation

The Commission on Jewish Education was created to implement these recommendations. Approximately 40 members were selected to represent a range of religious, educational, and agency affiliations, including 12 delegates from education-related agencies. Except for these delegates, most members were men who were major contributors and senior community leaders. A concern for representation of day schools led to a membership that was one-third Orthodox, a considerably higher proportion than their numbers in the community.

The commission began by creating subcommittees to make recommendations in and advocate for four areas: day school education, supplementary education, informal education, and higher education. The first three subcommittees reported in summer 1991. A dispute involving the Baltimore Hebrew University stopped the fourth subcommittee, and the plan waited on university reform.

Following are excerpts from three commission meetings held during the period after three subcommittee reports were submitted and the commission awaited the fourth report. The first two meetings involve discussions of educational priorities, while the third involves budgetary decision making. The meetings reveal educational, social, and religious disagreements. They show how members and staff address these conflicts. Comments come from notes and are close to the original text. Some remarks have been omitted, with their place indicated by dots (...). The names are pseudonyms.

Meeting one: talking about education priorities   Staff sent commission members a draft "Introduction to the Strategic Plan for Jewish Education" for discussion and possible approval. The text asserted the equality of formal and informal education. It was accompanied by a "Conceptual Framework/Planning Grid" to organize the disparate subcommittee recommendations. At the left of the grid was a list of potential client groups distinguished by age. Three other columns on the grid were labeled personnel, educational programs/initiatives, and special populations.

Commission members, most advocates for specific interests or programs, faced two challenges. The first was to examine their differences. The second was to find common interests and values from which to frame a plan. The chair and a staff member began by emphasizing that the draft was tentative and urged members to think about commonalities between formal and informal education.

Eugene Hammerman (the leading Orthodox advocate for day schools):   There is not enough in this document about Jewish education in Baltimore. We must define Jewish education in terms of what has been successful in increasing Jewish identity. Informal Jewish education has not been successful. Successful, for example, in stopping the intermarriage rate. Outreach [largely informal education] to the unaffiliated [who do not belong to synagogues] is not the same as Jewish education.

Louis Greenspan (a secular, non-Orthodox community leader):   There is a policy question. Are the unaffiliated our clients?

Max Neustadt (another secular, non-Orthodox leader, a strong advocate for informal education):   I am for the unaffiliated. Formal and informal, it is all education....

Harold Weiss (an Orthodox advocate for traditional Jewish education): The document, in being all-inclusive, is too neutral and meaningless. It doesn't identify a direction and make choices.

William Silver (chair):   Staff can't make these decisions; the Commission must.

Ruth Chernov (agency representative):   Even the affiliated are not a homogeneous group. Many nominally affiliated need Jewish education to increase their affiliation....

Rachel Eisenman (agency representative):   There are dangers in focusing on the core of affiliated groups, especially when many of their children become less affiliated. I have informal education programs in my agency, and they work in pulling in the unaffiliated.

Weiss: Okay, but informal education is only bait for the real thing, ... intensive Jewish education.

Roger Kobrin (non-Orthodox day school advocate):   More important than interested and connected people, as the informal education people emphasize, are educated and knowledgeable people. Not civil Jews, but Jewish Jews....

Esther Davidoff (agency representative):   The key is to focus on Torah-based Jewish education, whether formal or informal. I would propose to eliminate the words *formal* and *informal*, and to focus on what is learned....

Saul Aaronson (staff):   This is a draft. Read the observation that Jewish education is a lifelong enterprise. Keep in mind that The Associated funds only part of Jewish education, and that is what we are talking about. Please give me any written comments you have on the draft. For now, I would like a formal signoff on the grid as a framework.

Weiss: I move that Saul complete the grid. [Second.] [Some hands raised.] Now that we have gotten past that, I would like to argue again for preparing the introduction at the end, rather than now.

Silver: We won't ask you to sign off on it now.

Weiss: Okay. Though it is too all-inclusive now.

Silver: We can amend it later.

Weiss: Okay....

Davidoff: I would like to ask that by the next meeting we have the grid filled in also with current budget figures for programs in each box [so we can see who now gets how much].

Aaronson: May be at a later meeting. We can't do it by next time.

Betty Stein (agency representative):   I feel that, after the talk about the relative importance of outreach and inreach [mainly formal education for the affiliated], there is no consensus on it.

Aaronson: Right. I don't hear consensus either on affiliated and unaffiliated.

Silver: Our aim is to include all – for example, outreach and inreach.

Neustadt: I want to reinforce Esther's request for budget figures. I'd like to see at least round numbers.

Aaronson: Okay. We can do it. I was just waiting to hear you say "great job."

Silver: I want to thank the staff for a good job, as always.

Meeting one: analysis   Disagreements about education reflect disagreements about community. The Orthodox want a community of religiously knowledgeable and observant people and consider formal day-schooling the means to this end. Most non-Orthodox think of a community constituted by feelings of belonging and advocate whatever will nurture these bonds. They emphasize the quantitative goals of outreach, while the Orthodox talk qualitatively of reaching in to those already in the fold.

Most members argue from their experiences, often as parents or as former students, sometimes just as observers. No one appeals to scientific knowledge. Even with disagreements about desired outcomes, educational research might shed light on how effectively different programs contribute to their goals. No one considers the possibility that research might focus deliberations. One reason is that most members have been chosen for political influence, not educational experience. The Board of Jewish Education has expertise, but in the commission was treated as only one of several agencies competing for funding.

Discussion moves among general statements about the value of programs, arguments about target populations, and allusions to characteristics of a good community. The confusion between programs and outcomes can be attributed to inexperience with education, but knowledgeable staff members do not push for clarity. Perhaps people are sensitive to the limitations in their knowledge and refrain from asking questions they cannot discuss. Probably people avoid talking about what education should do because they assume differences are irreconcilable, and talking specifically seems not only futile, but dangerous. Perhaps people believe eventual decisions will involve compromises conceding language and funds to everyone, and conceptual clarity does not matter.

The Associated emphasizes consensus. The chair and others talk about whether there is consensus on certain issues, whether, in effect, the staff is authorized to draft language and negotiate with parties. This is the context in which the staff hoped for formal signoff on the conceptual introduction and grid. Weiss criticizes the language as unacceptably inclusive. The chair throws the decision back to the commission. Later, Stein and a staff member agree they don't hear consensus on basic issues, but the staff is authorized to fill out the grid.

The 90-minute meeting is too brief for detailed deliberation, but no one asks for more. Discussions of consensus are ambiguous, leaving staff free to move within the bounds of what they can persuade commission members they want.

Meeting two: voting on priorities   Staff members next sent committee members a ballot listing every recommendation mentioned in any subcommittee report. Recommendations were grouped under personnel, programs, and special populations. Members were asked to check the top 5 of 9 listings for personnel, 12 of 26 for programs, and to note 3 for special populations. Only 20 members voted.

The removal of recommendations from the contexts of advocative reports to a conceptual grid, as well as mail balloting, were efforts to reduce public conflict and facilitate agreement. The chair introduced the meeting as "pivotal" and hoped the commission would pivot toward consensus.

Silver (chair): We'll discuss each category of proposals in turn. Let's spend 20 minutes on personnel.

Hammerman (Orthodox): [He began by reading a long letter he had sent the chair and staff after the last meeting. He continued:] We can't talk about formal and informal education in the same breath. Personnel, for example: they have different personnel needs. We must talk about each of them separately. Formal education is institutional, regularized. Informal education is ad hoc, both in what people ask for and how people respond to the requests. These are two different constituencies. . . .

Silver: I'm not surprised you are saying that. I think we would have great difficulty getting consensus from the committee by separating the two, because one would come out higher than the other. If we consider differences of opinion, we will never get consensus.

Weiss (Orthodox): Why are we doing this prioritizing? What does voting on priorities mean? Does it mean how dollars will be spent? Or does it just mean how things are valued? For example, trips to Israel, which everyone valued high, versus day schools. Trips to Israel might be valued high, but that doesn't mean that a great deal of money should be spent on them.

Yitzchak Weinstein (an educator): Note the emphasis on the word *schooling*. This is formal education. Then there is also communal education. And informal education. . . . Isn't Israel a school in itself? All three – schooling, communal, and informal – should be integrated. Let's deal with these issues by going through specific recommendations. . . .

Jerome Ornstein (a traditionally religious non-Orthodox leader): I think there is a continuum, formal and informal. One is not more important than the other. The valuation here is that all are equal.

Silver: Don't worry about money yet.

Weiss: [To those around him,] But that's what it is all about.

Silver: [He reads,] "Increase salaries and benefits": day schools will come in with a proposal that fits in. But there could be someone defined as a teacher at the Jewish Community Center.

Hammerman: Formal and informal education are not the ends of a continuum. They are different.

Silver: Let's avoid dividing up into formal and informal. Doing that would lead to conflict, no decision, no consensus. . . .

[At this point, a staff member distributed tallies from the voting, and people looked them over. The chair read the results. As discussion suggested, the votes favored non-Orthodox interests in informal education.]

Davidoff (agency): I discussed this with the staff already. Each of these recommendations is actually five, related to early childhood, childhood, adolescence, adulthood, and family [target populations]. When are we going to decide among these?

Silver: Later. . . .

Jacob Litwak (an educator): The priorities are inconsistent. Why did greater teacher recognition get only eight votes?

Weiss: People were given a fixed number of unweighted votes, and this is how it ended up.

Silver: Let's turn to programs. [He lists the priorities, which include a system manager.]

Alexandra Norman (non-Orthodox community leader):   Regarding the system manager, this would lead to money going to a big bureaucracy.

Silver: This was a high, high priority for the Informal Education Subcommittee.

Weiss: What is the meaning of 18 votes for experience in Israel?

Silver: It is not yet the top priority. It is only one of the priority items. There will be a further vote. . . .

Hammerman: We should limit the system manager to informal education. Or call it a "coordinator for Jewish education" for informal education.

[A long discussion followed regarding the system manager. Questions involved to whom the manager would be accountable and whether it would just collect and disseminate information or have power over programs.]

Fred Ginsburg (agency representative):   For example, the system manager would be responsible for "encouraging interagency collaboration on programming and reducing possible redundancies." What power would it have?

Abel Chechin (agency representative with allegiances to day schools):   I would suggest substituting "identifying opportunities for interagency collaboration." . . .

Silver: What about "information resource person"?

Ginsburg: Take out "empower" from "Empower a system manager."

Silver: Would you accept "Establish an informational resource"?

Aaronson (staff):   It is informing the community.

Silver: We are getting close to consensus on this entity. . . . I am trying to move to [recommendations on] specific populations. [Discussion continued to focus on programs, and ending time arrived.] We will convene the steering committee of the subcommittee chairs to draft this into the text of the plan. Well, we got through it!

Meeting two: analysis   The staff designed the survey to reach consensus among viewpoints by identifying agreements on specific recommendations. Weiss criticized it on methodological grounds, noting that votes could not express preference rankings or weights. But his stronger objection was that breaking down committee reports into discrete recommendations avoided a direct confrontation between the main positions.

The chair tried to avoid confrontation. Hammerman began by reading his long letter, suggesting formal and informal education be considered separately. The chair explicitly rejected the idea, insisting that the two types of education constituted ends of a continuum. Separating them, he argued, would force people to value one over the other, with some winners and others losers. Such an outcome would prevent consensus and was unacceptable. After the meeting, several people complained to staff members that Hammerman had taken too much time. They assumed people were supposed to refer briefly to their positions, but not advocate for them at length.

Members ignored anyone who said they should talk specifically about setting priorities, as did Weinstein and Davidoff at this meeting and Weiss at the earlier one. The only specifically discussed proposal was that of a system manager, proposed by the informal education subcommittee to coordinate informal education resources, but favored by Associated administration as a way of centrally managing all educational programs. Opposition came primarily from day school advocates who did not want outside control. Fearful of federation domination, they turned a system manager into an informational resource.

Near the end, the chair identified a consensus, and he finally assumed sufficient agreement to guide subcommittee chairs (though, in fact, they never drafted language). The survey and discussion suggested general agreement about giving more money to education, recruiting more students, and facilitating Israel trips, though there was no specific guidance for planning or budgetary decisions. Nevertheless, no one objected that the discussion had been incomplete (for example, in not getting to special populations) or that it had not led toward consensus on text. Probably members assumed important decisions would be made when the staff negotiated privately with influential parties and, therefore, were willing to turn initiative over to staff members.

Meeting three: passing an educational budget   The fiscal calendar forced the commission to shift to its budgetary role. That diverted the commission from policy issues, but forced it to decide on allocating money without a plan. The commission held three hearings on agency requests before a final meeting to allocate a new supplementary $300,000 Fund for Jewish Education, intended to support innovation. This was the first time the commission made a decision entailing priorities.

Five agencies requested a total of $488,403, with the Council on Day School Education asking for the most, $199,372 (two-thirds of the available fund, and 41% of total requests). Prior to the meeting, the staff negotiated with agencies to lower their requests, in order to make the agencies look realistic and magnanimous while avoiding a fight.

The chair, who had been party to the negotiations, called the meeting to order with a grin. He began by saying that the Board of Jewish Education "showed great fiscal management and great planning for 1993," summarized the agency's new position, and announced what The Associated leadership would give the agency in return. A staff member signaled he should wait until presentation of the agency's intentions before responding to them. The chair then introduced the agency reports.

All agencies except the Day School Council scaled back their requests. After the other four had compromised, the day school group subtracted their totals from $300,000 and lowered its request to equal the remainder. While it now asked for only $142,599, this became 48% of requests. Requests now equaled available funds, and conflict could be avoided.

At the end of presentations, an agency representative proposed to "give *koved* [respect] to the chair," and everyone applauded. The chair said he "would like to give a tribute to the staff. They make me look good." Everyone applauded. Then the chair called for a vote, and the new budget passed without objection.

After the meeting, an agency representative congratulated himself for contributing to a harmonious decision by lowering his request. The leading Orthodox day school advocate told the staff that the Baltimore federation was exceptional in America for such a conciliatory way of working. Staff members congratulated one another on the amicable outcome.

Meeting three: analysis   Absent a plan or consensus about the relative priority of formal and informal education, in a commission where Orthodox and other day school advocates represented a minority but refused to compromise, the commission gave almost half the budget for innovation to day schools, who proposed to use the money for routine expenses. No one discussed the merits of any request, and no one openly criticized the day schools for inflexibility. When the day school spokesman revised his request to equal the exact amount that would bring the total funds requested to $300,000 people laughed.

The meeting could have erupted in conflict. To prevent this, staff privately negotiated with agencies. The chairman's grin seems to reflect his appreciation of the intensity of potential conflict, his knowledge that deals have been made, and his recognition that others know of the bargains. The meeting would not be as it might appear, but it would end happily. The congratulatory comments and applause at meeting's end express a similar relief. This is the way in which the staff (by negotiating) makes the chair look good (in running a harmonious meeting).

The Politics and Psychology of Consensus

The Strategic Planning Committee produced only general recommendations after 18 months, and the Commission on Jewish Education had not agreed on a plan in two years. Budgeting, however, required specific decisions. Although budgeting implies agreement on priorities, dollars (unlike beliefs) are divisible. The process of reaching agreement on the Fund for Jewish Education budget reveals consensus decision making as it usually works, as well as the political and psychological meanings of consensus that hindered agreement on a plan.

A staff member explains what consensus is and why it is preferable to majority rule: "If we are 6–5, we offend five people. If we are 10–1, we only offend one." While a 6–5 vote would produce a decision, it could make problems. Half the parties would be angry. They might attack the federation or cut their gifts. These actions would challenge The Associated's claim to centrality in a unified community. Following this norm, the Commission on Jewish Education could not produce a strategic plan.

When budgeting required agreement, commission work moved behind the scenes, where federation staff negotiated with agency representatives. Such negotiations are so much a part of normal Associated politics, they are hardly private or hidden. Everyone expects them, and nearly everyone regards them as the real work. Top management is central, largely because of its influence over Associated and local Jewish foundation money. A staff member involved in brokering agreements talks of using persuasion, influence, and coalition building.

> I wouldn't say threats; I would say persuasion. I say they should think in terms of what is good for the overall community. I say that if they want something later on, they should go along on this issue.

Another speaks of occasionally buying someone off with a position or contribution to a program. Participation and power in negotiations, he says, follow the "Golden Rule":

> The politics is, he who has the gold rules. Where there is consensus in the purest sense is among those who have the gold. The consensus is built around the leadership of the organization [the biggest contributors, members of the Executive Committee]. Once the leadership agree on positions, the staff's job is taking this consensus and selling it to everyone else. The consensus is most important at the very top. It is less important lower

down on the rungs. Most of the time the people who are most important are the people with responsibility for resource development [contributing]. In the end, people will acquiesce because they know the big boys have signed off. They know the likelihood of fighting it is minimal. They will buy in in order to get a piece of the pie for themselves. People are intimidated by the leadership of the organization.

This is interest-group politics with the requirement of reaching public unanimity and presenting that as a result of reasoned search for agreement.

Some outside the leadership criticize the process. One complains that because decision making is behind the scenes, public meetings, particularly in large groups like the commission, "are a joke, and everybody knows they are a joke." There is no public debate on issues, decisions have already been made, and everyone comes just to rubber stamp them. Some, he says, believe they are making decisions, but many cynically do not.

Why does he not speak up when he disagrees, at least for the record? At small meetings, he says he does, but he would be seen as disruptive in large meetings. Staff would get angry. He wants to be a team player, supporting the party line in public to get something later on. Moreover, he knows how to play the game behind the scenes, and he works hard at it. This is more than prudent politics.

Many agree that public meetings rubber stamp decisions made elsewhere. The less powerful complain more openly. Top leaders acknowledge that decision making is not democratic. But no one moves to change the arrangement. More is involved than just the powerful holding on to procedures that benefit them. For example, at the end of meeting one, Neustadt, a powerful man, added his weight to the request for budget figures, sure to explicate and thus add to conflict. The staff member agreed to comply but first wanted a compliment for good work. His good work, as he saw it, was an effort to avoid conflict with a conceptual framework and a grid. The chair, also a powerful man, gave the compliment, and the meeting ended. After some disagreements at meeting two, the chair concluded with a sense of relief: "Well, we got through it!" – without a blowup. His grin during meeting three expressed similar satisfaction at the prospect of avoiding open conflict. Applause and self-congratulations afterward echoed this relief.

Behind-the-scenes politics makes this possible. Even powerful community leaders fear public conflict, and they displace conflict onto staff, expecting them to recognize and resolve differences. Publicly, community members can act as if there are no divisions and they have no community-rending disagreements. Politically, this arrangement benefits the elite.

But psychologically it protects everyone from anxiety about splitting the community. In consensus politics, Associated management and leadership try to get as near unanimity as possible. Agreement normally starts with the leadership, but those who are not team players harm others as well as themselves. They make themselves losers and can make the majority feel guilty. More than that, they make it impossible for the participants to feel as though they are members (or leaders) of a cohesive community. Both winners and losers may feel guilty and anxious.

Participants are likely to explain unanimity by saying that constituencies have sufficiently overlapping interests and enough good sense to discover reasonable solutions to problems. In reality, many begin with the emotional assumption that unanimity is intrinsically good and will go along with either the leaders or a strong minority to affirm and create emotional unity (Mansbridge 1983). Behind-the-scenes politics helps avoid guilt about acting aggressively and shame about failing. Instead, people can bask in the warmth of caring for and feeling cared for by other members of a unified community. On the other hand, the managers who negotiate backstage agreements are exhausted, not just by the effort, but also by taking on the anxiety, guilt, and shame community members push onto them.

The contrast between the self-interested logrolling and the intense emphasis on a unanimous community interest parallels the private and public accounts of the community. In reality, negotiations are necessary because there are group differences and conflicts. However, the broad public agreement allows the fantasy that there was unity all along.

The Costs of Consensus: Reality and Fantasy

Decision norms that lead to broad public agreement have political and emotional benefits, but also costs. Where there is intense, even anxious, concern for unanimity, an intransigent minority can get its way or block the majority. This is especially true where the minority has special moral standing. Thus the history of strategic planning for Jewish education shows four years in which the majority could neither come to agreement with the minority nor defeat them. In a rare specific decision, the majority agreed to give half the budget to a minority who said they would not use the money for its intended purpose.

Strategic planning was an effort to subsume the politics of budgetary interests under agreed-on principles and priorities. Instead, political and psychological interests in unanimity led the non-Orthodox majority to move their conflicts with the largely Orthodox minority behind the scenes to a realm of interest-group politics. Bargaining the appearance of unity against budgetary demands, the day school interests took a position the majority would not publicly challenge. The non-Orthodox majority wanted consensus so badly that they agreed to a substantive decision they did not like.

The strengths and weaknesses of these politics mirror the inner conflicts of community members. Avowedly, they want to examine and improve reality, but many anxiously want to avoid confronting their differences. Where these aims conflict, consensus politics favors the second over the first. While the rhetoric of strategic planning implies rationality, the reality of frightening differences and unacknowledged emotions drives politics. Participants become cynical about formal, public decision making; planning; the community organization; and themselves.

People often blame Associated staff members or leaders for controlling things to get unanimity and not dealing with real issues. Yet these politics also serve to obscure a psychological reality. Many think of the world dualistically, not only contrasting a threatening outside society with the safety of their community, but also worrying that anyone within the community who is different is a potential defector and enemy. When even small differences arouse anxiety, it is easier to attack right-wing Orthodox, civil Jews, unaffiliated, or intermarried as dangers to the community than it is to grapple with a mixture of similarities and differences. Modern non-Orthodox and traditional Orthodox, for example, cannot see how they resemble one another because they have stakes in finding differences (Klein 1948; Volkan 1988). So long as people unconsciously insist on these benefits, they will be unable to create politics that better fit social realities.

Lessons for Strategic Planning

Advocates of strategic planning hesitate to say that their methods readily fit community organizations. This case illustrates reasons for caution by showing how social, cultural, and psychological dynamics reflect and create a complicated web of stakeholders. Yet it is too easy to see communities as different from formal organizations. In comparison with organizations, communities are usually larger, less formal, and less definitely bounded. In general, not only do communities have less control over money, but they have less control over members or, indeed, whether someone is a member. Moreover, people often enter communities as whole persons, with all their beliefs and feelings becoming part of the community, while organization members are expected to occupy segmented roles (but see Baum 1990).

In general, these contrasts hold, but they conceal similarities between organizations and communities by exaggerating the degree to which organizations are susceptible to managerial order. Strategic planning manuals, both by their words and by the length and detail of their task lists, suggest that strategic planning can bring an organization under control. This was the psychological promise of comprehensive rationality. In fact, the lessons of this community strategic planning effort apply, as well, to organizational strategic planning. Members chose to act according to fantasies about how they wanted the entity to be, rather than plan realistically to address different interests and preferences. General Motors and NASA are as good as any examples of organizations brought down by similar fantasies (Schwartz 1990).

The first lesson for any strategic planning is that organizations and communities must overtly acknowledge and address differences if they are to plan realistically. This means creating settings that support members in taking political and psychological risks in discussing what they know but do not normally say, in order to find new ways of thinking about both differences and similarities among members (Diamond 1993). Otherwise, people may act on partial, distorted, or erroneous beliefs about others, even if doing so leads to unsatisfying outcomes, as in this case, because they exaggerate the risks (Argyris and Schön 1978; Argyris 1982); even when not talking prevents decisions everyone would like (Schön 1982); even when anxious agreement preserves the appearance of consensus but leads to unrealistic decisions, of which the Challenger disaster is a tragic example (Schwartz 1990).

Second, decision rules should correspond to the extent and intensity of real group differences. Concepts or procedures that assume nonexistent agreement do not eliminate differences, cannot build commitment to collective action, and encourage cynical withdrawal. Majority vote can accommodate widely varying positions, particularly when it follows honest presentation of interests, but when differences are extreme or undiscussed, formal voting may produce decisions without creating sanction for them. No specific procedure is more important than a process that recognizes the difficulty but necessity of examining differences.

Strategic planning, as any planning, depends on taking people, organizations, and communities seriously, analyzing not only what they say, but what they feel, what they fear, what they desire, and how they act.

ACKNOWLEDGMENT

I have benefited greatly from the extraordinarily thoughtful comments of three anonymous reviewers of the manuscript.

REFERENCES

Argyris, C. 1982. *Reasoning, Learning, and Action*. San Francisco, California: Jossey-Bass.

Argyris, C., and D. A. Schön. 1978. *Organizational Learning*, Reading, Massachusetts: Addison-Wesley.

Baum, H. S. 1987. *The Invisible Bureaucracy*. New York: Oxford University Press.

Baum, H. S. 1990. *Organizational Membership*. Albany, New York: SUNY Press.

Bryce, H. 1992. *Financial & Strategic Management for Nonprofit Organizations*. 2nd ed. Englewood Cliffs, New Jersey: Prentice-Hall.

Bryson, J. M. 1988. *Strategic Planning for Public and Nonprofit Organizations*. San Francisco, California: Jossey-Bass.

Bryson, J. M., and R. C. Einsweiler. 1987. Introduction. *Journal of the American Planning Association* 53: 6–8.

Bryson, J. M., and W. D. Roering. 1987. Applying private-sector strategic planning in the public sector. *Journal of the American Planning Association* 53: 9–22.

Diamond, M. A. 1993. *The Unconscious Life of Organizations*. Westport, Connecticut: Quorum Books.

Espy, S. N. 1986. *Handbook of Strategic Planning for Nonprofit Organizations*. New York: Praeger.

Fein, I. M. 1971. *The Making of an American Jewish Community*. Philadelphia, Pennsylvania: Jewish Publication Society of America.

Heilman, S. 1992. *Defenders of the Faith*. New York: Schocken Books.

Heilman, S. C., and S. M. Cohen. 1989. *Cosmopolitans & Parochials*. Chicago, Illinois: University of Chicago Press.

Hirschhorn, L. 1988. *The Workplace Within*. Cambridge, Massachusetts: MIT Press.

Hirschhorn, L., and C. K. Barnett, eds. 1993. *The Psychodynamics of Organizations*. Philadelphia, Pennsylvania: Temple University Press.

Kaplan, M. M. [1934] 1981. *Judaism as a Civilization*. Philadelphia, Pennsylvania, and New York: Jewish Publication Society of America and Reconstructionist Press.

Kaufman, J. L., and H. M. Jacobs. 1987. A public planning perspective on strategic planning. *Journal of the American Planning Association* 53: 23–33.

Kets de Vries, M. F. R., and Associates. 1991. *Organizations on the Couch*. San Francisco, California: Jossey-Bass.

Klein, M. 1948. *Contributions to Psychoanalysis, 1921–1945*. London: Hogarth Press and Institute of Psychoanalysis.

Kosmin, B. A., S. Goldstein, J. Waksberg, N. Lerer, A. Keysar, and J. Scheckner. 1991. *Highlights of the CJF 1990 National Jewish Population Survey*. New York: Council of Jewish Federations.

Levin, M. S., and W. S. Bernstein. 1991. Community in concert: Baltimore's vision toward the year 2000. *Journal of Jewish Communal Service* 67: 194–204.

Liebman, C. S. 1973. *The Ambivalent American Jew*. Philadelphia, Pennsylvania: Jewish Publication Society of America.

Liebman, C. S. 1988. *Deceptive Images*. New Brunswick, New Jersey: Transaction Books.

Mansbridge, J. J. 1983. *Beyond Adversary Democracy*. Chicago, Illinois: University of Chicago Press.

Miller, L. E., ed. 1989. *Managing Human Service Organizations*. New York: Quorum Books.

Mitroff, I. I. 1983. *Stakeholders of the Organizational Mind*. San Francisco, California: Jossey-Bass.

Nutt, P. C., and R. W. Backoff. 1992. *Strategic Management of Public and Third Sector Organizations*. San Francisco, California: Jossey-Bass.

Schön, D. A. 1982. Some of what a planner knows: A case study of knowing-in-practice. *Journal of the American Planning Association* 48: 351–364.

Schwartz, H. S. 1990. *Narcissistic Process and Corporate Decay*. New York: New York University Press.

Strategic Planning Committee, Associated Jewish Charities and Welfare Fund. 1989. *Building a Stronger Community: Toward the Year 2000*, volume 1. Baltimore, Maryland: Associated Jewish Charities and Welfare Fund.

Tobin, G. A. 1986. *Jewish Population Study of Greater Baltimore*. Baltimore: Associated Jewish Charities and Welfare Fund.

Volkan, V. D. 1988. *The Need to Have Enemies and Allies*. Northvale, New Jersey: Jason Aronson.

16

Popular Planning: Coin Street, London

Tim Brindley, Yvonne Rydin, and Gerry Stoker

Popular planning is planning by local communities in their own neighborhoods. It involves both the formulation of planning proposals and their implementation by local community organizations. This rests on close collaboration between the community and the local planning authority, which has to be persuaded to adopt the popular plan as official policy. But the essence of popular planning is that local residents retain a high degree of direct control over the whole process.

For our case study of popular planning we have chosen to look at a small area of Central London known as Coin Street, which was the scene of a protracted fight between a major developer and a local community. In 1984 this struggle culminated in what has been described as "one of the most extraordinary victories ever by a community group" (Cowan 1986, p. 6), when local residents gained control of the site and began to implement their own development scheme, since when many of the community's plans have been realized. In itself this makes Coin Street a classic case of popular planning, since few such plans have ever got this far – it may indeed come to be seen as "the" classic case.

Coin Street and Waterloo

The area known as Coin Street is situated on the South Bank of the Thames in London, near the National Theatre (Figure 16.1). It consists of a string of sites, some 13 acres in area, lying mainly between Upper Ground and Stamford Street, which stretch from Waterloo Road through to the Thames at Stamford Wharf, with its famous "Oxo" tower. Like much of the South Bank, it has long remained on the

From Tim Brindley, Yvonne Rydin, and Gerry Stoker, *Remaking Planning: The Politics of Urban Change in the Thatcher Years*, pp. 74–95. Copyright © the authors, 1989. "update" from 2nd edn (1996), pp. 205–11.

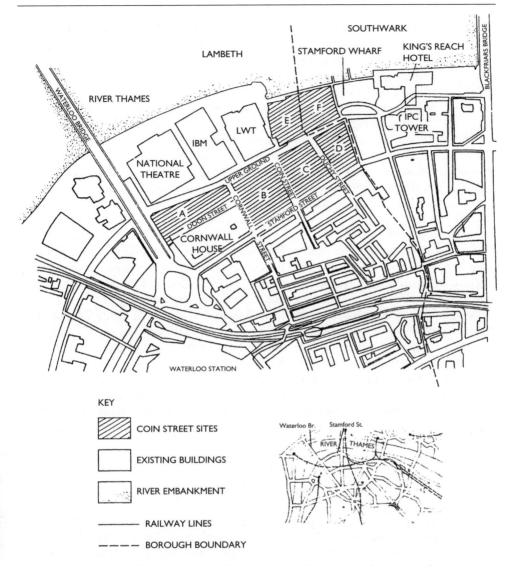

Fig. 16.1 Map of the Coin Street area, showing places referred to in the case study

periphery of London's major land and property markets and can justifiably be described as a marginal area in economic terms. Before redevelopment began in 1986, most of the Coin Street area had been vacant for many years. The few remaining buildings were largely abandoned and the open land was used for temporary car parks. About half of the area was owned by the [Greater London Council] (GLC), having been acquired by the London County Council (LCC) in 1953. Most of the remainder, including Stamford Wharf and the Eldorado Cold Store, was owned by the Vestey family through various companies, either freehold or on LCC/GLC leases. When this story began Coin Street represented one of the largest remaining undeveloped areas in Central London.

The Coin Street sites straddle the boundary between the London Boroughs of Southwark and Lambeth, falling mostly in the latter. The area forms part of the neighborhood known as Waterloo which, like several other neighborhoods in Central London, grew up around the station, completed in 1848. The main residential areas of Waterloo lie to the east and south of the station and comprise tenanted estates of the former GLC, the London Borough of Lambeth, the Peabody Trust and the Church Commissioners. Much of this housing was built on redevelopment sites between the wars, so little of the nineteenth-century stock remains. Where there are Victorian and Georgian terraced houses these have attracted middle-class owner-occupiers. There is some local industry, particularly printing and distribution, mostly in small firms located under the arches of the elevated Waterloo and Charing Cross railway lines. Most residents of Waterloo work locally or in nearby parts of Central London and there are local shopping centers at Lower Marsh and The Cut. The Waterloo District Plan (London Borough of Lambeth 1977) remarks on the strong feeling of community among the remaining local population, down by half since 1961 to about 5,000 in 1981. It is in the main a low-income, working-class community, with relatively high proportions of unskilled and semi-skilled workers and elderly households, not untypical of many inner-city areas today.

As well as having its local community, Waterloo is a part of Central London. It includes major office complexes, such as County Hall and the Shell Centre, St Thomas's Hospital, Lambeth Palace and the South Bank arts complex – the Festival Hall, the Hayward Gallery and the National Theatre. Waterloo Station itself is a dominant feature, covering some seven acres. Consequently, most people who work in and visit Waterloo come from outside the area. Although this gives Waterloo its attractive metropolitan character, it is the tension between the needs of local residents and the demands of outside interests which underlies the main planning conflicts in its recent history.

The Initial Conflict

The background to the popular plan for Coin Street can be found in a basic conflict over the future of Waterloo which came to a head in the 1970s. The conflict was between a future as part of the commercial expansion of Central London, through the speculative development of offices and hotels, and a future for the local community in the form of social rented housing and local employment and amenities. Before the 1970s, attempts to encourage commercial development in the area had been largely unsuccessful. In 1955 the South Bank was designated a Comprehensive Development Area (CDA), covering all of the Waterloo district between the railways and the Thames, and including about a quarter of the area's housing south of Stamford Street. Although the CDA was zoned for "central area" uses, Waterloo was hardly touched by the office building boom of the late 1950s. London's Initial Development Plan of 1962 zoned the area for "West End" uses, but again little new development occurred. It was not until the Greater London Development Plan of 1969 identified the South Bank as one of several "preferred locations" for offices that any interest in redevelopment was stimulated.

The early 1970s saw the first commercial developments around Coin Street, but even in the midst of London's second major office boom, very little of this was speculative. The King's Reach hotel was built as a speculative venture but never completed, because its intended operator went into receivership (although the building was later converted into offices). However, there was further speculative interest in some of the Coin Street sites, and in 1971 the Heron Corporation was granted planning permission for an hotel on the site behind the National Theatre.

The same period saw the first organized responses from the local community. It appears that what first stirred the residents of Waterloo was a proposal to extend the Imperial War Museum into the adjacent public park. A welfare rights stall in the local market had identified various problems in the area, including a shortage of open space and play facilities. The extension to the museum would have taken up some of the existing open space, and so a campaign was launched to oppose it. This issue became a focus for community action and led to the formation in 1972 of the Waterloo Community Development Group (WCDG). The success of the campaign in stopping the museum extension inspired the WCDG to embark on the major step of developing a planning strategy for the Waterloo area.

Preparing a Local Plan

Commencing in 1973, the WCDG organized a series of public meetings and invited councillors and planners from the London Borough of Lambeth. The meetings discussed a wide range of local issues, including the changing types of shops related to new office developments, the closure of schools as the resident population declined and aged, and the shortage of low-cost housing. Housing seemed to hold the key, since it was needed to bring families back to the area and thus regenerate the demand for schools and shops, and Coin Street offered some obvious sites.

The GLC, which was the planning authority for the South Bank CDA, came under Labour control in 1973, and a similar series of meetings was held with GLC councillors and planning officers. As a result of the public meetings, both Lambeth and the GLC prepared independent reports on planning options for their respective areas of responsibility – Waterloo and the wider South Bank area. The reports offered a choice between private-sector office development with negotiated planning gains, public-sector housing development for local needs, or combinations of the two. In Lambeth the planners, like their colleagues in neighbouring Southwark, tended to favor office development in riverside areas, but the public's preference was for housing. Lambeth's politicians, unlike their Southwark counterparts, accepted this for most of Waterloo and it became the basis of the Borough's *Waterloo draft planning strategy*, adopted by the council in 1975 (London Borough of Lambeth 1975). The GLC adopted a similar policy in 1976, and this was published as *The future of the South Bank* (GLC 1976).

Lambeth was further persuaded by the WCDG to prepare a statutory local plan for Waterloo on the basis of the *Draft planning strategy*, and in 1977 the *Waterloo district plan* became the first local plan to be officially adopted in London (London Borough of Lambeth 1977). As a result Lambeth regained official responsibility for the Coin Street area from the GLC. Although not quite a popular plan, the *Waterloo district plan* 'bore the stamp of strong local approval and virtually no dissent' (Self 1979), following widespread public consultation. It included a policy of severe restraint on further office development and earmarked most of the Coin Street sites for housing and a public park.

The mid-1970s, the period during which these planning strategies were being prepared, was a time of retrenchment for the property development industry in London. The oil crisis of 1973–74, with its dramatic effects on interest rates and inflation, resulted in the virtual collapse of the speculative property market and the failure of several smaller banks (Rees and Lambert 1985). At Coin Street, the fate of the King's Reach hotel was only typical of other Central London developments, including the notorious Centrepoint office block, which remained unoccupied for years. Further interest in commercial development at Coin Street therefore subsided. The GLC broke off negotiations with the Heron Corporation and pressed ahead with the design of a housing scheme. In February 1977, the GLC gave scheme approval for some 200 dwellings on the two available sites in its ownership, the first stage of a plan to develop the whole Coin Street area for housing and open space.

The first phase of the Coin Street story underlines its relatively marginal position in the London property market. Commercial land uses were barely established on this part of the South Bank, with the exception of a few purpose-built complexes such as the London Weekend Television building and the International Publishing Corporation tower at King's Reach. Speculative property development had been tried on a small scale and had largely failed, and so remaining speculative interest appeared to have died away. Without very much effort, the field seemed open for the GLC to fulfil the objectives of the local plan and build housing for rent on some low-value redevelopment sites which it already owned. And this might well have been the end of the story: as *Coin Street News* put it:

> People would by now be living on Coin Street again had a new Tory GLC admin-istration not axed the housing scheme and backed plans for a massive hotel and office project put forward by the Heron Corporation and Lord Vestey's Commercial Properties.   (September 1984)

Property Developers and Popular Planners

The election of a Conservative administration to the GLC in May 1977, under the leadership of Horace Cutler, heralded a new phase of property speculation at Coin Street, as in other parts of Central London. The respite of the mid-1970s had seen steady progress towards community goals – preparation of the anti-office local plan and the GLC housing scheme. But after toying with the idea of housing for sale, the new politicians at the GLC scrapped the housing scheme and, by expressing support for 'appropriate mixed developments' at Coin Street (Sudjic and Wood 1981), effectively declared their intention, as the major landowners, of ignoring the *Water-loo district plan*. This prompted Harry Dobin, a director of Heron, to declare: 'With the change of control at the GLC we thought we would get our plans out and dust them off' (*Tribune* June 1 1979).

Political support for commercial development at Coin Street came not only from the predictable quarter of the Conservative GLC but from the less predictable minority Labour government. As Secretary of State for the Environment, Peter

Shore contrived in August 1978 both to confirm the statutory status of the *Waterloo district plan* with its pro-housing, anti-office policies; and simultaneously to grant speculative office development permits to the Heron Corporation and the Vestey company, Commercial Properties, for over a million square feet of offices and a skyscraper hotel on the Coin Street sites. Since this positively invited planning applications contrary to Lambeth's declared policies, in the view of one commentator Shore had "sold the pass" on the local community (Self 1979).

The community, however, was not standing still. In 1976, the large number of community groups in the area, including the WCDG, had formed an umbrella organization, the Association of Waterloo Groups (AWG), which was recognized by Lambeth as a neighborhood council. The election of the Tory GLC prompted the formation of an active campaign group, the Coin Street Action Group (CSAG), to oppose the hotel/office proposals and promote housing and open space. Lambeth took over a version of the GLC scheme for Coin Street, consisting of 251, mainly low-rise, dwellings, to which it added schemes for the other two sites within the Borough boundary, and applied for a compulsory purchase order to acquire the sites from the GLC. The CSAG, however, was not satisfied that this scheme met the wishes of the local community and decided to prepare its own scheme for 360 low-rise dwellings, a riverside walk and park, shops and other facilities for all eight Coin Street sites, including those in Southwark.

In the confusion of competing and conflicting development proposals now seeking planning permission at Coin Street, in October 1978 the Secretary of State called in all the applications for his consideration at a public inquiry. Even between this announcement and the start of the inquiry further proposals came forward. These included the community scheme, just mentioned; Heron's plans for an even taller skyscraper hotel – at 458 ft, potentially the tallest in Europe; London Weekend Television's application to extend its existing premises; and a third major mixed development proposal hurriedly tabled by a newcomer, Greycoat London Estates Limited (Greycoats). All of these applications were called in for consideration at the inquiry, which opened on May 22 1979.

The popular plan for Coin Street emerged out of a complex sequence of events over the next few years. The first public inquiry extended over 64 days and concluded in November 1979. Described by *The Times* (September 10 1984) as "one of the longest, costliest and most important and confused planning inquiries ever held in Britain", perhaps its main achievement was to narrow the field and sharpen the conflicts. On the developers' side, Greycoats came out much the strongest contender. During the course of the inquiry, Greycoats submitted a revised scheme for the whole Coin Street area, designed by the international architect Richard Rogers. When it also acquired the freehold of the Boots factory and other leaseholds for around £2 million, Heron pulled out, leaving its partner, Commercial Properties, "rather high and dry" (Milne 1979).

The community's development scheme for Coin Street was prepared by the CSAG. The Action Group worked by dividing its tasks among a large number of subgroups and calling on whatever sources of professional and technical help it could muster. These included the architect of the original GLC housing scheme; a worker in a local housing co-operative; lawyers attached to local law projects; a planner in Southwark; Shelter Housing Aid Centre; the Society for Co-operative Dwellings; and many other individuals. Publicity and public relations were central to their strategy:

the Action Group produced a four-weekly bulletin and an occasional newspaper (*Coin Street News*), issued press releases, and organized exhibitions, a tape-slide show, street theatre and social events.

The community case was presented at the inquiry in a number of different ways. The formal planning application was submitted by the AWG, represented by a lawyer. Formal presentations of evidence in support of the community scheme were therefore made under the auspices of the AWG (hence it was generally known as "the AWG scheme"). In making its case, the AWG was able to draw on a wide range of professionals and experts, including many of those who had helped in the preparation of the scheme. It also presented a unique analysis of supply and demand in the office market in Central London, commissioned from a planning consultant, in order to challenge the office location policy of the GLDP and to demonstrate that no more offices were needed. In parallel with the official proceedings the CSAG ran an action campaign, including a petition, publicity and demonstrations. Three or four people from the community groups also attended the inquiry full-time.

In July 1980 all the applications were refused by the new Conservative Environment Secretary, Michael Heseltine, who described the office proposals as "massive and over-dominant", while criticizing the housing proposals because they "failed to exploit the employment potential of the sites" (*Journal of Planning and Environment Law* 1983). Instead, he called for a mixed development which would combine housing and employment. Heseltine appeared to be defining a new planning policy for the area which incorporated elements from both the GLDP and the Waterloo District Plan but deviated significantly from both. In effect, he had thrown out a challenge to each set of developers, Greycoats and the AWG, to come back with comprehensive schemes which met the revised criteria.

Greycoats responded by joining forces with jilted Commercial Properties, to form Greycoat Commercial Estates Limited (for brevity, we will continue to refer to this company as Greycoats). This consolidated the private landholdings in the area, giving the new company control over about half the sites through a mix of freeholds and leaseholds. A revised scheme was published in March 1980 and submitted for planning approval in December. It consisted of a string of cluster blocks of varying height, linked by a glazed pedestrian mall and connected to a new Thames footbridge. Described by the architect as "an open-ended flexible infrastructure capable of fostering a wide range of local and metropolitan activities" (Richard Rogers & Partners 1981, p. 52), the concept was much praised in the architectural press, while others nicknamed it "The Dinosaur" and "The Berlin Wall". It amounted to a million square feet of offices (slightly less than the earlier version), housing, shopping, light industrial workshops and other facilities, including public open space. Almost immediately it was called in and a second public inquiry became inevitable.

The AWG's revised proposal for a mixed development, comprising 400 dwellings, managed workshops, shopping and other facilities, and public open space, appeared early in 1980. It goes without saying that while both schemes included apparently similar elements, they represented radically different approaches to the development. The Greycoats scheme was a purely commercial venture which offered some social amenities as a planning gain, and was based on conventional institutional sources of funding. The AWG scheme was a thoroughgoing community project, which would provide low-rent housing for local people in need, funded either by the local authorities or a co-operative housing association; the managed workshops were mainly for light industrial uses, and were intended to extend the range of employment opportunities in Inner London; the shops would include a supermarket to supplement existing local facilities. The only common feature was public open space on the waterfront, and even here the two developments would have been unlikely to appeal to the same groups of users. There was no compromise between such diametrically opposed types of development, and it looked as if a conflict was about to become a battle.

When the second Coin Street inquiry opened on April 7 1981, it was indeed "amid scenes reminiscent of the worst motorway inquiries of the 70s" (*Building Design* April 10 1981). The protestors, mainly local residents, were incensed that the AWG scheme was not on the agenda, and that the inquiry should be starting before the May elections for the GLC, when a Labour victory was (correctly) anticipated. The result was an adjournment until June and the inclusion of the AWG scheme to be examined alongside Greycoats' proposals. After a further adjournment on a technicality had again postponed the start of the inquiry until September, it ran for 88 days and closed in March 1982.

In the interval between the publication of the revised development schemes and the much-delayed start of the inquiry, two events, both involving the GLC, significantly changed the balance of forces in the field. The first was a deal concluded between the outgoing Tory GLC and Greycoats, in the form of a conditional Agreement for Sale which gave Greycoats an option to acquire all the GLC's freehold interests at Coin Street on condition that it secured all necessary planning and other permissions within three years. Greycoats maintained that this controversial deal was purely a commercial decision, to give them sufficient basis on which to proceed with their development. The GLC imposed restrictive conditions on the deal, in an attempt to ensure that the site was in fact developed, but GLC officers were clearly unhappy about making this agreement prior to the granting of detailed planning permission (GLC 1981a). It is hard to avoid the inference that the land deal was a political manoeuvre designed to prevent the successor administration at the GLC from blocking Greycoats' plans.

Whatever interpretation is put on it, the land deal neatly anticipated the second important event, namely the Labour victory at the GLC elections just mentioned, and the new administration's immediate decision to back the AWG scheme for Coin Street. By July the GLC had published a statement of its new policy, *The future of the South Bank wider area* (GLC 1981b). This aimed "to limit the expansion of Central London activities into the South Bank. Housing should be the major land use with other supporting activities, such as industry." Office development was to be restricted to sites specified in approved local plans, such as the *Waterloo district plan*. The new administration at the GLC also provided more practical support for the AWG, which suddenly found its resources boosted by the full-time secondment of an architect and almost unlimited use of copying and printing facilities.

As these moves imply, one of the first priorities of the new administration at the GLC was to protect all the working-class communities in Central and Inner London from the blighting effects of commercial development pressures. From July 1981 the Council began to set out its Community Areas Policy. Building on the South Bank initiative, this policy aimed to resist commercial development and gentrification in the old neighborhoods surrounding the City and the West End, and to promote rented housing, community facilities and local employment, drawing for funds on the GLC's development programme. The areas covered by the policy ranged from Hammersmith to Spitalfields, and from King's Cross to Battersea. The South Bank, including Coin Street, was therefore defined as a Community Area and selected for funding from 1982–83 (GLC 1985).

The Community Victory

The second Coin Street inquiry ranged over much the same ground as the first one, with both the AWG and Greycoats claiming that their proposals conformed with statutory planning policies for the area and with Heseltine's demand for suitable mixed development. The Secretary of State's decision was announced in December, just before his departure for the Ministry of Defence, and granted outline planning permission to both Greycoats and the AWG. The decision letter explained that both schemes were acceptable as comprehensive, mixed developments. This seemingly even-handed decision was widely seen to favor Greycoats, since it appeared to raise the value of the land beyond what the GLC could reasonably pay for housing and industry. But, undaunted, the AWG, under the headline "Full Speed Ahead!", boldly announced its intention "to start construction on site towards the end of 1984" (*Coin Street News* April 1983).

Greycoats' three-year purchase option had just over a year to run and it still needed road closure agreements and permission to demolish the Stamford Wharf building, since 1983 in a declared Conservation Area. Meanwhile the GLC, the London Boroughs of Lambeth and Southwark and the AWG jointly went to the High Court in an attempt to have Greycoats' planning permission quashed. Their contention was that the Secretary of State had acted improperly, in particular by failing to consider the supply and demand for offices, the provisions of the statutory local plan and the policies of the local planning authorities, of which all three now backed the AWG. Rejecting these arguments, Mr. Justice Stephen Brown ruled in July that:

> the issue was not a question of "housing against offices"; it was a question of whether the application proposals achieved an acceptable balance of a mixture of uses set in an appropriate architectural context, in accordance with the Minister's stated policy.
> (*Journal of Planning and Environment Law* 1983, p. 797)

An appeal to the Court of Appeal in December was similarly dismissed and a petition to the House of Lords was rejected, leaving Greycoats' planning permission intact but with the deadline on its purchase option rapidly approaching.

February 1984 saw the inquiry into the road closures required by the Greycoats scheme, actively opposed by the AWG and all three planning authorities, along with some 400 other individuals and groups, including King's Reach Developments. But no sooner did the inquiry close than Greycoats made a dramatic move:

> With its option on the GLC-owned land about to expire, no funding or tenants for its wall of offices, and demoralised by the persistent opposition to its scheme, Greycoat Commercial Estates and associated companies finally admitted defeat and sold their land interests to the GLC on March 29 1984.   (*Coin Street News* September 1984)

Greycoats appear in the end to have endorsed the view proclaimed on a banner strung across Stamford Wharf, that this was "A Community Victory". The developers were defeated by the combination of an extraordinarily effective local campaign and the considerable muscle of the GLC. In addition to failing to obtain all the necessary permissions to force the GLC to sell the rest of the site, notably consent to demolish Stamford Wharf itself, Greycoats realized that it would face community opposition all the way. The CSAG had threatened to organize further action, even a union Green Ban, which could seriously hamper the development. Greycoats did consider holding on to the site and blocking the AWG scheme but decided instead to sell up and concentrate its efforts in other, less contentious parts of Central London.

In fact, the developer's position had always looked rather precarious. Greycoats was only prepared to start construction once the offices had been pre-let, ideally with one tenant for each of the eight linked blocks of the scheme. As events dragged on into 1984, it was observed that the developer "still has no firm potential tenants" and, even more critically, no sign of major sources of development investment (Milne 1984). Greycoats' change of heart was probably not uninfluenced by the start on site of the St Martin's Group development at Hay's Wharf, and by the fact that the company had recently secured two other major development projects in Central London. It sold its interests in the Boots site, Stamford and Nelson's wharves, and other smaller sites (amounting in total to some 6.5 acres) for £2.7 million.

George Nicholson, chair of the GLC Planning Committee, summed up the sense of euphoria which now came over the local campaigners:

> This is a landmark. It's the culmination of a long and determined battle by local people. The development we shall now see on this important London site is the people's plan – planning for the people and by the people. (GLC 1985a, p. 12)

Implementing the Popular Plan

With the whole of Coin Street in GLC freehold ownership, the AWG found itself in the spring of 1984 on the brink of realizing its popular plan. Although the tables appeared to have turned quite suddenly in its favor, the AWG and the GLC had been working for some time on a contingency plan. In 1983 a Joint Advisory Committee was formed, consisting of representatives from the GLC, the Boroughs of Lambeth and Southwark, and the AWG, with the aim of progressing the outline planning permission granted to the community scheme. There was an initial disagreement over who should act as overall developer. The GLC proposed that it should have this role, bringing in the Boroughs under joint committee and financing arrangements. Lambeth, in spite of its serious conflict with central government over spending levels and ratecapping, proposed that it should buy the sites and manage the development itself. However, neither of these arrangements was satisfactory to the AWG. It did not regard GLC ownership of the sites as secure, given the authority's imminent demise, while Lambeth councillors were fighting the government over ratecapping, and in any case were known to be opposed to co-operatives and wanted to develop conventional council housing. Drawing on grass-roots support in the Labour Party, the AWG was able to block both of these plans and take on the development role itself.

In December 1983, with the withdrawal of Greycoats looking more and more likely, it began the process of setting up a non-profit limited company to purchase the sites from the GLC once it had control of all the freeholds. In order to achieve a site valuation which the community group could afford, the GLC imposed restrictive covenants on the freeholds, effectively limiting the use of the land to the AWG scheme. By this means it was able to sell all the freeholds at an agreed value of £750,000 to the new company, Coin Street Community Builders (CSCB), formed jointly by members of the AWG and the North Southwark Community Development Group, in June 1984. CSCB financed the purchase with the aid of two mortgages, one from the GLC and one from the Greater London Enterprise Board, the repayments being covered by temporary income from car parks and advertising hoardings. The ownership of the freeholds and the income they generated gave CSCB the advantage of independence. It was able to employ five full-time workers; a company secretary and officers responsible for finance, housing and social facilities, commercial development and administration. A sixth full-time worker, an information officer, was funded by a small grant from Lambeth and Southwark.

The local community now owned 13 acres of Central London and, true to its ambitious prediction, the AWG actually had its project on site before the end of 1984, as demolition of the Eldorado Cold Store. The scheme fell into three distinct parts with different problems of implementation: the housing, the river wall and walk and other public open space, and the other land uses (industry, shopping and leisure). The intention was to develop and manage the housing through co-operative housing associations. To achieve this, the housing sites were initially sold to the Society for Co-operative Dwellings (SCD), at the nominal value of £1, which acted as development agent while CSCB set up new primary and secondary housing co-ops. A mortgage was raised from Lambeth and Southwark Boroughs to finance the first scheme on Site C (Fig. 16.1). A final design was prepared, granted detailed planning permission by Lambeth and scheme approval by the DoE, and the first houses commenced on site in June 1986. It consisted of three-storey, six-person houses for families, including two eight-person units, and mostly with gardens.

The detailed arrangements for the development were complicated but critical to the future of this controversial scheme. The freeholds of all the housing sites were transferred to a new secondary housing co-operative, called Axle, and the lease for the first scheme to a primary co-operative, Mulberry. Apart from conforming with CSCB's co-operative principles, this form of ownership and management carried added advantages. For one thing it was exempt from the "right to buy" under the 1980 Housing Act. If the housing had been developed by a local authority or conventional housing association, tenants would have had the right to purchase their own houses or flats at a discount, so taking them out of social ownership and beyond the means of households in need. It was also calculated to minimize the risk of the government finding some way to intervene and force the sale of the sites for commercial development.

AWG's planning permission required the construction of a new river wall and extension to the riverside walk before any buildings could be occupied. The GLC undertook to do this, together with the development of Sites D and F as public open space (Fig. 16.1), at an estimated cost of £4.5 million (GLC 1983). This also commenced in June 1986 on the basis of £2 million of forward funding from the GLC, agreed with the government prior to the authority's demise in April of that year. The successor to the GLC, the London Residuary Body (LRB), was unable to evade this financial commitment and the new walkway was opened in the autumn of 1987.

The other elements in the outline planning permission were 126,000 sq. ft of light industrial workshops and 67,000 sq. ft of shopping and leisure facilities, including a restaurant and museum in the restored Stamford Wharf building. Various sources of funding were explored for the estimated £6.75 million construction costs, in the public and private sectors (GLC 1983). Although it was operated as a charitable trust, the wharf was costing money to maintain and generating no income, so it was selected for the second phase of the development. In 1986 CSCB invited proposals for the use of the lower floors of the wharf, to supplement the 75 flats planned for the upper floors. Offices and luxury flats were ruled out, and tenders were invited to include workshops and a museum. Out of some 85 proposals two were shortlisted, one a children's museum, similar to the Halifax "Eureka" project, and the other a Museum of the Thames. Both proposals came with independent development finance. At the same time one of the later housing sites in the program (site E, Fig. 16.1) was designated for a temporary crafts market and workshops, modelled on Camden Lock. This left the greatest challenge for the co-operative developers in the planned third phase of the development, the managed workshops on the site behind the National Theatre. The scheme which they envisaged had implications for rent levels, lettings policy and training provision which were unlikely to be acceptable to a conventional institutional investor. Possible sources of finance included large private companies such as Shell or BAT, which had funded small, start-up workshops elsewhere, and the Greater London Enterprise Board. But, whatever the problems, CSCB was confident of its ability to realize the project and looked in a strong position to do so.

Popular Planning as a Planning Style

Coin Street stands as a classic example of popular planning in the 1980s. There have been other cases of successful community opposition to major development schemes and a handful of local plans prepared in full consultation with local residents. The *Covent Garden action area plan* (GLC 1977), approved in 1977, which was largely based on a document prepared by local community groups, was perhaps the first example of a popular plan, but since then the community has not played a major role in its implementation. The *People's plan for the Royal Docks* (Newham Docklands Forum 1983), although it was a full local plan drawn up by Newham residents, only really stood as a statement of opposition to the LDDC and the STOLport proposal. But at Coin Street community involvement has passed through all the stages, from opposition through consultation and active participation, to the implementation of large-scale development within the framework of a popular plan. The Coin Street case study therefore provides unique insights into the processes of popular planning, its strengths and weaknesses, and its conflicts and tensions.

Institutional arrangements

The characteristic organizational form of popular planning is the community forum. The Skeffington report of 1969 first advocated the setting up of community forums for consultation with local residents in the preparation of local plans. One of the first was created in Covent Garden in 1973 as a "representative" body, with members elected from among local residents, workers and property owners (Christensen 1979). In 1974 the Docklands Forum was created as an "umbrella" organization for local community and interest groups. More recently, Sheffield set up a number of forums for consultation on its city centre plan (Alty and Darke 1987).

Although they vary in their style and range of activities, community forums have played a major role in planning consultation, acting as a focal point for a number of community groups and bringing them into the planning process. However, as an institutional form the community forum has some limitations. It exists essentially as a focus of communication between, on one side, the diverse social groups which form the community and, on the other side, the local authority. As such, the forum tends to be trapped in a "consultative" role, invited to respond to local authority proposals but not expected to have any of its own. In trying to be representative it is not well placed to make positive decisions and move into active campaigning and real participation. In Covent Garden, this led to a split between the Forum and the Action Group, with the latter breaking away to engage in a more active campaign of positive planning. The Docklands Forum, although it has become a more active body since the designation of the LDDC, has also had campaign groups, such as the Joint Docklands Action Group, form around it. Generally, Skeffington-type consultative groups have suffered the fate of incorporation into local authority procedures, unable to take an independent critical line.

Significantly, Coin Street did not start with a Skeffington-type forum, set up by the local authorities for formal consultation with "the public". The initiative for a forum appears to have come instead from within the community, which put pressure on the local authorities (principally Lambeth and the GLC) to engage in consultation. The North Lambeth Multi-Services Group first identified local needs and opposed the War Museum extension, leading in 1972 to the formation of the Waterloo Community Development Group. This group, which paralleled another in the adjacent borough of Southwark (North Southwark Community Development Group), then became the main "forum" for consultation on planning policy. At that stage it seems to have adopted a role similar to that of other community forums, receiving and commenting on the local authorities' documents and proposals. This group, then, carried the process of popular planning through the stages of opposition and consultation.

The formation of the Association of Waterloo Groups in 1976 was a further significant step. The AWG was established as an umbrella organization, with some 32 affiliated groups including the WCDG. While it took over the role of consultative "forum", the Coin Street Action Group was set up specifically to fight the new commercial development proposals then emerging. It is interesting that many of the same people were actively involved in WCDG, AWG and CSAG, but that the different groups were used for different purposes. The AWG generally took on the mantle of the formal or quasi-official community group. We have seen how it presented the community case at the public inquiries, through a lawyer, and submitted planning applications for community proposals. The CSAG, on the other hand, was the activist wing, staging demonstrations and publicity events. The separation of these two organizations helped to maintain both the legitimacy of the AWG, in its relations with local authorities and formal planning procedures, and the independent voice of the CSAG. This tactic helped to sustain the impetus and dynamism of the active participation stage of the popular plan, leading to the relatively successful outcome of the 1981 inquiry.

Almost immediately after the AWG scheme was granted planning permission, along with the Greycoats scheme, a new phase of popular planning stimulated a further realignment of the community groups and their relationship with the local authorities. Initially, implementation depended on a closer relationship with these authorities (Lambeth, Southwark and the GLC) which would be the main sources of initial funding as well as the statutory planning authorities for detailed planning permissions. The authorities formed a member-level Joint Advisory Committee (initially within the GLC but later transferred to Lambeth), including representatives of the AWG, "to co-ordinate and progress the proposals for the Coin Street site". The committee worked on contingency plans for implementing the AWG scheme and tried to resolve the question of who should have overall responsibility for the development. As we have seen, the AWG won this important political skirmish, with the result that Coin Street Community Builders took over the freeholds of the development sites. In its turn, CSCB helped to set up a new consultative body, the Coin Street Development Group, to involve the community in the detailed implementation of the scheme, and established a series of primary and secondary co-operatives to develop the housing sites.

This rather convoluted history of community organization in the Coin Street case study shows that it is almost impossible to generalize about the institutional form of popular planning. The community forum advocated by Skeffington was never wholly successful, except as a consensual consultative body. At Coin Street, community activists demonstrated a rather sophisticated understanding of the roles of different kinds of community groups, which could represent various degrees of formality and informality, participation and opposition, in changing circumstances. They were aware both of the need for a formal relationship with the local authorities and of the dangers of political incorporation, and adopted what might be described as a "horses for courses" approach to organization. Popular planning may well depend on this kind of organizational flexibility, based on a formally recognized umbrella organization such as the AWG but able to diversify and reform into a range of more specialized groups at different stages in the process.

Politics and decision-making

The Coin Street case involved a large number of interest groups, each having different kinds and degrees of power and each pursuing different objectives for the development of the area. Decisions came out of a shifting pattern of alliances, with groups forming and dissolving, and with frequent changes of political leadership in the respective public authorities. This form of decision-making can be described as "imperfect pluralism", since not every interest is equally organized or represented, and decisions tend to be unpredictable and pragmatic. The eventual outcome of the events at Coin Street was not only unpredicted but regularly dismissed as unachievable, even by sympathetic commentators. The case illustrates a rather confused struggle for power in a situation where no one group, in the public or the private sector, held the upper hand for very long.

The idea of pluralism, however "imperfect", suggests a political process to which all interests have access and no one is systematically excluded. In the case of popular planning, the obvious question is just how "popular" is it? The apparent degree of pluralism suggested by the large number of community organizations involved at various stages may be exaggerated. Since many of the same people regularly reappear in different roles in different groups, it would seem that the community interest was being articulated by a fairly small group of activists. In spite of the large number of organizations in the area, a social survey in 1974 reported that only 6% of a random sample of local residents attended tenants' or residents' associations and 7% attended community associations (London Borough of Lambeth 1977, p. 19).

The representativeness of those involved has been an issue for the AWG and its offshoots. In a briefing note for local councillors the CSCB commented that the management committee of the first housing co-operative, Mulberry,

> is composed of six men and six women. They broadly represent the social make-up of the local community: two are printers, two retired, two unemployed, one is a teacher, one a receptionist, one a docker, one an administrator, one a housing advisor and one works full-time at Coin Street.   (Coin Street Community Builders 1986, p. 10)

It was also reported that positive action was being taken to recruit a black committee member. However, while the sex, race and class of community representatives are undeniably important for their credibility and legitimacy, it goes without saying that they are no guarantee of socially progressive attitudes. Rather, what stands out in the case study is the consistent efforts of the AWG and other groups to achieve both wide participation and popular control, for example in their insistence on developing the housing as mutual co-operatives. The representativeness of the community groups is ultimately reflected in their consistent aims and achievements, which were always to do with the needs of the mainly working-class residents of Waterloo and the surrounding area.

The local authorities, with wider constituencies to serve, never had the same single-minded commitment to meeting such local needs. Through the mid-1970s, Lambeth and the GLC under Labour control supported community goals and planned to build council housing on some of the Coin Street sites. Southwark remained in favor of office development on Thames-side sites until 1982 when a new council was elected that was more sympathetic to local communities. Under Conservative control from 1977 to 1981, the GLC actively promoted office development. But after 1981 it was the Labour GLC which became the principal ally of the local community, much more committed to their cause than even Lambeth. (It was only after most Lambeth councillors were disqualified from office and a new council elected in 1986 that the authority came to support the idea of housing co-operatives, for example, and then rather tentatively.) The eventual success of the popular plan for Coin Street was uniquely due to the support and intervention of Ken Livingstone's administration at the GLC. Its Community Areas Policy established the principle of defending local communities in Central and Inner London against the threat of commercial development and gentrification. This policy was later incorporated in proposed alterations to the GLDP which were submitted to the Secretary of State but never approved (GLC 1984b). Nevertheless, it led to the funding of many small projects through the GLC's development program, including some housing schemes. The Coin Street project received considerable assistance and effectively became the flagship of Community Areas Policy, a major rebuff to a large commercial developer and a demonstration of what could be achieved, apparently against all the odds. It was also, of course, one of the GLC's grandest swansongs.

Conflicts and tensions in popular planning

Although it might appear to be a consensual process within the community, popular planning also generates conflicts and tensions. Generally, the wider the involvement in decision-making, the more potentially conflicting needs will be identified. At Coin Street there seems to have been a remarkably consistent view within the local community of what was needed. When a few of the Lambeth sites were being considered in the early 1970s, the consensus was for housing, principally houses with gardens. When the idea of a larger scheme emerged during the public inquiries, open space, workshops and social amenities were added to the original housing proposal. The community itself does not therefore seem to have been in conflict over what to do with Coin Street. But conflicting demands have arisen in the sense of who should benefit from the popular plan and who should control its implementation.

The key tension at Coin Street emerged in the relationship of the community organizations with the local planning authorities. At various times and with various authorities this was a straight conflict of directly opposed aims: for example, with the Tory GLC and to a slightly lesser extent with Southwark before 1982. But even where the community and the local authority appeared to share the same goals, tensions emerged. The first housing scheme at Coin Street was funded jointly by Lambeth and Southwark, out of their Housing Investment Programme allocations. Although 90% of these loans would be repaid on completion of the scheme, through a Housing Association Grant, Lambeth insisted on 100% nomination of the initial tenancies from its own waiting list. To some extent this was an issue of who should benefit, the residents of Waterloo who had fought for ten years or people from other parts of Lambeth who might be in objectively greater housing need. It has been suggested that racial tensions were also involved, which the National Front attempted to exploit; Waterloo is a mainly white area and Lambeth had a policy of allocating at least 30% of new housing to black people (*City Limits* March 29 – April 4 1985). The CSCB conceded the principle of nomination for the first scheme, but in order to be able to set up a mutual co-operative among the new tenants it insisted on nominations being made six months in advance of occupation and a full co-operative training programme.

The fact that at Coin Street the community has become the developer puts it in a unique relation to the planning authorities, and yet it is a position which is not dissimilar to that of any commercial developer. On the one hand the community owns the land and has an outline planning permission, but on the other hand it still needs detailed permissions and, perhaps more significantly, financial support from the authorities. Where commercial developers might only need publicly provided infrastructure, CSCB needs more direct help in the form of housing loans and the provision of social facilities. Some of the Coin Street development will be independently financed, like a commercial development, but there will always be an element of dependence on the local authorities and therefore tension over policy decisions. This would seem to be an inevitable characteristic of popular planning.

A further tension can be seen in the Coin Street case which is also characteristic of popular planning generally, and that is the question of the longer-term future of the plan. National government policies have been stacked against popular planning since 1979, if not before. The increased emphasis on market criteria in development control decisions, the 'right to buy' social rented housing, and the abolition of the GLC all worked to the disadvantage of the AWG scheme. Highly conscious of this problem, the AWG sought to maximize its independence and therefore control over the implementation of the scheme, with remarkable success. It also stuck firmly to the principle of housing co-operatives, which fall outside the "right to buy". In fact, the future of Coin Street looks reasonably secure at the time of writing (1987). Interest in speculative office development has waned on the South Bank, with the construction of London Bridge City in North Southwark and the shift of attention to Docklands and Canary Wharf. For the time being, the pressure is off and CSCB is able to get on with the development.

Update (1996): Nine Years Later

Coin Street and the South Bank

Popular planning emerged from the activities of oppositional groups fighting for local interests, principally against the threat of commercial fighting for local interests, principally against the threat of commercial development but also against the imposition of insensitive or ill-considered projects by the central or local state. It had no formal role, but operated in the interstices of the planning and development system where it had to define its own role and functions. These changed in response to the outcomes of campaigns – mostly lost but a few won – and to new opportunities. Coin Street was a standard bearer of the popular planning movement largely because it moved on from confrontation and campaigning to become a new type of entity, a community developer, with the remit of implementing a popular plan. Since the late 1980s, Coin Street Community Builders have been working out what a community developer can do and how it can remain true to its popular roots. In the process, they have moved away from radicalism and forged common interests with a range of commercial, governmental and quasi-governmental organizations. While they continue to pursue popular planning goals, their new activities have extended the range of partnership planning.

By the end of the 1980s Coin Street Community Builders were a well-established presence on the South Bank, with all of their initial developments completed. The first co-operative housing scheme, Mulberry, was completed in March 1988. The temporary market on Gabriel's Wharf also opened in the Spring of 1988 with craft workshop and retail units, a garden centre, cafés and restaurants. The conversion scheme for Stamford Wharf had been chosen, including cafés, bars, a rooftop restaurant, and retail and workshop units, with 80 co-operative flats on the upper floors. They continued to pursue the objectives of the popular plan in the 1990s, with the completion of a second co-operative housing project, on Broadwall, to an award-winning design by architects Lifschutz Davison. The same architects took on the complex Stamford Wharf conversion, which became a prominent symbol of the regeneration of the area. A change of name to Oxo Tower Wharf, based on its landmark tower, emphasized the central place of this building in CSCB's popular image. At the time of writing, Oxo Tower Wharf had its first residents in co-operative flats, and the lower floors were due to open in 1996. CSCB was left with three major sites for future development, based on their original planning consent: the remaining large car park, scheduled for housing; the site of the Coin Street Design Centre, for work spaces; and Gabriel's Wharf, eventually intended for housing. It therefore saw its role as community developer continuing for some years.

However, the South Bank and Waterloo were changing around CSCB. While the defeat of Greycoats in 1984 had kept the property developers at bay for a few years, by 1989 several new developments were being planned for the South Bank which would have an impact on the Coin Street area. These began with the new terminal for Channel Tunnel trains at Waterloo Station, which opened in 1994; a major commercial development by P & O on York Road; the conversion of County Hall into a family hotel by its new Japanese owners, Shirayama; and improvements to the external spaces of the unpopular South Bank arts complex, based on a dramatic "Crystal Palace" design by Sir Richard Rogers. Other schemes came along, including the Jubilee Line Extension (approved in 1993), with two stations in the area; and the British Film Institute (BFI) plan for an IMAX cinema on the 'bullring' site at the southern end of Waterloo Bridge. To the west of the area, there were new plans to develop the Effra site at Vauxhall Bridge; and to the east the Tate Gallery's proposal to convert Bankside Power Station into a Museum of Modern Art, with the Globe Theatre nearing completion in the same area. In the early 1990s, the South Bank was no longer a backwater but a central focus for the regeneration of London's urban environment.

Therefore, at the start of the 1990s, Coin Street entered a new phase in which CSCB's plans for social and public uses on the South Bank faced new types of threat from new quarters. Their response illustrates many of the significant trends in planning styles which have emerged in the first half of this decade. There are two main points to note: first, the development of a broader role for the organization than simply that of land owner and developer of specific projects; and second, related to this changing role, the emergence of tensions between CSCB and other community organizations in the Waterloo area. The changing role of the community builders is seen most clearly in the establishment, on their initiative, of the South Bank Employers' Group (SBEG). At first this was a relatively informal group of organizations based at the South Bank who recognized their common interest in the quality of the urban environment. The initial members were Shell International, The South Bank Centre (i.e. the arts complex), London Weekend Television, the British Film Institute, the Royal National Theatre, IBM, HM Customs and Excise (who had moved into Sea Containers House in 1988), IPC Magazines and J Sainsbury. Later they were joined by the various railway companies operating out of Waterloo International and several other firms.

SBEG began by commissioning studies of the South Bank area from planning and urban design consultants. They progressed from studies to proposals, including a new piazza in front of the Victory Arch at Waterloo Station, a 'spine route' along Upper Ground, and extensive landscaping, signage and street furniture. They bid for government funding for four projects through the Single Regeneration Budget (SRB) (at the time of writing, a start is due to be made on the Upper Ground improvements early in 1996). SBEG also joined with central and local government bodies to form a public/private sector partnership for the South Bank. With this increase in support, from both local organizations and the government, SBEG put itself on a more permanent footing with the appointment in 1995 of a chief executive and an administrator, based at CSCB's Upper Ground offices.

The changed role and interests of CSCB started to create tensions in its relations with other community organizations, notably the WCDG. An incident involving a proposal by LWT to build an office block on its Prince's Wharf site, leased from CSCB, caused a rift between the two groups. By initially supporting the scheme, in exchange for a "planning gain" deal for community facilities on another site, CSCB appeared to have become pro-offices. WCDG saw this as a betrayal of the popular plan's central principle of opposition to office development at Coin Street. In the event the scheme collapsed, but it had affected the perception of CSCB in parts of the local community. In an interview with *Time Out* in 1994, Margaret Mellor of WCDG said that the South Bank had "turned its back on the rest of Waterloo", and that CSCB "has become like any other developer". Not all of the current wave of new developments were accepted by local residents either, particularly the speculative or commercial projects which seemed to have little relevance to local needs. The IMAX cinema, for example, although welcomed by CSCB and Mulberry Co-op, and granted planning permission by Lambeth, was condemned by WCDG as an "eyesore" and heavily criticized by other groups for its likely impact on rough sleepers under Waterloo Bridge.

As the South Bank became the focus of all kinds of development interests, the planning process was changing around it. Southwark and Lambeth prepared their Unitary Development Plans, and plans for Coin Street remained essentially unchanged from the popular plan. However, local MPs and councillors saw the need to broaden consultation on the increasing proposals for change on the South Bank and in October 1994 the South Bank Forum was established. Planning was proceeding on the basis of much wider consultation between the various development agencies, public and private, political representatives and potential "users". At the same time, many of the agencies were attempting to work together in a variety of partnership arrangements. As well as SBEG, other partnerships included a joint bid for SRB funding by Lambeth, Southwark and the local TEC; a Cross-River Partnership comprising Lambeth, Southwark, Westminster and the Corporation of London, which also put in SRB bids; and the all-embracing South Bank Partnership, with representation from central government (the Government Office for London), local government (Lambeth and Southwark), elected representatives (ward councillors and local MPs), and local business (SBEG).

The events of the early 1990s show that there has been a marked shift in the style of planning at Coin Street, as the popular plan of the mid-1980s has been gradually implemented and new development pressures have emerged on the South Bank. When the local community won its famous "victory" over the speculators, it represented an island of regeneration in a relatively stagnant area. By the mid-1990s, the South Bank was the site of a host of new projects and improvement schemes, involving the public and private sectors, separately and together, and Coin Street had been redefined as both a model development and a catalyst for wider change.

This seems to reflect a shift from a modernist concept of regeneration, based on planned provision for measurable local need – the GLC's "community areas" concept – to the essentially postmodernist concept of "cultural regeneration", where arts and culture provide a focus for change and renewal (Bianchini and Parkinson 1993).

In this context, two components of Coin Street stand out for particular note. The first is the gradual redefinition of building types from the original (unbuilt) schemes of the 1970s to the award-winning architectural projects of the 1990s. The original schemes were essentially conventional council housing, designed according to the prevailing models of low-rise, high density (Scoffham 1982), and this resulted in the Mulberry Co-op scheme. The 1990s schemes, in marked contrast, are manifestations of an entirely different urban architectural language. The Broadwall housing employs striking contemporary forms, including an ironic "tower block", and is intentionally open to the surrounding area in opposition to the defensive enclosure of the Mulberry scheme. Oxo Tower Wharf includes apartments on the upper floors which, although relatively conventional, are redolent of the "loft living" (Zukin 1982) trend which is spreading rapidly across London. This conversion provides a complex mix of uses and users, in the manner of the antimodernist city championed by Jane Jacobs (1961), Leon Krier (1978) and others. Mixed use is a way of undoing the land-use segregation which modernist planning brought about and which helped to destroy the pre-existing urban vitality. At Coin Street, it is intended to bring "life" back to the South Bank and the Waterloo neighborhood, with a varied mix of working, living, shopping, eating, relaxing, and a diversity of cultural activities.

The second postmodernist trend seen at Coin Street is the explosion of design and spectacle, and the emphasis on image and appearance. The mundane architecture of the GLC and the provincial architects who began the Stamford Wharf conversion was exchanged at the earliest opportunity for the eye-catching style of Lifschutz Davison. As well as attracting the attention of cultural critics and consumers (Coin Street began to be featured in *Time Out* and visited by restaurant critics), this gave CSCB a credible basis on which to engage in debate with other operators on the South Bank. Gabriel's Wharf, as well as being a focus for new, "cultural" uses in the area, became the site of the successful annual Coin Street Festival from 1990. All of this gives the message that Coin Street is as much about design, culture and the arts as any other South Bank organization, and that this is now leading the direction of regeneration. Those who do not wish to go down this road, and this would appear to include the WCDG, are left behind in the dust of modernism and its old-fashioned concepts and values.

Coin Street illustrates a further trend of the 1990s, which is the fragmentation of planning amongst many agents, combined with a consultative, consensus-building approach which attempts to lock these agents into pragmatic partnerships to achieve particular, local goals. The community builders have spawned several agencies, including Coin Street Secondary (CSS), the "mother" housing co-op, and Coin Street Management Services, which manages the open space, to become a partnership themselves. Also they have established the wider partnership with local employers, SBEG. Both CSCB and SBEG have joined other partnerships to carry out studies and reviews, and to bid for regeneration funding, involving government, quasi-government and non-government agencies, as well as commercial interests. This is a manifestation of a decentralized, polyphonous style of planning in which the voices of the "community" have become some amongst many, rather than a unified and dominant voice in a specific locale. The old language of popular planning, with its references to "community struggle" and "community victory", is now an outmoded rhetorical style. Regeneration at Coin Street is no longer a zero-sum game, with clear winners and losers, but something more akin to a permanent revolution, with constant opportunities for the various players to advance and change. While some will lose out in this new forum, those who fail to engage in the debate are unlikely to advance beyond "go". The question of accountability, which is inevitably raised by this competitive and disjointed approach to planning, has also fallen off the agenda: CSCB now asks to be judged not by to whom it is "answerable" but by its contribution to the regeneration of a central London neighborhood. This will be partly in terms of housing, jobs and amenities – the conventional planning criteria – but also in terms of how it has helped to redefine the experience of urban living in this part of the city.

Popular planning has lost its radical edge at the same time as popular opinion has been drawn into the planning of urban regeneration. The populist dimension of planning is now central to the partnership style, in which a greater number of community groups are consulted or work as full partners in regeneration projects and funding bids. The oppositional politics of planning still has a vigorous life, but it remains on the ground it started from, resisting road building or environmental destruction by direct action and lobbying. At one level, it could be argued that the popular planners have been incorporated in the formal processes of planning, while the true radicals remain outside and against the system. However, this would be to ignore the wider changes in planning, which has moved away from a strictly formal and procedural approach to a more open and flexible approach which responds to many influences. Popular voices have more chance of being heard in this style of planning than they did in the past, and community groups have found that they can influence outcomes, at least at the local level. To protest and resist is to define oneself outside the scope of partnership, but to develop popular plans and to work with other agencies gives at least some chance of success.

REFERENCES

Alty, R. and R. Darke 1987. A city center for people: involving the community in planning for Sheffield's central area. *Planning Practice and Research* 3, September, 7–12.

Bianchini, F. and M. Parkinson 1993. *Cultural policy and urban regeneration*. Manchester: Manchester University Press.

Christensen, T. 1979. *Neighbourhood Survival*. London: Prism.

Coin Street Community Builders 1986. *The Coin Street development: briefing for council members*. London: Coin Street Community Builders.

Cowan, R. 1986. The penny drops at Coin Street. *Roof* 11(2), March/April, 6–7.

GLC (Greater London Council) 1976. *The future of the South Bank*. London: GLC.

GLC 1977. *Covent Garden action area plan*. London: GLC.

GLC 1981a. *Report of a meeting of the Planning and Communications Policy Committee*. 11 March, PC 772.

GLC 1981b. *The future of the South Bank wider area*. London: GLC.

GLC 1983. *Report of a meeting of the Joint Advisory Committee for Coin Street*, 11 October.

GLC 1984. *The Greater London development plan – as proposed to be altered by the Greater London Council*. London: GLC.

GLC 1985. *Community areas policy: a record of achievement*. London: GLC.

Jacobs, J. 1961. *The death and life of great American cities*. New York: Random House.

Journal of Planning and Environment Law 1983. Notes of cases: *GLC et al. v. Secretary of State for the Environment and Greycoat Commercial Estates Ltd. Journal of Planning and Environment Law*, December, 793–9.

Krier, L. et al. 1978. *Rational architecture*. Brussels: Editions Archives d' Architecture Moderne.

London Borough of Lambeth 1975. *Waterloo draft planning strategy*. London: London Borough of Lambeth.

London Borough of Lambeth 1977. *Waterloo district plan*. London: London Borough of Lambeth.

Milne, R. 1979. The battle of Coin Street. *Estates Gazette* no. 252, 22/29 December, 1167–9.

Milne, R. 1984. Lords plea as Coin Street scheme struggles. *Planning* no. 550, 6 January, 6.

Newham Docklands Forum 1983. *The people's plan for the Royal Docks*. London: Newham Docklands Forum.

Rees, G. and J. Lambert 1985. *Cities in crisis: the political economy of urban development*. London: Edward Arnold.

Richard Rogers and Partners 1981. *Coin Street development*. Architectural Design nos 3–4, 52–5.

Scoffham, E. R. 1982. *The shape of British housing*. London: George Godwin.

Self, P. 1979. The siege of Coin Street. *Town and Country Planning*, 48, August, 149–50.

Sudjic, D. and S. Wood 1981. Last chance for the Thames. *Sunday Times Magazine*, 19 April, 21–31.

Zukin, S. 1982. *Loft living: culture and capital in urban change*. Baltimore: Johns Hopkins University Press.

17

Rationality and Power

Bent Flyvbjerg

Democratic contrivances are quarantine measures against that ancient plague, the lust for power: as such, they are very necessary and very boring.   *Friedrich Nietzsche*

Aalborg as Metaphor

The Aalborg Project may be interpreted as a metaphor of modern politics, modern administration and planning, and of modernity itself. The basic idea of the project was comprehensive, coherent, and innovative, and it was based on rational and democratic argument. During implementation, however, when idea met reality, the play of Machiavellian princes, Nietzschean will to power, and Foucauldian rationality-as-rationalization resulted in the fragmentation of the project. It disintegrated into a large number of disjointed subprojects, many of which had unintended, unanticipated, and undemocratic consequences. The grand, unifying, and prize-winning policy and plan degenerated into [a] string of petty incidents.... Planners, administrators, and politicians thought that if they believed in their project hard enough, rationality would emerge victorious; they were wrong. The Aalborg Project, designed to substantially restructure and democratically improve the downtown environment, was transformed by power and *Realrationalität* into environmental degradation and social distortion. Institutions that were supposed to represent what they themselves call the "public interest" were revealed to be deeply embedded in the hidden exercise of power and the protection of special interests. This is the story of modernity and democracy in practice, a story repeated all too often for comfort for a democrat. The problems with the Aalborg Project do not derive from Aalborg being especially plagued by corrupt policies or incompetent planning and administration.

From Bent Flyvbjerg, *Rationality and Power: Democracy in Practice*, trans. Steven Sampson, pp. 225–36, 272–5. © 1998 by The University of Chicago.

Most people interested in politics know one or more "Aalborg Stories," and the policy studies literature is replete with examples of failed policies, confused administration, and unbalanced planning. "You don't get to comfort yourself very long with the thought that they aren't too smart in Aalborg," observed one commentator on previously published results from the Aalborg study. "The description of what went wrong and why contains many elements familiar to anyone who works with planning in practice."[1] At a more general level, the Aalborg case confirms Charles Taylor's observation that central tenets of the Enlightenment legacy can be maintained primarily as goals and hope but not as reality.[2]

One such tenet is Francis Bacon's famous "Knowledge is power." Bacon's statement encapsulates one of the most fundamental ideas of modernity and of the Enlightenment: the more rationality, the better. Our study of the Aalborg Project certainly demonstrates the relevance of Bacon's statement. Yet it also shows that power and knowledge cannot be separated from each other in the way Bacon does; and even if one were to speak in Bacon's terms, the Aalborg study shows that the relationship between knowledge and power is commutative: not only is knowledge power, but, more important, power is knowledge. Power determines what counts as knowledge, what kind of interpretation attains authority as the dominant interpretation. Power procures the knowledge which supports its purposes, while it ignores or suppresses that knowledge which does not serve it. Moreover, the *relations* between knowledge and power are decisive if one seeks to understand the kinds of processes affecting the dynamics of politics, administration, and planning. There is a long tradition from Thucydides over Machiavelli and Nietzsche to Foucault for providing such an understanding. The case study of Aalborg was carried out in this tradition, and in our conclusions we will remain within it. Thus, the principal question to be addressed [here] is, "What basic relations of rationality and power have shaped the Aalborg Project and have led to its lack of balance, fragmentation, and lack of goal achievement?"[3]

This question will be elucidated by summarizing ten propositions about rationality and power.... [W]e will use the ten propositions to construct a "grounded theory," understood as theory inductively founded upon concrete phenomenology. While the propositions obviously derive from the case of Aalborg, and thus cannot be seen as general theory, they can serve as useful guidelines for researching rationality and power in other settings. The ten propositions may also serve as a phenomenology for testing, refining, and further developing the classical statements about power, knowledge, and rationality found in Bacon, Machiavelli, Kant, Nietzsche, and more recently in Michel Foucault, Jürgen Habermas, Richard Rorty, and others.

The order of presentation of the ten propositions will begin with a focus on the rationality of power and gradually move toward describing the power of rationality.

PROPOSITION 1: *Power defines reality*

Power concerns itself with defining reality rather than with discovering what reality "really" is. This is the single most important characteristic of the rationality of power, that is, of the strategies and tactics employed by power in relation to rationality. Defining reality by defining rationality is a principal means by which power exerts itself. This is not to imply that power seeks out rationality and knowledge *because* rationality and knowledge are power. Rather, power *defines* what counts as rationality and knowledge and thereby what counts as reality. The evidence of the Aalborg case confirms a basic Nietzschean insight: interpretation is not only commentary, as is often the view in academic settings, "interpretation is itself a means of becoming master of something" – in this case master of the Aalborg Project – and "all subduing and becoming master involves a fresh interpretation."[4] Power does not limit itself, however, to simply defining a given interpretation or view of reality, nor does power entail only the power to render a given reality authoritative. Rather, power defines, and creates, concrete physical, economic, ecological, and social realities.

PROPOSITION 2: *Rationality is context-dependent, the context of rationality is power, and power blurs the dividing line between rationality and rationalization*

Philosophy and science often present rationality as independent of context; for example, in universal philosophical, ethical, or scientific imperatives, a current example being the "theory of communicative rationality" and "discourse ethics" of Habermas. If these imperatives are followed, the result is supposed to be rational and generally acceptable actions. Our study of politics, administration, and planning in Aalborg shows rationality to be a discourse of power. Rationality is context-dependent, the context often being power. Rationality is penetrated by power, and it becomes meaningless, or misleading – for politicians, administrators, and research-ers alike – to operate with a concept of rationality in which power is absent. This holds true for substantive as well as communicative rationality. Communication is more typically characterized by nonrational rhetoric and maintenance of interests than by freedom from domination and consensus seeking. In rhetoric, the "validity" and effect of communication is established via the mode of communication – for example, eloquence, hidden control, rationalization, charisma, using dependency relations between participants – rather than through rational arguments concerning the matter at hand. Seen from this perspective, Habermas cuts himself off from understanding real communication when, in developing his theory of communica-tive rationality and discourse ethics, he distinguishes between "successful" and "distorted" utterances in human conversation; success in rhetoric that is not based on rational argument is associated precisely with distortion, a phenomenon demon-strated repeatedly in the Aalborg study.[5] The assertion of Harold Garfinkel and other ethnomethodologists that the rationality of a given activity is produced "in action" by participants via that activity is supported by the Aalborg case. In add-ition, we have seen that whenever powerful participants require rationalization and not rationality, such rationalization is produced. Rationalization is a pervasive feature of the Aalborg Project and is practiced by all key actors.

PROPOSITION 3: *Rationalization presented as rationality is a principal strategy in the exercise of power*

In the same way that political science, following Machiavelli and Ludwig von Rochau, distinguishes between formal politics and *Realpolitik*, evidence from the Aalborg study indicates the need for the study of politics, administration, planning, and modernity, to distinguish between formal rationality and *Realrationalität*, real rationality. The freedom to interpret and use "rationality" and "rationalization" for the purposes of power is a crucial element in enabling power to define reality and, hence, an essential feature of the rationality of power.

The relationship between rationality and rationalization is often what Erving Goffman calls a "front-back" relationship. "Up front" rationality dominates, frequently as rationalization presented as rationality. The front is open to public scrutiny, but it is not the whole story and, typically, not even its most important part. Backstage, hidden from public view, it is power and rationalization which dominate. A rationalized front does not necessarily imply dishonesty. It is not unusual to find individuals, organizations, and whole societies actually believing their own rationalizations. Nietzsche, in fact, claims this self-delusion to be part of the will to power. For Nietzsche, rationalization is necessary to survival.

Even though rationalization is a principal strategy in the rationality of power, and even though several of the most important events in the Aalborg Project have been profoundly affected by rationalization, the case study indicates that the freedom to rationalize is neither universal, inevitable, nor unlimited. All political and administrative activity cannot be reduced to rationalization; different degrees of rationalization exist; and rationalizations can be challenged – both rationally and by means of other rationalizations.

While it is possible to challenge rationalizations, this seldom occurs in the Aalborg Project. The "untouchable" position of rationalizations may be due to the fact that rationalizations are often difficult to identify and penetrate: they are presented as rationality, and, as demonstrated in the case study, often only a thorough deconstruction of an ostensibly rational argument can reveal whether it is a rationalization. In other cases, actors may be prevented from revealing a rationalization because so much power lies behind it that critique and clarification may become futile. A final explanation for actors' unwillingness to reveal rationalizations is that doing so may be dangerous: attempts at deconstruction and critique may lead to confrontations, to the destabilization of the decision-making process, or to negative sanctions on those actors who reveal rationality as rationalization.

PROPOSITION 4: *The greater the power, the less the rationality*

Kant said, "The possession of power unavoidably spoils the free use of reason."[6] On the basis of the Aalborg study, we may expand on Kant by observing that the possession of more power appears to spoil reason even more.

One of the privileges of power, and an integral part of its rationality, is the freedom to define reality. The greater the power, the greater the freedom in this respect, and the less need for power to understand how reality is "really" constructed. The absence of rational arguments and factual documentation in support of certain actions may be more important indicators of power than arguments and documentation produced. Power knows that which Nietzsche calls "the doctrine of Hamlet," that is, the fact that often "[k]nowledge kills action; action requires the veils of illusion."[7] A party's unwillingness to present rational argument or documentation may quite simply indicate its freedom to act and its freedom to define reality.

In a democratic society, rational argument is one of the few forms of power the powerless still possess. This may explain the enormous appeal of the Enlightenment project to those outside power. Machiavelli, however, places little trust in rational persuasion. "We must distinguish," he says in *The Prince*, "between ... those who to achieve their purpose can force the issue and those who must use persuasion. In the second case, they always come to grief."[8] "Always" may be somewhat exaggerated, and much has changed in terms of Enlightenment and modernity since Machiavelli.

Nevertheless, Machiavelli's analysis certainly applies to the Aalborg Project, which in this sense is premodern and predemocratic.

Nietzsche puts an interesting twist on the proposition "the greater the power, the less the rationality" by directly linking power and stupidity: "Coming to power is a costly business," Nietzsche says, "power *makes stupid*" (emphasis in original).[9] Nietzsche adds that "politics devours all seriousness for really intellectual things." In a critique of Charles Darwin, Nietzsche further points out that for human beings the outcome of the struggle for survival will be the opposite of that "desired" by Darwinism because "Darwin forgot the mind," and because "[h]e who possesses strength divests himself of mind."[10] Nietzsche identified the marginalization of mind and intellect by power as a central problem for the German *Reich*, and on this basis he predicted – correctly, we now know – the fall of the *Reich*.[11] Aalborg's mayor also suffered from the marginalization of mind by power, something which ultimately cost him his political life. Will to power is a will to life, but it may well lead to self-destruction.

In sum, what we see in Aalborg is not only, and not primarily, a general "will to knowledge" but also "a far more powerful will: the will to ignorance, to the uncertain, to the untrue! Not as [will to knowledge's] opposite but – as its refinement!"[12] Power, quite simply, often finds ignorance, deception, self-deception, rationalizations, and lies more useful for its purposes than truth and rationality. Yet Nietzsche is wrong when he says, "Who alone has good reason to lie his way out of reality? He who suffers from it. But to suffer from reality is to be a piece of reality that has come to grief."[13] What makes Nietzsche wrong here is the "alone" in the first sentence of the quote. In Aalborg, we have come across other groups that have good reasons to lie and rationalize, groups that do not suffer from reality. These are groups that stand to gain from propagating certain interpretations, rationalizations, and lies about reality and that use politics to create the reality they want. When it comes to politics, even Plato – the ultimate defender of rationality – recommended the "noble lie," that is, the lie which would be told to the citizens of his model state in order to support its moral and political order.[14]

PROPOSITION 5: *Stable power relations are more typical of politics, administration, and planning than antagonistic confrontations*

Michel Foucault characterizes power relations as dynamic and reciprocal: stable power relations can at any time evolve into antagonistic confrontations, and vice versa. The data from Aalborg confirm Foucault's conclusion, but we must also modify it by noting that the reciprocal relationship between stable power relations and antagonistic confrontations is asymmetrical: stable power relations are far more typical than antagonistic confrontations, much as peace is more typical than war in modern societies. Antagonistic confrontations are actively avoided. When such confrontations take place, they are quickly transformed into stable power relations. The result is that the issues shaping politics, administration, and planning are defined more by stable power relations than by antagonistic confrontations.

Because confrontations often are more visible than stable power relations, confrontations tend to be frequent topics of research on power and of public debate and press coverage. Concentration on the most visible aspects of power, however, results in an incomplete and biased picture of power relations.

PROPOSITION 6: *Power relations are constantly being produced and reproduced*

Even the most stable power relations, those with historical roots going back several centuries, are not immutable in form or content. Power relations are constantly changing. They demand constant maintenance, cultivation, and reproduction. In the Aalborg case (as described in the volume from which this chapter is drawn) the business community was much more conscious of this – and substantially more skilled and persevering – than were politicians, administrators, and planners. Through decades and centuries of careful maintenance, cultivation, and reproduction of power relations, business created a semi-institutionalized position for itself with more aptitude to influence governmental rationality than was found with democratically elected bodies of government.

PROPOSITION 7: *The rationality of power has deeper historical roots than the power of rationality*

From the historical perspective of what Fernand Braudel and the French *Annales* school call the *longue durée*, ideas like democracy, rationality, and neutrality, all central to modern institutions, are young and fragile when compared to traditions of class and privilege. In the Aalborg study, centuries of daily practice have made the latter so firmly entrenched in social institutions that they have become part of modern institutions. Policy, administration, and planning in the Aalborg Project are marked as much by premodern relations of power as by modern rationality, by tribalism as much as by democracy. This is despite the fact that the very raison d'être of modernity has been to eliminate, or attenuate, the influence of tradition, tribe, class, and privilege, and even though modernization has been going on for more than two centuries. One consequence of this state of affairs is what by modern standards is called the "abuse of power" in modern institutions.

Modern institutions and modern ideas such as democracy and rationality remain in large part ideals or hope. Such ideals cannot be implemented once and for all. We again need to remember that to call governments "democratic" is always a misleading piece of propaganda.[15] We may want the democratic element in government to grow greater, but it is still only an element. Efforts at implementing democracy are a constant, never-ending task existing in conflict with traditions and modernist initiatives gives rise to new traditions. In this sense, modernity and democracy must be seen as part of power, not the end points of power. Modernity and democracy do not "liberate man in his own being," nor do they free individuals from being governed, as Foucault says. Modernity and democracy undermine religion and tradition and compel man "to face the task of producing himself," and of practicing government that will not obstruct, but will instead advance, "the undefined" – and never-ending – "work of freedom."[16]

PROPOSITION 8: *In open confrontation, rationality yields to power*

Foucault says that knowledge–power and rationality–power relations exist everywhere. This is confirmed by our study, but modified by the finding that where power relations take the form of open, antagonistic confrontations, power-to-power relations dominate over knowledge–power and rationality–power relations; that is, knowledge and rationality carry little or no weight in these instances. As the proverb has it, "Truth is the first casualty of war."

In an open confrontation, actions are dictated by what works most effectively to defeat the adversary in the specific situation. In such confrontations, use of naked power tends to be more effective than any appeal to objectivity, facts, knowledge, or rationality, even though feigned versions of the latter, that is, rationalizations, may be used to legitimize naked power.

The proposition that rationality yields to power in open confrontations may be seen as an extreme case of proposition no.4, "the greater the power, the less the rationality": Rationality yields completely, or almost completely, to power in open, antagonistic confrontation because it is here that naked power can be exercised most freely.

PROPOSITION 9: *Rationality–power relations are more characteristic of stable power relations than of confrontations*

Interactions between rationality and power tend to stabilize power relations and often even constitute them. This stabilization process can be explained by the fact that decisions taken as part of rationality–power relations may be rationally informed, thereby gaining more legitimacy and a higher degree of consensus than "decisions" based on naked power-to-power confrontations.

Stable power relations, however, are not necessarily *equally balanced* power relations, understood as relations in which the involved parties act on equal terms. In other words, stability does not imply justice, and stable power relations imply neither "noncoercive [*zwanglos*] communication" nor "communicative rationality," to use Habermas's terms. Stable power relations may entail no more than a working consensus with unequal relations of dominance, which may lead to distortions in the production and use of rational or quasi-rational arguments. Where rational considerations play a role, however, they typically do so in the context of stable power relations.

PROPOSITION 10: *The power of rationality is embedded in stable power relations rather than in confrontations*

Confrontations are part of the rationality of power, not the power of rationality. Because rationality yields to power in open, antagonistic confrontations, the power of rationality, that is, the force of reason, is weak or nonexistent here. The force of reason gains maximum effect in stable power relations characterized by negotiations and consensus seeking. Hence, the power of rationality can be maintained only insofar as power relations are kept nonantagonistic and stable.

Special interest groups have substantially more freedom to use and to benefit from the full gamut of instruments in naked power play than do democratically elected governments. Democratic government of the modern Western variety is formally and legally based on rational argument and is constrained to operate within the framework of stable power relations, even when dealing with antagonistic interest groups, unless such groups go on to break the law and trigger police or military intervention. This difference in the mode of operation of governments and interest groups results in an unequal relationship between governmental rationality and private power, and between formal politics and *Realpolitik*, such that governmental rationality and formal politics end up in the weaker position. Inequality between rationality and power can be seen as a general weakness of democracy in the short-run struggle over specific policies and outcomes. It is a weakness, however, that cannot be overcome by resorting to the instruments of naked power, and modern democracy's ability to limit its use of naked power can be seen as its general strength.

The fact that the power of rationality emerges mostly in the absence of confrontation and naked power makes rationality appear as a relatively fragile phenomenon; the power of rationality is weak. If we want the power of reasoned argument to increase in the local, national, or international community, then rationality must be secured. Achieving this increase involves long term strategies and tactics which would constrict the space for the exercise of naked power and *Realpolitik* in social and political affairs. Rationality, knowledge, and truth are closely associated. "The problem of truth," says Foucault, is "the most general of political problems."[17] The task of speaking the truth is "endless," according to Foucault, who adds that "no power can avoid the obligation to respect this task in all its complexity, unless it imposes silence and servitude."[18] Herein lies the power of rationality.

The Challenge to Democracy

In sum, while power produces rationality and rationality produces power, their relationship is asymmetrical. Power has a clear tendency to dominate rationality in the dynamic and overlapping relationship between the two. Paraphrasing Pascal, one could say that power has a rationality that rationality does not know. Rationality, on the other hand, does not have a power that power does not know.

Modernity relies on rationality as the main means for making democracy work. But if the interrelations between rationality and power are even remotely close to the asymmetrical relationship depicted above – which Aalborg and the tradition from Thucydides, Machiavelli, and Nietzsche tell us they are – then rationality is such a weak form of power that democracy built on rationality will be weak, too. The asymmetry between rationality and power described in the ten propositions makes for a fundamental weakness of modernity and modern politics, administration and planning. The normative emphasis on rationality leaves the modern project ignorant of how power works and therefore open to being dominated by power. Relying on rationality therefore risks exacerbating the very problems modernity attempts to solve. Given the problems and risks of our time – environmental, social, demographic; globally and locally – I suggest we consider whether we can afford to continue this fundamental weakness of modernity. The first step in moving beyond the modern weakness is to understand power, and when we understand power we see that we cannot rely solely on democracy based on rationality to solve our problems.

Let us probe this point at a more concrete level. Constitution writing and institutional reform are the main means of action, in theory as well as in practice, in the modernist strategy of developing democracy by relying on rationality against power.[19] Whereas constitution writing and institutional reform may often be essential to democratic development, the idea that such reform alters practice is a hypothesis, not an axiom. The problem with many advocates of institutional reform is that they reverse the axiom and the hypothesis: they take for granted that which should be subjected to empirical and historical test. In Aalborg such testing showed us that even the police – supposedly the guard of the law – refused to follow and enforce the constitutional principles institutionalists rely upon to promote democracy, not to speak of the many other actors in the case who again and again, for personal and group advantage, violated the principles of democratic behavior they were supposed to honor as civil servants, politicians, and citizens in one of the oldest democracies in the world. We saw, in fact, that political actors are expert at judging how far a democratic constitution can be bent and used, or simply ignored, in nondemocratic ways. Such findings demonstrate that the question of how existing constitutions and their associated institutions can be utilized more democratically may frequently be more pressing than the question of how to establish more democratic constitutions and institutions as such. The Aalborg study certainly confirms Robert Putnam's general observation that "[t]wo centuries of constitution-writing around the world warn us...that designers of new institutions are often writing on water."[20]

Putnam's study of civic traditions in modern Italy is one of the few other studies of the practices of democracy combining a micro approach with the historical perspective of the *longue durée*, the very long run. Like the Aalborg study, Putnam and his associates find that social context and history profoundly condition the effectiveness of institutions; premodern social practices that go back several centuries drastically limit the possibilities for implementing modern democratic reform. Such conditioning is not only a problem for democracy in Italy and Denmark. In most societies entrenched practices of class and privilege form part of the social and political context and limit the possibilities of democratic change. Putnam notes that the effect of deep historical roots on the possibilities of modern democracy is a "depressing observation" for those who view constitutional and institutional reform as the main strategy for political change.[21] Nevertheless, such is currently the evidence. This does not mean, needless to say, that changing formal institutions cannot change political practice. It does mean, however, that institutional change typically moves much more slowly and circuitously than is often assumed by legal writers and institutional reformists.

But looking at democracy in the time perspective of the *longue durée* is only depressing to those impatient for instant change. For it is also by employing this time perspective that we begin to see what it takes to make democracy work in practice. It is in this perspective we see that people working for more democracy form part of a century-long and remarkably successful practical tradition that focuses on more participation, more transparency, and more civic reciprocity in public decision making. The fact that progress has generally been slow within the tradition by no means makes such progress less significant; quite the opposite. The tradition shows us that forms of participation that are practical, committed, and ready for conflict provide a superior paradigm of democratic virtue than forms of participation that are discursive, detached, and consensus-dependent, that is, rational. We see that in order to enable democratic thinking and the public sphere to make a real contribution to democratic action, one has to tie them back to precisely what they cannot accept in much of modern democratic theory: power, conflict, and partisanship, as has been done with the Aalborg study.[22]

In the *longue durée*, we see that in practice democratic progress is chiefly achieved not by constitutional and institutional reform alone but by facing the mechanisms of power and the practices of class and privilege more directly, often head-on: if you want to participate in politics but find the possibilities for doing so constricting, then you team up with like-minded people and you fight for what you want, utilizing the means that work in your context to undermine those who try to limit participation. If you want to know what is going on in politics but find little transparency, you do the same. If you want more civic reciprocity in political affairs, you work for civic virtues becoming worthy of praise and others becoming undesirable. At times direct power struggle over specific issues works best; on other occasions changing the ground rules for such struggle is necessary, which is where constitutional and institutional reform come in; and sometimes writing genealogies and case histories like the Aalborg study, that is, laying open the relationships between rationality and power, will help achieve the desired results. More often it takes a combination of all three, in addition to the blessings of beneficial circumstance and pure luck. Democracy in practice is that simple and that difficult.

Let us return one final time to Machiavelli's warning about the dangers of the normative attitude: "[A] man who neglects what is actually done for what should be done learns the way to self-destruction."[23] The focus of modernity and modern democracy has always been on "what should be done," on normative rationality. What I suggest is a reorientation toward the first half of Machiavelli's dictum, "what is actually done," toward *verita effettuale*. We need to rethink and recast the projects of modernity and democracy, and of modern politics, administration, and planning, in terms of not only rationality but of rationality and power, *Realrationalität*. Instead of thinking of modernity and democracy as rational means for dissolving power, we need to see them as practical attempts at regulating power and domination. When we do this we obtain a better grasp of what modernity and democracy are in practice and what it takes to change them for the better....

NOTES

1   Svend Søholt, "Miljø, Trafik og Demokrati," *Byplan* 42, no. 2 (1990), p. 60.
2   Charles Taylor, "Interpretation and the Sciences of Man," in Paul Rabinow and William M. Sullivan, eds., *Interpretive Social Science: A Second Look* (Berkeley: University of California Press, 1987), p. 72.
3   Robert Dahl and most other students of power, be they pluralist, elitist, or Marxist in their orientation, begin their analyses by posing the Weberian question, "Who governs?" [Here] we ask, "What 'governmental rationalities' are at work when those who govern govern?" This does not mean that we evade the Weberian question.... the fate of the Aalborg Project was decided by a tiny elite of top-level politicians, high-ranking civil servants, and business community leaders. The study uncovered an informal, hidden business–government "council" in which decisions about the Aalborg Project – and about other policies and plans of interest to the business community – were negotiated and enacted in corporative fashion before anyone else had a say over such decisions. Business interests also gained special weight in the Aalborg Project because of strong and coordinated support by the local press and the police. This is not to say that all decisions benefited the business community. Nevertheless, the trend in the overall pattern of decisions that comprise the Aalborg Project – from its genesis, through design and ratification, to implementation and operation – indicates a clear and irrefutable preference for business interests as a result of the initiatives by the business community. Democratically elected bodies of government such as the City Council, the magistrate, and political committees had very little influence. They merely rubber-stamped decisions already made elsewhere. Other community groups beside the business community lacked influence on outcomes, as did the general public. In sum, by democratic standards, and understood in terms of conventional power theory, decisions regarding the Aalborg Project were made by too few and the wrong parties. Read in this way, the Aalborg case can be seen as refuting pluralist power theories of the type propounded by Dahl and others and as corroborating

theories of a more elitist and corporatist orientation such as those developed by C. Wright Mills, Floyd Hunter, and Nicolas Poulantzas (Robert A. Dahl, *Who Governs?: Democracy and Power in an American City* (New Haven: Yale University Press, 1961). See also Dahl's updated reflections in "Rethinking *Who Governs?*: New Haven Revisited," in Robert Waste, ed., *Community Power: Directions for Future Research* (Beverly Hills: Sage, 1986); C. Wright Mills, *The Power Elite* (Oxford: Oxford University Press, 1956); Floyd Hunter, *Community Power Structure* (Chapel Hill: University of North Carolina Press, 1953), and Hunter, *Community Power Succession: Atlanta's Policy Makers Revisited* (Chapel Hill: University of North Carolina Press, 1980). See also G. William Domhoff, *Who Really Rules? New Haven and Community Power Reexamined* (Santa Monica, Calif.: Goodyear Publishing Company, 1978); Nicolas Poulantzas, *Political Power and Social Classes* (London: NLB, 1973); Poulantzas, *State, Power, Socialism* (London: NLB, 1979)). The question of "Who governs?" has been addressed in numerous other studies, many of which have emerged with similar conclusions. This is one reason why [here], instead of focusing mainly on the "who" and "where" of power, we have focused on the more dynamic question of "how" power is exercised and on the relationships between rationality and power. The latter questions have been studied and answered much less frequently than "Who governs?"

4   Friedrich Nietzsche, *The Will to Power* (New York: Vintage Books, 1968), p. 342 (§643); Friedrich Nietzsche, *On the Genealogy of Morals* (New York: Vintage Books, 1969), p. 77 (§2.12).

5   Jürgen Habermas, *The Philosophical Discourse of Modernity: Twelve Lectures* (Cambridge, Mass.: MIT Press, 1987), pp. 297–98. Habermas sees consensus seeking and freedom from domination as universally inherent as forces in human communication, and he emphasizes these particular aspects in his discourse ethics. Other important social thinkers have tended to emphasize the exact opposite. Machiavelli, e.g., whom students of politics do not hesitate to call a "most worthy humanist" and "distinctly modern," and whom, like Habermas, is concerned with "the business of good government," states: "One can make this generalization about men: they are ungrateful, fickle, liars, and deceivers" (Bernard Crick, "Preface" and "Introduction" to Niccolò Machiavelli, *The Discourses* (Harmondsworth: Penguin, 1983), pp. 12, 17; Machiavelli, *The Prince* (Harmondsworth: Penguin, 1984), p. 96 (chap. 17). Less radically, but still in clear contrast to Habermas, are observations by Nietzsche, Foucault, Derrida, and others that communication is at all times already penetrated by power. Whether the communicative or rhetorical position is "correct" is not the most important starting point for understanding rationality and power, even though the Aalborg study clearly supports the latter. What is decisive, rather, is that a nonidealistic point of departure must take account of the fact that in actual communication both positions are possible, and even simultaneously possible. In an empirical-scientific context, the question of communicative rationality versus rhetoric must therefore remain open for test. To assume either position ex ante based on a Kierkegaardian "leap of faith," to universalize it, and build a theory upon it makes for speculative philosophy and social science. Without placing Habermas's discourse ethics in the same league as Marxism, it may be said that the problem with discourse ethics is similar to that of some forms of Marxism in the sense that when it comes to organizing a better society, both Marx and Habermas have no account of how to deal with human evil; both assume that the good in human beings will dominate. In effect, this assumption tends to turn both lines of thinking into dogma. It is also what makes them potentially dangerous. History teaches us that assuming the nonexistence of evil may instead give free reign to evil. Nietzsche acutely observes about "[t]his mode of thought" that it "advises taking the side of the good, it desires that the good should renounce and oppose the evil down to its ultimate roots – it therewith actually denies life, which has in all its instincts both Yes and No." "Perhaps," says Nietzsche, "there has

never before been a more dangerous ideology – than this will to good" (*The Will to Power*, pp. 192–93 (§351)). The evidence of the Aalborg case is on the side of Foucault when, in a comment on Habermas, he observes that the problem is not one of trying to dissolve relations of power in the "utopia of a perfectly transparent communication" but to give the rules of law, the techniques of management, and also the ethics which would "allow these games of power to be played with a minimum of domination" (Michel Foucault, "The Ethic of Care for the Self as a Practice of Freedom," in James Bernauer and David Rasmussen, eds., *The Final Foucault* (Cambridge, Mass.: MIT Press, 1988), p. 18). For more on the issues covered in this note, see my paper, "Empowering Civil Society: Habermas, Foucault, and the Question of Conflict," paper for symposium in Celebration of John Friedmann, School of Public Policy and Social Research, University of California, Los Angeles, April 11–13, 1996.

6 Here quoted from Timothy Garton Ash, "Prague: Intellectuals and Politicians," *New York Review of Books* 42, no. 1 (1995), p. 39.

7 Friedrich Nietzsche, *The Birth of Tragedy* (New York: Vintage Books, 1967), p. 60 (§7).

8 Machiavelli, *The Prince*, pp. 51–52 (chap. 6).

9 Friedrich Nietzsche, *Twilight of the Idols* (Harmondsworth: Penguin, 1968), p. 60 (§1).

10 Ibid., p. 76 (§14).

11 Ibid.

12 Friedrich Nietzsche, *Beyond Good and Evil* (New York: Vintage Books, 1966), p. 35 (§24).

13 Friedrich Nietzsche, *The Antichrist*, in Walter Kaufmann, ed., *The Portable Nietzsche* (New York: Penguin, 1968), p. 582 (§15).

14 "[T]he rulers of our community: they can lie for the good of the community," from Plato, *Republic* (Oxford: Oxford University Press, 1993), p. 83 (bk. 3, sec. 389).

15 Bernard Crick, "Introduction" to Machiavelli, *The Discourses*, p. 27.

16 Michel Foucault, "What Is Enlightenment?," in Paul Rabinow, ed., *The Foucault Reader* (New York: Pantheon, 1984), pp. 42, 46.

17 Michel Foucault, "Questions of Method: An Interview," *I&C*, no. 8 (Spring 1981), p. 11.

18 Michel Foucault, "The Regard for Truth," *Art and Text*, no. 16 (1984), p. 31.

19 A prominent current example of the reliance on constitution writing and institutional reform for democratic progress is Habermas's trust in *Vervassungspatriotismus* (constitutional patriotism) as a main means to have the democratic principles of his discourse ethics take root in society. See Habermas, *Justification and Application: Remarks on Discourse Ethics* (Cambridge, Mass.: MIT Press, 1993); "Burdens of the Double Past," *Dissent* 41, no. 4; and Habermas, *Between Facts and Norms: Contributions to a Discourse Theory of Law and Democracy* (Cambridge: Polity, 1996). For an analysis of Habermas's *Vervassungspatriotismus*, see my "Empowering Civil Society."

20 Robert D. Putnam with Robert Leonardi and Raffaella Y. Nanetti, *Making Democracy Work: Civic Traditions in Modern Italy* (Princeton: Princeton University Press, 1993), p. 17.

21 Ibid., p. 183.

22 For more on this point, see my "Empowering Civil Society." See also Charles Spinosa, Fernando Flores, and Hubert Dreyfus, "Disclosing New Worlds: Entrepreneurship, Democratic Action, and the Cultivation of Solidarity," *Inquiry* 38, nos. 1–2 (June 1995).

23 Machiavelli, *The Prince*, p. 91 (chap. 15).

Part V

Race, Gender, and City Planning

Introduction

We begin with a chapter excerpted from Iris Marion Young's important book, *Justice and the Politics of Difference*. In "City Life and Difference," Young reconsiders the social ties that bind people together in a city. Young is critical of capitalist liberal democracy as a basis for urban social relations. But she also rejects the communitarian alternative. She offers a strong critique of participatory democratic theory, which tries to get around social difference by appealing to an ideal of community. Young provocatively questions our soft, fuzzy acceptance of the intrinsic value of "community", which can be xenophobic and anti-urban, enforce homogeneity, and exclude people with whom the community cannot or will not identify. (These concerns echo the criticisms directed at New Urbanist communitarianism.)

Young proposes a third path between liberal individualism and communitarianism: a vision of urban life in which social relations affirm group differences, rather than fusing into a single identity. City life is "the being together of strangers," and its vigor lies in its alternative to both atomistic solitude and village-scale community. Cities offer the potential for variety, eroticism, publicity (public life, public spaces), and social differentiation without exclusion. The challenge of urban politics is to construct this third path and allow people to get along in a city without forming a community. The answer, for Young, is creating the "politics of difference" (hence her book title), which reconciles diversity, empowerment, and social justice.[1]

June Manning Thomas continues this theme by examining how the planning discipline can more constructively teach diversity to its students. She offers a hopeful but sobering assessment of the progress already achieved in planning, and the great strides that still need to be taken. She recognizes the significant advances attained by women in planning, but bemoans the scarcity of African-Americans and other minorities at the management and faculty levels. Thomas outlines three historical stages of cultural politics for planning: monoculturalism, disjointed pluralism, and unified diversity. Though the field has generally moved on from a monocentric view of planning and society, it is still largely stuck in a disjointed pluralism, characterized by the occasional and often isolated use of materials on diversity. This marginalized function of diversity education mirrors the very problems that contemporary American cities face: fragmentation, polarization, and isolation from the rest of society. Thomas advocates a progression to the third stage of cultural politics, when issues of race and gender are integrated across the curricula with an eye to practical, effective reform, leading to "unified diversity for social action."

Gender politics has emerged as a powerful and transformative theme in urban planning in recent years. The forces behind an emerging feminist planning theory are numerous, including the larger feminist movement, women entering the labor force in large numbers, more women planners and professors, parallels between the civil rights movement and the feminist movement, and links with intellectual movements such as postmodernism and multiculturalism. The feminist perspective addresses many issues of urbanism: the differing uses of urban space by men and women; threats to personal safety of women in cities; structural discrimination against women in economic development; the transportation needs of women beyond the traditional "journey to work"; more fluid boundaries between the personal and the political (e.g. between home and wage work); and the connections between the experience of gender differences, racial differences, and the cultural politics of diversity.

Dolores Hayden, in "Nurturing: Home, Mom and Apple Pie," (excerpted from her book *Redesigning the American Dream*), traces the connections between gender roles, family life, and the structure of American neighborhoods. Specifically, she argues that the traditional suburban model was built for a nineteenth-century nuclear family structure no longer appropriate to contemporary society, and that the perpetuation of this housing pattern undermines progress for women and non-traditional households. To trace the suburban model historically, Hayden articulates three prototypes of organizing household work: home as haven, the industrial strategy, and the neighborhood strategy. The haven approach is to increase the efficiency of household work, glorify woman's traditional sphere of work in the home, and isolate a woman (housewife) in a suburban cottage in a garden, far from the toils of the city and its wage economy. At the other end of the scale is the industrial strategy, which views housework as a vestige of the pre-industrial craft production era, requiring modernization through mass production, standardization, and separation of home and work. That is, it shifts traditional housework (cooking, laundry, education, and child care) into a factory setting.

Hayden takes the middle path between these two extremes. She advocates the neighborhood strategy, with producer cooperatives, shared child care, and other household work activity done at the neighborhood scale. This third path seeks to empower women while retaining local initiative and to balance scale economies (of the industrial strategy) with the benefits of personalized nurturing and child rearing (of the home as haven strategy). The challenge for planners and architects is to design communities – and to retrofit existing suburbs – to encourage cooperation and collaboration at this decentralized scale. (Interestingly, in her combined social, environmental, and design critique of suburbia, and in her choice of the neighborhood scale, Hayden's 1984 writings anticipate many of the New Urbanist ideals.)

We conclude with a brief essay by Leonie Sandercock on her idea of cosmopolis. Following the three authors before her, Sandercock examines how cities can better accommodate a great diversity of people, cultures, and life-styles, and how urban planners can promote this agenda. She joins the chorus of critics opposed to the modernist tradition in planning, which embraced positivistic social sciences after the war and neglected a broader vision of planning. In the process, a rich array of urban qualities was neglected or forgotten altogether: identity, meaning, the arts (rather than science), memory, and desire. Planning became the practice of social control, of regulating these desires (especially of women) and their corresponding social spaces. Planners, it seemed, could talk about needs but found it hard to talk about desire.

To correct this, Sandercock advocates an expanded language for planning, as well as a broader design vocabulary to promote the city of desire: public spaces that encourage the mix of anonymity, longing, and chance encounters – that is, "an eroticism of city life." She also argues for the renewal of the city of spirit, encouraging female spiritual landscapes (with strong ties to the land) to flourish as an alternative to male industrial landscapes. Overall, one needs diversity of places, both loud and quiet, stimulating and reflective, some apart from commerce, with spaces for memory, desire, and the sacred. (Some readers may fault this view of planning as a preoccupation with the soft, cultural fringe of urban issues, rather than the main issues of jobs, land use, and environmental quality. But this may be the very crux of her argument: that planning has for too long only considered legitimate this narrow, technocratic view of functional city planning.)

NOTE

1 One sees a similar theme in David Harvey's efforts to reconcile the multiple voices of postmodernism and the need for social justice, contained in the companion volume to this one (Fainstein and Campbell, 2002).

REFERENCE

Fainstein, Susan S. and Scott Campbell. 2002. *Readings in Urban Theory,* 2nd edn. Oxford: Blackwell.

18

City Life and Difference

Iris Marion Young

The tolerance, the room for great differences among neighbors – differences that often go far deeper than differences in color – which are possible and normal in intensely urban life, but which are so foreign to suburbs and pseudosuburbs, are possible and normal only when streets of great cities have built-in equipment allowing strangers to dwell in peace together on civilized but essentially dignified and reserved terms.

Jane Jacobs

One important purpose of critical normative theory is to offer an alternative vision of social relations which, in the words of Marcuse, "conceptualizes the stuff of which the experienced world consists . . . with a view to its possibilities, in the light of their actual limitation, suppression, and denial" (Marcuse, 1964, p. 7). Such a positive normative vision can inspire hope and imagination that motivate action for social change. It also provides some of the reflective distance necessary for the criticism of existing social circumstances.

Many philosophers and political theorists criticize welfare capitalist society for being atomistic, depoliticized, fostering self-regarding interest-group pluralism and bureaucratic domination. The most common alternative vision offered by such critics is an ideal of community. Spurred by appeals to community as an alternative to liberal individualism made by Michael Sandel, Alasdair MacIntyre, and others, in recent years political theorists have debated the virtues and vices of communitarianism as opposed to liberalism (Gutmann, 1985; Hirsch, 1986; Buchanan, 1989). Many socialists, anarchists, feminists, and others critical of welfare capitalist society formulate their vision of a society free from domination and oppression in terms of an ideal of community. Much of this discussion would lead us to think that liberal individualism and communitarianism exhaust the possibilities for conceiving social relations.

...I share many of the communitarian criticisms of welfare capitalist liberal democratic theory and society. I shall argue [here], however, that the ideal of community fails to offer an appropriate alternative vision of a democratic polity. The ideal of community exemplifies the logic of identity....This ideal expresses a desire for the fusion of subjects with one another which in practice operates to exclude those with whom the group does not identify. The ideal of community denies and represses social difference, the fact that the polity cannot be thought of as a unity in which all participants share a common experience and common values. In its privileging of face-to-face relations, moreover, the ideal of community denies difference in the form of the temporal and spatial distancing that characterizes social process.

As an alternative to the ideal of community, I develop in this chapter an ideal of city life as a vision of social relations affirming group difference. As a normative ideal, city life instantiates social relations of difference without exclusion. Different groups dwell in the city alongside one another, of necessity interacting in city spaces. If city politics is to be democratic and not dominated by the point of view of one group, it must be a politics that takes account of and provides voice for the different groups that dwell together in the city without forming a community.

City life as an openness to unassimilated otherness, however, represents only an unrealized social ideal. Many social injustices exist in today's cities. Cities and the people in them are relatively powerless before the domination of corporate capital and state bureaucracy. Privatized decisionmaking processes in cities and towns reproduce and exacerbate inequalities and oppressions. They also produce or re-inforce segregations and exclusions within cities and between cities and towns, which contribute to exploitation, marginalization, and cultural imperialism.

Many democratic theorists respond to these ills of city life by calls for the creation of decentralized autonomous communities where people exercise local control over their lives and neighborhoods on a human scale. Such calls for local autonomy, I argue in conclusion, reproduce the problems of exclusion that the ideal of community poses. I offer a conceptual distinction between autonomy and empowerment, and sketch out some parameters of democratic empowerment in large-scale regional government.

The Opposition between Individualism and Community

Crities of liberalism frequently invoke a conception of community as an alternative to the individualism and abstract formalism they attribute to liberalism (cf. Wolff, 1968, chap. 5; Bay, 1981, chap. 5). They reject the image of persons as separate and self-contained atoms, each with the same formal rights, rights to keep others out, separate. For such writers, the ideal of community evokes the absence of the self-interested competitiveness of modern society. In this ideal, crities of liberalism find an alternative to the abstract, formal methodology of liberalism. Existing in community with others entails more than merely respecting their rights; it entails attending to and sharing in the particularity of their needs and interests.

In his rightly celebrated critique of Rawls, for example, Michael Sandel (1982) argues that liberalism's emphasis on the primacy of justice presupposes a conception of the self as an antecedent unity existing prior to its desires and goals, whole unto itself, separated and bounded. This is an unreal and incoherent conception of the self, he argues. It would be better replaced by a conception of the self as the product of an identity it shares with others, of values and goals that are not external and willed, as liberalism would have it, but constitutive of the self. This constitutive conception of the self is expressed by the concept of community.

Benjamin Barber (1984) also uses the idea of community to evoke a vision of social life that does not conceive the person as an atomistic, separated individual. Liberal political theory represents individuals as occupying private and separate spaces, as propelled only by their own private desires. This is a consumer-oriented conception of human nature, in which social and political relations can be understood only as goods instrumental to the achievement of individual desires, and not as intrinsic goods. This atomistic conception generates a political theory that presumes conflict and competition as characteristic modes of interaction. Like Sandel, Barber appeals to an ideal of community to invoke a conception of the person as socially constituted, actively oriented toward affirming relations of mutuality, rather than oriented solely toward satisfying private needs and desires (cf. Ackelsberg, 1988).

... I share these critiques of liberalism. Liberal social ontology, I have argued, has no place for a concept of social groups. I have characterized a social group as the relational outcome of interactions, meanings, and affinities according to which people identify one another. The self is indeed a product of social relations in profound and often contradictory ways. A person's social group identities, moreover, are in some meaningful sense shared with others of the group.

I have also criticized liberalism's consumer-oriented presuppositions about human nature, and agree with Barber that these lead to an instrumentalist understanding of the function of politics. With Barber and other new republican theorists, I too reject the privatization of politics in liberal pluralist processes, and call for the institution of democratic publics. I think, however, that all these criticisms of liberalism can and should be made without embracing community as a political ideal.

Too often contemporary discussion of these issues sets up an exhaustive dichotomy between individualism and community. Community appears in the oppositions individualism/community, separated self/shared self, private/public. But like most such terms, individualism and community have a common logic underlying their polarity, which makes it possible for them to define each other negatively. Each entails a denial of difference and a desire to bring multiplicity and heterogeneity into unity, though in opposing ways. Liberal individualism denies difference by positing the self as a solid, self-sufficient unity, not defined by anything or anyone other than itself. Its formalistic ethic of rights also denies difference by bringing all such separated individuals under a common measure of rights. Proponents of community, on the other hand, deny difference by positing fusion rather than separation as the social ideal. They conceive the social subject as a relation of unity or mutuality composed by identification and symmetry among individuals within a totality. Communitarianism represents an urge to see persons in unity with one another in a shared whole.

For many writers, the rejection of individualism logically entails the assertion of community, and conversely any rejection of community entails that one necessarily supports individualism. In their discussion of a debate between Jean Elshtain and Barbara Ehrenreich, for example, Harry Boyte and Sara Evans (1984) claim that Ehrenreich promotes individualism because she rejects the appeal to community that Elshtain makes. Recent accounts of the debate among political theorists generated by communitarian critiques of Rawls all couch that debate in terms of a dichotomy between liberal individualism and community, suggesting that these two categories are indeed mutually exclusive and exhaust all possible social ontologies and conceptions of the self (see Hirsch, 1986; Cornell, 1987). Thus even when the discussants recognize the totalizing and circular character of this debate, and seek to take a position outside its terms, they tend to slide into affirming one or the other "side" of the dichotomy because that dichotomy, like the dichotomy *a*/not-*a*, is conceived as exhausting all logical possibilities.

The Rousseauist Dream

The ideal of community... expresses an urge to unity, the unity of subjects with one another. The ideal of community expresses a longing for harmony among persons, for consensus and mutual understanding, for what Foucault calls the Rousseauist dream of

> a transparent society, visible and legible in each of its parts, the dream of there no longer existing any zones of darkness, zones established by the privileges of royal power or the prerogative of some corporation, zones of disorder. It was the dream that each individual, whatever position he occupied, might be able to see the whole of society, that men's hearts should communicate, their vision be unobstructed by obstacles, and that the opinion of all reign over each.   (Foucault, 1980, p. 152)

Whether expressed as shared subjectivity or common consciousness, on the one hand, or as relations of mutuality and reciprocity, the ideal of community denies, devalues, or represses the ontological difference of subjects, and seeks to dissolve social inexhaustibility into the comfort of a self-enclosed whole.

Sandel is explicit about defining community as shared subjectivity. The difference between his own constitutive meaning of community and the instrumental and sentimental meanings he finds in Rawls is precisely that in constitutive community subjects share a common self-understanding (Sandel, 1982, pp. 62–63, 173). He is also explicit about social transparency as the meaning and goal of community:

> And in so far as our constitutive self-understandings comprehend a wider subject than the individual alone, whether a family or tribe or city or class or nation or people, to this extent they define a community in the constitutive sense. And what marks such a community is not merely a spirit of benevolence, or the prevalence of communitarian values, or even certain "shared final ends" alone, but a common vocabulary of discourse and a background of implicit practices and understandings within which the opacity of the participants is reduced if never finally dissolved. In so far as justice depends for its pre-eminence on the separatedness or boundedness of persons in the cognitive sense, its priority would diminish as that opacity faded and this community deepened.
> (Sandel, 1982, pp. 172–73)

Barber also takes shared subjectivity as the meaning of community. Through political participation individuals confront one another and adjust their wants and desires, creating a "common ordering of individual needs and wants into a single vision of the future in which all can share." Strong democracy seeks to reach a "creative consensus" which through common talk and common work creates a "common consciousness and political judgment" (Barber, 1984, p. 224).

Some theorists of community, on the other hand, replace commonness in the meaning of community with mutuality and reciprocity, the recognition by each individual of the individuality of all the others (see Cornell, 1987). Seyla Benhabib, for example, regards a standpoint that emphasizes the commonness of persons as that of an ethic of rights and justice of the sort that Rawls represents, which she calls the standpoint of the "generalized other." Moral theory must also express a complementary point of view which Benhabib calls the standpoint of the "concrete other." Benhabib refers to this as a vision of a community of needs and solidarity, in contrast to the community of rights and entitlements envisaged by liberalism:

> The standpoint of the "concrete other," by contrast, requires us to view each and every rational being as an individual with a concrete history, identity, and affective-emotional constitution. In assuming this standpoint, we abstract from what constitutes our commonality and seek to understand the distinctiveness of the other. We seek to comprehend the needs of the other, their motivations, what they search for, and what they desire. Our relation to the other is governed by the norm of *complementary reciprocity*: each is entitled to expect and to assume from the other forms of behavior through which the other feels recognized and confirmed as a concrete, individual being with specific needs, talents, and capacities.... The moral categories that accompany such interactions are those of responsibility, bonding, and sharing. The corresponding moral feelings are those of love, care, sympathy, and solidarity, and the vision of community is one of needs and solidarity.   (Benhabib, 1986, p. 341)

Despite the apparent divergence of Sandel's and Barber's language of shared subjectivity and Benhabib's language of complementary reciprocity, I think all three express a similar ideal of social relations as the *copresence of subjects* (cf. Derrida, 1976, pp. 137–39). Whether expressed as common consciousness or as mutual understanding, the ideal is one of the transparency of subjects to one another. In this ideal each understands the others and recognizes the others in the same way that they understand themselves, and all recognize that the others understand them as they understand themselves. This ideal thus submits to what Derrida calls the metaphysics of presence, which seeks to collapse the temporal difference inherent in language and experience into a totality that can be comprehended in one view. This ideal of community denies the ontological difference within and between subjects.

In community persons cease to be other, opaque, not understood, and instead become mutually sympathetic, understanding one another as they understand themselves, fused. Such an ideal of the transparency of subjects to one another denies the difference, or basic asymmetry, of subjects. As Hegel first brought out and Sartre's analysis deepened, persons necessarily transcend one another because subjectivity is negativity. The regard of the other is always objectifying. Other persons never see the world from my perspective, and in witnessing the other's objective grasp of my body, actions, and words, I am always faced with an experience of myself different from the one I have.

This mutual intersubjective transcendence, of course, makes sharing between us possible, a fact that Sartre notices less than Hegel. The sharing, however, is never complete mutual understanding and reciprocity. Sharing, moreover, is fragile. At the next moment the other person may understand my words differently from the way I meant them, or carry my actions to consequences I do not intend. The same difference that makes sharing between us possible also makes misunderstanding, rejection, withdrawal, and conflict always possible conditions of social being.

Because the subject is not a unity, it cannot be present to itself, know itself. I do not always know what I mean, need, want, desire, because meanings, needs, and desires do not arise from an origin in some transparent ego. Often I express my desire in gesture or tone of voice, without meaning to do so. Consciousness, speech, expressiveness, are possible only if the subject always surpasses itself, and is thus necessarily unable to comprehend itself. Subjects all have multiple desires that do not cohere; they attach layers of meanings to objects without always being aware of each layer or the connections between them. Consequently, any individual subject is a play of difference that cannot be completely comprehended.

If the subject is heterogeneous process, never fully present to itself, then it follows that subjects cannot make themselves transparent, wholly present to one another. Consequently the subject also eludes sympathetic comprehension by others. I cannot understand others as they understand themselves, because they do not completely understand themselves. Indeed, because the meanings and desires they express may outrun their own awareness or intention, I may understand their words or actions more fully than they.

The ideal of community expresses a desire for social wholeness, symmetry, a security and solid identity which is objectified because affirmed by others unambiguously. This is an understandable dream, but a dream nevertheless, and, as I shall now argue, one with serious political consequences.

Privileging Face-to-Face Relations

The ideal of community as a pure copresence of subjects to one another receives political expression in a vision of political life that privileges local face-to-face direct democracy. Critics of welfare capitalist society repeatedly invoke such a model of small group relations as a political ideal. The anarchist tradition expresses these values most systematically, but they retain their form in other political soils as well. This model of politics as founded in face-to-face relations poses as the alternative to the impersonality, alienation, commodification, and bureaucratization of governance in existing mass societies:

> The incarnation of this project is the immediate, indeed unmediated, community that enters so profoundly into the fashioning of our humanity. This is the community in which we genuinely encounter each other, the public world that is only a bare step above our private world, in short, our towns, neighborhoods, and municipalities.
> (Bookchin, 1987, p. 267; cf. Manicas, 1974, pp. 246–50; Bay, 1981, chaps. 5 and 6)

Several problems arise when a community that privileges face-to-face relations is taken as the ideal of the polity. The ideal presumes a myth of unmediated social relations, and wrongly identifies mediation with alienation. It denies difference in the sense of temporal and spatial distancing. It implies a model of the good society as consisting of decentralized small units which is both unrealistic and politically undesirable, and which avoids the political question of just relations among such decentralized communities.

As the above quotation indicates, theorists of community privilege face-to-face relations because they conceive them as *immediate*. Immediacy is better than mediation because immediate relations have the purity and security longed for in the Rousseauist dream: we are transparent to one another, purely copresent in the same time and space, close enough to touch, and nothing comes between us to obstruct our vision of one another.

This ideal of the immediate copresence of subjects, however, is a metaphysical illusion. Even a face-to-face relation between two people is mediated by voice and gesture, spacing and temporality. As soon as a third person enters the interaction the possibility arises of the relation between the first two being mediated through the third, and so on. The mediation of relations among persons by the speech and actions of other persons is a fundamental condition of sociality. The richness, creativity, diversity, and potential of a society expand with growth in the scope and means of its media, linking persons across time and distance. The greater the time and distance, however, the greater the number of persons who stand between other persons.

I am not arguing that there is no difference between small groups in which persons relate to one another face-to-face and other social relations, nor am I denying a unique value to such face-to-face groups. Just as the intimacy of living with a few others in the same household has unique dimensions that are humanly valuable, so existing with others in communities of mutual regard has specific characteristics of warmth and sharing that are humanly valuable. There is no question either that bureaucratized capitalist patriarchal society discourages and destroys such communities of mutual friendship, just as it pressures and fragments families. A vision of the good society surely should include institutional arrangements that nurture the specific experience of mutual friendship which only relatively small groups interacting in a plurality of contexts can produce. But recognizing the value and specificity of such face-to-face relations is different from privileging them and positing them as a model for the institutional relations of a whole society.

In my view, a model of the good society as composed of decentralized, economically self-sufficient face-to-face communities functioning as autonomous political entities does not purify politics, as its proponents think, but rather avoids politics. First, it is wildly utopian. To bring it into being would require dismantling the urban character of modern society, a gargantuan overhaul of living space, workplaces, places of trade and commerce. A model of a transformed society must begin from the material structures that are given to us at this time in history, and in the United States those are large-scale industry and urban centers.

More important, however, this model of the good society as usually articulated leaves completely unaddressed the question of how such small communities relate to one another. Frequently the ideal projects a level of self-sufficiency and decentralization which suggests that proponents envision few relations among these communities except occasional friendly visits. Surely it is unrealistic, however, to assume that such decentralized communities need not engage in extensive relations of exchange of resources, goods, and culture.

Proponents frequently privilege face-to-face relations in reaction to the alienation and domination produced by huge, faceless bureaucracies and corporations, whose actions and decisions affect most people, but are out of their control. Appeals to community envision more local and direct control. A more participatory democratic society should indeed encourage active publics at the local levels of neighborhood and workplace. But the important political question is how relations among these locales can be organized so as to foster justice and minimize domination and oppression. Invoking a mystical ideal of community does not address this question, but rather obscures it. Politics must be conceived as a relationship of strangers who do not understand one another in a subjective and immediate sense, relating across time and distance.

Undesirable Political Consequences of the Ideal of Community

I have argued that the ideal of community denies the difference between subjects and the social differentiation of temporal and spatial distancing. The most serious political consequence of the desire for community, or for copresence and mutual identification with others, is that it often operates to exclude or oppress those experienced as different. Commitment to an ideal of community tends to value and enforce homogeneity (cf. Hirsch, 1986).

In ordinary speech in the United States, the term community refers to the people with whom one identifies in a specific locale. It refers to neighborhood, church, schools. It also carries connotations of ethnicity, race, and other group identifications. For most people, insofar as they consider themselves members of communities at all, a community is a group that shares a specific heritage, a common self-identification, a common culture and set of norms.... [S]elf-identification as a member of such a community also often occurs as an oppositional differentiation from other groups, who are feared, despised, or at best devalued. Persons feel a sense of mutual identification only with some persons, feel in community only with those, and fear the difference others confront them with because they identify with a different culture, history, and point of view on the world. The ideal of community, I suggest, validates and reinforces the fear and aversion some social groups exhibit toward others. If community is a positive norm, that is, if existing together with others in relations of mutual understanding and reciprocity is the goal, then it is understandable that we exclude and avoid those with whom we do not or cannot identify.

Richard Sennett (1970, chap. 2) discusses how a "myth of community" operates perpetually in American society to produce and implicitly legitimate racist and classist behavior and policy. In many towns, suburbs, and neighborhoods people do have an image of their locale as one in which people all know one another, have the same values and life style, and relate with feelings of mutuality and love. In modern American society such an image is almost always false; while there may be a dominant group with a distinct set of values and life style, within any locale one can usually find deviant individuals and groups. Yet the myth of community operates strongly to produce defensive exclusionary behavior: pressuring the Black family that buys a house on the block to leave, beating up the Black youths who come into "our" neighborhood, zoning against the construction of multiunit dwellings.

The exclusionary consequences of valuing community, moreover, are not restricted to bigots and conservatives. Many radical political organizations founder on the desire for community. Too often people in groups working for social change take mutual friendship to be a goal of the group, and thus judge themselves wanting as a group when they do not achieve such commonality (see Mansbridge, 1980, chap. 21; Breines, 1982, esp. chap. 4). Such a desire for community often channels energy away from the political goals of the group, and also produces a clique atmosphere which keeps groups small and turns potential members away. Mutual identification as an implicit group ideal can reproduce a homogeneity that usually conflicts with the organization's stated commitment to diversity. In recent years most socialist and feminist organizations, for example, have taken racial, class, age, and sexual diversity as an important criterion according to which the success of political organizations should be evaluated. To the degree that they take mutual understanding and identification as a goal, they may be deflected from this goal of diversity.

The exclusionary implications of a desire for face-to-face relations of mutual identification and sharing present a problem for movements asserting positive group difference.... [T]he effort of oppressed groups to reclaim their group identity, and to form with one another bonds of positive cultural affirmation around their group specificity, constitutes an important resistance to the oppression of cultural imperialism. It shifts the meaning of difference from otherness and exclusion to variation and specificity, and forces dominant groups to acknowledge their own group specificity. But does not such affirmation of group identity itself express an ideal of community, and is it not subject to exclusionary impulses?

Some social movements asserting positive group difference have found through painful confrontation that an urge to unity and mutual identification does indeed have exclusionary implications. Feminist efforts to create women's spaces and women's culture, for example, have often assumed the perspective of only a particular subgroup of women – white, or middle class, or lesbian, or straight – thus implicitly excluding or rendering invisible those women among them with differing identifications and experiences (Spelman, 1988). Similar problems arise for any movement of group identification, because in our society most people have multiple group identifications, and thus group differences cut across every social group.

These arguments against community are not arguments against the political project of constructing and affirming a positive group identity and relations of group solidarity, as a means of confronting cultural imperialism and discovering things about oneself and others with whom one feels affinity. Critique of the ideal of community, however, reveals that even in such group-specific contexts affinity cannot mean the transparency of selves to one another. If in their zeal to affirm a positive meaning of group specificity people seek or try to enforce a strong sense of mutual identification, they are likely to reproduce exclusions similar to those they confront. Those affirming the specificity of a group affinity should at the same time recognize and affirm the group and individual differences within the group.

City Life as a Normative Ideal

Appeals to community are usually antiurban. Much sociological literature diagnoses modern history as a movement to the dangerous bureaucratized *Gesellschaft* from the manageable and safe *Gemeinschaft*, nostalgically reconstructed as a world of lost origins (Stein, 1960; Nisbet, 1953). Many others follow Rousseau in romanticizing the ancient *polis* and the medieval Swiss *Bürger*, deploring the commerce, disorder, and unmanageable mass character of the modern city (Ellison, 1985; cf. Sennett, 1974, chaps. 7–10). Throughout the modern period, the city has often been decried as embodying immorality, artificiality, disorder, and danger – as the site of treasonous conspiracies, illicit sex, crime, deviance, and disease (Mosse, 1985, pp. 32–33, 137–38; Gilman, 1985, p. 214). The typical image of the modern city finds it expressing all the disvalues that a reinstantiation of community would eliminate.

Yet urbanity is the horizon of the modern, not to mention the postmodern, condition. Contemporary political theory must accept urbanity as a material given for those who live in advanced industrial societies. Urban relations define the lives not only of thos who live in the huge metropolises, but also of those who live in suburbs and large towns. Our social life is structured by vast networks of temporal and spatial mediation among persons, so that nearly everyone depends on the activities of seen and unseen strangers who mediate between oneself and one's associates, between oneself and one's objects of desire. Urbanites find themselves relating geographically to increasingly large regions, thinking little of traveling seventy miles to work or an hour's drive for an evening's entertainment. Most people frequently and casually encounter strangers in their daily activities. The material surroundings and structures available to us define and presuppose urban relationships. The very size of populations in our society and most other nations of the world, coupled with a continuing sense of national or ethnic identity with millions of other people, supports the conclusion that a vision of dismantling the city is hopelessly utopian.

Starting from the given of modern urban life is not simply necessary, moreover; it is desirable. Even for many of those who decry the alienation, bureaucratization, and mass character of capitalist patriarchal society, city life exerts a powerful attraction. Modern literature, art, and film have celebrated city life, its energy, cultural diversity, technological complexity, and the multiplicity of its activities. Even many of the most staunch proponents of decentralized community love to show visiting friends around the Boston or San Francisco or New York in or near which they live, climbing up towers to see the glitter of lights and sampling the fare at the best ethnic restaurants.

I propose to construct a normative ideal of city life as an alternative to both the ideal of community and the liberal individualism it criticizes as asocial. By "city life" I mean a form of social relations which I define as the being together of strangers. In the city persons and groups interact within spaces and institutions they all experience themselves as belonging to, but without those interactions dissolving into unity or commonness. City life is composed of clusters of people with affinities – families, social group networks, voluntary associations, neighborhood networks, a vast array of small "communities." City dwellers frequently venture beyond such familiar enclaves, however, to the more open public of politics, commerce, and festival, where strangers meet and interact (cf. Lofland, 1973). City dwelling situates one's own identity and activity in relation to a horizon of a vast variety of other activity, and the awareness that this unknown, unfamiliar activity affects the conditions of one's own.

City life is a vast, even infinite, economic network of production, distribution, transportation, exchange, communication, service provision, and amusement. City dwellers depend on the mediation of thousands of other people and vast organizational resources in order to accomplish their individual ends. City dwellers are thus together, bound to one another, in what should be and sometimes is a single polity. Their being together entails some common problems and common interests, but they do not create a community of shared final ends, of mutual identification and reciprocity.

A normative ideal of city life must begin with our given experience of cities, and look there for the virtues of this form of social relations. Defining an ideal as unrealized possibilities of the actual, I extrapolate from that experience four such virtues.

(1) *Social differentiation without exclusion.* City life in urban mass society is not inconsistent with supportive social networks and subcultural communities. Indeed, for many it is their necessary condition. In the city social group differences flourish. Modernization theory predicted a decline in local, ethnic, and other group affiliations as universalist state institutions touch people's lives more directly and as people encounter many others with identifications and life styles different from their own. There is considerable evidence, however, that group differences are often reinforced by city life, and that the city even encourages the formation of new social group affinities (Fischer, 1982, pp. 206–30; Rothschild, 1981). Deviant or minority groups find in the city both a cover of anonymity and a critical mass unavailable in the smaller town. It is hard to imagine the formation of gay or lesbian group affinities, for example, without the conditions of the modern city (D'Emilio, 1983). While city dwelling as opposed to rural life has changed the lives and self-concepts of Chicanos, to take another example, city life encourages group identification and a desire for cultural nationalism at the same time that it may dissolve some traditional practices or promote assimilation to Anglo language and values (Jankowski, 1986). In actual cities many people express violent aversions to members of groups with which they do not identify. More than those who live in small towns, however, they tend to recognize social group difference as a given, something they must live with (Fischer, 1982, pp. 206–40).

In the ideal of city life freedom leads to group differentiation, to the formation of affinity groups, but this social and spatial differentiation of groups is without exclusion. The urban ideal expresses difference . . . a side-by-side particularity neither reducible to identity nor completely other. In this ideal groups do not stand in relations of inclusion and exclusion, but overlap and intermingle without becoming homogeneous. Though city life as we now experience it has many borders and exclusions, even our actual experience of the city also gives hints of what differentiation without exclusion can be. Many city neighborhoods have a distinct ethnic identity, but members of other groups also dwell in them. In the good city one crosses from one distinct neighborhood to another without knowing precisely where one ended and the other began. In the normative ideal of city life, borders are open and undecidable.

(2) *Variety.* The interfusion of groups in the city occurs partly because of the multiuse differentiation of social space. What makes urban spaces interesting, draws people out in public to them, gives people pleasure and excitement, is the diversity of activities they support. When stores, restaurants, bars, clubs, parks, and offices are sprinkled among residences, people have a neighborly feeling about their neighbor-

hood, they go out and encounter one another on the streets and chat. They have a sense of their neighborhood as a "spot" or "place," because of that bar's distinctive clientele, or the citywide reputation of the pizza at that restaurant. Both business people and residents tend to have more commitment to and care for such neighborhoods than they do for single-use neighborhoods. Multifunctional streets, parks, and neighborhoods are also much safer than single-use functionalized spaces because people are out on the streets during most hours, and have commitment to the place (Jacobs, 1961, chap. 8; Sennett, 1970, chap. 4; cf. Whyte, 1988, chaps. 9, 22–25).

(3) *Eroticism*. City life also instantiates difference as the erotic, in the wide sense of an attraction to the other, the pleasure and excitement of being drawn out of one's secure routine to encounter the novel, strange, and surprising (cf. Barthes, 1986). The erotic dimension of the city has always been an aspect of its fearfulness, for it holds out the possibility that one will lose one's identity. But we also take pleasure in being open to and interested in people we experience as different. We spend a Sunday afternoon walking through Chinatown, or checking out this week's eccentric players in the park. We look for restaurants, stores, and clubs with something new for us, a new ethnic food, a different atmosphere, a different crowd of people. We walk through sections of the city that we experience as having unique characters which are not ours, where people from diverse places mingle and then go home.

The erotic attraction here is precisely the obverse of community. In the ideal of community people feel affirmed because those with whom they share experiences, perceptions, and goals recognize and are recognized by them; one sees oneself reflected in the others. There is another kind of pleasure, however, in coming to encounter a subjectivity, a set of meanings, that is different, unfamiliar. One takes pleasure in being drawn out of oneself to understand that there are other meanings, practices, perspectives on the city, and that one could learn or experience something more and different by interacting with them.

The city's eroticism also derives from the aesthetics of its material being: the bright and colored lights, the grandeur of its buildings, the juxtaposition of architecture of different times, styles, and purposes. City space offers delights and surprises. Walk around the corner, or over a few blocks, and you encounter a different spatial mood, a new play of sight and sound, and new interactive movement. The erotic meaning of the city arises from its social and spatial inexhaustibility. A place of many places, the city folds over on itself in so many layers and relationships that it is incomprehensible. One cannot "take it in," one never feels as though there is nothing new and interesting to explore, no new and interesting people to meet.

(4) *Publicity*. Political theorists who extol the value of community often construe the public as a realm of unity and mutual understanding, but this does not cohere with our actual experience of public spaces. Because by definition a public space is a place accessible to anyone, where anyone can participate and witness, in entering the public one always risks encounter with those who are different, those who identify with different groups and have different opinions or different forms of life. The group diversity of the city is most often apparent in public spaces. This helps account for their vitality and excitement. Cities provide important public spaces – streets, parks, and plazas – where people stand and sit together, interact and mingle, or

simply witness one another, without becoming unified in a community of "shared final ends."

Politics, the critical activity of raising issues and deciding how institutional and social relations should be organized, crucially depends on the existence of spaces and forums to which everyone has access. In such public spaces people encounter other people, meanings, expressions, issues, which they may not understand or with which they do not identify. The force of public demonstrations, for example, often consists in bringing to people who pass through public spaces those issues, demands, and people they might otherwise avoid. As a normative ideal city life provides public places and forums where anyone can speak and anyone can listen.

Because city life is a being together of strangers, diverse and overlapping neighbors, social justice cannot issue from the institution of an Enlightenment universal public. On the contrary, social justice in the city requires the realization of a politics of difference. This politics lays down institutional and ideological means for recognizing and affirming diverse social groups by giving political representation to these groups, and celebrating their distinctive characteristics and cultures. In the unoppressive city people open to unassimilated otherness. We all have our familiar relations and affinities, the people to whom we feel close and with whom we share daily life. These familial and social groups open onto a public in which all participate, and that public must be open and accessible to all. Contrary to the communitarian tradition, however, that public cannot be conceived as a unity transcending group differences, nor as entailing complete mutual understanding. In public life the differences remain unassimilated, but each participating group acknowledges and is open to listening to the others. The public is heterogeneous, plural, and playful, a place where people witness and appreciate diverse cultural expressions that they do not share and do not fully understand.

Cities and Social Injustice

An ideal can inspire action for social change only if it arises from possibilities suggested by actual experience. The ideals of city life I have proposed are realized incidentally and intermittently in some cities today. There is no doubt, however, that many large cities in the United States today are sites of decay, poverty, and crime. There is just as little doubt that the smaller towns and suburbs to which many people escape from these ills are strung along congested highways, are homogeneous, segregated, and privatized. In either case, an ideal of city life as eroticized public vitality where differences are affirmed in openness might seem laughably utopian. For on city streets today the depth of social injustice is apparent: homeless people lying in doorways, rape in parks, and cold-blooded racist murder are the realities of city life.

... [A] critical theory of social justice must consider not only distributive patterns, but also the processes and relationships that produce and reproduce those patterns. While issues of the distribution of goods and resources are central to reflections on social justice, issues of decision-making power and processes, the division of labor, and culture are just as important. Nowhere is this argument better illustrated than in the context of social injustice in the city. Inequalities of distribution can be read on the face of buildings, neighborhoods, and towns. Most cities have too many places where everyone would agree no one should have to live. These may be a stone's throw from opulent corporate headquarters or luxury condominiums. The correct principles and methods of distribution may be a subject of controversy, but as they wander through American city streets few would deny that something is wrong with existing distributions.

The social structures, processes, and relationships that produce and reproduce these distributions, however, are not visible on the surface of our cities. Yet normative theory must identify and evaluate them as well as their outcomes. In this section I shall discuss three aspects of these processes that contribute to domination and oppression: (a) centralized corporate and bureaucratic domination of cities; (b) decision-making structures in municipalities and their hidden mechanisms of redistribution; and (c) processes of segregation and exclusion, both within cities and between cities and suburbs.

(a) Corporate and city power once coincided. Firms started in a city and exploited the labor of the city's population, and the city grew and prospered with the success of its major firms. Industrial magnates ruled the cities, either directly as city officials, or more indirectly as behind-the-scenes framers of city policy. Having a self-serving paternal attitude toward these cities, the ruling families engaged in philanthropic projects, building museums, libraries, parks, plazas, and statues as gifts to the public and monuments to their wealth and entrepreneurial ingenuity. The captains of industry often ruled ruthlessly, keeping the majority of people in squalor and ignorance, but they had a sense of place, were tied economically, socially, and politically to one or a few cities.

Today corporate capital is homeless. The enterprises that rule the world economy are larger than many cities, some larger than many nations, with branches dotting the globe, and no center. Mergers, interlocking directorships, holding companies, and the dispersion of ownership through securities and stock market speculation mean that political and economic power is dislodged from place. Fast as a satellite signal, capital travels from one end of a continent to the other, from one end of the world to the other. Its direction depends on the pull of profit, and its directors rarely consider how its movement may affect local economies.

Municipalities are dependent on this flighty capital for the health of their economic infrastructure. They must sell bonds on the open market to raise funds for public works. Because there are no national or state policies for encouraging investment in particular cities or regions that need resources and industry for their economic health, cities must compete with one another to provide an attractive "investment climate" (cf. Elkin, 1987, pp. 30–31). They depend on private capital for housing, office, and commercial space, production facilities, public works, and with all this, of course, jobs. Their public funds depend on taxing the private investors doing business within their borders. Where cities once at least could hold the carrot of lordly power and prestige before corporate decision-makers, today cities are reduced to lowly suppliants, with little leverage for bargaining.

Cities are also relatively powerless before the state. Gerald Frug (1980) relates how American liberalism has always been hostile to a distinct and independent legal status for cities, and how gradually the law has removed most of the powers cities once had. Cities today have only those powers delegated to them by state governments, and these are usually rigorously limited by judicial interpretation. What decision-making authority cities have is restricted to matters deemed entirely local, and these are increasingly few. State laws not only regulate the kind and amount of taxes cities can levy, they also restrict the powers of cities to borrow money. Cities are limited in the kind of laws they can pass, which are generally restricted to "welfare improving regulatory services" (cf. Elkin, 1987, pp. 21–31).

Not only are city legal powers restricted and regulated by the state, but cities have become increasingly dependent on state and federal government for operating funds to provide their services, and increasingly come under the authority of state and federal government in the administration of services. Health, housing, and welfare services administered at the city level are usually regulated by state and federal bureaucracies, and cities depend on state and federal grants for their continued operation. Many local services, "such as education, transportation and health care, are provided not by cities but by special districts or public authorities organized to cut across city boundaries and over which cities have no control" (Frug, 1980, p. 1065). The "new federalism" of the past decade has not significantly altered the city's financial dependence on larger bureaucratic entities. It has somewhat increased cities' administrative responsibilities, often while reducing the resources with which they can administer.

The domination of centralized bureaucracies, whether public or private, over municipal economies tends to dissociate lived or experienced space from the commodified space of abstract planning and calculation (Gottdiener, 1985, pp. 290–97; Castells, 1983, chap. 31). Capitalist bureaucratic rationality fosters bird's-eye planning which encompasses vast regions including huge metropolitan areas, or even several states together. From this skytop vision, investors and planning bureaucrats determine the placement and design of highways, factories, shopping facilities, offices, and parks. They decide the most rational and efficient investment from the point of view of their portfolio and their centralized office operations, but not necessarily from the point of view of the locales in which they invest. Too often this bureaucratic rationality and efficiency results in a deadening separation of functions, with oppressive consequences that I will discuss shortly. It also often results in abrupt disinvestment in one region and massive disruptive speculation in another, each with significant consequences for the welfare of people in those locales.

The realization of the designers' plans creates an abstract space of efficiency and Cartesian rationality that often comes to dominate and displace the lived space of human movement and interaction:

> What tends to disappear is the meaning of places for people. Each place, each city, will receive its social meaning from its location in the hierarchy of a network whose control and rhythm will escape from each place and, even more, from the people in each place. Furthermore, people will be shifted according to the continuous restructuring of an increasingly specialized space.... The new space of a world capitalist system, combining the informational and the industrial modes of development, is a space of variable geometry, formed by locations hierarchically ordered in a continuously changing network of flows: flows of capital, labor, elements of production, commodities, infor-

mation, decisions, and signals. The new urban meaning of the dominant class is the absence of any meaning based on experience. The abstraction of production tends to become total. The new source of power relies on the control of the entire network of information. Space is dissolved into flows: cities become shadows that explode and disappear according to decisions that their dwellers will always ignore. The outer experience is cut off from the inner experience. The new tendential urban meaning is the spatial and cultural separation of people from their production and from their history.   (Castells, 1983, p. 314)

(b) Though city and town governments are seriously constrained by the domination of state and corporate imperatives, they nevertheless do make decisions, especially about land use and zoning. Decision-making structures and processes at the local level, however, often tend to create and exacerbate injustice.

... [P]olicy formation in welfare capitalist society tends to be depoliticized and operates through a relatively closed club of interest-group bargainers. Such depoliticization is perhaps even more typical at the municipal level than at state or national levels. Stephen Elkin argues that in most cities land use decisions, the local decisions that most affect the spatial environment of the city and its economic life, are a semiprivate process involving a triangle of capitalist developers, city bureaucrats, and elected city officials. The assumptions and interests of these groups set the basic parameters for such decisions, which are routine, usually unquestioned and rarely publicly discussed. This routine framework, Elkin argues, is usually biased toward growth and downtown development, emphasizing big, flashy, visible projects. The empirical record shows, however, that land use decision-making biased in these ways contributes to increasing inequalities (see Elkin, 1987, chap. 5; cf. Logan and Molotch, 1987, chaps. 3 and 4).

With the basic resources and institutional structure already given, interest groups in the city vie for and bargain over the distributive effects of city projects. Because some interests are better able to organize than others, have easier access to the major decision-makers and their information, and so on, this political process usually either reproduces initial distributions or increases inequalities (Harvey, 1973, pp. 73–79; Elkin, 1987, pp. 93–102).

The framework of privatized land use decision-making according to unquestioned routines, coupled with interest-group bargaining over the consequences of applying the framework, illustrates one of several "hidden mechanisms" that David Harvey (1973, esp. chap. 3) argues produce and reproduce social inequalities and oppression in cities. Policies to improve the lives and opportunities of the poor, the marginalized, or those otherwise disadvantaged will have little effect unless these hidden mechanisms are understood and restructured. Two other such mechanisms that Harvey cites are location and adaptability.

The location of land use projects often has serious redistributional impact on residents of a city. Some, usually the poor and unorganized, are displaced by projects. The location of production facilities, public services, transportation facilities, housing, and shopping areas affects different sectors of the population differently. Proximity to one facility may benefit some, by giving them easier or less costly access to a good or activity. Proximity to another kind of facility, on the other hand, may disadvantage some by imposing inconveniences such as dirt, noise, or environmental danger. Although a person's own material situation may remain constant, his or her life opportunities may nevertheless change significantly because of surrounding changes (Harvey, 1973, pp. 56–63). The losses caused by urban changes may involve not only monetary burdens, inconvenience, and loss of access to resources and services, but also the loss of the very environment that helps define a person's sense of self or a group's space and culture (Elkin, 1987, p. 90).

Another hidden mechanism of redistribution, according to Harvey, is the different adaptability of groups: some groups are better able than others to adjust to change in the urban environment. Thus one group's adjustment often lags behind another's, usually increasing inequality between them. Sometimes the disparity is caused by differences in initial levels of material resources. Just as often, however, the differences in ability to adjust have their sources in culture or life style (Harvey, 1973, pp. 62–64). Poverty, exploitation, marginalization, and cultural imperialism often determine that those less able to adapt to urban changes are more often required to do so (Elkin, 1987, p. 86).

(c) I have already noted how bureaucratic rationality imposes an abstract space of order and function over the lived space of multiuse interaction. The twentieth century has seen a steady increase in the functionalization and segregation of urban space. The earliest separation was the creation of residential districts spatially separated from manufacturing, retail, entertainment, commerce, and government. Recent decades, however, have seen a rapid increase in the spatial segregation of each of these other functions from one another. Each sort of activity occurs in its own walled enclaves, distinctly cut off from the others.

The separation of functions in urban space reduces the vitality of cities, making city life more boring, meaningless, and dangerous. Downtown districts bustling with people in the day hours become eerily deserted at night, when people swarm to the indoor shopping mall, which, despite the best efforts of designers, is boring and frenetic. Residential neighborhoods find few people on the streets either day or night, because there is nowhere to go and not much to look at without appearing to encroach on the privacy of others.

This separation of functions augments oppression and domination in several ways. The territorial separation of workplaces from residential communities divides the interest of working people between the shop floor, on the one hand, and consumer and neighborhood concerns, on the other. While corporate and state bureaucrats construct their bird's-eye view of cities and regions, citizens are unable to engage in significant collective action on the same scale, because the separation of home and work prevents them from constructing a larger pattern.

Territorial separation of residences from shopping centers, manufacturing, public plazas, and so on has specific damaging consequences for the lives of women, especially mothers. A full-time homemaker and mother who lives in a central city apartment within walking distance of stores, restaurants, offices, parks, and social services has a life very different from that of the woman who spends her day in a suburban house surrounded for miles by only houses and schools. The separation of urban functions forces homemaking women into isolation and boredom. It also makes their work – shopping, occupying children, taking them to activities, going to doctors, dentists, insurance agents, and so on – more difficult and time consuming. To the degree that they retain primary responsibility for children and other dependent family members, working women too suffer from the spatial separation of urban functions, which often limits their work opportunities to the few usually low-paying clerical and service jobs close to residential locations, or else forces them to traverse large spans of city space each day in a triangle or square, from home to child care to work to grocery store to child care to home (Hayden, 1983, pp. 49–59). The separation of functions and the consequent need for transportation to get to jobs and services also contributes directly to the increased marginality of old people, poor people, disabled people, and others who because of life situation as well as limited access to resources are less able to move independently in wide areas.

One aspect of the normative ideal of city life, I have said, is a social differentiation without exclusion. Groups will differentiate by affinities, but the borders will be undecidable, and there will be much overlap and intermingling. One of the most disturbing aspects of contemporary urban life is the depth and frequency of aversive behavior which occurs within it. Group segregation is produced by aversive perceptions that deprecate some groups, defining them as entirely other, to be shunned and avoided. Banks, real estate firms, city officials, newspapers, and residents all promote an image of neighborhoods as places where only certain kinds of people belong and others do not, deeply reinforcing aversive racism and the mechanism by which some groups are constructed as the depised Others. Zoning regulation enforces class segregation, and to a large degree racial segregation as well, by, for example, excluding multifamily dwellings from prosperous neighborhoods and even from entire municipalities. These group exclusions produce the conditions for harrassment of or violence against any persons found where they do not "belong." The myth of neighborhood community, of common values and life style, I have argued, fuels such exclusions.

The separation perhaps most far reaching in its effect on social justice is the legal separation of municipalities themselves. While social and economic processes have nearly obliterated any distinction between urban and rural life, and corporate and bureaucratic planning encompasses huge metropolitan regions, these same regions include scores of legally distinct municipalities, with their own local governments, ordinances, and public services. To avoid the ugliness, complexity, and dangers of contemporary city life, and often to avoid having to interact with certain kinds of people, many people seek community in the suburbs and small towns outside the city. The town's smallness and the fact that it is legally autonomous to make its own ordinances within the limits of state and federal regulation produce the illusion of local control. In fact the separation of towns renders them powerless against corporate and bureaucratic domination.

The legal and social separation of city and suburbs, moreover, contributes to social injustice. A direct relation of exploitation exists between most large American cities and their suburbs. Residents of the suburbs work in the city, use the city's services, and enjoy its life but, except in those rare cases where there is a city income or sales tax, pay no taxes to the city. Suburban municipalities usually benefit from their proximity to the city, but their legal autonomy ensures that they pay little or nothing for these benefits (Lowi, 1969, p. 197; Harvey, 1973, p. 94).

By means of their legal autonomy, some municipalities exclude certain kinds of people and certain kinds of activities from their borders. Because local governments generate funds to pay for local services by taxing residents, some towns and cities have far better schools and services than others. Because each municipality runs its own schools, police, fire department, and other public services, there is often an unjust and inefficient imbalance in the density and quality of services among different areas.

In the context of a large-scale and interdependent economic system under the control of private capital, "autonomy becomes a lead weight for the majority of cities, with only the most affluent towns able to create privilege from their formal independence. The political autonomy of places, as well as the planning power this entails, reproduces and exaggerates the inequalities between places rather than leveling them" (Logan and Molotch, 1987, p. 152).

These injustices have their primary source in the structural organization of decision-making. While all of the problems of city life I have discussed in this section involve distributive issues, the full extent of oppression and domination they involve can be understood only by considering culture and decision-making structures as they affect city geography, activities, and distributions.

REFERENCES

Ackelsberg, Martha. 1988. "Communities, Resistance and Women's Activism." In Ann Bookman and Sandra Morgen, eds., *Women and the Politics of Empowerment*. Philadelphia: Temple University Press.

Barber, Benjamin. 1984. *Strong Democracy*. Berkeley and Los Angeles: University of California Press.

Barthes, Roland. 1986. "Semiology and the urban." In M. Gottdiener and Alexandros P. Lagopoulos, eds., *The City and the Sign: An Introduction to Urban Semiotics*. New York: Columbia University Press.

Bay, Christian. 1981. *Strategies for Political Emancipation*. South Bend, Ind.: University of Notre Dame Press.

Benhabib, Seyla. 1986. *Critique, Norm and Utopia*. New York: Columbia University Press.

Bookchin, Murray. 1987. *The Rise of Urbanization and the Decline of Citizenship*. San Francisco: Sierra Club Books.

Boyte, Harry and Sara M. Evans. 1984. "Strategies in Search of America: Cultural Radicalism, Populism, and Democratic Culture." *Socialist Review*, May–August, pp. 73–100.

Breines, Wini. 1982. *Community and Organization in the New Left: 1962–68*. South Hadley, Mass.: Bergin.

Buchanan, Allen. 1989. "Assessing the Communitarian Critique of Liberalism." *Ethics* 99 (July): 852–82.

Castells, Manuel. 1983. *The City and the Grass Roots*. Berkeley and Los Angeles: University of California Press.

Cornell, Crucilla. 1987. "Two Lectures on the Normative Dimensions of Community in the Law." *Tennessee Law Review* 54 (Winter): 327–43.

D'Emilio, Joseph. 1983. *Sexual Politics, Sexual Communities*. Chicago: University of Chicago Press.

Derrida, Jacques. 1976. *Of Grammatology*. Baltimore: Johns Hopkins University Press.

Elkin, Stephen L. 1987. *City and Regime in the American Republic*. Chicago: University of Chicago Press.

Ellison, Charles. 1985. "Rousseau and the Modern City: The Politics of Speech and Dress." *Political Theory* 13 (November): 497–534.

Fischer, Claude. 1982. *To Dwell among Friends: Personal Networks in Town and City*. Chicago: University of Chicago Press.

Foucault, Michel. 1980. *Power/Knowledge*. New York: Pantheon.

Frug, Gerald. 1980. "The City as a Legal Concept." *Harvard Law Review* 93 (April): 1059–1154.

Gilman, Sander L. 1985. *Difference and Pathology: Stereotypes of Sexuality, Race and Madness*. Ithaca, N.Y.: Cornell University Press.

Gottdiener, Mark. 1985. *The Social Production of Urban Space*. Austin: University of Texas Press.

Gutmann, Amy. 1985. "Communitarian Critics of Liberalism." *Philosophy and Public Affairs* 14 (Summer): 308–22.

Harvey, David. 1973. *Social Justice and the City*. Baltimore: Johns Hopkins University Press.

Hayden, Delores. 1983. *Redesigning the American Dream*. New York: Norton.

Hirsch, H. N. 1986. "The Threnody of Liberalism: Constitutional Liberty and the Renewal of Community." *Political Theory* 14 (August): 423–49.

Jacobs, Jane. 1961. *The Death and Life of Great American Cities*. New York: Random House.

Jankowski, Martin Sanchez. 1986. *City Bound: Urban Life and Political Attitudes among Chicano Youth*. Albuquerque: University of New Mexico Press.

Lofland, Lynn H. 1973. *A World of Strangers: Order and Action in Urban Public Space*. New York: Basic Books.

Logan, John R. and Harvey L. Molotch. 1987. *Urban Fortunes: The Political Economy of Place*. Berkeley and Los Angeles: University of California Press.

Lowi, Theodore. 1969. *The End of Liberalism*. New York: Norton.

Manicas, Peter. 1974. *The Death of the State*. New York: Putnam.

Mansbridge, Jane. 1980. *Beyond Adversarial Democracy*. New York: Basic Books.

Marcuse, Herbert. 1964. *One-Dimensional Man*. Boston: Beacon.

Mosse, George. 1985. *Nationalism and Sexuality*. New York: Fertig.

Nisbet, Robert A. 1953. *The Quest for Community*. New York: Oxford University Press.

Rothschild, Joseph. 1981. *Ethnopolitics*. New York: Columbia University Press.

Sandel, Michael. 1982. *Liberalism and the Limits of Justice*. Cambridge: Cambridge University Press.

Sennett, Richard. 1970. *The Uses of Disorder*. New York: Knopf.

—— 1974. *The Fall of Public Man*. New York: Random House.

Spelman, Elizabeth V. 1988. *The Inessential Woman*. Boston: Beacon.

Stein, Maurice. 1960. *The Eclipse of Community*. Princeton: Princeton University Press.

Whyte, William. 1988. *City: Rediscovering the Center*. New York: Doubleday.

Wolff, Robert Paul. 1968. *The Poverty of Liberalism*. Boston: Beacon.

19

Educating Planners: Unified Diversity for Social Action

June Manning Thomas

One of the biggest tasks facing planning educators in the coming years is to develop learning environments that meet the challenge of diversity. Educators will need to bring fuller treatment of gender, race, and national origin into the training of planning professionals. They will have to become more adept at educating students who represent different backgrounds, become more responsive to the increasing diversity of the profession, and gain greater knowledge about the implications of race- and gender-related concerns for professional practice.

While some programs have focused upon recruitment and retention, diversity implies changing curriculum and course content, as well as understanding the variation in learning and teaching styles which diversity brings. Planning academia has followed a disjointed road toward incorporating diversity by race and gender. Part of the problem may be lack of a vision of a desired outcome. This chapter suggests such a vision: planning education characterized by unified diversity. The task is to reconstruct (rather than deconstruct) planning education so that it fosters the education of all students, more equitably reflects social realities and opportunities for social action, yet retains a sense of unity amidst difference. The need is for a model of diversity that reaches beyond disjointed pluralism and connects diversity with effective social action.

The need for such a paradigm is threefold:

to prepare students to function in multicultural work environments;

to develop more effective models of diversity in planning schools, eliminating existing points of ineffectiveness, disjointedness, or contradiction; and

to develop more effective ways of teaching planning students how to promote social action and reform of inequities.

Reprinted with permission from the *Journal of Planning Education and Research*, 15 (1996): 171–182. © 1996 Associated of Collegiate Schools of Planning.

These tasks may seem, at first glance, hopelessly complex. For some time, planning has experienced a grueling process of definition and redefinition. In 1974, Perloff noted that the prevailing "tensions" of planning education centered on recurring themes: whether to promote generalist or specialist skills; the movement to technical versus humanistic skills; the split between product (professional) and process (administrative) skills; and the two paths of professional versus scholarly approaches, among others (Perloff and Klett 1974). Time has only added to the length of the list.

Why add another layer of concern? Because it is necessary. The work force is changing dramatically. Societal inequities stemming from problems of discrimination and injustice linger. Multiculturalism – defined here to include race, ethnicity, gender, and nationality[1] – has affected the nature and quality of planning education, but with little clarity about how to handle it all. Embracing a stronger vision for diversity may in fact reduce current tensions and create a new focus for fragmented, conflicting efforts. This paper reflects upon the challenges, focusing in particular on issues concerning race and gender.

Planning Diversifies?

Planning scholars, as well as anyone else, recognize that a new era of pluralism or multiculturalism has dawned.[2] This is part of the postmodernism that now characterizes society. The postmodernist mode of thought questions conventional beliefs, distrusts universal truths, abandons dualistic beliefs, and encourages plurality and difference (Milroy 1991). Postmodernism has a down side, however: although it "gives voice to the disenfranchised," it can also undermine planning's reliance upon traditional social science techniques without specifying adequate replacements, or empower too many voices, providing little basis upon which to choose priorities (Feldman 1994, 98).

Even so, planning educators recognize that diversity is here to stay. When Friedmann and Kuester (1994) recently asked 32 educators what were the greatest national and local challenges facing planning education in North America, one of the top choices was racial, ethnic, and gender conflict within metropolitan areas. Respondents indicated that a key skill for planning education was the ability to plan for multicultural diversity within society.

The process of reaching diversity has been uneven and difficult, however. The profession is receiving more women, but academic programs are just beginning to acknowledge the contributions of women to the urban environment or the practical implications of gender for planning practice. Racial minority representation within the profession, faculty, and student body has stagnated, and little cohesion informs the treatment of race within the planning curriculum. International students face challenges as they strive to receive an appropriate education.

University planning programs often contain a large number of international students (Chatterjee 1990). The resulting challenges have generated a wealth of empirical studies, papers, and dialogue. Only a few key points will be mentioned here. First, agreement has not been reached about the extent of "the problem" or the means of resolving it (Sanyal and Jammal 1992). Although this issue arose because of concerns about how useful U.S. planning education is for international students

(Banerjee 1985; Heumann 1991; Niebanck 1988a, b), some empirical studies have suggested that a U.S. education is not a handicap, particularly in technical fields (Kihl 1990; Hinojosa et al. 1992). Some advocate a universal approach to planning education, but others argue that only dualism will work, since the specifics of operating within Third World countries will always require something other than "globalism" (Burayidi 1993; Sanyal 1990, p. 8).

Internationalists have raised valuable questions about the monocultural bias of U.S. planning education, however. They have called attention to the impact of differences in language or varying attitudes toward critical thinking (Dunlap 1990; Heumann 1991). And they have questioned the tendency to compel students to learn planning "the Western way," as if all knowledge stemmed from one country and one culture. Sanyal (1989) has called instead for mutual learning, whereby all students come to understand global linkages and common concerns.

The dialogue concerning diversity issues related to planning education for women and racial minorities is growing but, by comparison, less well developed. Yet these are the issues that most affect U.S. students, the base for U.S. planning programs.

Although growth in the number of women planners is strong, some bothersome issues linger. In 1968, 7.5% of U.S. planning program graduates were women; by 1978, that proportion had increased to 31% (Leavitt 1983); and by 1994, 45.4% of planning masters students were female (Contant et al. 1994, p. xv). In North American planning schools, women make up 41% of graduate programs and 32% of undergraduate programs (Mars and Springer 1993). Female membership of the American Planning Association rose from 18.2% in 1981 to 27.7% in 1991 (Getzel and Longhini 1982; Morris 1992). Nevertheless, upper ranks in the profession are largely male, since on the average women have fewer years of experience (Morris 1992). Faculty ranks are thin. In 1989, only 12% of directors and tenured faculty were women (Dalton 1993). In 1994, male planning faculty outnumbered female faculty five-to-one (Contant et al. 1994, p. xiv).

Graduates from planning programs – both male and female – may gain little information about the contributions of women to the profession. They may poorly understand the relationship between gender and poverty or between zoning ordinances and lack of social support for women and families (Sandercock and Forsyth 1992; Netter and Price 1983).

The record on race and ethnicity is even more discouraging. The percentage of African-Americans belonging to the American Planning Association has lingered under 3%, and other racial minorities do not fare much better. In North American planning schools, African-Americans make up 12.6% of master's students, but only 6.4% of doctoral students. Native Americans and Latinos are even fewer (Mars and Springer 1993). The number of African-American faculty has stagnated. From 1968 to 1976, 14 received full-time appointments; from 1977 to 1982, only five did (Ross 1990), and not many more have been added since.[3] During his travels to 12 prominent planning programs, Niebanck (1988b, 441) noted large numbers of women students, but "among neither student bodies nor faculties, are Blacks, Asians, Hispanics or Native Americans adequately represented, by any standard of fairness. . . . The situation is reprehensible, and it should embarrass us."

Just as embarrassing should be the disjointed way the planning literature and curriculum have dealt with matters of race (Catlin 1993a). Potential minority planning students may weather survey or introductory planning courses that give them precious little reason to become interested in planning. Planning history may give the impression that Blacks have had no role in improving cities – or a role only as victims (Thomas 1994) – and may mention other minorities not at all. Courses that stress land use planning and technical specialties may seem irrelevant at best, oppressive at worst, if they reinforce the existing social order of inequity and separatism.

This state of affairs is amazing considering how much racial disunity affects the work of urban planners. Scarcely is U.S. rural area or suburb so remote that it does not experience the social pressures of racial segregation. In metropolitan areas, where most of the U.S. population lives, historic and contemporary racial estrangement hinder urban improvement (Goldsmith and Blakely 1992). In large part, the true "urban problem" facing today's metropolitan areas is old-fashioned racial and income segregation (Rusk 1993; Massey and Denton 1993).

As Goldsmith (1991) pointed out in a critique of an Association of Collegiate Schools of Planning (ACSP) (1990) report, racial and ethnic diversity remains an important issue in planning education. Because it does, ACSP sponsored a series of reports exploring diversity in planning education (Committee on Recruitment and Retention 1990; Galindo et al. 1989; Grigsby 1988), which led to new accreditation standards for planning schools (Planning Accreditation Board (PAB) 1993).

Urban planning needs diversity, but far beyond faculty and student recruitment (Ross 1990; Hill 1990; Rodriguez 1993), or even minimum accreditation standards, is the need for a clearer understanding of why diversity is important. It is also important to train all students to work together on the job, since surveys suggest that the planning office is not exempt from discrimination. Minority and women planners experience salary disparities and lack of access to informal networks (Morris 1992; Hoch 1993). Planning schools should educate students to oppose racial discrimination, to promote the rights of all urban residents, and to bring about effective social change.

The Nonplanning Literature on Diversity

As planning educators respond to diversity, they can draw upon a wide range of sources. Very relevant guidance comes from the organizational literature, which focuses upon the workplace, and the educational literature, which address the classroom.

The literature on multicultural organizations is large and growing (Morrison and Crabtree 1992). Based largely upon corporate experience, this literature clarifies the positive results of diversity in the workplace and suggests ways to bring about positive organizational change so as to capitalize upon diversity.

Enthusiasm for multiculturalism is growing among corporations. Much of this "enthusiasm" comes because of the force of affirmative action laws (Gleckman et al. 1991; *Los Angeles Times* 3–5 Nov. 1991). But some firms act for broader reasons. Chief executives have reported that family and antidiscrimination policies increase productivity and employee retention (Lee and Mark 1990; Estrada 1992). African-American and Latino managers help their companies to compete profitably in ethnic markets. Race- and gender-sensitive policies reduce costs by eliminating turnover and generate higher levels of innovation and creativity (Morrison 1992; Loden and

Rosener 1991). International personnel offer an edge in a world of global markets (Johnston 1991). Women managers often lead differently, in a way that releases the participatory power of subordinates (Rosener 1990; Russell Reynolds Associates 1990). Successful firms understand that embracing diversity "enables us to fulfill our potential, activate our creativity, liberate our talents, enrich our teams, and make our organizations more fully human" (Garfield 1992, p. 305).

Several authors suggest stages of growth in the movement toward corporate diversity. Roosevelt Thomas (1990, 1991) identifies three stages for organizational change: affirmative action, "valuing differences," and "managing diversity." The last stage, a goal for progressive workplaces, modifies the core culture so that it works for everyone and increases workplace productivity. Cox (1991; Cox and Blake 1991) promotes the concept of the "multicultural organization." He too proposes three stages: monolithic organizations, which are homogeneous and expect assimilation by anyone in the minority; plural organizations, which are more heterogeneous but still rely on assimilation; and multicultural organizations, which include diverse workers, inclusion of minorities in networks and social activities, absence of prejudice and discrimination, and low levels of intergroup conflict.

The multicultural education field is also of great value to planning educators. This field is at least 30 years old and has already affected elementary, secondary, and university schooling in such countries as the U.S., Canada, Great Britain, and Australia (Lynch 1986; Nordquist 1992). In fact, the concept has become prominent enough to gain detractors, many of whom cling defensively to "Western civilization" and mainstream "American" values, and deny that multiculturalism has value. Other opponents of multicultural education charge that it is not radical enough (Horowitz 1991; Sleeter 1989; Ehrenreich 1991). Most useful about multicultural education for our purposes are its strong defense of diversity, its pedagogical suggestions, and its models for paradigm shifts in educational systems.

This field further clarifies why multicultural education is necessary and justified. Knowledge is not really objective or academically neutral; instead, it reflects the assumptions, biases, and culture of those who create it. When the creators are in positions of power, their vision of truth prevails. For example, a Eurocentric perspective on history will likely result if the only people writing and publishing history come from Eurocentric backgrounds and training. Multicultural education expands cultural vision, showing familiar issues from different perspectives, and granting credibility to cultures and perspectives often considered inferior (Auletta and Jones 1990).

Banks (1989a, p. 2) argues that multiculturalism improves educational performance. As he notes, "all students – regardless of their gender and social class, and their ethnic, racial, or cultural characteristics – [should] have an equal opportunity to learn in school." Schools tend to favor society's core culture. In North America, that culture values individual social mobility rather than group loyalty, and it rewards linear thinking, the kind of mentality that makes bureaucracies flourish. Although it is dangerous to typecast individuals, since variations abound, members of some microcultures do not function best according to these rules. In certain Latino, Native American, and African-American populations, the locus of reality is the group, so that individualistic learning environments may pose significant barriers (Banks 1989a). Similarly, women often experience different ways of knowing, thinking, and learning than do men (Gilligan 1982; Belenky et al. 1986).

Multicultural education, properly approached, can make learning easier for different races, nationalities, and ethnic minorities. It can enable students of all races and backgrounds to develop more positive attitudes toward different cultural, racial, and ethnic groups. It can "empower students from victimized groups [to] develop confidence in their ability to succeed academically," as well as help them "influence social, political, and economic institutions" (Banks 1989a, p. 20).

The multicultural education literature makes concrete suggestions for fostering such education. Some teachers have developed ingenious ways to teach undergraduates to value their own diversity – even if they come from supposedly homogeneous "White" backgrounds – and thus become more accepting of differences (Hollins 1990; Banks 1989b). Others have recommended administrative/institutional changes (Moses 1990) or mentoring programs to insure retention of women and people of color (Redmond 1990).

As with the organizational literature, multicultural education suggests phases of change. Tetreault (1989) offers five phases for inclusion of gender issues, ranging from (1) a strictly male-defined curriculum to one which (2) acknowledges the contributions of women, (3) presents women's concerns as dichotomized from males, (4) uses women's activities as the norm, and finally (5) balances concerns of women and of men. Banks (1989a; 1989b, p. 198) suggests expanding racial and ethnic issues via four phases: the first inserts ethnic heroes and artifacts into the curriculum; the second adds content and concepts about race, although in a poorly integrated fashion; the third enables students to view different themes and problems from different ethnic perspectives; and the last encourages students to become "reflective social critics" dedicated to social change.

Table 19.1 Selected models of educational multiculturalism. We have inferred Sanyal's stages from his text. (Sources: Tetreault (1989, p. 124–40); Banks (1989b, p. 192); Sanyal (1989). Ideas in last column developed by author.)

	Tetreault 1989	Banks 1989	Sanyal 1989	Thomas
Focus	Gender	Race and ethnicity	Internationalism	Race and gender
Phases	1. Male-defined	1. Contributions	1. Western dominance	1. Monoculture
	2. Contribution	2. Additive	2. Core/periphery, "alternative" theories	2. Pluralism: race, gender, international
	3. Bifocal	3. Transformation	3. Global education	3. Unified diversity for social action
	4. Women's 5. Gender-balanced	4. Social action		
Primary educational system	K–12	K–12, university	Planning education	Planning education

Planning Education Must Evolve

The challenge is to grow more consciously beyond traditional, mainstream-centered, male-dominated perspectives of planning and planning education. It will be necessary to do this in a way that does not destructively fragment the whole (hence the need for *unified* diversity), but rather supports effective planning and social reform. Adopting the simple technique of viewing diversity issues in paradigmatic stages helps clarify where we have come from and where we need to go. We might envision three phases of growth: monoculturalism, pluralism, and unified diversity. Table 19.1 summarizes how these phases compare with three other phased educational models, and Table 19.2 summarizes characteristics of each.

Monocultural planning education

Although monocultural elements survive in the present, this phase flourished from the beginning of U.S. planning education until the mid-1960s. This is not to deny that change occurred in that era. As an example, up until the 1950s, physical design was the bulwark of planning education, with a strong tendency to produce generalists rather than specialists (Schon and Nutt 1974; Perloff and Klett 1974; Adams 1954). Change came in the 1950s, with the influence of social science as promoted by the University of Chicago (Hemmens 1988; Kreditor 1990).

Lumping such changes into one phase is not meant to deny their importance, but merely to note that, from a multicultural perspective, this was a monocultural era. Planning reflected modernist thought and logical positivism: technical and supposedly value-neutral, governed by rational rules. Those international students who

Table 19.2   Paradigms of planning education.

	Monoculture	Pluralism	Unified diversity
Program administration/Goals	Technical	Eclectic, disjointed	Affirmative, reformist
Faculty membership	White, male	Interim levels of diversity by gender, ethnicity, and race	Diverse, cooperative, supportive
style	Hierarchical	Eclectic, contradictory	Interactive, dialogue-based
Student body	White male	Moderate diversity, segmented	Extensive diversity, cooperative
Academic environment	Not supportive of "differences"	More inclusionary, but incomplete support for those "different"; disjointed	Inclusionary, whole group identity, mentoring and support
Curriculum	Ethnocentric, rationalistic, monocultural	Contributional, bifocal, or additive; poorly integrated; occasional inclusion of diversity	Diverse, transformational, well-integrated, good preparation for effective social action

attended U.S. planning classes were obliged to accept U.S. knowledge as a given so as to help their countries "develop" (Sanyal 1989). The curriculum trained students in the fundamentals of land use and generalist planning without particular reference to race or gender. The faculty and student body were largely White and male, as were the authors of their texts.

Cities were certainly diverse, as was academia, to a limited extent. In the 1930s and 1940s it was difficult to study housing without acknowledging the work of Edith Elmer Wood, or to explore the origins of redevelopment legislation without listening to the voice of Catherine Bauer, later Wurster (Birch 1983a). Material feminists were already reshaping concepts of home and community (Spain 1995). Anyone wishing to explore the contributions of African-Americans to urbanism could have consulted Black scholars such as St. Clair Drake and Horace Cayton (1970), as well as other urban scholars. One could even find some treatment of the interaction of race and planning activity, particularly from Wurster (1946), or from others writing about public housing (Meyerson and Banfield 1955). But the planning academy was, on the whole, monocultural. Few women and racial minorities were even enrolled in planning schools, because of accepted practice or explicit bias against entrance (Birch 1983b).

Pluralist planning education

The pluralist era now prevails. It arrived in the 1960s, when Perloff and Klett (1974) noted an "exponential growth" in the number of minority students, when writers such as Altshuler began to question the rational paradigm, and when urban civil disorder and advocacy planning blew the old models of value-neutral planning to pieces (Klosterman 1981).

As planning education entered this era, one characteristic that emerged was endemic turbulence, or general confusion about planning theory. Major changes in the content of planning activity contributed to such turbulence, which can persist in wave-like motions for many years (Schon and Nutt 1974). One manifestation of this turbulence is discontinuity. During the pluralist phase, planning educators have experienced at least three waves of change related to the issue of diversity, concerning race, gender, and internationalism. The apparent exponential growth of minorities and minority issues in the 1960s did not last long. The 1970s and early 1980s produced vacillating concern for social, advocacy, and equity planning, all tied in some way to racial justice, but not quite the same thing. Then the feminist revolution brought a new wave of writing and research, which is still growing and evolving. Soon global education came to the fore. But advocates for these various movements remained remarkably disconnected.

Each of the three areas certainly made important contributions. We have already commented briefly on the role of the international dialogue. As the literature on racial conditions in U.S. metropolitan areas exploded, a dizzying array of urban studies issued forth concerning the interaction of race and employment, housing, social welfare, redevelopment, and other issues of critical importance. Several publications spoke particularly to issues of planning and of redevelopment (Altshuler 1965; Brooks and Stegman 1968; Meehan 1979; Bauman 1987; Krumholz 1982; Feld 1989). The heightened sensitivity to race transformed urban planning, pushing practitioners and scholars to consider issues of justice and equity, and forcing the evolution of social, advocacy, and equity planning (Thomas 1994). By the early 1990s, however, new literature on issues of planning and race appeared to diminish (Catlin 1993a); some urged planning academics instead to study Black writers far outside the stream of urban scholarship (Sandercock 1995).

In the meantime, production of materials on gender and planning increased. At first, much of this was in the contributional mode, as it "rescued" women from the abandoned heaps of history and made their contributions and visions known (Birch 1983a, b; Hayden 1981). But the literature soon shifted to a more critical phase of multiculturalism, moving toward bifocalism, especially with those authors who focused on bias against women in urban space or planning actions (Netter and Price 1983; Milroy 1991; Sandercock and Forsyth 1992; Ritzdorf 1993b; Pader 1994). Some recent writings resemble Tetreault's "women's curriculum" stage, such as Hendler's (1994, p. 125) call for "the substitution of feminist for traditional ethics" in planning education – an astonishing statement that would have been unimaginable a few years ago.

Several planning academics have also addressed issues of learning styles, since women often learn, interact, and think differently than do men (Belenky et al. 1986; Tannen 1990). One example is Ritzdorf's (1993b) effort to teach planning and public policy "in a different voice." As interactive skills become increasingly important in planning practice and education, the skills of women will become more valuable. Female planning educators may help tap the first-hand experiences of the learner, involving "the whole person in thinking, feeling, and acting" (Tyson and Low 1987). Disconnecting from the rational paradigm of thought should let planning educators value "those who use experience coupled with intuition, leadership, and brilliance [and] think of reason more philosophically as reflecting different ways of knowing or understanding the world" (Dalton 1986, p. 151).

But we are getting ahead of ourselves. Currently the field has not fully adopted such concepts and approaches (Sandercock and Forsyth 1992; Catlin 1993a). Few planning faculties seem persistently interested in the relationship between race and planning education. Only in recent years did the Faculty Women's Interest Group sponsor mini-seminars to consider race and gender in the curriculum. For many years, participation in seminars about internationalism included relatively few women and indigenous U.S. minorities (Sanyal and Jammal 1992).

At interim stages of pluralism, clashes between the old and new cultures can be crippling (Loden and Rosener 1991). Diverse faculty and student bodies may see things differently or face varying needs. Expecting women and racial minorities to sit passively in a planning classroom and study nothing about themselves and their life experiences may lead to discontent and uneven performance. Treating ethics as a matter of professional procedure, without instilling social values, may make the purpose and intent of planning unclear. Field projects which focus on the comfort of U.S. society's mainstream (middle-class White suburbia) may appear unexciting and send a strong message of conformity.

Students may become restless. Programs that went to great extremes to recruit women or minority students may lose them because of monocultural course content. Outnumbered women and minority faculty struggle to lead recruitment, mentor those students who might leave, and carry out their own research. These faculties may themselves leave, particularly if monocultural faculty networks shut them out. They may hear constant comments about how "different" their courses are than those of other faculties, in style as well as content, making the program appear disjointed.

These are all symptoms of disjointed pluralism, incompletely digested diversity. A planning program with such clashes, whether hidden or readily apparent, stands at a stage that multicultural experts suggest moving through.

Stronger accreditation requirements will doubtless lead to further pressure to promote diversity in planning education. These standards encourage recruitment of students and faculty and urge programs to address racial, ethnic, income, and gender topics in courses (Planning Accreditation Board 1993). Standards hardly tell academics how to do this, however. Requiring affirmative action, the organizational multicultural experience indicates, is merely a first step and could generate only half-hearted compliance.

Unified diversity for social action

We need to clearly identify a third stage, one that goes beyond monoculturalism and disjointed pluralism. This stage should be comparable in advancement of evolution to R. Thomas's third and highest stage, "managing diversity"; Cox's third stage, the "multicultural organization"; Tetreault's fifth stage, a "gender-balanced curriculum"; Banks's fourth stage, "social action approach"; and Sanyal's (implied) third stage, "one world" planning education.

This is a dizzying array of terms and options. What all of these higher stages have in common, first of all, is that they are visionary, describing desired states of being that may not yet exist completely. This concept is basic to planning and easy to grasp: good examples of organizations reflecting highest stages of diversity may be hard to find, but the point is to visualize them and aim toward creating them. In addition, each of these higher stages implies a degree of tolerance and cooperation (especially Cox, R. Thomas, Tetreault, and Sanyal), but also a higher level of organizational or educational quality and effectiveness than with previous levels (especially Cox, R. Thomas, Banks). Conflict falls to a minimum, and mutual learning rises to a maximum (especially Sanyal, Tetreault). These qualities are exactly those needed in planning education regarding diversity.

Banks (1989a, p. 192) chose the term *social action* to characterize his highest stage because he realized that the most powerful positive form of race and ethnic studies in the classroom was to enable students to "make decisions on important social issues and take actions to help solve them." The amalgamated term *unified diversity for social action* fits a culminating phase for multiculturalism in planning education because it acknowledges the role of diversity, but identifies its major purpose. Planning educators must never lose sight of that purpose, which is, as succinctly stated by Perloff, to respond effectively to the question: "How can we train the planners we need in our efforts to achieve a free, fruitful and peaceful life?" (cited in Feldman 1994, 99). This connects with the historical social reform agenda of planning (Hall 1989) and with the noble traditions of advocacy, social, equity, and redevelopment planning for improving urban society.

Based on the multicultural literature we have reviewed thus far, the following would seem to be important characteristics of academic urban planning programs exemplifying unified diversity for social action (summarized in Table 19.2).

Administration.   Leadership in and support for effective and unified diversity for social action. Active planning for improved program performance in recruitment, retention, and other areas of concern, simultaneously encouraging high standards of education, scholarship, and public service. Leadership in the concept of social action for reform in the urban and regional environment.

Faculty.   Diverse membership – of race, ethnicity, gender, and nationality – according to the limitations of program size and recruiting flexibility. Meaningful integration of pedagogical styles, with sharing and interactive improvement of techniques and approaches based on multicultural perspectives, all in the context of a curriculum that is balanced and complementary. Cooperation and comradeship among faculty, with no exclusion based on gender, race, or other exterior characteristics.

Students.   Again, diversity of race, ethnicity, gender, nationality according to the limitations of size and resources (although diversified student recruitment should be easier, that is more routine, than faculty recruitment). Admission according to typical criteria for educational achievement, but with dedication to improving or maintaining diversity, seeking in particular those with experience in, or potential dedication to, effective social action in the planning field.

Academic environment.   Support for a variety of cultures, backgrounds, and learning styles, along the continua of individualistic/group, rationalistic/holistic, etc. Inclusion of the cultural experiences of students in course and noncourse activities. Encouragement of group identity among planning students as a whole as opposed to oppositional or exclusionary cliques based on race, gender, or other characteristics (although voluntary, flexible groups may exist). Active mentoring between faculty and students, and older students or alumni and younger students.

Curriculum.   In general, the planning curriculum should reflect the best of multicultural knowledge about urban society and planning practice. It should also provide for meaningful social action in the context of superior skill enhancement, possibly in practicum or field studies courses, or in regular course components. (See the next section for more detail.)

   Although support exists for these points in the multicultural or planning literature, and although they are in keeping with planning concepts and accreditation standards, further research is needed to discern their specific characteristics concerning planning education. Part of this research could include examination of successful or unsuccessful case studies and dissemination of useful information concerning performance to other planning programs.

Initial thoughts on curriculum

It is not possible within the scope of this article to provide either an exhaustive annotated bibliography or a complete overview of the curriculum areas related to multiculturalism. Programs and instructors will have to tailor topics and materials to fit their classes, and in some cases may prefer to provide separate classes on race or gender. Presumably, however, most planning programs should move to a point where diversity issues are integrated within the regular curriculum. The following areas appear to offer particular opportunities for such integration in the context of changes related to diversity in accreditation requirements recently established by the PAB (1992, 1993).

Urban society   Students should gain knowledge of the city and its regional context for a range of subject areas, "including multicultural and gender dimensions" (PAB 1993, p. 1). Introductory courses on urbanization provide an excellent opportunity to draw upon the quite extensive literature that now exists concerning race, ethnicity, and gender in urban society, some of which is directly planning-related.

Planning history and theory   Accreditation requirements suggest attention to the history and theory of planning "in relation to . . . such characteristics as income, race, ethnicity, and gender" (PAB 1993, p. 2). Planning history offers an exceptional opportunity for more inclusion of subject material related to gender, race, and ethnicity (Thomas 1994, 1997; Thomas and Ritzdorf 1997; Birch 1983a, b; Ritzdorf 1994; Servon 1993, p. 20). One task is to move beyond the modes of "contribution" and description of existing conditions and attempt to provide "transformational" material (third stage of Banks model), which means helping students view issues from the perspective of diverse cultural, racial, and ethnic groups.

Planning theory is difficult to define – recent surveys suggest little consistency in course materials (Klosterman 1994) – but can include skill-building topics such as mediation and negotiation, or strategic planning. Such topics are of particular value for social action, with the addition of the somewhat less popular topics of citizen participation and social change (Klosterman 1994). Particular attention to planning reform traditions such as advocacy and equity planning could offer the opportunity to read about and discuss issues of social inequity and diversity, particularly of race. Connections between planning theory and feminist theory are well-documented and evolving as a field of study (Ritzdorf 1992, 1995; Servon 1993, p. 30–31).

Ethics   This area – included by some programs in planning theory courses – deserves special attention in relation to diversity. A fundamental requirement is for students to study and absorb those important provisions of the professional AICP code which relate to racial minorities, women, and the disadvantaged (American Institute of Certified Planners (AICP) 1994). Understanding the contributions of feminist ethics will be helpful (Hendler 1994), as will exploration of the ethical implications of society's racism (Feld 1989, Kaufman 1989). In spite of claims about the postmodernist era lacking universal values, planners can focus on one important value: social improvement. It is time to recapture the normative tradition in planning thought (Harper and Stein 1992) and to "develop a greater sense of moral obligation and social responsibility" (Kaufman 1981, p. 33; see also Kaufman 1993), lest we lose "our way in solving the important problems of our times" (Dalton 1993, p. 149).

Law/land use/zoning   Finding materials related to race and gender for planning law, land use, or zoning classes dovetails with other fields such as planning history.

Reference to the history of zoning, with particular reference to exclusion by race or family status, offers important background material for all planning students (Kayden and Harr 1989; Netter and Price 1983; Ritzdorf 1993a). Exploring modern cases of exclusion and court-ordered acceptance of subsidized housing, such as in Yonkers, New York, and Mt. Laurel, New Jersey, can help students prepare for the pressures that will face them in suburban or regional planning (Dennison 1990). Professors might also discuss the relationship between current metropolitan land use and effects upon women and families (Milroy 1991; Hayden 1981, 1984), or upon racial minorities (Rusk 1993).

Methods In spite of disclaimers, planners still use the rational paradigm, and so quantitative methods of analysis are important. Yet Dalton (1986, p. 151) has suggested guarding against judging other, more qualitative approaches as irrational, and urges us to learn to respect other modes, such as "experience coupled with intuition, leadership, and brilliance." She promotes humanitarian or empathetic understanding as valid, a point supported by feminist scholarship (Hendler 1994; Ritzdorf 1993a; Servon 1993, p. 8–10). Davidoff and Boyd (1983, p. 54) raised key points about the possibilities of addressing issues of racial inequity in analysis classes. They suggested that "distributional analysis of the allocation of resources, wealth, income, opportunity and knowledge in society should be a central component of planning analysis education." Two excellent recent examples of race- and ethnicity-sensitive planning analysis . . . used qualitative and quantitative approaches to illustrate important ways planners could improve practice (Pader 1994; Loukaitou-Sideris 1995).

Specialty areas Accreditation requirements indicate that a planning student should study at least one specialty area, which may include "housing, land use, economic development, urban design, the environment, and transportation," among others, but that, "wherever appropriate," areas should consider "racial, ethnic, income, and gender-related issues" (PAB 1993, p. 2). Although discussing the endless alternatives is impossible here, for each of the above specialty areas materials are assuredly available concerning race, ethnicity, and gender (Servon 1993; Ritzdorf 1994).

Field study, community service course modules, and guided internships This area is important because it allows educators to simplify the complexity implicit in the above dialogue through practice-based application. It is in the context of actual experience that theory comes to life (Forester 1987; Vakil et al. 1990; Goodrich and Resende 1993). Students can see for themselves the results of racial and income inequality and grapple with using planning tools to help address it. Experiential learning, which "involves the whole person in thinking, feeling, and acting," has some advantages over "learning acquired by listening to lectures, reading books, and analyzing statistics, all of which direct attention to 'them' at another time and in another place" (Tyson and Low 1987). And so one of the most effective techniques for helping students learn how to bring about social equity and effective action is to involve them in a guided experience that does just that.

A simple way to help planning students understand how to plan in a diversified world is to assign them to work with community groups in low-income mixed-race or minority neighborhoods. In this context, students learn more deeply the planning process concepts such as neighborhood, district, and master planning, as well as other concepts such as community development, community organizing, and re-development (Thomas 1993).

When I first began to develop field work courses in inner city Detroit, racial divisions posed challenges. One year, all the students were White or Asian, and all the residents were Black. The students did their best to overcome culture shock (as did the residents). They learned much about the common humanity of themselves with the residents and also gained creditable neighborhood planning skills. The possibilities for using planning to improve central cities opened up to them as they saw the dedication of people determined to do so and as they worked to help them. But the differences between that year and years when the students included African-Americans were palpable. The level of comfort increased, and the positive inter-active effects of several races of students, as well as both genders, seemed to heighten dedication and effectiveness.

The Vision

We have suggested that planning education has moved through a stage of mono-culturalism, and is moving through a disjointed, multiphased process of pluralism, but needs a stronger vision of a third stage: unified diversity for social action.

The vision is one of planning programs with extensive but harmonious diversity in the faculty, student body, and curriculum. As promoted by the organizational literature, in such planning programs people celebrate diversity as a source of strength and creativity. Picking up on Banks' educational ideas, in such programs monoculturalism poses no barriers to learning. Monoculturalism in course content would be rare, since course material would consider multiple perspectives on urban planning history, theory, and current practice. In such a program, the learning environment would be supportive of women and racial minorities. The focus on a common end – social justice and improvement for residents of urban and regional communities – would yield unity of purpose.

In a planning program characterized by unified diversity one would expect to see diverse students and faculty. Students would benefit from proper preparation for work in workplaces and metropolitan communities, having received strong overt and covert messages that all races and cultures are valuable, as are both genders, and that diversity is a strength to be nurtured rather than a requirement to be tolerated. As with Cox's multicultural organization, inclusion of minorities and females in networks and social activities would be extensive, absence of prejudice would be the norm, and little intergroup conflict would exist. These conditions would not come by means of wishful thinking, but by means of deliberate policies and procedures.

And the curriculum of planning programs characterized by unified diversity for social action would provide the best possible preparation for students to plan effective strategies for making a better urban and regional society.

Some have bemoaned the lack of coherence apparent in planning today. If one recalls the compelling need for urban reform, however, the directions in which the field should move are much clearer. Some of the most difficult problems facing North American metropolitan society relate to the fragmentation of the region, the decline of the central city, and the extremes of wealth and poverty (of individuals stratified by race and gender and of communities). The state of urban problems is such that, as a profession, we really cannot afford paralysis when so much work remains to be done.

A more diversified profession can offer new insights and creativity. With more planners of African-American and other minority backgrounds, who belong to the culture and understand the context of many city neighborhoods, we can perhaps design more effective strategies for improvement, or at least enhance trust between residents and planners. Such professionals may also gain greater connection with the minority mayors now firmly placed in city halls across the country (Catlin 1993b; Thomas 1997). Furthermore, bringing minority youth into the profession can assist upward mobility and professional growth among the oppressed races, a task shouldered disproportionately by planning programs at historically Black colleges and universities.

Women have already proven their worth within academia. The same level of creativity and innovation they have brought to campuses can help in the field of action. Women can enhance the quality of interaction and communication within the planning milieu, offer special skills in analysis and problem solving, and help visualize a new metropolis characterized by both compassion and justice. Fortified by the inclusion of individuals who broadly represent our nation's cities, the planning profession will have a better chance to have a positive impact on today's metropolis.

NOTES

1   It is quite common to include issues of gender and internationalism within the multicultural education and multicultural organizational dialogue, although this is not always done in the North American planning academy. See for examples Lynch (1986) and Banks (1989a).
2   Sometimes, within the planning literature, the term *pluralism* is used to mean plural streams of specialties within the planning profession, divorced from issues of race or gender. See for example Friedmann and Kuester (1994). In this article, *pluralism* refers to multiculturalism, as already defined, and to a particular stage of diversity, described later in the text.
3   I attempted to discern the number of African-American faculty in 1993 by compiling a list using personal knowledge, that of ACSP President Catherine Ross, and a "snowball" request for names of Black faculty teaching in accredited programs. That informal listing totaled 25.

REFERENCES

Adams, F. 1954. *Urban Planning Education in the U.S.* Cincinnati, Ohio: Alfred Bettman Foundation.

Altshuler, A. 1965. *Locating the Intercity Freeway.* Inter-University Case Program 88. Indianapolis, Indiana: Bobbs-Merrill Company, Inc. American Institute of Certified Planners. 1994. *1994–95 Roster.* Washington, D.C.

Association of Collegiate Schools of Planning, Commission on Undergraduate Education. 1990. Creating the future for undergraduate education in planning. *Journal of Planning Education and Research* 10: 15–26.

Auletta, G., and T. Jones. 1990. Reconstituting the inner circle. *American Behavioral Scientist* 34: 137–152.

Banerjee, T. 1985. Environmental design in the developing world: Some thoughts on design education. *Journal of Planning Education and Research* 5: 28–38.

Banks, J. 1989a. Multicultural education: Characteristics and goals. In *Multicultural Education: Issues and Perspectives*, ed. J. Banks and C. Banks. Needham Heights, Massachusetts: Allyn and Bacon.

Banks, J. 1989b. Integrating the curriculum with ethnic content: Approaches and guidelines. In *Multicultural Education: Issues and Perspectives*, ed. J. Banks and C. Banks. Needham Heights, Massachusetts: Allyn and Bacon.

Bauman, J. 1987. *Public Housing, Race, and Renewal: Urban Planning in Philadelphia, 1920–1974*. Philadelphia, Pennsylvania: Temple University Press.

Belenky, M., C. Blythe, N. Goldberger, and J. Tarule. 1986. *Women's Ways of Knowing*. New York: Basic Books.

Birch, E. 1983a. Woman-made America: The case of early public housing policy. In *The American Planner: Biographies and Recollections*, ed. D. Krueckeberg. New York: Methuen.

Birch, E. 1983b. From Civic worker to city planner: Women and planning, 1890–1980. In *The American Planner: Biographies and Recollections*, ed. D. Krueckeberg. New York: Methuem.

Brooks, M., and M. Stegman. 1968. Urban social policy, race, and the education of planners. *Journal of the American Institute of Planners* 34: 275–286.

Burayidi, M. 1993. Dualism and universalism: competing paradigms in planning education? *Journal of Planning Education and Research* 12: 223–229.

Catlin, R. 1993a. The planning profession and Blacks in the United States: A content analysis of academic and professional literature. *Journal of Planning Education and Research* 13: 26–32.

Catlin, R. 1993b. *Racial Politics and Urban Planning*. Lexington: University Press of Kentucky.

Chatterjee, J. 1990. Why new perspectives are needed. In *Breaking the Boundaries: A One-World Approach to Planning Education*, ed. B. Sanyal. New York: Plenum Press.

Committee on the Recruitment and Retention of Women and Minorities in Planning Education. 1990. The recruitment and retention of women faculty and faculty of color in planning education: Survey results. Madison. Wisconsin: Association of Collegiate Schools of Planning.

Contant, C., P. Fisher, and J. Kragt. 1994. *Guide to Graduate Education in Urban and Regional Planning*. Ninth edition. Association of Collegiate Schools of Planning. (Available from Planners Press, Chicago, Illinois.)

Cox, T. 1991. The multicultural organization. *Academy of Management Executive* 5: 34–47.

Cox, T., and S. Blake. 1991. Managing cultural diversity: Implications for organizational competitiveness. *Academy of Management Executive* 5: 45–54.

Dalton, L. 1986. Why the rational paradigm persists: The resistance of professional education and practice to alternative forms of planning. *Journal of Planning Education and Research* 5: 147–153.

Dalton, L. 1993. The dilemmas of the times. *Journal of the American Planning Association* 59: 149–152.

Davidoff, P., and L. Boyd. 1983. Peace and justice in planning education. *Journal of Planning Education and Research* 3: 54.

Dennison, M., ed. 1990. *1990 Zoning and Planning Law Handbook*. New York: Clark Boardman Company, Ltd.

Drake, St. C., and H. Cayton. 1970. *Black Metropolis*, Vol. 1: *A Study of Negro Life in a Northern City*. New York: Harcourt, Brace and World, Inc.

Dunlap, L. 1990. Language and power: Teaching writing to third World graduate students. In *Breaking the Boundaries: A One- World Approach to Planning Education*, ed. B. Sanyal. New York: Plenum Press.

Ehrenreich. B. 1991. The challenge for the left. *Democratic Left*, July/August: 3–4.

Estrada, A. 1992. CEP Roundtable on workforce diversity. *Hispanic*, January/February: 28–34.

Feld, M. 1989. The Yonkers case and its implications for the teaching and practice of planning. *Journal of Planning Education and Research* 8: 169–176.

Feldman, M. 1994. Perloff revisited: Reassessing planning education in postmodern times. *Journal of Planning Education and Research* 13: 89–103.

Forester, J. 1987. Teaching and studying planning practice: An analysis of the 'Planning and Institutional Processes' course at MIT. *Journal of Planning Education and Research* 6: 116–137.

Friedmann, J., and C. Kuester. 1994. Planning education for the late twentieth century: An initial inquiry. *Journal of Planning Education and Research* 14: 55–64.

Galindo, Y., M. B. Welch, and S. Wirka. 1987. Accepting the challenge: gender, race, and disability in urban planning education. Unpublished report to the Association of Collegiate Schools of Planning Executive Board Meeting.

Garfield, C. 1992. *Second to None: How Our Smartest Companies Put People First*. Homewood, Illinois: Business One Irwin.

Getzel, J., and G. Longhini. 1982. *Planners' Salaries, Reports and Trends, 1981*. Planners Advisory Service Report #366. Chicago, Illinois: American Planning Association.

Gilligan, C. 1982. *In a Different Voice*. Cambridge, Massachusetts: Harvard University Press.

Gleckman, H., T. Smart, P. Dwyer, T. Segal, and J. Weber. 1991. Race in the Workplace: Is affirmative action working? *Business Week* 14(3221): 50–63.

Goldsmith, W. 1991. Remarks on the Niebanck Commission Report on Undergraduate Education. *Journal of Planning Education and Research* 11: 75–77.

Goldsmith, W., and E. Blakely. 1992. *Separate Societies: Poverty and Inequality in U.S. Cities*. Philadelphia, Pennsylvania: Temple University Press.

Goodrich, K. and L. Resende. 1993. Participatory action research in East St. Louis. *Colloqui* 8: 40–47.

Grigsby, J. E., III. 1988. Minority education in planning schools. Unpublished report.

Hall, P. 1989. *Cities of Tomorrow: An Intellectual History of Urban Planning and Design in the Twentieth Century*. Oxford: Basil Blackwell.

Harper, T., and S. Stein. 1992. The centrality of normative ethical theory to contemporary planning theory. *Journal of Planning Education and Research* 11: 105–116.

Hayden, D. 1981. *The Grand Domestic Revolution: A History of Feminist Designs for American Homes, Neighborhoods, and Cities*. Cambridge, Massachusetts: M.I.T. Press.

Hayden, D. 1984. *Redesigning the American Dream: The Future of Housing, Work, and Family Life*. New York: W. W. Norton.

Hemmens, G. 1988. Thirty years of planning education. *Journal of Planning Education and Research* 7: 85–91.

Hendler, S. 1994. Feminist planning ethics. *Journal of Planning Literature* 9: 115–127.

Hendler, S., ed. 1995. *Planning Ethics*. New Brunswick, New Jersey: Center for Urban Policy Research.

Heumann, L. 1991. It is time to take stock of the education of foreign students in N. American planning Ph.D. programs. *Journal of Planning Education and Research* 10: 154–156.

Hill, E. 1990. Increasing minority representation in the planning professorate. *Journal of Planning Education and Research* 9: 139–142.

Hinojosa, R., T. Lyons, and F. Zinn. 1992. The relevance of North American Planning education for overseas practice: A survey of graduates. *Journal of Planning Education and Research* 12: 32–38.

Hoch, C. 1993. Racism and planning. *Journal of the American Planning Association* 59: 451–460.

Hollins, E. 1990. Debunking the myth of a monolithic white American culture; or, moving toward cultural inclusion. *American Behavioral Scientist* 34: 201–209.

Horowitz, I. 1991. The new nihilism. *Society* 29: 27–33.

Johnston, W. B. 1991. Global work force 2000: The new world labor market. *Harvard Business Review* 69: 115–128.

Kaufman, J. 1981. Teaching planning ethics. *Journal of Planning Education and Research* 1: 29–35.

Kaufman, J. 1989. U.S. vs. Yonkers: A tale of three planners. *Journal of Planning Education and Research* 8: 189–192.

Kaufman, J. 1993. Reflections on teaching three versions of a planning ethics course. *Journal of Planning Education and Research* 12: 107–115.

Kayden, J. and Harr, C. 1989. *Zoning and the American Dream*. Chicago, Illinois: Planners Press.

Kihl, M. 1990. Design education for international practice: The alumni perspective. *Journal of Planning Education and Research* 9: 142–146.

Klosterman, R. 1981. Contemporary planning theory education: Results of a course survey. *Journal of Planning Education and Research* 11: 1–11.

Klosterman, R. 1994. Planning theory education in the 1980s: Results of a second Course survey. *Journal of planning Education and Research* 11: 130–140.

Kreditor, A. 1990. The neglect of urban design in the American academic succession. *Journal of Planning Education and Research* 9: 155–163.

Krumholz, N. 1982. A retrospective view of equity planning: Cleveland 1969–1979. *Journal of the American Planning Association* 48: 163–178.

Leavitt, J. 1983. The gender gap: Making planning education relevant. *Journal of Planning Education and Research* 3: 55–56.

Lee, W., and R. Mark. 1990. Family, minority motivation requires highest CEO priority. *Financier* 14: 27–31.

Loden, M., and J. Rosener. 1991. *Workforce America! Managing Employee Diversity as a Vital Resource Tool*. Homewood, Illinois.: Business One Irwin.

Loukaitou-Sideris, A. 1995. Urban form and social context: Cultural differentiation in the uses of urban parks. *Journal of Planning Education and Research* 14: 89–102.

Lynch, J. 1986. *Multicultural Education: Principles and Practice*. London: Routledge & Kegan Paul.

Mars, J. H., and J. Springer. 1993. Who are we serving? A comparison of the students in graduate and undergraduate planning programs. Paper presented to the Association of Collegiate Schools of Planning, Philadelphia, Pennsylvania, October 29.

Massey, D., and N. Denton. 1993. *American Apartheid: Segregation and the Making of the Underclass*. Cambridge, Massachusetts: Harvard University Press.

Meehan, E. 1979. *The Quality of Federal Policymaking: Programmed Failure in Public Housing*. Columbia: University of Missouri Press.

Meyerson, M., and E. Banfield. 1955. *Politics, Planning and the Public Interest*. Glencoe, Illinois: The Free Press.

Milroy, B. M. 1991. Taking stock of planning, space, and gender. *Journal of Planning Literature* 6: 3–15.

Morris, M. 1992. *Planners Salaries and Employment Trends*, 1991. Planner Advisory Service #439. Chicago, Illinois: American Planning Association.

Morrison, A. 1992. *The New Leaders: Guidelines on Leadership Diversity in America*. San Francisco, California: Jossey-Bass Publishers.

Morrison, A., and K. Crabtree. 1992. *Developing Diversity in Organizations: A Digest of Selected Literature*. Greensboro, North Carolina: Center for Creative Leadership.

Moses, Y. 1990. The challenge of diversity: Anthropological perspectives on university culture. *Education and Urban Society* 22: 402–412.

Netter, E., and R. Price. 1983. Zoning and the nouveau poor. *Journal of the American Planning Association* 49: 171–181.

Niebanck, P. 1988a. Preparing leadership for the twenty-first century: Report of the Santa Cruz Conference on planning education. *Journal of Planning Education and Research* 7: 121–124.

Niebanck, P. 1988b. Unleashing the future. *Journal of the American Institute of Planning* 54: 432–443.

Nordquist, J. 1992. *The Multicultural Education Debate in the University: A Bibliography.* No. 25. Santa Cruz, California: Reference and Research Services.

Pader, E-J. 1994. Spatial relations and housing policy: Regulations that discriminate against Mexican-origin households. *Journal of Planning Education and Research* 13: 119–135.

Perloff, H., and F. Klett. 1974. The evolution of planning education. In *Learning from Turbulence,* ed. D. Godschalk. Washington, D.C.: American Institute of Planners.

Planning Accreditation Board. 1992. *The Accreditation Document: Criteria and Procedures.* Washington. D.C.: PAB.

Planning Accreditation Board. 1993. Accreditation Criteria changes in *The Accreditation Document.* Handout based on changes approved at May 7–8, 1992 PAB meeting. Distributed at the Association of Collegiate Schools of Planning conference, Philadelphia, Pennsylvania.

Redmond, S. 1990. Mentoring and cultural diversity in academic settings. *American Behavioral Scientist* 34: 188–200.

Ritzdorf, M. 1992. Feminist thoughts on the theory and practice of planning. *Planning Theory Newsletter,* No. 7–8: 13–20.

Ritzdorf, M. 1993a. Land use, local control, and social responsibility: The child care example. *Journal of Urban Affairs* 15: 79–92.

Ritzdorf, M. 1993b. The fairy's tale: Teaching planning and public policy in a different voice. *Journal of Planning Education and Research* 12: 99–106.

Ritzdorf, M. 1994. Diversifying the planning curriculum: A modest bibliography. Unpublished annotated bibliography. (Available from Ritzdorf at Blacksburg, Virginia Polytechnic Institute and State University.)

Ritzdorf, M. 1995. Feminist contributions to the theory and practice of planning. In *Planning Ethics,* ed. S. Hendler. New Brunswick, New Jersey: Center for Urban Policy Research.

Rodriguez, S. 1993. Schools for today, graduates for tomorrow. *Journal of American Planning Association* 59: 152–153.

Rosener, J. 1990. Ways women lead. *Harvard Business Review,* November–December: 119–125.

Ross, C. 1990. Increasing minority and female representation in the profession: A call for diversity. *Journal of Planning Education and Research* 9: 135–138.

Rusk, D. 1993. *Cities Without Suburbs.* Baltimore, Maryland: Johns Hopkins Press.

Russell Reynolds Associates, Inc. 1990. *Men, Women, and Leadership in the American Corporation.* New York: Russell Reynolds Associates, Inc.

Sandercock, L. 1995. Voices from the borderlands: A meditation on a metaphor. *Journal of Planning Education and Research* 14: 77–88.

Sandercock, L., and A. Forsyth. 1992. A gender agenda: New directions for planning theory. *Journal of the American Planning Association* 58: 49–59.

Sanyal, B. 1989. Poor countries' students in rich countries' universities: Possibilities of planning education for the twenty-first century. *Journal of Planning Education and Research* 8: 139–156.

Sanyal, B., ed. 1990. *Breaking the Boundaries: A One-World Approach to Planning Education.* New York: Plenum Press.

Sanyal, B., and I. Jammal. 1992. Growing pains or a fruitless endeavor? Retrospective notes on the Buffalo conference on global approaches to planning education. *Journal of Planning Education and Research* 11: 152–156.

Schon, D., and T. Nutt. 1974. Endemic turbulence: The future for planning education. In *Planning in America: Learning from Turbulence,* ed. D. Godschalk. Washington, D.C.: American Institute of Planners.

Servon, L. 1993. *The Intersection of Planning with Gender Issues*. Council of Planning Librarians Bibliography #303. Atlanta, Georgia: American Planning Association.

Sleeter, C. 1989. Multicultural education as a form of resistance to oppression. *Journal of Education* 171: 51–71.

Spain, D. 1995. Sustainability, feminist visions, and the utopian tradition. *Journal of Planning Literature* 9: 362–369.

Tannen, D. 1990. *You Just Don't Understand: Men and Women in Conversation*. New York: Morrow.

Tetreault, M. 1989. Integrating content about women and gender into the curriculum. In *Multicultural Education: Issues and Perspectives*, ed. J. Banks and C. Banks. Needham Heights, Massachusetts: Allyn and Bacon.

Thomas, R. 1990. From affirmative action to affirming diversity. *Harvard Business Review* 68: 107–117.

Thomas, J. 1993. Race, poverty and planning: An academic agenda. *Colloqui* 8: 34–36.

Thomas, J. 1994. Planning history and the Black urban experience. *Journal of Planning Education and Research* 14: 1–11.

Thomas, J. 1997. *Planning a Finer City: Redevelopment and Race in Postwar Detroit*. Baltimore, Maryland: Johns Hopkins University Press.

Thomas, J., and M. Ritzdorf, ed. 1997. *Urban Planning and the African American Community*. Thousand Oaks, California: Sage.

Thomas, R. 1991. *Beyond Race and Gender: Unleashing the Power of Your Total Work Force by Managing Diversity*. New York: American Management Association.

Tyson, B. and N. Low. 1987. Experiential learning in planning education. *Journal of Planning Education and Research* 7: 15–27.

Vakil, A., R. Marans, and M Feld. 1990. Integrative planning workshops: The Michigan experience. *Journal of Planning Education and Research* 10: 61–69.

Wurster, C. B. 1946. Is urban redevelopment possible under existing legislation? In *Planning 1946*. Chicago, Illinois: American Society of Planning Officials.

20

Nurturing: Home, Mom, and Apple Pie

Dolores Hayden

HOME FIRES ARE BRIGHTEST,
HOME TIES ARE STRONGEST,
HOME LIVES ARE HAPPIEST,
HOME LOVES ARE DEAREST.   *American sampler*
M IS FOR THE MANY THINGS SHE GAVE US,
O IS BECAUSE SHE'S THE ONLY ONE...   *Alberta Hunter*

Home is where the heart is. Home, sweet home. Whoever speaks of housing must also speak of home. The word embraces both physical space and the nurturing that takes place within it. Few of us can separate the ideal of home from thoughts of mom and apple pie, mother love and home cooking. Rethinking home life involves rethinking the spatial, technological, cultural, social, and economic dimensions of sheltering, nurturing, and feeding people. These activities, often discussed by men as if they had existed unchanged from the beginning of time, unsmirched by capitalist development, technological manipulation, or social pressures, require expert analysis. Sociologist Arlie Hochschild's *The Second Shift* and economist Nancy Folbre's *The Invisible Heart* break new ground in analyzing the complexities of domestic work.[1] Yet among feminist activists, mother love and home cooking have long been celebrated targets. It is understood that "Home, sweet home has never meant housework, sweet housework," as Charlotte Perkins Gilman put it in the 1890s. It has also been clear that mothering is political. Lily Braun, the German socialist feminist, wrote: "After the birth of my son, the problems of women's liberation were no longer mere theories. They cut into my own flesh."[2] That was 1901. The United States has been slower than the rest of the world to reach a more egalitarian political position on domestic life. Most industrialized nations have developed complex legislation to support women workers with paid maternity leave and quality child care. The U.S. has not.

Nurturing men and children has traditionally been women's work. A brief accounting reveals the many separate tasks involved. Home cooking requires meals prepared to suit the personal likes and dislikes of family members. It is also one of the most satisfying and creative aesthetic activities for many women and men. Housecleaning requires sweeping, vacuuming, washing, polishing, and tidying the living space. Laundry requires sorting, washing, drying, folding or ironing, and putting away clean clothes and linens. Health care begins at home, where home remedies and prescribed medicines are distributed. Mental health also begins at home, when homemakers provide emotional support so that all family members make successful connections and adjustments to the larger society. This is crucial not only for the education of [the] young, but also for adults, who must sustain the pressures of earning a living, and for the elderly, who need emotional support in their frail years.

Equally important are those ties to kin and community that maintain the social status and ethnic identity of the household. Maintenance of these ties often includes cultural rituals – the preparation of Thanksgiving dinners, Seders, Cinco de Mayo celebrations – with all the food, clothing, and special objects associated with each event. Recreation is another home task: arranging for children's play, team sports, birthday parties, and family vacations. In urban societies, recreation also means arranging family experiences of nature, such as visits to parks or camping trips.

Economist Heidi Hartmann has estimated that a good home life for a family of four requires about sixty hours of nurturing work per week.[3] That work may have been more physically arduous in the past, but never more complex. Beyond the house and the immediate neighborhood, home life includes the management of extensive relationships with stores, banks, and other commercial service facilities, and with public institutions such as schools, hospitals, clinics, and government offices. Part of homemaking involves seeing that each family member's myriad personal needs are fully met. The new dress must be the right size. The new fourth grade teacher must understand a child's history of learning difficulties. Sometimes relationships with stores or institutions turn into adversarial ones. If the new car is a lemon, if the grade school isn't teaching reading fast enough, if the hospital offers an incorrect diagnosis, if the social security benefit check is late, then the stressful nature of the homemaker's brokering work between home, market, and state is exacerbated.

Italian social theorist Laura Balbo has written brilliantly about the key roles women play in sustaining these three sectors of modern society. Not only do homemakers make the bridge between commercial services, government bureaucracies, and the family, they are also low-paid providers of service performing heroic feats of overtime in the commercial or state sectors.[4] Much women's nurturing work requires a high level of skill, understanding, judgment, and patience. Yet when this work is conducted in the private home, women's time and skills often go unrecognized. Traditionally, marriage has been a homemaker's labor agreement – and a rather vague one at that – to provide personal service and nurturing to a man and children in exchange for financial support. Homemakers, as the one group of workers for whom no legal limits on hours, pension benefits, health insurance, or paid vacations have ever applied, have often found that the only time their work of cooking, cleaning, and nurturing compelled attention was when it was *not* done.

While "man's home is his castle," a woman often lacks any private space in her home. Society defines the ideal home as a warm, supportive place for men and children, but for homemakers it has always been a workplace, where a "woman's work is never done." While women may have gourmet kitchens, sewing rooms, and so-called master bedrooms to inhabit, even in these spaces the homemaker's role is to service, not to claim autonomy and privacy. There has been little nurturing for homemakers themselves unless they break down. In crises, women have looked to other women for emotional support. This may be the informal help acknowledged by homemaker and author Erma Bombeck, who dedicated one of her books to the other homemakers in her car pool: the women who, "when I was drowning in a car pool threw me a line. . . . always a funny one."[5] Women's support may also come from mothers, sisters, female friends, and female kin, who traditionally rally in crises. It may come from the range of services provided by the feminist movement, such as discussion groups, crisis centers, health centers, and hostels. Or it may come from husbands and children who finally notice when their wives and mothers break down.

American urban design, social policy planning, and housing design have seldom taken the complexity of homemaking into account. To rethink private life, it is essential to be explicit about the range of needs that homes and homemakers fulfill. Home life is the source of great cultural richness and diversity in an immigrant nation. Home life is also the key to social services – education, health, mental health. And home life is the key to successful urban design, in the patterning of residential space, commercial space, and institutional space, so that the linkages between home, market, and state can be sustained without undue hardship.

Yet in the last half-century, the cultural strength of home has been debated. The success of the family in providing socialization for children has been challenged. The failure of many residential neighborhoods has been noted.[6] A conservative movement for "family values" has been mounted, without much interest in defining this term. In light of the extensive literature on such topics as divorce and family violence, it is surprising to see how few alternative models of home life are discussed in a serious, sustained way. Many critics fail to distinguish between the traditional male-headed family and other models of family life. Others welcome new models but fail to record the struggles to transform the male-headed family that feminists have waged for at least two hundred years.[7] Innovative, egalitarian housing strategies that lead to new forms of housing cannot be developed without a reformulation of the traditional family and its gender division of work. Americans interested in debating these issues can consider the history of three alternative models of home.

Three Models of Home

In the years between 1870 and 1930, home life provoked a phenomenal amount of political debate. Because this topic linked the Woman Question to the Labor Question, it attracted the attention of housewives, feminist activists, domestic servants, inventors, economists, architects, urban planners, utopian novelists, visionaries, and efficiency experts. Housework, factory work, and home were all susceptible to restructuring in the industrial city. Women and men of all political persuasions generally agreed that burdensome household work, as it had been carried out in the pre-industrial houses of the first half of the nineteenth century, left most women little time to be good wives and mothers. Industrial development was transforming all other work and workplaces, and it was expected that domestic work and residential environments would be transformed as well. Activists raised fundamental questions about the relationships between women and men, households and servants. They explored the economic and social definitions of "woman's work." They also raised basic questions about household space, public space, and the relationship between economic policies and family life concretized in domestic architecture and residential neighborhoods.

Many proposed solutions drew, in one way or another, on the possibilities suggested by new aspects of urban and industrial life: new forms of specialization and division of labor, new technologies, new concentrations of dwelling units in urban apartment houses or suburban neighborhoods. But domestic theorists also had to deal with a number of unwelcome consequences of these new developments: hierarchy in the workplace, replacement of handcraft skills by mechanization, erosion of privacy in crowded urban dwellings, and development of conspicuous domestic consumption in bourgeois neighborhoods. Although life in the isolated household was burdensome, inefficient, and stifling, many reformers feared that the socialization of domestic work would deprive industrial society of its last vestige of uncapitalized, uncompetitive, skilled work. That is, they worried about mother love and home cooking.

For the most part, the major domestic strategies of the time have been ignored or misunderstood by both historians and political theorists. William O'Neill, in his popular book *Everyone Was Brave*, scathingly condemned the leaders of the American nineteenth-century woman's movement as "weak and evasive" activists, completely unable to tackle the difficult ideological problem of the family. He called them frustrated women who never understood that a revolution in domestic life was needed to achieve feminist aims.[8] Betty Friedan, in her 1981 book *The Second Stage*, reiterated O'Neill's views approvingly, as support for her mistaken belief that twentieth-century feminists were the first to introduce serious concern for domestic life into political organizing.[9] Some contemporary writers still dismiss any serious theoretical concern with housework as a waste of time; they look to wage work to liberate women, much as Bebel did in 1883 and Lenin in 1919.[10]

Almost all American women involved in politics between 1870 and 1930 saw domestic work and family life as important theoretical and practical issues. The material feminists argued that no adequate theory of political economy could develop without full consideration of domestic work.[11] They debated both businessmen and Marxists with an eloquence that has rarely been equaled. The years between 1870 and 1930 produced three major strategies for domestic reform: Catharine Beecher's capitalist haven strategy, a Marxist industrial strategy, and the material feminists' neighborhood strategy. Finding a new approach requires that all of these strategies, and the experiences of trying to implement them, are clearly understood.

The haven strategy

The leading exponent of the home as haven, Catharine Beecher, explained the technological and architectural basis of a refined suburban home beginning in the 1840s.... she proposed to increase the effectiveness of the isolated housewife and to glorify woman's traditional sphere of work. Beecher devoted her energy to better design. The housewife would be equipped with an efficient kitchen, adequate running water, and effective home heating and ventilation. She would have a better stove. In *The American Woman's Home*, Beecher suggested that the housewife devote more of her labor to becoming an emotional support for her husband and an inspiring mother for her children. Self-sacrifice would be her leading virtue. The home, a spiritual and physical shelter from the competition and exploitation of industrial capitalist society, and a training ground for the young, would become a haven in a heartless world. Beecher believed this division of labor between men and women would blunt the negative effects of industrial society on male workers. She argued that both rich and poor women, removed from competition with men in paid work, would find gender a more engrossing identification than class.

For Beecher, it was extremely important that the housewife do nurturing work with her own two hands. As she performed many different tasks each day, she was to be a sacred figure, above and beyond the cash nexus. Her personal services as wife and mother were beyond price. The biological mother was presented as the only focus for her children's needs. The virtuous wife was presented as the only one who could meet her husband's needs as well. The spatial envelope for all of this exclusive nurturing was a little cottage in a garden. Nature surrounding the home reinforced belief in a woman's natural, biologically determined role within it. Beecher also showed how domesticity could be adapted to a tenement apartment or a single teacher's residence.

The industrial strategy

The German Marxist, August Bebel, in his classic book *Women Under Socialism* (1883), wanted to move most traditional household work into the factory, abolishing women's domestic sphere entirely. Bebel argued: "The small private kitchen is, just like the workshop of the small master mechanic, a transition stage, an arrangement by which time, power and material are senselessly squandered and wasted... in the future the domestic kitchen is rendered wholly superfluous by all the central institutions for the preparation of food."[12] He also predicted that just as factory kitchens would prepare dinners, and large state bakeries would bake pies, so mechanical laundries would wash clothes and cities would provide central heating. Children would be trained in public institutions from their earliest years. Women would take up industrial employment outside the household, and the household would lose control of many private activities. The effects of industrialization would be general, and women would share in the gains and losses with men, although their new factory work would probably be occupationally segregated labor in the laundry or the pie factory. A life of dedication to greater industrial production and the socialist state would reward personal sacrifice in the Marxist version of the industrial strategy.

In Bebel's version of home life, both nature and biology disappear in favor of industrial efficiency. Bebel believed that nurturing work should be done by women, but he tended to see women as interchangeable service workers. The demand that women nurture with a personal touch, so central to Beecher, was replaced by a sense that any day-care worker could offer a substitute for mother love and any canteen worker could serve up a substitute for home cooking. The spatial container for this interchangeable, industrial nurturing was to be the apartment house composed of industrial components and equipped with large mess halls, recreation clubs, child-care centers, and kitchenless apartments. Of course, service workers would need to be constantly on duty to keep these residential complexes running, but Bebel did not consider this service as labor of any particular value or skill. He underestimated the importance of the socialized home as workplace, even as he recognized the private home as workshop.

The neighborhood strategy

Midway between the haven strategy and the industrial strategy, there was a third strategy. The material feminists led by Melusina Fay Peirce wanted to socialize housework under women's control through neighborhood networks. In contrast to the advocates of the haven approach, who praised woman's traditional skills but denied women money, or the advocates of the industrial approach, who denied women's traditional skills but gave women wages, the material feminists argued that women should be paid for what they were already doing. As Jane Cunningham Croly put it in Stanton and Anthony's newspaper, *The Revolution*: "I demand for the wife who acts as cook, as nursery-maid, or seamstress, or all three, fair wages, or her rightful share in the net income. I demand that the bearing and rearing of children, the most exacting of employments, shall be the best paid work in the world."[13]

Material feminists agreed that women were already doing half the necessary labor in industrial society and should receive half the wages. They believed that women would have to reorganize their labor to gain these demands. The first reason for organizing was to present a united front; the second was to utilize the possibility of new technologies and the specialization and division of labor, in order to perfect their skills and to shorten their hours. Peirce argued that "it is just as necessary, and just as honorable for a wife to earn money as it is for her husband," but she criticized the traditional arrangement of domestic work as forcing the housewife to become a "jack-of-all-trades."[14]

Peirce's proposed alternative was the producers' cooperative. She envisioned former housewives and former servants doing cooking, baking, laundry, and sewing in one well-equipped neighborhood workplace. Women would send the freshly baked pies, the clean laundry, and the mended garments back to their own husbands (or their former male employers) for cash on delivery. Peirce planned to overcome the isolation and economic dependency inherent in the haven approach, and the alienation inherent in the industrial approach. While revering woman's traditional nurturing skills and neighborhood networks as the material basis of women's sphere, Peirce proposed to transform these skills and networks into a new kind of economic power for women by elevating nurturing to the scale of several dozen united households.

Peirce also overcame another great flaw in the haven approach. In the early 1870s, there were very few appliances, aside from Beecher's own inventions and architectural refinements, to help the housewife who worked alone. Almost all of the major advances, such as clothes-washing machines, dishwashers, refrigerators, and new kinds of stoves, were being developed for commercial laundries, breweries, hotels, hospitals, and apartment houses. They were designed to serve fifty to five hundred people, not one family. Peirce proposed, like Bebel, to use this technology, but to use it at the neighborhood scale, in a community workplace.

Peirce understood economic activity as both industrial production and human reproduction. She argued that her cooperative housekeeping strategies would lead to complete economic equality for women, because men could sustain farming and manufacturing while women ran the new, expanding areas of retail activity and service industries, in addition to their old standby, household production.[15] Thus she retained a gender division of labor but planned to revise national measures of productive economic activity. In this part of her analysis, Peirce anticipated Richard Ely, Helen Campbell, and Ellen Swallow Richards, who attempted, beginning in the 1880s and 1890s, to introduce home economics (or domestic economy) into academic debates and public policy as the "economics of consumption" on an equal plane with the economics of production.[16] All of the material feminists knew what many later Marxist and neoclassical economists alike have tended to forget: it is not the wage that defines work, it is the labor.

When Catharine Beecher, August Bebel, and Melusina Peirce framed their views of what the industrial revolution should mean to domestic life, they set up models of women's work and family life marked by all the hopes and fears of the mid-nineteenth century. They accepted gender stereotypes so strong that not one of these three models incorporated any substantial male responsibility for housework and child care. Yet Beecher's and Bebel's models of home continued to shape home life and public policy for over a century. The haven strategy and the industrial strategy became the ruling paradigms for domestic life in capitalist and in state socialist societies where the paid employment of women was a fact, not a hope or a fear.[17] Neither model of home life incorporated any substantial critique of male exclusion from the domestic scene. Both models disconnected household space from other parts of the industrial city and its economy. Attempts to repair their conceptual difficulties accelerated in the years after World War I, but neither model has undergone the total revision that would enable planners of housing, jobs, and services to create the spatial settings for modern societies where the paid employment of women is essential.

As a result, women have become disadvantaged workers in both capitalist and state socialist societies. If we look at the evolution of these two models, we see that there have been many ingenious modifications and ideological surprises as capitalists attempted to industrialize the haven strategy or state socialists attempted to domesticate the industrial strategy. The neighborhood strategy of Peirce met a rather different fate. Its adherents advanced their cause effectively in the United States and Europe, creating many interesting small experiments. As a result, they extended their argument for justice and women's liberation, but never had to provide a framework for government policy.

The evolution of all three models of home in different societies during the twentieth century reveals a great deal about capitalism and the role of the state in advanced capitalist societies, socialism and the role of the state in state socialist societies, and feminism and the persistence of male economic control of female labor. It is a story far too complex to be told in full here, yet a brief review may provoke readers of many different political persuasions. While the story does not deal at all with the fate of home life in economically developing nations, it may be read as a cautionary tale for any nation just beginning to make policies about housing and the employment of women. In the American context, the history of the three models of home may suggest ways to salvage the housing stock we now have while leaving the Victorian conventions of gender behind.

Modifying Beecher's Haven Strategy

Miniaturized technology and Household engineering

The first to modify the house as haven were manufacturers who introduced industrially produced appliances and products into the home. These were profitable extensions of the market economy, presented as aids to the hardworking homemaker. What is astonishing is that these inventions eroded the autonomy of women at least as much as they contributed to saving women's labor. Eventually the haven strategy produced not a skilled housewife happy at home, supported by her husband's "family" wage, but a harried woman constantly struggling to keep up standards.

The years since 1900 have seen the production of privately owned clothes washers, clothes dryers, refrigerators, gas and electric stoves, freezers, dishwashers, toasters, blenders, electric ovens, food processors, vacuum cleaners, and electric brooms.[18] Many of these appliances were the result of an extended campaign to miniaturize earlier hotel technology in the post–World War I era, and their potential for lightening household labor was tremendous. Unfortunately manufacturers began their sales of all such appliances and home improvements by advertising in women's magazines with themes of fear and guilt.[19] "For the health of your family...keep your foods sweet and pure, free from odors, impurities, and contamination," read the copy for McCray Sanitary Refrigerators. "Don't apologize for your toilet! Modernize it," said Pfau Manufacturing Company. Women were also told that liberation could be bought: "Electricity has brought to women a new freedom [represented by the figure of Liberty, wearing a crown and classical drapery]...the easy scientific method of cleaning with the Western Electric Vacuum cleaner."[20] The "laboratory-clean home" was what the housewife had to achieve.

In the first three decades of the twentieth century, industrial engineers and home economists joined forces to show housewives how to apply Frederick Taylor's factory-oriented, time-and-motion studies to their tasks at home. Since there had been no division and specialization of labor in the home, the industrial paraphernalia of task analysis with stopwatches made housewives into split personalities. They were the "managers" supervising their own speedup. As Christine Frederick put it, "Today, the woman in the home is called upon to be an executive as well as a manual laborer."[21] Or as one woman complained, "The role of the housewife is, therefore, analogous to that of the president of a corporation who would not only determine policies and make overall plans but also spend the major part of his time and energy in such activities as sweeping the plant and oiling the machines."[22]

Household engineers made women feel guilty for not doing tasks fast enough. Advertisers made both men and women feel guilty through emotional blackmail. Men were told that if they loved their wives, they owed it to them to buy particular appliances. Women were told that if they bought certain items, men would love them more. "Man seeks no club, when the home has a Hub," wrote one stove manufacturer. The American response to such ad campaigns was extensive purchasing, but research-ers who have studied time budgets find that conflicts within the home continued and the work of the "haven" housewives was still "never done." Jo Ann Vanek reported in her 1974 survey in *Scientific American* that household standards had risen but women's time had not been saved.[23] To take just one example, Vanek showed that the full-time urban or rural housewife spent more hours doing laundry in the 1970s than in the 1920s, despite all the new washing machines, dryers, bleaches, and detergents. Why? Her family had more clothes and wanted them cleaner. The classic "ring around the collar" commercials of the 1960s dramatized the issue. A husband and his five-year-old son jeered at a woman for using a detergent that could not remove the stains on their shirt collars. Her response – to buy a new product – exemplified the ways that conflict within a family was exploited. Manufacturers often present ownership of multiple appliances as an integral part of a rising standard of living. This is misleading: many appliances require more labor than they save.

The popularity of gourmet cooking, the expansion of houses, and the increasing complexity of home furnishings have also contributed to an increasing demand for female labor hours in the home. Another development launched in the 1920s, which continued into the twenty-first century, was the creation of a culture of mothering that demanded intense attention to children at every stage of their development. Although the numbers of children were shrinking, mothers were expected to spend more time with each one. When American manufacturers introduced television, many households used it as a baby-sitting machine. However, television created as many problems as it solved, since children listened to endless commercials for candy and toys. Some inventions are better eliminated from home life.

Commercial services

When increasing numbers of American housewives and mothers entered the paid labor force in the 1960s and 1970s, and commercial services became a fast-growing sector of the economy, there was a second major modification of the haven strategy. In 1978, it was estimated that Americans spent a third of their food budgets in restaurants and fast-food establishments. From 1970, when Americans spent $6 billion on fast food, until 2000, when they spent over $110 billion (an almost twenty-fold increase), fast-food logo buildings have lined the highways.[24] The proportion of restaurant food eaten by two-earner couples was, as might be expected, higher than for one-earner couples with a full-time housewife. A McDo-nald's slogan, "A Mom making time," captured the mood of some customers. "It's nice to feel so good about a meal," sang Colonel Sanders' chorus. "We're cooking dinner in your neighborhood," ran the folksy copy line for a California chain of fast-food restaurants. Happy family life and the consumption of industrially produced meals have collided, just as political liberation for women and the purchase of electrical appliances meshed as themes in the 1920s.

Harland Sanders, the goateed Kentucky colonel dressed in a white suit with a black string tie, smiles at motorists from the street corners and roadsides of America. A man who started his career in 1929, running a small cafe behind a gas station in Corbin, Kentucky, he became the king of the take-out chicken business in the late 1950s. By 2000, Colonel Sanders' Kentucky Fried Chicken franchised 10,800 businesses doing $8.9 billion worth of fast food annually, worldwide.[25] When fast food came of age as one of many commercial services supported by working women and their families, Sanders became a hero as an entrepreneur. When Sanders died in 1980, his body lay in the rotunda of the state capitol in Frankfort. In Louisville, his hometown, the flags on city buildings were flown at half-staff. But was Sanders a hero to women? His franchises employed thousands of non-union women at low wages to prepare and serve his industrial food products. These commercial services and products filled in for home cooking, but they drained a woman's salary. One woman's precarious haven was sustained by the products of another woman's small wages in this fast-growing sector of the market economy. Those theorists who argued that such commercial services "liberated" women considered only the consumer and not the producer. Of course, the quality and price of commercial fast food varies greatly, as do the costs and conditions of production. In 2000, upscale businesses run by professional cooks, with catchy names like "A Moveable Feast" and "Perfect Parties," offer a range of carefully prepared soups, main courses, and desserts to affluent households whose members have no time to create elegant dinners.

Almost as common as the fast-food place on the corner is the commercial child-care facility. Profit-making child care is also big business. Most are independent operations run by licensed day-care providers. The fastest growing group are more carefully calculated to run as franchises, such as the Kinder Care chain, with 1,240 centers in thirty-nine states and the United Kingdom. Their education director in 1980 was an ex–Air Force colonel who designed a program for children in the chain's standardized plastic schoolhouses.[26] At the high end, expensive day-care services may provide development child care for the children of affluent families. At the low end, many in-home, "family" day-care centers exist.

Other types of profitable, personalized commercial services now offered to the home-as-haven include private cooks, nurses, maids, baby-sitters (long employed by the affluent), and Internet grocery-shopping services. One, called nyerrands.com, advertised in 2001, "Give us your to do list." Their fees are $30 per hour for waiting around for home deliveries, 20 percent of the bill for drugstore or grocery errands, and 25 percent of the bill for category-killer discount stores like Costco. Should you require "life management" assistance such as cleaning your closets or organizing your refrigerator, services in most big cities will provide a price quote on demand. The bargain end of the spectrum on personal service is the maid franchise operation. Such services pay workers extremely low wages. When author Barbara Ehrenreich went on assignment as a maid, she received $6.65 an hour, while customers were charged $25 an hour.[27]

Employer benefits and state services

American employers may provide services to workers who are mothers when there are bonanza profits to be made; the state intervenes to provide services to employed women when there are wartime labor shortages. These crisis times reveal just how much can be gained by supporting women's economic activities. . . . Kaiser Shipyards in Vanport City, Oregon, was an impressive demonstration of how employers could make a difference for women. In less than one year, Kaiser management created a dazzling array of inducements for mothers with children to take on jobs as welders, riveters, and heavy construction workers. Almost sixty years later, American women workers still lack national legislation requiring that all employers treat women as valued workers and offer similar programs.

In 1993, the United States enacted the Family and Medical Leave Act. It requires employers with over fifty workers to provide up to twelve weeks of unpaid leave for "certain family and medical reasons," including childbirth, adoption, and the need to care for a spouse, child, or parent who is seriously ill, as well as a serious health condition of the worker. An international study of 152 countries in 1998 showed that 80 percent offered *paid* maternity leave. A European official commented sadly on the U.S., "it's a do-it-yourself maternity plan."[28] Since employers provide no pay, only affluent workers would be able to take time off. Mother and fathers who want a year off to bond with a new baby and create a secure attachment are out of luck.

The child-care situation is no better. A national day-care bill was passed by both houses of Congress in 1971, only to be vetoed by Richard Nixon, who argued that he was defending the American family. The need for developmental child care has been fought by conservatives, who fail to appreciate that while 65 percent of the mothers of children under six are in the paid labor force, only a small percent of the children of employed mothers enjoy quality child care.[29] Most parents have to struggle to find anything. Latch-key children are on the rise. When the topic turns to welfare mothers, the lack of day care becomes a clear example of inept policy. Welfare reformers in the Clinton era told women they must get off welfare and find paid employment. Often there was no public day care and no adequate provision for commercial child-care expenses, which might take a third or half of a woman's pay.

Experiments in flex-time, or flexible work schedules, have been heavily publicized as employers' initiatives to help employed parents at little cost to themselves. So have experiments in telecommuting, or work at home on the Internet. Such arrangements do not eliminate the double day, they merely make it less logistically stressful. Flexible work schedules are worth campaigning for, but trade unions and women's groups recognize they are only a small part of a broader solution to women's double workload.

Swedish Parent Insurance

It is instructive to mention Swedish benefits, which guarantee women and men workers more rights to economic support for parenting. Gender equality was not the only motivation for their legislation. Politicians agreed that more Swedish women in the paid labor force were preferable to large numbers of guest workers (migrant laborers) for political reasons. So, during the 1960s and 1970s, elaborate maternity insurance, child-care provisions, and incentives to employers evolved in order to avoid bringing guest workers from Southern Europe into the country in large numbers. Eventually, by 1999, 70 percent of Swedish women had joined the paid labor force; Swedish Parent Insurance was a monument to their economic importance to the nation, and to their role as mothers.

Swedish Parent Insurance, established in 1974, provides for economic benefits and leaves from paid work for either new mothers or new fathers. As Sheila Kamerman, a specialist in the comparative analysis of social welfare programs, has described it, "this is a universal, fully paid, wage-related, taxable cash benefit." It now covers the year after childbirth. Either parent can remain home to care for the infant. Kamerman explains how it might work: "A woman might use the benefit to cover four months of full time leave and stay home. Then each might, in turn, work two months at half time, followed by two months at three-quarter time (a six-hour day). Employers are required to accept part-time employment as part of this benefit, for childcare purposes." When only 10 percent of the eligible men used this benefit in 1976, the Swedish government appointed a Father's Commission to recommend changes. New legislation added thirty days of leave for fathers only. Men had to use it during the child's first year, or lose it. Men also got an additional benefit which provided ten days leave at the time of birth, and eighteen days of paid leave per child for either parent to care for sick children at home. In some parts of Sweden, Kamerman notes that workers will also come to the house to care for a sick child so that both parents may go to work, and another Swedish program has offered state subsidies for employers who hire women in fields dominated by men, or hire men in fields dominated by women. Sweden has recognized that there may be economic disruption caused by giving equal work to women and men, where jobs previously were segregated. This legislation makes it possible for employers to recoup some of the cost of this social change.[30] This is the kind of economic equity that can improve the lives of both women and men.

Male participation

One last attempt to modify the round of tasks for the housewife in the U.S. has been the call for male participation. Training boys for housework and child care, and insisting that adult men take part, educates them and improves their skills. Imaginative projects along these lines include grade-school courses for boys on how to take care of babies and YWHA play groups for fathers and children.[31] Both traditional consciousness-raising and these new courses reveal to men and boys the skills needed for nurturing, the time involved, and the role that space plays in isolating the nurturer. They find that kitchens are often designed for one worker, not two; that supermarkets are designed for the longest possible trip, not the shortest; and that men's rooms, like women's rooms, need a safe place where a diaper can be changed. Men who do housework and parenting then begin to see the patterns of private and public life in the divided American city.

In the United States, we have had active struggle for male participation in housework since the 1970s. Yet sociological studies suggest that American men do only 10 percent to 15 percent of household work (a smaller percentage than children contribute) and women still bear the brunt of 70 percent, even when both members of a couple are in the paid labor force. Sociologist Arlie Hochschild reported in *The Second Shift* that employed women averaged 15 hours more of housework and child care per week than men, a finding consistent from the 1980s through the 1990s. Indeed, economist Heidi Hartmann suggests that men actually demand eight hours more service per week than they contribute.[32] Other studies have found that the work week of American and Canadian women is 21 hours longer than that of men.[33]

A closer look at male behavior in different classes reveals common gender stereotypes underlying the struggle over housework within the family. Men pretend to be incompetent or they call the jobs trivial.[34] They may also have very heavy overtime (whether at executive or blue-collar jobs) and argue that their time is always worth more than a woman's time. Men may also find that even if they do participate, a couple with young children still can't manage alone if both partners are employed full-time. An even more insurmountable problem to male participation is the absence of men in many households.[35] Men's reluctance to take part in nurturing the next generation is only part of the problem. In many cases the ideal of male involvement has blinded many angry women to the severe logistical problems presented by the house itself. Women's hope for male cooperation, some time in the distant future, obscures the need for sweeping spatial and economic reforms.

Modifying Bebel's Industrial Strategy

In the same way that Beecher's haven strategy of keeping domestic work out of the market economy was slowly eroded, so Bebel's ideal strategy for the state socialist world has also been betrayed by the retention of a second shift of private life and home cooking. Bebel argued that only a comprehensive program of industrial development for all women, including the design of new services and new housing forms, could improve women's position.[36] This has never been realized. Domestic drudgery accompanied industrial work for women; it did not wither away under the "dictatorship of the proletariat," just as the state did not.

Between the 1950s and the 1990s, one might have expected more comprehensive planning of services in state socialist countries such as Cuba, China, and the former Soviet Union, where the state owned the factories, ran the shops, ran the day care, ran the transit, and owned the housing. At the state's discretion, day care and other services could be located in the factory or in the residential neighborhood. Indeed, day care, other social services, and even the factory itself could be placed in the residential neighborhood. Despite this potential ability to meet employed women's needs, such decisions were not usually made in ways that increased women's autonomy.

The house for the new way of life

The first opportunity for fulfilling Bebel's ideal occurred in the Soviet Union, after the October Revolution of 1917. Lenin and Alexandra Kollontai led Bolshevik support for housing and services for employed women. They argued for the transformation of the home by the state and experimented with these ideas as the basis for national housing policy. Lenin, in *The Great Initiative*, wrote about the need for housing with collective services in order to involve women in industrial production:

"Are we devoting enough attention to the germs of communism that already exist in this area [of the liberation of women]? No and again no. Public dining halls, creches, kindergartens – these are exemplary instances of these germs, these are those simple, everyday means, free of all bombast, grandiloquence and pompous solemnity, which, however, are *truly* such that they can *liberate women*, truly such that they can decrease and do away with her inequality vis-a-vis man in regard to her role in social production and public life." Lenin conceded that, "these means are not new, they have (like all the material prerequisites of socialism) been created by large-scale capitalism, but under capitalism they have firstly remained a rarity, secondly – and particularly important – they were either hucksterish enterprises, with all the bad sides of speculation, of profit-making, of deception, of falsification or else they were a 'trapeze act' of bourgeois charity, rightly hated and disclaimed by the best workers."[37] Following Lenin's encouragement, the new regime developed a program of building multifamily housing with collective services, beginning with competitions by architects to generate new designs for the "House for the New Way of Life."

While the competition had a strong intellectual impact on designers of mass housing all over the world, ultimately, few of the projects were built as intended. The USSR lacked the technology and the funds to follow through on its commitment to urban housing under Lenin. Under Stalin, the commitment itself dissolved. Stalin's ascendancy in the 1930s ended the official policy of women's liberation. Divorce and abortion were made difficult; "Soviet motherhood" was exalted, and experiments in collective living and new kinds of housing ended. Only the most minimal support for women's paid labor-force participation was provided: day care in large, bureaucratic centers stressing obedience, discipline, and propaganda.

Soviet motherhood

As a result, women in the USSR were encouraged to join the paid labor force without recognition of their first job in the home. In 1980, Anatole Kopp, a specialist in Soviet housing, concluded that "Soviet society today has but little connection with the fraternal, egalitarian, and self-managing society dreamed of by a few during the short period of cultural explosion which followed the Revolution." Workers lived in small private apartments in dreary, mass housing projects, where miles and miles of identical buildings had been constructed with industrialized building systems. Individual units were cramped and inconvenient. Appliances were minimal. Laundry was done in the sink; cooking on a two-burner countertop unit without oven. Refrigerators were rare status symbols for the favored elite. "Soviet architecture today well reflects daily life in the USSR.... It reflects the real condition of women in the Soviet Union – a far cry from the idyllic pictures once painted by Alexandra Kollontai."[38]

Research on the time budgets of women and men in the former Soviet Union showed the extent of inequality: 90 percent of all Soviet women between the ages of twenty and forty-nine were in the paid labor force. While women's housework time decreased somewhat between 1923 and 1966, men's time spent in housework did not increase. As a result, women's total work week was still seventeen hours longer than men's.[39] Moscow was one of the few cities in the world to provide enough day care for the children of all employed mothers, but while this allowed women to function as full-time paid workers (51 percent of the Soviet Union's labor force), their housing was not designed to include either Bebel's industrialized housekeeping services or American kitchen appliances.[40] So, one could compare women's work in the United States and the former Soviet Union. The USSR emphasized state subsidized day care and women's involvement in industrial production. The U.S. emphasized commercial day care and women's consumption of appliances and commercial services. In both cultures, the majority of married women had two jobs, worked 17–21 hours per week more than men, and earned about 60 to 75 percent of what men earned. The "new way of life" in the USSR was as elusive as the "new woman" in the U.S.

Housewives' Factories in Cuba and China

The situation for employed women has been quite similar in other state socialist countries whose economic development was influenced by the Soviet Union. Given that standing in long lines to purchase scarce food supplies and consumer goods has long been a problem for housewives in state socialist societies, Cuba developed the Plan Jaba or Shopping Bag Plan in the early 1970s to permit employed women to go to the head of lines in crowded stores. However pragmatic the Plan Jaba was, as a solution to the woman's double day as paid worker and mother, and as a solution to the hours of queuing, one could hardly call it a major theoretical innovation. The publicity given to it as a fine example of socialist liberation for women was overdone. In much the same vein, Cuba also offered employed women special access to rationed goods and factory laundry services.[41] Such services cannot correct more basic problems. The location of factories in neighborhoods was not a service to women but a disservice when the well-located factories offered only low-paid work for women. In Cuba, a textile factory staffed primarily by low-paid women was located in the Alamar housing project outside Havana; a shoe factory staffed by low-paid women was placed in the José Martí neighborhood in Santiago. In addition, the large and well-designed day-care centers in housing projects employed only women as day-care workers, at low salaries, because child care was considered a woman's job.

Chinese examples of residential quarter planning for employed women are similar. During the Great Leap Forward, so-called housewives' factories were located in residential neighborhoods. The female workers received low wages and worked in relatively primitive industrial conditions. All this was justified for some time as a transitional stage of national economic development. However, in 1980, the Chinese planned an entire new town, which included new housewives' factories, to accompany a large new steel plant for male workers who would earn much higher wages.[42] Chinese residential neighborhoods, like the Cuban ones, have also employed women as day-care workers and community-health workers at very low wages. So, while the socialization of traditional women's work proceeded at a rapid rate to support women's involvement in industrial production, both the industrial workers and the service workers remained in female ghettos, and female responsibility for nurturing work remained the norm.

During the last three decades, women in state socialist countries have raised the issue of male participation, as have their counterparts in the United States. Cuban women developed a strong critique of what they call the "second shift," or their responsibility for housework once the paid shift is over. A cartoon shows an agricultural worker with a mound of sugar cane she has just cut, saying "Finished! Now to cook, wash, and iron!" As a result of such campaigns, the Cuban Family Code of 1974 was written. In principle, it aimed at having men share what was formerly "women's work." In practice, the law depended upon private struggle between husband and wife for day-to-day enforcement. Men feigned incompetence, especially in the areas of cooking and cleaning. The gender stereotyping of low-paid jobs for women outside the home, in day-care centers for example, only reinforced the problem at home. Some Cuban men made an effort, but many argued that domestic sharing could wait for the next generation. While Communist Party policy urged male cadres to assume half the domestic chores, Heidi Steffens, a writer for *Cuba Review*, recounted a popular mid-1970s anecdote. A well-known member of the Central Committee of the party took over the job of doing the daily laundry, but he insisted that his wife hang it out and bring it in from the line, since he didn't want the neighbors to see his loss of *machismo*.[43] The power of *machismo* was also evident when men cited pressure to do "women's" work as one of their reasons for emigration.[44]

In China, where there have also been general political policies that housework should be shared, the ambience is even less supportive. Sometimes the elderly – more often a grandmother than a grandfather – will fill in. The history of party pronouncements on housework can be correlated with the need to move women into or out of the paid labor force. When a party directive instructed male members not to let themselves be henpecked into too much domestic activity at the expense of their very important political work, it was clear that full male participation in housework was a distant goal rather than a reality.[45] In state socialist countries, as in capitalist ones, the hope of male participation hides the inadequacy of the basic model concerning work and home. It encourages both women and men to think that the next generation might negotiate a better solution, rather than to consider the overall inadequacies of spatial and economic planning.

Modifying Peirce's Neighborhood Strategy

While the haven strategy and the industrial strategy suffered slow disintegration into the double day, Melusina Peirce's neighborhood strategy of material feminism never became mainstream. Like Bebel and Beecher, she failed to incorporate male participation in housework and child care, but at least she had a strong economic reason for the exclusion. Peirce wanted to overcome the isolation of housewives, the lack of specialization of tasks, the lack of labor-saving technology, and the lack of financial security for any woman who had spent a lifetime in domestic labor. She saw men as a threat to women's traditional economic activities and wanted women to defend and expand their household activities on their own terms, rather than have them taken over by men's commercial enterprises.

In 1868, Peirce herself organized a bakery, laundry, grocery, and sewing service in Cambridge, Massachusetts.[46] In the next half-century, dozens of other experiments were conducted, including a family dining club in Warren, Ohio, from 1903 to 1923, and a Cleaning Club in Northbrook, Illinois, in the late 1940s. In Massachusetts, between 1926 and 1931, Ethel Puffer Howes made an even more ambitious experiment, providing models of community-run services: a cooperative dinner kitchen for the home delivery of hot food, a cooperative nursery school, a home helpers' bureau, and a job placement advisory service for Smith graduates. As the head of the Institute for the Coordination of Women's Interests at Smith College, Howes believed that her model institutions could be recreated throughout the nation by housewives who also wished to enter paid employment. Unfortunately, during the Depression, prejudice against women's employment, combined with the Smith College faculty's suspicions that Howes' ideas were unacademic, ended this project after five years of successful operation.

Recruiting adequate capital to initiate change was a consistent problem for all of these neighborhood experiments. Some housewives' experiments failed because husbands found their wives demands for pay too expensive – they believed that marriage was a labor contract, making housewives' labor free. Other experiments – including some that lasted the longest – relied on ties between neighbors and kin but involved little money changing hands. This tradition of housewives' neighborly sharing of tasks moved too slowly for many nineteenth-century feminists who attempted to push the neighborhood strategy in the direction of more businesslike enterprises run by professional women. They believed that the increasing employment of women outside the home could provide the paid jobs and paying customers necessary to transform traditional domesticity. Yet while more cash was a resource, the neighborhood organization of women suffered as a result.

In the 1890s the idea of neighborhood domestic reform as "good business" became quite popular when the American feminist Charlotte Perkins Gilman proposed the construction of special apartment houses for employed women and their families. In *Women and Economics*, she noted that employed women required day care and cooked-food service to enjoy home life after a day of paid work, and argued that if any astute business woman were to construct an apartment hotel with these facilities for professional women and their families, it would be filled at once. She believed that female entrepreneurs would find this "one of the biggest businesses on earth."[47]

Service houses, collective houses, and cooperative quadrangles

Gilman's work was translated into several European languages, and her argument was taken up by many European women and men looking for a better approach to housing. The builder Otto Fick constructed the first "service house" in Copenhagen in 1903, a small apartment house occupied by tenants who enjoyed food service, cleaning, and laundry service. The building was explicitly designed for married women in the paid labor force, but Fick thought career and motherhood incompatible and prohibited children.[48] A second fault can be seen in Fick's claim that he was the "inventor of a new mode of living which simultaneously has all the features of a profitable business venture."[49] His claim depended upon residents paying the service personnel low wages and making a profit on the market price of shares in the residents' association when they sold out. Nevertheless, Fick achieved a level of social and technological innovation that Gilman had only proposed, and his project operated until 1942.[50]

Another successful design for live/work housing was developed in Sweden in the 1930s. In 1935, feminist Alva Myrdal (later awarded the Nobel Prize for her work on world peace) collaborated with architect Sven Markelius to create housing with work space, food service, and child care. Their project in the center of Stockholm included fifty-seven small apartments of very elegant design. Some of them could also be used as offices or studios. Not only did Markelius design these, he moved into the building himself and served as an unofficial handyman for thirty years, in order to make sure everything about the building worked, and to demonstrate his commitment to social housing.[51]

In 1945, *Life* magazine praised this project as a model for post–World War II reorganization of American housing: the reporter suggested that Americans should copy its design for women in the wartime labor force who wished to continue their careers.[52] The only disadvantage was that most residents did not wish to leave after their children were grown, and new parents could not find space in the building. The day-care center ultimately had to take in neighborhood children as well as residents' children to stay in business. The restaurant food became less economically competitive when cheap eating places appeared in large numbers in the city.

Olle Enkvist, a Stockholm contractor who became involved with the combination of housing and services, built the collective houses Marieberg (1944), Nockebyhove (1951), Blackeberg (1952), and Hasselby (1955–56). All had restaurants and full child care. Unlike Fick, who believed in joint stock ownership by a residents' association, Enkvist owned these buildings as benign landlord. His success was measured in long waiting lists of prospective tenants. After his death there were numerous tenant confrontations with the new management, especially when, in the 1970s, the new management wished to close the collective dining rooms because they didn't generate as much profit as the rental apartments. This probably would have seemed most ironic to Enkvist, who decided against delivery systems for cooked food (such as the elevators Fick had used for food) on the grounds that a large dining room with private family tables was more conducive to social contacts. Hasselby tenants did prove they could cater for themselves without losing money (serving about one hundred people daily for three years), but management found this level of participation cumbersome and decided to eject the tenants. The turmoil of decollectivization then led to the impression that these projects were social or financial failures, although many functioned smoothly for thirty years. Their main failure was that the landlord did not turn a high profit.[53]

In England, Gilman's arguments were taken up by Ebenezer Howard, founder of the Garden Cities movement, who proposed the "cooperative quadrangle" as the basis of new town planning in 1898.[54] Howard's cooperative quadrangles were to be composed of garden apartments served by a collective kitchen, dining room, and open space. They were designed to release women from household drudgery in the private home, and between 1911 and 1930 several of these projects were built for various constituencies, including single female professionals and the elderly, as well as two-earner couples. Howard himself lived in Homesgarth, a cooperative triangle at Letchworth. The quadrangles never became the standard housing available in the Garden Cities, but they did provide some very successful alternative projects within these new towns. In time, their dining rooms also seemed expensive compared to local restaurants. After World War I, Clementina Black of London argued for the postwar adoption of "Domestic Federations" similar to Howard's designs.[55] After World War II, Sir

Charles Reilly, Member of Parliament and head of the School of Architecture at Liverpool University, also proposed a plan for reconstruction that incorporated many of the features of Howard's cooperative quadrangles.[56] He organized neighborhoods of duplex houses around nurseries, community kitchens, and open spaces.

Apartment hotels

In the United States, Gilman's ideas were reflected in the apartment hotels built between 1898 and 1930 in major cities. Mary Beard, the well-known historian, lived in one such apartment hotel with her husband and children; they were located on the bus line to the New York Public Library. Knowing that three meals a day would be served to her family, she was able to hop on the bus and tend to her research. Georgia O'Keefe lived in a similar hotel with good light for painting. For less affluent women, Finnish and Jewish workers' housing cooperatives provided child care, bed-sitting rooms for the elderly, and tea rooms adjacent to family apartments.[57] The Workers Cooperative Colony in the Bronx, organized and owned by workers in the needle trades, was an early example of this kind of project in the mid-1920s. Again, the cost of providing services with well-paid unionized service workers made competition with commercial groceries, restaurants, and laundries difficult.

Cash or community?

All these attempts to define supportive residential communities for employed women and their families ran into two related economic difficulties. First, the economic value of housework was never adequately understood. Second, the economic value of the new services was unclear, in relation both to the old-fashioned system of hiring personal servants and the new commercial services and industrial products developed for haven housewives. Such services, when produced by low-paid female workers, were cheaper, if less intimate and desirable, than community-generated alternatives. Economies of scale worked in favor of the nationally distributed products and services, even if they were impersonal. Once the substitution of cash for personal participation by residents had been arranged, the difference between industrial and neighborhood services might be difficult to discern. So professional women, if they attempted to buy services, had to be very careful to treat the women service workers well. Otherwise, they wound up closer to Colonel Sanders, year by year.

Family allowances and wages for housework   In much the same way, housewives struggling for economic independence through the neighborhood strategy found themselves closer to the haven strategy if they focused on wages and omitted the ideal of reshaping household work in community form. Eleanor Rathbone, an economist, feminist, and Member of Parliament in England, formed a club to lobby for wages for wives as early as 1918.[58] Some Americans also supported this cause in the 1940s.[59] Rathbone started by seeking a decent wage for housework; in the late 1940s, she won for mothers the Family Allowance: a small subsidy for a second child and any additional ones. Inspired by the concept of Family Allowances, and the potential of organizing to increase them, some British feminists revived the idea of larger payments for housework in the early 1970s. Led by Selma James, a group called Wages for Housework demanded that the state pay wages to all women for their housework. To attract supporters, the organizers ran skits about women's work in urban neighborhoods on market days. They passed out free potholders with their slogan to remind women of the campaign for wages every time they picked up a hot pot. They used union techniques of insisting on wages, wages, wages. "Just give us the money. All we want is the money," James incanted at one meeting.

Wages for Housework organized effectively among welfare recipients and single-parent mothers. They created special suborganizations: Lesbians for Wages for Housework, and Black Women for Wages for Housework. The campaign developed successful recruiting tactics, but there was no mass movement. Organizers demonstrated the value of a housewife's day but their emphasis was on cash. Their campaigns had some of the weaknesses of American welfare-rights organizing of the 1960s. Wages for Housework did not confront the isolated home as haven, the setting for housework. They accepted females as domestic workers and identified the welfare state (rather than employers or husbands) as the primary target of their activities. Furthermore, they included sexual services as "all in a day's work" for the housewife. This made it easy to organize angry women who felt sexually exploited, but the model of wife as paid maid and prostitute made it difficult to articulate a more sophisticated position on male-female relationships.

Wages for Housework never lacked vitality, even if it lacked subtlety. A china bank in the shape of a rolling pin, made in the 1940s, carried the message of the earlier British feminists, "If women were paid for all they do, there'd be a lot of wages due."[60] But just as Rathbone had found a wage for haven housewives politically impossible in the 1940s, so it was in the 1970s. Even if they had won, financial recognition from the state for the work of homemaking would not have been enough to transform the haven housewife's situation.

Trade-A-Maid   Gary Trudeau's *Doonesbury* cartoon on "Trade-A-Maid" schemes, in which American haven housewives swap chores, points out this problem as well. As Nichole, the "Alternate Life Stylist," explains it, "Housewife A and her best friend, Housewife B, spend weekdays cleaning each other's home. Their respective husbands pay for their services, just as they would for those of a first-class maid."[61] The employed wives then become eligible for Social Security and for tax deductions on cleaning equipment. They receive cash but neither husband suffers loss of family income since the swap means both wives are paid equally. However, they still work in isolation, since receiving a wage for housework (whether paid by individual husbands or by the state) does not transform the home as haven, nor does it utilize the full range of technologies available in twentieth-century society. "It's illegal, though, right?" worries the interviewer. "Not yet," says Nichole.

NICHE   Another American proposal captures the essence of the neighborhood strategy and avoids the question of industrial technologies by stressing the value of women offering social services to each other in the neighborhood. In 1977, Nona Glazer, Lindka Mjaka, Joan Acker, and Christine Bose suggested institutionalizing housewives' cooperative services by establishing government funding for Neighbors in Community Helping Environments (NICHE).[62] In *Women in a Full Employment Economy*, they explained how to start Neighborhood Service Houses, where women would supervise children's play, care for sick children, facilitate repair service to homes, encourage bartering, distribute hot meals, and work with battered women, abused children, and rape victims. In return for providing these family and community services, women would receive at least a minimum wage. This proposal recognized that women's cooperation to socialize homemaking tasks could transform women's experience. NICHE also saw economic recognition of domestic labor as essential, but it did not involve proposals for male participation. Since NICHE was relying on the state to provide the wages, they had selected almost as difficult a program as the Wages for Housework campaigns. In a Democratic administration concerned about full employment the proposal looked possible; when Republicans took office and slashed social services, the proposal looked even more relevant, but funding appeared impossible.

Complexity

All of these campaigns to transform models of home life underscore the need for complex social, economic, and environmental innovations. Successful solutions would reward housework and parenting as essential to society, incorporate male responsibility for nurturing, build on existing networks of neighbors, kin, and friends, and incorporate new technologies, in order to promote equality for women within a more caring society. Yet before any specific policy changes can be proposed, it is essential to recognize the consistent economic and spatial failures that marred previous attempts. Beecher's and Bebel's models were too simplistic. If Beecher's glorification of the homemaker attempted to recover a pre-industrial past, Bebel's rejection of the homemaker embraced the fantasy of a totally industrial future. As public policy, these strategies led to ironies compounded upon ironies; after a century, women had gotten the worst of both worlds, having been economically disadvantaged by the double day and spatially manipulated by the refusal of designers and planners to treat the home as a workplace.

Yet the most humiliating aspect of women's experience as nurturers was not their economic or spatial frustration, but the suppression of the neighborhood approach to home life, in order that the haven and industrial strategies could be presented as modern. The advocates of neighborhood networks were attacked as socialist sympathizers in the United States in the 1920s, and as bourgeois deviationists who should be expelled from the Communist Party in Germany and the USSR. Women have had warmed-over Beecher presented to them as women's liberation through Western Electric vacuum cleaners and Colonel Sanders; warmed-over Bebel presented as women's liberation through the Plan Jaba and the housewives' factories. Full recognition of what women actually contribute to society in the current century is essential to recover nurturing from the domain of corporate or bureaucratic planning. No one has put the problem of nurturing more succinctly than Melusina Peirce: "Two things women must do somehow, as the conditions not only of the future happiness, progress, and elevation of their sex, but of its bare respectability and morality. 1st. They *must* earn their own living. 2nd. They *must* be organized among themselves."[63] If this is still the best advice to women about how to deal with their traditional work, two huge areas of concern remain, architecture and economics. The three models of home life that have characterized nurturing have also had strong implications for housing design and for economic productivity, as house forms and systems of national accounting have reflected underlying ideas about the nature of home.

NOTES

1   Ellen Malos, ed., *The Politics of Housework* (London: Virago Press, 1980); Nancy Folbre, *The Invisible Heart: Economics and Family Values* (New York: The New Press, 2001); Arlie Russell Hochschild, *The Second Shift* (1989; New York: Avon Books, 1997), includes a bibliography of recent scholarship.

2   Lily Braun, *Frauenarbeit und Hauswirtschaft* (Berlin, 1901); Dolores Hayden, *The Grand Domestic Revolution: A History of Feminist Designs for American Homes, Neighborhoods, and Cities* (Cambridge, Mass.: MIT Press, 1981), 291–305.

3   Hartmann has pioneered the analysis of women's labor time in the home, as the basis for her analysis of the family as a site of class and gender conflict usually ignored by liberal theorists. Heidi I. Hartmann, "The Family as the Locus of Gender, Class, and Political Struggle: The Example of Housework," *Signs: Journal of Women in Culture and Society* 6 (Spring, 1981), 366–94.

4   Laura Balbo, "The Servicing Work of Women and the Capitalist State," in *Political Power and Social Theory* (New York: Basic Books, 1981); Laura Balbo, "Crazy Quilts: Rethinking the Welfare State Debate from a Woman's Perspective," mimeographed, GRIFF, Milan, Italy, 1981; Laura Balbo and Renate Siebert Zahar, *Interferenze* (Milan: Feltrinelli, 1979).

5   Erma Bombeck, *The Grass is Always Greener Over the Septic Tank* (New York: Fawcett, 1977), 5. Billed as "the exposé to end all exposés – the truth about the suburbs," this book can be read as a bunch of little jokes, or as an unconscious but revealing indictment of numerous planning and design failures, and housewives' struggles to overcome them. A more serious attack is John Keats, *The Crack in the Picture Window* (Boston: Houghton Mifflin, 1957).

6   Literature on the family is reviewed in Hartmann, "The Family as the Locus of Gender, Class, and Political Struggle," 365–8.

7   Among the traditional family's defenders is Christopher Lasch, *Haven in a Heartless World: The Family Besieged* (New York: Basic Books, 1976).

8   William O'Neill, *Everyone Was Brave: A History of Feminism in America* (1969; New York: Quadrangle, 1971), 358.

9   Betty Friedan, *The Second Stage* (New York: Summit, 1981), 43, 83.

10 August Bebel, *Women under Socialism*, tr. Daniel De Leon (1883; New York: Schocken, 1971), 338–9; V. I. Lenin, *The Emanicipation of Women* (New York: Progress Publishers, 1975), 69.

11 Hayden, *Grand Domestic Revolution*, 3–5.

12 Bebel, *Women Under Socialism*, 338–9.

13 Jane Cunningham Croly, letter to Elizabeth Cady Stanton, printed in *The Revolution* 3 (May 27, 1869), 324.

14 Melusina Fay Peirce, "Cooperative Housekeeping II" (second of five articles), *Atlantic Monthly* 22 (Dec. 1868), 684.

15 Melusina Fay Peirce, "Cooperative Housekeeping III," *Atlantic Monthly* 23 (Jan. 1869), 29–30.

16   Mari Jo Buhle, "A Republic of Women: Feminist Theory in the Gilded Age," paper read at the 1981 meeting of the American Historical Association, 4–7; also *Lake Placid Conference on Home Economics, Proceedings* (Lake Placid, N.Y., 1903, 1907).

17   Thomas Kuhn, *The Structure of Scientific Revolutions* (1962; Chicago: University of Chicago Press, 1973); "Second Thoughts on Paradigms," in *The Essential Tension: Selected Studies in Scientific Tradition and Change* (Chicago: University of Chicago Press, 1977), 293–319.

18   Susan Strasser, *Never Done: A History of American Housework* (New York: Pantheon Books, 1982), is an excellent work.

19   Ruth Schwartz Cowan, "The 'Industrial' Revolution in the Home: Household Technology and Social Change in the 20th Century," *Technology and Culture* 17 (Jan. 1976), 1–23.

20   Carol Miles, "The Craftsman Ideal of Home Life," unpublished paper, 1981.

21   Christine Frederick, *Household Engineering: Scientific Management in the Home* (Chicago: American School of Home Economics, 1920), 92.

22   Edith Mendel Stern, "Women Are Household Slaves," *American Mercury* (Jan. 1949), 71.

23   Jo Anne Vanek, "Time Spent in Housework," *Scientific American* (Nov. 1974), 116–20.

24   "U.S. Dines Out Despite Prices," *Boston Globe* (Oct. 25, 1978), 75; Eric Schlosser, *Fast Food Nation: The Dark Side of the All-American Meal* (Boston: Houghton Mifflin, 2001), 3.

25   Kentucky Fried Chicken Website, http://www.kfc.com/about/kfcfacts.htm (June 2001); Edith Evans Asbury, "Col. Harland Sanders, Founder of Kentucky Fried Chicken Dies," *New York Times* (Dec. 17, 1980), 29.

26   Kinder Care Web site, http://www.kindercare.com (June 2001); "A Big, Big Business," *Southern Exposure* 8 (Fall 1980), 36–40; Joseph Lelyveld, "Drive-in Day Care," *New York Times Magazine* (June 5, 1977), 110.

27   Barbara Ehrenreich, *Nickel and Dimed: On [Not] Getting By in America* (New York: Metropolitan Books, 2001), 72.

28   U.S. Department of Labor, "FMLA Compliance Guide," http://www.dol.gov/esa/public/regs/compliance/whd/1421.htm (July 2001); "U.S. Maternity Plans Pale in Comparison to Other Nations," *Washington Post* (Feb. 15, 1998), http://www.chron.com/content/chronicle/nation/98/02/16/ maternityleave.2-0.html (July 2001).

29   Kristin Moore and Sandra Hofferth, "Women and Their Children," in R. Smith, ed., *The Subtle Revolution: Women at Work* (Washington, D.C.: Urban Land Institute, 1979), 125–58; U.S. Department of Labor, Bureau of Labor Statistics, "Employment Characteristics of Families in 2000," April 2001, ftp://ftp.bls.gov/pub/news.release/famee.txt (June 2001); Nancy S. Barrett, "Women in the Job Market: Unemployment and Work Schedules," in Smith, ed., *The Subtle Revolution*, 88–90.

30   Sheila B. Kamerman, "Work and Family in Industrialized Societies," *Signs* 4 (Summer 1979), 644–5; Statistics Sweden, "Employment Rates for EU Member States, 1999," March 2001, http://www.scb.se/eng/omscb/eu/syssel sattning.asp (June 2001); Ann Crittenden, *The Price of Motherhood* (New York: Metropolitan Books, 2001), 244–6.

31   Ari Korpivaara, "Play Groups for Dads," and Alison Herzig and Jane Mali, "Oh, Boy! Babies!" in *Ms.* 10 (Feb. 1982), 52–8.

32   Sarah Fenstermaker Berk, "The Household as Workplace," in G. Wekerle, ed., *New Space for Women* (Boulder, Colo.: Westview, 1980), 70; Nona Glazer-Malbin, "Review Essay: Housework," *Signs* 1 (Summer 1976), 905–22; Nadine Brozan, "Men and Housework: Do They or Don't They?," *New York Times* (Nov. 1, 1980), 52; Clair Vickery, "Women's Economic Contribution to the Family," in Smith, ed., *The Subtle Revolution*, 159–200; Arlie Hochschild and Anne Machung, "Afterwood" to the 1997 edition of *The Second Shift* (1989; New York: Avon, 1997), 279; Nona Glazer, *Women's Paid and*

Unpaid Labor: The Work Transfer in Health Care and Retailing (Philadelphia: Temple University Press, 1993); Hartmann, "The Family as the Locus of Gender, Class, and Political Struggle," 383.

33 Hartmann, "The Family as Locus," 380; Crittenden, *The Price of Motherhood*, 22.

34 Mainardi, "The Politics of Housework," in Robin Morgan, ed., *Sisterhood Is Powerful* (New York: Vintage, 1970), 447–54.

35 The majority of American men stop paying child support within two years of a divorce settlement, according to Kathryn Kish Sklar, "Women, Work, and Children, 1600–1980," paper read at the Third Annual Conference on Planning and Women's Needs, UCLA, Urban Planning Program, Feb. 21, 1981.

36 Bebel, *Women under Socialism*, 344–9.

37 Vladmir I. Lenin, *The Great Initiative*, quoted in Vladimir Zelinski, "Architecture as a Tool of Social Transformation," *Women and Revolution* 11 (Spring 1976), 6–14.

38 Anatole Kopp, "Soviet Architecture Since the 20th Congress of the C.P.S.U.," paper delivered at the Second World Congress of Soviet and East European Studies, 1980, 12–13.

39 Michael Paul Sacks, "Unchanging Times: A Comparison of the Everyday Life of Soviet Working Men and Women between 1923 and 1966," *Journal of Marriage and the Family* 39 (Nov. 1977), 793–805.

40 Alice H. Cook, *The Working Mother: A Survey of Problems and Programs in Nine Countries*, 2nd ed. (1978; Ithaca, N.Y.: New York State School of Industrial and Labor Relations, 1975), 8.

41 Carollee Benglesdorf and Alice Hageman, "Women and Work," in "Women in Transition," special issue of *Cuba Review* 4 (Sept. 1974), 9.

42 I was shown this project by planners in April 1980 when I visited China as a guest of the Chinese Architectural Society.

43 Heidi Steffens, "A Woman's Place," *Cuba Review* 4 (Sept. 1974), 29.

44 Geoffrey E. Fox, "Honor, Shame, and Women's Liberation in Cuba: Views of Working-Class Emigré Men," in A. Pescatello, ed., *Female and Male in Latin America* (Pittsburgh: University of Pittsburgh Press, 1973). I visited Cuba in 1979 and also observed male refusal to do housework in many situations.

45 Delia Davin, *Woman-Work: Women and the Party in Revolutionary China* (Oxford, England: Clarendon Press, 1976); Elisabeth J. Croll, "Women in Rural Production and Reproduction in the Soviet Union, China, Cuba, and Tanzania: Case Studies," in *Signs*, special issue on Development and the Sexual Division of Labor, 7 (Winter 1981), 375–99.

46 Hayden, *Grand Domestic Revolution*, 66–89, 208–27, 266–77.

47 Charlotte Perkins Gilman, *Women and Economics* (Boston: Maynard and Small, 1898); Hayden, *Grand Domestic Revolution*, 182–205. An early translation of Gilman in an architectural journal is "La Maison de Demain," *La Construction Moderne* 5 (Nov. 1914), 66–8.

48 Erwin Muhlestein, "Kollektives Wohnen gestern und heute," *Architese* 14 (1975), 4–5.

49 Otto Fick, "The Apartment House Up To Date," *Architectural Record* 22 (July 1907), 68–71.

50 Dick Urban Vestbro, "Collective Housing Units in Sweden," *Current Sweden*, Svenska Institutet, Stockholm, publication no. 234 (Sept. 1976), (6), 6–7.

51 Ibid.

52 "Sweden's Model Apartments: Stockholm Building is Wonderful for Wives Who Work," *Life* 18 (Mar. 12, 1945), 112–14.

53 Muhlestein, "Kollektives," 6–8; Vestbro, "Collective Housing," 8–11.

54 Hayden, *Grand Domestic Revolution*, 230–7.

55 Clementina Black, *A New Way of Housekeeping* (London: W. Collins Sons, 1918).

56 Lawrence Wolfe, *The Reilly Plan* (London: Nicholson and Watson, 1945).
57 Hayden, *Grand Domestic Revolution*, 251–61.
58 Ann Oakley, *Woman's Work: The Housewife Past and Present* (New York: Pantheon, 1974), 227–9.
59 Kay Hanly Bretnall, "Should Housewives Be Paid a Salary?," *American Home* 37 (Feb. 1947), 15–16.
60 Wages for Housework Collective, *All Work and No Pay* (London: Falling Wall Press, 1975), 5; also see Malos, ed., *The Politics of Housework*, for a full analysis of this movement.
61 Gary B. Trudeau, *Doonesbury*, "And Now, Here's Nichole," in Ann E. Beaudry, ed., *Women in the Economy* (Washington, D.C.: Institute for Policy Studies, 1978), 61.
62 Nona Glazer, Lindka Mjaka, Joan Acker, Christine Bose, *Women in a Full Employment Economy* (1977), mimeo.
63 Melusina Fay Peirce, "Cooperative Housekeeping," *Atlantic Monthly* 23 (March 1869), 297.

21

Towards Cosmopolis: Utopia as Construction Site

Leonie Sandercock

In the late 1990s the world of planning education and practice uneasily straddles an old planning paradigm, and one that is struggling to be born, in a way that is evocative of Matthew Arnold's great mid-nineteenth-century image of wandering between two worlds, one lost, the other yet to be found. The old planning served modernist cities in a project that was, in part, dedicated to the eradication of difference. Metaphorically, this planning can be linked with the machine images of the great Fritz Lang film, *Metropolis*. The emerging planning is dedicated to a social project in which difference can flourish.

The metaphorical image of cosmopolis is meant to suggest that diversity. To ensure planning's continued relevance into the next century as a significant social project, contributing to the creation of cosmopolis, it is important to give more flesh to these bones. I do this by developing three notions: the importance of an expanded language for planning (involving a relinking with the design professions); of an epistemology of multiplicity; and of a transformative politics of difference. This extract can deal only with the first of these. My personal vision is for a profession embracing concerns for social and environmental justice, for human community, for cultural diversity and for the spirit. In postwar planning's rush to join the (positivist) social sciences, some of its capacity to address these concerns was lost because it turned its back on questions of values, of meaning, and of the arts (rather than science) of city-building. The language, and the mental and emotional universe of planning were thus constricted. We can expand this universe by talking about the city of memory, the city of desire and the city of spirit.

Reprinted with permission of *Architectural Design* 68(1–2) (1998): ii–v.

City of Memory

Why do we visit graves? Why do we erect sculptures to dead leaders or war heroes or revolutionaries? Why do we save love letters for thirty or forty years or more? Why do we make photo albums, home movies, write diaries and journals? Why do we visit the sites of cave paintings at Lascaux, at Kakadu? Because memory, both individual and collective, is deeply important to us. It locates us as part of something bigger than our individual existences, perhaps makes us seem less insignificant, sometimes gives us at least partial answers to questions like, "Who am I?" and "Why am I like I am?". Memory locates us, as part of a family history, as part of a tribe or community, as a part of city-building and nation-making. Loss of memory is, basically, loss of identity. People suffering from amnesia or Alzheimer's are adrift in a sea of confusion. To take away a person's memories is to steal a large part of their identity. The past dwells in us and gives us our sense of continuity, anchoring us even as we move on.

Cities are the repositories of memories, and they are one of memory's texts. We revisit the house(s) we grew up in, we show our new lover the park where, as a kid, we had our first kiss, or where students were killed by police in an anti-war demonstration... Our lives and struggles, and those of our ancestors, are written into places, houses, neighborhoods, cities, investing them with meaning and significance.

Modernist planners became thieves of memory. Faustian in their eagerness to erase all traces of the past in the interest of forward momentum, of growth in the name of progress, their 'drive-by' windscreen surveys of neighborhoods that they had already decided (on the basis of objective census and survey data, of course) to condemn to the bulldozer, have been, in their own way, as deadly as the more recent drive-by gang shootings in Los Angeles. Modernist planners, embracing the ideology of development as progress, have killed whole communities, by evicting them, demolishing their houses, and dispersing them to edge suburbs or leaving them homeless. They have killed communities and destroyed individual lives by not understanding the loss and grieving that go along with losing one's home and neighborhood and friends and memories. Since nobody knows how to put a dollar value on memory, or on a sense of connection and belonging, it always gets left out of the model.

This is not an argument against change. (Decaying and growing, cities can't choose to stay the same. They have to choose all the time between alternative changes – blight or renewal, replacements or additions, extensions outwards or upwards, new congestions or new expenditures.) It is rather an argument for the importance of memory, for the need to pay attention to it, to understand that communities can and do go through grieving processes, to acknowledge these in some sort of ritual way. We need to remind ourselves of the importance of memory, and of ritual in dealing with loss. If we need to destroy, as part of our city-building, we also need to heal.

Recent work by planner-historians like Gail Dubrow, Dolores Hayden and John Kuo Wei Tchen, among others, indicates that there is a new multicultural sensibility at work in planning in the 1990s. Hayden's *The Power of Place* dwells on the ways in which public space can help to nurture a sense of cultural belonging and at the same time acknowledge and respect diversity.[1] She writes of the power of ordinary urban landscapes to nurture citizens' public memory, and notes that this power remains untapped for most working people's neighborhoods in most American cities, and for most ethnic history and women's history. Urban landscapes are storehouses for individual and collective social memories. Both individuals and communities need to find ways to connect to the larger urban narrative. Some urban planners are now working with artists, anthropologists, landscape architects, archaeologists and communities to do just that in public history and public art, community mapping and urban landscape projects that seek a more socially and culturally inclusive approach to our urban memories.

City of Desire

Why do we enjoy sitting alone in a coffee shop, or outdoor cafe, or on a park bench, apparently day-dreaming? If city dwelling is in part about the importance of memory and belonging, it is also about the pleasures of anonymity and of not having to belong. These are closely related to desire, to sexual desires and fantasies. We sit on a bus, empty seat beside us, watching new passengers come on board, wondering whether anyone will sit next to us, and if so, who? This is the thrill and the fear of the chance encounter.[2] We sit on the beach or stroll through a park, watching others and being watched, and in that watching are hidden fantasies and desires, sometimes unacknowledged, other times a conscious searching. This is the eroticism of city life, in the broad sense of our attraction to others, the pleasure and excitement of being drawn out of one's secure routine to encounter the novel, the strange, the surprising. We may not want to partake. But we enjoy the parade. If city life is a coming together, a "being together of strangers", as Iris Young suggests in *Justice and the Politics of Difference*, we need to create public spaces that encourage this parade, that acknowledge our need for spectacle – not the authorised spectacle of the annual parade or the weekly football game, but the spontaneous spectacle of strangers and chance encounters.[3] Yet the opposite is happening. Planners are systematically demolishing such spaces in the name of the flip side of desire – fear.

The city of desire – and its place in city planning – is one of the aspects of city life that has only just begun to (re)surface in writings about the city. (It was certainly there in Walter Benjamin's writings in the 1920s and 1930s.) There are many themes to be unraveled and stories yet to be told relating to desire and the city, to sexuality and space. Elizabeth Wilson's *The Sphinx in the City* argues that the anonymity of big cities has been liberating for women (at the same time as it increases our jeopardy from sexual assault);[4] and George Chauncey makes the same point with respect to gay men, in his history of gay New York, noting how many gays have moved from the oppressive, homophobic atmosphere of small towns to the anonymity of New York.[5]

In Barbara Hooper's account of the origins of modern planning in nineteenth-century Paris, "The Poem of Male Desires", the role of desire on the one hand, and fear of it on the other, produces the desire to control desire, which Hooper argues has been a central organizing theme of planning practice.[6] Hers is a story of "bodies, cities, and social order, and more particularly of female bodies and their production as a threat to male/social order".[7] Hooper investigates planning's texts and uncovers the theme of "disorderly bodies". 'Significantly, this list of disorderly bodies includes not only prostitutes, but lesbians, excessive masturbators, nymphomaniacs, and hysterics – also suffragettes, female socialists, feminists, independent wage-earners.'[8] She argues that planning developed in the late nineteenth century as a participant in new forms of social control directed at women.

In making the hitherto invisible visible – that is, the significance of desire, of eros, in urban life – we also make it discussable. In breaking the taboo, the silence, we move slowly towards a richer understanding of urban life and of what has been left out of planners' models and histories. Billboards are an ongoing issue for planners, especially those advertising billboards that explicitly link sex/desire/the body with the sale of merchandise. As the ads get more explicit and provocative, there are pressures on city councils and planners to ban such displays. The pressures come from left and right, from feminists objecting to the objectification of the female body, to fundamentalist religions objecting to any public acknowledgment of eros. This conflict over billboards is, then, more than an aesthetic issue. It is about the (unresolved and unresolvable) "problem" of desire in the city.

But there is much more to the city of desire than eros, as philosopher Iris Young has suggested:

> The city's eroticism also derives from the aesthetics of its material being: the bright and colored lights, the grandeur of its buildings, the juxtaposition of architecture of different times, styles and purposes. City space offers delights and surprises. Walk around the corner, or over a few blocks, and you encounter a different spatial mood, a new play of sight and sound, and new interactive movement. The erotic meaning of the city arises from its social and spatial inexhaustibility. A place of many places, the city folds over on itself in so many layers and relationships that it is incomprehensible. One cannot "take it in", one never feels as though there is nothing new and interesting to explore, no new and interesting people to meet.[9]

The city of desire is also an imagined city of excitement, opportunity, fortune. It is what brings millions of people from the countryside to the big city – Nordestinos to São Paolo, Turks to Frankfurt, Anatolians to Istanbul, Michoacans to San Diego, the Hmong to Chicago, the people of the Maghreb to Paris. It fuels dreams. By not understanding the power of such dreams, or by dismissing them as irrational, planners' own dreams of rational control of migration processes, of orderly human settlements, will remain just that – dreams. The daily stories of border-crossings from Mexico into the United States, crossings in which people all too often risk, and sometimes lose, their lives, illustrates the point. Such is the power of the city of desire, a power strikingly rendered in Gregory Nava's movie, El Norte, and John Sayles' Lone Star, both of which also show how easily the city of desire may become the inferno. One symptom of the narrowness of modernist planners' horizons is the fact that they find it very hard to focus on desires rather than needs. A need is supposedly an objectifiable entity, identified in "needs surveys": "I need a more frequent bus service"; "I need more police patrols in my neighborhood". A desire, by contrast, involves the subconscious, a personal engagement, dreams and feelings, an ability to intuit the atmosphere and feeling of a place. How does the city of desire translate into planning? Perhaps by giving more attention to places of encounter, specifically those which are not commercialized – the street, the square – and which are not placed under the gaze of surveillance technologies. Perhaps also by recognizing that some places of encounter must necessarily be appropriated, and not trying to regulate the uses of all public spaces.

City of Spirit

What draws many of us to visit places like Machu Picchu, Stonehenge, the Dome of the Rock or the Wailing Wall in Jerusalem, the Kaaba stone at Mecca, Chartres, or Uluru, in the apparently empty center of Australia? Why do certain mountains, springs, trees, rocks, and other features of landscape assume symbolic and sacred values to certain peoples and cultures? Historically we have invested our surroundings, urban as well as non-urban, with sacred or spiritual values, and we have built shrines of one sort or another as an acknowledgment of the importance of the sacred, the spiritual, in human life. The completely profane world, the wholly desacralized cosmos, is a recent deviation in the history of the human spirit. Beginning perhaps in the nineteenth century we have created landscapes, cityscapes, devoid of the sacred, devoid of spirit. The tall chimneys that arose in the nineteenth-century factory landscape (Mumford's "Coketown") and the skyscrapers of the late twentieth-century city, perhaps symbolise the excessive dominance of the masculine yang force and its values. From East Germany and Russia to California or the Mississippi Delta, parts of the devastated countryside are left sterile and dead, a monument to the consequences of human rapacity unchecked by considerations of spirit. We are so deadened by our Western industrial landscapes that we now go in search of comfort to Aboriginal songlines or Native American sacred places.

The environmental message is clear. It is time to re-introduce into our thinking about cities and their regions the importance of the sacred, of spirit. In his superb book about black and white Australians' relationship to the Australian landscape, *Edge of the Sacred*, David Tacey calls for such a 'resacralization' as a social and political necessity.[10] "White Man Got No Dreaming" was the partial title of a book by anthropologist W E H Stanner.[11] The Aboriginal Dreaming and Western rationality stand to each other as thesis to antithesis. What the one affirms, the other denies. In Aboriginal cosmology, landscape is a living field of spirits and metaphysical forces.[12] Our English word landscape, as the poet Judith Wright has pointed out, is wholly inadequate to describe the "earth-sky-water-tree-spirit-human continuum", which is the existential ground of the Aboriginal Dreaming. Obviously white Australians cannot appropriate Aboriginal cosmology, tacking it on to their own overly-rational consciousness, and nor can alienated North Americans adopt the cosmology of Native Americans (although much of so-called new age spirituality, the world over, seems to be attempting something very much like that). But there are Western traditions of re-enchantment to which we might connect. The point is that perhaps our modernist/progressive longing for freedom from the non-rational is inherently flawed; out of date and out of touch with the real needs of our time.

How can cities/human settlements nurture our unrequited thirst for the spirit, for the sacred? In the European Middle Ages, it was in the building of cities around cathedrals. But that was long ago. In the more secular cities of today, at least in the West, life does not revolve around the cathedral, although in many communities the church, synagogue or mosque continues to play a vital role in social organization.

But if we look at cities as centers of spontaneous creativity and festival, then we get a different sense of the presence of spirit around us. Our deepest feelings about city and community are expressed on special occasions such as carnivals and festivals. Our highest levels of creativity are seen in art galleries or heard in symphony halls. But the nourishing of the spirit, or soul, also needs daily space and has everyday expressions: two women on a park bench "gossiping"; a group of students in a coffee shop discussing plans for a protest; an old Chinese man practising his *tai chi* on the beach or in a park; amateur musicians busking in front of cafés and museums; an old woman tending her garden; kids skateboarding among the asphalt landscaping of sterile bank plazas ... Rational planners have been obsessed with controlling how and when and which people use public as well as private space. Meanwhile, ordinary people continue to find creative ways of appropriating spaces and creating places, in spite of planning, to fulfil their desires as well as their needs, to tend the spirit as well as take care of the rent.

There is another dimension to the city of spirit which has begun to actively engage some planners, in collaboration with artists and communities. That is the process of identifying what we might call sacred places in the urban landscape. The works of Hayden,[13] Dubrow,[14] and Kenney,[15] are suggestive. Kenney's work in mapping gay and lesbian activism in Los Angeles reveals the connections between place and collective identity which are at the heart of gay and lesbian experience of the city. Kenney evokes Stonewall – the scene of three days of rioting in Greenwich Village in 1969 in protest at police entrapment and harassment in a bar frequented by African-American and Puerto Rican drag queens – as essentially a sacred site for the gay and lesbian movement. The labor movement, the women's movement, African-Americans and Native Americans could each name such 'sacred urban places', and have begun to do so, and to commemorate such sites.

What the above discussion suggests is the need for a diversity of spaces and places in the city: places loaded with visual stimulation, but also places of quiet contemplation, uncontaminated by commerce, where the deafening noise of the city can be kept out so that we can listen to the 'noise of stars' or the wind or water, and the voice(s) within ourselves. An essential ingredient of planning beyond the modernist paradigm – planning for cosmopolis – is a reinstatement of inquiry about and recognition of the importance of memory, desire, and the spirit (or the sacred) as vital dimensions of healthy human settlements and a sensitivity to cultural differences in the expressions of each.

NOTES

1 Dolores Hayden, *The Power of Place: Urban Landscape as Public History*, MIT Press (Cambridge, Mass.), 1995.
2 Dora Epstein, "Afraid/NOT: Psychoanalytic Directions for Planning Historiography", in Leonie Sandercock (ed), *Making the Invisible Visible: A Multicultural History of Planning*, University of California Press (Berkeley), 1998.
3 Iris Marion Young, *Justice and the Politics of Difference*, Princeton University Press (Princeton, NJ), 1990.

4   Elizabeth Wilson, *The Sphinx in the City: Urban Life, the Control of Disorder and Women*, University of California Press (Berkeley), 1991.

5   George Chauncey, *Gay New York: Gender, Urban Culture, and the Making of the Gay Male World 1890–1940*, Basic Books (New York), 1994, p 135.

6   Barbara Hooper, 'The Poem of Male Desires: Female Bodies, Modernity, and "Paris: Capital of the Nineteenth Century"', *Planning Theory* 13, 1995.

7   Ibid, p 105.

8   Ibid, p 120.

9   Iris Marion Young, op cit, p 240.

10 David Tacey, *Edge of the Sacred*, Harper Collins (Melbourne), 1995.

11 W E H Stanner, *White Man Got No Dreaming: Essays, 1938–1973*, ANU Press (Canberra), 1979.

12 David Tacey, op cit, p 148.

13 Dolores Hayden, op cit.

14 Gail Dubrow, "Redefining the Place of Historic Preservation in Planning Education", *Planning Theory* 13, 1995, pp 89–104.

15 Moira Kenney, "Remember, Stonewall was a Riot: Understanding Gay and Lesbian Experience in the City", *Planning Theory* 13, 1995, pp 73–88.

Part VI

Ethics, the Environment, and Conflicting Priorities

Introduction

This final section includes three readings on planning ethics, community participation, and sustainability. Each addresses a shortcoming of the traditional, rational-comprehensive model of planning, whether it is its simplistic notion of serving the public interest, its lack of subtlety about ethical conflicts, its presumption of privileged expert knowledge, or its shortcomings in dealing with the complex challenge of sustainable development.

A profession is characterized by a common set of expert knowledge and methods, professional autonomy, and internal control over the certification and disciplining of colleagues. It also shares a set of ethics, both implicit and explicit. This is true for planning as well. We begin with the ethical principles of the American Planning Association, and a critique of them by William Lucy. Lucy admires the good intentions of the stated ethics, yet is troubled by the simplistic and antiquated planning theory assumptions that underlie these principles. At the heart of the principles is the premise that the planner's primary obligation is to serve the public interest. Yet for years planners have challenged the "public interest" as being a naive, overly simplistic ideal. Serving the public interest often clashes with the planner's obligation to serve the client, the profession, and the planner's self-responsibility. Lucy also challenges the simple call for greater citizen participation and comprehensiveness. He faults these ethical principles for neglecting the real conflicts, dissent, and trade-offs that exist in planning. The vagueness and technocratic optimism in these principles do not always coincide with the competitive and messy political realities of planning.

In addition to ethical questions, planners face basic choices about what value should be placed on public health and the quality of life. In particular, the growing interest in environmental protection requires planners to address environmental risks. Though there is no scientific consensus on the level of risk for various environmental hazards, much of the current effort in risk assessment is a technocratic quest to define "acceptable risk." Frank Fischer challenges this standard model on both technical and political grounds. By integrating concepts of citizen participation and social communication with a critique of technical rationality, Fischer argues for a participatory approach to risk assessment. This alternative is not just risk communication, in which scientific experts present their privileged information to the lay public. Instead, this risk assessment process integrates the public in defining the agenda, setting values and discount rates, and giving legitimacy to the process. The result is a participatory methodology that both avoids some of the risk assessment failures of technocratic institutions and includes a wider range of political interests and social concerns.

We conclude the anthology of readings with a discussion of the growing interest in sustainability development in planning. In "Green Cities, Growing Cities, Just Cities? Urban Planning and the Contradictions of Sustainable Development," Campbell questions whether the idea of sustainability is a useful rallying cry for the urban planning profession. Its broad promises attract a wide and hopeful following, but also undercut its strategic credibility. The remarkable consensus for the idea is encouraging but also reason for skepticism, since sustainability can mean many things to many people without requiring commitment to any specific policies. The danger is that in the end, though all will endorse the principle of sustainability, few will actually practice it. The result would be simply superficial, feel-good solutions: by merely adding "sustainable" to existing planning documents (sustainable zoning, sustainable economic development, sustainable transportation planning, sustainable housing, and so on), this would create the illusion that we are actually doing sustainable planning. (This is reminiscent of the addition of the term "comprehensive" to planning 40 years ago – or "strategic" planning in the 1980s.)

The author argues for a broader definition of sustainability. He develops the idea of the "planner's triangle" to distinguish the field's three fundamental goals – economic development, environmental protection, and social justice – and more importantly, to articulate the resulting conflicts over property, resources, and development. At the theoretical center of this triangle lies the sustainable city, but the path to this elusive center is neither direct nor simple; instead, as the struggle for sustainability becomes more advanced, it will also become more sharply contentious, since it will involve increasingly explicit and sobering trade-offs between interest groups in society.

22

APA's Ethical Principles Include Simplistic Planning Theories

William H. Lucy

I am pleased that the American Planning Association (APA) has addressed the issue of ethical principles for planning. I am skeptical, however, about the appropriateness of the first five of the thirteen principles that the APA board of directors adopted.

Principles 1 through 5 concern me for several reasons. First, they deal with some of the most difficult subjects of political and planning theory. Second, in some instances they reduce complex subjects to a single sentence and thus run the risk of trivializing the profession. Third, some of the principles are contradictory, either within a single principle or between principles. Fourth, some of the subjects should not be included in a statement of ethical principles, because of the oversimplification that brevity requires, the controversial philosophical issues they address, and the questionable conclusions they express. A statement in the July 1987 issue of *Planning* (p. 35) heightens my concern about those matters. The statement reads as follows: "APA encourages the adoption of the principles in this Statement by legislatures through ordinances or statutes, by public planning bodies through incorporation into bylaws, and by employers of planners, who may include them in personnel manuals and other employment policy documents."

I can explain my concerns most clearly by commenting on each ethical principle in sequence.

I Serve the Public Interest

APA quite properly advocates serving the public interest, but I do not know what APA intends by that. The most prominent opinion among political theorists seems to be that "the public interest" is a phantom, unless the phrase means only an accumulation of individual wants, the merits of which others have no public right to judge.

Reprinted by permission of the *Journal of the American Planning Association*, 54 (2) (1988): 147–9.

That is not my view of the public interest. Defending a concept of public interest that one cannot define solely as an accumulation of individual wants is a major task of political philosophy. The single sentence in the APA statement of principles about serving the public interest may seem harmless, but I question whether it is useful unless we elaborate on it. Such elaboration, however, would elucidate the complexity of the task and thereby raise doubts about whether APA should really include it in a statement of principles. I believe debate about the public interest is essential to the future of the planning profession and to the nation. The statement of principles may discourage such debate, because some will conclude from the simplicity of its expression there that nothing remains to be discussed.

2 Support Citizen Participation in Planning

Citizens should have some participatory role between elections, including opportunities to initiate proposals and to review and comment on the proposals of others; but planners should be wary of the common defects in citizen participation. Participation usually does not come from a representative sample of the population. Often it reflects narrow self-interests rather than any larger sense of public concern, and more often than not it expresses the views of the wealthier and better-educated strata of society. APA's omission of any reference to the role of elections is unfortunate. While elections have many faults – including being too unfocused on planning issues to provide clear guidance – they do offer the widest forum for participation. They also lead to election of representatives whose functions include deliberation. One hopes that deliberation by elected representatives will at least occasionally produce greater insight than, say, a poll of a random sample of not very interested citizens. The appropriate role for elections, deliberative representation, leadership by chief executives and political parties, and participation by citizens by various means between elections are fundamental subjects for discussion and debate. We would do better to deal with those subjects in analysis and essays than in a brief statement of ethical principles.

3 Recognize the Comprehensive and Long-Range Nature of Planning Decisions

One problem with the formulation of the planning process in principle 3 is that comprehensive and long-range planning are not consistent with serving a public interest that is "continuously modified" (a characterization given in principle 2) since broad and long-range planning intentions must adhere to more stable values. Perhaps APA's intent in principle 3 was to emphasize balance between careful attention to breadth and length of vision and the responsiveness that principle 2 emphasizes. The notions of balance and responsiveness are stretched beyond possibility by the additional injunctions in principle 3 to "continuously gather and consider *all* (emphasis mine) relevant facts, alternatives, and means of accomplishing them" and to "explicitly evaluate *all* (emphasis mine) consequences before making a recommendation or decision." Critics of "idealized" planning have consistently attacked such unrealistic demands as impossible to accomplish because planners have limited time, money, expertise, and decision-processing capacity. In addition, planners cannot consider all consequences, because there are no predictive theories about some consequences, theories about other consequences are inadequate, and knowledge needed to asses still other consequences is not available. Perhaps APA intended to present some notion of sufficiency. Indeed, principle 7 encourages such a hope, saying, "If the official has not sufficiently reviewed relevant facts and advice affecting a public planning decision, the official must not participate in that decision." Principle 3, on the other hand, suggests an image of ivory tower planners far removed from arenas in which officials must make decisions with insufficient time, information, or expertise, as usually happens with important decisions. Certainly it is excessive to make an impossible assignment an ethical injunction; but that is precisely what principle 3 does. APA should at least revise that principle to make it consistent with the "sufficiency" spirit of principle 7.

4 Expand Choice and Opportunity for all Persons

My own political preferences include expanding choices for disadvantaged persons, as suggested in principle 4, and doing so by changing restrictive policies, institutions, and decisions. But that requires restricting the choices of some persons rather than expanding them. If the material pie is expanding more slowly than the population is increasing, as has been occurring in recent years, that trend calls for some redistribution of benefits and some limitations on choices accompanying the redistribution if we are to expand opportunities for the disadvantaged. Furthermore, environmental conservation in particular requires limiting choices, and those limitations must apply to the disadvantaged as well as to the advantaged.

5 Facilitate Coordination through the Planning Process

This principle at first seems intended merely to encourage open and timely dissemination of information. But I also infer from it that it assumes an unrealistically pleasant and cooperative context for planning. It promotes cooperation as a planning ideal. But the adjustments on behalf of the disadvantaged, which principle 4 advocates, may call for some public officials, including planners, to develop coalitions of support on behalf of change. Planners have finally begun to pay more attention to the importance of devising strategies to cope with opposition in competitive contexts. We should not place a label of "unethical" on strategies to overcome opposition to low-income housing, landfill sites, homes for retarded citizens, neighborhood parks, annexation, and progressive taxation, merely because those strategies recognize that voluntary cooperation may not produce the desired results. Sometimes we best promote the public interest by coping with competition and opposition. Emphasizing coordination as a planning ideal may reflect avoidance of competitive political realities.

I hope that APA will give the statement of ethical principles additional deliberation and that APA officials will consider revising or eliminating principles 1 through 5.

APA Ethical Principles for Planning

1   *Serve the public interest.* The primary obligation of planners and public planning officials is to serve the public interest.

2   *Support citizen participation in planning.* Because the definition of the public interest is continuously modified, the planner and public planning official must recognize the right of citizens to influence planning decisions that affect their well-being. They should advocate a forum for meaningful citizen participation and expression in the planning process and assist in the clarification of community goals, objectives, and policies in plan-making.

3   *Recognize the comprehensive and long-range nature of planning decisions.* The planner and public planning official must recognize and have special concern for the comprehensive and long-range nature of planning decisions. The planner and official must balance and integrate physical (including historical, cultural, and natural), economic, and social characteristics of the community or area affected by those decisions. The planner and official must continuously gather and consider all relevant facts, alternatives, and means of accomplishing them. The planner and official should explicitly evaluate all consequences before making a recommendation or decision.

4   *Expand choice and opportunity for all persons.* The planner and public planning official must strive to expand choice and opportunity for all persons, recognize a special responsibility to plan for the needs of disadvantaged people, and urge changing policies, institutions, and decisions that restrict their choices and opportunities.

5   *Facilitate coordination through the planning process.* The planner and public planning official must facilitate coordination. The planning process should enable all those concerned with an issue to learn what other participants are doing, thus permitting coordination of activities and efforts and accommodation of interests. The planner and official must ensure that individuals and public and private agencies possibly affected by a prospective planning decision receive adequate information far enough in advance of the decision.

6   *Avoid conflict of interest.* To avoid conflict of interest and even the appearance of impropriety, the public planning official who may receive some private benefit from a public planning decision must not participate in that decision. The private benefit may be direct or indirect, create a material personal gain, or provide an advantage to relations, friends, groups, or associations that hold a significant share of the official's loyalty. An official with a conflict of interest must make that interest public, abstain from voting on the matter, not participate in any deliberations on the matter, and leave any chamber in which such deliberations are to take place. The official must not discuss the matter privately with any other official voting on the matter. A private sector planner who has previously worked for a public planning body on a plan or project should not appear before that body representing a private client in connection with proposals affecting that plan or project for one year after the planner's last date of employment with the planning body.

7   *Render thorough and diligent planning service.* The planner and public planning official must render thorough and diligent planning service. Should the planner

or official believe s/he can no longer render such service in a thorough and diligent manner, s/he should resign from the position. If the official has not sufficiently reviewed relevant facts and advice affecting a public planning decision, the official must not participate in that decision.

8 *Not seek or offer favors.* The public sector planner and public planning official must seek no favor. The planner and official must not directly or indirectly solicit any gift or accept or receive any gift (whether in money, services, loans, travel, entertainment, hospitality, promises, or in some other form) under circumstances in which it could be reasonably inferred that the gift was intended or could reasonably be expected to influence them in the performance of their duties or was intended as a reward for any recommendation or decision on their part. The private sector planner must not offer any gifts or favors to influence the recommendation or decision of a public sector planner or public planning official. The private sector planner should oppose such action by a client.

9 *Not disclose or improperly use confidential information for financial gain.* The planner and public planning official must not disclose or improperly use confidential information for financial gain. The planner and official must not disclose to others confidential information acquired in the course of their duties or use it to further a personal interest. Exceptions to this requirement of non-disclosure may be made only when (a) required by process of law, or (b) required to prevent a clear violation of law, or (c) required to prevent substantial injury to the public. Disclosure pursuant to (b) and (c) must not be made until after the planner or official has verified the facts and issues involved, has exhausted efforts to obtain reconsideration of the matter, and has sought separate opinions on the issue from other planners or officials.

10 *Ensure access to public planning reports and studies on an equal basis.* The public planning official must ensure that reports and records of the public planning body are open equally to all members of the public. All non-confidential information available to the official must be made available in the same form to the public in a timely manner at reasonable or no cost.

11 *Ensure full disclosure at public hearings.* The public planning official must ensure that the presentation of information on behalf of any party to a planning question occurs only at the scheduled public hearing on the question, not in private, unofficially, or with other interested parties absent. The official must make partisan information regarding the question received in the mail or by telephone or other communication part of the public record.

12 *Maintain public confidence.* The public planning official must conduct himself/herself publicly so as to maintain public confidence in the public planning body, the official's unit of government, and the official's performance of the public trust.

13 *Respect professional codes of ethics and conduct.* The planner and public planning official must respect the professional codes of ethics and conduct established by the American Institute of Certified Planners (AICP) Commission and by several professions related to the practice of planning. Professional codes commonly establish standards of professional conduct and include provisions that protect the integrity of professional judgment and describe the professional's responsibility to the public, clients, employers, and colleagues.

23

Risk Assessment and Environmental Crisis: Toward an Integration of Science and Participation

Frank Fischer

Introduction

It is commonplace today to say that we live in an advanced techno-industrial, or high-tech society. Science and technology now literally drive the modern industrial economy and, furthermore, have spread into every area of social and political life. To be sure, the advance of technological development has brought with it much of what we accept as good in modern society. Technological artifacts have become so much a part of everyday life that we take them for granted. In this respect the belief in technological progress has itself become one of the basic modern world views, an ideology cutting across the traditional categories of both capitalism and socialism (Fischer 1990).

Many of the most ardent enthusiasts of this ideology, particularly the so-called postindustrial theorists, see its beliefs to be the rationale for the ascent of a new technocratic elite destined to guide our political and our economic systems (Bell 1973; Brzezinski 1976). These writers see the need to extend science fully into the realm of political decision making (Platt 1969). The function of the technocratic elite would be to replace democratic political decision processes (based on conflicting interests) with a more technically informed discussion (based on scientific decision-making techniques). In the process, political issues would increasingly be trans-formed into technically defined ends that can be pursued through administrative means (Stanley 1978).

Although technocratic elites still remain formally subordinate to political and economic elites, their world view and decision techniques now play prominent roles in the governance of modern corporate-bureaucratic institutions, the dominant power

Reprinted with permission from the *Industrial Crisis Quarterly*, 5(2) (1991): 113–32.

structures of modern society (Galbraith 1967). This essay is about one of these technocratic methodologies: risk assessment. Before turning to the methodology, however, it is essential first to elaborate on the political context to which it is applied, namely, the increasing concern about technological hazards and their impact on the environment. Toward this end, the chapter proceeds in the following fashion: after first examining the central importance of technological progress and its fundamental crisis, the discussion develops the concept of "acceptable risk" as the techno-industrial response to the current situation. The technocratic character of the risk assessment methodology is then criticized in the context of a broader sociological perspective. The result is a proposal to examine the possibility of restructuring risk assessment to include a wider range of participants. The chapter closes with a call for the innovation of a participatory methodology and briefly explores some of the institutional and political implications of such an approach for expertise more generally.

Technological Progress and the Environmental Crisis

In spite of the aforementioned enthusiasm for technological progress, during the past two decades there has also been a growing recognition that advanced technologies have brought with them many dangers. Indeed, in various quarters of society there is a growing distrust of modern techno-industrial progress (National Research Council 1989: 54–71). In the face of nuclear power catastrophes, the death of oceans and rivers due to oil spills and other disasters, greater structural unemployment owing to computerized work, pollution and the greenhouse effect, the pervasiveness of toxic wastes, the rise of cancer rates, and the like, we have come to recognize that one of the prices paid for this technological advance has been a dramatic increase in risk, or at least the awareness of risk (Slovic et al. 1980; National Research Council 1989).

Such events have given both credibility and political influence to the environmental movement, which emerged in the 1970s as a response to these and other related events (Douglas and Wildavsky 1982). The result has been a much greater awareness of the impacts of modern technologies on the environment, coupled with a questioning of our blind acceptance of technological progress. Indeed, the more radical ecological groups in the environmental movement have raised basic questions about our very way of life. Proponents of the "green" philosophy see the solution in a return to smaller, less hierarchical technological systems, with a much greater role for people (Porritt 1984).

In terms of environmental and technological risks, these two competing world views have divided one of the most critical issues of our time into two deeply entrenched and opposing camps: those who argue that we live in "the safest of times," and those who see it as "the riskiest of times" (National Research Council 1989). The first of these views, the technocratic view largely proffered by industrial and political leaders, takes life expectancy to be the best overall measure of risk to health and safety, points to substantial increases in this measure, and shows that these increases run parallel over time with the growing use of risky chemicals and dangerous technologies. In fact, they argue that many of the contemporary hazards have decreased overall risk by replacing more dangerous ones. People are seen as becoming more and more worried about less significant risks.

By contrast, the number of people who believe that we live in the riskiest of times has increased dramatically over the past two decades. For these people, particularly those of the green persuasion, the world is on the brink of ecological disaster. Modern technology is seen to constantly generate new threats to the earth's life-support systems and thus in turn to the stability of social systems. Especially important to this argument are the synergistic effects of these problems. It is not just the appearance of new problems but rather the emergence of countless serious problems at the same time, for example, overconsumption of the earth's energy resources, the ozone hole, the toxic waste problem, contamination of rivers and oceans, the dangers of nuclear radiation, the rise of cancer rates, the destruction of rain forests, the rise of the earth's temperatures, escalating population growth, and so on. Even though people are seldom exposed to one risk in isolation from the others, there exists little empirical information on the interactive effects of these dangers. For such reasons, those who see a dramatic increase in risks call for tighter control over technology, including the abandonment of some technologies considered to be particularly risky (such as nuclear power and genetic engineering) and the need for the development and intro-duction of more environmentally benign technologies.

Despite this fundamental disagreement, or perhaps because of it, the struggle over this question has elevated the "search for safety" to the top of the political agenda (Wildavsky 1988). The quest for safety has emerged as one of the paramount political issues of our time, both as a prominent public concern and a leading topic in intellectual discourse (Fischer and Wagner 1990). In Germany, for example, it has led sociologist Ulrich Beck (1986) literally to define the postindustrial society as the "Risk Society."

The Techno-Industrial Response: Acceptable Risk

Such concerns have forced the proponents of large-scale technological progress, corporate and governmental leaders in particular, to pay much greater attention to the regulation of advanced technologies. Indeed, the future of many new technolo-gies today is believed virtually to depend upon the ability of regulatory institutions to restore public confidence in them. Numerous industrial and political leaders, in fact, express their concern about an emerging environmental philosophy that would oppose the introduction of all new technologies – even tested technologies – without *absolute* prior proof that they pose no risks, a view exemplified by such radical ecologists as Jeremy Rifkin (Tivnan 1988: 38).

This concern often reflects very concrete experiences, the nuclear energy industry being the example *par excellence* (Rosenbaum 1985: 227–34). What started out as one of the magnificent peacetime wonders of modern technology has been brought to a virtual standstill in the United States by the environmental movement and the assistance of such events as the accidents at Three Mile Island and Chernobyl. Sweden, moreover, now plans a total phase-out of nuclear energy altogether in the 1990s, thanks to powerful environmental agitation.

Stated straightforwardly, the stakes in this struggle are high, and the mandarins of technology have recognized the challenge. The primary response has been an at-tempt to shift the political discourse to the search for "acceptable risk." Toward this end, supporters of the modern techno-industrial complex argue that risk must be seen as a mixed phenomenon, always producing both danger and opportunity. Too often, they argue, the debate revolves purely around potential dangers (all too often centering on high-impact accidents with low probability, for example, nuclear meltdowns or runaway genetic mutations). Risk taking, in contrast, must be seen as necessary for successful technological change and economic growth, as well as the overall resiliency and health of modern society.

Playing it safe thus actually tends to reduce opportunities to benefit from new entrepreneurial chances. Even further, risk taking is itself said to be a fundamental source of safety. Like joggers who routinely risk heart attacks to improve overall health, societies must run short-term risks in order to expand future wealth and security (Wildavsky 1988). Moreover, the resulting expansion of wealth is said to make it possible for society to absorb the impact of greater disasters, thus directly increasing its overall levels of safety. In short, risk raises issues fundamental to the future of Western industrial societies and has ushered in a deep-seated political struggle to shape the very way we think and talk about it.

The basic strategy of industrial and scientific leaders has been to focus the risk debate on technical factors (Wynne 1987; Schwarz and Thompson 1990: pp. 103–20). The approach is grounded in the view that technological dangers have been grossly exaggerated (particularly by the Luddites in the environmental movement said to harbor a vested political interest in exploiting the public's fears). The result, it is argued, is a high degree of ignorance in the general public about technological risks. The layperson thus tends to worry a great deal about the safety of air travel but thinks nothing of driving his car to the airport, which statistics demonstrate to be much more dangerous (Lopes 1987). Because this uncontrolled expansion of "irrational" beliefs is quite threatening to technological progress, often specifically manifested in the issue of financial investment, managerial elites have seen the need to counter this antitechnology trend driven by the ecological movement.

The answer is to supply the public with more objective (technical) information about the levels of risks themselves. That is, the "irrationality" of contemporary political arguments must be countered with rationally demonstrable scientific data. The solution is to provide more information – standardized scientific information – to offset the irrationalities plaguing uninformed thinkers, namely, the proverbial "man on the street." More recently, in fact, the task has become the focus of a new subspecialty of risk management known as "risk communication" (National Research Council 1989).

The task of generating such information has fallen to the most likely candidate, the managerially oriented decision sciences. These sciences are themselves largely the by-products of large-scale technological systems and their managerial requirements. Developed to help steer and manage such systems, they can appropriately be seen as the methodological embodiment of the technocratic world view and its strategies.

Risk Assessment as Technocratic Methodology

Risk assessment, then, is the modern technocratic response to the contemporary technology and environmental crisis. It is a methodological strategy designed to supply a technically rational basis for centralized regulatory decision making. The practice first emerged to deal with two different types of risks: geological risks concerned with the probabilities of earthquakes and their damages; and technological risk problems confronted by the U.S. space program (which, it must be remembered, was as much an organizational and managerial project as it was a technical feat). Its more contemporary methodological manifestations are largely by-products of its adoption and use by the nuclear power industry (Mazur 1980).

As a scientific model of rational decision making, risk assessment reflects an amalgam of managerial and engineering methodologies. The goal of risk analysis is to provide objectively standardized quantitative information about the reliability of a technology's performance (Coppock 1984: pp. 53–146). Toward this end, it defines risk in terms of the physical properties of a technology and its environment. Like the engineering model upon which it is largely based, risk assessment proceeds from a fundamental assumption, namely, that a technological system (defined as an integration of physical and human factors) can be rigorously defined with a unitary concept of technical rationality (Schwarz and Thompson 1989: pp. 102–22).

This means, more specifically, that physical risks exist separately from the symbolic context in which they are socially situated and that social perceptions of technological systems and their risks can be strictly excluded. Indeed, social perceptions are "irrationalities" that have little or nothing to do with technical knowledge. The goal, in short, is to isolate and measure the objective probabilities of technical failure in terms of intrinsic and extrinsic physical properties.

In analytical terms, risk is quantitatively expressed as the product of the estimated degree of harm (death or damage) a given technical failure would cause and its probabilities of occurrence (Wynne 1987; Irwin and Smith 1982; Covello and Menkes 1985). In complicated technological systems, probabilistic risk assessment involves first breaking the system down into various measurable components – materials, pipes, pumps, seals, coolants, fail-safe mechanisms; second, measuring the statistical probability of a failure of each of these dimensions – using past performance data, experimental assessments, and expert judgments; third, it means an examination of crucial environmental factors that might either precipitate or exacerbate a technical failure, such as geological fault lines (which might cause earthquakes), or climatic conditions such as wind patterns (which would influence the spread of dangerous particles, for example, radiation). Fourth, the foregoing factors, stated statistically as multiple probabilities, must be integrated through a modeling process based on decision-oriented event and fault trees. After calculating the various chains of probabilities to provide an overall estimate of system failure, the figure must be multiplied by the estimated damages. For example, the health effects of human exposure to the release of dangerous substances, such as chemicals or radioactive particles, are estimated with epidemiological, medical, and actuarial data to determine the long- and short-run damages to human well-being, latent as well as delayed.

The result is a set of objective statements that are to be the focus of regulatory deliberations about risk, thus replacing risk "perceptions" divined – so to say – by technically uninformed social actors, particularly those who lead environmental movements (Andrews, 1990). Indeed, the U.S. Environmental Protection Agency established quantitative risk assessment as the primary methodology for agency decision making (Russell and Gruber 1987).

Methodological Critique: Bringing in the Social Dimension

The method proved to be anything but a success. Although it produced a mountain of quantitative data, it altogether failed to reassure the public. Indeed, in many ways it has only worsened the situation. There are, in this regard, two problems: one formally grounded in technical considerations, the other in political realities. Both, it is argued here, result from the technocratic framing of the risk problem.

First, the technical problem. Given the complexity of technological systems, the task of generating quantitatively standardized estimates of risk requires the use of very narrowly specified empirical assumptions and analytical concepts, including the very definition of what constitutes a technology. This is not the place to go into technical details (concerning such matters as data limitations, units of analysis, issues concerning the delineation of various technical subprocesses, security of safety components, levels of professional expertise, and the like). Suffice it to say that analysts are forced to make many uncertain assumptions – sometimes even heroic assumptions – which are later masked by the precision of their risk statements. As Wynne (1987) puts it, the price paid for precision is often a high degree of hidden ignorance about the safety of technical systems (Conrad 1980).

This glossing over of empirical and analytical uncertainties has given rise to a good deal of disagreement among the experts themselves. Indeed, their judgments about these statistics often range from completely reliable to totally useless. Almost needless to say, this display of technical disagreements – featuring counterexperts criticizing experts – does nothing to assuage the public of its fears (Collingridge and Reeve 1986). Indeed, there is little doubt that the open display of disagreement among experts has only heightened public worries. To put it bluntly, risk assessment – on its own terms – has not only failed as a technical tool, it has also in the process exacerbated the very doubts it set out to assuage (Schwarz and Thompson 1990; Wynne 1987).

This brings us to regulatory decision making and the role of social and political factors. Technocratic contentions to the contrary, the argument that social factors are irrelevant to the objective assessment of risk is sociologically uninformed. There are three interrelated points to make in this regard. The first concerns the goal of regulation itself. Despite a history of attempts to technocratically control regulatory decision processes, regulation in a democratic system necessarily remains an interplay between technical issues and social concerns. Once risk assessment's technical estimates are formally introduced as the basis for regulatory rule making, the methodology encounters a fundamental decision problem – namely, that the very social context it holds constant becomes a key focus in regulatory deliberations.

The regulatory process, in other words, seeks to examine the effects of technologies and risks not only in terms of their physical magnitudes and probabilities but also in terms of how these have a specific impact on the social and institutional contexts in which the technologies are embedded, both internally (the workplace) and externally (the social and natural environments). In more recent years, risk assessment has attempted to confront this problem more directly through the empirical identification of rules for determining acceptable risk (Slovic et al. 1982). The idea is to determine empirically the levels and types of risks people have already learned to live with and then to posit these as objective standards of "acceptable risk." Regulatory rules, then, can be objectively determined by empirical comparisons of risk estimates and the standards of risk acceptance. This, in fact, shores up the technocratic mission; people's subjective perceptions of risk, as well as their individual comparisons of risk, need not be directly solicited. The entire rule-making process can thus be governed by the techno-analytic methodologies of the decision sciences (Wynne 1987).

This reluctance to consider contextual factors directly, however, breeds major problems. The method is greeted with public distrust, even suspicion. It comes to be seen – correctly – as a managerial decision methodology strategically employed to gloss over and hide important social and political issues. The result is a political legitimacy problem. By denying legitimacy to the values and anxieties that arise from the social contexts in which technologies are situated, those who seek to regulate risk seriously jeopardize their own credibility by saying to people that their social experiences and searches for meaning do not count (Wynne 1987; Schwarz and Thompson 1990).

In contrast to the engineering orientation, then, the regulatory task of risk assessment in a democratic society has to approach its object of investigation in a very different way, which brings the discussion to the second point. The first step toward a solution is to be found in the theoretical redefinition of large-scale technological systems. Rather than a complicated set of technically oriented relationships, we must much more broadly recognize such systems to be socio-institutional phenomena (Joerges 1988). Actually, large-scale technological systems are integrated sets of techno-institutional relationships embedded in both historical and contemporary social processes. They are complicated technical processes functionally woven together by networks of socio-organizational controls (Perrow 1984).

This reality bears directly on the empirical estimation of risk *and* the social perceptions of acceptable risk. With regard to the social perception of risk, much to the chagrin of the risk analysts, these institutional factors are discovered to play an essential role in the layperson's perception of technological systems. Social perceptions and understandings of large technological systems – those of workers and citizens in particular – are fundamentally rooted in their concrete social experiences with decision-making institutions and their historically conditioned relationships. Any single technical "event" or "decision" is in fact located within a continual socio-institutional process, which is itself an integral dimension of the large-scale technological system. For example, sociological evidence (as well as common sense) shows that workers cannot altogether divorce their responses to physical risks from their attitudes toward social relations in the plant, particularly those pertaining to managerial practices. If the workers' social relations with management are pervaded by mistrust and hostility, the ever-present uncertainties of physical risks in the plant are amplified.

For risk analysts, this amplification is subjectively irrational behavior (sometimes portrayed as rooted in a neurotic pathology). The cynics among them see this inclusion of social perceptions to be the result of a simple fact, namely that the social dimension is the only aspect of such systems that people are capable of understanding. The technical dimensions are beyond their intellectual reach (Douglas and Wildavsky 1982; Wynne 1987). This judgment has in fact led to a line of behavioral research concerned with the psychology of risk perceptions (Slovic et al. 1982; Slovic 1984). Researchers seek to determine how and why people attach social meaning – irrational meanings – to specific technologies. Why, for example, has nuclear power – in the face of favorable risk assessments – attracted such negative images?

But really how "irrational" is this behavior? Which brings us to the third point. Here I want to underscore the most obvious empirical perception pertinent to this issue, that is, the fact that over the past fifteen years we have more and more recognized the sources of technological hazards and catastrophes frequently to have been the result of institutional failures (Paté-Cornell 1990; Clarke 1989). The examination of such accidents as occurred at Three Mile Island and Bhopal, the explosion of the space shuttle *Challenger*, or the Exxon oil spill in Alaska, show them to be the consequences of untrustworthy or irresponsible organizational and managerial systems. Indeed it becomes increasingly difficult to find crises in which this is not at least partly the case (Dobrzynski 1988; Lambright 1989; Vaughan 1990). Such events have scarcely contributed to the public's trust and confidence in management's ability to ensure reliably personal and environmental protection.

Thus, institutional and managerial factors are themselves very real sources of technological risk and uncertainty; and people often correctly perceive this, even if formal risk assessment chooses not to. As Wynne (1980: p. 218) nicely puts it, "uncertainties which are not acknowledged and dealt with full-frontally have a way of creeping back into social perceptions, perhaps dressed in a different language." From this perspective, social perceptions can just as easily be seen as sources of experiential knowledge that must be taken seriously (Fietkau 1990). This is particularly the case when they pertain to the kinds of situational circumstances that escape the broad social generalities typically sought by risk perception research.

To the degree that risk assessment has miscast this problem, it becomes itself a source of technological risk. Rather than being a technical issue plagued by social perceptions, the risk problem turns out to be as much a social question related to technical issues. Not only does the abstract language of risk assessment underplay the institutional-managerial context of technological systems, it also fails to recognize that they reflect larger normative concerns rooted in the society itself (Schwarz and Thompson 1990). Some, in fact, argue that a lack of credibility in our institutions and leaders is, in reality, the central factor driving the fear of technological systems, an argument central to the environmental movement.

Restructuring Risk Assessment: Toward a Participatory Approach

One should not underestimate the problem posed here: the search for a more democratic form of risk assessment confronts a number of the most sophisticated political and epistemological problems of our time. In epistemological terms, it is nothing less than the question of how to relate empirical data to norms and values – a very old question that continues to occupy philosophers (Hawkesworth 1988). In political terms, this question asks how we are to transform our increasingly techno-bureaucratic institutions into less hierarchical democratic structures (Fischer 1990). Indeed, in an age of technocratic expertise the question is critical; one can justifiably argue that the very future of democracy depends on it (Petersen 1984).

Within the scope of this chapter I cannot, of course, adequately supply answers to these challenging questions. I will thus attempt only to point risk assessment in a direction suggested by the foregoing critique. The first step, which should be apparent by now, is to move beyond the idea that technical knowledge, coupled with improved communications of empirical findings, can alone answer questions posed in the social and political world. Put more bluntly, it is finally time to recognize this to be the technocratic ideology that it is (Fischer 1990).

The challenge is to find ways to integrate technical and social data more comprehensively and meaningfully in both analytical inquiry and public discussion. In the case of the latter, I mean something more than calling for new forums in which experts present and discuss their findings with the public, largely the contemporary approach to risk communication (National Research Council 1989). In this scenario, science presents something of a *fait accompli*. By virtue of their "exalted" method, scientists command the privileged position in such forums; the intimidated public is relegated to the role of passive listener largely closed out of the discussion. In the end, as experience shows, the process only further breeds the kind of alienation that already presents risk assessment with its legitimacy problem (Nelkin 1984; Petersen 1984).

The solution is to be found in the invention of new institutional forums and methodological approaches capable of opening up the risk assessment process to nonexperts. Laypersons must be integrated into the process as part of a discussion of the social and institutional issues upon which quantitative and technical risk assessment calculations rest. This means building the much-needed social discourse into the phases of scientific research itself (Eldon 1981). Consider some more specific illustrations.

At the outset of risk assessment, a wider range of stakeholders must be built into the initial discussions of what the risk problem is in the first place: they must again be built into the search for risks; then again when it comes to the determination of the relative importance of risks and benefits and how they might be most meaningfully quantified and measured. Finally, their perspectives on the interpretations of the resulting risk estimates must be elicited. It is important to elaborate somewhat on each of these phases.

First, building the participants into decisions about problem definition is essential to an effective strategy of risk assessment, especially once we recognize the fundamentally social nature of technological systems. Important in the definitional problem, for instance, are questions concerning what the technology actually is, what are its significant components and connections, and what are its boundaries and external contexts.

For instance, in a complex techno-institutional system such as hazardous waste disposal (involving a cycle of activities ranging from production, collection, transportation, treatment and storage), how do we determine which actors and institutions are in the system and which are out? In some cases, of course, the answer is easy: The incinerator, for example, is an essential component of the system. But what about the production process? How much of that, if any, is to be included in the definition of the hazardous waste system? Some argue that we cannot adequately understand the process without including the industry that produces the waste, although analysis typically ignores this dimension.

Perhaps even more critical, once we recognize that the social dimension is itself a fundamental source of risk, it is again important to bring the social actors themselves into the process of identification and search for risks. In particular, workers familiar with the everyday operations of a plant have important experiential knowledge about how the socio-institutional structures and processes of the system actually function. Such concrete knowledge is of critical importance in the search for alternative sources of risk. Information of this type often cannot be obtained from management, and it certainly cannot be gleaned from the kind of abstract statistical analysis that has typically characterized risk assessment (Wynne 1987).

While the assignment of weights to risks and benefits sounds like a highly technical task, this process too is grounded in a large number of normative considerations. How, for example, are risks and benefits to be counted? If a benefit is intangible or not traded in markets, how should we establish price values for it? If the benefits will occur far into the future, how should their values be "discounted" to accord with the fact that money available only in the future is typically worth less than money available immediately?

Or, how does one attach numbers to the value of lives saved by a safety procedure? Should the value of each life be the expected future earnings of each person? Should we count as part of the program's costs all of the future medical expenses of the people saved? Should we add their children's schooling and medical costs – children they would not have had if they would have died without the vaccine? Should we count as benefits the taxes paid by the people we rescued?

Finally, citizens and workers must have important inputs into the process of interpreting the meaning and uses of an analysis. Especially important in this respect is the relationship of the findings to the specific circumstances to which they are to be applied. The production of generalized information about the risks of a technological system can never be more than guidelines that must be interpreted within the specific contexts to which they are applied. Wynne (1987), for example, has shown how centrally established regulatory rules about risk often produce enormous problems in their implementation. Because each technological system is located in a different geographical area with varying physical and social characteristics, there is no possibility for the rule to apply directly to specific facilities. In each case, then, the meaning of the data must be socially negotiated between the central authorities and the local officials. Without such normative negotiations, central rules are seen often to do more harm than good. Not only do they create a great deal of frustration among local participants, they themselves also become the sources of risks.

These are typical of the kinds of normative questions that underlie an otherwise technical analysis. The processes of empirical measurement, data collection and mathematical analysis – the processes typically identified as scientific risk assessment – are seen to be founded on a very wide range of crucial normative judgments. Rather than questions and issues merely brought to the scientific process by concerned social and political participants, they are in fact an inherent part of scientific risk assessment. Although scientists must grapple with these judgments, such issues can only be established by social judgments. In this realm, scientists have no epistemologically privileged position over the other members of society, although in fact they frequently make such judgments in the name of science (Stone 1990). These are societal questions and can be legitimately dealt with only through societal processes.

The advantage of such an integration rests on two fundamentally important contributions. First, it builds into the analytical process the stakeholders' pragmatic experiential knowledge about technical and institutional risks, and second, it addresses the essential issues of public legitimation and motivation. By involving them in these normative dimensions of the scientific process as it proceeds, stakeholders become cooperative participants in the formation of scientific arguments rather than mere passive listeners, the result of which is greater commitment to the analytical conclusions. That is the very objective risk assessment has been unable to accomplish.

Institutional Innovations

Clearly such an approach will depend on institutional and political change. Risk assessment, as a decision strategy, is a product of a bureaucratic system of governance; it is a tool designed to inform and guide hierarchically structured decision-making processes. The success of a more democratically structured practice of expertise ultimately depends on a more participatory set of institutions.

Experimentation with such participatory structures for risk assessment is not an altogether new idea in the United States. The 1970s showed a wide range of experiments in this direction. Important in this respect was the rise of the public interest science movement and such institutions as the Center for Science in the Public Interest. To support such efforts, the National Science Foundation established a program to foster the development of citizens' science. Largely judged to be successful, the program was designed to help develop and facilitate projects that sought to incorporate diverse points of view into science and technology projects, thus helping to assure the representation of all groups with substantial interests in project matters.

The most widely discussed, if not the most important, effort of this type was the city of Cambridge's Experimental Review Board, established to examine the risks of biotechnological research at Harvard University and the Massachusetts Institute of Technology. In this case, the Cambridge City Council appointed a broadly representative group of nonscientific citizens to assess the risks involved in recombinant DNA research within the city's boundaries. After many months of intensive work, the group issued a report that stunned the scientific community. As a Harvard Nobel Prize-winning biologist and critic of the citizens' commission asserted, "the result was a very thoughtful, sober and conscientious report" (Dutton 1984: p. 148). It was widely agreed, independently of disagreements over the commission's final conclusions (which largely supported the continuation of such research), that a representative group of nonscientists could grapple with a profoundly complex science policy issue and develop recommendations widely seen to be intelligent and responsible. As Dutton (1984: p. 154) put it, "such a twist in science policymaking was as unprecedented as the research itself."

During the same period, Congress formulated national legislation to bring science research policy more fully into the public domain. Precipitated in large part by widespread worries about genetic research, as well as by the public attention received by the Cambridge review project, Congress worked out plans for a freestanding national commission dominated by nonscientists to make regulatory decisions and to consider long-range policy implications. Senator Edward Kennedy, for example, stated at a Senate hearing in 1977 that "the assessment of risk and the judgment of how to balance risk against benefit of recombinant DNA research are responsibilities that clearly rest in the public domain. And it follows that these issues must be decided through public processes" (Dutton 1984). Although the legislation ultimately failed to become law, it had strong Congressional support and was widely seen to be model legislation for the public interest science movement. As the *New York Times* noted, politicians and public interest groups were now recognizing that the regulation of risk was too important to be left to the scientists alone.

Regrettably, such innovative efforts were beaten back by scientific lobbies and conservative politicians during the Reagan years of the 1980s. The argument was always the same: The layman simply cannot understand and responsibly judge complex technological issues. Such participation is said to be unrealistic, if not utopian. As a former president of the National Academy of Sciences put it, "most members of the public usually don't know enough about any given complicated technical matter to make meaningful judgments. And that includes scientists and engineers who work in unrelated areas" (Handler 1980). There is truth in such statements, but they tend unfortunately to refer to the purely technical aspects of such problems, obscuring the wide range of normative social judgments upon which such technical matters depend. Even more important, experiments such as those of the Cambridge Review Board and the National Science Foundation show this view to be premature, if not simply false.

It is also important to mention several efforts designed to supply deliberative methodologies that incorporate a wider range of stakeholders into the decision processes. One approach is "constructive technology assessment" (CTA), particularly as developed and employed in the Netherlands Organization for Technology Assessment. CTA is an attempt to find ways to open up the technological design process as it unfolds, rather than focusing attention solely on the impacts of a technology after they have appeared. Toward this end, CTA theorists have sought an approach to build a wider range of stakeholders into the various discussion phases involved in the development of new technological systems. Although too limited in scope to fully constitute a participatory research methodology, this work offers important insights into how to identify the points at which social discourse can effectively be introduced in technical design processes (Schwarz and Thompson 1990: pp. 143–51; Smits et al. 1987).

As yet, CTA theorists have offered few methodological details on how the discourse around these decision points might be structured. The question of how to organize and conduct such discourses has itself in recent years begun to receive attention in other disciplines, particularly in the advancing field of conflict and dispute resolution. Especially important in this respect have been the efforts to develop mediation techniques for structuring and facilitating dialogues between contending stakeholders (Susskind and Cruikshank 1987). Indeed, there has been much experimentation with dispute resolution methodologies, especially in the settlement of environmental disputes.

Such dispute mediation techniques are essentially efforts "to use informal face-to-face negotiations and consensus-building to resolve disputes" (Amy 1990: p. 212). Typically, the practice involves the use of a neutral mediator to bring together the various interests deemed party to a dispute – community members, businesspeople, environmental activists, and government officials, among others – in an effort to shape a compromise agreement among the relevant participants. As an informal process designed to get contentious parties to sit down and talk through their differences, this approach has made some real advances. Experience has shown that it can in fact lead to better communication, cooperation, and consensus building.

But the methodology is not without problems. Careful investigation shows the technique to harbor a number of hidden biases. One important disadvantage concerns the problem of access to the mediation process. The supporters of the technique offer it "as a new form of citizen participation open to all who want to participate," although it is far from obvious that equal access in fact exists in practice. Mediators, it is discovered, frequently "play a pivotal role in deciding who is invited to participate, and they often opt to keep the number as small as possible to facilitate the process of coming to agreement" (Amy 1990: p. 222). Moreover, the criteria that they typically use to select the participants is their relative power. Powerful interest groups, particularly those capable of later impeding negotiated agreements, are encouraged to participate, while the less influential tend to be ruled out, if not ignored. Beyond the problem of access, power also provides some of the participants with fundamental advantages at the bargaining table. One of the most important is the ability of those with the most resources to avail themselves of the best forms of scientific, technical, and legal expertise. As Amy (1990) sums it up, "despite the appearance of a purely informal process where people sit down to talk to equals," in practice it is often quite similar to "other political decision-making processes in which the special interests with the most power and resources have the most advantages" (p. 224). The outcome is thus often a form of cooptation ratified in the name of participatory consensus. The issue, then, is less with the deliberatory techniques than with the legitimacy of the underlying balance of power. This suggests the need for a more radical orientation toward the distribution of power, the implications of which we take up in the next and final section.

Participatory Expertise

For those interested in democratizing the risk decision-making processes, the in-equitable distribution of power and resources that differentiate the participants poses a fundamental challenge. As we have already seen, risk assessment, as a managerial decision science, is a product of a bureaucratic system; it is a tool designed to guide hierarchically structured decision-making processes. A more democratically structured practice of expertise would similarly require a more participatory set of institutions. This means new political innovations that can be brought about only through political struggles, particularly of the type advanced by participatory-oriented social movements, such as the ecology movement, grounded in a very different set of values (Friedmann 1987; Fischer 1990).

In the absence of a full-blown participatory social movement, we ask in this final section what kinds of political innovation the experts themselves might introduce to help overcome the barriers to participation. Toward this end, the first and most essential requirement would have to be a professional commitment, at least on the part of those committed to social change, to the furtherance of democratic partici-pation and public empowerment. Such a commitment, of course, is not the sort of thing most scientists are accustomed to, or would even willingly welcome, as it clearly represents a challenge to their privileges and status. But as the sociology of science has made clear, social commitments are already imported into the research process (a point even more applicable to an applied goal-directed science such as risk assessment). A commitment to participation is therefore as much a matter of changing a social practice as it is disturbing the epistemological requirements of science (Weingart 1990).

Beyond the commitment must be the innovation of new methodological techniques capable of facilitating the development of participatory institutions and their prac-tices. Here I refer to the kinds of discussion that take place in a public interest science center or a citizens' technology review board, as well as to the possibility of extending such participatory discourses to other societal institutions. Such a method would provide a format and a set of procedures for organizing the interactions between experts and the citizens they would seek to assist. One promising movement in this direction is the development of "participatory research" (Fischer 1990). Participatory research is a practice that has begun to take shape among alternative social move-ments, including alternative technology and ecological movements, especially in the

Third World. Indeed, there is an international network of participatory research with its own publications (Society for Participatory Research in Asia 1982).

To many conventionally trained scientists, both physical and social, the idea of participatory research sounds outrageously unscientific. But actually, in most ways it is only the scientific method made more time-consuming and perhaps more expensive, at least in the short run. Fundamentally, it is a progressive version of something already accepted as a methodology in the managerial sciences, namely, action research (Argyris 1985). Like action research, participatory research is designed as a methodology for integrating social learning and goal-oriented decision making. Where the former was eventually coopted by the managerial sciences to serve the rather narrowly defined needs of bureaucratic reform (typically defined as participatory management), participatory research is largely an effort to carry through on action research's earlier commitment to democratic participation (Reason and Rowan 1981; Fernandes and Tandon 1981; Kassam and Mustafa 1982; Merrifield 1989).

To be sure, participatory research is scarcely appropriate to all scientific contexts. Its most important applications pertain to problems involving a mixture of social and technical factors. Within this context it has emerged as an effort to restructure expertise to serve the requirements of democratic empowerment. Rather than providing technical answers designed to bring political discussions to an end, the task is to assist citizens in their efforts to examine their own interests and to make their own decisions (Hirschhorn 1979). Toward this end, it conceptualizes the expert as a "facilitator" of public learning and empowerment. Beyond merely providing data, the facilitator must also become an expert in how people learn, clarify, and decide for themselves (Fischer 1990). This includes coming to grips with the basic languages of public normative argumentation, as well as knowledge about the kinds of environmental and intellectual conditions within which citizens can formulate their own ideas. It involves the creation of institutional and intellectual conditions that help people pose questions and examine technical analyses in their own ordinary (or everyday) languages and decide which issues are important to them.

A particularly important feature of this integration process must be a better understanding of the relation of technical languages to public normative languages. For example, public debates, we are beginning to recognize, proceed more as social narratives than as formal inferential logics (Mink 1978; Fisher 1984; Stone 1989). While public narrative languages encompass elements of formal logic, in structure they are more like stories grounded in questions concerning the motivations and values of the political actors and technical experts involved in the ongoing deliberation, the way in which they conceive and behave in respect to the conflict, and so on (Weiss 1990). Such considerations, it will be recalled, are the very sorts of social concerns that risk assessors have failed to appreciate (Wynne 1987).

To be sure, those who practice participatory research almost always underscore the difficulties that it encounters (Eldon 1981). Most of the problems, however, are social and interpersonal rather than scientific per se: it takes, in short, a lot of time, political commitment and interpersonal skill to build people into complex decision process.

But its practitioners also point to two important payoffs. One, it identifies very real and important dangers that hide behind the generalities buried in the technocrats' calculations. That is, it brings to the fore the very problems that have been overlooked by technocratic risk assessment. Every bit as important, participation in decision making helps to build both credibility and acceptance of research findings (Dutton 1984; Friedmann 1987), the most critical failure facing the contemporary risk assessment approach.

Finally, it is important to note that participatory research is already beginning to emerge in the assessment of hazardous risks. In recent years there have been a number of efforts to develop a community-based approach to risk assessment. Designed to facilitate empowerment, such experiments attempt to integrate citizen information methodologically into the analytical process (Wartenberg 1989: p. 23) The goal, as Chess and Sandman (1989) put it, is to avoid conducting "risk assessments in isolation from community concerns." Toward this end, community groups systematically "provide information to risk assessors about routes of exposure and the history of the environmental problem that can both increase the validity of the risk assessment." The results, as preliminary evidence suggests, are more effective identification and documentation of community concerns; a better understanding of the nature and degree of the hazardous risks confronting the community; an improved capacity to set action-oriented priorities; and greater input into public decision-making processes (Chess and Sandman 1989; Merrifield 1989).

By way of closing, it must be recognized that such a proposal will be criticized by many industrial leaders, politicians and scientists, as this approach will be seen as expensive, time consuming, inefficient and unscientific (the first three of which are surely true in the short run). But the long run suggests a different assessment. Given the failures of the technocratic approach, coupled with a way of legitimating new technologies, it would appear that a participatory approach may open the only avenue to a successful solution to this pressing problem.

REFERENCES

Amy, J., 1990. Environmental dispute resolution: the promise and the pitfalls. In: N. J. Vig and M. E. Kraft (editors), *Environmental Policy in the 1990s*. Congressional Quarterly Press, Washington, DC: 211–234.

Andrews, R. N. L, 1990. Risk assessment: regulation and beyond. In: N. J. Vig and M. E. Kraft (editors), *Environmental Policy in the 1990s*. Congressional Quarterly Press, Washington, DC: 167–186.

Argyris, C., 1985. *Action Science*. Harvard University Press, Cambridge, MA.

Beck, U., 1986. *Risikogesellschaft: Auf dem Weg in eine andere Moderne*. Surkamp, Frankfurt.

Bell, D., 1973. *The Coming of Post-Industrial Society*. Basic Books, New York.

Brzezinski, Z., 1976. *Between the Ages: America's Role in the Technetronic Era*. Viking, New York.

Chess, C. and Sandman, P., 1989. Community use of risk assessment. *Science for the People*, January/February: 20.

Clarke, L., 1989. *Acceptable Risk? Making Decisions in a Toxic Environment*. University of California Press, Berkeley, CA.

Collingridge, D. and Reeve. C., 1986. *Science Speaks to Power*. St. Martins Press, New York.

Conrad, J. 1980 (ed.). *Society, Technology and Risk Assessment*. Academic Press, New York.

Coppock, R., 1984. *Social Constraints on Technological Progress*. Gower, Hampshire.

Covello, V. and Menkes, J., 1985. *Risk Assessment and Risk Assessment Methods: The State-of-the-Art*. National Science Foundation, Washington, DC.

Dobrzynski, J., 1988. Morton Thiokol: reflections on the Shuttle disaster. *Business Week*, March 14: 82–91.

Douglas, M. and Wildavsky, A., 1982. *Risk and Culture*. University of California Press, Berkeley, CA.

Dutton, D., 1984. The impact of public participation in biomedical policy: evidence from four case studies. In: J. C. Peterson (editor), *Citizen Participation in Science Policy*. University Press, Amherst, MA: 147–181.

Eldon, M., 1981. Sharing the research work: participatory research and its role demands. In: P. Reason and J. Rowan (editors), *Human Inquiry: a Sourcebook of New Paradigm Research*. Wiley, New York.

Fernandes, W. and Tandon, R., 1981 (editors). *Participatory Research and Evaluation: Experiments in Research as a Process of Liberation*. Indian Social Institute, New Delhi.

Fietkau, H. J., 1990. Accident prevention and risk communication in environmental protection: a sociopsychological perspective. *Industrial Crisis Quarterly*, 4: 277–289.

Fischer, F., 1990. *Technocracy and the Politics of Expertise*. Sage, Newbury Park, CA.

Fischer, F. and Wagner, P., 1990 (editors). Technological risk and political conflict: perspectives from West Germany. *Industrial Crisis Quarterly*, 4: 149–154.

Fisher, W. R., 1984. Narration as a human communications paradigm: the case of public moral argument. *Communications Monographs*, 51 (March): 1–22.

Friedmann, J., 1987. *Planning in the Public Domain*. Princeton University Press, Princeton, NJ.

Galbraith, J. K., 1967. *The New Industrial State*. Houghton Mifflin, Boston, MA.

Handler, P., 1980. In science, 'no advances without risks.' *U. S. News and World Report*, Sept. 15: 60.

Hawkesworth, M.E., 1988. *Theoretical Issues in Policy Research*. State University of New York Press, Albany, NY.

Hirschhorn, L., 1979. Alternative services and the crisis of the professions. In: J. Case and R. C. R. Taylor (editors), *Coops, Communes and Collectives: Experiments in Social Change in the 1960s and 1970s*. Pantheon, New York: 153–159.

Irwin, A. and Smith, D. et al., 1982. Risk analysis and public policy for major hazards. *Physics and Technology*, 13: 258–265.

Joerges, B., 1988. Large technical systems: concepts and systems. In: R. Mayntz and T. P. Hughes (editors), *The Development of Large Technical Systems*. Westview, Boulder, CO: 9–36.

Kassam, Y. and Mustafa, K., 1982 (editors). *Participatory Research: an Emerging Alternative in Social Science Research*. African Adult Education Association, Nairobi.

Lambright, H. W., 1989. Government–industry relations in the context of disaster lessons from *Apollo* and *Challenger*. Paper presented at the Second International Conference on Industrial and Organizational Crisis Management. New York University, Stern School of Business.

Lopes, L. L., 1987. The rhetoric of irrationality. Paper presented at the Colloquium on Mass Communications. University of Wisconsin, Nov. 19.

Mazur, A., 1980. Societal and scientific causes of the historical development of risk assessment. In: J. Conrad (editor), *Society, Technology and Risk Assessment*. Academic Press, New York: 151–157.

Merrifield, J., 1989. *Putting the Scientists in their Place: Participatory Research in Environmental and Occupational Health*. Highlander Center, New Market, TN.

Mink, L. P., 1978. Narrative form as cognitive instrument. In: R. H. Canary and H. Kozick (editors), *The Writing of History: Literary Form and Historical Understanding*. University of Wisconsin Press, Madison, WI: 20–49.

National Research Council, 1989. *Improving Risk Communication*. National Academy Press, Washington, DC.

Nelkin, D., 1984. Science and technology policy and the democratic process. In: C. Peterson (editor), *Citizen Participation in Science Policy*. University of Massachusetts Press, Amherst, MA: 18–39.

Paté-Cornell, E., 1990. Organizational aspects of engineering system safety: the case of offshore platforms. *Science*, Nov. 30: 1210–1217.

Perrow, C., 1984. Normal accidents. In: F. Fischer and C. Sirianni (editors), *Critical Studies in Organization and Bureaucracy*. Temple University Press, Philadelphia, PA: 287–305.

Petersen, J. C., 1984. Citizen participation in science policy. In: J. C. Peterson (editor), *Citizen Participation in Science Policy*. University of Massachusetts Press, Amherst, MA: 1–17.

Platt, J., 1969. What we must do? *Science*, 28 (Nov.): 1178.

Porritt, J., 1984. *Seeing Green*. Blackwell, Oxford.

Reason, P. and Rowan, J. (editors), 1981. *Human Inquiry: a Sourcebook of New Paradigm Research*. Wiley, New York.

Rosenbaum, W. A., 1985. *Environmental Politics and Policy*. Congressional Quarterly Press, Washington, DC.

Russell, M. and Gruber, M., 1987. Risk assessment in environmental policy-making. *Science*, 236 (April 17): 286–290.

Schwarz, M. and Thompson, M., 1990. *Divided We Stand: Redefining Politics, Technology and Social Choice*. Harvester & Wheatsheaf, Hertfordshire.

Slovic, P., 1984. Behavioral decision theory perspectives on risk and safety. *Acta Psychologica*, 56: 183–203.

Slovic, P. and Fischoff, B. et al., 1980. Facts and fears: understanding perceived risk. In: R. Schwing and W. A. Albers (editors), *Social Risk Assessment: How Safe Is Safe Enough?* Plenum, New York: 75–98.

Slovic, P. et al., 1982. *Acceptable Risk*. Cambridge University Press, Cambridge.

Society for Participatory Research in Asia, 1982. *Participatory Research: An Introduction*. Rajkamal Electric Press, New Delhi.

Smits, R. E. H. M. et al., 1987. The possibilities and limitations of technology assessment: in search of a useful approach. In: *Technology Assessment: An Opportunity for Europe*, vol. 1. Dutch Ministry of Education and Science/Commission of the European Communities/FAST, The Hague: 120–143.

Stanley, M., 1978. *The Technological Conscience: Survival and Dignity in an Age of Expertise*. University of Chicago Press, Chicago, IL.

Stone, D. A., 1990. Causal stories and the formation of policy agendas. *Political Science Quarterly*, 104(2): 281–300.

Susskind, L. and Cruikshank, J., 1987. *Breaking the Impasse: Consensual Approaches to Resolving Public Disputes*. Basic Books, New York.

Tivnan, E., 1988. Jeremy Rifkin just says no. *New York Times*, Oct. 18: 38.

Vaughan, D., 1990. Antonomy, independence and social control: NASA and the space shuttle challenge. *Administrative Science Quarterly*, 35 (3): 225–257.

Wartenberg, D., 1989. Quantitative risk assessment. *Science for the People*, January/February: 19–23.

Weingart, P., 1990. Science abused – challenging the legend. Paper presented at the Seminar on Sociology of Science at the Inter-University Centre, Dubrovnik, May 7–21.

Weiss, A., 1990. Scientific information, causal stories and the ozone hole controversy. Paper presented at the Seminar on the Sociology of Science at the Inter-University Centre, Dubrovnik, May 7–21.

Wildavsky, A., 1988. *Searching for Safety*. Rutgers University Press, New Brunswick, NJ.

Wynne, B., 1980. Technology risk and participation under uncertainty. In: J. Conrad (editor), *Society, Technology and Risk Assessment*. Academic Press, New York: 200–230.

Wynne, B., 1987. *Risk Management and Hazardous Waste: Implementation and the Dialectics of Credibility*. Springer, Berlin.

24

Green Cities, Growing Cities, Just Cities? Urban Planning and the Contradictions of Sustainable Development

Scott Campbell

In the coming years planners face tough decisions about where they stand on protecting the green city, promoting the economically growing city, and advocating social justice. Conflicts among these goals are not superficial ones arising simply from personal preferences. Nor are they merely conceptual, among the abstract notions of ecological, economic, and political logic, nor a temporary problem caused by the untimely confluence of environmental awareness and economic recession. Rather, these conflicts go to the historic core of planning, and are a leitmotif in the contemporary battles in both our cities and rural areas, whether over solid waste incinerators or growth controls, the spotted owls or nuclear power. And though sustainable development aspires to offer an alluring, holistic way of evading these conflicts, they cannot be shaken off so easily.

This chapter uses a simple triangular model to understand the divergent priorities of planning. My argument is that although the differences are partly due to misunderstandings arising from the disparate languages of environmental, economic, and political thought, translating across disciplines alone is not enough to eliminate these genuine clashes of interest. The socially constructed view of nature put forward here challenges the view of these conflicts as a classic battle of "man versus nature" or its current variation, "jobs versus the environment." The triangular model is then used to question whether sustainable development, the current object of planning's fascination, is a useful model to guide planning practice. I argue that the current concept of sustainability, though a laudable holistic vision, is vulnerable to the same criticism of vague idealism made thirty years ago against comprehensive planning. In this case, the idealistic fascination often builds upon a

Reprinted with permission from the *Journal of the American Planning Association*, 62 (3) (Summer 1996): 296–312. © American Planning Association, Chicago, IL.

romanticized view of pre-industrial, indigenous, sustainable cultures – inspiring visions, but also of limited modern applicability. Nevertheless, sustainability, if redefined and incorporated into a broader understanding of political conflicts in industrial society, can become a powerful and useful organizing principle for planning. In fact, the idea will be particularly effective if, instead of merely evoking a misty-eyed vision of a peaceful ecotopia, it acts as a lightning rod to focus conflicting economic, environmental, and social interests. The more it stirs up conflict and sharpens the debate, the more effective the idea of sustainability will be in the long run.

The paper concludes by considering the implications of this viewpoint for planning. The triangle shows not only the conflicts, but also the potential complementarity of interests. The former are unavoidable and require planners to act as mediators, but the latter area is where planners can be especially creative in building coalitions between once-separated interest groups, such as labor and environmentalists, or community groups and business. To this end, planners need to combine both their procedural and their substantive skills and thus become central players in the battle over growth, the environment, and social justice.

The Planner's Triangle: Three Priorities, Three Conflicts

The current environmental enthusiasm among planners and planning schools might suggest their innate predisposition to protect the natural environment. Unfortunately, the opposite is more likely to be true: our historic tendency has been to promote the development of cities at the cost of natural destruction: to build cities we have cleared forests, fouled rivers and the air, leveled mountains. That is not the complete picture, since planners also have often come to the defense of nature, through the work of conservationists, park planners, open space preservationists, the Regional Planning Association of America, greenbelt planners, and modern environmental planners. Yet along the economic–ecological spectrum, with Robert Moses and Dave Foreman (of *Earth First!*) standing at either pole, the planner has no natural home, but can slide from one end of the spectrum to the other; moreover, the midpoint has no special claims to legitimacy or fairness.

Similarly, though planners often see themselves as the defenders of the poor and of socio-economic equality, their actions over the profession's history have often belied that self-image (Harvey 1985). Planners' efforts with downtown redevelopment, freeway planning, public–private partnerships, enterprise zones, smokestack-chasing and other economic development strategies don't easily add up to equity planning. At best, the planner has taken an ambivalent stance between the goals of economic growth and economic justice.

In short, the planner must reconcile not two, but at least three conflicting interests: to "grow" the economy, distribute this growth fairly, and in the process not degrade the ecosystem. To classify contemporary battles over environmental racism, pollution-producing jobs, growth control, etc., as simply clashes between economic growth and environmental protection misses the third issue, of social justice. The "jobs versus environment" dichotomy (e.g., the spotted owl versus Pacific Northwest timber jobs) crudely collapses under the "economy" banner the often differing interests of workers, corporations, community members, and the national public.

The intent of this chapter's title is to focus planning not only for "green cities and growing cities," but also for "just cities."

In an ideal world, planners would strive to achieve a balance of all three goals. In practice, however, professional and fiscal constraints drastically limit the leeway of most planners. Serving the broader public interest by holistically harmonizing growth, preservation, and equality remains the ideal; the reality of practice restricts planners to serving the narrower interests of their clients, that is, authorities and bureaucracies (Marcuse 1976), despite efforts to work outside those limitations (Hoffman 1989). In the end, planners usually represent one particular goal – planning perhaps for increased property tax revenues, or more open space preservation, or better housing for the poor – while neglecting the other two. Where each planner stands in the triangle depicted in figure 24.1 defines such professional bias. One may see illustrated in the figure the gap between the call for integrative, sustainable development planning (the center of the triangle) and the current fragmentation of professional practice (the edges). This point is developed later.

The points (corners) of the triangle: the economy, the environment, and equity

The three types of priorities lead to three perspectives on the city: The economic development planner sees the city as a location where production, consumption, distribution, and innovation take place. The city is in competition with other cities for markets and for new industries. Space is the economic space of highways, market areas, and commuter zones.

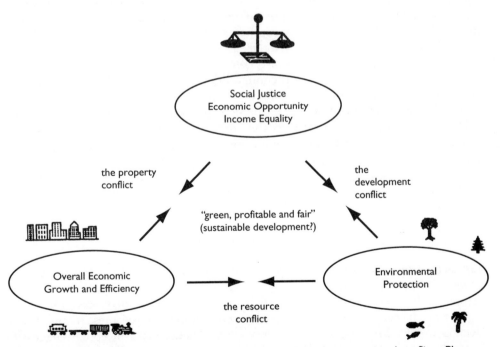

Fig. 24.1 The triangle of conflicting goals for planning, and the three associated conflicts. Planners define themselves, implicitly, by where they stand on the triangle. The elusive ideal of sustainable development leads one to the center.

The environmental planner sees the city as a consumer of resources and a producer of wastes. The city is in competition with nature for scarce resources and land, and always poses a threat to nature. Space is the ecological space of greenways, river basins, and ecological niches.

The equity planner sees the city as a location of conflict over the distribution of resources, of services, and of opportunities. The competition is within the city itself, among different social groups. Space is the social space of communities, neighborhood organizations, labor unions: the space of access and segregation.

Certainly there are other important views of the city, including the architectural, the psychological, and the circulatory (transportation); and one could conceivably construct a planner's rectangle, pentagon, or more complex polygon. The triangular shape itself is not propounded here as the underlying geometric structure of the planner's world. Rather, it is useful for its conceptual simplicity. More importantly, it emphasizes the point that a one-dimensional "man versus environment" spectrum misses the social conflicts in contemporary environmental disputes, such as loggers versus the Sierra Club, farmers versus suburban developers, or fishermen versus barge operators (Reisner 1987; Jacobs 1989; McPhee 1989; Tuason 1993).[1]

Triangle axis 1: the property conflict

The three points on the triangle represent divergent interests, and therefore lead to three fundamental conflicts. The first conflict – between economic growth and equity – arises from competing claims on and uses of property, such as between management and labor, landlords and tenants, or gentrifying professionals and long-time residents. This growth–equity conflict is further complicated because each side not only resists the other, but also needs the other for its own survival. The contradictory tendency for a capitalist, democratic society to define property (such as housing or land) as a private commodity, but at the same time to rely on government intervention (e.g., zoning, or public housing for the working class) to ensure the beneficial social aspects of the same property, is what Richard Foglesong (1986, and see chap. 5 above) calls the "property contradiction." This tension is generated as the private sector simultaneously resists and needs social intervention, given the intrinsically contradictory nature of property. Indeed, the essence of property in our society is the tense pulling between these two forces. The conflict defines the boundary between private interest and the public good.

Triangle axis 2: the resource conflict

Just as the private sector both resists regulation of property, yet needs it to keep the economy flowing, so too is society in conflict about its priorities for natural resources. Business resists the regulation of its exploitation of nature, but at the same time needs regulation to conserve those resources for present and future demands. This can be called the "resource conflict." The conceptual essence of natural resources is therefore the tension between their economic utility in industrial society and their ecological utility in the natural environment. This conflict defines the boundary between the developed city and the undeveloped wilderness, which is symbolized by the "city limits." The boundary is not fixed; it is a dynamic and contested boundary between mutually dependent forces.

Is there a single, universal economic–ecological conflict underlying all such disputes faced by planners? I searched for this essential, Platonic notion, but the diversity of examples – water politics in California, timber versus the spotted owl in the pacific Northwest, tropical deforestation in Brazil, park planning in the Adirondacks, greenbelt planning in Britain, to name a few – suggests otherwise. Perhaps there is an *Ur-Konflikt*, rooted in the fundamental struggle between human civilization and the threatening wilderness around us, and expressed variously over the centuries. However, the decision must be left to anthropologists as to whether the essence of the spotted owl controversy can be traced back to Neolithic times. A meta-theory tying all these multifarious conflicts to an essential battle of "human versus nature" (and, once tools and weapons were developed and nature was controlled, "human versus human") – that invites skepticism. In this discussion, the triangle is used simply as a template to recognize and organize the common themes; to examine actual conflicts, individual case studies are used.[2]

The economic–ecological conflict has several instructive parallels with the growth–equity conflict. In the property conflict, industrialists must curb their profit-increasing tendency to reduce wages, in order to provide labor with enough wages to feed, house, and otherwise "reproduce" itself – that is, the subsistence wage. In the resource conflict, the industrialists must curb their profit-increasing tendency to increase timber yields, so as to ensure that enough of the forest remains to "reproduce" itself (Clawson 1975; Beltzer and Kroll 1986; Lee, Field, and Burch 1990). This practice is called "sustained yield," though timber companies and environmentalists disagree about how far the forest can be exploited and still be "sustainable." (Of course, other factors also affect wages, such as supply and demand, skill level, and discrimination, just as lumber demand, labor prices, transportation costs, tariffs, and other factors affect how much timber is harvested.) In both cases, industry must leave enough of the exploited resource, be it human labor or nature, so that the resource will continue to deliver in the future. In both cases, how much is "enough" is also contested.

Triangle axis 3: the development conflict

The third axis on the triangle is the most elusive: the "development conflict," lying between the poles of social equity and environmental preservation. If the property conflict is characterized by the economy's ambivalent interest in providing at least a subsistence existence for working people, and the resource conflict by the economy's ambivalent interest in providing sustainable conditions for the natural environment, the development conflict stems from the difficulty of doing both at once. Environment–equity disputes are coming to the fore to join the older dispute about economic growth versus equity (Paehlke 1994, pp. 349–50). This may be the most challenging conundrum of sustainable development: how to increase social equity and protect the environment simultaneously, whether in a steady-state economy (Daly 1991) or not. How could those at the bottom of society find greater economic opportunity if environmental protection mandates diminished economic growth? On a global scale, efforts to protect the environment might lead to slowed economic growth in many countries, exacerbating the inequalities between rich and poor nations. In effect, the developed nations would be asking the poorer nations to forgo rapid development to save the world from the greenhouse effect and other global emergencies.

This development conflict also happens at the local level, as in resource-dependent communities, which commonly find themselves at the bottom of the economy's hierarchy of labor. Miners, lumberjacks, and mill workers see a grim link between environmental preservation and poverty, and commonly mistrust environmentalists as elitists. Poor urban communities are often forced to make the no-win choice between economic survival and environmental quality, as when the only economic opportunities are offered by incinerators, toxic waste sites, landfills, and other noxious land uses that most neighborhoods can afford to oppose and do without (Bryant and Mohai 1992; Bullard 1990, 1993). If, as some argue, environmental protection is a luxury of the wealthy, then environmental racism lies at the heart of the development conflict. Economic segregation leads to environmental segregation: the former occurs in the transformation of natural resources into consumer products; the latter occurs as the spoils of production are returned to nature. Inequitable development takes place at all stages of the materials cycle.

Consider this conflict from the vantage of equity planning. Norman Krumholz, as the planning director in Cleveland, faced the choice of either building regional rail lines or improving local bus lines (Krumholz et al. 1982). Regional rail lines would encourage the suburban middle class to switch from cars to mass transit; better local bus service would help the inner-city poor by reducing their travel and waiting time. One implication of this choice was the tension between reducing pollution and making transportation access more equitable, an example of how bias toward social inequity may be embedded in seemingly objective transit proposals.

Implications of the Planner's Triangle Model

Conflict and complementarity in the triangle

Though I use the image of the triangle to emphasize the strong conflicts among economic growth, environmental protection, and social justice, no point can exist alone. The nature of the three axial conflicts is mutual dependence based not only on opposition, but also on collaboration.

Consider the argument that the best way to distribute wealth more fairly (i.e., to resolve the property conflict) is to increase the size of the economy, so that society will have more to redistribute. Similarly, we can argue that the best way to improve environmental quality (i.e., to resolve the resource conflict) is to expand the economy, thereby having more money with which to buy environmental protection. The former is trickle-down economics; can we call the latter "trickle-down environmentalism"? One sees this logic in the conclusion of the Brundtland Report: "If large parts of the developing world are to avert economic, social, and environmental catastrophes, it is essential that global economic growth be revitalized" (World Commission on Environment and Development 1987). However, only if such economic growth is more fairly distributed will the poor be able to restore and protect their environment, whose devastation so immediately degrades their quality of life. In other words, the development conflict can be resolved only if the property conflict is resolved as well. Therefore, the challenge for planners is to deal with the conflicts between competing interests by discovering and implementing complementary uses.

The triangle's origins in a social view of nature

One of the more fruitful aspects of recent interdisciplinary thought may be its linking the traditionally separate intellectual traditions of critical social theory and environmental science/policy (e.g., Smith 1990; Wilson 1992; Ross 1994). This is also the purpose of the triangle figure presented here: to integrate the environmentalist's and social theorist's world views. On one side, an essentialist view of environmental conflicts ("man versus nature") emphasizes the resource conflict. On another side, a historical materialist view of social conflicts (e.g., capital versus labor) emphasizes the property conflict. By simultaneously considering both perspectives, one can see more clearly the social dimension of environmental conflicts, that is, the development conflict. Such a synthesis is not easy: it requires accepting the social construction of nature but avoiding the materialistic pitfall of arrogantly denying any aspects of nature beyond the labor theory of value.

Environmental conflict should not, therefore, be seen as simply one group representing the interests of nature and another group attacking nature (though it often appears that way).[3] Who is to say that the lumberjack, who spends all his or her days among trees (and whose livelihood depends on those trees), is any less close to nature than the environmentalist taking a weekend walk through the woods? Is the lumberjack able to cut down trees only because s/he is "alienated" from the "true" spirit of nature – the spirit that the hiker enjoys? In the absence of a forest mythology, neither the tree cutter nor the tree hugger – nor the third party, the owner/lessee of the forest – can claim an innate kinship to a tree. This is not to be an apologist for clear-cutting, but rather to say that the merits of cutting versus preserving trees cannot be decided according to which persons or groups have the "truest" relationship to nature.

The crucial point is that all three groups have an interactive relationship with nature: the differences lie in their conflicting *conceptions* of nature, their conflicting *uses* of nature, and how they incorporate nature into their systems of values (be they community, economic, or spiritual values). This clash of human values reveals how much the ostensibly separate domains of community development and environmental protection overlap, and suggests that planners should do better in combining social and environmental models. One sees this clash of values in many environmental battles: between the interests of urban residents and those of subsidized irrigation farmers in California water politics; between beach homeowners and coastal managers trying to control erosion; between rich and poor neighborhoods, in the siting of incinerators; between farmers and environmentalists, in restrictions by open space zoning. Even then-President George Bush weighed into such disputes during his 1992 campaign when he commented to a group of loggers that finally people should be valued more than spotted owls (his own take on the interspecies equity issue). Inequity and the imbalance of political power are often issues at the heart of economic–environmental conflicts.

Recognition that the terrain of nature is contested need not, however, cast us adrift on a sea of socially-constructed relativism where "nature" appears as an arbitrary idea of no substance (Bird 1987; Soja 1989). Rather, we are made to rethink the idea and to see the appreciation of nature as an historically evolved sensibility. I suspect that radical environmentalists would criticize this perspective as anthropocentric environmentalism, and argue instead for an ecocentric world view that puts the Earth first (Sessions 1992; Parton 1993). It is true that an anthropocentric view, if distorted, can lead to an arrogant optimism about civilization's ability to reprogram nature through technologies ranging from huge hydroelectric and nuclear plants down to genetic engineering. A rigid belief in the anthropocentric labor theory of value, Marxist or otherwise, can produce a modern-day Narcissus as a social-constructionist who sees nature as merely reflecting the beauty of the human aesthetic and the value of human labor. In this light, a tree is devoid of value until it either becomes part of a scenic area or is transformed into lumber. On the other hand, even as radical, ecocentric environmentalists claim to see "true nature" beyond the city limits, they are blind to how their own world view and their definition of nature itself are shaped by their socialization. The choice between an anthropocentric or an ecocentric world view is a false one. We are all unavoidably anthropocentric; the question is which anthropomorphic values and priorities we will apply to the natural and the social world around us.

Sustainable Development: Reaching the Elusive Center of the Triangle

If the three corners of the triangle represent key goals in planning, and the three axes represent the three resulting conflicts, then I will define the center of the triangle as representing sustainable development: the balance of these three goals. Getting to the center, however, will not be so easy. It is one thing to locate sustainability in the abstract, but quite another to reorganize society to get there.

At first glance, the widespread advocacy of sustainable development is astonishing, given its revolutionary implications for daily life (World Commission 1987; Daly and Cobb 1989; Rees 1989; World Bank 1989; Goodland 1990; Barrett and Bohlen 1991; Korten 1991; Van der Ryn and Calthorpe 1991). It is getting hard to refrain from sustainable development; arguments against it are inevitably attached to the strawman image of a greedy, myopic industrialist. Who would now dare to speak up in opposition? Two interpretations of the bandwagon for sustainable development suggest themselves. The pessimistic thought is that sustainable development has been stripped of its transformative power and reduced to its lowest common denominator. After all, if both the World Bank and radical ecologists now believe in sustainability, the concept can have no teeth: it is so malleable as to mean many things to many people without requiring commitment to any specific policies. Actions speak louder than words, and though all endorse sustainability, few will actually practice it. Furthermore, any concept fully endorsed by all parties must surely be bypassing the heart of the conflict. Set a goal far enough into the future, and even conflicting interests will seem to converge along parallel lines. The concept certainly appears to violate Karl Popper's requirement that propositions be falsifiable, for to reject sustainability is to embrace nonsustainability – and who dares to sketch that future? (Ironically, the nonsustainable scenario is the easiest to define: merely the extrapolation of our current way of life.)

Yet there is also an optimistic interpretation of the broad embrace given sustainability: the idea has become hegemonic, an accepted meta-narrative, a given. It has shifted from being a variable to being the parameter of the debate, almost certain to be integrated into any future scenario of development. We should therefore neither be surprised that no definition has been agreed upon, nor fear that this reveals a fundamental flaw in the concept. In the battle of big public ideas, sustainability has won: the task of the coming years is simply to work out the details, and to narrow the gap between its theory and practice.

Is sustainable development a useful concept?

Some environmentalists argue that if sustainable development is necessary, it therefore must be possible. Perhaps so, but if you are stranded at the bottom of a deep well, a ladder may be impossible even though necessary. The answer espoused may be as much an ideological as a scientific choice, depending on whether one's loyalty is to Malthus or Daly. The more practical question is whether sustainability is a useful concept for planners. The answer here is mixed. The goal may be too far away and holistic to be operational: that is, it may not easily break down into concrete, short-term steps. We also might be able to *define* sustainability yet be unable ever to actually measure it or even know, one day in the future, that we had achieved it. An old eastern proverb identifies the western confusion of believing that to name something is to know it. That may be the danger in automatically embracing sustainable development: a facile confidence that by adding the term "sustainable" to all our existing planning documents and tools (sustainable zoning, sustainable economic development, sustainable transportation planning), we are *doing* sustainable planning. Conversely, one can do much beneficial environmental work without ever devoting explicit attention to the concept of sustainability.

Yet sustainability can be a helpful concept in that it posits the long-term planning goal of a social–environmental system in balance. It is a unifying concept, enormously appealing to the imagination, that brings together many different environmental concerns under one overarching value. It defines a set of social priorities and articulates how society values the economy, the environment, and equity (Paehlke 1994, p. 360). In theory, it allows us not only to calculate whether we have attained sustainability, but also to determine how far away we are. (Actual measurement, though, is another, harder task.) Clearly, it can be argued that, though initially flawed and vague, the concept can be transformed and refined to be of use to planners.

History, equity, and sustainable development

One obstacle to an accurate, working definition of sustainability may well be the historical perspective that sees the practice as pre-existing, either in our past or as a Platonic concept. I believe instead that our sustainable future does not yet exist, either in reality or even in strategy. We do not yet know what it will look like; it is being socially constructed through a sustained period of conflict negotiation and resolution. This is a process of innovation, not of discovery and converting the nonbelievers.

This point brings us to the practice of looking for sustainable development in pre-industrial and nonwestern cultures (a common though not universal practice). Searching for our future in our indigenous past is instructive at both the philosophical and the practical level (Turner 1983; Duerr 1985). Yet it is also problematical, tapping into a myth that our salvation lies in the pre-industrial sustainable culture. The international division of labor and trade, the movement of most people away from agriculture into cities, and exponential population growth lead us irrevocably down a unidirectional, not a circular path: the transformation of pre-industrial, indigenous settlements into mass urban society is irreversible. Our modern path to sustainability lies forward, not behind us.

The key difference between those indigenous, sustainable communities and ours is that they had no choice but to be sustainable. Bluntly stated, if they cut down too many trees or ruined the soil, they would die out. Modern society has the options presented by trade, long-term storage, and synthetic replacements; if we clear-cut a field, we have subsequent options that our ancestors didn't. In this situation, we must *voluntarily choose* sustainable practices, since there is no immediate survival or market imperative to do so. Although the long-term effects of a nonsustainable economy are certainly dangerous, the feedback mechanisms are too long-term to prod us in the right direction.

Why do we often romanticize the sustainable past? Some are attracted to the powerful spiritual link between humans and nature that has since been lost. Such romanticists tend, however, to overlook the more harsh and unforgiving aspects of being so dependent on the land. Two hundred years ago, Friedrich Schiller (1965, p. 28) noted the tendency of utopian thinkers to take their dream for the future and posit it as their past, thus giving it legitimacy as a cyclical return to the past.[4] This habit is not unique to ecotopians (Kumar 1991); some religious fundamentalists also justify their utopian urgency by drawing on the myth of a paradise lost. Though Marxists don't glorify the past in the same way, they, too, manage to anticipate a *static* system of balance and harmony, which nonetheless will require a cataclysmic, revolutionary social transformation to reach. All three ideologies posit some basic flaw in society – be it western materialism, original sin, or capitalism – whose identification and cure will free us from conflict. Each ideology sees a fundamental alienation as the danger to overcome: alienation from nature, from god, or from work. Each group is so critical of existing society that it would seem a wonder we have made it this far; but this persistence of human society despite the dire prognoses of utopians tells us something.

What is the fallout from such historical thinking? By neglecting the powerful momentum of modern industrial and postindustrial society, it both points us in the wrong direction and makes it easier to marginalize the proponents of sustainable development. It also carries an anti-urban sentiment that tends to neglect both the centrality and the plight of megacities. Modern humans are unique among species in their propensity to deal with nature's threats, not only through flight and burrowing and biological adaptation, nor simply through spiritual understanding, but also through massive population growth, complex social division of labor, and the fundamental, external transformation of their once-natural environment (the building of cities). Certainly the fixation on growth, industry, and competition has degraded the environment. Yet one cannot undo urban-industrial society. Rather, one must continue to innovate through to the other side of industrialization, to reach a more sustainable economy.

The cyclical historical view of some environmentalists also hinders a critical understanding of equity, since that view attributes to the environment a natural state of equality rudely upset by modern society. Yet nature is inherently neither equal nor unequal, and at times can be downright brutal. The human observer projects a sense of social equity onto nature, through a confusion, noted by Schiller, of the idealized future with myths about our natural past. To gain a sense of historical legitimacy, we project our socially constructed sense of equality onto the past, creating revisionist history in which nature is fair and compassionate. Society's path to equality is perceived not as an uncertain progress from barbarism to justice, but rather as a return to an original state of harmony as laid out in nature. In this thinking, belief in an ecological balance and a social balance, entwined in the pre-industrial world, conjures up an eco-Garden of Eden "lost" by modern society.[5]

It will be more useful to let go of this mythic belief in our involuntary diaspora from a pre-industrial, ecotopian Eden.[6] The conflation of ecological diasporas and utopias constrains our search for creative, urban solutions to social–environmental conflict. By relinquishing such mythic beliefs, we will understand that notions of equity were not lying patiently in wait in nature, to be first discovered by indigenous peoples, then lost by colonialists, and finally rediscovered by modern society in the late twentieth century. This is certainly not to say that nature can teach us nothing. The laws of nature are not the same thing, however, as natural law, nor does ecological equilibrium necessarily generate normative principles of equity. Though we turn to nature to understand the context, dynamics, and effects of the economic–environmental conflict, we must turn to social norms to decide what balance is fair and just.

How, then, do we define what is fair? I propose viewing social justice as the striving towards a more equal distribution of resources among social groups across the space of cities and of nations – a definition of "fair" distribution. It should be noted that societies view themselves as "fair" if the *procedures* of allocation treat people equally, even if the *substantive* outcome is unbalanced. (One would hope that equal treatment is but the first step towards narrowing material inequality.) The environmental movement expands the space for this "equity" in two ways: (1) intergenerationally (present versus future generations) and (2) across species (as in animal rights, deep ecology, and legal standing for trees). The two added dimensions of equity remain essentially abstractions, however, since no one from the future or from other species can speak up for their "fair share" of resources. Selfless advocates (or selfish ventriloquists) "speak for them."

This expansion of socio-spatial equity to include future generations and other species not only makes the concept more complex; it also creates the possibility for contradictions among the different calls for "fairness." Slowing worldwide industrial expansion may preserve more of the world's resources for the future (thereby increasing intergenerational equity), but it may also undermine the efforts of the underdeveloped world to approach the living standards of the west (thereby lowering international equity). Battles over Native American fishing practices, the spotted owl, and restrictive farmland preservation each thrust together several divergent notions of "fairness." It is through resolving the three sorts of conflicts on the planner's triangle that society iteratively forms its definition of what is fair.

The path towards sustainable development

There are two final aspects of the fuzzy definition of sustainability: its path and its outcome. The basic premise of sustainable development is one that, like the long-term goal of a balanced U.S. budget, is hard not to like. As with eliminating the national debt, however, two troubling questions about sustainable development remain: How are you going to get there? Once you get there, what are the negative consequences? Planners don't yet have adequate answers to these two questions; that is, as yet they have no concrete strategies to achieve sustainable development, nor do they know how to counter the political resistance to it.

On the *path* towards a sustainable future, the steps are often too vague, as with sweeping calls for a "spiritual transformation" as the prerequisite for environmental transformation. Sometimes the call for sustainable development seems to serve as a vehicle for sermonizing about the moral and spiritual corruption of the industrial world (undeniable). Who would not want to believe in a holistic blending of economic and ecological values in each of our planners, who would then go out into the world and, on each project, internally and seamlessly merge the interests of jobs and nature, as well as of social justice? That is, the call to planners would be to stand at every moment at the center of the triangle.

But this aim is too reminiscent of our naive belief during the 1950s and 1960s in comprehensive planning for a single "public interest," before the incrementalists and advocacy planners pulled the rug out from under us (Lindblom 1959; Altshuler 1965; Davidoff 1965; Fainstein and Fainstein 1971). I suspect that planners' criticisms of the sustainable development movement in the coming years will parallel the critique of comprehensive planning thirty years ago: The incrementalists will argue that one cannot achieve a sustainable society in a single grand leap, for it requires too much social and ecological information and is too risky. The advocacy planners will argue that no common social interest in sustainable development exists, and that bureaucratic planners will invariably create a sustainable development scheme that neglects the interests both of the poor and of nature. To both groups of critics, the prospect of integrating economic, environmental and equity interests will seem forced and artificial. States will require communities to prepare "Sustainable Development Master Plans," which will prove to be glib wish lists of goals and suspiciously vague implementation steps. To achieve consensus for the plan, language will be reduced to the lowest common denominator, and the pleasing plans will gather dust.

An alternative is to let holistic sustainable development be a long-range goal; it is a worthy one, for planners do need a vision of a more sustainable urban society. But during the coming years, planners will confront deep-seated conflicts among economic, social and environmental interests that cannot be wished away through admittedly appealing images of a community in harmony with nature. One is no more likely to abolish the economic–environmental conflict completely by achieving sustainable bliss than one is to eliminate completely the boundaries between the city and the wilderness, between the public and private spheres, between the haves and have-nots. Nevertheless, one can diffuse the conflict, and find ways to avert its more destructive fall-out.

My concern about the *ramifications* of a sustainable future is one that is often expressed: steady-state, no-growth economics would be likely to relegate much of the developing world – and the poor within the industrialized world – to a state of persistent poverty. The advocates of sustainable development rightly reject as flawed the premise of conventional economics that only a growth economy can achieve social redistribution. And growth economics has, indeed, also exacerbated the environment's degradation. However, it is wishful thinking to assume that a sustainable economy will automatically ensure a socially just distribution of resources.[7] The vision of no-growth (commonly thought not universally assumed to characterize sustainable development) raises powerful fears, and planners should be savvy to such fears. Otherwise, they will understand neither the potential dangers of steady-state economics nor the nature of the opposition to sustainable development.

Rethinking/redefining sustainable development

Despite the shortcomings in the current formulation of sustainable development, the concept retains integrity and enormous potential. It simply needs to be redefined and made more precise. First, one should avoid a dichotomous, black-and-white view of sustainability. We should think of American society not as a corrupt, wholly unsustainable one that has to be made pure and wholly sustainable, but rather as a hybrid of both sorts of practices. Our purpose, then, should be to move further towards sustainable practices in an evolutionary progression.

Second, we should broaden the idea of "sustainability." If "crisis" is defined as the inability of a system to reproduce itself, then sustainability is the opposite: the long-term ability of a system to reproduce. This criterion applies not only to natural ecosystems, but to economic and political systems as well. By this definition, western society already does much to sustain itself: economic policy and corporate strategies (e.g., investment, training, monetary policy) strive to reproduce the macro- and micro-economies. Similarly, governments, parties, labor unions, and other political agents strive to reproduce their institutions and interests. Society's shortcoming is that as it strives to sustain its political and economic systems, it often neglects to sustain the ecological system. The goal for planning is therefore a broader agenda: to sustain, simultaneously and in balance, these three sometimes competing, sometimes complementary systems.[8]

Third, it will be helpful to distinguish initially between two levels of sustainability: specific versus general (or local versus global). One might fairly easily imagine and achieve sustainability in a single sector and/or locality, for example, converting a Pacific Northwest community to sustained-yield timber practices. Recycling, solar power, cogeneration, and conservation can lower consumption of nonsustainable resources. To achieve complete sustainability across all sectors and/or all places, however, requires such complex restructuring and redistribution that the only feasible path to global sustainability is likely to be a long, incremental accumulation of local and industry-specific advances.

What this incremental, iterative approach means is that planners will find their vision of a sustainable city developed best at the conclusion of contested negotiations over land use, transportation, housing, and economic development policies, not as the premise for beginning the effort. To first spend years in the hermetic isolation of universities and environmental groups, perfecting the theory of sustainable development, before testing it in community development is backwards. That approach sees sustainable development as an ideal society outside the conflicts of the planner's triangle, or as the tranquil "eye of the hurricane" at the triangle's center. As with the ideal comprehensive plan, it is presumed that the objective, technocratic merits of a perfected sustainable development scheme will ensure society's acceptance. But one cannot reach the sustainable center of the planner's triangle in a single, holistic leap to a pre-ordained balance.

The Task Ahead for Planners: Seeking Sustainable Development within the Triangle of Planning Conflicts

The role of planners is therefore to engage the current challenge of sustainable development with a dual, interactive strategy: (1) to manage and resolve conflict; and (2) to promote creative technical, architectural, and institutional solutions. Planners must both negotiate the procedures of the conflict and promote a substantive vision of sustainable development.

Procedural paths to sustainable development: conflict negotiation

In negotiation and conflict resolution (Bingham 1986; Susskind and Cruikshank 1987; Crowfoot and Wondolleck 1990), rather than pricing externalities, common ground is established at the negotiation table, where the conflicting economic, social, and environmental interests can be brought together. The potential rewards are numerous: not only an outcome that balances all parties, but avoidance of heavy legal costs and long-lasting animosity. Negotiated conflict resolution can also lead to a better understanding of one's opponent's interests and values, and even of one's own interests. The very process of lengthy negotiation can be a powerful tool to mobilize community involvement around social and environmental issues. The greatest promise, of course, is a win–win outcome: finding innovative solutions that would not have come out of traditional, adversarial confrontation. Through skillfully led, back-and-forth discussion, the parties can separate their initial, clashing substantive demands from their underlying interests, which may be more compatible. For example, environmentalists and the timber industry could solve their initial dispute over building a logging road through alternative road design and other mitigation measures (Crowfoot and Wondolleck 1990, pp. 32–52).

However, conflict resolution is no panacea. Sometimes conflicting demands express fundamental conflicts of interest. The either-or nature of the technology or ecology may preclude a win–win outcome, as in an all-or-nothing dispute over a proposed hydroelectric project (Reisner 1987) – you either build it or you don't. An overwhelming imbalance of power between the opposing groups also can thwart resolution (Crowfoot and Wondolleck 1990, p. 4). A powerful party can simply refuse to participate. It is also hard to negotiate a comprehensive resolution for a large number of parties.

Planners are likely to have the best success in using conflict resolution when there is a specific, concise dispute (rather than an amorphous ideological clash); all interested parties agree to participate (and don't bypass the process through the courts); each party feels on equal ground; there are a variety of possible compromises and innovative solutions; both parties prefer a solution to an impasse; and a skilled third-party negotiator facilitates. The best resolution strategies seem to include two areas of compromise and balance: the procedural (each party is represented and willing to compromise); and the substantive (the solution is a compromise, such as multiple land uses or a reduced development density).

Procedural paths to sustainable development: redefining the language of the conflict

A second strategy is to bridge the chasms between the languages of economics, environmentalism, and social justice. Linguistic differences, which reflect separate value hierarchies, are a major obstacle to common solutions. All too often, the economists speak of incentives and marginal rates, the ecologists speak of carrying capacity and biodiversity, the advocate planners speak of housing rights, empowerment, and discrimination, and each side accuses the others of being "out of touch" (Campbell 1992).

The planner therefore needs to act as a translator, assisting each group to understand the priorities and reasoning of the others. Economic, ecological and social thought may at a certain level be incommensurable, yet a level may still be found where all three may be brought together. To offer an analogy, a Kenyan Gikuyu text cannot be fully converted into English without losing something in translation; a good translation, nevertheless, is the best possible way to bridge two systems of expression that will never be one, and it is preferable to incomprehension.

The danger of translation is that one language will dominate the debate and thus define the terms of the solution. It is essential to exert equal effort to translate in each direction, to prevent one linguistic culture from dominating the other (as English has done in neocolonial Africa). Another lesson from the neocolonial linguistic experience is that it is crucial for each social group to express itself in its own language before any translation. The challenge for planners is to write the best translations among the languages of the economic, the ecological, and the social views, and to avoid a quasi-colonial dominance by the economic *lingua franca*, by creating equal two-way translations.[9]

For example, planners need better tools to understand their cities and regions not just as economic systems, or static inventories of natural resources, but also as *environmental systems* that are part of regional and global networks trading goods, information, resources and pollution. At the conceptual level, translating the economic vocabulary of global cities, the spatial division of labor, regional restructuring, and technoburbs/edge cities into environmental language would be a worthy start; at the same time, of course, the vocabulary of biodiversity, landscape linkages, and carrying capacity should be translated to be understandable by economic interests.

This bilingual translation should extend to the empirical level. I envision extending the concept of the "trade balance" to include an "environmental balance," which covers not just commodities, but also natural resources and pollution. Planners should improve their data collection and integration to support the environmental trade balance. They should apply economic–ecological bilingualism not only to the content of data, but also to the spatial framework of the data, by rethinking the geographic boundaries of planning and analysis. Bioregionalists advocate having the spatial scale for planning reflect the scale of *natural* phenomena (e.g., the extent of a river basin, vegetation zones, or the dispersion range of metropolitan air pollution); economic planners call for a spatial scale to match the *social* phenomena (e.g., highway networks, municipal boundaries, labor market areas, new industrial districts). The solution is to integrate these two scales and overlay the economic and ecological geographies of planning. The current merging of environmental Raster (grid-based) and infrastructural vector-based data in Geographic Information Systems (GIS) recognizes the need for multiple layers of planning boundaries (Wiggins 1993).

Translation can thus be a powerful planner's skill, and interdisciplinary planning education already provides some multilingualism. Moreover, the idea of sustainability lends itself nicely to the meeting on common ground of competing value systems. Yet translation has its limits. Linguistic differences often represent real, intractable differences in values. An environmental dispute may arise not from a misunderstanding alone; both sides may clearly understand that their vested interests fundamentally clash, no matter how expressed. At this point, translation must give way to other strategies. The difficulties are exacerbated when one party has greater power, and so shapes the language of the debate as well as prevailing in its outcome. In short, translation, like conflict negotiation, reveals both the promises and the limitations of communication-based conflict resolution.

Other procedural paths

Two other, more traditional approaches deserve mention. One is political pluralism: let the political arena decide conflicts, either directly (e.g., a referendum on an open space bond act, or a California state proposition on nuclear power), or indirectly (e.g., elections decided on the basis of candidates' environmental records and promised legislation). The key elements here, political debate and ultimately the vote, allow much wider participation in the decision than negotiation does. However, a binary vote cannot as easily handle complex issues, address specific land-use conflicts, or develop subtle, creative solutions. Choosing the general political process as a strategy for deciding conflict also takes the process largely out of the hands of planners.

The other traditional strategy is to develop market mechanisms to link economic and environmental priorities. Prices are made the commonality that bridges the gap between the otherwise noncommensurables of trees and timber, open space and real estate. The marketplace is chosen as the arena where society balances its competing values. This economistic approach to the environment reduces pollution to what the economist Edwin Mills (1978, p. 15) called "a problem in resource allocation." This approach can decide conflicts along the economic–environmental axis (the resource conflict), but often neglects equity. However, the market does seem to be dealing better with environmental externalities than it did ten or twenty years ago. Internalizing externalities, at the least, raises the issues of social justice and equity: e.g., who will pay for cleaning up abandoned industrial sites or compensate for the loss of fishing revenues due to oil spills. The recent establishment of a pollution credit market in the South Coast Air Quality Management District, for example, is a step in the right direction – despite criticism that the pollution credits were initially given away for free (Robinson 1993).

The role of the planner in all four of these approaches is to arrange the procedures for making decisions, not to set the substance of the actual outcomes. In some cases, the overall structure for decision-making already exists (the market and the political system). In other cases, however, the planner must help shape that structure (a mediation forum; a common language), which, done successfully, gives the process credibility. The actual environmental outcomes nevertheless remain unknowable: you don't know in advance if the environment will actually be improved. For example, environmentalists and developers heralded the Coachella Valley Fringe-Toed Lizard Habitat Conservation Plan as a model process to balance the interests of development and conservation; yet the actual outcome may not adequately protect the endangered lizard (Beatley 1992, pp. 15–16). Similarly, although the New Jersey State Development Plan was praised for its innovative cross-acceptance procedure, the plan itself arguably has not altered the state's urban sprawl.

The final issue that arises is whether the planner should play the role of neutral moderator, or of advocate representing a single party; this has been a long-standing debate in the field. Each strategy has its virtues.

Substantive paths to sustainable development: land use and design

Planners have substantive knowledge of how cities, economies, and ecologies interact, and they should put forth specific, farsighted designs that promote the sustainable city. The first area is traditional planning tools of land-use design and control. The potential for balance between economic and environmental interests exists in design itself, as in a greenbelt community (Elson 1986). Sometimes the land-use solution is simply to divide a contested parcel into two parcels: a developed and a preserved. This solution can take crude forms at times, such as the "no-net-loss" policy that endorses the dubious practice of creating wetlands. A different example, Howard's turn-of-the-century Garden City (1965), can be seen as a territorially symbolic design for balance between the economy and the environment, though its explicit language was that of town–country balance. It is a design's articulated balance between the built development and the unbuilt wilderness that promises the economic–environmental balance. Designs for clustered developments, higher densities, and live-work communities move toward such a balance (Rickaby 1987; Commission of the European Communities 1990; Hudson 1991; Van der Ryn and Calthorpe 1991). Some dispute the inherent benefits of the compact city (Breheny 1992). A further complication is that not all economic–environmental conflicts have their roots in spatial or architectural problems. As a result, ostensible solutions may be merely symbols of ecological–economic balance, without actually solving the conflict.

Nevertheless, land-use planning arguably remains the most powerful tool available to planners, who should not worry too much if it does not manage all problems. The trick in resolving environmental conflicts through land-use planning is to reconcile the conflicting territorial logics of human and of natural habitats. Standard real estate development reduces open space to fragmented, static, green islands – exactly what the landscape ecologists deplore as unable to preserve bio-diversity. Wildlife roam and migrate, and require large expanses of connected landscape (Hudson 1991). So both the ecological and the economic systems require the interconnectivity of a critical mass of land to be sustainable. Though we live in a three-dimensional world, land is a limited resource with essentially two dimensions (always excepting air and burrowing/mining spaces). The requirement of land's spatial interconnectivity is thus hard to achieve for both systems in one region: the continuity of one system invariably fragments continuity of the other.[10] So the guiding challenge for land-use planning is to achieve simultaneously spatial/territor-ial integrity for both systems. Furthermore, a sustainable development that aspires to social justice must also find ways to avoid the land-use manifestations of uneven development: housing segregation, unequal property-tax funding of public schools, jobs–housing imbalance, the spatial imbalance of economic opportunity, and un-equal access to open space and recreation.

Substantive paths to sustainable development: bioregionalism

A comprehensive vision of sustainable land use is bioregionalism, both in its 1920s articulation by the Regional Planning Association of America (Sussman 1976) and its contemporary variation (Sale 1985; Andrus et al. 1990; Campbell 1992). The movement's essential belief is that rescaling communities and the economy according to the ecological boundaries of a physical region will encourage sustain-ability. The regional scale presumably stimulates greater environmental awareness: it is believed that residents of small-scale, self-sufficient regions will be aware of the causes and effects of their environmental actions, thereby reducing externalities. Regions will live within their means, and bypass the environmental problems caused by international trade and exporting pollution.

The bioregional vision certainly has its shortcomings, including the same fuzzy, utopian thinking found in other writing about sustainable development. Its ecological determinism also puts too much faith in the regional "spatial fix": no geographic scale can, in itself, eliminate all conflict, for not all conflict is geographic. Finally, the call for regional self-reliance – a common feature of sustainable development concepts (Korten 1991, p. 184) – might relegate the regional economy to underdevelopment in an otherwise nationally and internationally interdependent world. Yet it can be effective to visualize sustainable regions within an interdependent world full of trade, migration, information flows and capital flows, and to know the difference between *healthy interdependence* and *parasitic dependence*, that is, a dependence on other regions' resources that is equivalent to depletion. Interdependence does not always imply an imbalance of power, nor does self-sufficiency guarantee equality. Finally, the bioregional perspective can provide a foundation for understanding conflicts among a region's interconnected economic, social and ecological networks.

Other substantive paths

One other approach is technological improvement, such as alternative fuels, conser-vation mechanisms, recycling, alternative materials, and new mass transit design.

Stimulated by competition, regulation, or government subsidies, such advances reduce the consumption of natural resources per unit of production and thereby promise to ameliorate conflict over their competing uses, creating a win–win solution. However, this method is not guaranteed to serve those purposes, for gains in conservation are often cancelled out by rising demand for the final products. The overall increase in demand for gasoline despite improvements in automobile fuel efficiency is one example of how market forces can undermine technologically-achieved environmental improvements. Nor, importantly, do technological improvements guarantee fairer distribution.

The role of the planner in all these substantive strategies (land use, bioregionalism, technological improvement) is to design outcomes, with less emphasis on the means of achieving them. The environmental ramifications of the solutions are known or at least estimated, but the political means to achieve legitimacy are not. There also is a trade-off between comprehensiveness (bioregions) and short-term achievability (individual technological improvements).

Merging the substantive and procedural

The individual shortcomings of the approaches described above suggest that combining them can achieve both political and substantive progress in the environmental–economic crisis. The most successful solutions seem to undertake several different resolution strategies at once. For example, negotiation among developers, city planners, and land-use preservationists can produce an innovative, clustered design for a housing development, plus a per-unit fee for preserving open space. Substantive vision combined with negotiating skills thus allows planners to create win–win solutions, rather than either negotiating in a zero-sum game or preparing inert, ecotopian plans. This approach is not a distant ideal for planners: they already have, from their education and experience, both this substantive knowledge and this political savvy.

In the end, however, the planner must also deal with conflicts where one or more parties have no interest in resolution. One nonresolution tactic is the NIMBY, Not In My Back Yard, response: a crude marriage of local initiative and the age-old externalizing of pollution. This "take it elsewhere" strategy makes no overall claim to resolve conflict, though it can be a productive form of resistance rather than just irrational parochialism (Lake 1993). Nor does eco-terrorism consider balance. Instead, it replaces the defensive stance of NIMBY with offensive, confrontational, symbolic action. Resolution is also avoided out of cavalier confidence that one's own side can manage the opposition through victory, not compromise ("My side will win, so why compromise?"). Finally, an "I don't care" stance avoids the conflict altogether. Unfortunately, this ostensible escapism often masks a more pernicious NIMBY or "my side will win" hostility, just below the surface.

Planners: Leaders or Followers in Resolving Economic–Environmental Conflicts?

I turn finally to the question of whether planners are likely to be leaders or followers in resolving economic–environmental conflicts. One would think that it would be natural for planners, being interdisciplinary and familiar with the three goals of balancing social equity, jobs, and environmental protection, to take the lead in resolving such conflicts. Of the conflict resolution scenarios mentioned above, those most open to planners' contributions involve the built environment and local resources: land use, soil conservation, design issues, recycling, solid waste, water treatment. Even solutions using the other approaches – environmental economic incentives, political compromise, and environmental technology innovations – that are normally undertaken at the state and federal levels could also involve planners if moved to the local or regional level.

But the planners' position at the forefront of change is not assured, especially if the lead is taken up by other professions or at the federal, not the local, level. The lively debate on whether gasoline consumption can best be reduced through higher-density land uses (Newman and Kenworthy 1989) or through energy taxes (Gordon and Richardson 1990) not only reflected an ideological battle over interpreting research results and the merits of planning intervention, but also demonstrated how local planning can be made either central or marginal to resolving environmental–economic conflicts. To hold a central place in the debate about sustainable development, planners must exploit those areas of conflict where they have the greatest leverage and expertise.

Certainly planners already have experience with both the dispute over economic growth versus equity and that over economic growth versus environmental protection. Yet the development conflict is where the real action for planners will be: seeking to resolve both environmental and economic equity issues at once. Here is where the profession can best make its unique contribution. An obvious start would be for community development planners and environmental planners to collaborate more (an alliance that an internal Environmental Protection Agency memo found explosive enough for the agency to consider defusing it) (Higgins 1993, 1994). One possible joint task is to expand current public–private partnership efforts to improve environmental health in the inner city. This urban-based effort would help planners bypass the danger of environmental elitism that besets many suburban, white-oriented environmental organizations.

If planners move in this direction, they will join the growing environmental justice movement, which emerged in the early 1980s and combined minority community organizing with environmental concerns (Higgins 1993, 1994). The movement tries to reduce environmental hazards that directly affect poor residents, who are the least able to fight pollution, be it the direct result of discriminatory siting decisions or the indirect result of housing and employment discrimination. The poor, being the least able to move away, are especially tied to place and therefore to the assistance or neglect of local planners. Understandably, local civil rights leaders have been pre-occupied for so long with seeking economic opportunity and social justice that they have paid less attention to inequities in the local environment. The challenge for poor communities is now to expand their work on the property conflict to address the development conflict as well, that is, to challenge the false choice of jobs over the environment. An urban vision of sustainable development, infused with a belief in social and environmental justice, can guide these efforts.

Yet even with the rising acceptance of sustainable development, planners will not always be able, on their own, to represent and balance social, economic, and environmental interests simultaneously. The professional allegiances, skills, and bureaucracies of the profession are too constraining to allow that. Pretending at all times to be at the center of the planner's triangle will only make sustainability a hollow term. Instead, the trick will be for individual planners to identify their specific loyalties and roles in these conflicts accurately: that is, to orient themselves in the triangle. Planners will have to decide whether they want to remain outside the conflict and act as mediators, or jump into the fray and promote their own visions of ecological-economic development, sustainable or otherwise. Both planning behaviors are needed.

ACKNOWLEDGMENT

The author thanks Elizabeth Mueller, Susan Fainstein, Diane Massell, Jonathan Feldman, Karen Lowry, Jessica Sanchez, Harvey Jacobs, Michael Greenberg, Renée Sieber, Robert Higgins, the Project on Regional and Industrial Economics (PRIE) Seminar, and three anonymous reviewers for their comments.

NOTES

1 A curious comparison to this equity–environment–economy triangle is the view of Arne Naess (1993), the radical environmentalist who gave Deep Ecology its name in the 1970s, that the three crucial postwar political movements were the social justice, radical environmental, and peace movements, whose goals might overlap but could not be made identical.

2 Perhaps one can explain the lack of a universal conflict in the following way: if our ideas of the economy, equity, and the environment are socially/culturally constructed, and if cultural society is local as well as global, then our ideas are locally distinct rather than universally uniform.

3 For planners, if one is simply "planning for place," then the dispute about suburban housing versus wetlands does indeed reflect a conflict between an economic and an environmental use of a specific piece of land. But if one sees this conflict in light of "planning for people," then the decision lies between differing social groups (e.g., environmentalists, fishermen, developers) and between their competing attempts to incorporate the piece of land into their system and world view. (This classic planning distinction between planning for people or for place begs the question: Is there a third option, "planning for nonpeople, i.e., nature"?)

4 Schiller, using Kant's logic, recognized 200 years ago this human habit of positing the future on the past: "He thus artificially retraces his childhood in his maturity, forms for himself a *state of Nature* in idea, which is not indeed given him by experience but is the necessary result of his rationality, borrows in this ideal state an ultimate aim which he never knew in his actual state of Nature, and a choice of which he was capable, and proceeds now exactly as though he were starting afresh...."

5 Some radical ecologists take this lost world a step further and see it not as a garden, but as wilderness (e.g., Parton 1993).

6 I use the term diaspora to mean the involuntary dispersal of a people from their native home, driven out by a greater power (Hall 1992). The curious nature of the diaspora implied by the environmental world view is that it is ambiguously voluntary: western positivistic thinking is the villain that we developed, but that eventually enslaved us. Then, too, diasporas invariably combine dislocations across both time and space, but the mythic "homeland" of this environmental diaspora is only from an historical era, but from no specific place.

7   The reverse may also not be automatic. David Johns (1992, p. 63), in advocating a broad interspecies equity, reminds us that not all forms of equity go hand-in-hand: "The nature of the linkages between various forms of domination is certainly not settled, but deep ecology may be distinct in believing that the resolution of equity issues among humans will not automatically result in an end to human destruction of the biosphere. One can envision a society without class distinctions, without patriarchy, and with cultural autonomy, that still attempts to manage the rest of nature in utilitarian fashion with resulting deterioration of the biosphere. . . . But the end of domination in human relations is not enough to protect the larger biotic community. Only behavior shaped by a biocentric view can do that."

8   The ambiguity of the term sustainable development is therefore not coincidental, given that reasonable people differ on which corner of the triangle is to be "sustained": a fixed level of natural resources? current environmental quality? current ecosystems? a hypothetical pre-industrial environmental state? the current material standards of living? long-term economic growth? political democracy?

9   These issues of language and translation were raised by Ngũgi wa Thiong-o and Stuart Hall in separate distinguished lectures at the Center for the Critical Analysis of Contemporary Cultures, Rutgers University (March 31 and April 15, 1993).

10 Conservationists have in fact installed underpasses and overpasses so that vulnerable migrating species can get around highways.

REFERENCES

Altshuler, Alan. 1965. The Goals of Comprehensive Planning. *Journal of the American Institute of Planning* 31, 3: 186–94.

Andrus, Van, et al., eds. 1990. *Home: A Bioregional Reader*. Philadelphia and Santa Cruz: New Catalyst/New Society.

Barrett, Gary W., and Patrick J. Bohlen. 1991. Landscape Ecology. In *Landscape Linkages and Biodiversity*, edited by Wendy E. Hudson. Washington, DC and Covelo, CA: Island Press.

Beatley, Timothy. 1992. Balancing Urban Development and Endangered Species: The Coachella Valley Habitat Conservation Plan. *Environmental Management* 16, 1: 7–19.

Beltzer, Dena, and Cynthia Kroll. 1986. *New Jobs for the Timber Region: Economic Diversification for Northern California*. Berkeley: Institute of Governmental Studies, University of California.

Bingham, Gail. 1986. *Resolving Environmental Disputes: A Decade of Experience*. Washington, DC: The Conservation Foundation.

Bird, Elizabeth Ann R. 1987. The Social Construction of Nature: Theoretical Approaches to the History of Environmental Problems. *Environmental Review* 11, 4: 255–64.

Breheny, M. J., ed. 1992. *Sustainable Development and Urban Form*. London: Pion.

Bryant, Bunyan, and Paul Mohai, eds. 1992. *Race and the Incidence of Environmental Hazards*. Boulder, CO: Westview Press.

Bullard, Robert D. 1990. *Dumping in Dixie: Race, Class, and Environmental Quality*. Boulder, CO: Westview Press.

Bullard, Robert D., ed. 1993. *Confronting Environmental Racism: Voices from the Grassroots*. Boston: South End Press.

Campbell, Scott. 1992. Integrating Economic and Environmental Planning: The Regional Perspective. Working Paper No. 43, Center for Urban Policy Research, Rutgers University.

Clawson, Marion. 1975. *Forests: For Whom and For What?* Washington, DC: Resources for the Future.

Commission of the European Communities. 1990. *Green Paper on the Urban Environment*. Brussels: EEC.

Crowfoot, James E., and Julia M. Wondolleck. 1990. *Environmental Disputes: Community Involvement in Conflict Resolution*. Washington, DC and Covelo, CA: Island Press.

Daly, Herman E. 1991. *Steady State Economics*. 2nd edition, with new essays. Washington, DC and Covelo, CA: Island Press.

Daly, Herman E., and John B. Cobb, Jr. 1989. *For the Common Good: Redirecting the Economy toward Community, the Environment, and a Sustainable Future*. Boston: Beacon Press.

Davidoff, Paul. 1965. Advocacy and Pluralism in Planning. *Journal of the American Institute of Planners* 31, 4: 544–55.

Duerr, Hans Peter. 1985. *Dreamtime: Concerning the Boundary between Wilderness and Civilization*. Oxford: Basil Blackwell.

Elson, Martin J. 1986. *Green Belts: Conflict Mediation in the Urban Fringe*. London: Heinemann.

Fainstein, Susan S., and Norman I. Fainstein. 1971. City Planning and Political Values. *Urban Affairs Quarterly* 6, 3: 341–62.

Foglesong, Richard E. 1986. *Planning the Capitalist City*. Princeton: Princeton University Press.

Goodland, Robert. 1990. Environmental Sustainability in Economic Development – with Emphasis on Amazonia. In *Race to Save the Tropics: Ecology and Economics for a Sustainable Future*, edited by Robert Goodland. Washington, DC and Covelo, CA: Island Press.

Gordon, Peter, and Harry Richardson. 1990. Gasoline Consumption and Cities – A Reply. *Journal of the American Planning Association*. 55, 3: 342–5.

Hall, Stuart. 1992. Cultural Identity and Diaspora. *Framework* 36.

Harvey, David. 1985. *The Urbanization of Capital*. Baltimore: Johns Hopkins University Press.

Higgins, Robert R. 1993. Race and Environmental Equity: An Overview of the Environmental Justice Issue in the Policy Process. *Polity*, 26, 2 (Winter): 281–300.

Higgins, Robert R. 1994. Race, Pollution, and the Mastery of Nature. *Environmental Ethics*, 16, 3 (Fall): 251–64.

Hoffman, Lily. 1989. *The Politics of Knowledge: Activist Movements in Medicine and Planning*. Albany: SUNY Press.

Howard, Ebenezer. 1965. *Garden Cities of To-Morrow* (first published in 1898 as *To-Morrow: A Peaceful Path to Real Reform*). Cambridge, MA: MIT Press.

Hudson, Wendy E., ed. 1991. *Landscape Linkages and Biodiversity*. Washington, DC and Covelo, CA: Island Press.

Jacobs, Harvey. 1989. Social Equity in Agricultural Land Protection. *Landscape and Urban Planning* 17, 1: 21–33.

Johns, David. 1992. The Practical Relevance of Deep Ecology. *Wild Earth* 2, 2.

Korten, David C. 1991. Sustainable Development. *World Policy Journal* 9, 1: 157–90.

Krumholz, Norman, et al. 1982. A Retrospective View of Equity Planning: Cleveland, 1969–1979, and Comments. *Journal of the American Planning Association* 48, 2: 163–83.

Kumar, Krishan. 1991. *Utopia and Anti-Utopia in Modern Times*. Oxford and Cambridge, MA: Basil Blackwell.

Lake, Robert. 1993. Rethinking NIMBY. *Journal of the American Planning Association* 59, 1: 87–93.

Lee, Robert G., Donald R. Field, and William R. Burch, Jr., eds. 1990. *Community and Forestry: Continuities in the Sociology of Natural Resources*. Boulder, CO: Westview Press.

Lindblom, C. E. 1959. The Science of Muddling Through. *Public Administration Review* 19 (Spring): 79–88.

Marcuse, Peter. 1976. Professional Ethics and Beyond: Values in Planning. *Journal of the American Institute of Planning* 42, 3: 264–74.

McPhee, John. 1989. *The Control of Nature*. New York: Farrar, Straus, Giroux.

Mills, Edwin S. 1978. *The Economics of Environmental Quality*. New York: Norton.

Naess, Arne. 1993. The Breadth and the Limits of the Deep Ecology Movement. *Wild Earth* 3, 1: 74–5.

Newman, Peter W. G., and Jeffrey R. Kenworthy. 1989. Gasoline Consumption and Cities – A Comparison of U. S. Cities with a Global Survey. *Journal of the American Planning Association* 55, 1: 24–37.

Paehlke, Robert C. 1994. Environmental Values and Public Policy. In *Environmental Policy in the 1990s*, 2nd edition, edited by Norman J. Vig and Michael E. Kraft. Washington, DC: Congressional Quarterly Press.

Parton, Glenn. 1993. Why I am a Primitivist. *Wild Earth* 3, 1: 12–14.

Rees, William. 1989. *Planning for Sustainable Development*. Vancouver, BC: UBC Centre for Human Settlements.

Reisner, Marc. 1987. *Cadillac Desert: The American West and its Disappearing Water*. New York: Penguin Books.

Rickaby, P. A. 1987. Six Settlement Patterns Compared. *Environment and Planning B: Planning and Design* 14: 193–223.

Robinson, Kelly. 1993. The Regional Economic Impacts of Marketable Permit Programs: The Case of Los Angeles. In *Cost Effective Control of Urban Smog*, Federal Reserve Bank of Chicago (November): 166–88.

Ross, Andrew. 1994. *The Chicago Gangster Theory of Life: Ecology, Culture, and Society*. London and New York: Verso.

Sale, Kirkpatrick. 1985. *Dwellers in the Land: The Bioregional Vision*. San Francisco: Sierra Club Books.

Schiller, Friedrich. 1965. *On the Aesthetic Education of Man* [translated by Reginald Snell]. Originally published in 1795 as *Über die Ästhetische Erziehung des Menschen in einer Reihe von Briefen*. New York: Friedrich Unger.

Sessions, George. 1992. Radical Environmentalism in the 90s. *Wild Earth* 2, 3: 64–7.

Smith, Neil. 1990. *Uneven Development: Nature, Capital and the Production of Space*. Oxford, UK: Blackwell.

Soja, Edward. 1989. *Postmodern Geographies: The Resurrection of Space in Critical Social Theory*. London and New York: Verso.

Susskind, Lawrence, and Jeffrey Cruikshank. 1987. Mediated Negotiation in the Public Sector: The Planner as Mediator. *Journal of Planning Education and Research* 4: 5–15.

Sussman, Carl, ed. 1976. *Planning the Fourth Migration: The Neglected Vision of the Regional Planning Association of America*. Cambridge, MA: MIT Press.

Tuason, Julie A. 1993. Economic/Environmental Conflicts in 19th-Century New York: Central Park, Adirondack State Park, and the Social Construction of Nature. Unpublished manuscript, Dept. of Geography, Rutgers University.

Turner, Frederick W. 1983. *Beyond Geography: The Western Spirit Against the Wilderness*. New Brunswick, NJ: Rutgers University Press.

Van der Ryn, Sim, and Peter Calthorpe. 1991. *Sustainable Communities: A New Design Synthesis for Cities, Suburbs and Towns*. San Francisco: Sierra Club Books.

Wiggins, Lyna. 1993. Geographic Information Systems. Lecture at the Center for Urban Policy Research, Rutgers University, April 5.

Wilson, Alexander. 1992. *The Culture of Nature: North American Landscape from Disney to the Exxon Valdez*. Cambridge, MA and Oxford, UK: Blackwell.

World Bank. 1989. *Striking a Balance: The Environmental Challenge of Development*. Washington, DC.

World Commission on Environment and Development (The Brundtland Commission). 1987. *Our Common Future*. Oxford: Oxford University Press.

Index